THE LITURGY DOCUMENTS
ESSENTIAL DOCUMENTS
FOR PARISH WORSHIP

VOLUME ONE

THE LITURGY DOCUMENTS

ESSENTIAL DOCUMENTS
FOR PARISH WORSHIP

Volume One

Fifth Edition

LITURGY
TRAINING
PUBLICATIONS

Nihil Obstat
Very Rev. Daniel A. Smilanic, JCD
Vicar for Canonical Services
Archdiocese of Chicago
June 22, 2012

Imprimatur
Rev. Msgr. John F. Canary, STL, DMIN
Vicar General
Archdiocese of Chicago
June 22, 2012

Please note that some liturgical documents in this resource were promulgated and published prior to the promulgation and publication of the 2010 *General Instruction of the Roman Missal* (GIRM). As such, the footnotes in these older documents may reference different citations from the GIRM. If you have questions, please contact Liturgy Training Publications or your local Office for Divine Worship.

23 22 21 20 19   3 4 5 6 7

ISBN: 978-1-61671-062-0
LD1V5

For the liturgy, "making the work of our redemption a present actuality," most of all in the divine sacrifice of the eucharist, is the outstanding means whereby the faithful may express in their lives and manifest to others the mystery of Christ and the real nature of the true Church.

—*Constitution on the Sacred Liturgy*, 2
Quoting *The Roman Missal*, Prayer over the Gifts,
Holy Thursday and the Second Sunday in Ordinary Time

CONTENTS

ABBREVIATIONS

Many texts listed here appear in *Documents on the Liturgy, 1963–1979: Conciliar, Papal and Curial Texts* (DOL) (Collegeville, MN: The Liturgical Press, 1982). This list is not all-inclusive of liturgical documents promulgated after the Second Vatican Council.

AAS	*Acta apostolicae sedis*
AG	*Ad gentes divinitus*
BB	Book of Blessings
BCDW	Bishops' Committee on Divine Worship
BCL	Bishops' Committee on the Liturgy
BG	Book of the Gospels
BLS	Built of Living Stones: Art, Architecture, and Worship
c.; cc.	canon; canons
CB	Ceremonial of Bishops
CCC	Catechism of the Catholic Church
CCCB	Canadian Conference of Catholic Bishops
CCEC	Code of Canons of the Eastern Churches *(Codex canonum ecclesiarum orientalium)*
CCL	*Corpus christianorum,* Series Latina
CD	*Christus dominus*
CDF	Congregation for the Doctrine of the Faith
CDWDS	Congregation for Divine Worship and the Discipline of the Sacraments
CEILT	Criteria for the Evaluation of Inclusive Language Translations of Scriptural Texts Proposed for Liturgical Use
CI	Christian Initiation, General Introduction
CIC	1983 Code of Canon Law *(Codex iuris canonici)*
1917 CIC	1917 Code of Canon Law *(Codex iuris canonici)*

CMBVM(L)	Collection of Masses of the Blessed Virgin Mary: Lectionary
CMBVM(M)	Collection of Masses of the Blessed Virgin Mary: Missal
CP	*Comme le prévoit*
CR	Congregation of Rites
CSEL	*Corpus scriptorum ecclesiasticorum latinorum*
CSL	Constitution on the Sacred Liturgy
CT	*Catechesi tradendae*
DD	*Dies Domini*
DE	Directory for the Application of Principles and Norms on Ecumenism
DedCh	Dedication of a Church and an Altar
DMC	Directory for Masses with Children
DSCAP	Directory on Sunday Celebrations in the Absence of a Priest
DV	*Dei verbum*
EACW	Environment and Art in Catholic Worship
EE	*Ecclesia de Eucharistia*
EM	*Eucharisticum mysterium*
FYH	Fulfilled in Your Hearing: The Homily in the Sunday Assembly
GCSPD	Guidelines for the Celebration of the Sacraments with Persons with Disabilities
GILOH	General Instruction of the Liturgy of the Hours
GIRM	The General Instruction of the Roman Missal

GMEF	God's Mercy Endures Forever: Guidelines on the Presentation of Jews and Judaism in Catholic Preaching	PGR	Plenty Good Room: The Spirit and Truth of African American Catholic Worship
GSF	Gathered in Steadfast Faith: Statement of the Bishops' Committee on Liturgy on Sunday Worship in the Absence of a Priest	PL	*Patrologiae cursus completus: Series Latina*
GS	*Gaudium et spes*	PO	*Presbyterorum ordinis*
HCWEOM	Holy Communion and Worship of the Eucharist Outside Mass	PS	*Paschale solemnitatis*
		RBC	Rite of Baptism for Children
		RCIA	Rite of Christian Initiation of Adults
HLS	This Holy and Living Sacrifice: Directory for the Celebration and Reception of Communion under Both Kinds	RConf/ RC	Rite of Confirmation
		RMarr	Rite of Marriage
		RM/ RomM	The Roman Missal
IRL	Inculturation and the Roman Liturgy: Fourth Instruction for the Right Application of the Conciliar Constitution on the Liturgy	RP	Roman Pontifical
		RPen	Rite of Penance
		RS	*Redemptionis sacramentum*
		SacCar	*Sacramentum caritatis*
		SC	*Sacrosanctum concilium*
IST	In Spirit and Truth: Black Catholic Reflections on the Order of Mass	SCAP	Sunday Celebrations in the Absence of a Priest
		SCC	To Speak as a Christian Community: Pastoral Message on Inclusive Language
LA	*Liturgiam authenticam*		
LG	*Lumen gentium*		
LM	Lectionary for Mass	SCh	*Sources chrétiennes*
LMT	Liturgical Music Today	STL	Sing to the Lord: Music in Divine Worship
MCW	Music in Catholic Worship		
MS	*Musicam sacram*	UNLY	Universal Norms on the Liturgical Year and the General Roman Calendar
n.; nn.	number; numbers		
NCCB	National Conference of Catholic Bishops		
		UR	*Unitatis redintegratio*
NDRHC	Norms for the Distribution and Reception of Holy Communion Under Both Kinds in the Dioceses of the United States of America	USCCB	United States Conference of Catholic Bishops
		VQA	*Vicesimus quintus annus*
		WWHSH	What We Have Seen and Heard: A Pastoral Letter on Evangelization from the Black Bishops of the United States
NSC	National Statutes on the Catechumenate		
OCF	Order of Christian Funerals		
OE	*Orientalium ecclesiarum*		
OT	*Optatam totius*		
OEx	*Ordo Exsequiarum*, 1969		
PCS	Pastoral Care of the Sick: Rites of Anointing and Viaticum		
PG	*Patrologiae cursus completus: Series Graeca*		

GENERAL INTRODUCTION
Rev. Michael S. Driscoll

THE *ARS CELEBRANDI*

In the 2007 document *Sing to the Lord: Music in Divine Worship* (STL), the American bishops eloquently declared: "Faith grows when it is well expressed in celebration. Good celebrations can foster and nourish faith. Poor celebrations may weaken it."[1] What prophetic words! How far we have moved in a few short decades from an understanding of how the sacraments work *ex opere operato* (if you merely say the correct words using the proper elements, then the sacrament was automatically effected) to a greater appreciation of "full, conscious, and active participation"[2] of all the baptized, as was desired and mandated by the Second Vatican Council. Furthermore, the experience of celebrating the rites well has not been lost on the people. They come to know what constitutes good liturgy, particularly as good ritual experiences have transformed their lives, and many are in active search for liturgical celebrations that nourish their spiritual needs.

This volume is intended primarily for parish priests, deacons, pastoral associates, liturgists, music directors, teachers, catechists, and any other parish staff members responsible for the preparation of the liturgy, to help them craft good celebrations. But the bishops' statement begs the question as to what constitutes "good celebrations"?[3] What criteria are available by which one can judge whether a liturgical celebration is good or bad? Is it determined by the style of music or by the quality of preaching? Is good liturgy simply a matter of following rules?

If good celebrations were simply a matter of following rules, sometimes called a rubrical approach, then there would be good liturgy everywhere. But good celebrations require more than simply coloring within the lines. Good celebrations require an artful sense. At the eleventh Synod of Bishops dealing with the Eucharist (October 2005), three sorts of concerns were addressed: theological (doctrine and catechetical), ethical, and aesthetical. That the bishops were concerned about doctrinal and ethical aspects of the Eucharist does not come as any great surprise, but their expressed concern about the *ars celebrandi* marks a newfound interest in how the liturgy is celebrated beautifully. In his post-Synodal exhortation, *Sacramentum caritatis*, Pope Benedict XVI explores this last dimension:

> In the course of the Synod, there was frequent insistence on the need to avoid any antithesis between the *ars celebrandi*, the art of proper celebration, and the full, active and fruitful participation of all the faithful. The primary way to foster the participation of the People of God in the sacred rite is the proper celebration of the rite itself. The *ars celebrandi* is the best

---

1. *Sing to the Lord: Music in Divine Worship* (STL), 5.
2. *Constitution on the Sacred Liturgy* (CSL), 14.
3. STL, 5.

way to ensure their *actuosa participatio*. The *ars celebrandi* is the fruit of faithful adherence to the liturgical norms in all their richness . . . .[4]

Elsewhere, Bishop Albert Rouet of Poitier, France, strongly underscores this idea in his book *Liturgy and the Arts*, when he boldly states, "The liturgy *is* an art that uses other arts."[5] He goes on to demonstrate how art and liturgy, when they join forces, express transcendence. Of course, the most critical element for the *ars celebrandi* is well-celebrated rites. What does it mean to celebrate the rites well? What are the criteria that we use to judge? To celebrate the liturgy well requires doing the action and saying the prayers so beautifully that their meaning clearly emerges in an intelligible and compelling manner. Because liturgical signs are vehicles of communication and instruments of faith, they should be simple and accessible. In short, they must be humanly attractive. In a word, if the rites are to be fully effective, we must tend to the aesthetics of worship. Suffice it to say that good liturgy is an absolute prerequisite to rich symbolic participation and contemplation. Because liturgy deals so much with symbols, it opens our imagination to multiple layers of interpretation. But symbols can be destroyed when they are interpreted, no longer as symbols, but as laws to be followed slavishly. Good liturgy should not be reduced to rubrics. Because the liturgy is symbolic, however, does not mean that one can just do with it what one wants. It follows its own logic, thus there are liturgical norms to be taken into consideration. The most important point about liturgy is that it must be symbolically the bearer of the transcendent and as such it relates to both the divine and the human. In the recent past there was a tendency to translate the word *liturgy* from the Greek *leitourgia* (from *laos*, meaning "people" and *ergon*, meaning "work") as the "work of the people." A corrective must be added to emphasize that liturgy is also the work of God. The initiative must always originate on the side of God and worship is the human response to God's initiative. Therefore, liturgy is both an *opus Dei* and an *opus hominum (a "work of God" and a "work of the people")*.

Perhaps there is no aspect so important in the whole discussion of the transcendent and symbolic nature of liturgy as the role of the aesthetic experience or the *ars celebrandi*. The Church has always felt the importance of the artful element in the liturgical celebration. The aesthetic experience can be the instrument that assists the faithful to make the assent of faith. It is in the liturgy where we encounter the divine through the beauty of the rites, music, art, and architecture. Therefore, reducing the liturgy to a series of rubrics would be a grave mistake. An overly rubrical approach can lead to dead symbols and will fail to stir the faith in those celebrating. Pope Benedict XVI understands this well as he writes:

> . . . The liturgy is inherently linked to beauty: it is *veritatis splendor*. The liturgy is a radiant expression of the paschal mystery, in which Christ draws us to himself and calls us to communion. As Saint Bonaventure would say, in Jesus we contemplate beauty and splendor at their source. This is no mere aestheticism, but the concrete way in which the truth of

---

4. *Sacramentum caritatis* (SacCar), 38.
5. *Liutrgy and the Arts* (Liturgical Press, 1997), p. 1, emphasis mine.

God's love in Christ encounters us, attracts us and delights us, enabling us to emerge from ourselves and drawing us towards our true vocation, which is love.[6]

LITURGICAL ADAPTATION AND ACCOMMODATION

Rather than thinking of this volume as a rulebook, it might be more helpful to think of it as a collection of recipes. The principles that are enunciated in the various documents need to be read and interpreted in context—just as changes to recipes are sometimes needed. Good liturgy is not a one-size-fits-all proposition. Liturgy must always take into consideration who is praying, where the prayer is taking place, what time of day, what are the acoustical properties of the space, what are the spatial concerns, and so on. Therefore, good liturgy, like authentic religion, frees and empowers those who pray rather than restricting them to simply following rules blindly. Slavishly following rules would be as bad as totally disregarding liturgical law. But the law has to be understood in its proper context. Moreover, the idea of tailoring the liturgy to each particular situation is covered in the various *praenotanda* (introductions) to the sacramental rites under the principle of "liturgical adaptation." The phrase has several meanings in liturgical law: most frequently it is used to indicate a liturgical variation or option that the universal law permits. The conference of bishops makes the determination of this as particular law. But an individual bishop as the chief liturgist in his diocese also regulates the way the liturgy is celebrated in his diocese. Finally at the level of the priests and ministers, Canon Law makes provision for *accomodatio*, translated from Latin into English as adaptation. But for sake of clarity, a better distinction might be made between inculturation, adaptation, and accommodation. Inculturation refers to substantial change in the liturgy for a certain nation or region, as addressed in the *Constitution on the Sacred Liturgy*, article 40. In the second case, adaptation is also substantial and comes under the jurisdiction of the episcopal conferences, such as the *Adaptations of the General Instruction of the Roman Missal* for *the Dioceses of the United States of America* that was aproved by the United States Conference of Catholic Bishops (USCCB) on November 14, 2001 and eventually incorporated into the main body of the text issued in 2010.[7] Finally, accommodation happens at the local level as ministers make judgments, taking into consideration the concrete circumstances in which the liturgy is to be celebrated.

Accommodations by the ministers are usually concerned with choices among options provided for in the rites themselves. For example in the Rite of the Anointing of the Sick, the minister must determine the gravity of the illness and accommodate the prayers for the specific circumstances. But accommodation also happens almost unwittingly as ministers adjust the size of their actions and the volume of their voices to the size of the space, taking into consideration the space in which the liturgy is celebrated. For example, in preparing Holy Week one necessarily has to take into consideration the physical church space where the liturgies are to be celebrated and prepare accordingly.

---

6. SacCar, 35.

7. The 2010 *General Instruction of the Roman Missal* (GIRM) is found in the third edition of *The Roman Missal* approved in 2010 and promulgated for liturgical use on November 27, 2011.

Liturgy, simply put, is the official prayer of the Church. But in order for prayer truly to be of the Church, the Church must recognize it as its own. Liturgical law is not as important as the liturgy itself, but it helps regulate the prayer officially. Liturgical law is in service of the liturgy and not vice versa. The *Constitution on the Sacred Liturgy*, article 11, warns about this: "Pastors must therefore realize that when the liturgy is celebrated something more is required than the mere observance of the laws governing valid and lawful celebration; it is also their duty to ensure that the faithful take part fully aware of what they are doing, actively engaged in the rite, and enriched by its effects." Nevertheless, fidelity to the liturgical norms in keeping with sound principles of liturgical celebration will aid in the worthy celebration of the Church's rites. As the Second Vatican Council taught: "the liturgy is the summit toward which the activity of the Church is directed; at the same time it is the font from which all the Church's power flows."[8]

But people must understand that liturgical law is a complex system of practical norms ordering the rituals in and through which people are sanctified and worship God. Thus, a canonical study of the liturgy is important, but ministers who blindly follow the ritual directives in the reformed liturgical books will run the risk of a new form of liturgical rubricism that might be externally correct but spiritually dead.

In Volumes One and Two, there are many documents, each with its own pastoral overview explaining the meaning, authority, and purpose of the document. The touchstone document is still the *Constitution on the Sacred Liturgy*, which is why this document is included in both volumes. Even after fifty years, this is the basis for the liturgical reform and holds the greatest weight. All later documents need to be read in light of this *Constitution*. There is a tendency to think that later documents trump former ones, but this is not always the case. It is important to know and assess the relative weight of each document in order to interpret it properly. Without going into great depth about the nature of liturgical law, a word must be said about its form and function. In the past fifty years more than 400 documents have appeared that deal in whole or in part with the liturgy. Some have been published by Conferences of Bishops or by individual bishops, while many have issued from the Council itself or the consilium that was charged with the implementation of the conciliar reforms. Some of these documents have seen several revisions, so the question arises as to how they should be interpreted. However, in comparing later revisions, for example of *The General Instruction of the Roman Missal*, one is struck by the similarity of the various revisions. One readily concludes that liturgy by its nature is a conservative affair and that revisions usually involve reworking of pre-existing materials.

How then do we assess the weight of liturgical documents? With the appearance of the revised *General Instruction of the Roman Missal*, the American canonist, John Huels, wrote an informative article in *Worship* magazine entitled "Assessing the Weight of Documents on the Liturgy."[9] I will summarize the salient points that he makes and then apply these to the documents contained

---

8. CSL, 10.
9. 74.2 March, 2000.

in this volume. First, it is important to understand certain principles operative within the liturgical documents, otherwise the weight of a document cannot be ascertained. There are four questions that must be asked of the document: (1) Is it theological or juridical in nature? (2) Who is the authority issuing the document? (3) To whom it is addressed? (4) Is the document juridically binding?

IS THE DOCUMENT THEOLOGICAL OR JURIDICAL?

When bishops speak, they wear different hats. Sometimes they are speaking in their capacity to lead and govern and sometimes in their capacity to teach, and at other times in their capacity to sanctify. *Lumen gentium* addresses this in terms of threefold ministry (*munera*): to teach, to govern, and to sanctify.[10] But this raises a question about the type of document we are considering when there could possibly be an overlap of all three areas, particularly in considering liturgical documents. Nevertheless, when bishops exercise the teaching office (*munus docendi*), they are functioning as magisterium. When they exercise the ruling office (*munus regendi*), they are functioning as governance. This is a helpful distinction, because teaching is often confused with governance. When the function is teaching, then the interpretation is theological, whereas when the function is governance, then the interpretation looks to Canon Law. Some documents are easily identifiable as magisterial, such as apostolic letters, encyclical letters, decretal letters, post-Synodal apostolic exhortations, and apostolic exhortations. Thus, these are not juridical documents but teaching documents dealing with theological, moral, and pastoral matters, and should be interpreted as such. When a document is exclusively magisterial or juridical, the interpretation is easy following the distinction. But some documents straddle the two areas. For example, often a juridical document will begin with a theological introduction. Thus an apostolic constitution or an apostolic letter (*motu proprio*) from the pope or directories, instructions, circular letters from the Roman Curia must first be determined for the document type. In the case of the introductions to the rites (*praenotanda*), which function as juridical norms for the various sacraments, theology is interwoven in the statement. Within the various kinds of magisterial (teaching) and juridical (legal) documents there are also differing degrees of weight, depending upon whether the statement is dogmatic and requires an assent of faith. If the document is related to "revelation" then it is definitely binding. But if a statement is not central to the faith, then it merits less attention and it pertains to the discipline of theology to assess the weight. Documents originating in a teaching authority of the Church often speak to the liturgy. Nevertheless, these documents are not legally binding and do not establish juridical norms. Thus, before interpreting any document, it is first important to establish whether it is juridical or theological. If the document is theological, then it imposes no juridical obligations.

Who issues the document? In many governments, there are three distinct branches: legislative, executive, and juridical. So also this is true in the Church. The pope and the College of Bishops are the legislative branch. The pope individually is the supreme legislator, but he also works in concert with the bishops

---

10. See *Lumen gentium* (LG), 21.

in council or with the various Roman dicasteries. Bishops exercise their legislative authority globally in an ecumenical council, and particularly for a specific nation as an episcopal conference or a plenary council. A bishop within his own diocese is a legislator. Beginning with the pope, a cursory glance at the table of contents of the *Acta apostolicae sedis* (AAS; the official listing of all Vatican communications published by the Secretariat of State) for the recent past reveals that there are well over twenty-five different types of pronouncements made by recent popes. They range from solemn constitutions presented in the form of bulls to simple congratulatory messages sent by the Holy Father to the leaders of various countries. After studying the types of documents, brief reference must also be made to the mode of promulgation. For instance, some documents are issued in the form of bulls, other as briefs, others as rescripts. However, no decisive argument can be drawn from the form to substantiate the dogmatic or disciplinary value of an act. Rather, it is by the nature of the document and not its form that we will be able to determine if a specific text is doctrinal or legislative.

To whom is the document addressed? Legislative texts given for the community bind those for whom they are made. Therefore, the canons of the code on religious life are binding only for those people in religious institutes. Whereas administrative documents for the community, like many legislative texts, are acts of executive power and are given to the community binding those for whom they are made. The norms are virtually synonymous with law, although they are subservient to laws. For example, they cannot be contrary to the law, otherwise they lack all force, nor can they revoke contrary particular laws and legal customs already in existence.

In other cases, there are administrative documents intended for the executors of the law. In this instance the law is not intended for the community at large but is binding only to the executor and is intended for internal administration. Because they are addressed to bishops, major superiors, seminary rectors, and formation directors, among others, they are binding only to the administrators who are addressed.

Is the document binding? The Holy See issues public juridical documents intended to be binding for the Catholic faithful who have a canonical obligation to observe these norms. Sometimes, however, some documents lack binding force while treating matters that have a juridical nature. In this case, the dicastery wishes to be of service by offering pastoral advice but this should not be confused for law that is binding. For example, documents that are called pastoral guides, guidelines, and recommendations should be interpreted as just that. Sometimes, however, a form such as a letter may be ambiguous as to its legal force. In general, only public documents of the Church are binding, provided that these issue from competent ecclesiastical authorities who have the required legislative or executive power.

GENRES OF LEGISLATIVE LITURGICAL DOCUMENTS

A cursory glance at the documents contained in Volumes One and Two reveals varying degrees of authoritative weight, which is important when they are under consideration. Sometimes there is confusion about the kind of document it is and what authoritative weight should be granted to it. A number of documents and parts of documents originating at the Second Vatican Council are juridical in nature. Much of this was subsequently incorporated into the 1983 *Code of Canon Law* (CIC) and the liturgical books. Four different types of documents were prepared by the Council Fathers: *constitutions, decrees, declarations,* and *messages.* It is quite difficult to state precisely why one document is given a specific qualification rather than another. It would seem that the constitutions are addressed to the universal Church, while the decrees are directed more specifically to a given category of the faithful or to a special form of apostolate. The declarations are policy statements giving the ordinary teaching of the Church, while the messages are exhortations, addressed to various categories of people at the conclusion of the final session of the Council. It is probably the matter itself that determined whether a particular document was to be given a certain title. From this distinction, however, we can assess the weight of the *Constitution on the Sacred Liturgy* as being quite authoritative. The Council laid down laws that must be respected. But on other occasions, the Council formulated principles, criteria, desires which must be given concrete expression in new laws and instructions, in new organisms and offices, in spiritual, cultural, and moral movements, and in organizations. For example, the conciliar documents must be completed with the post-conciliar legislation.

Finally, there are documents issued by the Roman Curia. The types of documents issued by the Roman Congregations, Secretariates, and Offices are as varied as those used by the Holy Father in his teachings. Among those most often used are *decrees, instructions, declarations, circular letters, official responses,* and so on. Each of these documents should be studied in turn so that its legislative weight can be determined.

Decree is the term having many meanings according to the threefold division of executive, legislative, and juridical branches. In *executive* matters, it is applied to designate the decisions of the Roman dicasteries, the regulations of bishops or other prelates. In *legislative* matters, the term is given specifically to the disciplinary laws of the Ecumenical or particular Councils, to the decisions taken by groups which do not have the characteristics of perfect societies, and to acts which were formerly described as "general precepts." Finally in *juridical* matters, the various decisions taken by the judge throughout a hearing, which are not related directly to the object of the case nor to an individual's cause, are called. Many of the documents relating to the liturgical renewal are placed in this category. It can easily be stated that decrees are new laws, promulgated by the Congregations with the special approval of the Holy Father, and, consequently, have the same effect as the general laws of the *Code of Canon Law* (CIC).

Instructions are a common form of pronouncement by the Roman Curia. An instruction is a doctrinal explanation, or a set of rules, directive norms, recommendations, and admonitions. Perhaps the most publicized instructions were the five that implemented the conciliar *Constitution on the Sacred Liturgy*. It is this form of document, along with the declaration, that gave rise to the greatest difficulty in interpretation in the post-conciliar era. Because the texts are not strictly legislative—at least according to their nature—their application certainly allows for more leeway than in the case of a decree.

Declarations are another form of pronouncement used quite frequently in the past to interpret existing law or facts, or as a reply to a contested point of law. *Circular letters* are a relatively new form used by the Curia and are more difficult to circumscribe in legislative terms. The general legislation of the Church does not provide for circular letters as an authentic source of law. At times a circular letter will accompany a set of norms on a given subject. It is quite clear that the norms constitute the legislative portion of the communication, and the circular letter explains the intention and purpose of the rules.

Directories are another new type of act wherein guidelines are given for the application of accepted principles. The intent of a directory is to provide the basic principles of pastoral theology, taken from the Magisterium of the Church, and especially from the Second Vatican Council, by which pastoral action in the ministry can be more fittingly directed and governed. This outlook explains why the theoretical aspect is given primary emphasis in a directory, without neglecting the practical aspects. Consequently, directories are addressed more particularly to bishops to give assistance in practical matters. The Council had called for them to provide shepherds "with general directories concerning the care of souls be compiled for the use of both bishops and parish priests so that they may have definitive directives to guide them in the discharge of their particular pastoral function."[11]

Official responses also exist in addition to the various decrees and instructions of the Roman Curia, such as the answers issued by the Pontifical Commission for the Interpretation of the Acts of the Second Vatican Council, or the Consilium for Liturgy.

DOCUMENTS IN VOLUME ONE AND VOLUME TWO

The *Constitution on the Sacred Liturgy* from the Second Vatican Council is so important as the foundational document authorizing the liturgical reforms that it appears at the beginning of both volumes. At the end of both volumes is a very helpful Glossary in order to understand words that are not a part of our everyday vocabulary. Thirty-four liturgical documents are distributed throughout the two volumes. They fall into three genres as follows: Roman rituals, documents that accompany the liturgical books, and other liturgical documents and pastoral letters. The documents in Volume One represent the primary liturgical documents needed to prepare the Mass in its varied aspects while Volume Two deals with the sacraments and other major rites (blessings, Liturgy of the Hours). Following each document is the year of publication. When several years are noted, this signals that the document went through multiple revisions but the document in this volume represent the last date listed.

In Volume One dealing with the Eucharistic liturgy, there are also **documents that accompany the liturgical books** as follows (in the order in which they appear in the volume): *General Instruction of the Roman Missal, Norms for the Distribution and Reception of Holy Communion under Both Kinds for the Dioceses of the United States of America, Universal Norms on the Liturgical Year and the General Roman Calendar, Lectionary for Mass: Introduction, The Book of the Gospels: Introduction,* and the *Directory for Sunday Celebrations in the*

---

11. *Christus Dominus,* 44.

Absence of a Priest: Introduction. In the third category of **other liturgical documents and pastoral letters** we find the following: *Dies Domini: On Keeping the Lord's Day Holy, Ecclesia de Eucharistia, Redemptionis sacramentum, Sing to the Lord: Music in Divine Worship, Built of Living Stones,* and *Gathered in Steadfast Faith.*

Volume Two contains the **Roman rites** (other than the Mass) each with its own introduction (*praenotanda*), as follows in the order in which they appear in the volume: *Christian Initiation, Rite of Christian Initiation of Adults, Rite of Baptism of Children, Rite of Confirmation, Rite of Penance, Rite of Marriage, Pastoral Care of the Sick: Rites of Anointing and Viaticum, Order of Christian Funerals: General Introduction,* and *Ordo Exsequiarum, 1969.* There is additionally a *Collection of Masses for the Blessed Virgin Mary.*

In the second category of **documents that accompany the liturgical books** we find the following: *General Instruction of the Liturgy of the Hours,* and the *Book of Blessings: General Introduction.*

In the third category of other liturgical documents and pastoral letters we find the following: *Appendix for Cremation, Guidelines for the Celebration of the Sacraments with Persons with Disabilities, Directory for Masses with Children, Holy Communion and Worship of the Eucharist Outside Mass, Paschale solemnitatis,* and the *National Statutes for the Catechumenate.*

It might seem to some people that the Church has an over-abundance of legislation on liturgical matters. On the other hand, the large corpus of liturgical legislation attests to the importance of the liturgy for the life of the Church and witnesses to the firm belief that Christ endowed his Church this means of prayer to draw all who pray closer to God.

CONSTITUTION
ON THE
SACRED LITURGY

SACROSANCTUM CONCILIUM

SECOND VATICAN COUNCIL
DECEMBER 4, 1963

AN OVERVIEW OF THE *CONSTITUTION ON THE SACRED LITURGY*

Rev. Msgr. Richard B. Hilgartner

The publication of this collection of liturgical documents occurs at the intersection of two significant moments in the liturgical life of the Church: the fiftieth anniversary of the opening of the Second Vatican Council in 1962, and the implementation of the third edition of *The Roman Missal* in most of the English-speaking world in Advent, 2011—the latest step in the ongoing reform of the liturgy. The Council's *Constitution on the Sacred Liturgy* (CSL), was by no means the beginning of liturgical renewal within the Church, but it did formally articulate the principles and the agenda for the reform, inaugurating the real work of reform of the liturgy of the Roman Rite. These guiding principles still have much to say to the Church today.

It is not a coincidence that the Sacred Liturgy was the subject of the first major document of the Second Vatican Council. If the Council's aim was to renew and invigorate the life of the Church in light of the modern world, then there could be no more effective means to do so than the renewal of the Sacred Liturgy. This approach also sent a message regarding the pastoral nature of the Council, whose influence would reach beyond matters of policy and doctrine to the place where the faithful meet the Church most frequently and profoundly—the Mass.

The *Constitution* was approved and promulgated on December 4, 1963, by an almost unanimous vote of the Council (2147 for, 4 against). As a work of the College of Bishops gathered with the pope in an Ecumenical Council, this document has the highest teaching authority of any in the Church. The *Catechism of the Catholic Church* (CCC) states: "'The infallibility promised to the Church is also present in the body of bishops when, together with Peter's successor, they exercise the supreme Magisterium' (*Lumen gentium*, 25), above all in an Ecumenical Council."[1] The work of the liturgical reform was undertaken quickly as Pope Paul VI, in the *motu proprio, Sacram liturgiam* (January 25, 1964), announced the formation of the Consilium, the working commission that enacted the agenda set by the *Constitution*.

In the nearly fifty years since the *Constitution on the Sacred Liturgy* (CSL) was promulgated, it is not an overstatement to claim that liturgical life has changed substantially, if not radically. And yet the reforms of the Sacred Liturgy that the Council put into motion were not sudden, but can be viewed, in the words of Pope Benedict XVI, through a "hermeneutic of continuity." Among the principles of the liturgical movement and the *Constitution* as well, was a *ressourcement*, a "return to the sources," which immediately grounds the work of reform in the breadth and depth of tradition.

The *Constitution* is divided into seven chapters. The first, "General Principles for the Reform and Promotion of the Sacred Liturgy," presents the "big picture" of the agenda and plan for reform, while the remaining chapters speak in more

---

1. *Catechism of the Catholic Church* (CCC), 891.

concrete terms about the application of the agenda. Among the many principles, goals, and themes of the *Constitution*, three in particular are worthy of reflection here in terms of what has been accomplished and what remains to be explored further: Participation, the Paschal Mystery, and Inculturation.

PARTICIPATION

One of the most quoted texts of all the documents of the Second Vatican Council is article 14 of the *Constitution*: "The Church earnestly desires that all the faithful be led to that full, conscious, and active participation in liturgical celebrations called for by the very nature of the liturgy." As one of the guiding principles of the liturgical movement and the reform itself, it was not a new idea that came out of nowhere at the Council, but was already prevalent in scholarly writing and pastoral work. Pope Pius X brought the matter of participation to the forefront in his 1903 *motu proprio*, *Tra le sollecitudini*, in which he said, "active participation in the most holy mysteries and in the public and solemn prayer of the Church" is the "foremost and indispensable font" of the "true Christian spirit."

The call for active participation had a great influence on the reform of the rites. The normative celebration of the Mass today includes many forms of participation that engage the faithful in the act of worship. Caution about the recent implementation of the third edition of *The Roman Missal* demonstrates that people take very seriously their own participation. The changes in liturgical texts have, at least in the short term, hindered the external participation and interior consciousness of the mystery being celebrated because of unfamiliar prayers, responses, and acclamations. Liturgical music is evidence of great progress in terms of participation. Music in the liturgy is not understood as some form of ornamentation or window-dressing, but as essential to the very nature of worship. The celebration of the liturgy today is also marked by the actions of a great number of liturgical ministers, and those ministers symbolize the participation of the entire assembly in order to underscore that the Mass is not the responsibility of one person (the priest), but of all who gather to celebrate.

In light of accomplishments in the area of "active participation,"[2] there is still a need to continue to cultivate awareness that participation must first of all be conscious. Participation often takes on external forms, making use of the body, the voice, particular roles, and the like. Those external forms manifest what takes place in the heart, and they should encourage what takes place interiorly. The implementation of the new edition of *The Roman Missal* provided an opportunity to be more conscious: to pay more attention to what is being said and done.

THE PASCHAL MYSTERY

To understand the nature of the Paschal Mystery in the liturgy, one recalls the words of Saint Paul, which are so often taken up as words of praise in the Mass: "For as often as you eat this bread and drink the cup, you proclaim the Lord's death until he comes."[3] The *Constitution* articulated this sacramental and liturgical participation in the Paschal Mystery.[4] The liturgy is understood

2. *Constitution on the Sacred Liturgy* (CSL), 14.
3. 1 Corinthians 11:26.
4. See CSL, 6.

as an encounter with the living God and not merely a historical reenactment of the Last Supper or of the Cross, but as an encounter with the living God in Christ Jesus, present and active in a dynamic and sacramental way.

The liturgy is, in fact, the work of Christ himself, head and members, and active participation in the liturgy is a participation in the very work of Christ. In the liturgy, the real sacrifice being offered is not anything else but Christ himself continuing his sacrifice for the salvation of his people. Conscious participation in the liturgy must lead to the offering of one's whole self. The invitation to prayer, "Pray, brethren (brothers and sisters), / that my sacrifice and yours / may be acceptable to God, / the almighty Father" is meant to emphasize two things: the offering of the Mass does not belong to the priest alone, and the sacrifice of the Mass is not only bread and wine but the offering of one's whole self. The *Constitution* states:

> [The faithful] should be instructed by God's word and be nourished at the table of the Lord's body; they should give thanks to God; by offering the immaculate Victim, not only through the hands of the priest, but also with him, they should learn to offer themselves. . . .[5]

Ongoing catechesis about the nature of the liturgy as an encounter with the whole Christ in his Paschal Mystery is still important. Blessed John Paul II, in his final encyclical, *Ecclesia de Eucharistia* (EE), described the liturgical encounter with Christ as an encounter on the road to Emmaus: "Whenever the Church celebrates the Eucharist, the faithful can in some way relive the experience of the two disciples on the road to Emmaus: 'their eyes were opened and they recognized him' (Luke 24:31)."[6] The disciples, in that moment, experienced the total person of Jesus as he listened to them, spoke to them, fed them, and so prepared them to be witnesses. The liturgy does the same today, as worshippers participate not only in the sacrifice of the Cross but the whole life of Christ, including sending forth for mission: "Go and announce the Gospel of the Lord" and "Go in peace, glorifying the Lord by your life."

The liturgy—the Eucharist—is not only about here and now, but about the Kingdom of God as well. The hearts of the faithful always burn within them as they encounter the Lord—really and substantially present; Body, Blood, soul, and divinity—but at the same time their hearts are still longing and yearning for something more in the Kingdom of Heaven. The *Constitution on the Sacred Liturgy* states: "In the earthly liturgy we take part in a foretaste of that heavenly liturgy celebrated in the holy city of Jerusalem toward which we journey as pilgrims, where Christ is sitting at the right hand of God. . . ."[7]

INCULTURATION

One of the means by which the Second Vatican Council sought to inspire participation in the sacred mysteries was to make the liturgy accessible to the faithful and to see to the authentic transmission of the faith, particularly through various means of inculturation. The use of the vernacular in the liturgy became

---

5. Ibid., 48.
6. *Ecclesia de Eucharistia (EE)*, 6.
7. CSL, 8.

one of the most significant developments in this regard (though it is not the only one), and the notion of inculturation was not new at the Council. The Council of Trent was not absolutely opposed to the use of use of vernacular languages, though at the time the Latin liturgy was certainly maintained.

The *Constitution on the Sacred Liturgy* not only opened up the possibility of the use of the vernacular in the liturgy, even if perhaps the Council Fathers did not initially envision the extent to which it would be used, but it spoke about other matters of culture as well.[8] Today the liturgy is celebrated in diverse languages with various expressions of local cultures, and the breadth of the Body of Christ that is the Church is evident even within individual parishes. Music and other forms of expression of devotion and worship take on many forms, and while the essential unity of the liturgy is maintained, it is embodied in particular settings that are accessible to all (or at least that is the aim).

Many unanswered questions remain as the Church continues to address the challenge of inculturation. The sense of a global society is especially evident in the Church today. Should the liturgy strive for such uniformity that marked the Church's worship after the Tridentine Reform of the sixteenth century, or should the Church find new ways to appreciate and embrace the rich diversity of the catholic (small c, "universal") Church? Should worship be a melting pot where all the cultures blend, or should the gathered assembly form an elaborate mosaic, in which each piece is distinct yet forms part of a whole? In light of a society that is often marked by increasing secularism, materialism, and individualism, perhaps the Church should be taking a fresh approach to the question of inculturation: How can the liturgy shape culture?

In conclusion, the *Constitution on the Sacred Liturgy* itself presents the context and the motivation for the work of the reform of the liturgy, and these remain in force as ever today:

> This sacred Council has several aims in view: it desires to impart an ever increasing vigor to the Christian life of the faithful; to adapt more suitably to the needs of our own times those institutions that are subject to change; to foster whatever can promote union among all who believe in Christ; to strengthen whatever can help to call the whole of humanity into the household of the Church.[9]

The disciples on the road to Emmaus provide a model for the Church as it celebrates the liturgy.[10] Their journey was difficult: they were downcast as they went, and in their grief they probably didn't have much sense of where they were. In that moment Christ came and walked with them. He listened, he spoke, and he renewed their zeal giving them new direction. The Church experiences that same need and for the Lord and hunger for Eucharist so that it may be strengthened for mission. In this way the *Constitution* is a strong reminder of what the liturgy must be, and remains as relevant today as it did when it launched the reform of the liturgy fifty years ago.

---

8. See CSL, 37.
9. Ibid., 1.
10. See Luke 24:13–35.

OUTLINE

CONSTITUTION ON THE SACRED LITURGY
SACROSANCTUM CONCILIUM

1.   This Sacred Council has several aims in view: it desires to impart an ever increasing vigor to the Christian life of the faithful; to adapt more suitably to the needs of our own times those institutions that are subject to change; to foster whatever can promote union among all who believe in Christ; to strengthen whatever can help to call the whole of humanity into the household of the Church. The Council therefore sees particularly cogent reasons for undertaking the reform and promotion of the liturgy.

2.   For the liturgy, "making the work of our redemption a present actuality,"[1] most of all in the divine sacrifice of the eucharist, is the outstanding means whereby the faithful may express in their lives and manifest to others the mystery of Christ and the real nature of the true Church. It is of the essence of the Church to be both human and divine, visible yet endowed with invisible resources, eager to act yet intent on contemplation, present in this world yet not at home in it; and the Church is all these things in such wise that in it the human is directed and subordinated to the divine, the visible likewise to the invisible, action to contemplation, and this present world to that city yet to come which we seek.[2] While the liturgy daily builds up those who are within into a holy temple of the Lord, into a dwelling place for God in the Spirit,[3] to the mature measure of the fullness of Christ,[4] at the same time it marvelously strengthens their power to preach Christ and thus shows forth the Church to those who are outside as a sign lifted up among the nations,[5] under which the scattered children of God may be gathered together,[6] until there is one sheepfold and one shepherd.[7]

3.   Wherefore the Council judges that the following principles concerning the promotion and reform of the liturgy should be called to mind and practical norms established.

Among these principles and norms there are some that can and should be applied both to the Roman Rite and also to all the other rites. The practical norms that follow, however, should be taken as applying only to the Roman Rite, except for those that, in the very nature of things, affect other rites as well.

---

1. RomM, prayer over the gifts, Holy Thursday and 2d Sunday in Ordinary Time.
2. See Heb 13:14.
3. See Eph 2:21–22.
4. See Eph 4:13.
5. See Is 11:12.
6. See Jn 11:52.
7. See Jn 10:16.

4.   Lastly, in faithful obedience to tradition, the Council declares that the Church holds all lawfully acknowledged rites to be of equal right and dignity and wishes to preserve them in the future and to foster them in every way. The Council also desires that, where necessary, the rites be revised carefully in the light of sound tradition and that they be given new vigor to meet the circumstances and needs of modern times.

CHAPTER I
GENERAL PRINCIPLES FOR THE REFORM AND PROMOTION OF THE SACRED LITURGY

I. NATURE OF THE LITURGY AND ITS IMPORTANCE IN THE CHURCH'S LIFE

5.   God who "wills that all be saved and come to the knowledge of the truth" (1 Tm 2:4), "who in many and various ways spoke in times past to the fathers by the prophets" (Heb 1:1), when the fullness of time had come sent his Son, the Word made flesh, anointed by the Holy Spirit, to preach the Gospel to the poor, to heal the contrite of heart;[1] he is "the physician, being both flesh and of the Spirit,"[2] the mediator between God and us.[3] For his humanity, united with the person of the Word, was the instrument of our salvation. Therefore in Christ "the perfect achievement of our reconciliation came forth and the fullness of divine worship was given to us.[4]

The wonderful works of God among the people of the Old Testament were a prelude to the work of Christ the Lord. He achieved his task of redeeming humanity and giving perfect glory to God, principally by the paschal mystery of his blessed passion, resurrection from the dead, and glorious ascension, whereby "dying, he destroyed our death and, rising, he restored our life."[5] For it was from the side of Christ as he slept the sleep of death upon the cross that there came forth the sublime sacrament of the whole Church.[6]

6.   As Christ was sent by the Father, he himself also sent the apostles, filled with the Holy Spirit. Their mission was, first, by preaching the Gospel to every creature,[7] to proclaim that by his death and resurrection Christ has freed us from Satan's grip[8] and brought us into the Father's kingdom. But the work they

---

1. See Is 61:1; Lk 4:18.
2. Ignatius of Antioch, *To the Ephesians* 7, 2.
3. See 1 Tm 2:5.
4. *Sacramentarium Veronense* (ed. Mohlberg), no. 1265.
5. RomM, preface I of Easter.
6. RomM, prayer after the seventh reading, Easter Vigil.
7. See Mk 16:15.
8. See Acts 26:18.

preached they were also to bring into effect through the sacrifice and the sacraments, the center of the whole liturgical life. Thus by baptism all are plunged into the paschal mystery of Christ: they die with him, are buried with him, and rise with him;[9] they receive the spirit of adoption as children "in which we cry: Abba, Father" (Rom 8:15), and thus become true adorers whom the Father seeks.[10] In like manner, as often as they eat the supper of the Lord they proclaim the death of the Lord until he comes.[11] For that reason, on the very day of Pentecost when the Church appeared before the world, "those who received the word" of Peter "were baptized." And "they continued steadfastly in the teaching of the apostles and in the communion of the breaking of bread and in prayers . . . praising God and being in favor with all the people" (Acts 2:41–47). From that time onward the Church has never failed to come together to celebrate the paschal mystery: reading those things "which were in all the Scriptures concerning him" (Lk 24:27); celebrating the eucharist, in which "the victory and triumph of his death are again made present";[12] and at the same time giving thanks "to God for his inexpressible gift" (2 Cor 9:15) in Christ Jesus, "in praise of his glory" (Eph 1:12), through the power of the Holy Spirit.

7.   To accomplish so great a work, Christ is always present in his Church, especially in its liturgical celebrations. He is present in the sacrifice of the Mass, not only in the person of his minister, "the same now offering, through the ministry of priests, who formerly offered himself on the cross,"[13] but especially under the eucharistic elements. By his power he is present in the sacraments, so that when a man baptizes it is really Christ himself who baptizes.[14] He is present in his word, since it is he himself who speaks when the holy Scriptures are read in the Church. He is present, lastly, when the Church prays and sings, for he promised: "Where two or three are gathered together in my name, there am I in the midst of them" (Mt 18:20).

Christ always truly associates the Church with himself in this great work wherein God is perfectly glorified and the recipients made holy. The Church is the Lord's beloved Bride who calls to him and through him offers worship to the eternal Father.

Rightly, then, the liturgy is considered as an exercise of the priestly office of Jesus Christ. In the liturgy, by means of signs perceptible to the senses, human sanctification is signified and brought about in ways proper to each of these signs; in the liturgy the whole public worship is performed by the Mystical Body of Jesus Christ, that is, by the Head and his members.

From this it follows that every liturgical celebration, because it is an action of Christ the Priest and of his Body which is the Church, is a sacred action surpassing

---

9. See Rom 6:4; Eph 2:6; Col 3:1.

10. See Jn 4:23.

11. See 1 Cor 11:26.

12. Council of Trent, sess. 13, 11 Oct 1551, *Decree on the Holy Eucharist*, chap. 5.

13. Council of Trent, sess. 22, 17 Sept 1562, *Doctrine on the Holy Sacrifice of the Mass*, chap. 2.

14. See Augustine, *In Ioannis Evangelium Tractatus 6*, chap. 1, n. 7.

all others; no other action of the Church can equal its effectiveness by the same title and to the same degree.

8.   In the earthly liturgy we take part in a foretaste of that heavenly liturgy celebrated in the holy city of Jerusalem toward which we journey as pilgrims, where Christ is sitting at the right hand of God, a minister of the holies and of the true tabernacle;[15] we sing a hymn to the Lord's glory with the whole company of heaven; venerating the memory of the saints, we hope for some part and fellowship with them; we eagerly await the Savior, our Lord Jesus Christ, until he, our life, shall appear and we too will appear with him in glory.[16]

9.   The liturgy does not exhaust the entire activity of the Church. Before people can come to the liturgy they must be called to faith and to conversion: "How then are they to call upon him in whom they have not yet believed? But how are they to believe him whom they have not heard? And how are they to hear if no one preaches? And how are men to preach unless they be sent?" (Rom 10:14–15).

Therefore the Church announces the good tidings of salvation to those who do not believe, so that all may know the true God and Jesus Christ whom he has sent and may be converted from their ways, doing penance.[17] To believers, also, the Church must ever preach faith and penance, prepare them for the sacraments, teach them to observe all that Christ has commanded,[18] and invite them to all the works of charity, worship, and the apostolate. For all these works make it clear that Christ's faithful, though not of this world, are to be the light of the world and to glorify the Father in the eyes of all.

10.   Still, the liturgy is the summit toward which the activity of the Church is directed; at the same time it is the fount from which all the Church's power flows. For the aim and object of apostolic works is that all who are made children of God by faith and baptism should come together to praise God in the midst of his Church, to take part in the sacrifice, and to eat the Lord's Supper.

The liturgy in its turn moves the faithful, filled with "the paschal sacraments," to be "one in holiness";[19] it prays that "they may hold fast in their lives to what they have grasped by their faith";[20] the renewal in the eucharist of the covenant between the Lord and his people draws the faithful into the compelling love of Christ and sets them on fire. From the liturgy, therefore, particularly the eucharist, grace is poured forth upon us as from a fountain; the liturgy is the source for achieving in the most effective way possible human sanctification and God's glorification, the end to which all the Church's other activities are directed.

---

15. See Rv. 21:2; Col 3:1; Heb 8:2.
16. See Phil 3:20; Col 3:4.
17. See Jn 17:3; Lk 24:47; Acts 2:38.
18. See Mt 28:20.
19. RomM, prayer after communion, Easter Vigil.
20. RomM, opening prayer, Mass for Monday of Easter Week.

11.   But in order that the liturgy may possess its full effectiveness, it is necessary that the faithful come to it with proper dispositions, that their minds be attuned to their voices, and that they cooperate with divine grace, lest they receive it in vain.[21] Pastors must therefore realize that when the liturgy is celebrated something more is required than the mere observance of the laws governing valid and lawful celebration; it is also their duty to ensure that the faithful take part fully aware of what they are doing, actively engaged in the rite, and enriched by its effects.

12.   The spiritual life, however, is not limited solely to participation in the liturgy. Christians are indeed called to pray in union with each other, but they must also enter into their chamber to pray to the Father in secret;[22] further, according to the teaching of the Apostle, they should pray without ceasing.[23] We learn from the same Apostle that we must always bear about in our body the dying of Jesus, so that the life also of Jesus may be made manifest in our bodily frame.[24] This is why we ask the Lord in the sacrifice of the Mass that "receiving the offering of the spiritual victim," he may fashion us for himself "as an eternal gift."[25]

13.   Popular devotions of the Christian people are to be highly endorsed, provided they accord with the laws and norms of the Church, above all when they are ordered by the Apostolic See.

Devotions proper to particular Churches also have a special dignity if they are undertaken by mandate of the bishops according to customs or books lawfully approved.

But these devotions should be so fashioned that they harmonize with the liturgical seasons, accord with the sacred liturgy, are in some way derived from it, and lead the people to it, since, in fact, the liturgy, by its very nature far surpasses any of them.

II. PROMOTION OF LITURGICAL INSTRUCTION AND ACTIVE PARTICIPATION

14.   The Church earnestly desires that all the faithful be led to that full, conscious, and active participation in liturgical celebrations called for by the very nature of the liturgy. Such participation by the Christian people as "a chosen race, a royal priesthood, a holy nation, God's own people" (1 Pt 2:9; see 2:4–5) is their right and duty by reason of their baptism.

In the reform and promotion of the liturgy, this full and active participation by all the people is the aim to be considered before all else. For it is the primary and indispensable source from which the faithful are to derive the true

---

21. See 2 Cor 6:1.
22. See Mt 6:6.
23. See 1 Thes 5:17.
24. See 2 Cor 4:10 –11.
25. RomM, prayer over the gifts, Saturday after the 2d, 4th, and 6th Sundays of Easter.

Christian spirit and therefore pastors must zealously strive in all their pastoral work to achieve such participation by means of the necessary instruction.

Yet it would be futile to entertain any hopes of realizing this unless, in the first place, the pastors themselves become thoroughly imbued with the spirit and power of the liturgy and make themselves its teachers. A prime need, therefore, is that attention be directed, first of all, to the liturgical formation of the clergy. Wherefore the Council has decided to enact what follows.

15.   Professors appointed to teach liturgy in seminaries, religious houses of study, and theological faculties must be thoroughly trained for their work in institutes specializing in this subject.

16.   The study of liturgy is to be ranked among the compulsory and major courses in seminaries and religious houses of studies; in theological faculties it is to rank among the principal courses. It is to be taught under its theological, historical, spiritual, pastoral, and canonical aspects. Moreover, other professors, while striving to expound the mystery of Christ and the history of salvation from the angle proper to each of their own subjects, must nevertheless do so in a way that will clearly bring out the connection between their subjects and the liturgy, as also the underlying unity of all priestly training. This consideration is especially important for professors of dogmatic, spiritual, and pastoral theology and for professors of holy Scripture.

17.   In seminaries and houses of religious, clerics shall be given a liturgical formation in their spiritual life. The means for this are: proper guidance so that they may be able to understand the sacred rites and take part in them whole-heartedly; the actual celebration of the sacred mysteries and of other, popular devotions imbued with the spirit of the liturgy. In addition they must learn how to observe the liturgical laws, so that life in seminaries and houses of religious may be thoroughly permeated by the spirit of the liturgy.

18.   Priests, both secular and religious, who are already working in the Lord's vineyard are to be helped by every suitable means to understand ever more fully what it is they are doing in their liturgical functions; they are to be aided to live the liturgical life and to share it with the faithful entrusted to their care.

19.   With zeal and patience pastors must promote the liturgical instruction of the faithful and also their active participation in the liturgy both internally and externally, taking into account their age and condition, their way of life, and their stage of religious development. By doing so, pastors will be fulfilling one of their chief duties as faithful stewards of the mysteries of God; and in this matter they must lead their flock not only by word but also by example.

20.   Radio and television broadcasts of sacred rites must be marked by discretion and dignity, under the leadership and direction of a competent person appointed for this office by the bishops. This is especially important when the service to be broadcast is the Mass.

III. THE REFORM OF THE SACRED LITURGY

21. In order that the Christian people may more surely derive an abundance of graces from the liturgy, the Church desires to undertake with great care a general reform of the liturgy itself. For the liturgy is made up of immutable elements, divinely instituted, and of elements subject to change. These not only may but ought to be changed with the passage of time if they have suffered from the intrusion of anything out of harmony with the inner nature of the liturgy or have become pointless.

In this reform both texts and rites should be so drawn up that they express more clearly the holy things they signify and that the Christian people, as far as possible, are able to understand them with ease and to take part in the rites fully, actively, and as befits a community.

Wherefore the Council establishes tbe general norms that follow.

A. General Norms

22. § 1. Regulation of the liturgy depends solely on the authority of the Church, that is, on the Apostolic See and, accordingly as the law determines, on the bishop.

§ 2. In virtue of power conceded by the law, the regulation of the liturgy within certain defined limits belongs also to various kinds of competent territorial bodies of bishops lawfully established.

§ 3. Therefore, no other person, not even if he is a priest, may on his own add, remove, or change anything in the liturgy.

23. That sound tradition may be retained and yet the way remain open to legitimate progress, a careful investigation is always to be made into each part of the liturgy to be revised. This investigation should be theological, historical, and pastoral. Also the general laws governing the structure and meaning of the liturgy must be studied in conjunction with the experience derived from recent liturgical reforms and from the indults conceded to various places. Finally, there must be no innovations unless the good of the Church genuinely and certainly requires them; care must be taken that any new forms adopted should in some way grow organically from forms already existing.

As far as possible, marked differences between the rites used in neighboring regions must be carefully avoided.

24. Sacred Scripture is of the greatest importance in the celebration of the liturgy. For it is from Scripture that the readings are given and explained in the homily and that psalms are sung; the prayers, collects, and liturgical songs are scriptural in their inspiration; it is from the Scriptures that actions and signs derive their meaning. Thus to achieve the reform, progress, and adaptation of the liturgy, it is essential to promote that warm and living love for Scripture to which the venerable tradition of both Eastern and Western rites gives testimony.

25.   The liturgical books are to be revised as soon as possible; experts are to be employed in this task and bishops from various parts of the world are to be consulted.

B. Norms Drawn from the Hierarchic and Communal Nature of the Liturgy

26.   Liturgical services are not private functions, but are celebrations belonging to the Church, which is the "sacrament of unity," namely, the holy people united and ordered under their bishops.[26]

Therefore liturgical services involve the whole Body of the Church; they manifest it and have effects upon it; but they also concern the individual members of the Church in different ways, according to their different orders, offices, and actual participation.

27.   Whenever rites, according to their specific nature, make provision for communal celebration involving the presence and active participation of the faithful, it is to be stressed that this way of celebrating them is to be preferred, as far as possible, to a celebration that is individual and, so to speak, private.

This applies with special force to the celebration of Mass and the administration of the sacraments, even though every Mass has of itself a public and social character.

28.   In liturgical celebrations each one, minister or layperson, who has an office to perform, should do all of, but only, those parts which pertain to that office by the nature of the rite and the principles of liturgy.

29.   Servers, readers, commentators, and members of the choir also exercise a genuine liturgical function. They ought to discharge their office, therefore, with the sincere devotion and decorum demanded by so exalted a ministry and rightly expected of them by God's people.

Consequently, they must all be deeply imbued with the spirit of the liturgy, in the measure proper to each one, and they must be trained to perform their functions in a correct and orderly manner.

30.   To promote active participation, the people should be encouraged to take part by means of acclamations, responses, psalmody, antiphons, and songs, as well as by actions, gestures, and bearing. And at the proper times all should observe a reverent silence.

31.   The revision of the liturgical books must ensure that the rubrics make provision for the parts belonging to the people.

32.   The liturgy makes distinctions between persons according to their liturgical function and sacred orders and there are liturgical laws providing for due honors to be given to civil authorities. Apart from these instances, no special

---

26. Cyprian, *On the Unity of the Catholic Church* 7; see *Letter 66*, n. 8, 3.

honors are to be paid in the liturgy to any private persons or classes of persons, whether in the ceremonies or by external display.

C. Norms Based on the Teaching and Pastoral Character of the Liturgy

33. Although the liturgy is above all things the worship of the divine majesty, it likewise contains rich instruction for the faithful.[27] For in the liturgy God is speaking to his people and Christ is still proclaiming his gospel. And the people are responding to God by both song and prayer.

Moreover, the prayers addressed to God by the priest, who presides over the assembly in the person of Christ, are said in the name of the entire holy people and of all present. And the visible signs used by the liturgy to signify invisible divine realities have been chosen by Christ or the Church. Thus not only when things are read "that were written for our instruction" (Rom 15:4), but also when the Church prays or sings or acts, the faith of those taking part is nourished and their minds are raised to God, so that they may offer him their worship as intelligent beings and receive his grace more abundantly.

In the reform of the liturgy, therefore, the following general norms are to be observed.

34. The rites should be marked by a noble simplicity; they should be short, clear, and unencumbered by useless repetitions; they should be within the people's powers of comprehension and as a rule not require much explanation.

35. That the intimate connection between words and rites may stand out clearly in the liturgy:

1. In sacred celebrations there is to be more reading from holy Scripture and it is to be more varied and apposite.

2. Because the spoken word is part of the liturgical service, the best place for it, consistent with the nature of the rite, is to be indicated even in the rubrics; the ministry of preaching is to be fulfilled with exactitude and fidelity. Preaching should draw its content mainly from scriptural and liturgical sources, being a proclamation of God's wonderful works in the history of salvation, the mystery of Christ, ever present and active within us, especially in the celebration of the liturgy.

3. A more explicitly liturgical catechesis should also be given in a variety of ways. Within the rites themselves provision is to be made for brief comments, when needed, by the priest or a qualified minister; they should occur only at the more suitable moments and use a set formula or something similar.

4. Bible services should be encouraged, especially on the vigils of the more solemn feasts, on some weekdays in Advent and Lent, and on Sundays and holy days. They are particularly to be recommended in places where no priest is available; when this is the case, a deacon or some other person authorized by the bishop is to preside over the celebration.

---

27. See Council of Trent, sess. 22, 17 Sept 1562, *Doctrine on the Holy Sacrifice of the Mass,* chap. 8.

36. § 1. Particular law remaining in force, the use of the Latin language is to be preserved in the Latin rites.

§ 2. But since the use of the mother tongue, whether in the Mass, the administration of the sacraments, or other parts of the liturgy, frequently may be of great advantage to the people, the limits of its use may be extended. This will apply in the first place to the readings and instructions and to some prayers and chants, according to the regulations on this matter to be laid down for each case in subsequent chapters.

§ 3. Respecting such norms and also, where applicable, consulting the bishops of nearby territories of the same language, the competent, territorial ecclesiastical authority mentioned in art. 22, §2 is empowered to decide whether and to what extent the vernacular is to be used. The enactments of the competent authority are to be approved, that is, confirmed by the Holy See.

§ 4. Translations from the Latin text into the mother tongue intended for use in the liturgy must be approved by the competent, territorial ecclesiastical authority already mentioned.

D. Norms for Adapting the Liturgy to the Culture and Traditions of Peoples

37. Even in the liturgy the Church has no wish to impose a rigid uniformity in matters that do not affect the faith or the good of the whole community; rather, the Church respects and fosters the genius and talents of the various races and peoples. The Church considers with sympathy and, if possible, preserves intact the elements in these peoples' way of life that are not indissolubly bound up with superstition and error. Sometimes in fact the Church admits such elements into the liturgy itself, provided they are in keeping with the true and authentic spirit of the liturgy.

38. Provisions shall also be made, even in the revision of liturgical books, for legitimate variations and adaptations to different groups, regions, and peoples, especially in mission lands, provided the substantial unity of the Roman Rite is preserved; this should be borne in mind when rites are drawn up and rubrics devised.

39. Within the limits set by the *editio typica* of the liturgical books, it shall be for the competent, territorial ecclesiastical authority mentioned in art. 22, §2 to specify adaptations, especially in the case of the administration of the sacraments, the sacramentals, processions, liturgical language, sacred music, and the arts. This, however, is to be done in accord with the fundamental norms laid down in this Constitution.

40. In some places and circumstances, however, an even more radical adaptation of the liturgy is needed and this entails greater difficulties. Wherefore:

1. The competent, territorial ecclesiastical authority mentioned in art. 22, §2, must, in this matter, carefully and prudently weigh what elements from the traditions and culture of individual peoples may be appropriately admitted into

divine worship. They are to propose to the Apostolic See adaptations considered useful or necessary that will be introduced with its consent.

2. To ensure that adaptations are made with all the circumspection they demand, the Apostolic See will grant power to this same territorial ecclesiastical authority to permit and to direct, as the case requires, the necessary preliminary experiments within certain groups suited for the purpose and for a fixed time.

3. Because liturgical laws often involve special difficulties with respect to adaptation, particularly in mission lands, experts in these matters must be employed to formulate them.

IV. PROMOTION OF LITURGICAL LIFE IN DIOCESE AND PARISH

41. The bishop is to be looked on as the high priest of his flock, the faithful's life in Christ in some way deriving from and depending on him.

Therefore all should hold in great esteem the liturgical life of the diocese centered around the bishop, especially in his cathedral church; they must be convinced that the preeminent manifestation of the Church is present in the full, active participation of all God's holy people in these liturgical celebrations, especially in the same eucharist, in a single prayer, at one altar at which the bishop presides, surrounded by his college of priests and by his ministers.[28]

42. But because it is impossible for the bishop always and everywhere to preside over the whole flock in his Church, he cannot do otherwise than establish lesser groupings of the faithful. Among these the parishes, set up locally under a pastor taking the place of the bishop, are the most important: in some manner they represent the visible Church established throughout the world.

And therefore both in attitude and in practice the liturgical life of the parish and its relationship to the bishop must be fostered among the faithful and clergy; efforts must also be made toward a lively sense of community within the parish, above all in the shared celebration of the Sunday Mass.

V. PROMOTION OF PASTORAL-LITURGICAL ACTION

43. Zeal for the promotion and restoration of the liturgy is rightly held to be a sign of the providential dispositions of God in our time, a movement of the Holy Spirit in his Church. Today it is a distinguishing mark of the Church's life, indeed of the whole tenor of contemporary religious thought and action.

So that this pastoral-liturgical action may become even more vigorous in the Church, the Council decrees what follows.

44. It is advisable that the competent, territorial ecclesiastical authority mentioned in art. 22, §2 set up a liturgical commission, to be assisted by experts in

---

28. See Ignatius of Antioch, *To the Magnesians*, 7; *To the Philadelphians*, 4; *To the Smyrnians*, 8.

liturgical science, music, art, and pastoral practice. As far as possible the commission should be aided by some kind of institute for pastoral liturgy, consisting of persons eminent in these matters and including the laity as circumstances suggest. Under the direction of the aforementioned territorial ecclesiastical authority, the commission is to regulate pastoral-liturgical action throughout the territory and to promote studies and necessary experiments whenever there is question of adaptations to be proposed to the Apostolic See.

45.   For the same reason every diocese is to have a commission on the liturgy, under the direction of the bishop, for promoting the liturgical apostolate.

Sometimes it may be advisable for several dioceses to form among themselves one single commission, in order to promote the liturgy by means of shared consultation.

46.   Besides the commission on the liturgy, every diocese, as far as possible, should have commissions for music and art.

These three commissions must work in closest collaboration; indeed it will often be best to fuse the three of them into one single commission.

CHAPTER II
THE MOST SACRED MYSTERY OF THE EUCHARIST

47.   At the Last Supper, on the night when he was betrayed, our Savior instituted the eucharistic sacrifice of his body and blood. He did this in order to perpetuate the sacrifice of the cross throughout the centuries until he should come again and in this way to entrust to his beloved Bride, the Church, a memorial of his death and resurrection: a sacrament of love, a sign of unity, a bond of charity,[1] a paschal banquet "in which Christ is eaten, the heart is filled with grace, and a pledge of future glory given to us."[2]

48.   The Church, therefore, earnestly desires that Christ's faithful, when present at this mystery of faith, should not be there as strangers or silent spectators; on the contrary, through a good understanding of the rites and prayers they should take part in the sacred service conscious of what they are doing, with devotion and full involvement. They should be instructed by God's word and be nourished at the table of the Lord's body; they should give thanks to God; by offering the immaculate Victim, not only through the hands of the priest, but also with him, they should learn to offer themselves as well; through Christ the Mediator,[3] they should be formed day by day into an ever more perfect unity with God and with each other, so that finally God may be all in all.

---

1. See Augustine, *In Ioannis Evangelium Tractatus 36*, chap. 6, n. 13.
2. Liturgy of the Hours, antiphon for Canticle of Mary, evening prayer II, feast of Corpus Christi.
3. See Cyril of Alexandria, *Commentary on the Gospel of John*, book 11, chap. 11–12.

49.   Thus, mindful of those Masses celebrated with the assistance of the faithful, especially on Sundays and holy days of obligation, the Council makes the following decrees in order that the sacrifice of the Mass, even in its ritual forms, may become pastorally effective to the utmost degree.

50.   The Order of Mass is to be revised in a way that will bring out more clearly the intrinsic nature and purpose of its several parts, as also the connection between them, and will more readily achieve the devout, active participation of the faithful.

For this purpose the rites are to be simplified, due care being taken to preserve their substance; elements that, with the passage of time, came to be duplicated or were added with but little advantage are now to be discarded; other elements that have suffered injury through accident of history are now, as may seem useful or necessary, to be restored to the vigor they had in the traditions of the Fathers.

51.   The treasures of the Bible are to be opened up more lavishly, so that a richer share in God's word may be provided for the faithful. In this way a more representative portion of holy Scripture will be read to the people in the course of a prescribed number of years.

52.   By means of the homily the mysteries of the faith and the guiding principles of the Christian life are expounded from the sacred text during the course of the liturgical year; as part of the liturgy itself therefore, the homily is strongly recommended; in fact, at Masses celebrated with the assistance of the people on Sundays and holy days of obligation it is not to be omitted except for a serious reason.

53.   Especially on Sundays and holy days of obligation there is to be restored, after the gospel and the homily, "the universal prayer" or "the prayer of the faithful." By this prayer, in which the people are to take part, intercession shall be made for holy Church, for the civil authorities, for those oppressed by various needs, for all people, and for the salvation of the entire world.[4]

54.   With art. 36 of this Constitution as the norm, in Masses celebrated with the people a suitable place may be allotted to their mother tongue. This is to apply in the first place to the readings and "the universal prayer," but also, as local conditions may warrant, to those parts belonging to the people.

Nevertheless steps should be taken enabling the faithful to say or to sing together in Latin those parts of the Ordinary of the Mass belonging to them.

Wherever a more extended use of the mother tongue within the Mass appears desirable, the regulation laid down in art. 40 of this Constitution is to be observed.

55.   That more complete form of participation in the Mass by which the faithful, after the priest's communion, receive the Lord's body from the sacrifice, is strongly endorsed.

---

4. See 1 Tm 2:1–2.

The dogmatic principles laid down by the Council of Trent remain intact.[5] In instances to be specified by the Apostolic See, however, communion under both kinds may be granted both to clerics and religious and to the laity at the discretion of the bishops, for example, to the ordained at the Mass of their ordination, to the professed at the Mass of their religious profession, to the newly baptized at the Mass following their baptism.

56.   The two parts that, in a certain sense, go to make up the Mass, namely, the liturgy of the word and the liturgy of the eucharist, are so closely connected with each other that they form but one single act of worship. Accordingly this Council strongly urges pastors that in their catechesis they insistently teach the faithful to take part in the entire Mass, especially on Sundays and holy days of obligation.

57.   § 1. Concelebration, which aptly expresses the unity of the priesthood, has continued to this day as a practice in the Church of both East and West. For this reason it has seemed good to the Council to extend permission for concelebration to the following cases:

    1. a. on Holy Thursday, both the chrism Mass and the evening Mass;

       b. Masses during councils, bishops' conferences, and synods;

       c. the Mass at the blessing of an abbot.

    2. Also, with permission of the Ordinary, who is the one to decide whether concelebration is opportune, to:

       a. the conventual Mass and the principal Mass in churches, when the needs of the faithful do not require that all the priests on hand celebrate individually;

       b. Masses celebrated at any kind of meeting of priests, whether secular or religious.

    § 2. 1. The regulation, however, of the discipline of concelebration in the diocese pertains to the bishop.

       2. This, however, does not take away the option of every priest to celebrate Mass individually, not, however, at the same time and in the same church as a concelebrated Mass or on Holy Thursday.

58.   A new rite for concelebration is to be drawn up and inserted into the Roman Pontifical and Roman Missal.

---

5. Council of Trent, sess. 21, *Doctrine on Communion under Both Species*, chap. 1–3.

CHAPTER III
THE OTHER SACRAMENTS AND THE SACRAMENTALS

59.   The purpose of the sacraments is to make people holy, to build up the Body of Christ, and, finally, to give worship to God; but being signs they also have a teaching function. They not only presuppose faith, but by words and objects they also nourish, strengthen, and express it; that is why they are called "sacraments of faith." They do indeed impart grace, but, in addition, the very act of celebrating them disposes the faithful most effectively to receive this grace in a fruitful manner, to worship God rightly, and to practice charity.

It is therefore of the highest importance that the faithful should readily understand the sacramental signs and should with great eagerness frequent those sacraments that were instituted to nourish the Christian life.

60.   The Church has, in addition, instituted sacramentals. These are sacred signs bearing a kind of resemblance to the sacraments: they signify effects, particularly of a spiritual kind, that are obtained through the Church's intercession. They dispose people to receive the chief effect of the sacraments and they make holy various occasions in human life.

61.   Thus, for well-disposed members of the faithful, the effect of the liturgy of the sacraments and sacramentals is that almost every event in their lives is made holy by divine grace that flows from the paschal mystery of Christ's passion, death, and resurrection, the fount from which all sacraments and sacramentals draw their power. The liturgy means also that there is hardly any proper use of material things that cannot thus be directed toward human sanctification and the praise of God.

62.   With the passage of time, however, certain features have crept into the rites of the sacraments and sacramentals that have made their nature and purpose less clear to the people of today; hence some changes have become necessary as adaptations to the needs of our own times. For this reason the Council decrees what follows concerning the revision of these rites.

63.   Because the use of the mother tongue in the administration of the sacraments and sacramentals can often be of considerable help for the people, this use is to be extended according to the following norms:

a. With art. 36 as the norm, the vernacular may be used in administering the sacraments and sacramentals.

b. Particular rituals in harmony with the new edition of the Roman Ritual shall be prepared without delay by the competent, territorial ecclesiastical authority mentioned in art. 22, §2 of this Constitution. These rituals are to be adapted, even in regard to the language employed, to the needs of the different regions. Once they have been reviewed by the Apostolic See, they are to be used in the regions for which they have been prepared. But those who draw up these rituals or particular collections of rites must not leave out the prefatory instructions for the individual rites in the Roman Ritual, whether the instructions are pastoral and rubrical or have some special social bearing.

64.   The catechumenate for adults, divided into several stages, is to be restored and put into use at the discretion of the local Ordinary. By this means the time of the catechumentate, which is intended as a period of well-suited instruction, may be sanctified by sacred rites to be celebrated at successive intervals of time.

65.   With art. 37–40 of this Constitution as the norm, it is lawful in mission lands to allow, besides what is part of Christian tradition, those initiation elements in use among individual peoples, to the extent that such elements are compatible with the Christian rite of initiation.

66.   Both of the rites for the baptism of adults are to be revised: not only the simpler rite, but also the more solemn one, with proper attention to the restored catechumenate. A special Mass "On the Occasion of a Baptism" is to be incorporated into the Roman Missal.

67.   The rite for the baptism of infants is to be revised and it should be suited to the fact that those to be baptized are infants. The roles as well as the obligations of parents and godparents should be brought out more clearly in the rite itself.

68.   The baptismal rite should contain alternatives, to be used at the discretion of the local Ordinary, for occasions when a very large number are to be baptized together. Moreover, a shorter rite is to be drawn up, especially in mission lands, for use by catechists, but also by the faithful in general, when there is danger of death and neither a priest nor a deacon is available.

69.   In place of the rite called the "Order of Supplying What Was Omitted in the Baptism of an Infant," a new rite is to be drawn up. This should manifest more clearly and fittingly that an infant who was baptized by the short rite has already been received into the Church.

Similarly, a new rite is to be drawn up for converts who have already been validly baptized; it should express that they are being received into the communion of the Church.

70.   Except during the Easter season, baptismal water may be blessed within the rite of baptism itself by use of an approved, shorter formulary.

71.   The rite of confirmation is also to be revised in order that the intimate connection of this sacrament with the whole of Christian initiation may stand out more clearly; for this reason it is fitting for candidates to renew their baptismal promises just before they are confirmed.

Confirmation may be conferred within Mass when convenient; as for the rite outside Mass, a formulary is to be composed for use as an introduction.

72.   The rite and formularies for the sacrament of penance are to be revised so that they more clearly express both the nature and effect of the sacrament.

73.   "Extreme unction," which may also and more properly be called "anointing of the sick," is not a sacrament for those only who are at the point of death. Hence, as soon as any one of the faithful begins to be in danger of death from sickness or old age, the fitting time for that person to receive this sacrament has certainly already arrived.

74.   In addition to the separate rites for anointing of the sick and for viaticum, a continuous rite shall be drawn up, structured so that the sick person is anointed after confessing and before receiving viaticum.

75.   The number of the anointings is to be adapted to the circumstances; the prayers that belong to the rite of anointing are to be so revised that they correspond to the varying conditions of the sick who receive the sacrament.

76.   Both the ceremonies and texts of the ordination rites are to be revised. The address given by the bishop at the beginning of each ordination or consecration may be in the vernacular.

When a bishop is consecrated, all the bishops present may take part in the laying on of hands.

77.   The marriage rite now found in the Roman Ritual is to be revised and enriched in such a way that it more clearly signifies the grace of the sacrament and imparts a knowledge of the obligations of spouses.

"If any regions follow other praiseworthy customs and ceremonies when celebrating the sacrament of marriage, the Council earnestly desires that by all means these be retained."[1]

Moreover, the competent, territorial ecclesiastical authority mentioned in art. 22, §2 of this Constitution is free to draw up, in accord with art. 63, its own rite, suited to the usages of place and people. But the rite must always conform to the law that the priest assisting at the marriage must ask for and obtain the consent of the contracting parties.

78.   Marriage is normally to be celebrated within Mass, after the reading of the gospel and the homily and before "the prayer of the faithful." The prayer for the bride, duly emended to remind both spouses of their equal obligation to remain faithful to each other, may be said in the vernacular.

But if the sacrament of marriage is celebrated apart from Mass, the epistle and gospel from the nuptial Mass are to be read at the beginning of the rite and the blessing is always to be given to the spouses.

79.   The sacramentals are to be reviewed in the light of the primary criterion that the faithful participate intelligently, actively, and easily; the conditions of our own days must also be considered. When rituals are revised, in accord with art. 63, new sacramentals may also be added as the need for them becomes apparent.

---

1. Council of Trent, sess. 24, *Decree on Reform*, chap. 1. See also RomR, title 8, chap. 2, n. 6.

Reserved blessings shall be very few; reservations shall be in favor only of bishops and Ordinaries.

Let provision be made that some sacramentals, at least in special circumstances and at the discretion of the Ordinary, may be administered by qualified laypersons.

80.   The rite for the consecration to a life of virginity as it exists in the Roman Pontifical is to be revised.

A rite of religious profession and renewal of vows shall be drawn up with a view to achieving greater unity, simplicity, and dignity. Apart from exceptions in particular law, this rite should be adopted by those who make their profession or renewal of vows within Mass.

Religious profession should preferably be made within Mass.

81.   The rite of funerals should express more clearly the paschal character of Christian death and should correspond more closely to the circumstances and traditions of various regions. This applies also to the liturgical color to be used.

82.   The rite for the burial of infants is to be revised and a special Mass for the occasion provided.

CHAPTER IV
DIVINE OFFICE

83.   Christ Jesus, High Priest of the new and eternal covenant, taking human nature, introduced into this earthly exile the hymn that is sung throughout all ages in the halls of heaven. He joins the entire human community to himself, associating it with his own singing of this canticle of divine praise.

For he continues his priestly work through the agency of his Church, which is unceasingly engaged in praising the Lord and interceding for the salvation of the whole world. The Church does this not only by celebrating the eucharist, but also in other ways, especially by praying the divine office.

84.   By tradition going back to early Christian times, the divine office is so arranged that the whole course of the day and night is made holy by the praises of God. Therefore, when this wonderful song of praise is rightly performed by priests and others who are deputed for this purpose by the Church's ordinance or by the faithful praying together with the priest in the approved form, then it is truly the voice of a bride addressing her bridegroom; it is the very prayer that Christ himself, together with his Body, addresses to the Father.

85.   Hence all who render this service are not only fulfilling a duty of the Church, but also are sharing in the greatest honor of Christ's Bride, for by offering these praises to God they are standing before God's throne in the name of the Church, their Mother.

86.   Priests engaged in the sacred pastoral ministry will offer the praises of the hours with greater fervor the more vividly they realize that they must heed St. Paul's exhortation: "Pray without ceasing" (1 Thes 5:17). For the work in which they labor will effect nothing and bring forth no fruit except by the power of the Lord who said: "Without me you can do nothing" (Jn 15:5). That is why the apostles, instituting deacons, said: "We will devote ourselves to prayer and to the ministry of the word" (Acts 6:4).

87.   In order that the divine office may be better and more completely carried out in existing circumstances, whether by priests or by other members of the Church, the Council, carrying further the restoration already so happily begun by the Apostolic Sec, has seen fit to decree what follows concerning the office of the Roman Rite.

88.   Because the purpose of the office is to sanctify the day, the traditional sequence of the hours is to be restored so that once again they may be genuinely related to the hour of the day when they are prayed, as far as it is possible. Moreover, it will be necessary to take into account the modern conditions in which daily life has to be lived, especially by those who are called to labor in apostolic works.

89.   Therefore, when the office is revised, these norms are to be observed:

a. By the venerable tradition of the universal Church, lauds as morning prayer and vespers as evening prayer are the two hinges on which the daily office turns; hence they are to be considered as the chief hours and celebrated as such.

b. Compline is to be so composed that it will be a suitable prayer for the end of the day.

c. The hour known as matins, although it should retain the character of nocturnal praise when celebrated in choir, shall be adapted so that it may be recited at any hour of the day; it shall be made up of fewer psalms and longer readings.

d. The hour of prime is to be suppressed.

e. In choir the minor hours of terce, sext, and none are to be observed. But outside choir it will be lawful to choose whichever of the three best suits the hour of the day.

90.   The divine office, because it is the public prayer of the Church, is a source of devotion and nourishment also for personal prayer. Therefore priests and all others who take part in the divine office are earnestly exhorted in the Lord to attune their minds to their voices when praying it. The better to achieve this, let them take steps to improve their understanding of the liturgy and of the Bible, especially the psalms.

In revising the Roman office, its ancient and venerable treasures are to be so adapted that all those to whom they are handed on may more fully and readily draw profit from them.

91.   So that it may really be possible in practice to observe the course of the hours proposed in art. 89, the psalms are no longer to be distributed over just one week, but over some longer period of time.

The work of revising the psalter, already happily begun, is to be finished as soon as possible and is to take into account the style of Christian Latin, the liturgical use of psalms, including their being sung, and the entire tradition of the Latin Church.

92.   As regards the readings, the following shall be observed:

a. Readings from sacred Scripture shall be arranged so that the riches of God's word may be easily accessible in more abundant measure.

b. Readings excerpted from the works of the Fathers, doctors, and ecclesiastical writers shall be better selected.

c. The accounts of the martyrdom or lives of the saints are to be made to accord with the historical facts.

93.   To whatever extent may seem advisable, the hymns are to be restored to their original form and any allusion to mythology or anything that conflicts with Christian piety is to be dropped or changed. Also, as occasion arises, let other selections from the treasury of hymns be incorporated.

94.   That the day may be truly sanctified and the hours themselves recited with spiritual advantage, it is best that each of them be prayed at a time most closely corresponding to the true time of each canonical hour.

95.   In addition to the conventual Mass, communities obliged to choral office are bound to celebrate the office in choir every day. In particular:

a. Orders of canons, of monks and of nuns, and of other regulars bound by law or constitutions to choral office must celebrate the entire office.

b. Cathedral or collegiate chapters are bound to recite those parts of the office imposed on them by general or particular law.

c. All members of the above communities who are in major orders or are solemnly professed, except for lay brothers, are bound individually to recite those canonical hours which they do not pray in choir.

96.   Clerics not bound to office in choir, if they are in major orders, are bound to pray the entire office every day, either in common or individually, following the norms in art. 89.

97.   Appropriate instances are to be defined by the rubrics in which a liturgical service may be substituted for the divine office.

In particular cases and for a just reason Ordinaries may dispense their subjects wholly or in part from the obligation of reciting the divine office or may commute it.

98.   Members of any institute dedicated to acquiring perfection who, according to their constitutions, are to recite any parts of the divine office are thereby performing the public prayer of the Church.

They too perform the public prayer of the Church who, in virtue of their constitutions, recite any little office, provided this has been drawn up after the pattern of the divine office and duly approved.

99.   Since the divine office is the voice of the Church, that is, of the whole Mystical Body publicly praising God, those clerics who are not obliged to office in choir, especially priests who live together or who meet together for any purpose, are urged to pray at least some part of the divine office in common.

All who pray the divine office, whether in choir or in common, should fulfill the task entrusted to them as perfectly as possible: this refers not only to the internal devotion of their minds but also to their external manner of celebration.

It is advantageous, moreover, that the office in choir and in common be sung when there is an opportunity to do so.

100. Pastors should see to it that the chief hours, especially vespers, are celebrated in common in church on Sundays and the more solemn feasts. The laity, too, are encouraged to recite the divine office either with the priests, or among themselves, or even individually.

101. § 1. In accordance with the centuries-old tradition of the Latin rite, clerics are to retain the Latin language in the divine office. But in individual cases the Ordinary has the power of granting the use of a vernacular translation, prepared in accord with art. 36, to those clerics for whom the use of Latin constitutes a grave obstacle to their praying the office properly.

§ 2. The competent superior has the power to grant the use of the vernacular in the celebration of the divine office, even in choir, to nuns and to members of institutes dedicated to acquiring perfection, both men who are not clerics and women. The version, however, must be one that has been approved.

§ 3. Any cleric bound to the divine office fulfills his obligation if he prays the office in the vernacular together with a group of the faithful or with those mentioned in §2, provided the text of the translation has been approved.

CHAPTER V
THE LITURGICAL YEAR

102. The Church is conscious that it must celebrate the saving work of the divine Bridegroom by devoutly recalling it on certain days throughout the course of the year. Every week, on the day which the Church has called the Lord's Day, it keeps the memory of the Lord's resurrection, which it also celebrates once in the year, together with his blessed passion, in the most solemn festival of Easter.

Within the cycle of a year, moreover, the Church unfolds the whole mystery of Christ, from his incarnation and birth until his ascension, the day of Pentecost, and the expectation of blessed hope and of the Lord's return.

Recalling thus the mysteries of redemption, the Church opens to the faithful the riches of the Lord's powers and merits, so that these are in some way made present in every age in order that the faithful may lay hold on them and be filled with saving grace.

103. In celebrating this annual cycle of Christ's mysteries, the Church honors with special love Mary, the Mother of God, who is joined by an inseparable bond to the saving work of her Son. In her the Church holds up and admires the most excellent effect of the redemption and joyfully contemplates, as in a flawless image, that which the Church itself desires and hopes wholly to be.

104. The Church has also included in the annual cycle days devoted to the memory of the martyrs and the other saints. Raised up to perfection by the manifold grace of God and already in possession of eternal salvation, they sing God's perfect praise in heaven and offer prayers for us. By celebrating their passage from earth to heaven the Church proclaims the paschal mystery achieved in the saints, who have suffered and been glorified with Christ; it proposes them to the faithful as examples drawing all to the Father through Christ and pleads through their merits for God's favors.

105. Finally, in the various seasons of the year and according to its traditional discipline, the Church completes the formation of the faithful by means of devout practices for soul and body, by instruction, prayer, and works of penance and of mercy.

Accordingly the sacred Council has seen fit to decree what follows.

106. By a tradition handed down from the apostles and having its origin from the very day of Christ's resurrection, the Church celebrates the paschal mystery every eighth day, which, with good reason, bears the name of the Lord's Day or Sunday. For on this day Christ's faithful must gather together so that, by hearing the word of God and taking part in the eucharist, they may call to mind the passion, the resurrection, and the glorification of the Lord Jesus and may thank God, who "has begotten them again unto a living hope through the resurrection of Jesus Christ from the dead" (1 Pt 1:3). Hence the Lord's Day is the first holy day of all and should be proposed to the devotion of the faithful and taught to them in such a way that it may become in fact a day of joy and of freedom from

work. Other celebrations, unless they be truly of greatest importance, shall not have precedence over the Sunday, the foundation and core of the whole liturgical year.

original feast

107. The liturgical year is to be so revised that the traditional customs and usages of the sacred seasons are preserved or restored to suit the conditions of modern times; their specific character is to be retained, so that they duly nourish the devotion of the faithful who celebrate the mysteries of Christian redemption and above all the paschal mystery. If certain adaptations are considered necessary on account of local conditions, they are to be made in accordance with the provisions of art. 39 and 40.

108. The minds of the faithful must be directed primarily toward those feasts of the Lord on which the mysteries of salvation are celebrated in the course of the year. Therefore, the Proper of Seasons shall be given the precedence due to it over the feasts of the saints, in order that the entire cycle of the mysteries of salvation may be celebrated in the measure due to them.

109. Lent is marked by two themes, the baptismal and the penitential. By recalling or preparing for baptism and by repentance, this season disposes the faithful, as they more diligently listen to the word of God and devote themselves to prayer, to celebrate the paschal mystery. The baptismal and penitential aspects of Lent are to be given greater prominence in both the liturgy and liturgical catechesis. Hence:

a. More use is to be made of the baptismal features proper to the Lenten liturgy; some of those from an earlier era are to be restored as may seem advisable.

b. The same is to apply to the penitential elements. As regards catechesis, it is important to impress on the minds of the faithful not only the social consequences of sin but also the essence of the virtue of penance, namely, detestation of sin as an offense against God; the role of the Church in penitential practices is not to be neglected and the people are to be exhorted to pray for sinners.

110. During Lent penance should be not only inward and individual, but also outward and social. The practice of penance should be fostered, however, in ways that are possible in our own times and in different regions and according to the circumstances of the faithful; it should be encouraged by the authorities mentioned in art. 22.

Nevertheless, let the paschal fast be kept sacred. Let it be observed everywhere on Good Friday and, where possible, prolonged throughout Holy Saturday, as a way of coming to the joys of the Sunday of the resurrection with uplifted and welcoming heart.

111. The saints have been traditionally honored in the Church and their authentic relics and images held in veneration. For the feasts of the saints proclaim the wonderful works of Christ in his servants and display to the faithful fitting examples for their imitation.

Lest the feasts of the saints take precedence over the feasts commemorating the very mysteries of salvation, many of them should be left to be celebrated by a particular Church or nation or religious family; those only should be extended to the universal Church that commemorate saints of truly universal significance.

CHAPTER VI
SACRED MUSIC

112. The musical tradition of the universal Church is a treasure of inestimable value, greater even than that of any other art. The main reason for this preeminence is that, as sacred song closely bound to the text, it forms a necessary or integral part of the solemn liturgy.

Holy Scripture itself has bestowed praise upon sacred song[1] and the same may be said of the Fathers of the Church and of the Roman pontiffs, who in recent times, led by St. Pius X, have explained more precisely the ministerial function supplied by sacred music in the service of the Lord.

Therefore sacred music will be the more holy the more closely it is joined to the liturgical rite, whether by adding delight to prayer, fostering oneness of spirit, or investing the rites with greater solemnity. But the Church approves of all forms of genuine art possessing the qualities required and admits them into divine worship.

Accordingly, the Council, keeping the norms and precepts of ecclesiastical tradition and discipline and having regard to the purpose of sacred music, which is the glory of God and the sanctification of the faithful, decrees what follows.

113. A liturgical service takes on a nobler aspect when the rites are celebrated with singing, the sacred ministers take their parts in them, and the faithful actively participate.

As regards the language to be used, the provisions of art. 36 are to be observed; for the Mass, those of art. 54; for the sacraments, those of art. 63; for the divine office, those of art. 101.

114. The treasure of sacred music is to be preserved and fostered with great care. Choirs must be diligently developed, especially in cathedral churches; but bishops and other pastors of souls must be at pains to ensure that whenever a liturgical service is to be celebrated with song, the whole assembly of the faithful is enabled, in keeping with art. 28 and 30, to contribute the active participation that rightly belongs to it.

115. Great importance is to be attached to the teaching and practice of music in seminaries, in the novitiates and houses of study of religious of both sexes, and also in other Catholic institutions and schools. To impart this instruction, those in charge of teaching sacred music are to receive thorough training.

---

1. See Eph 5:19; Col 3:16.

It is recommended also that higher institutes of sacred music be established whenever possible.

Musicians and singers, especially young boys, must also be given a genuine liturgical training.

116. The Church acknowledges Gregorian chant as distinctive of the Roman liturgy; therefore, other things being equal, it should be given pride of place in liturgical services.

But other kinds of sacred music, especially polyphony, are by no means excluded from liturgical celebrations, provided they accord with the spirit of the liturgical service, in the way laid down in art. 30.

117. The *editio typica* of the books of Gregorian chant is to be completed and a more critical edition is to be prepared of those books already published since the reform of St. Pius X.

It is desirable also that an edition be prepared containing the simpler melodies for use in small churches.

118. The people's own religious songs are to be encouraged with care so that in sacred devotions as well as during services of the liturgy itself, in keeping with rubrical norms and requirements, the faithful may raise their voices in song.

119. In certain parts of the world, especially mission lands, people have their own musical traditions and these play a great part in their religious and social life. Thus, in keeping with art. 39 and 40, due importance is to be attached to their music and a suitable place given to it, not only in forming their attitude toward religion, but also in adapting worship to their native genius.

Therefore, when missionaries are being given training in music, every effort should be made to see that they become competent in promoting the traditional music of the people, both in schools and in sacred services, as far as may be practicable.

120. In the Latin Church the pipe organ is to be held in high esteem, for it is the traditional musical instrument that adds a wonderful splendor to the Church's ceremonies and powerfully lifts up the spirit to God and to higher things.

But other instruments also may be admitted for use in divine worship, with the knowledge and consent of the competent territorial authority and in conformity with art. 22, §2, art. 37 and art. 40. This applies, however, only on condition that the instruments are suitable, or can be made suitable, for sacred use, are in accord with the dignity of the place of worship, and truly contribute to the uplifting of the faithful.

121. Composers, filled with the Christian spirit, should feel that their vocation is to develop sacred music and to increase its store of treasures.

Let them produce compositions having the qualities proper to genuine sacred music, not confining themselves to works that can be sung only by large choirs, but providing also for the needs of small choirs and for the active participation of the entire assembly of the faithful.

The texts intended to be sung must always be consistent with Catholic teaching; indeed they should be drawn chiefly from holy Scripture and from liturgical sources.

CHAPTER VII
SACRED ART AND SACRED FURNISHINGS

122. The fine arts are deservedly ranked among the noblest activities of human genius and this applies especially to religious art and to its highest achievement, sacred art. These arts, by their very nature, are oriented toward the infinite beauty of God, which they attempt in some way to portray by the work of human hands. They are dedicated to advancing God's praise and glory to the degree that they center on the single aim of turning the human spirit devoutly toward God.

The Church has therefore always been the friend of the fine arts, has ever sought their noble help, and has trained artists with the special aim that all things set apart for use in divine worship are truly worthy, becoming, and beautiful, signs and symbols of the supernatural world. The Church has always regarded itself as the rightful arbiter of the arts, deciding which of the works of artists are in accordance with faith, with reverence, and with honored traditional laws and are thereby suited for sacred use.

The Church has been particularly careful to see that sacred furnishings worthily and beautifully serve the dignity of worship and has admitted changes in materials, design, or ornamentation prompted by the progress of the technical arts with the passage of time.

Wherefore it has pleased the Fathers to issue the following decrees on these matters.

123. The Church has not adopted any particular style of art as its very own but has admitted styles from every period, according to the proper genius and circumstances of peoples and the requirements of the many different rites in the Church. Thus, in the course of the centuries, the Church has brought into being a treasury of art that must be very carefully preserved. The art of our own days, coming from every race and region, shall also be given free scope in the Church, on condition that it serves the places of worship and sacred rites with the reverence and honor due to them. In this way contemporary art can add its own voice to that wonderful chorus of praise sung by the great masters of past ages of Catholic faith.

124. In encouraging and favoring art that is truly sacred, Ordinaries should strive after noble beauty rather than mere sumptuous display. This principle is to apply also in the matter of sacred vestments and appointments.

Let bishops carefully remove from the house of God and from other places of worship those works of artists that are repugnant to faith and morals and to

Christian devotion and that offend true religious sense either by their grotesqueness or by the deficiency, mediocrity, or sham in their artistic quality.

When churches are to be built, let great care be taken that they are well suited to celebrating liturgical services and to bringing about the active participation of the faithful.

125. The practice of placing sacred images in churches so that they may be venerated by the faithful is to be maintained. Nevertheless there is to be restraint regarding their number and prominence so that they do not create confusion among the Christian people or foster religious practices of doubtful orthodoxy.

126. When deciding on works of art, local Ordinaries shall give hearing to the diocesan commission on sacred art, and if need be, to others who are especially expert, as well as to the commissions referred to in art. 44, 45, and 46. Ordinaries must be very careful to see that sacred furnishings and valuable works of art are not disposed of or damaged, for they are the adornment of the house of God.

127. Bishops should have a special concern for artists, so as to imbue them with the spirit of sacred art and liturgy. This they may do in person or through competent priests who are gifted with a knowledge and love of art.

It is also recommended that schools or academies of sacred art to train artists be founded in those parts of the world where they seem useful.

All artists who, prompted by their talents, desire to serve God's glory in holy Church, should ever bear in mind that they are engaged in a kind of sacred imitation of God the Creator and are concerned with works intended to be used in Catholic worship, to uplift the faithful, and to foster their devotion and religious formation.

128. Along with the revision of the liturgical books, as laid down in art. 25, there is to be an early revision of the canons and ecclesiastical statutes regulating the supplying of material things involved in sacred worship. This applies in particular to the worthy and well-planned construction of places of worship, the design and construction of altars, the nobility, placement, and security of the eucharistic tabernacle, the practicality and dignity of the baptistry, the appropriate arrangement of sacred images and church decorations and appointments. Laws that seem less suited to the reformed liturgy are to be brought into harmony with it or else abolished; laws that are helpful are to be retained if already in use or introduced where they are lacking.

With art. 22 of this Constitution as the norm, the territorial bodies of bishops are empowered to make adaptations to the needs and customs of their different regions; this applies especially to the material and design of sacred furnishings and vestments.

129. During their philosophical and theological studies, clerics are to be taught about the history and development of sacred art and about the sound principles on which the production of its works must be grounded. In consequence they will be able to appreciate and preserve the Church's treasured monuments and

be in a position to offer good advice to artists who are engaged in producing works of art.

130. It is fitting that the use of pontifical insignia be reserved to those ecclesiastical persons who have either episcopal rank or some definite jurisdiction.

APPENDIX
DECLARATION OF THE SECOND VATICAN ECUMENICAL COUNCIL ON REVISION OF THE CALENDAR

131. The Second Vatican Ecumenical Council recognizes the importance of the wishes expressed by many on assigning the feast of Easter to a fixed Sunday and on an unchanging calendar and has considered the effects that could result from the introduction of a new calendar. Accordingly the Council issues the following declaration:

1. The Council is not opposed to the assignment of the feast of Easter to a particular Sunday of the Gregorian Calendar, provided those whom it may concern, especially other Christians who are not in communion with the Apostolic See, give their assent.

2. The Council likewise declares that it does not oppose measures designed to introduce a perpetual calendar into civil society.

Among the various systems being suggested to establish a perpetual calendar and to introduce it into civil life, only those systems are acceptable to the Church that retain and safeguard a seven-day week with Sunday and introduce no days outside the week, so that the present sequence of weeks is left intact, unless the most serious reasons arise. Concerning these the Apostolic See will make its own judgment.

The Fathers of the Council have given assent to all and to each part of the matters set forth in this Constitution. And together with the venerable Fathers, we, by the apostolic power given to us by Christ, approve, enact, and establish in the Holy Spirit each and all the decrees in this Constitution and command that what has been thus established in the Council be promulgated for the glory of God.

DIES DOMINI
ON KEEPING
THE LORD'S DAY HOLY

JOHN PAUL II

APOSTOLIC LETTER
MAY 31, 1998

AN OVERVIEW OF *DIES DOMINI:* *ON KEEPING THE LORD'S DAY HOLY*

Joyce Ann Zimmerman, CPPS

Well over a decade beyond the turn of this millennium, many of us have long forgotten the hopes and dreams, excitement and anticipation, and anxiety and worries that accompanied that turning of the calendar. On the threshold of the third millennium—but more importantly, on the threshold of the Great Jubilee of the Year 2000—on Pentecost Sunday, May 31, 1998—Pope John Paul II issued the apostolic letter, *Dies Domini: On Keeping the Lord's Day Holy* (DD). More timely than warnings about millennium doomsday, more challenging than fixing computer glitches, more engaging than expectations of novelty, this letter demands all the attention and response we can give it. The Holy Father invites us to reexamine our weekly rhythm of living, not just for the turn of the third millennium but for every day, every week, every year of our lives.

An apostolic letter is issued by a pope or by a Roman congregation in the pope's name and concerns some important topic. It carries the authority of the papal office, but is not primarily legislative in intent. *Dies Domini* underscores the canonical Sunday obligation,[1] but it does far more than that. It explores Sunday as a uniquely Christian day in the larger and richer context of creation, the Jewish Sabbath, and Christian salvation. The Holy Father especially emphasizes Sunday as a weekly Easter celebration and reminds us that Christ's Resurrection is at the very center of our belief and living. Rather than merely stressing Sunday observance as universal law, Pope John Paul beautifully presents the many dimensions of Sunday observance in such a way as to leave us eager for Sunday in order to discover ever new ways to make this day special each week.

SUNDAY'S MANY DIMENSIONS

Creatively playing on the word *Dies* (Latin for "day"), the Holy Father gives us a sense of the breadth of the richness of Sunday with the five chapter titles: *Dies Domini, Dies Christi, Dies ecclesiae, Dies hominis,* and *Dies dierum.*

CHAPTER I: *DIES DOMINI*

Dies Domini (the Lord's Day) is a meditation on God's work of creation in all its splendor: God's creation is good—*very* good. God's "joyous delight" in the work of creation is the background for God's resting on the seventh day. Rather than divine "inactivity," this rest is about the fullness of God's creating work and "God's lingering" before the work of creation in a "contemplative gaze."[2] The goodness and beauty of creation reveal for us the glory of God and find their

---

1. See *Dies Domini* (DD), 46–49.
2. Ibid., 11.

"fullest expression in Christ's death and resurrection" that usher in a new creation, a new revelation of glory "which shines on the face of the Risen Christ."[3]

CHAPTER 2: *DIES CHRISTI*

Dies Christi (Christ's Day) considers Sunday as the "weekly Easter"[4] and helps us focus on Sunday as the day when we celebrate the joy of risen life. It is the day of the Resurrection[5] as well as the day of Pentecost,[6] when the Holy Spirit descended upon the disciples. But Sunday is more than a Christological day, a day focused on Christ. It is also our day. From early Christianity this first day of the week was also called "the eighth day,"[7] a day out of time, a day when we celebrate our own journey toward eternal new life that is the Risen One's gift to us. Sunday is our defining day. It is the day we celebrate who we are in Christ.

CHAPTER 3: *DIES ECCLESIAE*

Dies ecclesiae (the Church's Day) takes us to the "heart of Sunday"[8] and the Eucharistic celebration. When we gather as the Eucharistic assembly, we are an "epiphany of the church."[9] Sunday is a day to celebrate community as the Body of Christ[10] and our unity.[11] From the double tables of Word[12] and Sacrament[13] we are nourished and then sent forth[14] to live what we have celebrated. That living begins on Sunday itself, and the Holy Father points to traditional values of "family life, social relationships, [and] moments of relaxation"[15] as already beginning to live what we have celebrated.

CHAPTER 4: *DIES HOMINIS*

Dies hominis (Man's [Human Being's] Day) is truly a reflection on how we become more human, more fully alive. As the disciples rejoiced at encountering the Risen Christ on that first Easter, so the pope reminds us that Sunday is primarily a day of joy,[16] a day of celebration. Rather than "shallow feelings of satisfaction and pleasure,"[17] deep Christian joy is a fruit of the Holy Spirit that gives expression to our covenantal love union with the Risen Christ. Our Sunday rest[18] affords us the opportunity to be in touch with this love union, which is not only directed

---

3. Ibid., 18.
4. Ibid., 28.
5. See ibid., 19.
6. See ibid., 28.
7. Ibid., 26.
8. Ibid., 46.
9. Ibid., 34.
10. See ibid., 35.
11. See ibid., 36.
12. See ibid., 39–41.
13. See ibid., 42–44.
14. Ibid., 45.
15. Ibid., 52.
16. See ibid., 55.
17. Ibid., 57.
18. See ibid., 64–68.

to our unity in the Body of Christ, but also our union in solidarity with all others.[19] We are reminded that from the Church's earliest days, charity and care for others were given concrete expression within the shape of the Eucharistic rite itself. Gifts were brought to the altar by the assembly, of which some of the bread and wine were used in the Eucharistic offering to be consecrated as the true Body and Blood of our Lord Jesus Christ. The other gifts were distributed to those in need. Thus care for those in need flows from the Eucharistic table itself. As God is gracious to us, so are we to be gracious to others.

CHAPTER 5: *DIES DIERUM*

Dies dierum (Days' Day) invites us to grasp each Sunday as an important point in a rhythm of celebrating the entire mystery of Christ over a given year.[20] Within this mystery, too, we celebrate Mary as the Holy Mother of God and the Mother of the Church, as well as all the saints throughout the Church's history who have modeled how we are to live the Gospel in deep faith and vivid commitment to discipleship. The pope warns about "the popular and cultural traditions"[21] that can so easily distract us from a true celebration of Sunday. Holy days and feasts are most often not supported by civil legislation, and those that are (for example, Christmas) can easily become simply holidays. Some days celebrating the mystery of Christ are so important (for example, the Solemnities of the Epiphany of the Lord, Ascension of the Lord, and the Most Holy Body and Blood of Christ)[22] that they have been transferred to Sunday so the faithful can celebrate them with full hearts.

CONCLUSION

In the Conclusion the Holy Father remarks that Sunday, when properly observed, "becomes the soul of the other days"[23] and "becomes a synthesis of the Christian life and a condition for living it well."[24] This is why throughout the letter Pope John Paul II raises the issue of Sunday obligation, and why he is so deeply concerned that the faithful understand the significance, beauty, and grace of keeping Sunday well. We observe Sunday as a day of liturgical celebration and rest not because we have to, but because we want to and need to. The Holy Father is leading us to embrace Sunday as a day to grow in our faith, love, commitment, joy, and peace.

SUNDAY'S MANY CHALLENGES

Would that each of us would internalize and live all the richness this apostolic letter offers us! This is a letter beautifully written from the pope's heart that easily lends itself to meditation and prayer. It might be tempting to glance through it and then put it aside. The first challenge in the Holy Father's message

---

19. See ibid., 69–73.

20. See ibid., 76–80.

21. Ibid., 80.

22. See ibid., 79. Please note that in some eccesiastical provinces the Solemnity of the Ascension of the Lord is celebrated on the Thursday before the Seventh Sunday of Easter.

23. Ibid., 83.

24. Ibid., 81.

is that Sunday is too important not to reflect regularly on its meaning, celebration, and demands. We cannot afford to put aside that to which this letter calls us because Sunday defines who we are as a people saved by Christ's life, Death, and Resurrection; celebrates our share in Christ's Risen Life; and sends us forth to sanctify all the days of our weeks and lives.

This first challenge is perhaps the most difficult, because Sunday is not hallowed in our society as it used to be. Traditionally a day of worship and family, Sunday now is all too often one more work day, one more day to shop and to finish chores, a day focused on sports and leisure that do not embody the deepest meaning of rest.

Two recurring themes in the letter are Resurrection and rest, which are defining aspects of Sunday. Both themes summon us to a deeper relationship with God. Sunday rest bids us to put aside all productive work, so that we become more aware that all we have and all we are is dependent upon God and God's goodness. Through our Sunday rest we recreate ourselves in the divine image in which we are made. We need this rest to keep our lives in perspective, to keep our focus on God as our center, and to prepare ourselves to journey more faithfully toward the eternal rest we will one day share in fullness with God. Sunday rest, then, is really directed to new life. It is a concrete expression of our desire to share more fully in the Risen Life of Christ. Without this rest Sunday can easily become simply the first day of the week, thereby losing all vestiges of its being the eighth day, a day when we celebrate risen life and our steady journey toward its final fulfillment in eternity.

A second challenge follows from the first. The celebration of Sunday liturgy cannot simply be a matter of fulfilling an obligation. Sunday Mass is a privileged entry into eternal rest—for a short bit of time—that makes concrete our baptismal, covenental belonging to God and each other. Although every celebration of liturgy does this, Sunday Mass (because it is on the Lord's Day, the day of Resurrection) enacts the Paschal Mystery in a most profound way. The secular day of the week intersects with the sacred day of eternity.

For this reason the preparation and celebration of Sunday Mass ought to be the primary intent of the entire parish—staff and parishioners alike. This is a particular challenge for parish staff, for whom Sunday is usually the most demanding day of the week. This is why it is so important to keep in perspective Sunday's focal point: the saving mystery of Christ risen. The care that goes into the preparation of Sunday Mass—the texts chosen, the ministries undertaken, the music sung, the prayers prayed, the environment enhanced, the processions danced, the offerings shared, the greetings exchanged, the intercessions raised, the Word proclaimed, the nourishment consumed, the mission pronounced—all work together to draw the assembly members into being who they are baptized to be: the Body of Christ carrying forth his saving mission. Care must be given in the celebration of liturgy to observe the prescribed (and judiciously chosen optional) silences. In these moments of rest we are equipped for divine encounter, a quiet that is fittingly carried over into all of Sunday as a day of rest.

Only when Sunday Mass is carefully prepared and celebrated can the assembly be drawn into this great mystery in which we are privileged to participate. Without surrender to the mystery being celebrated, there can be no fruitful sending forth. And with no fruitful sending forth, lives are not changed by liturgy;

instead we might become stagnant in who we are rather than joyfully embracing who we are becoming in Christ. And perhaps herein is the greatest challenge Sunday offers us: surrendering ourselves—our own wants and desires, our own perception of leisure and what refreshes us, our own construction of what is a gainful way to spend our time—to the incredible invitation by God to be in the divine presence, to be transformed more perfectly into being members of the Body of Christ, to grow in our love and care for each other.

The apostolic letter *Dies Domini* is caregiving by the Holy Father exercising his Good Shepherd ministry. In this letter Pope John Paul II makes clear his concern about Sunday slipping away from being at the center of our Christian lives. He calls us to continue or inaugurate a Sunday way of living that is at once refreshing and demanding, life-giving and life-surrendering, Easter joy and paschal dying. May we heed his call and enjoy the fruits of his writing: a Sunday restored to being the high point of our week, the day of encounter, the meeting of who we are with who we are becoming. May Sunday be the source from which we draw our every breath and celebrate our risen life.

OUTLINE

DIES DOMINI
ON KEEPING THE LORD'S DAY HOLY

INTRODUCTION

MY ESTEEMED BROTHERS IN THE EPISCOPATE AND THE PRIESTHOOD,
DEAR BROTHERS AND SISTERS!

1.   The Lord's Day—as Sunday was called from apostolic times[1]—has always been accorded special attention in the history of the church because of its close connection with the very core of the Christian mystery. In fact, in the weekly reckoning of time Sunday recalls the day of Christ's resurrection. It is *Easter* which returns week by week, celebrating Christ's victory over sin and death, the fulfillment in him of the first creation and the dawn of "the new creation" (cf. 2 Corinthians 5:17). It is the day which recalls in grateful adoration the world's first day and looks forward in active hope to "the last day," when Christ will come in glory (cf. Acts 1:11; 1 Thessalonians 4:13–17) and all things will be made new (cf. Revelation 21:5).

         Rightly, then, the psalmist's cry is applied to Sunday: "This day which the Lord has made: Let us rejoice and be glad in it" (Psalm 118:24). This invitation to joy, which the Easter liturgy makes its own, reflects the astonishment which came over the women who, having seen the crucifixion of Christ, found the tomb empty when they went there "very early on the first day after the Sabbath" (Mark 16:2). It is an invitation to relive in some way the experience of the two disciples of Emmaus, who felt their hearts "burn within them" as the Risen One walked with them on the road, explaining the scriptures and revealing himself in "the breaking of the bread" (cf. Luke 24:32, 35). And it echoes the joy—at first uncertain and then overwhelming—which the apostles experienced on the evening of that same day, when they were visited by the risen Jesus and received the gift of his peace and of his Spirit (cf. John 20:19–23).

2.   The resurrection of Jesus is the fundamental event upon which Christian faith rests (cf. 1 Corinthians 15:14). It is an astonishing reality, fully grasped in the light of faith, yet historically attested to by those who were privileged to see the Risen Lord. It is a wondrous event which is not only absolutely unique in human history, but which lies *at the very heart of the mystery of time*. In fact, "all time belongs to [Christ] and all the ages," as the evocative liturgy of the Easter Vigil recalls in preparing the paschal candle. Therefore, in commemorating the day of Christ's resurrection not just once a year but every Sunday, the

---

   1. Cf. Revelation 1:10: *"Kyriake heméra"*; cf. also the *Didache* 14, 1; Saint Ignatius of Antioch, *To the Magnesians* 9, 1–2; SCh 10, 88–89.

church seeks to indicate to every generation the true fulcrum of history, to which the mystery of the world's origin and its final destiny leads.

It is right, therefore, to claim, in the words of a fourth century homily, that "the Lord's Day" is "the lord of days."[2] Those who have received the grace of faith in the Risen Lord cannot fail to grasp the significance of this day of the week with the same deep emotion which led Saint Jerome to say: "Sunday is the day of the resurrection, it is the day of Christians, it is our day."[3] For Christians, Sunday is "the fundamental feast day,"[4] established not only to mark the succession of time but to reveal time's deeper meaning.

3. The fundamental importance of Sunday has been recognized through two thousand years of history and was emphatically restated by the Second Vatican Council: "Every seven days, the Church celebrates the Easter mystery. This is a tradition going back to the Apostles, taking its origin from the actual day of Christ's Resurrection—a day thus appropriately designated 'the Lord's Day.'"[5] Paul VI emphasized this importance once more when he approved the new General Roman Calendar and the Universal Norms which regulate the ordering of the liturgical year.[6] The coming of the third millennium, which calls believers to reflect upon the course of history in the light of Christ, also invites them to rediscover with new intensity the meaning of Sunday: its mystery, its celebration, its significance for Christian and human life.

I note with pleasure that in the years since the Council this important theme has prompted not only many interventions by you, dear brother bishops, as teachers of the faith, but also different pastoral strategies which—with the support of your clergy—you have developed either individually or jointly. On the threshold of the Great Jubilee of the Year 2000, it has been my wish to offer you this Apostolic Letter in order to support your pastoral efforts in this vital area. But at the same time I wish to turn to all of you, Christ's faithful, as though I were spiritually present in all the communities in which you gather with your pastors each Sunday to celebrate the eucharist and the Lord's Day. Many of the insights and intuitions which prompt this Apostolic Letter have grown from my episcopal service in Krakow and, since the time when I assumed the ministry of Bishop of Rome and Successor of Peter, in the visits to the Roman parishes which I have made regularly on the Sundays of the different seasons of the liturgical year. I see this letter as continuing the lively exchange which I am always happy to have with the faithful, as I reflect with you on the meaning of Sunday and underline the reasons for living Sunday as truly the Lord's Day, also in the changing circumstances of our own times.

4. Until quite recently, it was easier in traditionally Christian countries to keep Sunday holy because it was an almost universal practice and because, even in the organization of civil society, Sunday rest was considered a fixed part of

---

2. Pseudo-Eusebius of Alexandria, *Sermon* 16: PG 86, 416.
3. *In Die Dominica Paschae II*, 52: CCL 78, 550.
4. SC, 106.
5. *Ibid.*
6. Cf. Motu Proprio *Mysterii Paschalis* (14 February 1969): AAS 61 (1969), 222–226.

the work schedule. Today, however, even in those countries which give legal sanction to the festive character of Sunday, changes in socioeconomic conditions have often led to profound modifications of social behavior and hence of the character of Sunday. The custom of the weekend has become more widespread, a weekly period of respite, spent perhaps far from home and often involving participation in cultural, political or sporting activities which are usually held on free days. This social and cultural phenomenon is by no means without its positive aspects if, while respecting true values, it can contribute to people's development and to the advancement of the life of society as a whole. All of this responds not only to the need for rest, but also to the need for celebration which is inherent in our humanity. Unfortunately, when Sunday loses its fundamental meaning and becomes merely part of a weekend, it can happen that people stay locked within a horizon so limited that they can no longer see "the heavens."[7] Hence, though ready to celebrate, they are really incapable of doing so.

The disciples of Christ, however, are asked to avoid any confusion between the celebration of Sunday, which should truly be a way of keeping the Lord's Day holy, and the weekend, understood as a time of simple rest and relaxation. This will require a genuine spiritual maturity, which will enable Christians to "be what they are," in full accordance with the gift of faith, always ready to give an account of the hope which is in them (cf. 1 Peter 3:15). In this way, they will be led to a deeper understanding of Sunday, with the result that, even in difficult situations, they will be able to live it in complete docility to the Holy Spirit.

5.   From this perspective, the situation appears somewhat mixed. On the one hand, there is the example of some young churches, which shows how fervently Sunday can be celebrated, whether in urban areas or in widely scattered villages. By contrast, in other parts of the world, because of the sociological pressures already noted, and perhaps because the motivation of faith is weak, the percentage of those attending the Sunday liturgy is strikingly low. In the minds of many of the faithful, not only the sense of the centrality of the eucharist, but even the sense of the duty to give thanks to the Lord and to pray to him with others in the community of the church seems to be diminishing.

It is also true that both in mission countries and in countries evangelized long ago the lack of priests is such that the celebration of the Sunday eucharist cannot always be guaranteed in every community.

6.   Given this array of new situations and the questions which they prompt, it seems more necessary than ever *to recover the deep doctrinal foundations* underlying the church's precept, so that the abiding value of Sunday in the Christian life will be clear to all the faithful. In doing this, we follow in the footsteps of the age-old tradition of the church, powerfully restated by the Second Vatican Council in its teaching that on Sunday "Christian believers should come together, in order to commemorate the suffering, resurrection and glory of the Lord Jesus, by hearing God's word and sharing the eucharist, and to give thanks to God who

---

7. Cf. Pastoral Note of the Italian Episcopal Conference *"Il giorno del Signore"* (15 July 1984), 5: *Enchiridion* CEI 3, 1398.

has given them new birth to a living hope through the resurrection of Jesus Christ from the dead" (cf. 1 Peter 1:3).[8]

7.   The duty to keep Sunday holy, especially by sharing in the eucharist and by relaxing in a spirit of Christian joy and fraternity, is easily understood if we consider the many different aspects of this day upon which the present letter will focus our attention.

Sunday is a day that is at the very heart of the Christian life. From the beginning of my pontificate, I have not ceased to repeat: "Do not be afraid! Open, open wide the doors to Christ!"[9] In the same way, today I would strongly urge everyone to rediscover Sunday: *Do not be afraid to give your time to Christ!* Yes, let us open our time to Christ, that he may cast light upon it and give it direction. He is the One who knows the secret of time and the secret of eternity, and he gives us "his day" as an ever new gift of his love. The rediscovery of this day is a grace which we must implore, not only so that we may live the demands of faith to the full, but also so that we may respond concretely to the deepest human yearnings. Time given to Christ is never time lost, but is rather time gained, so that our relationships and indeed our whole life may become more profoundly human.

CHAPTER I
DIES DOMINI

THE CELEBRATION OF THE CREATOR'S WORK

"THROUGH HIM ALL THINGS WERE MADE" JOHN 1:3

8.   For the Christian, Sunday is above all an Easter celebration, wholly illumined by the glory of the Risen Christ. It is the festival of the "new creation." Yet, when understood in depth, this aspect is inseparable from what the first pages of scripture tell us of the plan of God in the creation of the world. It is true that the Word was made flesh in "the fullness of time" (Galatians 4:4); but it is also true that, in virtue of the mystery of his identity as the eternal Son of the Father, he is the origin and end of the universe. As John writes in the prologue of his gospel: "Through him all things were made, and without him was made nothing that was made" (1:3). Paul too stresses this in writing to the Colossians: "In him all things were created, in heaven and on earth, visible and invisible. . . . All things were created through him and for him" (1:16). This active presence of the Son in the creative work of God is revealed fully in the paschal mystery, in which Christ, rising as "the first fruits of those who had fallen asleep" (1 Corinthians 15:20), established the new creation and began the process which he himself will bring to completion when he returns in glory to "deliver the kingdom to God the Father . . . so that God may be everything to everyone" (1 Corinthians 15:24, 28).

---

8. SC, 106.

9. Homily for the Solemn Inauguration of the Pontificate (22 October 1978), 5: AAS 70 (1978), 947.

Already at the dawn of creation, therefore, the plan of God implied Christ's "cosmic mission." This *Christocentric perspective*, embracing the whole arc of time, filled God's well-pleased gaze when, ceasing from all his work, he "blessed the seventh day and made it holy" (Genesis 2:3). According to the priestly writer of the first biblical creation story, then was born the "Sabbath," so characteristic of the first covenant, which in some ways foretells the sacred day of the new and final covenant. The theme of God's rest (cf. Genesis 2:2) and the rest which he offered to the people of the Exodus when they entered the Promised Land (cf. Exodus 33:14; Deuteronomy 3:20; 12:9; Joshua 21:44; Psalm 95:11) is re-read in the New Testament in the light of the definitive Sabbath rest (Hebrews 4:9) into which Christ himself has entered by his resurrection. The People of God are called to enter into this same rest by persevering in Christ's example of filial obedience (cf. Hebrews 4:3–16). In order to grasp fully the meaning of Sunday, therefore, we must re-read the great story of creation and deepen our understanding of the theology of the Sabbath.

"IN THE BEGINNING, GOD CREATED THE HEAVENS AND THE EARTH" GENESIS 1:1

9.   The poetic style of the Genesis story conveys well the awe which people feel before the immensity of creation and the resulting sense of adoration of the One who brought all things into being from nothing. It is a story of intense religious significance, a hymn to the creator of the universe, pointing to him as the only Lord in the face of recurring temptations to divinize the world itself. At the same time, it is a hymn to the goodness of creation, all fashioned by the mighty and merciful hand of God.

"God saw that it was good" (Genesis 1:10, 12, etc.). Punctuating the story as it does, this refrain *sheds a positive light upon every element of the universe* and reveals the secret for a proper understanding of it and for its eventual regeneration: The world is good insofar as it remains tied to its origin and, after being disfigured by sin, it is again made good when, with the help of grace, it returns to the One who made it. It is clear that this process directly concerns not inanimate objects and animals but human beings, who have been endowed with the incomparable gift and risk of freedom. Immediately after the creation stories, the Bible highlights the dramatic contrast between the grandeur of humanity, created in the image and likeness of God, and the fall of humanity, which unleashes on the world the darkness of sin and death (cf. Genesis 3).

10.   Coming as it does from the hand of God, the cosmos bears the imprint of his goodness. It is a beautiful world, rightly moving us to admiration and delight, but also calling for cultivation and development. At the "completion" of God's work, the world is ready for human activity. "On the seventh day God finished his work which he had done, and he rested on the seventh day from all his work which he had done" (Genesis 2:2). With this anthropomorphic image of God's "work," the Bible not only gives us a glimpse of the mysterious relationship between the Creator and the created world, but also casts light upon the task of human beings in relation to the cosmos. The "work" of God is in some ways an example for men and women, called not only to inhabit the cosmos, but also to "build" it and thus become God's "co-workers." As I wrote in my encyclical

Laborem Exercens, the first chapters of Genesis constitute in a sense the first "gospel of work."[10] This is a truth which the Second Vatican Council also stressed: "Created in God's image, men and women were commissioned to subdue the earth and all it contains, to rule the world in justice and holiness, and, recognizing God as the creator of all things, to refer themselves and the totality of things to God so that with everything subject to God, the divine name would be glorified in all the earth."[11]

The exhilarating advance of science, technology and culture in their various forms—an ever more rapid and today even overwhelming development—is the historical consequence of the mission by which God entrusts to man and woman the task and responsibility of filling the earth and subduing it by means of their work, in the observance of God's Law.

SHABBAT: THE CREATOR'S JOYFUL REST

11.   If the first page of the Book of Genesis presents God's "work" as an example for men and women, the same is true of God's "rest": "On the seventh day God finished his work which he had done" (Genesis 2:2). Here too we find an anthropomorphism charged with a wealth of meaning.

It would be banal to interpret God's "rest" as a kind of divine "inactivity." By its nature, the creative act which founds the world is unceasing and God is always at work, as Jesus himself declares in speaking of the Sabbath precept: "My Father is working still, and I am working" (John 5:17). The divine rest of the seventh day does not allude to an inactive God, but emphasizes the fullness of what has been accomplished. It speaks, as it were, of God's lingering before the "very good" work (Genesis 1:31) which his hand has wrought in order to cast upon it *a gaze full of joyous delight*. This is a contemplative gaze which does not look to new accomplishments but enjoys the beauty of what has already been achieved. It is a gaze which God casts upon all things, but in a special way upon human beings, the crown of creation. It is a gaze which already discloses something of the nuptial shape of the relationship which God wants to establish with the creature made in his own image, by calling that creature to enter a pact of love. This is what God will gradually accomplish in offering salvation to all humanity through the saving covenant made with Israel and fulfilled in Christ. It will be the Word incarnate, through the eschatological gift of the Holy Spirit and the configuration of the church as his body and bride, who will extend to all humanity the offer of mercy and the call of the Father's love.

12.   In the Creator's plan, there is both a distinction and a close link between the order of creation and the order of salvation. This is emphasized in the Old Testament, when it links the *shabbat* commandment not only with God's mysterious "rest" after the days of creation (cf. Exodus 20:8–11), but also with the salvation which he offers to Israel *in the liberation from the slavery of Egypt* (cf. Deuteronomy 5:12–15). The God who rests on the seventh day, rejoicing in his creation, is the same God who reveals his glory in liberating his children

---

10. *Laborem excercens*, 25: AAS 73 (1981), 639.
11. GS, 34.

from Pharaoh's oppression. Adopting an image dear to the prophets, one could say that in both cases *God reveals himself as the bridegroom before the bride* (cf. Hosea 2:16–24; Jeremiah 2:2; Isaiah 54:4–8).

As certain elements of the same Jewish tradition suggest,[12] to reach the heart of the *shabbat*, of God's "rest," we need to recognize in both the Old and the New Testament the nuptial intensity that marks the relationship between God and his people. Hosea, for instance, puts it thus in this marvelous passage:

> I will make for you a covenant on that day with the beasts of the field, the birds of the air, and the creeping things of the ground; and I will abolish the bow, the sword, and war from the land; and I will make you lie down in safety. And I will betroth you to me for ever; I will betroth you to me in righteousness and in justice, in steadfast love and in mercy. I will betroth you to me in faithfulness; and you shall know the Lord. (2:18–20)

"GOD BLESSED THE SEVENTH DAY AND MADE IT HOLY" GENESIS 2:3

13. The Sabbath precept, which in the first covenant prepares for the Sunday of the new and eternal covenant, is therefore rooted in the depths of God's plan. This is why, unlike many other precepts, it is set not within the context of strictly cultic stipulations but within the Decalogue, the "ten words" that represent the very pillars of the moral life inscribed on the human heart. In setting this commandment within the context of the basic structure of ethics, Israel and then the church declare that they consider it not just a matter of community religious discipline but *a defining and indelible expression of our relationship with God,* announced and expounded by biblical revelation. This is the perspective within which Christians need to rediscover this precept today. Although the precept may merge naturally with the human need for rest, it is faith alone which gives access to its deeper meaning and ensures that it will not become banal and trivialized.

14. In the first place, therefore, Sunday is the day of rest because it is the day blessed by God and made holy by him, set apart from the other days to be, among all of them, "the Lord's Day."

In order to grasp fully what the first of the biblical creation accounts means by keeping the Sabbath holy, we need to consider the whole story, which shows clearly that every reality, without exception, must be referred back to God. Time and space belong to him. He is not the God of one day alone, but the God of all the days of humanity.

Therefore, if God sanctifies the seventh day with a special blessing and makes it his day *par excellence*, this must be understood within the deep dynamic of the dialogue of the covenant, indeed the dialogue of marriage. This is the dialogue of love which knows no interruption, yet is never monotonous. In fact,

---

12. For our Jewish brothers and sisters, a "nuptial" spirituality characterizes the Sabbath, as appears, for example, in texts of *Genesis Rabbah* such as X, 9 and XI, 8 (cf. J. Neusner, *Genesis Rabbah*, Atlanta: 1985, vol. I, pp. 107, 117). The song *Leka Dôdi* is also nuptial in tone: "Your God will delight in you, as the Bridegroom delights in the Bride . . . In the midst of the faithful of your beloved people, come O Bride, O Shabbat Queen" (cf. *Preghiera serale del sabato*, Rome: A. Toaff, 1968–69, p. 3).

it employs the different registers of love, from the ordinary and indirect to those more intense, which the words of scripture and the witness of so many mystics do not hesitate to describe in imagery drawn from the experience of married love.

15.   All human life, and therefore all human time, must become praise of the Creator and thanksgiving to him. But our relationship with God also *demands times of explicit prayer*, in which the relationship becomes an intense dialogue, involving every dimension of the person. The Lord's Day is the day of this relationship par excellence when men and women raise their song to God and become the voice of all creation.

This is precisely why it is also *the day of rest*. Speaking vividly as it does of renewal and detachment, the interruption of the often oppressive rhythm of work expresses the dependence of human beings and the cosmos upon God. *Everything belongs to God!* The Lord's Day returns again and again to declare this principle within the weekly reckoning of time. The Sabbath has therefore been interpreted evocatively as a determining element in the kind of sacred architecture of time which marks biblical revelation.[13] It recalls that *the universe and history belong to God*; and without a constant awareness of that truth, men and women cannot serve in the world as co-workers of the Creator.

TO "KEEP HOLY" BY "REMEMBERING"

16.   The commandment of the Decalogue by which God decrees the Sabbath observance is formulated in the Book of Exodus in a distinctive way: "Remember the Sabbath day in order to keep it holy" (20:8). And the inspired text goes on to give the reason for this, recalling as it does the work of God: "For in six days the Lord made heaven and earth, the sea, and all that is in them, and rested on the seventh day; therefore the Lord blessed the Sabbath day and made it holy" (v. 11). Before decreeing that something be *done*, the commandment urges that something be *remembered*. It is a call to awaken remembrance of the grand and fundamental work of God which is creation, a remembrance which must inspire our entire religious life and then fill the day on which men and women are called to *rest*. Rest therefore acquires a sacred value: The faithful are called to rest not only *as* God rested, but to rest in the Lord, bringing the entire creation to him, in praise and thanksgiving, intimate as a child and friendly as a spouse.

17.   The connection between Sabbath rest and the theme of remembering God's wonders is found also in the Book of Deuteronomy (5:12–15), where the precept is grounded less in the work of creation than in the work of liberation accomplished by God in the Exodus: "You shall remember that you were a slave in the land of Egypt, and the LORD your God brought you out from there with mighty hand and outstretched arm; therefore the LORD your God commanded you to keep the Sabbath day" (Deuteronomy 5:15).

This formulation complements the one we have already seen; and taken together, the two reveal the meaning of the Lord's Day within a single theological vision that fuses creation and salvation. Therefore, the main point of the

_____

13. Cf. A. J. Heschel, *The Sabbath: Its Meaning for Modern Man* (22nd ed., 1995), pp. 3–24.

precept is not just any kind of *interruption* of work, but the *celebration* of the marvels which God has wrought.

Insofar as this remembrance is alive, *full of thanksgiving and of the praise of God,* human rest on the Lord's Day takes on its full meaning. It is then that men and women enter the depths of God's rest and can experience a tremor of the Creator's joy when, after the creation, he saw that all he had made "was very good" (Genesis 1:31).

FROM THE SABBATH TO SUNDAY

18.   Because the Third Commandment depends upon the remembrance of God's saving works and because Christians saw the definitive time inaugurated by Christ as a new beginning, they made the first day after the Sabbath a festive day, for that was the day on which the Lord rose from the dead. The paschal mystery of Christ is the full revelation of the mystery of the world's origin, the climax of the history of salvation and the anticipation of the eschatological fulfilment of the world. What God accomplished in creation and wrought for his people in the Exodus has found its fullest expression in Christ's death and resurrection, though its definitive fulfillment will not come until the *Parousia,* when Christ returns in glory. In him, the spiritual meaning of the Sabbath is fully realized, as Saint Gregory the Great declares: "For us, the true Sabbath is the person of our Redeemer, our Lord Jesus Christ."[14] This is why the joy with which God, on humanity's first Sabbath, contemplated all that was created from nothing, is now expressed in the joy with which Christ, on Easter Sunday, appeared to his disciples, bringing the gift of peace and the gift of the Spirit (cf. John 20:19–23). It was in the paschal mystery that humanity, and with it the whole creation, "groaning in birth-pangs until now" (Romans 8:22), came to know its new exodus into the freedom of God's children who can cry out with Christ, "Abba, Father!" (Romans 8:15; Galatians 4:6). In the light of this mystery, the meaning of the Old Testament precept concerning the Lord's Day is recovered, perfected and fully revealed in the glory which shines on the face of the Risen Christ (cf. 2 Corinthians 4:6). We move from the "Sabbath" to the "first day after the Sabbath," from the seventh day to the first day: The *dies Domini* becomes the *dies Christi!*

CHAPTER II
DIES CHRISTI

THE DAY OF THE RISEN LORD
AND OF THE GIFT OF THE HOLY SPIRIT

THE WEEKLY EASTER

19.   "We celebrate Sunday because of the venerable resurrection of our Lord Jesus Christ, and we do so not only at Easter but also at each turning of the week": So wrote Pope Innocent I at the beginning of the fifth century,[15] testifying to an

---

14. *"Verum autem sabbatum ipsum redemptorem nostrum Iesum Christum Dominum habemus": Epist.* 13, 1: CCL 140A, 992.

15. *Ep. ad Decentium* XXV, 4, 7: PL 20, 555.

already well established practice which had evolved from the early years after the Lord's resurrection. Saint Basil speaks of "holy Sunday, honored by the Lord's Resurrection, the first fruits of all the other days";[16] and Saint Augustine calls Sunday "a sacrament of Easter."[17]

The intimate bond between Sunday and the resurrection of the Lord is strongly emphasized by all the churches of East and West. In the tradition of the Eastern churches in particular, every Sunday is the *anastasimos hemera*, the day of resurrection,[18] and this is why it stands at the heart of all worship.

In the light of this constant and universal tradition, it is clear that, although the Lord's Day is rooted in the very work of creation and even more in the mystery of the biblical rest of God, it is nonetheless to the resurrection of Christ that we must look in order to understand fully the Lord's Day. This is what the Christian Sunday does, leading the faithful each week to ponder and live the event of Easter, true source of the world's salvation.

20.   According to the common witness of the gospels, the resurrection of Jesus Christ from the dead took place on "the first day after the Sabbath" (Mark 16:2, 9; Luke 24:1; John 20:1). On the same day, the Risen Lord appeared to the two disciples of Emmaus (cf. Luke 24:13–35) and to the eleven apostles gathered together (cf. Luke 24:36; John 20:19). A week later—as the Gospel of John recounts (cf. 20:26)—the disciples were gathered together once again, when Jesus appeared to them and made himself known to Thomas by showing him the signs of his passion. The day of Pentecost—the first day of the eighth week after the Jewish Passover (cf. Acts 2:1), when the promise made by Jesus to the apostles after the resurrection was fulfilled by the outpouring of the Holy Spirit (cf. Luke 24:49; Acts 1:4–5)—also fell on a Sunday. This was the day of the first proclamation and the first baptisms: Peter announced to the assembled crowd that Christ was risen and "those who received his word were baptized" (Acts 2:41). This was the epiphany of the church, revealed as the people into which are gathered in unity, beyond all their differences, the scattered children of God.

THE FIRST DAY OF THE WEEK

21.   It was for this reason that, from apostolic times, "the first day after the Sabbath," the first day of the week, began to shape the rhythm of life for Christ's disciples (cf. 1 Corinthians 16:2). "The first day after the Sabbath" was also the day upon which the faithful of Troas were gathered "for the breaking of bread," when Paul bade them farewell and miraculously restored the young Eutychus to life (cf. Acts 20:7–12). The Book of Revelation gives evidence of the practice of calling the first day of the week "the Lord's Day" (1:10). This would now be a characteristic distinguishing Christians from the world around them. As early as the beginning of the second century, it was noted by Pliny the Younger, governor of Bithynia, in his report on the Christian practice "of gathering together

---

16. *Homiliae in Hexaemeron* II, 8: SCh 26, 184.

17. Cf. *In Io. Ev. Tractatus* XX, 20, 2: CCL 36, 203; *Epist.* 55, 2: CSEL 34, 170–171.

18. The reference to the resurrection is especially clear in Russian, which calls Sunday simply "Resurrection" *(Voskresenie).*

on a set day before sunrise and singing among themselves a hymn to Christ as to a god."[19] And when Christians spoke of the "Lord's Day," they did so giving to this term the full sense of the Easter proclamation: "Jesus Christ is Lord" (Philippians 2:11; cf. Acts 2:36; 1 Corinthians 12:3). Thus Christ was given the same title which the Septuagint used to translate what in the revelation of the Old Testament was the unutterable name of God: YHWH.

22.   In those early Christian times, the weekly rhythm of days was generally not part of life in the regions where the gospel spread, and the festive days of the Greek and Roman calendars did not coincide with the Christian Sunday. For Christians, therefore, it was very difficult to observe the Lord's Day on a set day each week. This explains why the faithful had to gather before sunrise.[20] Yet fidelity to the weekly rhythm became the norm, since it was based upon the New Testament and was tied to Old Testament revelation. This is eagerly underscored by the apologists and the Fathers of the church in their writings and preaching where, speaking of the paschal mystery, they use the same scriptural texts which, according to the witness of Saint Luke (cf. 24:27, 44–47), the Risen Christ himself would have explained to the disciples. In the light of these texts, the celebration of the day of the resurrection acquired a doctrinal and symbolic value capable of expressing the entire Christian mystery in all its newness.

GROWING DISTINCTION FROM THE SABBATH

23.   It was this newness that the catechesis of the first centuries stressed as it sought to show the prominence of Sunday relative to the Jewish Sabbath. It was on the Sabbath that the Jewish people had to gather in the synagogue and to rest in the way prescribed by the Law. The apostles, and in particular Saint Paul, continued initially to attend the synagogue so that there they might proclaim Jesus Christ, commenting upon "the words of the prophets which are read every Sabbath" (Acts 13:27). Some communities observed the Sabbath while also celebrating Sunday. Soon, however, the two days began to be distinguished ever more clearly, in reaction chiefly to the insistence of those Christians whose origins in Judaism made them inclined to maintain the obligation of the old Law. Saint Ignatius of Antioch writes:

> If those who were living in the former state of things have come to a new hope, no longer observing the Sabbath but keeping the Lord's Day, the day on which our life has appeared through him and his death . . . that mystery from which we have received our faith and in which we persevere in order to be judged disciples of Christ, our only Master, how could we then live without him, given that the prophets too, as his disciples in the Spirit, awaited him as master?[21]

Saint Augustine notes in turn: "Therefore the Lord too has placed his seal on his day, which is the third after the Passion. In the weekly cycle, however, it is the

---

19. *Epist.* 10, 96, 7.

20. Cf. *ibid.* In reference to Pliny's letter, Tertullian also recalls the *coetus antelucani in Apologeticum* 2, 6: CCL 1, 88; *De Corona* 3, 3: CCL 2, 1043.

21. *To the Magnesians* 9, 1–2: SCh 10, 88–89.

eighth day after the seventh, that is after the Sabbath, and the first day of the week."[22] The distinction of Sunday from the Jewish Sabbath grew ever stronger in the mind of the church, even though there have been times in history when, because the obligation of Sunday rest was so emphasized, the Lord's Day tended to become more like the Sabbath. Moreover, there have always been groups within Christianity which observe both the Sabbath and Sunday as "two brother days."[23]

THE DAY OF THE NEW CREATION

24.   A comparison of the Christian Sunday with the Old Testament vision of the Sabbath prompted theological insights of great interest. In particular, there emerged the unique connection between the resurrection and creation. Christian thought spontaneously linked the resurrection, which took place on "the first day of the week," with the first day of that cosmic week (cf. Genesis 1:1–2:4) which shapes the creation story in the Book of Genesis: the day of the creation of light (cf. 1:3–5). This link invited an understanding of the resurrection as the beginning of a new creation, the first fruits of which is the glorious Christ, "the first born of all creation" (Colossians 1:15) and "the first born from the dead" (Colossians 1:18).

25.   In effect, Sunday is the day above all other days that summons Christians to remember the salvation which was given to them in baptism and which has made them new in Christ. "You were buried with him in baptism, in which you were also raised with him through faith in the working of God, who raised him from the dead" (Colossians 2:12; cf. Romans 6:4–6). The liturgy underscores this baptismal dimension of Sunday, both in calling for the celebration of baptisms—as well as at the Easter Vigil—on the day of the week "when the Church commemorates the Lord's Resurrection,"[24] and in suggesting as an appropriate penitential rite at the start of Mass the sprinkling of holy water, which recalls the moment of baptism in which all Christian life is born.[25]

THE EIGHTH DAY: IMAGE OF ETERNITY

26.   By contrast, the Sabbath's position as the seventh day of the week suggests for the Lord's Day a complementary symbolism, much loved by the Fathers. Sunday is not only the first day, it is also "the eighth day," set within the sevenfold succession of days in a unique and transcendent position which evokes not only the beginning of time but also its end in "the age to come." Saint Basil explains that Sunday symbolizes that truly singular day which will follow the present time, the day without end which will know neither evening nor morning, the imperishable age which will never grow old; Sunday is the ceaseless

---

22. *Sermon 8 in the Octave of Easter* 4: PL 46, 841. This sense of Sunday as the first day is clear in the Latin liturgical calendar, where Monday is called *feria secunda*, Tuesday *feria tertia* and so on. In Portuguese, the days are named in the same way.

23. Saint Gregory of Nyssa, *De Castigatione:* PG 46, 309. The Maronite liturgy also stresses the link between the Sabbath and Sunday, beginning with the "mystery of Holy Saturday" (cf. M. Hayek, *Maronite [Eglise], Dictionnaire de spiritualité,* [1980] X, 632–644).

24. RBaptC, 9; cf. RCIA, 59.

25. Cf. RomM, Rite of Blessing and Sprinkling of Holy Water.

foretelling of life without end which renews the hope of Christians and encourages them on their way.[26] Looking toward the last day, which fulfills completely the eschatological symbolism of the Sabbath, Saint Augustine concludes the *Confessions* describing the *eschaton* as "the peace of quietness, the peace of the Sabbath, a peace with no evening."[27] In celebrating Sunday, both the "first" and the "eighth" day, the Christian is led toward the goal of eternal life.[28]

THE DAY OF CHRIST-LIGHT

27.   This Christocentric vision sheds light upon another symbolism which Christian reflection and pastoral practice ascribed to the Lord's Day. Wise pastoral intuition suggested to the church the christianization of the notion of Sunday as "the day of the sun," which was the Roman name for the day and which is retained in some modern languages.[29] This was in order to draw the faithful away from the seduction of cults that worshiped the sun, and to direct the celebration of the day to Christ, humanity's true "sun." Writing to the pagans, Saint Justin uses the language of the time to note that Christians gather together "on the day named after the sun,"[30] but for believers the expression had already assumed a new meaning which was unmistakably rooted in the gospel.[31] Christ is the light of the world (cf. John 9:5; also 1:4–5, 9), and, in the weekly reckoning of time, the day commemorating his resurrection is the enduring reflection of the epiphany of his glory. The theme of Sunday as the day illuminated by the triumph of the Risen Christ is also found in the Liturgy of the Hours[32] and is given special emphasis in the *Pannichida*, the vigil which in the Eastern liturgies prepares for Sunday. From generation to generation as she gathers on this day, the church makes her own the wonderment of Zechariah as he looked upon Christ, seeing in him the dawn which gives "light to those who sit in darkness and in the shadow of death" (Luke 1:78–79), and she echoes the joy of Simeon when he takes in his arms the divine Child who has come as the "light to enlighten the Gentiles" (Luke 2:32).

---

26. Cf. Saint Basil, *On the Holy Spirit*, 27, 66: SCh 17, 484–485. Cf. also *Letter of Barnabas* 15, 8–9: SC 172, 186–189; Saint Justin, *Dialogue with Trypho* 24, 138: PG 6, 528, 793; Origen, *Commentary on the Psalms*, Psalm 118 (119), 1: PG 12, 1588.

27. *"Domine, praestitisti nobis pacem quietis, pacem sabbati, pacemsine vespera"*: *Confess.*, 13, 50: CCL 27, 272.

28. Cf. Saint Augustine, *Epist.* 55, 17: CSEL 34, 188: *"Ita ergo erit octavus, qui primus, ut prima vita sed aeterna reddatur."*

29. Thus in English "Sunday" and in German *"Sonntag."*

30. *Apologia* I, 67: PG 6, 430.

31. Cf. Saint Maximus of Turin, *Sermo* 44, 1: CCL 23, 178; *Sermo* 53, 2: CCL 23, 219; Eusebius of Caesarea, *Comm. in Ps.* 91: PG 23, 1169–1173.

32. See, for example, the hymn of the Office of Readings: *"Dies aetasque ceteris octava splendet sanctior in te quam, Iesu, consecras primitiae surgentium"* (Week I); and also: *"Salve dies, dierum gloria, dies felix Christi victoria, dies digna iugi laetitia dies prima. Lux divina caecis irradiat, in qua Christus infernum spoliat, mortem vincit et reconciliat summis ima"* (Week II). Similar expressions are found in hymns included in the Liturgy of the Hours in various modern languages.

28.   Sunday, the day of light, could also be called the day of "fire," in reference to the Holy Spirit. The light of Christ is intimately linked to the "fire" of the Spirit, and the two images together reveal the meaning of the Christian Sunday.[33] When he appeared to the apostles on the evening of Easter, Jesus breathed upon them and said: "Receive the Holy Spirit. If you forgive the sins of any, they are forgiven; if you retain the sins of any, they are retained" (John 20:22–23). The outpouring of the Spirit was the great gift of the Risen Lord to his disciples on Easter Sunday. It was again Sunday when, fifty days after the resurrection, the Spirit descended in power, as "a mighty wind" and "fire" (Acts 2:2–3), upon the apostles gathered with Mary. Pentecost is not only the founding event of the church, but is also the mystery which for ever gives life to the church.[34] Such an event has its own powerful liturgical moment in the annual celebration which concludes "the great Sunday,"[35] but it also remains a part of the deep meaning of every Sunday because of its intimate bond with the paschal mystery. The "weekly Easter" thus becomes, in a sense, the "weekly Pentecost," when Christians relive the apostles' joyful encounter with the Risen Lord and receive the life-giving breath of his Spirit.

THE DAY OF FAITH

29.   Given these different dimensions which set it apart, Sunday appears as the supreme *day of faith*. It is the day when, by the power of the Holy Spirit, who is the church's living "memory" (cf. John 14:26), the first appearance of the Risen Lord becomes an event renewed in the "today" of each of Christ's disciples. Gathered in his presence in the Sunday assembly, believers sense themselves called like the apostle Thomas: "Put your finger here, and see my hands. Put out your hand, and place it in my side. Doubt no longer, but believe" (John 20:27). Yes, Sunday is the day of faith. This is stressed by the fact that the Sunday eucharistic liturgy, like the liturgy of other solemnities, includes the profession of faith. Recited or sung, the Creed declares the baptismal and paschal character of Sunday, making it the day on which in a special way the baptized renew their adherence to Christ and his gospel in a rekindled awareness of their baptismal promises. Listening to the word and receiving the Body of the Lord, the baptized contemplate the Risen Jesus present in the "holy signs" and confess with the apostle Thomas: "My Lord and my God!" (John 20:28).

AN INDISPENSABLE DAY!

30.   It is clear then why, even in our own difficult times, the identity of this day must be protected and above all must be lived in all its depth. An Eastern writer of the beginning of the third century recounts that as early as then the faithful in every region were keeping Sunday holy on a regular basis.[36] What

---

33. Cf. Clement of Alexandria, *Stromata*, VI, 138, 1–2: PG 9, 364.

34. Cf. John Paul II, Encyclical Letter *Dominum et Vivificantem* (18 May 1986), 22–26: AAS 78 (1986), 829–837.

35. Cf. Saint Athanasius of Alexandria, *Sunday Letters* 1, 10: PG 26, 1366.

36. Cf. Bardesanes, *Dialogue on Destiny*, 46: PS 2, 606–607.

began as a spontaneous practice later became a juridically sanctioned norm. The Lord's Day has structured the history of the church through two thousand years: How could we think that it will not continue to shape her future? The pressures of today can make it harder to fulfill the Sunday obligation; and, with a mother's sensitivity, the church looks to the circumstances of each of her children. In particular, she feels herself called to a new catechetical and pastoral commitment in order to ensure that, in the normal course of life, none of her children are deprived of the rich outpouring of grace which the celebration of the Lord's Day brings. It was in this spirit that the Second Vatican Council, making a pronouncement on the possibility of reforming the church calendar to match different civil calendars, declared that the church "is prepared to accept only those arrangements which preserve a week of seven days with a Sunday."[37] Given its many meanings and aspects, and its link to the very foundations of the faith, the celebration of the Christian Sunday remains, on the threshold of the third millennium, an indispensable element of our Christian identity.

CHAPTER III
DIES ECCLESIAE

THE EUCHARISTIC ASSEMBLY: HEART OF SUNDAY

THE PRESENCE OF THE RISEN LORD

31. "I am with you always, to the end of the age" (Matthew 28:20). This promise of Christ never ceases to resound in the church as the fertile secret of her life and the wellspring of her hope. As the day of resurrection, Sunday is not only the remembrance of a past event: It is a celebration of the living presence of the Risen Lord in the midst of his own people.

For this presence to be properly proclaimed and lived, it is not enough that the disciples of Christ pray individually and commemorate the death and resurrection of Christ inwardly, in the secrecy of their hearts. Those who have received the grace of baptism are not saved as individuals alone, but as members of the mystical body, having become part of the People of God.[38] It is important therefore that they come together to express fully the very identity of the church, the *ekklesia*, the assembly called together by the Risen Lord who offered his life "to reunite the scattered children of God" (John 11:52). They have become one in Christ (cf. Galatians 3:28) through the gift of the Spirit. This unity becomes visible when Christians gather together: It is then that they come to know vividly and to testify to the world that they are the people redeemed, drawn "from every tribe and language and people and nation" (Revelation 5:9). The assembly of Christ's disciples embodies from age to age the image of the first Christian community, which Luke gives as an example in the Acts of the Apostles when he recounts that the first baptized believers "devoted themselves to the apostles' teaching and fellowship, to the breaking of bread and the prayers" (2:42).

---

37. SC, Appendix: Declaration on the Reform of the Calendar.
38. Cf. LG, 9.

32.   The eucharist is not only a particularly intense expression of the reality of the church's life, but also in a sense its "fountainhead."[39] The eucharist feeds and forms the church: "Because there is one bread, we who are many are one body, for we all partake of the one bread" (1 Corinthians 10:17). Because of this vital link with the sacrament of the Body and Blood of the Lord, the mystery of the church is savored, proclaimed and lived supremely in the eucharist.[40]

This ecclesial dimension intrinsic to the eucharist is realized in every eucharistic celebration. But it is expressed most especially on the day when the whole community comes together to commemorate the Lord's resurrection. Significantly, the *Catechism of the Catholic Church* teaches that "the Sunday celebration of the Lord's Day and his eucharist is at the heart of the church's life."[41]

33.   At Sunday Mass, Christians relive with particular intensity the experience of the apostles on the evening of Easter when the Risen Lord appeared to them as they were gathered together (cf. John 20:19). In a sense, the People of God of all times were present in that small nucleus of disciples, the first fruits of the church. Through their testimony, every generation of believers hears the greeting of Christ, rich with the messianic gift of peace, won by his blood and offered with his Spirit: "Peace be with you!" Christ's return among them "a week later" (John 20:26) can be seen as a radical prefiguring of the Christian community's practice of coming together every seven days, on "the Lord's Day" or Sunday, in order to profess faith in his resurrection and to receive the blessing which he had promised: "Blessed are those who have not seen and yet believe" (John 20:29). This close connection between the appearance of the Risen Lord and the eucharist is suggested in the Gospel of Luke in the story of the two disciples of Emmaus, whom Christ approached and led to understand the scriptures and then sat with at table. They recognized him when he "took the bread, said the blessing, broke it and gave it to them" (24:30). The gestures of Jesus in this account are his gestures at the Last Supper, with the clear allusion to the "breaking of bread," as the eucharist was called by the first generation of Christians.

THE SUNDAY EUCHARIST

34.   It is true that, in itself, the Sunday eucharist is no different from the eucharist celebrated on other days, nor can it be separated from liturgical and sacramental life as a whole. By its very nature, the eucharist is an epiphany of the church;[42] and this is most powerfully expressed when the diocesan community gathers in prayer with its pastor: "The church appears with special clarity when the holy People of God, all of them, are actively and fully sharing in the same liturgical celebrations—especially when it is the same eucharist—sharing one prayer at one altar, at which the bishop is presiding, surrounded by his presbyters and

---

39. Cf. John Paul II, Letter *Dominicae Cenae* (24 February 1980), 4: AAS 72 (1980), 120; Encyclical Letter *Dominum et Vivificantem* (18 May 1986), 62–64: AAS 78 (1986), 889–894.

40. Cf. John Paul II, VQA, 9: AAS 81 (1989), 905–906.

41. CCC, 2177.

42. Cf. John Paul II, VQA 9: AAS 81 (1989), 905–906.

his ministers."[43] This relationship with the bishop and with the entire church community is inherent in every eucharistic celebration, even when the bishop does not preside, regardless of the day of the week on which it is celebrated. The mention of the bishop in the eucharistic prayer is the indication of this.

But because of its special solemnity and the obligatory presence of the community, and because it is celebrated "on the day when Christ conquered death and gave us a share in his immortal life,"[44] the Sunday eucharist expresses with greater emphasis its inherent ecclesial dimension. It becomes the paradigm for other eucharistic celebrations. Each community, gathering all its members for the "breaking of the bread," becomes the place where the mystery of the church is concretely made present. In celebrating the eucharist, the community opens itself to communion with the universal church,[45] imploring the Father to "remember the church throughout the world" and make her grow in the unity of all the faithful with the pope and with the pastors of the particular churches, until love is brought to perfection.

THE DAY OF THE CHURCH

35.   Therefore, the *dies Domini* is also the *dies Ecclesiae.* This is why on the pastoral level the community aspect of the Sunday celebration should be particularly stressed. As I have noted elsewhere, among the many activities of a parish, "none is as vital or as community-forming as the Sunday celebration of the Lord's Day and his eucharist."[46] Mindful of this, the Second Vatican Council recalled that efforts must be made to ensure that there is "within the parish, a lively sense of community, in the first place through the community celebration of Sunday Mass."[47] subsequent liturgical directives made the same point, asking that on Sundays and holy days the eucharistic celebrations held normally in other churches and chapels be coordinated with the celebration in the parish church, in order "to foster the sense of the church community, which is nourished and expressed in a particular way by the community celebration on Sunday, whether around the bishop, especially in the cathedral, or in the parish assembly, in which the pastor represents the bishop."[48]

36.   The Sunday assembly is the privileged place of unity: It is the setting for the celebration of the *sacramentum unitatis* which profoundly marks the church as a people gathered "by" and "in" the unity of the Father, of the Son and of the

---

43. SC, 41; cf. CD, 15.

44. These are the words of the embolism, formulated in this or similar ways in some of the eucharistic prayers of the different languages. They stress powerfully the paschal character of Sunday.

45. Cf. Congregation for the Doctrine of the Faith, Letter to the Bishops of the Catholic Church on Certain Aspects of the Church as Communion *Communionis Notio* (28 May 1992), 11–14: AAS 85 (1993), 844–847.

46. *Speech to the Third Group of the Bishops of the United States of America* (17 March 1998), 4: *L'Osservatore Romano*, 18 March 1998, 4.

47. SC, 42.

48. EM, 26: AAS 59 (1967), 555.

Holy Spirit.[49] For Christian families, the Sunday assembly is one of the most outstanding expressions of their identity and their "ministry" as "domestic churches,"[50] when parents share with their children at the one table of the word and of the bread of life. We do well to recall in this regard that it is first of all the parents who must teach their children to participate in Sunday Mass; they are assisted in this by catechists, who are to see to it that initiation into the Mass is made a part of the formation imparted to the children entrusted to their care, explaining the important reasons behind the obligatory nature of the precept. When circumstances suggest it, the celebration of Masses for children, in keeping with the provisions of the liturgical norms,[51] can also help in this regard.

At Sunday Masses in parishes, insofar as parishes are "eucharistic communities,"[52] it is normal to find different groups, movements, associations and even the smaller religious communities present in the parish. This allows everyone to experience in common what they share most deeply, beyond the particular spiritual paths which, by discernment of church authority,[53] legitimately distinguish them. This is why on Sunday, the day of gathering, small group Masses are not to be encouraged: It is not only a question of ensuring that parish assemblies are not without the necessary ministry of priests, but also of ensuring that the life and unity of the church community are fully safeguarded and promoted.[54] Authorization of possible and clearly restricted exceptions to this general guideline will depend upon the wise discernment of the pastors of the particular churches, in view of special needs in the area of formation and pastoral care, and keeping in mind the good of individuals or groups—especially the benefits which such exceptions may bring to the entire Christian community.

A PILGRIM PEOPLE

37.   As the church journeys through time, the reference to Christ's resurrection and the weekly recurrence of this solemn memorial help to remind us of *the pilgrim and eschatological character of the People of God.* Sunday after Sunday the church moves toward the final "Lord's Day," that Sunday which knows no end. The expectation of Christ's coming is inscribed in the very mystery of the church[55] and is evidenced in every eucharistic celebration. But, with its specific remembrance of the glory of the Risen Christ, the Lord's Day recalls with greater intensity the future glory of his "return." This makes Sunday the day on which the church, showing forth more clearly her identity as "Bride,"

---

49. Cf. Saint Cyprian, *De Orat. Dom.* 23: PL 4, 553; *De Cath. Eccl. Unitate,* 7: CSEL 31, 215; LG, 4; SC, 26.

50. Cf. John Paul II, Apostolic Exhortation *Familiaris Consortio* (22 November 1981), 57, 61: AAS 74 (1982), 151, 154.

51. Cf. DMC: AAS 66 (1974), 30–46.

52. Cf. EM, 26: AAS 59 (1967), 555–556; Sacred Congregation for Bishops, Directory for the Pastoral Ministry of Bishops *Ecclesiae Imago* (22 February 1973), 86c: *Enchiridion Vaticanum* 4, 2071.

53. Cf. John Paul II, Post-Synodal Apostolic Exhortation *Christifideles Laici* (30 December 1988), 30: AAS 81 (1989), 446–447.

54. Cf. Sacred Congregation for Divine Worship, Instruction *Masses for Particular Groups* (15 May 1969), 10: AAS 61 (1969), 810.

55. Cf. LG, 48–51.

anticipates in some sense the eschatological reality of the heavenly Jerusalem. Gathering her children into the eucharistic assembly and teaching them to wait for the "divine Bridegroom," she engages in a kind of "exercise of desire,"[56] receiving a foretaste of the joy of the new heavens and new earth, when the holy city, the new Jerusalem, will come down from God, "prepared as a bride adorned for her husband" (Revelation 21:2).

THE DAY OF HOPE

38. Viewed in this way, Sunday is not only the day of faith, but is also *the day of Christian hope*. To share in "the Lord's Supper" is to anticipate the eschatological feast of the "marriage of the Lamb" (Revelation 19:9). Celebrating this memorial of Christ, risen and ascended into heaven, the Christian community waits "in joyful hope for the coming of our Savior, Jesus Christ."[57] Renewed and nourished by this intense weekly rhythm, Christian hope becomes the leaven and the light of human hope. This is why the prayer of the faithful responds not only to the needs of the particular Christian community but also to those of all humanity; and the church, coming together for the eucharistic celebration, shows to the world that she makes her own "the joys and hopes, the sorrows and anxieties of people today, especially of the poor and all those who suffer."[58] With the offering of the Sunday eucharist, the church crowns the witness which her children strive to offer every day of the week by proclaiming the gospel and practicing charity in the world of work and in all the many tasks of life; thus she shows forth more plainly her identity "as a sacrament, or sign and instrument of intimate union with God and of the unity of the entire human race."[59]

THE TABLE OF THE WORD

39. As in every eucharistic celebration, the Risen Lord is encountered in the Sunday assembly at the twofold table of the word and of the bread of life. The table of the word offers the same understanding of the history of salvation and especially of the paschal mystery which the risen Jesus himself gave to his disciples: It is Christ who speaks, present as he is in his word "when sacred scripture is read in the church."[60] At the table of the bread of life, the Risen Lord becomes really, substantially and enduringly present through the memorial of his passion and resurrection, and the bread of life is offered as a pledge of future glory. The Second Vatican Council recalled that "the liturgy of the word and the liturgy of the eucharist are so closely joined together that they form a single act of worship."[61] The Council also urged that "the table of the word of God be more lavishly prepared for the faithful, opening to them more abundantly the

---

56. *"Haec est vita nostra, ut desiderando exerceamur"*: Saint Augustine, *In Prima Ioan. Tract.* 4, 6: SCh 75, 232.

57. RomM, embolism after the Lord's Prayer.

58. GS, 1.

59. LG, 1; cf. John Paul II, Encyclical Letter *Dominum et Vivificantem* (18 May 1986), 61–64: AAS 78 (1986), 888–894.

60. SC, 7; cf. 33.

61. *Ibid.*, 56; cf. *Ordo Lectionum Missae, Praenotanda*, 10.

treasures of the Bible."[62] It then decreed that, in Masses of Sunday and holy days of obligation, the homily should not be omitted except for serious reasons.[63] These timely decrees were faithfully embodied in the liturgical reform about which Paul VI wrote, commenting upon the richer offering of biblical readings on Sundays and holy days: "All this has been decreed so as to foster more and more in the faithful 'that hunger for hearing the word of the Lord' (Amos 8:11) which, under the guidance of the Holy Spirit, spurs the People of the New Covenant on toward the perfect unity of the church."[64]

40.   In considering the Sunday eucharist more than thirty years after the Council, we need to assess how well the word of God is being proclaimed and how effectively the People of God have grown in knowledge and love of sacred scripture.[65] There are two aspects of this—that of *celebration* and that of *personal appropriation*—and they are very closely related. At the level of celebration, the fact that the Council made it possible to proclaim the word of God in the language of the community taking part in the celebration must awaken a new sense of responsibility toward the word, allowing "the distinctive character of the sacred text" to shine forth "even in the mode of reading or singing."[66] At the level of personal appropriation, the hearing of the word of God proclaimed must be well prepared in the souls of the faithful by an apt knowledge of scripture and, where pastorally possible, by *special initiatives designed to deepen understanding of the biblical readings,* particularly those used on Sundays and holy days. If Christian individuals and families are not regularly drawing new life from the reading of the sacred text in a spirit of prayer and docility to the church's interpretation,[67] then it is difficult for the liturgical proclamation of the word of God alone to produce the fruit we might expect. This is the value of initiatives in parish communities that bring together during the week those who take part in the eucharist—priest, ministers and faithful[68]—in order to prepare the Sunday liturgy, reflecting beforehand upon the word of God that will be proclaimed. The objective sought here is that the entire celebration—praying, singing, listening, and not just the preaching—should express in some way the theme of the Sunday liturgy, so that all those taking part may be penetrated more powerfully by it. Clearly, much depends on those who exercise the ministry of the word. It is their duty to prepare the reflection on the word of the Lord by prayer and study of the sacred text, so that they may then express its contents faithfully and apply them to people's concerns and to their daily lives.

41.   It should also be borne in mind that the *liturgical proclamation of the word of God,* especially in the eucharistic assembly, is not so much a time for meditation and catechesis as *a dialogue between God and his people,* a dialogue in

62. SC, 51.

63. Cf. *ibid.,* 52; CIC, c. 767, 2; CCEC, c. 614.

64. Apostolic Constitution *Missale Romanum* (3 April 1969): AAS 61 (1969), 220.

65. The Council's Constitution *Sacrosanctum Concilium* speaks of *"suavis et vivus Sacrae Scripturae affectus"* (24).

66. John Paul II, Letter *Dominicae Cenae* (24 February 1980), 10: AAS 72 (1980), 135.

67. Cf. DV, 25.

68. Cf. *Ordo Lectionum Missae, Praenotanda,* Chap. III.

which the wonders of salvation are proclaimed and the demands of the covenant are continually restated. On their part, the People of God are drawn to respond to this dialogue of love by giving thanks and praise, also by demonstrating their fidelity to the task of continual conversion. The Sunday assembly commits us therefore to an inner renewal of our baptismal promises, which are in a sense implicit in the recitation of the Creed, and are an explicit part of the liturgy of the Easter Vigil and whenever baptism is celebrated during Mass. In this context, the proclamation of the word in the Sunday eucharistic celebration takes on the solemn tone found in the Old Testament at moments when the covenant was renewed, when the Law was proclaimed and the community of Israel was called—like the people in the desert at the foot of Sinai (cf. Exodus 19:7–8; 24:3, 7)—to repeat its "yes," renewing its decision to be faithful to God and to obey his commandments. In speaking his word, God awaits our response: a response which Christ has already made for us with his "Amen" (cf. 2 Corinthians 1:20–22), and which echoes in us through the Holy Spirit so that what we hear may involve us at the deepest level.[69]

THE TABLE OF THE BODY OF CHRIST

42.   The table of the word leads naturally to the table of the eucharistic bread and prepares the community to live its many aspects, which in the Sunday eucharist assume an especially solemn character. As the whole community gathers to celebrate "the Lord's Day," the eucharist appears more clearly than on other days as the great "thanksgiving" in which the Spirit-filled church turns to the Father, becoming one with Christ and speaking in the name of all humanity. The rhythm of the week prompts us to gather up in grateful memory the events of the days which have just passed, to review them in the light of God and to thank him for his countless gifts, glorifying him "through Christ, with Christ and in Christ, in the unity of the Holy Spirit." The Christian community thus comes to a renewed awareness of the fact that all things were created through Christ (cf. Colossians 1:16; John 1:3), and that in Christ, who came in the form of a slave to take on and redeem our human condition, all things have been restored (cf. Ephesians 1:10), in order to be handed over to God the Father, from whom all things come to be and draw their life. Then, giving assent to the eucharistic doxology with their "Amen," the People of God look in faith and hope toward the eschatological end, when Christ "will deliver the kingdom to God the Father . . . so that God may be everything to everyone" (1 Corinthians 15:24, 28).

43.   This ascending movement is inherent in every eucharistic celebration and makes it a joyous event, overflowing with gratitude and hope. But it emerges particularly at Sunday Mass because of its special link with the commemoration of the resurrection. By contrast, this eucharistic rejoicing that "lifts up our hearts" is the fruit of God's descending movement toward us, which remains for ever etched in the essential sacrificial element of the eucharist, the supreme expression and celebration of the mystery of the kenosis, the descent by which Christ "humbled himself, and became obedient unto death, even death on a Cross" (Philippians 2:8).

---

69. Cf. *Ordo Lectionum Missae, Praenotanda*, Chap. I, 6.

The Mass in fact *truly makes present the sacrifice of the cross*. Under the species of bread and wine, upon which has been invoked the outpouring of the Spirit who works with absolutely unique power in the words of consecration, Christ offers himself to the Father in the same act of sacrifice by which he offered himself on the cross. "In this divine sacrifice which is accomplished in the Mass, the same Christ who offered himself once and for all in a bloody manner on the altar of the Cross is contained and is offered in an unbloody manner."[70] To his sacrifice Christ unites the sacrifice of the church: "In the eucharist the sacrifice of Christ becomes also the sacrifice of the members of his Body. The lives of the faithful, their praise, sufferings, prayer and work, are united with those of Christ and with his total offering, and so acquire a new value."[71] The truth that the whole community shares in Christ's sacrifice is especially evident in the Sunday gathering, which makes it possible to bring to the altar the week that has passed, with all its human burdens.

EASTER BANQUET AND FRATERNAL GATHERING

44. The communal character of the eucharist emerges in a special way when it is seen as the Easter banquet in which Christ himself becomes our nourishment. In fact, "for this purpose Christ entrusted to the church this sacrifice: so that the faithful might share in it, both spiritually, in faith and charity, and sacramentally, in the banquet of holy communion. Sharing in the Lord's Supper is always communion with Christ, who offers himself for us in sacrifice to the Father."[72] This is why the church *recommends that the faithful receive communion when they take part in the eucharist*, provided that they are properly disposed and, if aware of grave sin, have received God's pardon in the sacrament of reconciliation,[73] in the spirit of what Saint Paul writes to the community at Corinth (cf. 1 Corinthians 11:27–32). Obviously, the invitation to eucharistic communion is more insistent in the case of Mass on Sundays and holy days.

It is also important to be ever mindful that communion with Christ is deeply tied to communion with our brothers and sisters. The Sunday eucharistic gathering is an *experience of brotherhood*, which the celebration should demonstrate clearly, while ever respecting the nature of the liturgical action. All this will be helped by gestures of welcome and by the tone of prayer, alert to the needs of all in the community. The sign of peace—in the Roman Rite significantly placed before eucharistic communion—is a particularly expressive gesture which the faithful are invited to make as a manifestation of the People of God's acceptance of all that has been accomplished in the celebration[74] and of the commitment to mutual love that is made in sharing the one bread, with the

---

70. Ecumenical Council of Trent, Session XXII, Doctrine and Canons on the Most Holy Sacrifice of the Mass, II: DS 1743; cf. CCC, 1366.

71. CCC, 1368.

72. EM, 3b: AAS 59 (1967), 541; cf. Pius XII, Encyclical Letter *Mediator Dei* (20 November 1947), II: AAS 39 (1947), 564–566.

73. Cf. CCC, 1385; cf. also Congregation for the Doctrine of the Faith, Letter to the Bishops of the Catholic Church concerning the Reception of Eucharistic Communion by Divorced and Remarried Faithful (14 September 1994): AAS 86 (1994), 974–979.

74. Cf. Innocent I, *Epist.* 25, 1 to Decentius of Gubbio: PL 20, 553.

demanding words of Christ in mind: "If you are offering your gift at the altar, and there remember that your brother has something against you, leave your gift there before the altar and go; first be reconciled with your brother, and then come and offer your gift" (Matthew 5:23–24).

45.   Receiving the bread of life, the disciples of Christ ready themselves to undertake with the strength of the Risen Lord and his Spirit *the tasks which await them in their ordinary life.* For the faithful who have understood the meaning of what they have done, the eucharistic celebration does not stop at the church door. Like the first witnesses of the resurrection, Christians who gather each Sunday to experience and proclaim the presence of the Risen Lord are called to *evangelize and bear witness* in their daily lives. Given this, the prayer after communion and the concluding rite—the final blessing and the dismissal—need to be better valued and appreciated, so that all who have shared in the eucharist may come to a deeper sense of the responsibility that is entrusted to them. Once the assembly disperses, Christ's disciples return to their everyday surroundings with the commitment to make their whole life a gift, a spiritual sacrifice pleasing to God (cf. Romans 12:1). They feel indebted to their brothers and sisters because of what they have received in the celebration, not unlike the disciples of Emmaus who, once they had recognized the Risen Christ "in the breaking of the bread" (cf. Luke 24:30–32), felt the need to return immediately to share with their brothers and sisters the joy of meeting the Lord (cf. Luke 24:33–35).

THE SUNDAY OBLIGATION

46.   Since the eucharist is the very heart of Sunday, it is clear why, from the earliest centuries, the pastors of the church have not ceased to remind the faithful of *the need to take part in the liturgical assembly.* "Leave everything on the Lord's Day," urges the third century text known as the *Didascalia,* "and run diligently to your assembly, because it is your praise of God. Otherwise, what excuse will they make to God, those who do not come together on the Lord's Day to hear the word of life and feed on the divine nourishment which lasts forever?"[75] The faithful have generally accepted this call of the pastors with conviction of soul and, although there have been times and situations when this duty has not been perfectly met, one should never forget the genuine heroism of priests and faithful who have fulfilled this obligation even when faced with danger and the denial of religious freedom, as can be documented from the first centuries of Christianity up to our own time.

In his *First Apology,* addressed to the Emperor Antoninus and the Senate, Saint Justin proudly described the Christian practice of the Sunday assembly, which gathered in one place Christians from both the city and the countryside.[76] When, during the persecution of Diocletian, their assemblies were banned with the greatest severity, many were courageous enough to defy the imperial decree and accepted death rather than miss the Sunday eucharist. This was the case of

---

75. II, 59, 2–3: ed. F. X. Funk, 1905, pp. 170–171.
76. Cf. *Apologia* I, 67, 3–5: PG 6, 430.

the martyrs of Abitina, in proconsular Africa, who replied to their accusers: "Without fear of any kind we have celebrated the Lord's Supper, because it cannot be missed; that is our law"; "We cannot live without the Lord's Supper." As she confessed her faith, one of the martyrs said: "Yes, I went to the assembly and I celebrated the Lord's Supper with my brothers and sisters, because I am a Christian."[77]

47.   Even if in the earliest times it was not judged necessary to be prescriptive, the church has not ceased to confirm this obligation of conscience, which rises from the inner need felt so strongly by the Christians of the first centuries. It was only later, faced with the half-heartedness or negligence of some, that the church had to make explicit the duty to attend Sunday Mass: More often than not, this was done in the form of exhortation, but at times the church had to resort to specific canonical precepts. This was the case in a number of local Councils from the fourth century onward (as at the Council of Elvira of 300, which speaks not of an obligation but of penalties after three absences)[78] and most especially from the sixth century onward (as at the Council of Agde in 506).[79] These decrees of local councils led to a universal practice, the obligatory character of which was taken as something quite normal.[80]

The Code of Canon Law of 1917 for the first time gathered this tradition into a universal law.[81] The present Code reiterates this, saying that "on Sundays and other holy days of obligation the faithful are bound to attend Mass."[82] This legislation has normally been understood as entailing a grave obligation: This is the teaching of the *Catechism of the Catholic Church*,[83] and it is easy to understand why if we keep in mind how vital Sunday is for the Christian life.

48.   Today, as in the heroic times of the beginning, many who wish to live in accord with the demands of their faith are being faced with difficult situations in various parts of the world. They live in surroundings that are sometimes decidedly hostile and at other times—more frequently in fact—indifferent and unresponsive to the gospel message. If believers are not to be overwhelmed, they must be able to count on the support of the Christian community. This is why they must be convinced that it is crucially important for the life of faith that they should come together with others on Sundays to celebrate the Passover of the Lord in the sacrament of the new covenant. It is the special responsibility

---

77. *Acta SS. Saturnini, Dativi et aliorum plurimorum Martyrum in Africa*, 7, 9, 10: PL 8, 707, 709–710.

78. Cf. Canon 21, Mansi, *Conc.* II, 9.

79. Cf. Canon 47, Mansi, *Conc.* VIII, 332.

80. Cf. the contrary proposition, condemned by Innocent XI in 1679, concerning the moral obligation to keep the feast day holy: DS 2152.

81. Canon 1248: *"Festis de praecepto diebus Missa audienda est"*; Canon 1247, 1: *"Dies festi sub praecepto in universa Ecclesia sunt . . . omnes et singuli dies dominici."*

82. CIC, c. 1247; CCEC, c. 881, 1, prescribes that "the Christian faithful are bound by the obligation to participate on Sundays and feast days in the Divine Liturgy or, according to the prescriptions or legitimate customs of their own Church *sui iuris*, in the celebration of the divine praises."

83. CCC, 2181: "Those who deliberately fail in this obligation commit a grave sin."

of the bishops, therefore, "to ensure that Sunday is appreciated by all the faithful, kept holy and celebrated as truly 'the Lord's Day,' on which the church comes together to renew the remembrance of the Easter mystery in hearing the word of God, in offering the sacrifice of the Lord, in keeping the day holy by means of prayer, works of charity and abstention from work."[84]

49.   Because the faithful are obliged to attend Mass unless there is a grave impediment, pastors have the corresponding duty to offer to everyone the real possibility of fulfilling the precept. The provisions of church law move in this direction, as for example in the faculty granted to priests, with the prior authorization of the diocesan bishop, to celebrate more than one Mass on Sundays and holy days,[85] the institution of evening Masses[86] and the provision that allows the obligation to be fulfilled from Saturday evening onwards, starting at the time of First Vespers of Sunday.[87] From a liturgical point of view, in fact, holy days begin with First Vespers.[88] Consequently, the liturgy of what is sometimes called the "vigil Mass" is in effect the "festive" Mass of Sunday, at which the celebrant is required to preach the homily and recite the prayer of the faithful.

Moreover, pastors should remind the faithful that when they are away from home on Sundays they are to take care to attend Mass wherever they may be, enriching the local community with their personal witness. At the same time, these communities should show a warm sense of welcome to visiting brothers and sisters, especially in places which attract many tourists and pilgrims, for whom it will often be necessary to provide special religious assistance.[89]

A JOYFUL CELEBRATION IN SONG

50.   Given the nature of Sunday Mass and its importance in the lives of the faithful, it must be prepared with special care. In ways dictated by pastoral experience and local custom in keeping with liturgical norms, efforts must be made to ensure that the celebration has the festive character appropriate to the day commemorating the Lord's resurrection. To this end, it is important to devote attention to the *songs used by the assembly,* since singing is a particularly apt way to express a joyful heart, accentuating the solemnity of the celebration and fostering the sense of a common faith and a shared love. Care must be taken to ensure the quality both of the texts and of the melodies so that what is proposed today as new and creative will conform to liturgical requirements and be worthy of the church's tradition which, in the field of sacred music, boasts a priceless heritage.

---

84. Sacred Congregation for Bishops, Directory for the Pastoral Ministry of Bishops Ecclesiae Imago (22 February 1973), 86a: *Enchiridion Vaticanum* 4, 2069.

85. Cf. CIC, c. 905, 2.

86. Cf. Pius XII, Apostolic Constitution *Christus Dominus* (6 January 1953): AAS 45 (1953), 15–24; Motu Proprio *Sacram Communionem* (19 March 1957): AAS 49 (1957), 177–178. Congregation of the Holy Office, Instruction on the Discipline concerning the Eucharistic Fast (6 January 1953): AAS 45 (1953), 47–51.

87. Cf. CIC, c. 1248, 1; CCEC, c. 881, 2.

88. Cf. GNLY, 3.

89. Cf. Sacred Congregation of Bishops, Directory for the Pastoral Ministry of Bishops *Ecclesiae Imago* (22 February 1973), 86: *Enchiridion Vaticanum* 4, 2069–2073.

51.   There is a need too to ensure that all those present, children and adults, take an active interest, by encouraging their involvement at those points where the liturgy suggests and recommends it.[90] Of course, it falls to only those who exercise the priestly ministry to effect the eucharistic sacrifice and to offer it to God in the name of the whole people.[91] This is the basis of the distinction, which is much more than a matter of discipline, between the task proper to the celebrant and that which belongs to deacons and the non-ordained faithful.[92] Yet the faithful must realize that, because of the common priesthood received in baptism, "they participate in the offering of the eucharist."[93] Although there is a distinction of roles, they still "offer to God the divine victim and themselves with him. Offering the sacrifice and receiving holy communion, they take part actively in the liturgy,"[94] finding in it light and strength to live their baptismal priesthood and the witness of a holy life.

OTHER MOMENTS OF THE CHRISTIAN SUNDAY

52.   Sharing in the eucharist is the heart of Sunday, but the duty to keep Sunday holy cannot be reduced to this. In fact, the Lord's Day is lived well if it is marked from beginning to end by grateful and active remembrance of God's saving work. This commits each of Christ's disciples to shape the other moments of the day— those outside the liturgical context: family life, social relationships, moments of relaxation—in such a way that the peace and joy of the Risen Lord will emerge in the ordinary events of life. For example, the relaxed gathering of parents and children can be an opportunity not only to listen to one another but also to share a few formative and more reflective moments. Even in lay life, when possible, why not make provision for special *times of prayer*—especially the solemn celebration of Vespers, for example—or *moments of catechesis*, which on the eve of Sunday or on Sunday afternoon might prepare for or complete the gift of the eucharist in people's hearts?

This rather traditional way of keeping Sunday holy has perhaps become more difficult for many people, but the church shows her faith in the strength of the Risen Lord and the power of the Holy Spirit by making it known that today more than ever she is unwilling to settle for minimalism and mediocrity at the level of faith. She wants to help Christians to do what is most correct and pleasing to the Lord. And despite the difficulties, there are positive and encouraging signs. In many parts of the church, a new need for prayer in its many forms is being felt, and this is a gift of the Holy Spirit. There is also a rediscovery of ancient religious practices, such as pilgrimages; often the faithful take advantage of Sunday rest to visit a shrine where, with the whole family perhaps, they can spend time in a more intense experience of faith. These are moments of

---

90. Cf. SC, 14, 26; VQA, 4, 6, 12: AAS 81 (1989), 900–901, 902, 909–910.

91. Cf. LG, 10.

92. Cf. Interdicasterial Instruction on Certain Questions concerning the Collaboration of Lay Faithful in the Ministry of Priests *Ecclesiae de Mysterio* (15 August 1997), 6, 8: AAS 89 (1997), 869, 870–872.

93. LG, 10: "*in oblationem Eucharistiae concurrunt.*"

94. *Ibid.*, 11.

grace that must be fostered through evangelization and guided by genuine pastoral wisdom.

SUNDAY ASSEMBLIES WITHOUT A PRIEST

53.   There remains the problem of parishes which do not have the ministry of a priest for the celebration of the Sunday eucharist. This is often the case in young churches, where one priest has pastoral responsibility for faithful scattered over a vast area. However, emergency situations can also arise in countries of long-standing Christian tradition, where diminishing numbers of clergy make it impossible to guarantee the presence of a priest in every parish community. In situations where the eucharist cannot be celebrated, the church recommends that the Sunday assembly come together even without a priest,[95] in keeping with the indications and directives of the Holy See which have been entrusted to the episcopal conferences for implementation.[96] Yet the objective must always remain the celebration of the sacrifice of the Mass, the one way in which the Passover of the Lord becomes truly present, the only full realization of the eucharistic assembly over which the priest presides *in persona Christi*, breaking the bread of the word and the eucharist. At the pastoral level, therefore, everything has to be done to ensure that the sacrifice of the Mass is made available as often as possible to the faithful who are regularly deprived of it, either by arranging the presence of a priest from time to time, or by taking every opportunity to organize a gathering in a central location accessible to scattered groups.

RADIO AND TELEVISION

54.   Finally, the faithful who because of sickness, disability or some other serious cause are prevented from taking part should as best they can unite themselves with the celebration of Sunday Mass from afar, preferably by means of the readings and prayers for that day from the Missal, as well as through their desire for the eucharist.[97] In many countries, radio and television make it possible to join in the eucharistic celebration broadcast from some sacred place.[98] Clearly, this kind of broadcast does not in itself fulfill the Sunday obligation, which requires participation in the fraternal assembly gathered in one place, where eucharistic communion can be received. But for those who cannot take part in the eucharist and who are therefore excused from the obligation, radio and television are a precious help, especially if accompanied by the generous service of extraordinary ministers who bring the eucharist to the sick, also bringing them the greeting and solidarity of the whole community. Sunday Mass thus produces rich fruits for these Christians too, and they are truly enabled to experience Sunday as the Lord's Day and the church's day.

---

95. Cf. CIC, c. 1248, 2.

96. Cf. Sacred Congregation for Divine Worship, Directory for Sunday Celebrations in the Absence of a Priest *Christi Ecclesia* (2 June 1988): *Enchiridion Vaticanum* 11, 442–468; Interdicasterial Instruction on Certain Questions concerning the Collaboration of Lay Faithful in the Ministry of Priests *Ecclesiae de Mysterio* (15 August 1997): AAS 89 (1997), 852–877.

97. Cf. CIC, c. 1248, 2; Congregation for the Doctrine of the Faith, Letter *Sacerdotium Ministeriale* (6 August 1983), III: AAS 75 (1983), 1007.

98. Cf. Pontifical Commission for Social Communications, Instruction *Communio et Progressio* (23 May 1971), 150–152, 157: AAS 63 (1971), 645–646, 647.

CHAPTER IV
DIES HOMINIS

SUNDAY: DAY OF JOY, REST AND SOLIDARITY

THE FULL JOY OF CHRIST

55.   "Blessed be he who has raised the great day of Sunday above all other days. The heavens and the earth, angels and people give themselves over to joy."[99] This cry of the Maronite liturgy captures well the intense acclamations of joy that have always characterized Sunday in the liturgy of both East and West. Moreover, historically—even before it was seen as a day of rest, which in any case was not provided for in the civil calendar—Christians celebrated the weekly day of the Risen Lord primarily as a day of joy. "On the first day of the week, you shall all rejoice," urges the *Didascalia.*[100] This was also emphasized by liturgical practice, through the choice of appropriate gestures.[101] Voicing an awareness widespread in the church, Saint Augustine describes the joy of the weekly Easter: "Fasting is set aside and prayers are said standing as a sign of the Resurrection, which is also why the alleluia is sung on every Sunday."[102]

56.   Beyond particular ritual forms, which can vary in time depending upon church discipline, there remains the fact that Sunday, as a weekly echo of the first encounter with the Risen Lord, is unfailingly marked by the joy with which the disciples greeted the Master: "The disciples rejoiced to see the Lord" (John 20:20). This was the confirmation of the words that Jesus spoke before the Passion and that resound in every Christian generation: "You will be sorrowful, but your sorrow will turn to joy" (John 16:20). Had not he himself prayed for this, that the disciples would have "the fullness of his joy" (cf. John 17:13)? The festive character of the Sunday eucharist expresses the joy that Christ communicates to his church through the gift of the Spirit. Joy is precisely one of the fruits of the Holy Spirit (cf. Romans 14:17; Galatians 5:22).

57.   Therefore, if we wish to rediscover the full meaning of Sunday, we must rediscover this aspect of the life of faith. Certainly, Christian joy must mark the whole of life, and not just one day of the week. But in virtue of its significance as *the day of the Risen Lord*, celebrating God's work of creation and "new creation," Sunday is the day of joy in a very special way, indeed the day most suitable for learning how to rejoice and to rediscover the true nature and deep roots of joy.

---

99. This is the deacon's proclamation in honor of the Lord's Day: cf. the Syriac text in the *Missal of the Church of Antioch of the Maronites* (edition in Syriac and Arabic), Jounieh (Lebanon) 1959, p. 38.

100. V, 20, 11: ed. F. X. Funk, 1905, p. 298; cf. *Didache* 14, 1: ed. F X. Funk, 1901, p. 32; Tertullian, *Apologeticum* 16, 11: CCL 1, 116. See in particular the *Epistle of Barnabas*, 15, 9: SCh 172, 188–189: "This is why we celebrate as a joyous feast the eighth day on which Jesus was raised from the dead and, after having appeared, ascended into heaven."

101. Tertullian, for example, tells us that on Sunday it was forbidden to kneel, since kneeling, which was then seen as an essentially penitential gesture, seemed unsuited to the day of joy. Cf. *De Corona* 3, 4: CCL 2, 1043.

102. *Ep.* 55, 28: CSEL 342, 202.

This joy should never be confused with shallow feelings of satisfaction and pleasure, which inebriate the senses and emotions for a brief moment, but then leave the heart unfulfilled and perhaps even embittered. In the Christian view, joy is much more enduring and consoling; as the saints attest, it can hold firm even in the dark night of suffering.[103] It is, in a certain sense, a virtue to be nurtured.

58.   Yet there is no conflict whatever between Christian joy and true human joys, which in fact are exalted and find their ultimate foundation precisely in the joy of the glorified Christ, the perfect image and revelation of humanity as God intended. As my revered predecessor Paul VI wrote in his Exhortation on Christian joy: "In essence, Christian joy is a sharing in the unfathomable joy, at once divine and human, found in the heart of the glorified Christ."[104] Pope Paul concluded his Exhortation by asking that, on the Lord's Day, the church should witness powerfully to the joy experienced by the apostles when they saw the Lord on the evening of Easter. To this end, he urged pastors to insist

> upon the need for the baptized to celebrate the Sunday eucharist in joy. How could they neglect this encounter, this banquet which Christ prepares for us in his love? May our sharing in it be most worthy and joyful! It is Christ, crucified and glorified, who comes among his disciples, to lead them all together into the newness of his resurrection. This is the climax, here below, of the covenant of love between God and his people: the sign and source of Christian joy, a stage on the way to the eternal feast.[105]

This vision of faith shows the Christian Sunday to be a true "time for celebration," a day given by God to men and women for their full human and spiritual growth.

THE FULFILLMENT OF THE SABBATH

59.   This aspect of the Christian Sunday shows in a special way how it is the fulfillment of the Old Testament Sabbath. On the Lord's Day, which—as we have already said—the Old Testament links to the work of creation (cf. Genesis 2:1–3; Exodus 20:8–11) and the Exodus (cf. Deuteronomy 5:12–15), the Christian is called to proclaim the new creation and the new covenant brought about in the paschal mystery of Christ. Far from being abolished, the celebration of creation becomes more profound within a Christocentric perspective, being seen in the light of the God's plan "to unite all things in [Christ], things in heaven and things on earth" (Ephesians 1:10). The remembrance of the liberation of the Exodus also assumes its full meaning as it becomes a remembrance of the universal redemption accomplished by Christ in his death and resurrection. More than a "replacement" for the Sabbath, therefore, Sunday is its fulfillment, and in a certain sense its extension and full expression in the ordered unfolding of the history of salvation, which reaches its culmination in Christ.

---

103. Cf. Saint Thérèse of the Child Jesus and the Holy Face, *Derniers entretiens*, 5–6 July 1897, in *Oeuvres complètes*, Paris: Cerf Desclée de Brouwer, 1992, pp. 1024–1025.
104. Apostolic Exhortation *Gaudete in Domino* (9 May 1975), II: AAS 67 (1975), 295.
105. *Ibid.* VII, l.c., 322.

60.   In this perspective, the biblical theology of the Sabbath can be recovered in full, without compromising the Christian character of Sunday. It is a theology which leads us ever anew and in unfailing awe to the mystery of the beginning, when the eternal Word of God, by a free decision of love, created the world from nothing. The work of creation was sealed by the blessing and consecration of the day on which God ceased "from all the work which he had done in creation" (Genesis 2:3). This day of God's rest confers meaning upon time, which in the sequence of weeks assumes not only a chronological regularity but also, in a manner of speaking, a theological resonance. The constant return of the *shabbat* ensures that there is no risk of time being closed in upon itself, since, in welcoming God and his *kairoi*—the moments of his grace and his saving acts—time remains open to eternity.

61.   As the seventh day blessed and consecrated by God, the *shabbat* concludes the whole work of creation and is therefore immediately linked to the work of the sixth day, when God made man and woman "in his image and likeness" (cf. Genesis 1:26). This very close connection between the "day of God" and the "day of humanity" did not escape the Fathers in their meditation on the biblical creation story. Saint Ambrose says in this regard:

> Thanks, then, to the Lord our God who accomplished a work in which he might find rest. He made the heavens, but I do not read that he found rest there; he made the stars, the moon, the sun, and neither do I read that he found rest in them. I read instead that he made man and woman and that then he rested, finding in them those to whom he could offer the forgiveness of sins.[106]

Thus there will be for ever a direct link between the "day of God" and the "day of humanity." When the divine commandment declares: "Remember the Sabbath day in order to keep it holy" (Exodus 20:8), the rest decreed in order to honor the day dedicated to God is not at all a burden imposed upon men and women, but rather an aid to help them to recognize their life-giving and liberating dependence upon the Creator, and at the same time their calling to cooperate in the Creator's work and to receive his grace. In honoring God's "rest," men and women fully discover themselves, and thus the Lord's Day bears the profound imprint of God's blessing (cf. Genesis 2:3), by virtue of which, we might say, it is endowed in a way similar to the animals and to humanity itself, with a kind of "fruitfulness" (cf. Genesis 1:22, 28). This fruitfulness is apparent above all in filling and, in a certain sense, "multiplying" time itself, deepening in men and women the joy of living and the desire to foster and communicate life.

62.   It is the duty of Christians therefore to remember that although the practices of the Jewish Sabbath are gone, surpassed as they are by the fulfillment that Sunday brings, the underlying reasons for keeping the Lord's Day holy—inscribed solemnly in the Ten Commandments—remain valid, though they need to be reinterpreted in the light of the theology and spirituality of Sunday:

---

106. *Hex.* 6, 10, 76: CSEL 321, 261.

Remember the Sabbath day to keep it holy, as the LORD your God commanded you. Six days you shall labor, and do all your work; but the seventh day is a Sabbath to the LORD your God. Then you shall do no work, you, or your son, or your daughter, or your servant, or your maid, or your ox, or your ass, or any of your beasts, or the foreigner within your gates, that your servant and maid may rest as well as you. You shall remember that you were a servant in the land of Egypt, and the LORD your God brought you out from there with a mighty hand and an outstretched arm. Therefore the LORD your God commanded that you keep the Sabbath day. (Deuteronomy 5:12–15)

Here the Sabbath observance is closely linked with the liberation which God accomplished for his people.

63.   Christ came to accomplish a new "exodus," to restore freedom to the oppressed. He performed many healings on the Sabbath (cf. Matthew 12:9–14 and parallels), certainly not to violate the Lord's Day, but to reveal its full meaning: "The Sabbath was made for people, not people for the Sabbath" (Mark 2:27). Opposing the excessively legalistic interpretation of some of his contemporaries and developing the true meaning of the biblical Sabbath, Jesus, as "Lord of the Sabbath" (Mark 2:28), restores to the Sabbath observance its liberating character, carefully safeguarding the rights of God and the rights of human beings. This is why Christians, called as they are to proclaim the liberation won by the blood of Christ, felt that they had the authority to transfer the meaning of the Sabbath to the day of the resurrection. The passover of Christ has in fact liberated human beings from a slavery more radical than any weighing upon an oppressed people—the slavery of sin, which alienates us from God, and alienates us from our very selves and from others, constantly sowing within history the seeds of evil and violence.

THE DAY OF REST

64.   For several centuries, Christians observed Sunday simply as a day of worship, without being able to give it the specific meaning of Sabbath rest. Only in the fourth century did the civil law of the Roman Empire recognize the weekly recurrence, determining that on "the day of the sun" the judges, the people of the cities and the various trade corporations would not work.[107] Christians rejoiced to see thus removed the obstacles which until then had sometimes made observance of the Lord's Day heroic. They could now devote themselves to prayer in common without hindrance.[108]

It would therefore be wrong to see in this legislation of the rhythm of the week a mere historical circumstance with no special significance for the church and which she could simply set aside. Even after the fall of the Empire, the Councils did not cease to insist upon the arrangements regarding Sunday rest. In countries where Christians are in the minority and where the festive days of the calendar do not coincide with Sunday, it is still Sunday that remains the Lord's Day, the day on which the faithful come together for the eucharistic assembly.

---

107. Cf. The Edict of Constantine, 3 July 321: *Codex Theodosianus* II, tit. 8, 1, ed. T. Mommsen, 12, p. 87; *Codex Iustiniani*, 3, 12, 2, ed. P. Krueger, p. 248.
108. Cf. Eusebius of Caesarea, *Life of Constantine*, 4, 18: PG 20, 1165.

But this involves real sacrifices. For Christians it is not normal that Sunday, the day of joyful celebration, should not also be a day of rest, and it is difficult for them to keep Sunday holy if they do not have enough free time.

65. By contrast, the link between the Lord's Day and the day of rest in civil society has a meaning and importance that go beyond the distinctly Christian point of view. The alternation between work and rest, built into human nature, is willed by God himself, as appears in the creation story in the Book of Genesis (cf. 2:2–3; Exodus 20:8–11): Rest is something sacred, because it is a way for men and women to withdraw from the sometimes excessively demanding cycle of earthly tasks in order to renew an awareness that everything is the work of God. There is a risk that the prodigious power over creation which God gives to human beings can lead them to forget that God is the Creator upon whom everything depends. It is all the more urgent to recognize this dependence in our own time, when science and technology have so incredibly increased the power that men and women exercise through their work.

66. Finally, it should not be forgotten that even in our own day work is very oppressive for many people, either because of miserable working conditions and long hours—especially in the poorer regions of the world—or because of the persistence in economically more developed societies of too many cases of injustice and exploitation. When, through the centuries, she has made laws concerning Sunday rest,[109] the church has had in mind above all the work of servants and workers, certainly not because this work was any less worthy when compared to the spiritual requirements of Sunday observance, but rather because it needed greater regulation to lighten its burden and thus enable everyone to keep the Lord's Day holy. In this matter, my predecessor Pope Leo XIII in his encyclical *Rerum Novarum* spoke of Sunday rest as a worker's right which the State must guarantee.[110]

In our own historical context there remains the obligation to ensure that everyone can enjoy the freedom, rest and relaxation that human dignity requires, together with the associated religious, family, cultural and interpersonal needs that are difficult to meet if there is no guarantee of at least one day of the week on which people can *both* rest and celebrate. Naturally, this right of workers to rest presupposes their right to work and, as we reflect on the question of the Christian understanding of Sunday, we cannot but recall with a deep sense of solidarity the hardship of countless men and women who, because of the lack of jobs, are forced to remain inactive on workdays as well.

67. Through Sunday rest, daily concerns and tasks can find their proper perspective: The material things about which we worry give way to spiritual values; in a moment of encounter and less pressured exchange, we see the true face of the people with whom we live. Even the beauties of nature—too often marred

---

109. The most ancient text of this kind is can. 29 of the Council of Laodicea (second half of the fourth century): Mansi, II, 569–570. From the sixth to the ninth century, many Councils prohibited *"opera ruralia."* The legislation on prohibited activities, supported by civil laws, became increasingly detailed.

110. Cf. Encyclical Letter *Rerum Novarum* (15 May 1891): *Acta Leonis XIII* 11 (1891), 127–128.

by the desire to exploit, which turns against us—can be rediscovered and enjoyed to the full. As the day on which people are at peace with God, with themselves and with others, Sunday becomes a moment when people can look anew upon the wonders of nature, allowing themselves to be caught up in that marvelous and mysterious harmony which, in the words of Saint Ambrose, weds the many elements of the cosmos in a "bond of communion and peace" by "an inviolable law of concord and love."[111] Men and women then come to a deeper sense, as the apostle says, that "everything created by God is good and nothing is to be rejected if it is received with thanksgiving, for then it is consecrated by the word of God and prayer" (1 Timothy 4:4–5). If after six days of work—reduced in fact to five for many—people look for time to relax and to pay more attention to other aspects of their lives, this corresponds to an authentic need which is in full harmony with the vision of the gospel message. Believers are therefore called to satisfy this need in a way consistent with the manifestation of their personal and community faith, as expressed in the celebration and sanctification of the Lord's Day.

Therefore, also in the particular circumstances of our own time, Christians will naturally strive to ensure that civil legislation respects their duty to keep Sunday holy. In any case, they are obliged in conscience to arrange their Sunday rest in a way that allows them to take part in the eucharist, refraining from work and activities that are incompatible with the sanctification of the Lord's Day, with its characteristic joy and necessary rest for spirit and body.[112]

68.   In order that rest may not degenerate into emptiness or boredom, it must offer spiritual enrichment, greater freedom, opportunities for contemplation and fraternal communion. Therefore, among the forms of culture and entertainment that society offers, the faithful should choose those that are most in keeping with a life lived in obedience to the precepts of the Gospel. Sunday rest then becomes prophetic, affirming not only the absolute primacy of God, but also the primacy and dignity of the person with respect to the demands of social and economic life, and anticipating in a certain sense the "new heavens and the new earth," in which liberation from slavery to needs will be final and complete. In short, the Lord's Day thus becomes in the truest sense *the day of humanity* as well.

A DAY OF SOLIDARITY

69.   Sunday should also give the faithful an opportunity to devote themselves to works of mercy, charity and apostolate. To experience the joy of the Risen Lord deep within is to share fully the love that pulses in his heart: There is no joy without love! Jesus himself explains this, linking the "new commandment" with the gift of joy: "If you keep my commandments, you will remain in my love, just as I have kept the Father's commandments and remain in his love. I have told you this that my own joy may be in you and your joy may be complete. This is my commandment: that you love one another as I have loved you" (John 15:10–12).

---

111. *Hex.* 2, 1, 1: CSEL 321, 41.
112. Cf. CIC, c. 1247; CCEC, c. 881, 1, 4.

The Sunday eucharist, therefore, not only does not absolve the faithful from the duties of charity, but on the contrary commits them even more "to all the works of charity, of mercy, of apostolic outreach, by means of which it is seen that the faithful of Christ are not of this world and yet are the light of the world, giving glory to the Father in the midst of the people."[113]

70.　Ever since apostolic times, the Sunday gathering has in fact been for Christians a moment of fraternal sharing with the very poor. "On the first day of the week, each of you is to put aside and save whatever extra you earn" (1 Corinthians 16:2), says Saint Paul, referring to the collection organized for the poor churches of Judaea. In the Sunday eucharist, the believing heart opens wide to embrace all aspects of the church. But the full range of the apostolic summons needs to be accepted: Far from trying to create a narrow "gift" mentality, Paul calls rather for a demanding *culture of sharing*, to be lived not only among the members of the community itself but also in society as a whole.[114] More than ever, we need to listen once again to the stern warning that Paul addresses to the community at Corinth, guilty of having humiliated the poor in the fraternal *agape* which accompanied "the Lord's Supper": "When you meet together, it is not the Lord's Supper that you eat. For in eating, each one goes ahead with his own meal, and one is hungry and another is drunk. What! Do you not have houses to eat and drink in? Or do you despise the church of God and humiliate those who have nothing?" (1 Corinthians 11:20–22). James is equally forceful in what he writes: "If a man with gold rings and in fine clothing comes into your assembly and a poor man in shabby clothing also comes in, and you pay attention to the one who wears the fine clothing and say, 'Take a seat here, please,' while you say to the poor man, 'Stand there,' or, 'Sit at my feet,' have you not made distinctions among yourselves, and become judges with evil thoughts?" (2:2–4).

71.　The teachings of the apostles struck a sympathetic chord from the earliest centuries, and evoked strong echoes in the preaching of the Fathers of the church. Saint Ambrose addressed words of fire to the rich who presumed to fulfill their religious obligations by attending church without sharing their goods with the poor, and who perhaps even exploited them: "You who are rich, do you hear what the Lord God says? Yet you come into church not to give to the poor but to take instead."[115] Saint John Chrysostom is no less demanding:

> Do you wish to honor the body of Christ? Do not ignore him when he is naked. Do not pay him homage in the temple clad in silk only then to neglect him outside where he suffers cold and nakedness. He who said: "This is my body," is the same One who said: "You saw me hungry and you gave me no food," and "Whatever you did to the least of my brothers you did also to me." . . . What good is it if the eucharistic table is overloaded with

---

113. SC, 9.

114. Cf. also Saint Justin, *Apologia* I, 67, 6: "Each of those who have an abundance and who wish to make an offering gives freely whatever he chooses, and what is collected is given to him who presides and he assists the orphans, the widows, the sick, the poor, the prisoners, the foreign visitors—in a word, he helps all those who are in need": PG 6, 430.

115. *De Nabuthae*, 10, 45: *"Audis, dives, quid Dominus Deus dicat? Et tu ad ecclesiam venis, non ut aliquid largiaris pauperi, sed ut auferas"*: CSEL 322, 492.

golden chalices, when he is dying of hunger? Start by satisfying his hunger, and then with what is left you may adorn the altar as well.[116]

These words effectively remind the Christian community of the duty to make the eucharist the place where fraternity becomes practical solidarity, where the last are the first in the minds and attention of the brothers and sisters, where Christ himself—through the generous gifts of the rich to the very poor—may somehow prolong in time the miracle of the multiplication of the loaves.[117]

72.   The eucharist is an event and program of true brotherhood. From the Sunday Mass there flows a tide of charity destined to spread into the whole life of the faithful, beginning by inspiring the very way in which they live the rest of Sunday. If Sunday is a day of joy, Christians should declare by their actual behavior that we cannot be happy "on our own." They look around to find people who may need their help. It may be that in their neighborhood or among those they know there are sick people, elderly people, children or immigrants, who precisely on Sundays feel more keenly their isolation, need and suffering. It is true that commitment to these people cannot be restricted to occasional Sunday gestures. But presuming a wider sense of commitment, why not make the Lord's Day a more intense time of sharing, encouraging all the inventiveness of which Christian charity is capable? Inviting to a meal people who are alone, visiting the sick, providing food for needy families, spending a few hours in voluntary work and acts of solidarity—these would certainly be ways of bringing into people's lives the love of Christ received at the eucharistic table.

73.   Lived in this way, not only the Sunday eucharist but the whole of Sunday becomes a great school of charity, justice and peace. The presence of the Risen Lord in the midst of his people becomes an undertaking of solidarity, a compelling force for inner renewal, an inspiration to change the structures of sin in which individuals, communities and at times entire peoples are entangled. Far from being an escape, the Christian Sunday is a prophecy inscribed on time itself, a prophecy obliging the faithful to follow in the footsteps of the One who came "to preach good news to the poor, to proclaim release to captives and new sight to the blind, to set at liberty those who are oppressed, and to proclaim the acceptable year of the Lord" (Luke 4:18–19). In the Sunday commemoration of Easter, believers learn from Christ, and remembering his promise, "I leave you peace, my peace I give you" (John 14:27), they become in their turn *builders of peace.*

---

116. *Homilies on the Gospel of Matthew,* 50, 3–4: PG 58, 508–509.
117. Saint Paulinus of Nola, *Ep.* 13, 11–12 to Pammachius: CSEL 29, 92–93. The Roman senator is praised because, by combining participation in the eucharist with distribution of food to the poor, he in a sense reproduced the gospel miracle.

CHAPTER V
DIES DIERUM

SUNDAY: THE PRIMORDIAL FEAST, REVEALING THE MEANING OF TIME

CHRIST THE ALPHA AND OMEGA OF TIME

74.   In Christianity time has a fundamental importance. Within the dimension of time the world was created; within it the history of salvation unfolds, finding its culmination in the "fullness of time" of the Incarnation, and its goal in the glorious return of the Son of God at the end of time. In Jesus Christ, the Word made flesh, time becomes a dimension of God, who is himself eternal.[118]

In the light of the New Testament, the years of Christ's earthly life truly constitute the *center of time*; this center reaches its apex in the resurrection. It is true that Jesus is God made human from the very moment of his conception in the womb of the Blessed Virgin, but only in the resurrection is his humanity wholly transfigured and glorified, thus revealing the fullness of his divine identity and glory. In his speech in the synagogue at Antioch in Pisidia (cf. Acts 13:33), Paul applies the words of Psalm 2 to the resurrection of Christ: "You are my son, this day I have begotten you" (v. 7). It is precisely for this reason that, in celebrating the Easter Vigil, the church acclaims the risen Christ as "the Beginning and End, the Alpha and Omega." These are the words spoken by the celebrant as he prepares the paschal candle, which bears the number of the current year. These words clearly attest that "Christ is the Lord of time; he is its beginning and its end; every year, every day and every moment are embraced by his incarnation and resurrection, and thus become part of the 'fullness of time.'"[119]

75.   Since Sunday is the weekly Easter, recalling and making present the day upon which Christ rose from the dead, it is also the day that reveals the meaning of time. It has nothing in common with the cosmic cycles according to which natural religion and human culture tend to impose a structure on time, succumbing perhaps to the myth of eternal return. The Christian Sunday is wholly other! Springing from the resurrection, it cuts through human time, the months, the years, the centuries, like a directional arrow that points them toward their target: Christ's Second Coming. Sunday foreshadows the last day, the day of the *Parousia*, which in a way is already anticipated by Christ's glory in the event of the resurrection.

In fact, everything that will happen until the end of the world will be no more than an extension and unfolding of what happened on the day when the battered body of the crucified Lord was raised by the power of the Spirit and became in turn the wellspring of the Spirit for all humanity. Christians know that there is no need to wait for another time of salvation, since, however long the world may last, they are already living in *the last times*. Not only the church,

---

118. John Paul II, Apostolic Letter *Tertio Millennio Adveniente* (10 November 1994), 10: AAS 87 (1995), 11.
119. *Ibid.*

but the cosmos itself and history are ceaselessly ruled and governed by the glorified Christ. It is this life-force that propels creation, "groaning in birth-pangs until now" (Romans 8:22), toward the goal of its full redemption. Humankind can have only a faint intuition of this process, but Christians have the key and the certainty. Keeping Sunday holy is the important witness that they are called to bear, so that every stage of human history will be upheld by hope.

SUNDAY IN THE LITURGICAL YEAR

76.   With its weekly recurrence, the Lord's Day is rooted in the most ancient tradition of the church and is vitally important for the Christian. But there was another rhythm that soon established itself: *the annual liturgical cycle.* Human psychology in fact desires the celebration of anniversaries, associating the return of dates and seasons with the remembrance of past events. When these events are decisive in the life of a people, their celebration generally creates a festive atmosphere that breaks the monotony of daily routine.

Now, by God's design, the great saving events upon which the church's life is founded were closely linked to the annual Jewish feasts of Passover and Pentecost, and were prophetically foreshadowed in them. Since the second century, the annual celebration of Easter by Christians—having been added to the weekly Easter celebration—allowed a more ample meditation on the mystery of Christ crucified and risen. Preceded by a preparatory fast, celebrated in the course of a long vigil, extended into the fifty days leading to Pentecost, the feast of Easter— "solemnity of solemnities"—became the day *par excellence* for the initiation of catechumens. Through baptism they die to sin and rise to a new life because Jesus "was put to death for our sins and raised for our justification" (Romans 4:25; cf. 6:3–11). Intimately connected to the paschal mystery, the solemnity of Pentecost takes on special importance, celebrating as it does the coming of the Holy Spirit upon the apostles gathered with Mary and inaugurating the mission to all peoples.[120]

77.   A similar commemorative logic guided the arrangement of the entire liturgical year. As the Second Vatican Council recalls, the church wished to extend throughout the year

> the entire mystery of Christ, from the Incarnation and Nativity to the Ascension, to the day of Pentecost and to the waiting in blessed hope for the return of the Lord. Remembering in this way the mysteries of redemption, the church opens to the faithful the treasury of the Lord's power and merits, making them present in some sense to all times, so that the faithful may approach them and be filled by them with the grace of salvation.[121]

After Easter and Pentecost, the most solemn celebration is undoubtedly the Nativity of the Lord, when Christians ponder the mystery of the incarnation and contemplate the Word of God who deigns to assume our humanity in order to give us a share in his divinity.

---

120. Cf. CCC, 731–732.
121. SC, 102.

78.   Likewise, "in celebrating this annual cycle of the mysteries of Christ, the holy church venerates with special love the Blessed Virgin Mary, Mother of God, united forever with the saving work of her Son."[122] In a similar way, by inserting into the annual cycle the commemoration of the martyrs and other saints on the occasion of their anniversaries, "the church proclaims the Easter mystery of the saints who suffered with Christ and with him are now glorified."[123] When celebrated in the true spirit of the liturgy, the commemoration of the saints does not obscure the centrality of Christ, but on the contrary extols it, demonstrating as it does the power of the redemption wrought by him. As Saint Paulinus of Nola sings, "All things pass, but the glory of the saints endures in Christ, who renews all things, while he himself remains unchanged."[124] The intrinsic relationship between the glory of the saints and that of Christ is built into the very arrangement of the liturgical year, and is expressed most eloquently in the fundamental and sovereign character of Sunday as the Lord's Day. Following the seasons of the liturgical year in the Sunday observance which structures it from beginning to end, the ecclesial and spiritual commitment of Christians comes to be profoundly anchored in Christ, in whom believers find their reason for living and from whom they draw sustenance and inspiration.

79.   Sunday emerges therefore as the natural model for understanding and celebrating these feast days of the liturgical year, which are of such value for the Christian life that the church has chosen to emphasize their importance by making it obligatory for the faithful to attend Mass and to observe a time of rest, even though these feast days may fall on variable days of the week.[125] Their number has been changed from time to time, taking into account social and economic conditions, and also how firmly they are established in tradition, and how well they are supported by civil legislation.[126]

The present canonical and liturgical provisions allow each episcopal conference, because of particular circumstances in one country or another, to reduce the list of holy days of obligation. Any decision in this regard needs to receive the special approval of the Apostolic See,[127] and in such cases the celebration of a mystery of the Lord, such as the Epiphany, the Ascension or the Solemnity of the Body and Blood of Christ, must be transferred to Sunday, in accordance with liturgical norms, so that the faithful are not denied the chance to meditate upon

---

122. *Ibid.*, 103.
123. *Ibid.*, 104.
124. *Carm.* XVI, 3–4: "*Omnia praetereunt, sanctorum gloria durat in Christo qui cuncta novat, dum permanet ipse*": CSEL 30, 67.
125. Cf. CIC, c. 1247; CCEC, c. 881, 1, 4.
126. By general law, the holy days of obligation in the Latin church are the feasts of the Nativity of the Lord, the Epiphany, the Ascension, the Body and Blood of Christ, Mary Mother of God, the Immaculate Conception, the Assumption, Saint Joseph, Saints Peter and Paul and All Saints: cf. CIC, c. 1246. The holy days of obligation in all the Eastern churches are the feasts of the Nativity of the Lord, the Epiphany, the Ascension, the Dormition of Mary Mother of God and Saints Peter and Paul: cf. CCEC, c. 880, 3.
127. Cf. CIC, c. 1246, 2; for the Eastern Churches, cf. CCEC, c. 880, 3.

the mystery.[128] Pastors should also take care to encourage the faithful to attend Mass on other important feast days celebrated during the week.[129]

80.   There is a need for special pastoral attention to the many situations where there is a risk that the popular and cultural traditions of a region may intrude upon the celebration of Sundays and other liturgical feast days, mingling the spirit of genuine Christian faith with elements that are foreign to it and may distort it. In such cases, catechesis and well-chosen pastoral initiatives need to clarify these situations, eliminating all that is incompatible with the gospel of Christ. At the same time, it should not be forgotten that these traditions—and, by analogy, some recent cultural initiatives in civil society—often embody values that are not difficult to integrate with the demands of faith. It rests with the discernment of pastors to preserve the genuine values found in the culture of a particular social context and especially in popular piety, so that liturgical celebration—above all on Sundays and holy days—does not suffer but rather may actually benefit.[130]

CONCLUSION

81.   The spiritual and pastoral riches of Sunday, as it has been handed on to us by tradition, are truly great. When its significance and implications are understood in their entirety, Sunday in a way becomes a synthesis of the Christian life and a condition for living it well. It is clear therefore why the observance of the Lord's Day is so close to the church's heart, and why in the church's discipline it remains a real obligation. Yet more than as a precept, the observance should be seen as a need rising from the depths of Christian life. It is crucially important that all the faithful should be convinced that they cannot live their faith or share fully in the life of the Christian community unless they take part regularly in the Sunday eucharistic assembly. The eucharist is the full realization of the worship which humanity owes to God, and it cannot be compared to any other religious experience. A particularly efficacious expression of this is the Sunday gathering of the entire community, obedient to the voice of the Risen Lord who calls the faithful together to give them the light of his word and the nourishment of his Body as the perennial sacramental wellspring of redemption. The grace flowing from this wellspring renews humankind, life and history.

82.   It is with this strong conviction of faith, and with awareness of the heritage of human values that the observance of Sunday entails, that Christians today must face the enticements of a culture that has accepted the benefits of rest and free time, but that often uses them frivolously and is at times attracted by morally questionable forms of entertainment. Certainly, Christians are no different from other people in enjoying the weekly day of rest; but at the same time they are keenly aware of the uniqueness and originality of Sunday, the day on which they are called to celebrate their salvation and the salvation of all humanity.

---

128. Cf. GNLY, 5, 7: *Enchiridion Vaticanum* 3, 895, 897.
129. Cf. *Caeremoniale Episcoporum*, ed. typica 1995, 230.
130. Cf. *ibid.*, 233.

Sunday is the day of joy and the day of rest precisely because it is the Lord's Day, the day of the risen Lord.

83.   Understood and lived in this fashion, Sunday in a way becomes the soul of the other days, and in this sense we can recall the insight of Origen that the perfect Christian "is always in the Lord's Day, and is always celebrating Sunday."[131] Sunday is a true school, an enduring program of church pedagog—an irreplaceable pedagogy, especially with social conditions now marked more and more by a fragmentation and cultural pluralism that constantly test the fidelity of individual Christians to the practical demands of their faith. In many parts of the world, we see a "diaspora" Christianity, which is put to the test because the scattered disciples of Christ can no longer easily maintain contact with one another, and lack the support of the structures and traditions proper to Christian culture. In a situation of such difficulty, the opportunity to come together on Sundays with fellow believers, exchanging gifts of brotherhood, is an indispensable help.

84.   Sustaining Christian life as it does, Sunday has the additional value of being a testimony and a proclamation. As a day of prayer, communion and joy, Sunday resounds throughout society, emanating vital energies and reasons for hope. Sunday is the proclamation that time, in which he who is the Risen Lord of history makes his home, is not the grave of our illusions but the cradle of an ever new future, an opportunity given to us to turn the fleeting moments of this life into seeds of eternity. Sunday is an invitation to look ahead; it is the day on which the Christian community cries out to Christ, *Marana tha:* Come, O Lord!" (1 Corinthians 16:22). With this cry of hope and expectation, the church is the companion and support of human hope. From Sunday to Sunday, enlightened by Christ, she goes forward toward the unending Sunday of the heavenly Jerusalem, which "has no need of the sun or moon to shine upon it, for the glory of God is its light and its lamp is the Lamb" (Revelation 21:23).

85.   As she strains toward her goal, the church is sustained and enlivened by the Spirit. It is he who awakens memory and makes present for every generation of believers the event of the resurrection. He is the inward gift uniting us to the Risen Lord and to our brothers and sisters in the intimacy of a single body, reviving our faith, filling our hearts with charity and renewing our hope. The Spirit is unfailingly present to every one of the church's days, appearing unpredictably and lavishly with the wealth of his gifts. But it is in the Sunday gathering for the weekly celebration of Easter that the church listens to the Spirit in a special way and reaches out with him to Christ in the ardent desire that he return in glory: "The Spirit and the Bride say, 'Come!'" (Revelation 22:17). Precisely in consideration of the role of the Spirit, I have wished that this exhortation aimed at rediscovering the meaning of Sunday should appear in this year which, in the immediate preparation for the Jubilee, is dedicated to the Holy Spirit.

86.   I entrust this Apostolic Letter to the intercession of the Blessed Virgin, that it may be received and put into practice by the Christian community. Without

---

131. *Contra Celsum* VIII, 22: SCh 150, 222–224.

in any way detracting from the centrality of Christ and his Spirit, Mary is always present in the church's Sunday. It is the mystery of Christ itself which demands this: Indeed, how could she who is *Mater Domini* and *Mater Ecclesiae* fail to be uniquely present on the day which is both *dies Domini* and *dies Ecclesiae?*

As they listen to the word proclaimed in the Sunday assembly, the faithful look to the Virgin Mary, learning from her to keep it and ponder it in their hearts (cf. Luke 2:19). With Mary, they learn to stand at the foot of the cross, offering to the Father the sacrifice of Christ and joining to it the offering of their own lives. With Mary, they experience the joy of the resurrection, making their own the words of the Magnificat, which extol the inexhaustible gift of divine mercy in the inexorable flow of time: "His mercy is from age to age upon those who fear him" (Luke 1:50). From Sunday to Sunday, the pilgrim people follow in the footsteps of Mary, and her maternal intercession gives special power and fervor to the prayer that rises from the church to the most holy Trinity.

87.   Dear brothers and sisters, the imminence of the Jubilee invites us to a deeper spiritual and pastoral commitment. Indeed, this is its true purpose. In the Jubilee year, much will be done to give it the particular stamp demanded by the ending of the second millennium and the beginning of the third since the incarnation of the Word of God. But this year and this special time will pass, as we look to other jubilees and other solemn events. As the weekly solemnity, however, Sunday will continue to shape the time of the church's pilgrimage, until that Sunday which will know no evening.

Therefore, dear brother bishops and priests, I urge you to work tirelessly with the faithful to ensure that the value of this sacred day is understood and lived ever more deeply. This will bear rich fruit in Christian communities, and will not fail to have a positive influence on civil society as a whole.

In coming to know the church, which every Sunday joyfully celebrates the mystery from which she draws her life, may the men and women of the third millennium come to know the risen Christ. And constantly renewed by the weekly commemoration of Easter, may Christ's disciples be ever more credible in proclaiming the gospel of salvation and ever more effective in building the civilization of love.

My blessing to you all!

From the Vatican, on 31 May, the Solemnity of Pentecost, in the year 1998, the twentieth of my pontificate.

THE GENERAL INSTRUCTION
OF THE
ROMAN MISSAL

INCLUDING ADAPTATIONS FOR THE DIOCESES OF
THE UNITED STATES OF AMERICA

CONGREGATION FOR DIVINE WORSHIP AND THE DISCIPLINE
OF THE SACRAMENTS

CURRENT LATIN EDITION
MARCH 17, 2002

CURRENT ENGLISH TRANSLATION APPROVED
MARCH 26, 2010

CURRENT ENGLISH TRANSLATION PROMULGATED FOR USE
IN THE DIOCESE OF THE UNITED STATES OF AMERICA
NOVEMBER 27, 2011

OVERVIEW OF *THE GENERAL INSTRUCTION OF THE ROMAN MISSAL*

Rev. Msgr. Joseph DeGrocco

The General Instruction of the Roman Missal (GIRM) is the *praenotanda*, or introductory document, to *The Roman Missal*, which is the ritual book that contains all the prayers and rubrics for the celebration of the Eucharist. As an instruction, the intention behind the document is that it be seen more as a pastoral and practical document rather than a juridic or dogmatic one. While authentic Eucharistic theology and doctrine are reflected in the document, its purpose is to be catechetical and pastoral. The text of the GIRM contained in this volume is the 2010 translation of the 2002 (Latin) / 2003 (English) edition. The third edition of *The Roman Missal* (*editio typica tertia*) was promulgated in Latin by Pope John Paul II in 2002, along with an updated revision of the GIRM. Provisional English translations of the GIRM were released in 2003 by the United States Conference of Catholic Bishops (USCCB) for use in the dioceses of the United States, and in subsequent years by bishops' conferences of various other English-speaking countries. In 2010 an official translation became available; the document contained herein is that translation. However, the GIRM also includes specific adaptations to be used in the dioceses of the United States of America—adaptations that have been voted on by the USCCB and approved by the Holy See. Previous editions of the GIRM contained these adaptations in a separate appendix, but in this edition they are contained within the text of the document.

As the *praenotanda*, or introduction, to *The Roman Missal*, the GIRM provides both a comprehensive description of the theological and spiritual meaning of the Mass and the official directives for its proper celebration. As such, it is an important document to be familiar with in order to have an in-depth understanding of the Church's celebration of the Eucharist. While much of the GIRM is indeed devoted to descriptions of procedures, the document as a whole should not be seen simply as a dry, rubrics-oriented "how-to" manual. Instead, the text should be appreciated for its full value as an important source through which the reader can explore the richness and depth of the Church's liturgical theology of the Eucharist. Thus, not only clergy should be thoroughly familiar with its contents, but indeed all liturgical ministers and all those who are involved in preparation or leadership roles in parish liturgy. In fact, since it applies to all who are involved in liturgy, including those who participate as members of the assembly, an argument could be made that every Catholic who attends Mass should be familiar with the content of this document. As such, the GIRM should ideally be considered to be a standard text not only in academic degree programs in liturgy, but in all parish adult education and leadership formation programs. It should be the first source consulted whenever questions arise concerning the celebration of the Eucharist.

Thus, in reading the GIRM, the reader will want to be attentive not only to the description of *what* is to be done, but more importantly to the questions of *why* the ritual should be enacted in that way and, therefore, *what it all means*. This is because liturgy is enacted theology: Liturgy expresses the faith of the Church through ritual bodily expression. Concern for proper celebration of the Eucharist is to be seen as something more than simple concern for outward ceremony; instead, proper celebration ensures that we are correctly expressing our communal faith. This is in keeping with an ancient adage in the Church that is often stated as *lex orandi, lex credendi*—generally speaking, "the law of prayer is the law of belief." The faith that is expressed in the celebration of the Eucharist is not personal belief, but the communal faith Tradition of the Body of Christ, the Church. Participants at Mass engage in the ritual actions of the Eucharist precisely as members of a body with a common faith that has been handed down through the generations. Additionally, to *lex orandi, lex credendi* is often added *lex vivendi*, "the law of life." This refers to the fact that the communal faith expressed in the celebration of the Eucharist remains, in a sense, an incomplete expression until it is lived out in everyday life. The offering made in union with Christ at the liturgical celebration must be replicated in the offering of self through acts of love and sacrifice made to one's brothers and sisters in the life that is lived outside the liturgical celebration, for the building up of the Kingdom of God. Then and only then is the communal faith truly fully expressed in all its fullness, so that life itself becomes an act of worship.

Some of the major themes that can be found running throughout the text of the GIRM include an overall theology of worship; a theology of the Eucharist, including the Eucharist as a sacrifice; what the various parts of the Mass mean and how they relate to each other; how the liturgy is celebrated by all, with each and every person, clergy or lay, liturgical minister or "person in the pew," having an important part to play according to his or her role; the meaning of "full, conscious, and active participation;"[1] and a theology of Church, especially as the Church is made manifest in the liturgical assembly. These theological themes are dealt with in a broader way at the beginning of the GIRM, especially in the "Introduction," in chapter 1 ("The Importance and Dignity of the Celebration of the Eucharist"), and in the first two sections of chapter 2 ("The Structure of the Mass, Its Elements, and Its Parts"): Section I, "The General Structure of the Mass," and Section II, "The Different Elements of the Mass." Then, with Section III of chapter 2, "The Individual Parts of the Mass," a more detailed description of the ritual actions begins. In fact, the overall structure of the GIRM might be seen as broadly moving from the more general foundational principles—*why* and *what it means*—into the more specific and detailed directives—*what* is to be done and what it all is *supposed to look like* (Chapter III deals with "Duties and Ministries in the Mass;" chapter 4 gives detailed instructions in "The Different Forms of Celebrating Mass;" chapter 5 discusses "The Arrangement and Ornamentation of Churches for the Celebration of the Eucharist;" chapter 6 specifies "The Requisites for the Celebration of Mass;" chapter 7 gives details for "The Choice of the Mass and Its Parts;" and chapter 8 deals specifically with "Masses and Prayers for Various Needs and Occasions and Masses for the Dead").

---

1. *Constitution on the Sacred Liturgy* (CSL), 14.

The "Introduction" is made up of the first fifteen articles of the GIRM. It is here that the theological foundations are laid down for what follows in the remainder of the text. Previous editions of the GIRM numbered these articles as 1–15, and then chapter 1 began again with article 1. This was because these first fifteen articles were added to the first edition of the GIRM after questions were raised by a small but vocal minority of curial officials in Rome about its validity. There were concerns, for example, that the document did not maintain the traditional Catholic understanding of the Real Presence and the ministerial priesthood, and that the "new Mass" broke with authentic Tradition. These concerns were addressed in these articles, which are arranged under the headings "Testimony of an Unaltered Faith" (2–5), "Uninterrupted Tradition" (6–9), and "Accommodation to New Conditions" (10–15). Thus, the legitimacy both of the liturgical reforms that were promulgated in the Second Vatican Council's *Constitution on the Sacred Liturgy* (CSL) and of the reforms that were implemented in its wake are affirmed.

Chapter I begins the elucidation of the foundational liturgical principles for the celebration of the Eucharist. Beginning here, and continuing in chapters 2 and 3, we find articles that present succinctly some profound liturgical and Eucharistic theology. Some of these topics might be noted as follows.

THE LITURGICAL ASSEMBLY

When the People of God are assembled for liturgy, the assembly is not just a collection of people who happen to be in the same place at the same time. Instead, the celebration of Mass is "the action of Christ and of the People of God arrayed hierarchically . . . ."[2] This means that all participate equally, but each person participates according to his or her role within the assembly. The liturgical action, therefore—the way in which the celebration of the Eucharist is enacted—must manifest that all who take part in it do so "according to the state proper to each."[3] This is not for the sake of mere external ritualism, however, but rather because the celebration of Mass is the center of the whole Christian life, and when the celebration is carried out in this way, each person may draw the abundant spiritual fruits that can be gained from participating in it. Additionally, the bishop, who is the chief shepherd and sign of unity, and the "moderator, promoter, and guardian of the whole of liturgical life,"[4] is seen as the one who directs all legitimate celebrations of the Eucharist, either personally or through priests. Thus, celebrations at which the bishop presides are to be given preeminence, because the bishop's leadership more clearly manifests the mystery of the Church, which is "the sacrament of unity."[5]

THEOLOGY OF PARTICIPATION

Participation in liturgy is both internal and external; full participation engages the person's mind, heart, and body. The GIRM is consistent in its vision that

---

2. *The General Instruction of the Roman Missal* (GIRM), 16.
3. Ibid., 17.
4. Ibid., 22; see also ibid., 91.
5. Ibid., 92; quoting CSL, 26.

the celebration of the Eucharist is not the action of the priest that the people "attend" or "watch"; rather, it is an action of the whole community, and the people's participation is not only presumed, but is also constitutive of an important meaning of the action. Thus, the GIRM notes how people's responses to the greetings, their participation in acclamations and responses, their role in the Penitential Act, the Profession of Faith, the Universal Prayer (Prayer of the Faithful), the Lord's Prayer, and so on are all important manifestations of their inward, spiritual participation. The goal is the interplay of both internal and external participation, never having one without the other. Participation at Mass should never solely be defined by the outward things that are done, nor can it be reduced simply to participation by silence and inward reflection and adoration on the part of the people. Additionally, the GIRM affirms that the goal of participation is to be found not in the liturgy itself, but in the living of the Christian life. Greater participation in the offering of oneself in love and sacrifice to God and to one's brothers and sisters in everyday life should be the fruit of the offering of oneself in "full, conscious, and active participation"[6] at Mass.

UNITY AND COMMUNAL ACTION

None of this takes place individually, however. Participation as a member of the body and handing oneself over to the communal actions are essential components of participation in the celebration. The GIRM is clear in asserting that it is the "common spiritual good of the People of God"[7] that must be served, not "private inclination or arbitrary choice."[8] Such communitarian action both expresses and fosters the spiritual intentions of the participants. Participation in Mass must lead to deeper union with God and with our brothers and sisters, and so the manner in which the celebration is enacted must be expressive of this union. Any appearance of "singularity or division"[9] must be carefully and unambiguously avoided.[10]

ROLES OF THE PRIEST AND THE DEACON

The role of the priest is described in the GIRM as the one who presides at the prayer over the people in the person of Christ—a designation which should be understood specifically in the priest's role as standing in the person of Christ *the Head of the Church*. The laity's participation in the rites should not be minimized, as they also act, in a proper sense, in the person of Christ as members of his Body. Thus is the communal nature of the action affirmed, as the priest presides "in the name of the entire holy people and of all present."[11] This presidential role is manifested through the specific prayers and actions that are entrusted to the priest as presidential functions. Most importantly, this is a role of service to the people, in which the priest envisions himself as a servant of the liturgy—thereby not taking it upon himself to add, change, or delete anything

---

6. CSL 14; see also GIRM 18, 35, 36, 91, and 95.

7. Ibid., 42, 352.

8. Ibid., 42.

9. Ibid., 95.

10. See also ibid., 16, 34, and 96 regarding unity and communal action.

11. Ibid., 30.

on his own initiative, and enacting his role with dignity and humility. The deacon functions not in any capacity as a presider, but as the chief minister, and therefore carries out various ministerial functions.[12]

SILENCE

The role of silence as part of the ritual action is mentioned several times in the GIRM and bears mention here as an important component in the art of celebration. Although the meaning of the silence varies according to the place at which it occurs, it is an essential component in nurturing inward participation and in fostering a sense of reverence and transcendence.[13]

THE MEANING OF THE PARTS OF THE MASS

In addition to giving specific directions for the celebration, the GIRM explains the broader significance of the major parts of the Mass, and also offers further clarification of the individual parts. The Introductory Rites, for example, not only begin the celebration, but also have the purpose of establishing communion among the people as the proper preparation for hearing the Word of God and celebrating the Eucharist.[14] The Liturgy of the Word is seen as God speaking to his people, and the people making God's Word their own.[15] The Liturgy of the Eucharist is explained using the fourfold actions of Christ's taking, giving thanks, breaking, and giving.[16] The Concluding Rites are described simply and directly.[17]

There are a number of clarifications and specifications that should be noted by those who have responsibility for preparing and enacting parish liturgy. One item is of particular interest and should be especially noted. The GIRM presumes that the faithful are receiving Eucharistic bread that has been consecrated at that same celebration, not from hosts reserved in the tabernacle. It explains the importance of this practice as stemming from the need to ritually express that the faithful, through the actual signs themselves, are truly participating in the sacrifice actually being celebrated.[18] Another clarification is that the priest celebrant is the ordinary minister of the Homily, and that when others preach (for example, a concelebrating priest or a deacon) it is not by right, but because the Homily has been "entrusted" to him by the priest celebrant.[19] Proper procedure for composing and enacting the Universal Prayer (Prayer of the Faithful),[20] the proper preparation of the altar before the presentation of the offerings (i.e.,

---

12. See also ibid., 22, 94, 100, 107.
13. See, for example, ibid., 45, 51, 55, 56, 66, 71, and 88.
14. See ibid., 46.
15. See ibid., 55.
16. See ibid., 72.
17. See ibid., 90.
18. See ibid., 85.
19. Ibid., 66.
20. See ibid., 69–71.

that none of the items needed should be on the altar beforehand),[21] the importance of singing[22] and the role of music ministers,[23] when genuflections and bows are to be done,[24] and proper procedures for incensation[25] are further examples of useful information that can be found in the GIRM.

Finally, although the GIRM is a Roman document issued by the Vatican Congregation for Divine Worship and the Discipline of the Sacraments (CDWDS) (and therefore universal), there are areas of the celebration of the Eucharist that are within the competence of the local bishop or of bishops' conferences to decide. Although the areas for possible adaptation are listed in chapter 9, the adaptations themselves that have been approved for use in the dioceses of the United States have been inserted into the proper place in the text where they apply (rather than in a separate appendix, as was the case in previous editions of the GIRM). Thus in several places the phrase "In the Dioceses of the United States" introduces those adaptations. The places in the rite where adaptations are possible are enumerated in article 390.[26]

To be sure, the GIRM contains a wealth of information about the Mass in its various theological, pastoral, spiritual, and canonical aspects. Yet even this document is not the last word; even as complete and detailed as it might seem, it must be read in concert with other documents about the liturgy, such as those contained in this volume. Nonetheless, the GIRM is an invaluable resource for all those involved in the celebration of the Eucharist in any way.

---

21. See GIRM, 73.

22. See ibid., 39–41.

23. See ibid., 102–104.

24. See ibid., 274–275.

25. See ibid., 276–277.

26. Some examples of adaptations specific to the United States include the following:

GIRM 43, that the assembly should kneel beginning after the Holy, Holy, Holy until after the Amen of the Eucharistic Prayer, unless prevented from doing so because of the large number of people present, or ill health, lack of space, or some other reasonable cause;

GIRM 48, 87, that there are four options (the antiphon from the Missal or the antiphon with its Psalm from the Graduale Romanum; the antiphon and Psalm of the Graduale Simplex for the liturgical time; a chant from another collection of Psalms and antiphons as approved by the Conference of Bishops or the Diocesan Bishop; or another liturgical chant [song] suited to the sacred action) for singing at the Entrance, Offertory, and Communion;

GIRM 283, all that pertains to Communion under both kinds, as described in *Norms for the Distribution and Reception of Holy Communion Under Both Kinds in the Dioceses of the United States of America*;

GIRM 301, that wood which is "dignified, solid, and well-crafted" may be used for the construction of the table of an altar, rather than stone.

OUTLINE

THE GENERAL INSTRUCTION
OF THE ROMAN MISSAL

INTRODUCTION

1.   As Christ the Lord was about to celebrate with the disciples the paschal supper in which he instituted the Sacrifice of his Body and Blood, he commanded that a large, furnished upper room be prepared (Lk 22:12). Indeed, the Church has always judged that this command also applied to herself whenever she decided about things related to the disposition of people's minds, and of places, rites and texts for the Celebration of the Most Holy Eucharist. The present norms, too, prescribed in keeping with the will of the Second Vatican Council, together with the new Missal with which the Church of the Roman Rite will henceforth celebrate the Mass, are again a demonstration of this same solicitude of the Church, of her faith and her unaltered love for the supreme mystery of the Eucharist, and also attest to her continuous and consistent tradition, even though certain new elements have been introduced.

TESTIMONY OF AN UNALTERED FAITH

2.   The sacrificial nature of the Mass, solemnly defended by the Council of Trent, because it accords with the universal tradition of the Church,[1] was once more stated by the Second Vatican Council, which pronounced these clear words about the Mass: "At the Last Supper, Our Savior instituted the Eucharistic Sacrifice of his Body and Blood, by which the Sacrifice of his Cross is perpetuated until he comes again; and till then he entrusts the memorial of his Death and Resurrection to his beloved spouse, the Church."[2]

What is taught in this way by the Council is consistently expressed in the formulas of the Mass. Moreover, the doctrine which stands out in the following sentence, already notable and concisely expressed in the ancient Sacramentary commonly called the Leonine—"for whenever the memorial of this sacrifice is celebrated the work of our redemption is accomplished"[3]—is aptly and exactly expounded in the Eucharistic Prayers; for as in these the Priest enacts the anamnesis, while turned towards God likewise in the name of all the people, he renders thanks and offers the living and holy sacrifice, that is, the Church's oblation

---

1. Ecumenical Council of Trent, Session XXII, September 17, 1562: Denzinger-Schönmetzer, nos. 1738–1759.
2. Second Ecumenical Council of the Vatican, Constitution on the Sacred Liturgy, *Sacrosanctum Concilium*, no. 47; cf. Dogmatic Constitution on the Church, *Lumen gentium*, nos. 3, 28; Decree on the Ministry and Life of Priests, *Presbyterorum ordinis*, nos. 2, 4, 5.
3. Evening Mass of the Lord's Supper, Prayer over the Offerings. Cf. *Sacramentarium Veronense*, L.C. Mohlberg editor, no. 93.

and the sacrificial Victim by whose death God himself willed to reconcile us to himself;[4] and the Priest also prays that the Body and Blood of Christ may be a sacrifice which is acceptable to the Father and which brings salvation to the whole world.[5]

So, in the new Missal the rule of prayer (*lex orandi*) of the Church corresponds to her perennial rule of faith (*lex credendi*), by which we are truly taught that the sacrifice of his Cross and its sacramental renewal in the Mass, which Christ the Lord instituted at the Last Supper and commanded his Apostles to do in his memory, are one and the same, differing only in the manner of their offering; and as a result, that the Mass is at one and the same time a sacrifice of praise, thanksgiving, propitiation, and satisfaction.

3.   Moreover, the wondrous mystery of the real presence of the Lord under the Eucharistic species, confirmed by the Second Vatican Council[6] and other teachings of the Church's Magisterium[7] in the same sense and with the same doctrine as the Council of Trent proposed that it must be believed,[8] is proclaimed in the celebration of the Mass, not only by the very words of consecration by which Christ is rendered present through transubstantiation, but also with a sense and a demonstration of the greatest reverence and adoration which strives for realization in the Eucharistic liturgy. For the same reason, the Christian people are led to worship this wondrous Sacrament through adoration in a special way on Thursday of the Lord's Supper in Holy Week and on the Solemnity of the Most Holy Body and Blood of Christ.

4.   In truth, the nature of the ministerial Priesthood proper to the Bishop and the Priest, who offer the Sacrifice in the person of Christ and who preside over the gathering of the holy people, shines forth in the form of the rite itself, on account of the more prominent place and function given to the Priest. The essential elements of this function are set out and explained clearly and extensively in the Preface for the Chrism Mass on Thursday of Holy Week, the day, namely, when the institution of the Priesthood is commemorated. For in the Preface is made clear how the conferral of Priestly power is accomplished through the laying on of hands; and, by the listing one by one of its duties, that power is described which is the continuation of the power of Christ, the High Priest of the New Testament.

5.   Moreover, by this nature of the ministerial Priesthood, something else is put in its proper light, something certainly to be held in great esteem, namely,

4. Cf. Eucharistic Prayer III.

5. Cf. Eucharistic Prayer IV.

6. Second Ecumenical Council of the Vatican, Constitution on the Sacred Liturgy, *Sacrosanctum Concilium*, nos. 7, 47; Decree on the Ministry and Life of Priests, *Presbyterorum ordinis*, nos. 5, 18.

7. Cf. Pius XII, Encyclical Letter, *Humani generis*, August 12, 1950: *Acta Apostolicae Sedis* 42 (1950), pp. 570-571; Paul VI, Encyclical Letter, *Mysterium fidei*, September 3, 1965: *Acta Apostolicae Sedis* 57 (1965), pp. 762-769; Paul VI, Solemn Profession of Faith, June 30, 1968, nos. 24–26: *Acta Apostolicae Sedis* 60 (1968), pp. 442–443; Sacred Congregation of Rites, Instruction, *Eucharisticum mysterium*, May 25, 1967, nos. 3f, 9: *Acta Apostolicae Sedis* 59 (1967), pp. 543, 547.

8. Cf. Ecumenical Council of Trent, Session XIII, October 11, 1551: Denzinger-Schönmetzer, nos. 1635–1661.

the royal Priesthood of the faithful, whose spiritual sacrifice is brought to completion through the ministry of the Bishop and the Priests, in union with the Sacrifice of Christ, the sole Mediator.[9] For the celebration of the Eucharist is the action of the whole Church, and in it each one should carry out solely but totally that which pertains to him, in virtue of the place of each within the People of God. The result of this is that greater consideration is also given to some aspects of the celebration that have sometimes been accorded less attention in the course of the centuries. For this people is the People of God, purchased by Christ's Blood, gathered together by the Lord, nourished by his word, the people called to present to God the prayers of the entire human family, a people that gives thanks in Christ for the mystery of salvation by offering his Sacrifice, a people, finally, that is brought together in unity by Communion in the Body and Blood of Christ. This people, though holy in its origin, nevertheless grows constantly in holiness by conscious, active, and fruitful participation in the mystery of the Eucharist.[10]

UNINTERRUPTED TRADITION

6.   When it set out its instructions for the renewal of the Order of Mass, the Second Vatican Council, using, namely, the same words as did St. Pius V in the Apostolic Constitution *Quo primum*, by which the Missal of Trent was promulgated in 1570, also ordered, among other things, that a number of rites be restored "to the original norm of the holy Fathers."[11] From the fact that the same words are used, it can be noted how the two *Roman Missals*, although four centuries have intervened, embrace one and the same tradition. Furthermore, if the inner elements of this tradition are reflected upon, it is also understood how outstandingly and felicitously the older *Roman Missal* is brought to fulfillment in the later one.

7.   In truly difficult times, when the Catholic faith in the sacrificial nature of the Mass, the ministerial Priesthood, and the real and perpetual presence of Christ under the Eucharistic species were called into question, St. Pius V was first of all concerned with preserving the more recent tradition, then unjustly assailed, introducing only very slight changes into the sacred rite. In fact, the Missal of 1570 differs very little from the very first printed edition of 1474, which in turn faithfully takes up again the Missal used in the time of Pope Innocent III. Moreover, manuscript books in the Vatican Library, even though they provided material for several textual emendations, by no means made it possible to pursue inquiry into "ancient and approved authors" further back than the liturgical commentaries of the Middle Ages.

8.   Today, however, innumerable writings of scholars have shed light on the "norm of the holy Fathers," which the revisers of the Missal of St. Pius V assiduously followed. For following the first publication in 1571 of the Sacramentary called the Gregorian, critical editions of other ancient Roman and Ambrosian

---

9. Cf. Second Ecumenical Council of the Vatican, Decree on the Ministry and Life of Priests, *Presbyterorum ordinis*, no. 2.

10. Cf. Second Ecumenical Council of the Vatican, Constitution on the Sacred Liturgy, *Sacrosanctum Concilium*, no. 11.

11. *Ibidem*, no. 50.

Sacramentaries were disseminated, often in printed form, as were ancient Hispanic and Gallican liturgical books; these editions brought to light numerous prayers of no slight spiritual value but previously unknown.

In the same way, traditions of the first centuries, before the rites of East and West were formed, are now better known because of the discovery of so many liturgical documents.

Furthermore, continuing progress in the study of the holy Fathers has also shed upon the theology of the mystery of the Eucharist the light brought by the doctrine of such illustrious Fathers of Christian antiquity as St. Irenaeus, St. Ambrose, St. Cyril of Jerusalem, and St. John Chrysostom.

9.   Hence, the "norm of the holy Fathers" requires not only the preservation of what our immediate forebears have handed on to us, but also an understanding and a more profound pondering of the Church's entire past ages and of all the ways in which her one faith has been expressed in forms of human and social culture so greatly differing among themselves, indeed, as those prevailing in the Semitic, Greek, and Latin regions. Moreover, this broader view allows us to see how the Holy Spirit endows the People of God with a marvelous fidelity in preserving the unalterable deposit of faith, even though there is a very great variety of prayers and rites.

ACCOMMODATION TO NEW CONDITIONS

10.   Hence, the new Missal, while bearing witness to the Roman Church's rule of prayer (*lex orandi*), also safeguards the deposit of faith handed down by the more recent Councils and marks in its turn a step of great importance in liturgical tradition.

For, when the Fathers of the Second Vatican Council reaffirmed the dogmatic pronouncements of the Council of Trent, they spoke at a far different time in world history, and, for that reason, were able to bring forward proposals and measures regarding pastoral life that could not have even been foreseen four centuries earlier.

11.   The Council of Trent had already recognized the great catechetical usefulness contained in the celebration of Mass but was unable to bring out all its consequences in regard to actual practice. In fact, many at that time requested that permission be given to use the vernacular in celebrating the Eucharistic Sacrifice. To such a request, the Council, by reason of the circumstances of that age, judged it a matter of duty to answer by insisting once more on the teaching of the Church as had been handed on, according to which the Eucharistic Sacrifice is in the first place the action of Christ himself, whose inherent efficacy is therefore unaffected by the manner in which the faithful participate in it. The Council for this reason stated in these firm and likewise measured words: "Although the Mass contains much instruction for the faithful people, it did not seem to the Fathers expedient, however, that it be celebrated indiscriminately in the

vernacular."[12] And the Council declared worthy of censure anyone maintaining that "the rite of the Roman Church, in which part of the Canon and the words of consecration are pronounced in a low voice, is to be condemned, or that the Mass must be celebrated only in the vernacular."[13] Nevertheless, at the same time as it prohibited the use of the vernacular in the Mass, it ordered, on the other hand, pastors of souls to put appropriate catechesis in its place: "Lest Christ's flock go hungry . . . the Holy Synod commands pastors and each and all of those others having the care of souls that frequently during the celebration of Mass, either personally or through others, they should explain what is read at Mass; and expound, among other things, something of the mystery of this most holy Sacrifice, especially on Sundays and feast days."[14]

12.   Hence, the Second Vatican Council, having come together in order to accommodate the Church to the requirements of her proper apostolic office precisely in these times, considered thoroughly, as had the Council of Trent, the catechetical and pastoral character of the Sacred Liturgy.[15] And since no Catholic would now deny a sacred rite celebrated in Latin to be legitimate and efficacious, the Council was also able to concede that "not rarely adopting the vernacular language may be of great usefulness for the people" and gave permission for it to be used.[16] The eagerness with which this measure was everywhere received has certainly been so great that it has led, under the guidance of the Bishops and the Apostolic See itself, to permission for all liturgical celebrations in which the people participate to be in the vernacular, so that the people may more fully understand the mystery which is celebrated.

13.   In this regard, although the use of the vernacular in the Sacred Liturgy is a means, admittedly of great importance, for expressing more clearly catechesis on the mystery, a catechesis inherent in the celebration itself, the Second Vatican Council ordered additionally that certain prescriptions of the Council of Trent that had not been followed everywhere be brought to fruition, such as the Homily to be given on Sundays and feast days[17] and the faculty to interject certain explanations during the sacred rites themselves.[18]

Above all, the Second Vatican Council, which recommended "that more perfect form of participation in the Mass by which the faithful, after the Priest's Communion, receive the Lord's Body from the same Sacrifice,"[19] called for another desire of the Fathers of Trent to be put into effect, namely, that for the sake of a fuller participation in the Holy Eucharist "at each Mass the faithful present

---

12. Ecumenical Council of Trent, Session XXII, *Doctrina de ss. Missae sacrificio*, chapter 8, September 17, 1562: Denzinger-Schönmetzer, no.1749.

13. *Ibidem*, chapter 9: Denzinger-Schönmetzer, no. 1759.

14. *Ibidem*, chapter 8: Denzinger-Schönmetzer, no. 1749.

15. Cf. Second Ecumenical Council of the Vatican, Constitution on the Sacred Liturgy, *Sacrosanctum Concilium*, no. 33.

16. *Ibidem*, no. 36.

17. *Ibidem*, no. 52.

18. *Ibidem*, no. 35, 3.

19. *Ibidem*, no. 55.

should communicate not only by spiritual desire but also by sacramental reception of the Eucharist."[20]

14. Prompted by the same intention and pastoral zeal, the Second Vatican Council was able to give renewed consideration to what was established by Trent on Communion under both kinds. And indeed, since nowadays the doctrinal principles on the complete efficacy of Eucharistic Communion received under the species of bread alone are not in any way called into question, the Council gave permission for the reception on occasion of Communion under both kinds, because this clearer form of the sacramental sign offers a particular opportunity for understanding more deeply the mystery in which the faithful participate.[21]

15. In this manner the Church, while remaining faithful to her office as teacher of truth, safeguarding "things old," that is, the deposit of tradition, fulfills at the same time the duty of examining and prudently adopting "things new" (cf. Mt 13:52).

For part of the new Missal orders the prayers of the Church in a way more open to the needs of our times. Of this kind are above all the Ritual Masses and Masses for Various Needs, in which tradition and new elements are appropriately brought together. Thus, while a great number of expressions, drawn from the Church's most ancient tradition and familiar through the many editions of the *Roman Missal*, have remained unchanged, numerous others have been accommodated to the needs and conditions proper to our own age, and still others, such as the prayers for the Church, for the laity, for the sanctification of human labor, for the community of all nations, and certain needs proper to our era, have been newly composed, drawing on the thoughts and often the very phrasing of the recent documents of the Council.

On account, moreover, of the same attitude toward the new state of the world as it now is, it seemed to cause no harm at all to so revered a treasure if some phrases were changed so that the language would be in accord with that of modern theology and would truly reflect the current state of the Church's discipline. Hence, several expressions regarding the evaluation and use of earthly goods have been changed, as have several which alluded to a certain form of outward penance which was proper to other periods of the Church's past.

In this way, finally, the liturgical norms of the Council of Trent have certainly been completed and perfected in many particulars by those of the Second Vatican Council, which has carried into effect the efforts to bring the faithful closer to the Sacred Liturgy that have been taken up these last four centuries and especially those of recent times, and above all the attention to the Liturgy promoted by St. Pius X and his Successors.

---

20. Ecumenical Council of Trent, Session XXII, *Doctrina de ss. Missae sacrificio*, chapter 6: Denzinger-Schönmetzer, no. 1747.

21. Cf. Second Ecumenical Council of the Vatican, Constitution on the Sacred Liturgy, *Sacrosanctum Concilium*, no. 55.

CHAPTER I
THE IMPORTANCE AND DIGNITY OF THE CELEBRATION OF THE EUCHARIST

16.   The celebration of Mass, as the action of Christ and of the People of God arrayed hierarchically, is the center of the whole of Christian life for the Church both universal and local, as well as for each of the faithful individually.[22] For in it is found the high point both of the action by which God sanctifies the world in Christ and of the worship that the human race offers to the Father, adoring him through Christ, the Son of God, in the Holy Spirit.[23] In it, moreover, during the course of the year, the mysteries of redemption are celebrated so as to be in some way made present.[24] As to the other sacred actions and all the activities of the Christian life, these are bound up with it, flow from it, and are ordered to it.[25]

17.   It is, therefore, of the greatest importance that the celebration of the Mass or the Lord's Supper be so ordered that the sacred ministers and the faithful taking part in it, according to the state proper to each, may draw from it more abundantly[26] those fruits, to obtain which, Christ the Lord instituted the Eucharistic Sacrifice of his Body and Blood and entrusted it as the memorial of his Passion and Resurrection to the Church, his beloved Bride.[27]

18.   This will fittingly come about if, with due regard for the nature and other circumstances of each liturgical assembly, the entire celebration is arranged in such a way that it leads to a conscious, active, and full participation of the faithful, namely in body and in mind, a participation fervent with faith, hope, and charity, of the sort which is desired by the Church and which is required by the very nature of the celebration and to which the Christian people have a right and duty in virtue of their Baptism.[28]

19.   Even though it is on occasion not possible to have the presence and active participation of the faithful, which manifest more clearly the ecclesial nature of the celebration,[29] the celebration of the Eucharist is always endowed with its

---

22. Cf. Second Ecumenical Council of the Vatican, Constitution on the Sacred Liturgy, *Sacrosanctum Concilium*, no. 41; Dogmatic Constitution on the Church, *Lumen gentium*, no. 11; Decree on the Ministry and Life of Priests, *Presbyterorum ordinis*, nos. 2, 5, 6; Decree on the Pastoral Office of Bishops, *Christus Dominus*, no. 30; Decree on Ecumenism, *Unitatis redintegratio*, no. 15; Sacred Congregation of Rites, Instruction, *Eucharisticum mysterium*, May 25, 1967, nos. 3e, 6: *Acta Apostolicae Sedis* 59 (1967), pp. 542, 544–545.

23. Cf. Second Ecumenical Council of the Vatican, Constitution on the Sacred Liturgy, *Sacrosanctum Concilium*, no. 10.

24. Cf. *ibidem*, no. 102.

25. Cf. Second Ecumenical Council of the Vatican, Constitution on the Sacred Liturgy, *Sacrosanctum Concilium*, no. 10; cf. Decree on the Ministry and Life of Priests, *Presbyterorum ordinis*, no. 5.

26. Cf. Second Ecumenical Council of the Vatican, Constitution on the Sacred Liturgy, *Sacrosanctum Concilium*, nos. 14, 19, 26, 28, 30.

27. Cf. *ibidem*, no. 47.

28. Cf. *ibidem*, no. 14.

29. Cf. *ibidem*, no. 41.

own efficacy and dignity, since it is the act of Christ and of the Church, in which the Priest fulfills his own principal function and always acts for the sake of the people's salvation.

Hence the Priest is recommended to celebrate the Eucharistic Sacrifice, in so far as he can, even daily.[30]

20. Since, however, the celebration of the Eucharist, like the entire Liturgy, is carried out by means of perceptible signs by which the faith is nourished, strengthened, and expressed,[31] the greatest care is to be taken that those forms and elements proposed by the Church are chosen and arranged, which, given the circumstances of persons and places, more effectively foster active and full participation and more aptly respond to the spiritual needs of the faithful.

21. Hence this Instruction aims both to offer general lines for a suitable ordering of the celebration of the Eucharist and to explain the rules by which individual forms of celebration may be arranged.[32]

22. The celebration of the Eucharist in a particular Church is of the utmost importance.

For the Diocesan Bishop, the prime steward of the mysteries of God in the particular Church entrusted to his care, is the moderator, promoter, and guardian of the whole of liturgical life.[33] In celebrations that take place with the Bishop presiding, and especially in the celebration of the Eucharist by the Bishop himself with the Presbyterate, the Deacons, and the people taking part, the mystery of the Church is manifest. Hence, solemn celebrations of Mass of this sort must be exemplary for the entire diocese.

The Bishop should therefore be determined that the Priests, the Deacons, and the lay Christian faithful grasp ever more deeply the genuine significance of the rites and liturgical texts, and thereby be led to the active and fruitful celebration of the Eucharist. To that end, he should also be vigilant in ensuring that the dignity of these celebrations be enhanced and, in promoting such dignity,

---

30. Cf. Second Ecumenical Council of the Vatican, Decree on the Ministry and Life of Priests, *Presbyterorum ordinis*, no. 13; *Code of Canon Law*, can. 904.

31. Cf. Second Ecumenical Council of the Vatican, Constitution on the Sacred Liturgy, *Sacrosanctum Concilium*, no. 59.

32. Special celebrations of Mass should observe the guidelines established for them: For Masses with particular groups, cf. Sacred Congregation for Divine Worship, Instruction, *Actio pastoralis*, May 15, 1969: *Acta Apostolicae Sedis* 61 (1969), pp. 806–811; for Masses with children, cf. Sacred Congregation for Divine Worship, *Directory for Masses with Children*, November 1, 1973: *Acta Apostolicae Sedis* 66 (1974), pp. 30–46; for the manner of joining the Hours of the Office with the Mass, cf. Sacred Congregation for Divine Worship, *General Instruction of the Liturgy of the Hours*, nos. 93–98; for the manner of joining certain blessings and the crowning of an image of the Blessed Virgin Mary with the Mass, cf. Rituale Romanum, *De Benedictionibus*, editio typica, 1984, Praenotanda, no. 28; *Ordo coronandi imaginem beatae Mariae Virginis*, editio typica, 1981, nos. 10 and 14.

33. Cf. Second Ecumenical Council of the Vatican, Decree on the Pastoral Office of Bishops, *Christus Dominus*, no. 15; cf. also Constitution on the Sacred Liturgy, *Sacrosanctum Concilium*, no. 41.

the beauty of the sacred place, of the music, and of art should contribute as greatly as possible.

23.   Moreover, in order that such a celebration may correspond more fully to the prescriptions and spirit of the Sacred Liturgy, and also in order that its pastoral effectiveness be enhanced, certain accommodations and adaptations are set out in this *General Instruction* and in the Order of Mass.

24.   These adaptations consist, for the most part, in the choice of certain rites or texts, that is, of the chants, readings, prayers, explanatory interventions, and gestures capable of responding better to the needs, the preparation, and the culture of the participants and which are entrusted to the Priest Celebrant. However, the Priest will remember that he is the servant of the Sacred Liturgy and that he himself is not permitted, on his own initiative, to add, to remove, or to change anything in the celebration of Mass.[34]

25.   In addition, at the proper place in the Missal are indicated certain adaptations which in accordance with the Constitution on the Sacred Liturgy pertain respectively to the Diocesan Bishop or to the Conference of Bishops[35] (cf. below nos. 387, 388–393).

26.   As for variations and the more profound adaptations which give consideration to the traditions and culture of peoples and regions, to be introduced in accordance with article 40 of the Constitution on the Sacred Liturgy, for reasons of usefulness or necessity, those norms set out in the *Instruction on the Roman Liturgy and Inculturation*[36] and below in nos. 395–399 are to be observed.

CHAPTER II
THE STRUCTURE OF THE MASS,
ITS ELEMENTS, AND ITS PARTS

I. THE GENERAL STRUCTURE OF THE MASS

27.   At Mass or the Lord's Supper the People of God is called together, with a Priest presiding and acting in the person of Christ, to celebrate the memorial of the Lord or Eucharistic Sacrifice.[37] In an outstanding way there applies to such a local gathering of the holy Church the promise of Christ: "Where two or three are gathered in my name, there am I in their midst" (Mt 18:20). For in the celebration

---

34. Cf. Second Ecumenical Council of the Vatican, Constitution on the Sacred Liturgy, *Sacrosanctum Concilium*, no. 22.

35. Cf. Second Ecumenical Council of the Vatican, Constitution on the Sacred Liturgy, *Sacrosanctum Concilium*, nos. 38, 40; Paul VI, Apostolic Constitution, *Missale Romanum*, above.

36. Congregation for Divine Worship and the Discipline of the Sacraments, Instruction, *Varietates legitimae*, January 25, 1994: *Acta Apostolicae Sedis* 87 (1995), pp. 288–314.

37. Cf. Second Ecumenical Council of the Vatican, Decree on the Ministry and Life of Priests, *Presbyterorum ordinis*, no. 5; Constitution on the Sacred Liturgy, *Sacrosanctum Concilium*, no. 33.

of Mass, in which the Sacrifice of the Cross is perpetuated,[38] Christ is really present in the very assembly gathered in his name, in the person of the minister, in his word, and indeed substantially and uninterruptedly under the Eucharistic species.[39]

28. The Mass consists in some sense of two parts, namely the Liturgy of the Word and the Liturgy of the Eucharist, these being so closely interconnected that they form but one single act of worship.[40] For in the Mass is spread the table both of God's Word and of the Body of Christ, and from it the faithful are to be instructed and refreshed.[41] There are also certain rites that open and conclude the celebration.

II. THE DIFFERENT ELEMENTS OF THE MASS

READING AND EXPLAINING THE WORD OF GOD

29. When the Sacred Scriptures are read in the Church, God himself speaks to his people, and Christ, present in his word, proclaims the Gospel.

Therefore, the readings from the Word of God are to be listened to reverently by everyone, for they are an element of the greatest importance in the Liturgy. Although in the readings from Sacred Scripture the Word of God is addressed to all people of whatever era and is understandable to them, a fuller understanding and a greater efficaciousness of the word is nevertheless fostered by a living commentary on the word, that is, by the Homily, as part of the liturgical action.[42]

THE PRAYERS AND OTHER PARTS PERTAINING TO THE PRIEST

30. Among those things assigned to the Priest, the prime place is occupied by the Eucharistic Prayer, which is the high point of the whole celebration. Next are the orations, that is to say, the Collect, the Prayer over the Offerings, and the Prayer after Communion. These prayers are addressed to God by the Priest who presides over the assembly in the person of Christ, in the name of the entire holy people and of all present.[43] Hence they are rightly called the "presidential prayers."

---

38. Cf. Ecumenical Council of Trent, Session XXII, *Doctrina de ss. Missae sacrificio*, chapter 1: Denzinger-Schönmetzer, no. 1740; Paul VI, Solemn Profession of Faith, June 30, 1968, no. 24: *Acta Apostolicae Sedis* 60 (1968), p. 442.

39. Cf. Second Ecumenical Council of the Vatican, Constitution on the Sacred Liturgy, *Sacrosanctum Concilium*, no. 7; Paul VI, Encyclical Letter, *Mysterium fidei*, September 3, 1965: *Acta Apostolicae Sedis* 57 (1965), p. 764; Sacred Congregation of Rites, Instruction, *Eucharisticum mysterium*, May 25, 1967, no. 9: *Acta Apostolicae Sedis* 59 (1967), p. 547.

40. Cf. Second Ecumenical Council of the Vatican, Constitution on the Sacred Liturgy, *Sacrosanctum Concilium*, no. 56; Sacred Congregation of Rites, Instruction, *Eucharisticum mysterium*, May 25, 1967, no. 3: *Acta Apostolicae Sedis* 59 (1967), p. 542.

41. Cf. Second Ecumenical Council of the Vatican, Constitution on the Sacred Liturgy, *Sacrosanctum Concilium*, nos. 48, 51; Dogmatic Constitution on Divine Revelation, *Dei Verbum*, no. 21; Decree on the Ministry and Life of Priests, *Presbyterorum ordinis*, no. 4.

42. Cf. Second Ecumenical Council of the Vatican, Constitution on the Sacred Liturgy, *Sacrosanctum Concilium*, nos. 7, 33, 52.

43. Cf. *ibidem*, no. 33.

31.   Likewise it is also for the Priest, in the exercise of his office of presiding over the gathered assembly, to offer certain explanations that are foreseen in the rite itself. Where this is laid down by the rubrics, the celebrant is permitted to adapt them somewhat so that they correspond to the capacity for understanding of those participating. However, the Priest should always take care to keep to the sense of the explanatory text given in the Missal and to express it in just a few words. It is also for the presiding Priest to regulate the Word of God and to impart the final blessing. He is permitted, furthermore, in a very few words, to give the faithful an introduction to the Mass of the day (after the initial Greeting and before the Penitential Act), to the Liturgy of the Word (before the readings), and to the Eucharistic Prayer (before the Preface), though never during the Eucharistic Prayer itself; he may also make concluding comments regarding the entire sacred action before the Dismissal.

32.   The nature of the "presidential" parts requires that they be spoken in a loud and clear voice and that everyone listen to them attentively.[44] Therefore, while the Priest is pronouncing them, there should be no other prayers or singing, and the organ or other musical instruments should be silent.

33.   For the Priest, as the one who presides, expresses prayers in the name of the Church and of the assembled community; but at times he prays only in his own name, asking that he may exercise his ministry with greater attention and devotion. Prayers of this kind, which occur before the reading of the Gospel, at the Preparation of the Gifts, and also before and after the Communion of the Priest, are said quietly.

OTHER FORMULAS OCCURRING DURING THE CELEBRATION

34.   Since the celebration of Mass by its nature has a "communitarian" character,[45] both the dialogues between the Priest and the assembled faithful, and the acclamations are of great significance;[46] for they are not simply outward signs of communal celebration but foster and bring about communion between Priest and people.

35.   The acclamations and the responses of the faithful to the Priest's greetings and prayers constitute that level of active participation that is to be made by the assembled faithful in every form of the Mass, so that the action of the whole community may be clearly expressed and fostered.[47]

---

44. Cf. Sacred Congregation of Rites, Instruction, *Musicam sacram*, March 5, 1967, no. 14: *Acta Apostolicae Sedis* 59 (1967), p. 304.

45. Cf. Second Ecumenical Council of the Vatican, Constitution on the Sacred Liturgy, *Sacrosanctum Concilium*, nos. 26–27; Sacred Congregation of Rites, Instruction, *Eucharisticum mysterium*, May 25, 1967, no. 3d: *Acta Apostolicae Sedis* 59 (1967), p. 542.

46. Cf. Second Ecumenical Council of the Vatican, Constitution on the Sacred Liturgy, *Sacrosanctum Concilium*, no. 30.

47. Cf. Sacred Congregation of Rites, Instruction, *Musicam sacram*, March 5, 1967, no. 16a: *Acta Apostolicae Sedis* 59 (1967), p. 305.

36.   Other parts, most useful for expressing and fostering the active participation of the faithful, and which are assigned to the whole gathering, include especially the Penitential Act, the Profession of Faith, the Universal Prayer, and the Lord's Prayer.

37.   Finally, among other formulas:

  a) Some constitute an independent rite or act, such as the *Gloria in excelsis (Glory to God in the highest)*, the Responsorial Psalm, the *Alleluia* and Verse before the Gospel, the *Sanctus (Holy, Holy, Holy)*, the Memorial Acclamation, and the chant after Communion;

  b) Others, on the other hand, accompany some other rite, such as the chants at the Entrance, at the Offertory, at the fraction *(Agnus Dei, Lamb of God)* and at Communion.

THE MANNER OF PRONOUNCING THE DIFFERENT TEXTS

38.   In texts that are to be pronounced in a loud and clear voice, whether by the Priest or the Deacon, or by a reader, or by everyone, the voice should correspond to the genre of the text itself, that is, depending upon whether it is a reading, a prayer, an explanatory comment, an acclamation, or a sung text; it should also be suited to the form of celebration and to the solemnity of the gathering. Consideration should also be given to the characteristics of different languages and of the culture of different peoples.

    Therefore, in the rubrics and in the norms that follow, words such as "say" and "proclaim" are to be understood either of singing or of reciting, with due regard for the principles stated here above.

THE IMPORTANCE OF SINGING

39.   The Christian faithful who come together as one in expectation of the Lord's coming are instructed by the Apostle Paul to sing together Psalms, hymns, and spiritual canticles (cf. Col 3:16). Singing is the sign of the heart's joy (cf. Acts 2:46). Thus St. Augustine says rightly, "Singing is for one who loves,"[48] and there is also an ancient proverb: "Whoever sings well prays twice over."

40.   Great importance should therefore be attached to the use of singing in the celebration of the Mass, with due consideration for the culture of peoples and abilities of each liturgical assembly. Although it is not always necessary (e.g., in weekday Masses) to sing all the texts that are in principle meant to be sung, every care should be taken that singing by the ministers and the people not be absent in celebrations that occur on Sundays and on Holydays of Obligation.

    However, in the choosing of the parts actually to be sung, preference is to be given to those that are of greater importance and especially to those which

---

48. St. Augustine of Hippo, *Sermo* 336, 1: PL 38: 1472.

are to be sung by the Priest or the Deacon or a reader, with the people replying, or by the Priest and people together.[49]

41.   The main place should be given, all things being equal, to Gregorian chant, as being proper to the Roman Liturgy. Other kinds of sacred music, in particular polyphony, are in no way excluded, provided that they correspond to the spirit of the liturgical action and that they foster the participation of all the faithful.[50]

Since the faithful from different countries come together ever more frequently, it is desirable that they know how to sing together at least some parts of the Ordinary of the Mass in Latin, especially the Profession of Faith and the Lord's Prayer, according to the simpler settings.[51]

GESTURES AND BODILY POSTURE

42.   The gestures and bodily posture of both the Priest, the Deacon, and the ministers, and also of the people, must be conducive to making the entire celebration resplendent with beauty and noble simplicity, to making clear the true and full meaning of its different parts, and to fostering the participation of all.[52] Attention must therefore be paid to what is determined by this *General Instruction* and by the traditional practice of the Roman Rite and to what serves the common spiritual good of the People of God, rather than private inclination or arbitrary choice.

A common bodily posture, to be observed by all those taking part, is a sign of the unity of the members of the Christian community gathered together for the Sacred Liturgy, for it expresses the intentions and spiritual attitude of the participants and also fosters them.

43.   The faithful should stand from the beginning of the Entrance Chant, or while the Priest approaches the altar, until the end of the Collect; for the *Alleluia* Chant before the Gospel; while the Gospel itself is proclaimed; during the Profession of Faith and the Universal Prayer; and from the invitation, *Orate, fratres (Pray, brethren),* before the Prayer over the Offerings until the end of Mass, except at the places indicated here below.

The faithful should sit, on the other hand, during the readings before the Gospel and the Responsorial Psalm and for the Homily and during the Preparation of the Gifts at the Offertory; and, if appropriate, they may sit or kneel during the period of sacred silence after Communion.

---

49. Cf. Sacred Congregation of Rites, Instruction, *Musicam sacram,* March 5, 1967, nos. 7, 16: *Acta Apostolicae Sedis* 59 (1967), pp. 302, 305.

50. Cf. Second Ecumenical Council of the Vatican, Constitution on the Sacred Liturgy, *Sacrosanctum Concilium,* no. 116; cf. also no. 30.

51. Cf. Second Ecumenical Council of the Vatican, Constitution on the Sacred Liturgy, *Sacrosanctum Concilium,* no. 54; Sacred Congregation of Rites, Instruction, *Inter Oecumenici,* September 26, 1964, no. 59: *Acta Apostolicae Sedis* 56 (1964), p. 891; Instruction, *Musicam sacram,* March 5, 1967, no. 47: *Acta Apostolicae Sedis* 59 (1967), p. 314.

52. Cf. Second Ecumenical Council of the Vatican, Constitution on the Sacred Liturgy, *Sacrosanctum Concilium,* nos. 30, 34; cf. also no. 21.

In the dioceses of the United States of America, they should kneel beginning after the singing or recitation of the *Sanctus (Holy, Holy, Holy)* until after the *Amen* of the Eucharistic Prayer, except when prevented on occasion by ill health, or for reasons of lack of space, of the large number of people present, or for another reasonable cause. However, those who do not kneel ought to make a profound bow when the Priest genuflects after the Consecration. The faithful kneel after the *Agnus Dei (Lamb of God)* unless the Diocesan Bishop determines otherwise.[53]

For the sake of uniformity in gestures and bodily postures during one and the same celebration, the faithful should follow the instructions which the Deacon, a lay minister, or the Priest gives, according to what is laid down in the Missal.

44. Among gestures are included also actions and processions, by which the Priest, with the Deacon and ministers, goes to the altar; the Deacon carries the Evangeliary or *Book of the Gospels* to the ambo before the proclamation of the Gospel; the faithful bring up the gifts and come forward to receive Communion. It is appropriate that actions and processions of this sort be carried out with decorum while the chants proper to them are sung, in accordance with the norms laid down for each.

SILENCE

45. Sacred silence also, as part of the celebration, is to be observed at the designated times.[54] Its nature, however, depends on the moment when it occurs in the different parts of the celebration. For in the Penitential Act and again after the invitation to pray, individuals recollect themselves; whereas after a reading or after the Homily, all meditate briefly on what they have heard; then after Communion, they praise God in their hearts and pray to him.

Even before the celebration itself, it is a praiseworthy practice for silence to be observed in the church, in the sacristy, in the vesting room, and in adjacent areas, so that all may dispose themselves to carry out the sacred celebration in a devout and fitting manner.

III. THE INDIVIDUAL PARTS OF THE MASS

A) The Introductory Rites

46. The rites that precede the Liturgy of the Word, namely, the Entrance, the Greeting, the Penitential Act, the *Kyrie*, the *Gloria in excelsis (Glory to God in the highest)* and Collect, have the character of a beginning, an introduction, and a preparation.

---

53. Cf. *ibidem*, no. 40; Congregation for Divine Worship and the Discipline of the Sacraments, Instruction, *Varietates legitimae*, January 25, 1994, no. 41: *Acta Apostolicae Sedis* 87 (1995), p. 304.

54. Cf. Second Ecumenical Council of the Vatican, Constitution on the Sacred Liturgy, *Sacrosanctum Concilium*, no. 30; Sacred Congregation of Rites, Instruction, *Musicam sacram*, March 5, 1967, no. 17: *Acta Apostolicae Sedis* 59 (1967), p. 305.

Their purpose is to ensure that the faithful, who come together as one, establish communion and dispose themselves properly to listen to the Word of God and to celebrate the Eucharist worthily.

In certain celebrations that are combined with Mass according to the norms of the liturgical books, the Introductory Rites are omitted or take place in a particular way.

THE ENTRANCE

47.   When the people are gathered, and as the Priest enters with the Deacon and ministers, the Entrance Chant begins. Its purpose is to open the celebration, foster the unity of those who have been gathered, introduce their thoughts to the mystery of the liturgical time or festivity, and accompany the procession of the Priest and ministers.

48.   This chant is sung alternately by the choir and the people or similarly by a cantor and the people, or entirely by the people, or by the choir alone. In the Dioceses of the United States of America there are four options for the Entrance Chant: (1) the antiphon from the Missal or the antiphon with its Psalm from the *Graduale Romanum* as set to music there or in another setting; (2) the antiphon and Psalm of the *Graduale Simplex* for the liturgical time; (3) a chant from another collection of Psalms and antiphons, approved by the Conference of Bishops or the Diocesan Bishop, including Psalms arranged in responsorial or metrical forms; (4) another liturgical chant that is suited to the sacred action, the day, or the time of year, similarly approved by the Conference of Bishops or the Diocesan Bishop.

If there is no singing at the Entrance, the antiphon given in the Missal is recited either by the faithful, or by some of them, or by a reader; otherwise, it is recited by the Priest himself, who may even adapt it as an introductory explanation (cf. no. 31).

REVERENCE TO THE ALTAR AND GREETING OF THE ASSEMBLED PEOPLE

49.   When they have arrived at the sanctuary, the Priest, the Deacon, and the ministers reverence the altar with a profound bow.

Moreover, as an expression of veneration, the Priest and Deacon then kiss the altar itself; the Priest, if appropriate, also incenses the cross and the altar.

50.   When the Entrance Chant is concluded, the Priest stands at the chair and, together with the whole gathering, signs himself with the Sign of the Cross. Then by means of the Greeting he signifies the presence of the Lord to the assembled community. By this greeting and the people's response, the mystery of the Church gathered together is made manifest.

After the greeting of the people, the Priest, or the Deacon, or a lay minister may very briefly introduce the faithful to the Mass of the day.

THE PENITENTIAL ACT

51.   After this, the Priest calls upon the whole community to take part in the Penitential Act, which, after a brief pause for silence, it does by means of a formula of general confession. The rite concludes with the Priest's absolution, which, however, lacks the efficacy of the Sacrament of Penance.

From time to time on Sundays, especially in Easter Time, instead of the customary Penitential Act, the blessing and sprinkling of water may take place as a reminder of Baptism.[55]

THE *KYRIE, ELEISON*

52.   After the Penitential Act, the *Kyrie, eleison (Lord, have mercy)*, is always begun, unless it has already been part of the Penitential Act. Since it is a chant by which the faithful acclaim the Lord and implore his mercy, it is usually executed by everyone, that is to say, with the people and the choir or cantor taking part in it.

Each acclamation is usually pronounced twice, though it is not to be excluded that it be repeated several times, by reason of the character of the various languages, as well as of the artistry of the music or of other circumstances. When the *Kyrie* is sung as a part of the Penitential Act, a "trope" precedes each acclamation.

THE *GLORIA IN EXCELSIS*

53.   The *Gloria in excelsis (Glory to God in the highest)* is a most ancient and venerable hymn by which the Church, gathered in the Holy Spirit, glorifies and entreats God the Father and the Lamb. The text of this hymn may not be replaced by any other. It is intoned by the Priest or, if appropriate, by a cantor or by the choir; but it is sung either by everyone together, or by the people alternately with the choir, or by the choir alone. If not sung, it is to be recited either by everybody together or by two choirs responding one to the other.

It is sung or said on Sundays outside Advent and Lent, and also on Solemnities and Feasts, and at particular celebrations of a more solemn character.

THE COLLECT

54.   Next the Priest calls upon the people to pray and everybody, together with the Priest, observes a brief silence so that they may become aware of being in God's presence and may call to mind their intentions. Then the Priest pronounces the prayer usually called the "Collect" and through which the character of the celebration finds expression. By an ancient tradition of the Church, the Collect prayer is usually addressed to God the Father, through Christ, in the Holy Spirit,[56]

---

55. Cf. below, pp. 1453–1456.

56. Cf. Tertullian, *Adversus Marcionem*, IV, 9: *Corpus Christianorum, Series Latina* 1, p. 560; Origen, *Disputatio cum Heracleida*, no. 4, 24: *Sources chrétiennes* 67, p. 62; *Statuta Concilii Hipponensis Breviata*, no. 21: *Corpus Christianorum, Series Latina* 149, p. 39.

and is concluded with a Trinitarian ending, or longer ending, in the following manner:

- If the prayer is directed to the Father: *Through our Lord Jesus Christ, your Son, who lives and reigns with you in the unity of the Holy Spirit, one God, for ever and ever;*

- If it is directed to the Father, but the Son is mentioned at the end: *Who lives and reigns with you in the unity of the Holy Spirit, one God, for ever and ever;*

- If it is directed to the Son: *Who live and reign with God the Father in the unity of the Holy Spirit, one God, for ever and ever.*

The people, joining in this petition, make the prayer their own by means of the acclamation *Amen.*

At Mass only a single Collect is ever said.

B) The Liturgy of the Word

55.   The main part of the Liturgy of the Word is made up of the readings from Sacred Scripture together with the chants occurring between them. As for the Homily, the Profession of Faith, and the Universal Prayer, they develop and conclude it. For in the readings, as explained by the Homily, God speaks to his people,[57] opening up to them the mystery of redemption and salvation, and offering spiritual nourishment; and Christ himself is present through his word in the midst of the faithful.[58] By silence and by singing, the people make this divine word their own, and affirm their adherence to it by means of the Profession of Faith; finally, having been nourished by the divine word, the people pour out their petitions by means of the Universal Prayer for the needs of the whole Church and for the salvation of the whole world.

SILENCE

56.   The Liturgy of the Word is to be celebrated in such a way as to favor meditation, and so any kind of haste such as hinders recollection is clearly to be avoided. In the course of it, brief periods of silence are also appropriate, accommodated to the assembled congregation; by means of these, under the action of the Holy Spirit, the Word of God may be grasped by the heart and a response through prayer may be prepared. It may be appropriate to observe such periods of silence, for example, before the Liturgy of the Word itself begins, after the First and Second Reading, and lastly at the conclusion of the Homily.[59]

---

57. Cf. Second Ecumenical Council of the Vatican, Constitution on the Sacred Liturgy, *Sacrosanctum Concilium*, no. 33.

58. Cf. *ibidem*, no. 7.

59. Cf. Missale Romanum, *Ordo lectionum Missae*, editio typica altera, 1981, no. 28.

57.   In the readings, the table of God's Word is spread before the faithful, and the treasures of the Bible are opened to them.[60] Hence, it is preferable that the arrangement of the biblical readings be maintained, for by them the unity of both Testaments and of salvation history is brought out. Nor is it lawful to replace the readings and Responsorial Psalm, which contain the Word of God, with other, non-biblical texts.[61]

58.   In the celebration of the Mass with the people, the readings are always read from the ambo.

59.   The function of proclaiming the readings is by tradition not presidential but ministerial. Therefore the readings are to be read by a reader, but the Gospel by the Deacon or, in his absence, by another Priest. If, however, a Deacon or another Priest is not present, the Priest Celebrant himself should read the Gospel, and moreover, if no other suitable reader is present, the Priest Celebrant should also proclaim the other readings as well.

After each reading, whoever reads it pronounces the acclamation, and by means of the reply the assembled people give honor to the Word of God that they have received in faith and with gratitude.

60.   The reading of the Gospel constitutes the high point of the Liturgy of the Word. The Liturgy itself teaches the great reverence that is to be shown to this reading by setting it off from the other readings with special marks of honor, by the fact of which minister is appointed to proclaim it and by the blessing or prayer with which he prepares himself; and also by the fact that through their acclamations the faithful acknowledge and confess that Christ is present and is speaking to them and stand as they listen to the reading; and by the mere fact of the marks of reverence that are given to the *Book of the Gospels*.

THE RESPONSORIAL PSALM

61.   After the First Reading follows the Responsorial Psalm, which is an integral part of the Liturgy of the Word and which has great liturgical and pastoral importance, since it fosters meditation on the Word of God.

The Responsorial Psalm should correspond to each reading and should usually be taken from the Lectionary.

It is preferable for the Responsorial Psalm to be sung, at least as far as the people's response is concerned. Hence the psalmist, or cantor of the Psalm, sings the Psalm verses at the ambo or another suitable place, while the whole congregation sits and listens, normally taking part by means of the response, except when the Psalm is sung straight through, that is, without a response. However, in order that the people may be able to sing the Psalm response more easily, texts

---

60. Cf. Second Ecumenical Council of the Vatican, Constitution on the Sacred Liturgy, *Sacrosanctum Concilium*, no. 51.

61. Cf. John Paul II, Apostolic Letter, *Vicesimus quintus annus*, December 4, 1988, no. 13: *Acta Apostolicae Sedis* 81 (1989), p. 910.

of some responses and Psalms have been chosen for the different times of the year or for the different categories of Saints. These may be used instead of the text corresponding to the reading whenever the Psalm is sung. If the Psalm cannot be sung, then it should be recited in a way that is particularly suited to fostering meditation on the Word of God.

In the Dioceses of the United States of America, instead of the Psalm assigned in the Lectionary, there may be sung either the Responsorial Gradual from the *Graduale Romanum*, or the Responsorial Psalm or the *Alleluia* Psalm from the *Graduale Simplex*, as described in these books, or an antiphon and Psalm from another collection of Psalms and antiphons, including Psalms arranged in metrical form, providing that they have been approved by the Conference of Bishops or the Diocesan Bishop. Songs or hymns may not be used in place of the Responsorial Psalm.

THE ACCLAMATION BEFORE THE GOSPEL

62.   After the reading that immediately precedes the Gospel, the *Alleluia* or another chant laid down by the rubrics is sung, as the liturgical time requires. An acclamation of this kind constitutes a rite or act in itself, by which the gathering of the faithful welcomes and greets the Lord who is about to speak to them in the Gospel and profess their faith by means of the chant. It is sung by everybody, standing, and is led by the choir or a cantor, being repeated as the case requires. The verse, on the other hand, is sung either by the choir or by a cantor.

a) The *Alleluia* is sung in every time of year other than Lent. The verses are taken from the Lectionary or the *Graduale*.

b) During Lent, instead of the *Alleluia*, the Verse before the Gospel as given in the Lectionary is sung. It is also possible to sing another Psalm or Tract, as found in the *Graduale*.

63.   When there is only one reading before the Gospel:

a) during a time of year when the *Alleluia* is prescribed, either an *Alleluia* Psalm or the Responsorial Psalm followed by the *Alleluia* with its verse may be used;

b) during a time of year when the *Alleluia* is not foreseen, either the Psalm and the Verse before the Gospel or the Psalm alone may be used;

c) the *Alleluia* or the Verse before the Gospel, if not sung, may be omitted.

64.   The Sequence which, except on Easter Sunday and on Pentecost Day, is optional, is sung before the *Alleluia*.

THE HOMILY

65.   The Homily is part of the Liturgy and is highly recommended,[62] for it is necessary for the nurturing of the Christian life. It should be an explanation of

---

62. Cf. Second Ecumenical Council of the Vatican, Constitution on the Sacred Liturgy, *Sacrosanctum Concilium*, no. 52; *Code of Canon Law*, can. 767 §1.

some aspect of the readings from Sacred Scripture or of another text from the Ordinary or the Proper of the Mass of the day and should take into account both the mystery being celebrated and the particular needs of the listeners.[63]

66.   The Homily should ordinarily be given by the Priest Celebrant himself or be entrusted by him to a concelebrating Priest, or from time to time and, if appropriate, to the Deacon, but never to a lay person.[64] In particular cases and for a just cause, the Homily may even be given by a Bishop or a Priest who is present at the celebration but cannot concelebrate.

On Sundays and Holydays of Obligation there is to be a Homily at every Mass that is celebrated with the people attending, and it may not be omitted without a grave reason. On other days it is recommended, especially on the weekdays of Advent, Lent, and Easter Time, as well as on other festive days and occasions when the people come to church in greater numbers.[65]

It is appropriate for a brief period of silence to be observed after the Homily.

THE PROFESSION OF FAITH

67.   The purpose of the Creed or Profession of Faith is that the whole gathered people may respond to the Word of God proclaimed in the readings taken from Sacred Scripture and explained in the Homily and that they may also honor and confess the great mysteries of the faith by pronouncing the rule of faith in a formula approved for liturgical use and before the celebration of these mysteries in the Eucharist begins.

68.   The Creed is to be sung or said by the Priest together with the people on Sundays and Solemnities. It may be said also at particular celebrations of a more solemn character.

If it is sung, it is intoned by the Priest or, if appropriate, by a cantor or by the choir. It is then sung either by everybody together or by the people alternating with the choir.

If it is not sung, it is to be recited by everybody together or by two choirs responding one to the other.

THE UNIVERSAL PRAYER

69.   In the Universal Prayer or Prayer of the Faithful, the people respond in some sense to the Word of God which they have received in faith and, exercising the office of their baptismal Priesthood, offer prayers to God for the salva-

---

63. Cf. Sacred Congregation of Rites, Instruction, *Inter Oecumenici*, September 26, 1964, no. 54: *Acta Apostolicae Sedis* 56 (1964), p. 890.

64. Cf. *Code of Canon Law*, can. 767 §1; Pontifical Commission for the Authentic Interpretation of the *Code of Canon Law*, response to *dubium* regarding can. 767 §1: *Acta Apostolicae Sedis* 79 (1987), p. 1249; Interdicasterial Instruction on certain questions regarding the collaboration of the non-ordained faithful in the sacred ministry of Priests, *Ecclesiae de mysterio*, August 15, 1997, art. 3: *Acta Apostolicae Sedis* 89 (1997), p. 864.

65. Cf. Sacred Congregation of Rites, Instruction, *Inter Oecumenici*, September 26, 1964, no. 53: *Acta Apostolicae Sedis* 56 (1964), p. 890.

tion of all. It is desirable that there usually be such a form of prayer in Masses celebrated with the people, so that petitions may be offered for holy Church, for those who govern with authority over us, for those weighed down by various needs, for all humanity, and for the salvation of the whole world.[66]

70. The series of intentions is usually to be:

a) for the needs of the Church;

b) for public authorities and the salvation of the whole world;

c) for those burdened by any kind of difficulty;

d) for the local community.

Nevertheless, in any particular celebration, such as a Confirmation, a Marriage, or at a Funeral, the series of intentions may be concerned more closely with the particular occasion.

71. It is for the Priest Celebrant to regulate this prayer from the chair. He himself begins it with a brief introduction, by which he calls upon the faithful to pray, and likewise he concludes it with an oration. The intentions announced should be sober, be composed with a wise liberty and in few words, and they should be expressive of the prayer of the entire community.

They are announced from the ambo or from another suitable place, by the Deacon or by a cantor, a reader, or one of the lay faithful.[67]

The people, for their part, stand and give expression to their prayer either by an invocation said in common after each intention or by praying in silence.

C) The Liturgy of the Eucharist

72. At the Last Supper Christ instituted the Paschal Sacrifice and banquet, by which the Sacrifice of the Cross is continuously made present in the Church whenever the Priest, representing Christ the Lord, carries out what the Lord himself did and handed over to his disciples to be done in his memory.[68]

For Christ took the bread and the chalice, gave thanks, broke the bread and gave it to his disciples, saying: Take, eat and drink: this is my Body; this is the chalice of my Blood. Do this in memory of me. Hence, the Church has arranged the entire celebration of the Liturgy of the Eucharist in parts corresponding to precisely these words and actions of Christ, namely:

---

66. Cf. Second Ecumenical Council of the Vatican, Constitution on the Sacred Liturgy, *Sacrosanctum Concilium*, no. 53.

67. Cf. Sacred Congregation of Rites, Instruction, *Inter Oecumenici*, September 26, 1964, no. 56: *Acta Apostolicae Sedis* 56 (1964), p. 890.

68. Cf. Second Ecumenical Council of the Vatican, Constitution on the Sacred Liturgy, *Sacrosanctum Concilium*, no. 47; Sacred Congregation of Rites, Instruction, *Eucharisticum mysterium*, May 25, 1967, no. 3a, b: *Acta Apostolicae Sedis* 59 (1967), pp. 540–541.

a) At the Preparation of the Gifts, bread and wine with water are brought to the altar, the same elements, that is to say, which Christ took into his hands.

b) In the Eucharistic Prayer, thanks is given to God for the whole work of salvation, and the offerings become the Body and Blood of Christ.

c) Through the fraction and through Communion, the faithful, though many, receive from the one bread the Lord's Body and from the one chalice the Lord's Blood in the same way that the Apostles received them from the hands of Christ himself.

THE PREPARATION OF THE GIFTS

73. At the beginning of the Liturgy of the Eucharist the gifts which will become Christ's Body and Blood are brought to the altar.

First of all, the altar or Lord's table, which is the center of the whole Liturgy of the Eucharist,[69] is made ready when on it are placed the corporal, purificator, Missal, and chalice (unless this last is prepared at the credence table).

The offerings are then brought forward. It is a praiseworthy practice for the bread and wine to be presented by the faithful. They are then accepted at an appropriate place by the Priest or the Deacon to be carried to the altar. Even though the faithful no longer bring from their own possessions the bread and wine intended for the liturgy as was once the case, nevertheless the rite of carrying up the offerings still keeps its spiritual efficacy and significance.

Even money or other gifts for the poor or for the Church, brought by the faithful or collected in the church, are acceptable; given their purpose, they are to be put in a suitable place away from the Eucharistic table.

74. The procession bringing the gifts is accompanied by the Offertory Chant (cf. no. 37 b), which continues at least until the gifts have been placed on the altar. The norms on the manner of singing are the same as for the Entrance Chant (cf. no. 48). Singing may always accompany the rite at the Offertory, even when there is no procession with the gifts.

75. The bread and wine are placed on the altar by the Priest to the accompaniment of the prescribed formulas; the Priest may incense the gifts placed on the altar and then incense the cross and the altar itself, so as to signify the Church's offering and prayer rising like incense in the sight of God. Next, the Priest, because of his sacred ministry, and the people, by reason of their baptismal dignity, may be incensed by the Deacon or by another minister.

76. Then the Priest washes his hands at the side of the altar, a rite in which the desire for interior purification finds expression.

---

69. Cf. Sacred Congregation of Rites, Instruction, *Inter Oecumenici*, September 26, 1964, no. 91: *Acta Apostolicae Sedis* 56 (1964), p. 898; Instruction, *Eucharisticum mysterium*, May 25, 1967, no. 24: *Acta Apostolicae Sedis* 59 (1967), p. 554.

77.   Once the offerings have been placed on the altar and the accompanying rites completed, by means of the invitation to pray with the Priest and by means of the Prayer over the Offerings, the Preparation of the Gifts is concluded and preparation made for the Eucharistic Prayer.

At Mass, a single Prayer over the Offerings is said, and it ends with the shorter conclusion, that is: *Through Christ our Lord*. If, however, the Son is mentioned at the end of this prayer, the conclusion is: *Who lives and reigns for ever and ever*.

The people, joining in this petition, make the prayer their own by means of the acclamation *Amen*.

THE EUCHARISTIC PRAYER

78.   Now the center and high point of the entire celebration begins, namely, the Eucharistic Prayer itself, that is, the prayer of thanksgiving and sanctification. The Priest calls upon the people to lift up their hearts towards the Lord in prayer and thanksgiving; he associates the people with himself in the Prayer that he addresses in the name of the entire community to God the Father through Jesus Christ in the Holy Spirit. Furthermore, the meaning of this Prayer is that the whole congregation of the faithful joins with Christ in confessing the great deeds of God and in the offering of Sacrifice. The Eucharistic Prayer requires that everybody listens to it with reverence and in silence.

79.   The main elements of which the Eucharistic Prayer consists may be distinguished from one another in this way:

   a) The *thanksgiving* (expressed especially in the Preface), in which the Priest, in the name of the whole of the holy people, glorifies God the Father and gives thanks to him for the whole work of salvation or for some particular aspect of it, according to the varying day, festivity, or time of year.

   b) The *acclamation*, by which the whole congregation, joining with the heavenly powers, sings the *Sanctus (Holy, Holy, Holy)*. This acclamation, which constitutes part of the Eucharistic Prayer itself, is pronounced by all the people with the Priest.

   c) The *epiclesis*, in which, by means of particular invocations, the Church implores the power of the Holy Spirit that the gifts offered by human hands be consecrated, that is, become Christ's Body and Blood, and that the unblemished sacrificial Victim to be consumed in Communion may be for the salvation of those who will partake of it.

   d) The *Institution narrative and Consecration*, by which, by means of the words and actions of Christ, that Sacrifice is effected which Christ himself instituted during the Last Supper, when he offered his Body and Blood under the species of bread and wine, gave them to the Apostles to eat and drink, and leaving with the latter the command to perpetuate this same mystery.

e) The *anamnesis*, by which the Church, fulfilling the command that she received from Christ the Lord through the Apostles, celebrates the memorial of Christ, recalling especially his blessed Passion, glorious Resurrection, and Ascension into heaven.

f) The *oblation*, by which, in this very memorial, the Church, in particular that gathered here and now, offers the unblemished sacrificial Victim in the Holy Spirit to the Father. The Church's intention, indeed, is that the faithful not only offer this unblemished sacrificial Victim but also learn to offer their very selves,[70] and so day by day to be brought, through the mediation of Christ, into unity with God and with each other, so that God may at last be all in all.[71]

g) The *intercessions*, by which expression is given to the fact that the Eucharist is celebrated in communion with the whole Church, of both heaven and of earth, and that the oblation is made for her and for all her members, living and dead, who are called to participate in the redemption and salvation purchased by the Body and Blood of Christ.

h) The *concluding doxology*, by which the glorification of God is expressed and which is affirmed and concluded by the people's acclamation *Amen*.

THE COMMUNION RITE

80. Since the celebration of the Eucharist is the Paschal Banquet, it is desirable that in accordance with the Lord's command his Body and Blood should be received as spiritual food by those of the faithful who are properly disposed. This is the sense of the fraction and the other preparatory rites by which the faithful are led more immediately to Communion.

THE LORD'S PRAYER

81. In the Lord's Prayer a petition is made for daily bread, which for Christians means principally the Eucharistic Bread, and entreating also purification from sin, so that what is holy may in truth be given to the holy. The Priest pronounces the invitation to the prayer, and all the faithful say the prayer with him; then the Priest alone adds the embolism, which the people conclude by means of the doxology. The embolism, developing the last petition of the Lord's Prayer itself, asks for deliverance from the power of evil for the whole community of the faithful.

The invitation, the Prayer itself, the embolism, and the doxology by which the people conclude these things are sung or are said aloud.

---

70. Cf. Second Ecumenical Council of the Vatican, Constitution on the Sacred Liturgy, *Sacrosanctum Concilium*, no. 48; Sacred Congregation of Rites, Instruction, *Eucharisticum mysterium*, May 25,1967, no. 12: *Acta Apostolicae Sedis* 59 (1967), pp. 548–549.

71. Cf. Second Ecumenical Council of the Vatican, Constitution on the Sacred Liturgy, *Sacrosanctum Concilium*, no. 48; Decree on the Ministry and Life of Priests, *Presbyterorum ordinis*, no. 5; Sacred Congregation of Rites, Instruction, *Eucharisticum mysterium*, 25 May 1967, no. 12: *Acta Apostolicae Sedis* 59 (1967), pp. 548–549.

82.   There follows the Rite of Peace, by which the Church entreats peace and unity for herself and for the whole human family, and the faithful express to each other their ecclesial communion and mutual charity before communicating in the Sacrament.

As for the actual sign of peace to be given, the manner is to be established by the Conferences of Bishops in accordance with the culture and customs of the peoples. However, it is appropriate that each person, in a sober manner, offer the sign of peace only to those who are nearest.

THE FRACTION OF THE BREAD

83.   The Priest breaks the Eucharistic Bread, with the assistance, if the case requires, of the Deacon or a concelebrant. The gesture of breaking bread done by Christ at the Last Supper, which in apostolic times gave the entire Eucharistic Action its name, signifies that the many faithful are made one body (1 Cor 10:17) by receiving Communion from the one Bread of Life, which is Christ, who for the salvation of the world died and rose again. The fraction or breaking of bread is begun after the sign of peace and is carried out with proper reverence, and should not be unnecessarily prolonged or accorded exaggerated importance. This rite is reserved to the Priest and the Deacon.

The Priest breaks the Bread and puts a piece of the host into the chalice to signify the unity of the Body and Blood of the Lord in the work of salvation, namely, of the Body of Jesus Christ, living and glorious. The supplication *Agnus Dei (Lamb of God)* is usually sung by the choir or cantor with the congregation replying; or at least recited aloud. This invocation accompanies the fraction of the bread and, for this reason, may be repeated as many times as necessary until the rite has been completed. The final time it concludes with the words *grant us peace.*

COMMUNION

84.   The Priest prepares himself by a prayer, said quietly, so that he may fruitfully receive the Body and Blood of Christ. The faithful do the same, praying silently.

Then the Priest shows the faithful the Eucharistic Bread, holding it over the paten or over the chalice, and invites them to the banquet of Christ; and along with the faithful, he then makes an act of humility, using the prescribed words from the Gospels.

85.   It is most desirable that the faithful, just as the Priest himself is bound to do, receive the Lord's Body from hosts consecrated at the same Mass and that, in the cases where this is foreseen, they partake of the chalice (cf. no. 283), so

that even by means of the signs Communion may stand out more clearly as a participation in the sacrifice actually being celebrated.[72]

86.   While the Priest is receiving the Sacrament, the Communion Chant is begun, its purpose being to express the spiritual union of the communicants by means of the unity of their voices, to show gladness of heart, and to bring out more clearly the "communitarian" character of the procession to receive the Eucharist. The singing is prolonged for as long as the Sacrament is being administered to the faithful.[73] However, if there is to be a hymn after Communion, the Communion Chant should be ended in a timely manner.

Care should be taken that singers, too, can receive Communion with ease.

87.   In the Dioceses of the United States of America, there are four options for singing at Communion: (1) the antiphon from the Missal or the antiphon with its Psalm from the *Graduale Romanum*, as set to music there or in another musical setting; (2) the antiphon with Psalm from the *Graduale Simplex* of the liturgical time; (3) a chant from another collection of Psalms and antiphons, approved by the Conference of Bishops or the Diocesan Bishop, including Psalms arranged in responsorial or metrical forms; (4) some other suitable liturgical chant (cf. no. 86) approved by the Conference of Bishops or the Diocesan Bishop. This is sung either by the choir alone or by the choir or a cantor with the people.

However, if there is no singing, the antiphon given in the Missal may be recited either by the faithful, or by some of them, or by a reader; otherwise, it is recited by the Priest himself after he has received Communion and before he distributes Communion to the faithful.

88.   When the distribution of Communion is over, if appropriate, the Priest and faithful pray quietly for some time. If desired, a Psalm or other canticle of praise or a hymn may also be sung by the whole congregation.

89.   To bring to completion the prayer of the People of God, and also to conclude the whole Communion Rite, the Priest pronounces the Prayer after Communion, in which he prays for the fruits of the mystery just celebrated.

At Mass a single Prayer after Communion is said, and it ends with the shorter conclusion; that is:

– if the prayer is directed to the Father: *Through Christ our Lord;*

– if it is directed to the Father, but the Son is mentioned at the end: *Who lives and reigns for ever and ever;*

– if it is directed to the Son: *Who live and reign for ever and ever.*

---

72. Cf. Sacred Congregation of Rites, Instruction, *Eucharisticum mysterium*, May 25, 1967, nos. 31, 32: *Acta Apostolicae Sedis* 59 (1969), pp. 558–559; Sacred Congregation for the Discipline of the Sacraments, Instruction, *Immensae caritatis*, January 29, 1973, no. 2: *Acta Apostolicae Sedis* 65 (1973), pp. 267–268.

73. Cf. Sacred Congregation for the Sacraments and Divine Worship, Instruction, *Inestimabile donum*, April 3, 1980, no. 17: *Acta Apostolicae Sedis* 72 (1980), p. 338.

The people make the prayer their own by means of the acclamation *Amen*.

D) The Concluding Rites

90. To the Concluding Rites belong the following:

    a) brief announcements, should they be necessary;

    b) the Priest's Greeting and Blessing, which on certain days and occasions is expanded and expressed by the Prayer over the People or another more solemn formula;

    c) the Dismissal of the people by the Deacon or the Priest, so that each may go back to doing good works, praising and blessing God;

    d) the kissing of the altar by the Priest and the Deacon, followed by a profound bow to the altar by the Priest, the Deacon, and the other ministers.

CHAPTER III
DUTIES AND MINISTRIES IN THE MASS

91. The celebration of the Eucharist is the action of Christ and of the Church, namely, of the holy people united and ordered under the Bishop. It therefore pertains to the whole Body of the Church, manifests it, and has its effect upon it. Indeed, it also affects the individual members of the Church in a different way, according to their different orders, functions, and actual participation.[74] In this way, the Christian people, "a chosen race, a royal Priesthood, a holy nation, a people for his own possession," expresses its cohesion and its hierarchical ordering.[75] All, therefore, whether ordained ministers or lay Christian faithful, in fulfilling their function or their duty, should carry out solely but totally that which pertains to them.[76]

I. THE DUTIES OF THOSE IN HOLY ORDERS

92. Every legitimate celebration of the Eucharist is directed by the Bishop, either in person or through Priests who are his helpers.[77]

When the Bishop is present at a Mass where the people are gathered, it is most fitting that he himself celebrate the Eucharist and associate Priests with himself in the sacred action as concelebrants. This is done not for the sake of adding outward solemnity to the rite, but to signify more vividly the mystery of the Church, "the sacrament of unity."[78]

---

74. Cf. Second Ecumenical Council of the Vatican, Constitution on the Sacred Liturgy, *Sacrosanctum Concilium*, no. 26.

75. Cf. *ibidem*, no. 14.

76. Cf. *ibidem*, no. 28.

77. Cf. Second Ecumenical Council of the Vatican, Dogmatic Constitution on the Church, *Lumen gentium*, nos. 26, 28; Constitution on the Sacred Liturgy, *Sacrosanctum Concilium*, no. 42.

78. Cf. Second Ecumenical Council of the Vatican, Constitution on the Sacred Liturgy, *Sacrosanctum Concilium*, no. 26.

If, on the other hand, the Bishop does not celebrate the Eucharist but has assigned it to someone else to do this, then it is appropriate that he should preside over the Liturgy of the Word, wearing the pectoral cross, stole, and cope over an alb, and that he should give the blessing at the end of Mass.[79]

93. A Priest, also, who possesses within the Church the sacred power of Orders to offer sacrifice in the person of Christ,[80] presides by this fact over the faithful people gathered here and now, presides over their prayer, proclaims to them the message of salvation, associates the people with himself in the offering of sacrifice through Christ in the Holy Spirit to God the Father, and gives his brothers and sisters the Bread of eternal life and partakes of it with them. Therefore, when he celebrates the Eucharist, he must serve God and the people with dignity and humility, and by his bearing and by the way he pronounces the divine words he must convey to the faithful the living presence of Christ.

94. After the Priest, the Deacon, in virtue of the sacred Ordination he has received, holds first place among those who minister in the celebration of the Eucharist. For the sacred Order of the Diaconate has been held in high honor in the Church even from the early time of the Apostles.[81] At Mass the Deacon has his own part in proclaiming the Gospel, from time to time in preaching God's Word, in announcing the intentions of the Universal Prayer, in ministering to the Priest, in preparing the altar and in serving the celebration of the Sacrifice, in distributing the Eucharist to the faithful, especially under the species of wine, and from time to time in giving instructions regarding the people's gestures and posture.

II. THE FUNCTIONS OF THE PEOPLE OF GOD

95. In the celebration of Mass the faithful form a holy people, a people of God's own possession and a royal Priesthood, so that they may give thanks to God and offer the unblemished sacrificial Victim not only by means of the hands of the Priest but also together with him and so that they may learn to offer their very selves.[82] They should, moreover, take care to show this by their deep religious sense and their charity toward brothers and sisters who participate with them in the same celebration.

They are consequently to avoid any appearance of singularity or division, keeping in mind that they have only one Father in heaven and that hence are all brothers or sisters one to the other.

---

79. Cf. *Caeremoniale Episcoporum*, editio typica, 1984, nos. 175–186.

80. Cf. Second Ecumenical Council of the Vatican, Dogmatic Constitution on the Church, *Lumen gentium*, no. 28; Decree on the Ministry and Life of Priests, *Presbyterorum ordinis*, no. 2.

81. Cf. Paul VI, Apostolic Letter, *Sacrum Diaconatus Ordinem*, June 18, 1967: *Acta Apostolicae Sedis* 59 (1967), pp. 697–704; Pontificale Romanum, *De Ordinatione Episcopi, presbyterorum et diaconorum*, editio typica altera, 1989, no. 173.

82. Cf. Second Ecumenical Council of the Vatican, Constitution on the Sacred Liturgy, *Sacrosanctum Concilium*, no. 48; Sacred Congregation of Rites, Instruction, *Eucharisticum mysterium*, May 25, 1967, no. 12: *Acta Apostolicae Sedis* 59 (1967), pp. 548–549.

96.   Moreover, they are to form one body, whether in hearing the Word of God, or in taking part in the prayers and in the singing, or above all by the common offering of the Sacrifice and by participating together at the Lord's table. This unity is beautifully apparent from the gestures and bodily postures observed together by the faithful.

97.   The faithful, moreover, should not refuse to serve the People of God in gladness whenever they are asked to perform some particular service or function in the celebration.

III. PARTICULAR MINISTRIES

THE MINISTRY OF THE INSTITUTED ACOLYTE AND LECTOR

98.   The acolyte is instituted for service at the altar and to assist the Priest and Deacon. It is his place principally to prepare the altar and the sacred vessels and, if necessary, to distribute the Eucharist to the faithful as an extraordinary minister.[83]

   In the ministry of the altar, the acolyte has his own proper functions (cf. nos. 187–193), which he must carry out in person.

99.   The lector is instituted to proclaim the readings from Sacred Scripture, with the exception of the Gospel. He may also announce the intentions for the Universal Prayer and, in the absence of a psalmist, recite the Psalm between the readings.

   In the celebration of the Eucharist, the lector has his own proper function (cf. nos. 194–198), which he himself must carry out.

OTHER FUNCTIONS

100. In the absence of an instituted acolyte, there may be deputed lay ministers to serve at the altar and assist the Priest and the Deacon; these carry the cross, the candles, the thurible, the bread, the wine, and the water, or who are even deputed to distribute Holy Communion as extraordinary ministers.[84]

101. In the absence of an instituted lector, other lay people may be deputed to proclaim the readings from Sacred Scripture, people who are truly suited to carrying out this function and carefully prepared, so that by their hearing the readings from the sacred texts the faithful may conceive in their hearts a sweet and living affection for Sacred Scripture.[85]

---

83. Cf. *Code of Canon Law*, can. 910 §2; cf. also the Interdicasterial Instruction on certain questions regarding the collaboration of the non-ordained faithful in the sacred ministry of Priests, *Ecclesiae de mysterio*, August 15, 1997, art. 8: *Acta Apostolicae Sedis* 89 (1997), p. 871.

84. Cf. Sacred Congregation for the Discipline of the Sacraments, Instruction, *Immensae caritatis*, January 29, 1973, no. 1: *Acta Apostolicae Sedis* 65 (1973), pp. 265–266; *Code of Canon Law*, can. 230 §3.

85. Cf. Second Ecumenical Council of the Vatican, Constitution on the Sacred Liturgy, *Sacrosanctum Concilium*, no. 24.

102. It is the psalmist's place to sing the Psalm or other biblical canticle to be found between the readings. To carry out this function correctly, it is necessary for the psalmist to be accomplished in the art of singing Psalms and have a facility in public speaking and elocution.

103. Among the faithful, the *schola cantorum* or choir exercises its own liturgical function, its place being to take care that the parts proper to it, in keeping with the different genres of chant, are properly carried out and to foster the active participation of the faithful by means of the singing.[86] What is said about the *schola cantorum* also applies, with due regard for the relevant norms, to other musicians, and especially the organist.

104. It is fitting that there be a cantor or a choir director to direct and support the people's singing. Indeed, when there is no choir, it is up to the cantor to direct the different chants, with the people taking the part proper to them.[87]

105. A liturgical function is also exercised by:

a) The sacristan, who diligently arranges the liturgical books, the vestments, and other things that are necessary for the celebration of Mass.

b) The commentator, who, if appropriate, provides the faithful briefly with explanations and exhortations so as to direct their attention to the celebration and ensure that they are better disposed for understanding it. The commentator's remarks should be thoroughly prepared and notable for their restraint. In performing this function the commentator stands in a suitable place within sight of the faithful, but not at the ambo.

c) Those who take up the collections in the church.

d) Those who, in some regions, welcome the faithful at the church doors, seat them appropriately, and marshal them in processions.

106. It is desirable, at least in cathedrals and in larger churches, to have some competent minister or master of ceremonies, to see to the appropriate arrangement of sacred actions and to their being carried out by the sacred ministers and lay faithful with decorum, order, and devotion.

107. Liturgical functions that are not proper to the Priest or the Deacon and are mentioned above (nos. 100–106) may even be entrusted by means of a liturgical blessing or a temporary deputation to suitable lay persons chosen by the pastor or the rector of the church.[88] As to the function of serving the Priest at the altar, the norms established by the Bishop for his diocese should be observed.

---

86. Cf. Sacred Congregation of Rites, Instruction, *Musicam sacram*, March 5, 1967, no. 19: *Acta Apostolicae Sedis* 59 (1967), p. 306.

87. Cf. *ibidem*, no. 21: pp. 306–307.

88. Cf. Pontifical Commission for the Interpretation of Legal Texts, response to *dubium* regarding can. 230 §2: *Acta Apostolicae Sedis* 86 (1994), p. 541.

IV. THE DISTRIBUTION OF FUNCTIONS AND
THE PREPARATION OF THE CELEBRATION

108. One and the same Priest must always exercise the presidential function in all of its parts, except for those parts which are proper to a Mass at which the Bishop is present (cf. above no. 92).

109. If there are several present who are able to exercise the same ministry, nothing forbids their distributing among themselves and performing different parts of the same ministry or duty. For example, one Deacon may be assigned to execute the sung parts, another to serve at the altar; if there are several readings, it is well to distribute them among a number of readers, and the same applies for other matters. However, it is not at all appropriate that several persons divide a single element of the celebration among themselves, e.g., that the same reading be proclaimed by two readers, one after the other, with the exception of the Passion of the Lord.

110. If at a Mass with the people only one minister is present, that minister may exercise several different functions.

111. There should be harmony and diligence among all those involved in the effective preparation of each liturgical celebration in accordance with the Missal and other liturgical books, both as regards the rites and as regards the pastoral and musical aspects. This should take place under the direction of the rector of the church and after consultation with the faithful in things that directly pertain to them. However, the Priest who presides at the celebration always retains the right of arranging those things that pertain to him.[89]

CHAPTER IV
THE DIFFERENT FORMS OF CELEBRATING MASS

112. In the local Church, first place should certainly be given, because of its significance, to the Mass at which the Bishop presides, surrounded by his Presbyterate, Deacons, and lay ministers,[90] and in which the holy People of God participate fully and actively, for it is there that the principal manifestation of the Church is found.

At a Mass celebrated by the Bishop or at which he presides without celebrating the Eucharist, the norms found in the *Caeremoniale Episcoporum (Ceremonial of Bishops)* should be observed.[91]

113. Great importance should also be given to a Mass celebrated with any community, but especially with the parish community, inasmuch as it represents

---

89. Cf. Second Ecumenical Council of the Vatican, Constitution on the Sacred Liturgy, *Sacrosanctum Concilium*, no. 22.

90. Cf. Second Ecumenical Council of the Vatican, Constitution on the Sacred Liturgy, *Sacrosanctum Concilium*, no. 41.

91. Cf. *Caeremoniale Episcoporum*, editio typica, 1984, nos. 119–186.

the universal Church at a given time and place, and chiefly in the common Sunday celebration.[92]

114. Moreover, among those Masses celebrated by some communities, a particular place belongs to the Conventual Mass, which is a part of the daily Office, or the "community" Mass. Although such Masses do not involve any special form of celebration, it is nevertheless most fitting that they be celebrated with singing, especially with the full participation of all members of the community, whether of religious or of canons. Therefore, in these Masses all should exercise their function according to the Order or ministry they have received. Hence, it is desirable that all the Priests who are not obliged to celebrate individually for the pastoral benefit of the faithful concelebrate in so far as possible at the conventual or community Mass. In addition, all Priests belonging to the community who are obliged, as a matter of duty, to celebrate individually for the pastoral benefit of the faithful may also on the same day concelebrate at the conventual or community Mass.[93] For it is preferable that Priests who are present at a celebration of the Eucharist, unless excused for a just reason, should usually exercise the function proper to their Order and hence take part as concelebrants, wearing sacred vestments. Otherwise, they wear their proper choir dress or a surplice over a cassock.

I. MASS WITH THE PEOPLE

115. By Mass with the people is meant a Mass celebrated with the participation of the faithful. Moreover, it is appropriate, in so far as possible, and especially on Sundays and Holydays of Obligation, that the celebration take place with singing and with a suitable number of ministers.[94] It may, however, take place even without singing and with only one minister.

116. If at any celebration of Mass a Deacon is present, he should exercise his function. Furthermore, it is desirable that an acolyte, a reader, and a cantor should usually be there to assist the Priest Celebrant. Indeed, the rite described below foresees an even greater number of ministers.

THINGS TO BE PREPARED

117. The altar is to be covered with at least one white cloth. In addition, on or next to the altar are to be placed candlesticks with lighted candles: at least two in any celebration, or even four or six, especially for a Sunday Mass or a Holyday

---

92. Cf. Second Ecumenical Council of the Vatican, Constitution on the Sacred Liturgy, *Sacrosanctum Concilium*, no. 42; Dogmatic Constitution on the Church, *Lumen gentium*, no. 28; Decree on the Ministry and Life of Priests, *Presbyterorum ordinis*, no. 5; Sacred Congregation of Rites, Instruction, *Eucharisticum mysterium*, May 25, 1967, no. 26: *Acta Apostolicae Sedis* 59 (1967), p. 555.

93. Cf. Sacred Congregation of Rites, Instruction, *Eucharisticum mysterium*, May 25, 1967, no. 47: *Acta Apostolicae Sedis* 59 (1967), p. 565.

94. Cf. Sacred Congregation of Rites, Instruction, *Eucharisticum mysterium*, May 25, 1967, no. 26: *Acta Apostolicae Sedis* 59 (1967), p. 555; Instruction, *Musicam sacram*, March 5, 1967, nos. 16, 27: *Acta Apostolicae Sedis* 59 (1967), pp. 305, 308.

of Obligation, or if the Diocesan Bishop celebrates, then seven candlesticks with lighted candles. Likewise, on the altar or close to it, there is to be a cross adorned with a figure of Christ crucified. The candles and the cross with the figure of Christ crucified may also be carried in the procession at the Entrance. On the altar itself may be placed a *Book of the Gospels* distinct from the book of other readings, unless it is carried in the Entrance Procession.

118. Likewise these should be prepared:

   a) next to the Priest's chair: the Missal and, if appropriate, a hymnal;

   b) at the ambo: the Lectionary;

   c) on the credence table: the chalice, corporal, purificator, and, if appropriate, the pall; the paten and, if needed, ciboria; bread for the Communion of the Priest who presides, the Deacon, the ministers, and the people; cruets containing the wine and the water, unless all of these are presented by the faithful in the procession at the Offertory; the vessel of water to be blessed, if the sprinkling of holy water takes place; the Communion-plate for the Communion of the faithful; and whatever is needed for the washing of hands.

   It is a praiseworthy practice for the chalice to be covered with a veil, which may be either of the color of the day or white.

119. In the sacristy, according to the various forms of celebration, there should be prepared the sacred vestments (cf. nos. 337–341) for the Priest, the Deacon, and other ministers:

   a) for the Priest: the alb, the stole, and the chasuble;

   b) for the Deacon: the alb, the stole, and the dalmatic; the latter may be omitted, however, either out of necessity or on account of a lesser degree of solemnity;

   c) for the other ministers: albs or other lawfully approved attire.[95]

   All who wear an alb should use a cincture and an amice unless, due to the form of the alb, they are not needed.

   When the Entrance takes place with a procession, the following are also to be prepared: a *Book of the Gospels*; on Sundays and festive days, a thurible and incense boat, if incense is being used; the cross to be carried in procession; and candlesticks with lighted candles.

---

95. Cf. the Interdicasterial Instruction on certain questions regarding the collaboration of the non-ordained faithful in the sacred ministry of Priests, *Ecclesiae de mysterio*, August 15, 1997, art. 6: *Acta Apostolicae Sedis* 89 (1997), p. 869.

A) Mass without a Deacon

120. When the people are gathered, the Priest and ministers, wearing the sacred vestments, go in procession to the altar in this order:

    a) the thurifer carrying a smoking thurible, if incense is being used;

    b) ministers who carry lighted candles, and between them an acolyte or other minister with the cross;

    c) the acolytes and the other ministers;

    d) a reader, who may carry a *Book of the Gospels* (though not a Lectionary), slightly elevated;

    e) the Priest who is to celebrate the Mass.

If incense is being used, before the procession begins, the Priest puts some into the thurible and blesses it with the Sign of the Cross without saying anything.

121. During the procession to the altar, the Entrance Chant takes place (cf. nos. 47–48).

122. When they reach the altar, the Priest and ministers make a profound bow.

The cross adorned with a figure of Christ crucified, and carried in procession, may be placed next to the altar to serve as the altar cross, in which case it must be the only cross used; otherwise it is put away in a dignified place. As for the candlesticks, these are placed on the altar or near it. It is a praiseworthy practice for the *Book of the Gospels* to be placed on the altar.

123. The Priest goes up to the altar and venerates it with a kiss. Then, if appropriate, he incenses the cross and the altar, walking around the latter.

124. Once all this has been done, the Priest goes to the chair. When the Entrance Chant is concluded, with everybody standing, the Priest and faithful sign themselves with the Sign of the Cross. The Priest says: *In the name of the Father, and of the Son, and of the Holy Spirit.* The people reply, *Amen.*

Then, facing the people and extending his hands, the Priest greets the people, using one of the formulas indicated. The Priest himself or some other minister may also very briefly introduce the faithful to the Mass of the day.

125. The Penitential Act follows. After this, the *Kyrie* is sung or said, in accordance with the rubrics (cf. no. 52).

126. For celebrations where it is prescribed, the *Gloria in excelsis (Glory to God in the highest)* is either sung or said (cf. no. 53).

127. The Priest then calls upon the people to pray, saying, with hands joined, *Let us pray.* All pray silently with the Priest for a brief time. Then the Priest, with hands extended, says the Collect, at the end of which the people acclaim, *Amen.*

128. After the Collect, all sit. The Priest may, very briefly, introduce the faithful to the Liturgy of the Word. Then the reader goes to the ambo and, from the Lectionary already placed there before Mass, proclaims the First Reading, to which all listen. At the end, the reader pronounces the acclamation *The word of the Lord*, and all reply, *Thanks be to God*.

Then a few moments of silence may be observed, if appropriate, so that all may meditate on what they have heard.

129. Then the psalmist or the reader proclaims the verses of the Psalm and the people make the response as usual.

130. If there is to be a Second Reading before the Gospel, the reader proclaims it from the ambo. All listen and at the end reply to the acclamation, as noted above (no. 128). Then, if appropriate, a few moments of silence may be observed.

131. After this, all rise, and the *Alleluia* or other chant is sung as the liturgical time requires (cf. nos. 62–64).

132. During the singing of the *Alleluia* or other chant, if incense is being used, the Priest puts some into the thurible and blesses it. Then, with hands joined, he bows profoundly before the altar and quietly says the prayer *Munda cor meum (Cleanse my heart)*.

133. If the *Book of the Gospels* is on the altar, the Priest then takes it and approaches the ambo, carrying the *Book of the Gospels* slightly elevated. He is preceded by the lay ministers, who may carry the thurible and the candles. Those present turn towards the ambo as a sign of special reverence for the Gospel of Christ.

134. At the ambo, the Priest opens the book and, with hands joined, says, *The Lord be with you*, to which the people reply, *And with your spirit*. Then he says, *A reading from the holy Gospel*, making the Sign of the Cross with his thumb on the book and on his forehead, mouth, and breast, which everyone else does as well. The people acclaim, *Glory to you, O Lord*. The Priest incenses the book, if incense is being used (cf. nos. 276–277). Then he proclaims the Gospel and at the end pronounces the acclamation *The Gospel of the Lord*, to which all reply, *Praise to you, Lord Jesus Christ*. The Priest kisses the book, saying quietly the formula *Per evangelica dicta (Through the words of the Gospel)*.

135. If no reader is present, the Priest himself proclaims all the readings and the Psalm, standing at the ambo. If incense is being used, he puts some incense into the thurible at the ambo, blesses it, and, bowing profoundly, says the prayer *Munda cor meum (Cleanse my heart)*.

136. The Priest, standing at the chair or at the ambo itself or, if appropriate, in another worthy place, gives the Homily. When the Homily is over, a period of silence may be observed.

137. The Symbol or Creed is sung or recited by the Priest together with the people (cf. no. 68) with everyone standing. At the words *et incarnatus est, etc. (and by the Holy Spirit . . . and became man)* all make a profound bow; but on the Solemnities of the Annunciation and of the Nativity of the Lord, all genuflect.

138. After the recitation of the Symbol or Creed, the Priest, standing at the chair with his hands joined, by means of a brief address calls upon the faithful to participate in the Universal Prayer. Then the cantor, the reader, or another person announces the intentions from the ambo or from some other suitable place while facing the people. The latter take their part by replying in supplication. At the very end, the Priest, with hands extended, concludes the petitions with a prayer.

THE LITURGY OF THE EUCHARIST

139. When the Universal Prayer is over, all sit, and the Offertory Chant begins (cf. no. 74).

An acolyte or other lay minister places the corporal, the purificator, the chalice, the pall, and the Missal on the altar.

140. It is desirable that the participation of the faithful be expressed by an offering, whether of bread and wine for the celebration of the Eucharist or of other gifts to relieve the needs of the Church and of the poor.

The offerings of the faithful are received by the Priest, assisted by the acolyte or other minister. The bread and wine for the Eucharist are carried to the Celebrant, who places them on the altar, while other gifts are put in another suitable place (cf. no. 73).

141. The Priest accepts the paten with the bread at the altar, holds it slightly raised above the altar with both hands and says quietly, *Benedictus es, Domine (Blessed are you, Lord God).* Then he places the paten with the bread on the corporal.

142. After this, as the minister presents the cruets, the Priest stands at the side of the altar and pours wine and a little water into the chalice, saying quietly, *Per huius aquae (By the mystery of this water).* He returns to the middle of the altar and with both hands raises the chalice a little, and says quietly, *Benedictus es, Domine (Blessed are you, Lord God).* Then he places the chalice on the corporal and, if appropriate, covers it with a pall.

If, however, there is no Offertory Chant and the organ is not played, in the presentation of the bread and wine the Priest may say the formulas of blessing aloud and the people acclaim, *Blessed be God for ever.*

143. After placing the chalice on the altar, the Priest bows profoundly and says quietly, *In spiritu humilitatis (With humble spirit).*

144. If incense is being used, the Priest then puts some in the thurible, blesses it without saying anything, and incenses the offerings, the cross, and the altar.

While standing at the side of the altar, a minister incenses the Priest and then the people.

145. After the prayer *In spiritu humilitatis (With humble spirit)* or after the incensation, the Priest washes his hands standing at the side of the altar and, as the minister pours the water, says quietly, *Lava me, Domine (Wash me, O Lord).*

146. Returning to the middle of the altar, and standing facing the people, the Priest extends and then joins his hands, and calls upon the people to pray, saying, *Orate, fratres (Pray, brethren).* The people rise and make the response *May the Lord accept the sacrifice, etc.* Then the Priest, with hands extended, says the Prayer over the Offerings. At the end the people acclaim, *Amen.*

147. Then the Priest begins the Eucharistic Prayer. In accordance with the rubrics (cf. no. 365), he selects a Eucharistic Prayer from those found in the *Roman Missal* or approved by the Apostolic See. By its very nature, the Eucharistic Prayer requires that only the Priest say it, in virtue of his Ordination. The people, for their part, should associate themselves with the Priest in faith and in silence, as well as by means of their interventions as prescribed in the course of the Eucharistic Prayer: namely, the responses in the Preface dialogue, the *Sanctus (Holy, Holy, Holy),* the acclamation after the Consecration, the acclamation *Amen* after the concluding doxology, as well as other acclamations approved by the Conference of Bishops with the *recognitio* of the Holy See.

It is most appropriate that the Priest sing those parts of the Eucharistic Prayer for which musical notation is provided.

148. As he begins the Eucharistic Prayer, the Priest extends his hands and sings or says, *The Lord be with you.* The people reply, *And with your spirit.* As he continues, saying, *Lift up your hearts,* he raises his hands. The people reply, *We lift them up to the Lord.* Then the Priest, with hands extended, adds, *Let us give thanks to the Lord our God,* and the people reply, *It is right and just.* After this, the Priest, with hands extended, continues the Preface. At its conclusion, he joins his hands and, together with all those present, sings or says aloud the *Sanctus (Holy, Holy, Holy)* (cf. no. 79 b).

149. The Priest continues the Eucharistic Prayer in accordance with the rubrics that are set out in each of the Prayers.

If the celebrant is a Bishop, in the Prayers, after the words *N., our Pope,* he adds, *and me, your unworthy servant.* If, however, the Bishop is celebrating outside his own diocese, after the words *with . . . N., our Pope,* he adds, *my brother N., the Bishop of this Church, and me, your unworthy servant;* or after the words *especially . . . N., our Pope,* he adds, *my brother N., the Bishop of this Church, and me, your unworthy servant.*

The Diocesan Bishop, or one who is equivalent to the Diocesan Bishop in law, must be mentioned by means of this formula: *together with your servant N., our Pope, and N., our Bishop (or Vicar, Prelate, Prefect, Abbot).*

It is permitted to mention Coadjutor Bishop and Auxiliary Bishops in the Eucharistic Prayer, but not other Bishops who happen to be present. When several are to be mentioned, this is done with the collective formula: *N., our Bishop and his assistant Bishops.*

In each of the Eucharistic Prayers, these formulas are to be adapted according to the requirements of grammar.

150. A little before the Consecration, if appropriate, a minister rings a small bell as a signal to the faithful. The minister also rings the small bell at each elevation by the Priest, according to local custom.

If incense is being used, when the host and the chalice are shown to the people after the Consecration, a minister incenses them.

151. After the Consecration when the Priest has said, *The mystery of faith,* the people pronounce the acclamation, using one of the prescribed formulas.

At the end of the Eucharistic Prayer, the Priest takes the paten with the host and the chalice and elevates them both while pronouncing alone the doxology *Through him.* At the end the people acclaim, *Amen.* After this, the Priest places the paten and the chalice on the corporal.

152. After the Eucharistic Prayer is concluded, the Priest, with hands joined, says alone the introduction to the Lord's Prayer, and then with hands extended, he pronounces the prayer together with the people.

153. After the Lord's Prayer is concluded, the Priest, with hands extended, says alone the embolism *Libera nos (Deliver us, Lord).* At the end, the people acclaim, *For the kingdom.*

154. Then the Priest, with hands extended, says aloud the prayer *Domine Iesu Christe, qui dixisti (Lord Jesus Christ, who said to your Apostles)* and when it is concluded, extending and then joining his hands, he announces the greeting of peace, facing the people and saying, *The peace of the Lord be with you always.* The people reply, *And with your spirit.* After this, if appropriate, the Priest adds, *Let us offer each other the sign of peace.*

The Priest may give the Sign of Peace to the ministers but always remains within the sanctuary, so that the celebration is not disrupted. In the Dioceses of the United States of America, for a good reason, on special occasions (for example, in the case of a funeral, a wedding, or when civic leaders are present), the Priest may offer the Sign of Peace to a small number of the faithful near the sanctuary. According to what is decided by the Conference of Bishops, all express to one another peace, communion, and charity. While the Sign of Peace is being given, it is permissible to say, *The peace of the Lord be with you always,* to which the reply is *Amen.*

155. After this, the Priest takes the host, breaks it over the paten, and places a small piece in the chalice, saying quietly, *Haec commixtio (May this mingling).*

Meanwhile the *Agnus Dei (Lamb of God)* is sung or said by the choir and by the people (cf. no. 83).

156. Then the Priest, with hands joined, says quietly the prayer for Communion, either *Domine Iesu Christe, Fili Dei vivi (Lord Jesus Christ, Son of the living God)* or *Perceptio Corporis et Sanguinis tui (May the receiving of your Body and Blood).*

157. When the prayer is concluded, the Priest genuflects, takes a host consecrated at the same Mass, and, holding it slightly raised above the paten or above the chalice, facing the people, says, *Ecce Agnus Dei (Behold the Lamb of God)* and together with the people he adds, *Lord, I am not worthy.*

158. After this, standing facing the altar, the Priest says quietly, *Corpus Christi custodiat me in vitam aeternam (May the Body of Christ keep me safe for eternal life),* and reverently consumes the Body of Christ. Then he takes the chalice, saying quietly, *Sanguis Christi custodiat me in vitam aeternam (May the Blood of Christ keep me safe for eternal life),* and reverently partakes of the Blood of Christ.

159. While the Priest is receiving the Sacrament, the Communion Chant begins (cf. no. 86).

160. The Priest then takes the paten or ciborium and approaches the communicants, who usually come up in procession.

It is not permitted for the faithful to take the consecrated Bread or the sacred chalice by themselves and, still less, to hand them on from one to another among themselves. The norm established for the Dioceses of the United States of America is that Holy Communion is to be received standing, unless an individual member of the faithful wishes to receive Communion while kneeling (Congregation for Divine Worship and the Discipline of the Sacraments, Instruction *Redemptionis Sacramentum*, March 25, 2004, no. 91).

When receiving Holy Communion, the communicant bows his or her head before the Sacrament as a gesture of reverence and receives the Body of the Lord from the minister. The consecrated host may be received either on the tongue or in the hand, at the discretion of each communicant. When Holy Communion is received under both kinds, the sign of reverence is also made before receiving the Precious Blood.

161. If Communion is given only under the species of bread, the Priest raises the host slightly and shows it to each, saying, *The Body of Christ.* The communicant replies, *Amen,* and receives the Sacrament either on the tongue or, where this is allowed, in the hand, the choice lying with the communicant. As soon as the communicant receives the host, he or she consumes the whole of it.

If, however, Communion is given under both kinds, the rite prescribed in nos. 284–287 is to be followed.

162. In the distribution of Communion the Priest may be assisted by other Priests who happen to be present. If such Priests are not present and there is a truly large

number of communicants, the Priest may call upon extraordinary ministers to assist him, that is, duly instituted acolytes or even other faithful who have been duly deputed for this purpose.[96] In case of necessity, the Priest may depute suitable faithful for this single occasion.[97]

These ministers should not approach the altar before the Priest has received Communion, and they are always to receive from the hands of the Priest Celebrant the vessel containing the species of the Most Holy Eucharist for distribution to the faithful.

163. When the distribution of Communion is over, the Priest himself immediately and completely consumes at the altar any consecrated wine that happens to remain; as for any consecrated hosts that are left, he either consumes them at the altar or carries them to the place designated for the reservation of the Eucharist.

Upon returning to the altar, the Priest collects the fragments, should any remain, and he stands at the altar or at the credence table and purifies the paten or ciborium over the chalice, and after this purifies the chalice, saying quietly the formula *Quod ore sumpsimus, Domine (What has passed our lips)*, and dries the chalice with a purificator. If the vessels are purified at the altar, they are carried to the credence table by a minister. Nevertheless, it is also permitted to leave vessels needing to be purified, especially if there are several, on a corporal, suitably covered, either on the altar or on the credence table, and to purify them immediately after Mass, after the Dismissal of the people.

164. After this, the Priest may return to the chair. A sacred silence may now be observed for some time, or a Psalm or other canticle of praise or a hymn may be sung (cf. no. 88).

165. Then, standing at the chair or at the altar, and facing the people with hands joined, the Priest says, *Let us pray*; then, with hands extended, he recites the Prayer after Communion. A brief period of silence may precede the prayer, unless this has been already observed immediately after Communion. At the end of the prayer the people acclaim, *Amen*.

THE CONCLUDING RITES

166. When the Prayer after Communion is concluded, brief announcements should be made to the people, if there are any.

167. Then the Priest, extending his hands, greets the people, saying, *The Lord be with you*. They reply, *And with your spirit*. The Priest, joining his hands again and then immediately placing his left hand on his breast, raises his right

---

96. Cf. Sacred Congregation for the Sacraments and Divine Worship, Instruction, *Inaestimabile donum*, April 3, 1980, no. 10: *Acta Apostolicae Sedis* 72 (1980), p. 336; Interdicasterial Instruction on certain questions regarding the collaboration of the non-ordained faithful in the sacred ministry of Priests, *Ecclesiae de mysterio*, August 15, 1997, art. 8: *Acta Apostolicae Sedis* 89 (1997), p. 871.

97. Cf. Roman Missal, Appendix III, Rite of Deputing a Minister to Distribute Holy Communion on a Single Occasion.

hand and adds, *May almighty God bless you* and, as he makes the Sign of the Cross over the people, he continues, *the Father, and the Son, and the Holy Spirit.* All reply, *Amen.*

On certain days and occasions this blessing, in accordance with the rubrics, is expanded and expressed by a Prayer over the People or another more solemn formula.

A Bishop blesses the people with the appropriate formula, making the Sign of the Cross three times over the people.[98]

168. Immediately after the Blessing, with hands joined, the Priest adds, *Ite, missa est (Go forth, the Mass is ended)* and all reply, *Thanks be to God.*

169. Then the Priest venerates the altar as usual with a kiss and, after making a profound bow with the lay ministers, he withdraws with them.

170. If, however, another liturgical action follows the Mass, the Concluding Rites, that is, the Greeting, the Blessing, and the Dismissal, are omitted.

B) Mass with a Deacon

171. When he is present at the celebration of the Eucharist, a Deacon should exercise his ministry, wearing sacred vestments. In fact, the Deacon:

   a) assists the Priest and walks at his side;

   b) ministers at the altar, both as regards the chalice and the book;

   c) proclaims the Gospel and may, at the direction of the Priest Celebrant, give the Homily (cf. no. 66);

   d) guides the faithful people by giving appropriate instructions, and announces the intentions of the Universal Prayer;

   e) assists the Priest Celebrant in distributing Communion, and purifies and arranges the sacred vessels;

   f) carries out the duties of other ministers himself, if necessary, when none of them is present.

THE INTRODUCTORY RITES

172. Carrying the *Book of the Gospels* slightly elevated, the Deacon precedes the Priest as he approaches the altar or else walks at the Priest's side.

173. When he reaches the altar, if he is carrying the *Book of the Gospels*, he omits the sign of reverence and goes up to the altar. It is a praiseworthy practice for him to place the *Book of the Gospels* on the altar, after which, together with the Priest, he venerates the altar with a kiss.

---

98. Cf. *Caeremoniale Episcoporum*, editio typica, 1984, nos. 1118–1121.

If, however, he is not carrying the *Book of the Gospels*, he makes a profound bow to the altar with the Priest in the customary way and with him venerates the altar with a kiss.

Lastly, if incense is being used, he assists the Priest in putting some into the thurible and in incensing the cross and the altar.

174. Once the altar has been incensed, the Deacon goes to the chair together with the Priest and there stands at the Priest's side and assists him as necessary.

THE LITURGY OF THE WORD

175. During the singing of the *Alleluia* or other chant, if incense is being used, the Deacon ministers to the Priest as he puts incense into the thurible. Then, bowing profoundly before the Priest, he asks for the blessing, saying in a low voice, *Your blessing, Father*. The Priest blesses him, saying, *May the Lord be in your heart*. The Deacon signs himself with the Sign of the Cross and replies, *Amen*. Having bowed to the altar, he then takes up the *Book of the Gospels* which was placed on it and proceeds to the ambo, carrying the book slightly elevated. He is preceded by a thurifer carrying a smoking thurible and by ministers with lighted candles. At the ambo the Deacon greets the people, with hands joined, saying, *The Lord be with you*. After this, at the words *A reading from the holy Gospel*, he signs with his thumb the book and then himself on his forehead, mouth, and breast. He incenses the book and proclaims the Gospel reading. When this is done, he acclaims, *The Gospel of the Lord*, and all reply, *Praise to you, Lord Jesus Christ*. He then venerates the book with a kiss, saying quietly the formula *Per evangelica dicta (Through the words of the Gospel)*, and returns to the Priest's side.

When the Deacon is assisting the Bishop, he carries the book to him to be kissed, or else kisses it himself, saying quietly the formula *Per evangelica dicta (Through the words of the Gospel)*. In more solemn celebrations, if appropriate, the Bishop may impart a blessing to the people with the *Book of the Gospels*.

Lastly, the Deacon may carry the *Book of the Gospels* to the credence table or to another suitable and dignified place.

176. Moreover, if there is no other suitable reader present, the Deacon should proclaim the other readings as well.

177. After the introduction by the Priest, it is the Deacon himself who announces the intentions of the Universal Prayer, usually from the ambo.

THE LITURGY OF THE EUCHARIST

178. After the Universal Prayer, while the Priest remains at the chair, the Deacon prepares the altar, assisted by the acolyte, but it is the Deacon's place to take care of the sacred vessels himself. He also assists the Priest in receiving the people's gifts. After this, he hands the Priest the paten with the bread to be consecrated, pours wine and a little water into the chalice, saying quietly, *By the mystery of this water, etc.*, and after this presents the chalice to the Priest. He

may also carry out the preparation of the chalice at the credence table. If incense is being used, the Deacon assists the Priest during the incensation of the offerings, the cross, and the altar; and after this the Deacon himself or the acolyte incenses the Priest and the people.

179. During the Eucharistic Prayer, the Deacon stands near the Priest, but slightly behind him, so that when necessary he may assist the Priest with the chalice or the Missal.

From the epiclesis until the Priest shows the chalice, the Deacon usually remains kneeling. If several Deacons are present, one of them may place incense in the thurible for the Consecration and incense the host and the chalice at the elevation.

180. At the concluding doxology of the Eucharistic Prayer, the Deacon stands next to the Priest, and holds the chalice elevated while the Priest elevates the paten with the host, until the people have acclaimed, *Amen.*

181. After the Priest has said the prayer for the Rite of Peace and the greeting *The peace of the Lord be with you always* and the people have replied, *And with your spirit*, the Deacon, if appropriate, says the invitation to the Sign of Peace. With hands joined, he faces the people and says, *Let us offer each other the sign of peace.* Then he himself receives the Sign of Peace from the Priest and may offer it to those other ministers who are nearest to him.

182. After the Priest's Communion, the Deacon receives Communion under both kinds from the Priest himself and then assists the Priest in distributing Communion to the people. If Communion is given under both kinds, the Deacon himself administers the chalice to the communicants; and, when the distribution is over, standing at the altar, he immediately and reverently consumes all of the Blood of Christ that remains, assisted, if the case requires, by other Deacons and Priests.

183. When the distribution of Communion is over, the Deacon returns to the altar with the Priest, collects the fragments, should any remain, and then carries the chalice and other sacred vessels to the credence table, where he purifies them and arranges them as usual, while the Priest returns to the chair. Nevertheless, it is also permitted to leave vessels needing to be purified on a corporal, suitably covered, on the credence table, and to purify them immediately after Mass, following the Dismissal of the people.

THE CONCLUDING RITES

184. Once the Prayer after Communion has been said, the Deacon makes brief announcements to the people, if indeed any need to be made, unless the Priest prefers to do this himself.

185. If a Prayer over the People or a formula of Solemn Blessing is used, the Deacon says, *Bow down for the blessing.* After the Priest's blessing, the Deacon,

with hands joined and facing the people, dismisses the people, saying, *Ite, missa est (Go forth, the Mass is ended).*

186. Then, together with the Priest, the Deacon venerates the altar with a kiss, makes a profound bow, and withdraws in a manner similar to the Entrance Procession.

C) The Functions of the Acolyte

187. The functions that the acolyte may carry out are of various kinds and several may occur at the same moment. Hence, it is desirable that these duties be suitably distributed among several acolytes. If, in fact, only one acolyte is present, he should perform the more important duties while the rest are to be distributed among several ministers.

THE INTRODUCTORY RITES

188. In the procession to the altar, the acolyte may carry the cross, walking between two ministers with lighted candles. Upon reaching the altar, however, the acolyte places the cross upright near the altar so that it may serve as the altar cross; otherwise, he puts it away in a dignified place. Then he takes his place in the sanctuary.

189. Through the entire celebration, it is for the acolyte to approach the Priest or the Deacon, whenever necessary, in order to present the book to them and to assist them in any other way required. Thus it is appropriate that, in so far as possible, the acolyte should occupy a place from which he can easily carry out his ministry either at the chair or at the altar.

THE LITURGY OF THE EUCHARIST

190. In the absence of a Deacon, after the Universal Prayer and while the Priest remains at the chair, the acolyte places the corporal, the purificator, the chalice, the pall, and the Missal on the altar. Then, if necessary, the acolyte assists the Priest in receiving the gifts of the people and, if appropriate, brings the bread and wine to the altar and hands them to the Priest. If incense is being used, the acolyte presents the thurible to the Priest and assists him while he incenses the offerings, the cross, and the altar. Then the acolyte incenses the Priest and the people.

191. A duly instituted acolyte, as an extraordinary minister, may, if necessary, assist the Priest in distributing Communion to the people.[99] If Communion is given under both kinds, in the absence of a Deacon, the acolyte administers the chalice to the communicants or holds the chalice if Communion is given by intinction.

192. Likewise, after the distribution of Communion is complete, a duly instituted acolyte helps the Priest or Deacon to purify and arrange the sacred vessels. In the absence of a Deacon, a duly instituted acolyte carries the sacred vessels

---

99. Paul VI, Apostolic Letter, *Ministeria quaedam*, August 15, 1972: *Acta Apostolicae Sedis* 64 (1972), p. 532.

to the credence table and there purifies them, wipes them, and arranges them as usual.

193. After the celebration of Mass, the acolyte and other ministers return together with the Deacon and the Priest in procession to the sacristy, in the same manner and in the same order in which they entered.

D) The Functions of the Reader

INTRODUCTORY RITES

194. In the procession to the altar, in the absence of a Deacon, the reader, wearing approved attire, may carry the *Book of the Gospels*, slightly elevated. In that case, the reader walks in front of the Priest but otherwise walks along with the other ministers.

195. Upon reaching the altar, the reader makes a profound bow with the others. If he is carrying the *Book of the Gospels*, he approaches the altar and places the *Book of the Gospels* upon it. Then the reader takes his own place in the sanctuary with the other ministers.

THE LITURGY OF THE WORD

196. The reader reads from the ambo the readings that precede the Gospel. In the absence of a psalmist, the reader may also proclaim the Responsorial Psalm after the First Reading.

197. In the absence of a Deacon, the reader, after the introduction by the Priest, may announce the intentions of the Universal Prayer from the ambo.

198. If there is no singing at the Entrance or at Communion and the antiphons given in the Missal are not recited by the faithful, the reader may read them at an appropriate time (cf. nos. 48, 87).

II. CONCELEBRATED MASS

199. Concelebration, by which the unity of the Priesthood, of the Sacrifice, and also of the whole People of God is appropriately expressed, is prescribed by the rite itself for the Ordination of a Bishop and of Priests, at the Blessing of an Abbot, and at the Chrism Mass.

It is recommended, moreover, unless the good of the Christian faithful requires or suggests otherwise, at:

    a) the Evening Mass of the Lord's Supper;

    b) the Mass during Councils, gatherings of Bishops, and Synods;

    c) the Conventual Mass and the principal Mass in churches and oratories;

    d) Masses at any kind of gathering of Priests, either secular or religious.[100]

---

100. Cf. Second Ecumenical Council of the Vatican, Constitution on the Sacred Liturgy, *Sacrosanctum Concilium*, no. 57; *Code of Canon Law*, can. 902.

Every Priest, however, is allowed to celebrate the Eucharist individually, though not at the same time as a concelebration is taking place in the same church or oratory. However, on Holy Thursday, and for the Mass of the Easter Vigil, it is not permitted to celebrate Mass individually.

200. Visiting Priests should be gladly admitted to concelebration of the Eucharist, provided their Priestly standing has been ascertained.

201. When there is a large number of Priests, concelebration may take place even several times on the same day, where necessity or pastoral advantage commend it. However, this must be done at different times or in distinct sacred places.[101]

202. It is for the Bishop, in accordance with the norm of law, to regulate the discipline for concelebration in all churches and oratories of his diocese.

203. To be held in particularly high regard is that concelebration in which the Priests of any given diocese concelebrate with their own Bishop at a stational Mass, especially on the more solemn days of the liturgical year, at the Ordination Mass of a new Bishop of the diocese or of his Coadjutor or Auxiliary, at the Chrism Mass, at the Evening Mass of the Lord's Supper, at celebrations of the Founder Saint of a local Church or the Patron of the diocese, on anniversaries of the Bishop, and, lastly, on the occasion of a Synod or a pastoral visitation.

In the same way, concelebration is recommended whenever Priests gather together with their own Bishop whether on the occasion of a retreat or at any other gathering. In these cases the sign of the unity of the Priesthood and also of the Church inherent in every concelebration is made more clearly manifest.[102]

204. For a particular reason, having to do either with the significance of the rite or of the festivity, the faculty is given to celebrate or concelebrate more than once on the same day in the following cases:

a) a Priest who has celebrated or concelebrated the Chrism Mass on Thursday of Holy Week may also celebrate or concelebrate the Evening Mass of the Lord's Supper;

b) a Priest who has celebrated or concelebrated the Mass of the Easter Vigil may celebrate or concelebrate Mass during the day on Easter Sunday;

c) on the Nativity of the Lord (Christmas Day), all Priests may celebrate or concelebrate three Masses, provided the Masses are celebrated at their proper times of day;

d) on the Commemoration of All the Faithful Departed (All Souls' Day), all Priests may celebrate or concelebrate three Masses, provided that the

---

101. Cf. Sacred Congregation of Rites, Instruction, *Eucharisticum mysterium*, May 25, 1967, no. 47: *Acta Apostolicae Sedis* 59 (1967), p. 566.
102. Cf. *ibidem*, no. 47: p. 565.

celebrations take place at different times, and with due regard for what has been laid down regarding the application of second and third Masses;[103]

e) a Priest who concelebrates with the Bishop or his delegate at a Synod or pastoral visitation, or concelebrates on the occasion of a gathering of Priests, may celebrate Mass again for the benefit of the faithful. This holds also, with due regard for the prescriptions of law, for groups of religious.

205. A concelebrated Mass, whatever its form, is arranged in accordance with the norms commonly in force (cf. nos. 112–198), observing or adapting however what is set out below.

206. No one is ever to join a concelebration or to be admitted as a concelebrant once the Mass has already begun.

207. In the sanctuary there should be prepared:

a) seats and texts for the concelebrating Priests;

b) on the credence table: a chalice of sufficient size or else several chalices.

208. If a Deacon is not present, the functions proper to him are to be carried out by some of the concelebrants.

If other ministers are also absent, their proper parts may be entrusted to other suitable faithful laypeople; otherwise, they are carried out by some of the concelebrants.

209. The concelebrants put on in the vesting room, or other suitable place, the sacred vestments they customarily wear when celebrating Mass individually. However, should a just cause arise (e.g., a more considerable number of concelebrants or a lack of vestments), concelebrants other than the principal celebrant may omit the chasuble and simply wear the stole over the alb.

THE INTRODUCTORY RITES

210. When everything has been properly arranged, the procession moves as usual through the church to the altar. The concelebrating Priests walk ahead of the principal celebrant.

211. On arriving at the altar, the concelebrants and the principal celebrant, after making a profound bow, venerate the altar with a kiss, then go to their designated seats. As for the principal celebrant, if appropriate, he incenses the cross and the altar and then goes to the chair.

THE LITURGY OF THE WORD

212. During the Liturgy of the Word, the concelebrants remain at their places, sitting or standing whenever the principal celebrant does.

---

103. Cf. Benedict XV, Apostolic Constitution, *Incruentum altaris sacrificium*, August 10, 1915: *Acta Apostolicae Sedis* 7 (1915), pp. 401–404.

When the *Alleluia* is begun, all rise, except for a Bishop, who puts incense into the thurible without saying anything and blesses the Deacon or, in the absence of a Deacon, the concelebrant who is to proclaim the Gospel. However, in a concelebration where a Priest presides, the concelebrant who in the absence of a Deacon proclaims the Gospel neither requests nor receives the blessing of the principal celebrant.

213. The Homily is usually given by the principal celebrant or by one of the concelebrants.

THE LITURGY OF THE EUCHARIST

214. The Preparation of the Gifts (cf. nos. 139–146) is carried out by the principal celebrant, while the other concelebrants remain at their places.

215. After the Prayer over the Offerings has been said by the principal celebrant, the concelebrants approach the altar and stand around it, but in such a way that they do not obstruct the execution of the rites and that the sacred action may be seen clearly by the faithful. Nor should they obstruct the Deacon whenever he needs to approach the altar by reason of his ministry.

The Deacon exercises his ministry near the altar, assisting whenever necessary with the chalice and the Missal. However, in so far as possible, he stands back slightly, behind the concelebrating Priests standing around the principal celebrant.

THE MANNER OF PRONOUNCING THE EUCHARISTIC PRAYER

216. The Preface is sung or said by the principal Priest Celebrant alone; but the *Sanctus (Holy, Holy, Holy)* is sung or recited by all the concelebrants, together with the people and the choir.

217. After the *Sanctus (Holy, Holy, Holy)*, the concelebrating Priests continue the Eucharistic Prayer in the way described below. Only the principal celebrant makes the gestures, unless other indications are given.

218. The parts pronounced by all the concelebrants together and especially the words of Consecration, which all are obliged to say, are to be recited in such a manner that the concelebrants speak them in a low voice and that the principal celebrant's voice is heard clearly. In this way the words can be more easily understood by the people.

It is a praiseworthy practice for the parts that are to be said by all the concelebrants together and for which musical notation is provided in the Missal to be sung.

EUCHARISTIC PRAYER I, OR THE ROMAN CANON

219. In Eucharistic Prayer I, or the Roman Canon, the *Te igitur (To you, therefore, most merciful Father)* is said by the principal celebrant alone, with hands extended.

220. It is appropriate that the commemoration (*Memento*) of the living and the *Communicantes (In communion with those)* be assigned to one or other of the concelebrating Priests, who then pronounces these prayers alone, with hands extended, and in a loud voice.

221. The *Hanc igitur (Therefore, Lord, we pray)* is said once again by the principal celebrant alone, with hands extended.

222. From the *Quam oblationem (Be pleased, O God, we pray)* up to and including the *Supplices (In humble prayer we ask you, almighty God)*, the principal celebrant alone makes the gestures, while all the concelebrants pronounce everything together, in this manner:

> a) the *Quam oblationem (Be pleased, O God, we pray)*, with hands extended toward the offerings;
>
> b) the *Qui pridie (On the day before he was to suffer)* and the *Simili modo (In a similar way)* with hands joined;
>
> c) the words of the Lord, with each extending his right hand toward the bread and toward the chalice, if this seems appropriate; and at the elevation looking toward them and after this bowing profoundly;
>
> d) the *Unde et memores (Therefore, O Lord, as we celebrate the memorial)* and the *Supra quae (Be pleased to look upon)* with hands extended;
>
> e) for the *Supplices (In humble prayer we ask you, almighty God)* up to and including the words *through this participation at the altar*, bowing with hands joined; then standing upright and crossing themselves at the words *may be filled with every grace and heavenly blessing*.

223. It is appropriate that the commemoration (*Memento*) of the dead and the *Nobis quoque peccatoribus (To us, also, your servants)* be assigned to one or other of the concelebrants, who pronounces them alone, with hands extended, and in a loud voice.

224. At the words *To us, also, your servants, who though sinners*, of the *Nobis quoque peccatoribus*, all the concelebrants strike their breast.

225. The *Per quem haec omnia (Through whom you continue)* is said by the principal celebrant alone.

EUCHARISTIC PRAYER II

226. In Eucharistic Prayer II, the part *You are indeed Holy, O Lord* is pronounced by the principal celebrant alone, with hands extended.

227. In the parts from *Make holy, therefore, these gifts* to the end of *Humbly we pray*, all the concelebrants pronounce everything together as follows:

> a) the part *Make holy, therefore, these gifts*, with hands extended toward the offerings;

b) the parts *At the time he was betrayed* and *In a similar way* with hands joined;

c) the words of the Lord, with each extending his right hand toward the bread and toward the chalice, if this seems appropriate; and at the elevation looking toward them and after this bowing profoundly;

d) the parts *Therefore, as we celebrate* and *Humbly we pray* with hands extended.

228. It is appropriate that the intercessions for the living, *Remember, Lord, your Church*, and for the dead, *Remember also our brothers and sisters*, be assigned to one or other of the concelebrants, who pronounces them alone, with hands extended, and in a loud voice.

EUCHARISTIC PRAYER III

229. In Eucharistic Prayer III, the part *You are indeed Holy, O Lord* is pronounced by the principal celebrant alone, with hands extended.

230. In the parts from *Therefore, O Lord, we humbly implore you* to the end of *Look, we pray upon the oblation*, all the concelebrants pronounce everything together as follows:

a) the part *Therefore, O Lord, we humbly implore you* with hands extended toward the offerings;

b) the parts *For on the night he was betrayed* and *In a similar way* with hands joined;

c) the words of the Lord, with each extending his right hand toward the bread and toward the chalice, if this seems appropriate; and at the elevation looking toward them and after this bowing profoundly;

d) the parts *Therefore, O Lord, as we celebrate the memorial* and *Look, we pray, upon the oblation* with hands extended.

231. It is appropriate that the intercessions *May he make of us an eternal offering to you*, and *May this Sacrifice of our reconciliation*, and *To our departed brothers and sisters* be assigned to one or other of the concelebrants, who pronounces them alone, with hands extended, and in a loud voice.

EUCHARISTIC PRAYER IV

232. In Eucharistic Prayer IV, the part *We give you praise, Father most holy* up to and including the words *he might sanctify creation to the full* is pronounced by the principal celebrant alone, with hands extended.

233. In the parts from *Therefore, O Lord, we pray* to the end of *Look, O Lord, upon the Sacrifice*, all the concelebrants pronounce everything together as follows:

a) the part *Therefore, O Lord, we pray* with hands extended toward the offerings;

b) the parts *For when the hour had come* and *In a similar way* with hands joined;

c) the words of the Lord, with each extending his right hand toward the bread and toward the chalice, if this seems appropriate; and at the elevation looking toward them and after this bowing profoundly;

d) the parts *Therefore, O Lord, as we now celebrate* and *Look, O Lord, upon the Sacrifice* with hands extended.

234. It is appropriate that the intercessions *Therefore, Lord, remember now* and *To all of us, your children* be assigned to one or other of the concelebrants, who pronounces them alone, with hands extended, and in a loud voice.

235. As for other Eucharistic Prayers approved by the Apostolic See, the norms laid down for each one are to be observed.

236. The concluding doxology of the Eucharistic Prayer is pronounced solely by the principal Priest Celebrant or together, if this is desired, with the other concelebrants, but not by the faithful.

THE COMMUNION RITE

237. Then the principal celebrant, with hands joined, says the introduction to the Lord's Prayer. Next, with hands extended, he says the Lord's Prayer itself together with the other concelebrants, who also pray with hands extended, and together with the people.

238. The *Libera nos (Deliver us)* is said by the principal celebrant alone, with hands extended. All the concelebrants, together with the people, pronounce the concluding acclamation *For the kingdom*.

239. After the Deacon or, in the absence of a Deacon, one of the concelebrants, has given the instruction *Let us offer each other the sign of peace*, all give one another the Sign of Peace. Those concelebrants nearer the principal celebrant receive the Sign of Peace from him before the Deacon does.

240. During the *Agnus Dei (Lamb of God)*, the Deacons or some of the concelebrants may help the principal celebrant to break the hosts for the Communion of both the concelebrants and the people.

241. After the commingling, the principal celebrant alone, with hands joined, quietly says either the prayer *Domine Iesu Christe, Fili Dei vivi (Lord Jesus Christ, Son of the living God)* or the prayer *Perceptio Corporis et Sanguinis tui (May the receiving of your Body and Blood)*.

242. Once the prayer for Communion has been said, the principal celebrant genuflects and steps back a little. Then one after another the concelebrants come to the middle of the altar, genuflect, and reverently take the Body of Christ from the altar. Then holding it in their right hand, with the left hand placed underneath, they return to their places. However, the concelebrants may remain in

their places and take the Body of Christ from the paten held for them by the principal celebrant or held by one or more of the concelebrants passing in front of them, or they may do so by handing the paten one to another, and so to the last of them.

243. Then the principal celebrant takes a host consecrated in the same Mass, holds it slightly raised above the paten or the chalice, and, facing the people, says the *Ecce Agnus Dei (Behold the Lamb of God)*. With the concelebrants and the people he continues, saying the *Domine, non sum dignus (Lord, I am not worthy)*.

244. Then the principal celebrant, facing the altar, says quietly, *Corpus Christi custodiat me in vitam aeternam (May the Body of Christ keep me safe for eternal life)*, and reverently receives the Body of Christ. The concelebrants do likewise, giving themselves Communion. After them the Deacon receives the Body and Blood of the Lord from the principal celebrant.

245. The Blood of the Lord may be consumed either by drinking from the chalice directly, or by intinction, or by means of a tube or a spoon.

246. If Communion is consumed by drinking directly from the chalice, one of these procedures may be followed:

a) The principal celebrant, standing at the middle of the altar, takes the chalice and says quietly, *Sanguis Christi custodiat me in vitam aeternam (May the Blood of Christ keep me safe for eternal life)*. He consumes a little of the Blood of Christ and hands the chalice to the Deacon or a concelebrant. He then distributes Communion to the faithful (cf. nos. 160–162).

   The concelebrants approach the altar one after another or, if two chalices are used, two by two. They genuflect, partake of the Blood of Christ, wipe the rim of the chalice, and return to their seats.

b) The principal celebrant consumes the Blood of the Lord standing as usual at the middle of the altar.

   The concelebrants, however, may partake of the Blood of the Lord while remaining in their places and drinking from the chalice presented to them by the Deacon or by one of the concelebrants, or even passed from one to the other. The chalice is always wiped either by the one who drinks from it or by the one who presents it. After each has communicated, he returns to his seat.

247. The Deacon reverently drinks at the altar all of the Blood of Christ that remains, assisted, if the case requires, by some of the concelebrants. He then carries the chalice to the credence table and there he or a duly instituted acolyte purifies it, wipes it, and arranges it as usual (cf. no. 183).

248. The Communion of the concelebrants may also be arranged in such a way that each communicates from the Body of the Lord at the altar and, immediately afterwards, from the Blood of the Lord.

In this case the principal celebrant receives Communion under both kinds in the usual way (cf. no. 158), observing, however, the rite chosen in each particular instance for Communion from the chalice; and the other concelebrants should do the same.

After the principal celebrant's Communion, the chalice is placed at the side of the altar on another corporal. The concelebrants approach the middle of the altar one by one, genuflect, and communicate from the Body of the Lord; then they move to the side of the altar and partake of the Blood of the Lord, following the rite chosen for Communion from the chalice, as has been remarked above.

The Communion of the Deacon and the purification of the chalice take place as described above.

249. If the concelebrants' Communion is by intinction, the principal celebrant partakes of the Body and Blood of the Lord in the usual way, but making sure that enough of the precious Blood remains in the chalice for the Communion of the concelebrants. Then the Deacon, or one of the concelebrants, arranges the chalice together with the paten containing particles of the host, if appropriate, either in the center of the altar or at the side on another corporal.

The concelebrants approach the altar one by one, genuflect, and take a particle, intinct it partly into the chalice, and, holding a purificator under their mouth, consume the intincted particle. They then return to their places as at the beginning of Mass.

The Deacon also receives Communion by intinction and to the concelebrant's words, *Corpus et Sanguis Christi (The Body and Blood of Christ)* replies, *Amen*. Moreover, the Deacon consumes at the altar all that remains of the Precious Blood, assisted, if the case requires, by some of the concelebrants. He carries the chalice to the credence table and there he or a duly instituted acolyte purifies it, wipes it, and arranges it as usual.

THE CONCLUDING RITES

250. Everything else until the end of Mass is done by the principal celebrant in the usual way (cf. nos. 166–168), with the other concelebrants remaining at their seats.

251. Before leaving the altar, the concelebrants make a profound bow to the altar. For his part the principal celebrant, along with the Deacon, venerates the altar as usual with a kiss.

III. MASS AT WHICH ONLY ONE MINISTER PARTICIPATES

252. At a Mass celebrated by a Priest with only one minister to assist him and to make the responses, the rite of Mass with the people is followed (cf. nos. 120–169), the minister saying the people's parts if appropriate.

253. If, however, the minister is a Deacon, he performs his proper functions (cf. nos. 171–186) and likewise carries out the other parts, that is, those of the people.

254. Mass should not be celebrated without a minister, or at least one of the faithful, except for a just and reasonable cause. In this case, the greetings, the instructions, and the blessing at the end of Mass are omitted.

255. Before Mass, the necessary vessels are prepared either at the credence table or on the right hand side of the altar.

THE INTRODUCTORY RITES

256. The Priest approaches the altar and, after making a profound bow along with the minister, venerates the altar with a kiss and goes to the chair. If he wishes, the Priest may remain at the altar; in which case, the Missal is also prepared there. Then the minister or the Priest says the Entrance Antiphon.

257. Then the Priest, standing, makes with the minister the Sign of the Cross as the Priest says, *In the name of the Father, etc.* Facing the minister, he greets him, choosing one of the formulas provided.

258. Then the Penitential Act takes place, and, in accordance with the rubrics, the *Kyrie* and the *Gloria in excelsis (Glory to God in the highest)* are said.

259. Then, with hands joined, the Priest pronounces, *Let us pray,* and after a suitable pause, with hands extended, he pronounces the Collect. At the end the minister acclaims, *Amen.*

THE LITURGY OF THE WORD

260. The readings should, in so far as possible, be proclaimed from the ambo or a lectern.

261. After the Collect, the minister reads the First Reading and Psalm, the Second Reading, when it is to be said, and the verse of the *Alleluia* or other chant.

262. Then the Priest, bowing profoundly, says the prayer *Munda cor meum (Cleanse my heart)* and after this reads the Gospel. At the end he says, *The Gospel of the Lord,* to which the minister replies, *Praise to you, Lord Jesus Christ.* The Priest then venerates the book with a kiss, saying quietly the formula *Per evangelica dicta (Through the words of the Gospel).*

263. After this, the Priest says the Symbol or Creed, in accordance with the rubrics, together with the minister.

264. The Universal Prayer follows, which may be said even in this form of Mass. The Priest introduces and concludes it, with the minister announcing the intentions.

THE LITURGY OF THE EUCHARIST

265. In the Liturgy of the Eucharist, everything is done as at Mass with the people, except for the following.

266. After the acclamation at the end of the embolism that follows the Lord's Prayer, the Priest says the prayer *Domine Iesu Christe, qui dixisti (Lord Jesus Christ, who said to your Apostles)*. He then adds, *The peace of the Lord be with you always*, to which the minister replies, *And with your spirit*. If appropriate, the Priest gives the Sign of Peace to the minister.

267. Then, while he says the *Agnus Dei (Lamb of God)* with the minister, the Priest breaks the host over the paten. After the *Agnus Dei (Lamb of God)*, he performs the commingling, saying quietly the prayer *Haec commixtio (May this mingling)*.

268. After the commingling, the Priest quietly says either the prayer *Domine Iesu Christe, Fili Dei vivi (Lord Jesus Christ, Son of the living God)* or the prayer *Perceptio Corporis et Sanguinis tui (May the receiving of your Body and Blood)*. Then he genuflects, takes the host, and, if the minister is to receive Communion, turns to the minister and, holding the host a little above the paten or the chalice, says the *Ecce Agnus Dei (Behold the Lamb of God)*, adding with the minister, *Lord, I am not worthy*. Then facing the altar, the Priest partakes of the Body of Christ. If, however, the minister does not receive Communion, the Priest, after genuflecting, takes the host and, facing the altar, says quietly, *Lord, I am not worthy, etc.*, and the *Corpus Christi custodiat me in vitam aeternam (May the Body of Christ keep me safe for eternal life)*, and consumes the Body of Christ. Then he takes the chalice and says quietly, *Sanguis Christi custodiat me in vitam aeternam (May the Blood of Christ keep me safe for eternal life)*, and consumes the Blood of Christ.

269. Before Communion is given to the minister, the Communion Antiphon is said by the minister or by the Priest himself.

270. The Priest purifies the chalice at the credence table or at the altar. If the chalice is purified at the altar, it may be carried to the credence table by the minister or may be arranged once again on the altar, at the side.

271. After the purification of the chalice, the Priest should observe a brief pause for silence, and after this he says the Prayer after Communion.

THE CONCLUDING RITES

272. The Concluding Rites are carried out as at a Mass with the people, but the *Ite, missa est (Go forth, the Mass is ended)* is omitted. The Priest venerates the altar as usual with a kiss and, after making a profound bow with the minister, withdraws.

IV. SOME GENERAL NORMS FOR ALL FORMS OF MASS

VENERATION OF THE ALTAR AND THE BOOK OF THE GOSPELS

273. According to traditional practice, the veneration of the altar and of the *Book of the Gospels* is done by means of a kiss. However, where a sign of this kind is not in harmony with the traditions or the culture of some region, it is

for the Conference of Bishops to establish some other sign in its place, with the consent of the Apostolic See.

274. A genuflection, made by bending the right knee to the ground, signifies adoration, and therefore it is reserved for the Most Blessed Sacrament, as well as for the Holy Cross from the solemn adoration during the liturgical celebration on Good Friday until the beginning of the Easter Vigil.

During Mass, three genuflections are made by the Priest Celebrant: namely, after the elevation of the host, after the elevation of the chalice, and before Communion. Certain specific features to be observed in a concelebrated Mass are noted in their proper place (cf. nos. 210–251).

If, however, the tabernacle with the Most Blessed Sacrament is situated in the sanctuary, the Priest, the Deacon, and the other ministers genuflect when they approach the altar and when they depart from it, but not during the celebration of Mass itself.

Otherwise, all who pass before the Most Blessed Sacrament genuflect, unless they are moving in procession.

Ministers carrying the processional cross or candles bow their heads instead of genuflecting.

275. A bow signifies reverence and honor shown to the persons themselves or to the signs that represent them. There are two kinds of bow: a bow of the head and a bow of the body.

a) A bow of the head is made when the three Divine Persons are named together and at the names of Jesus, of the Blessed Virgin Mary, and of the Saint in whose honor Mass is being celebrated.

b) A bow of the body, that is to say, a profound bow, is made to the altar; during the prayers *Munda cor meum (Cleanse my heart)* and *In spiritu humilitatis (With humble spirit)*; in the Creed at the words *et incarnatus est (and by the Holy Spirit . . . and became man)*; in the Roman Canon at the *Supplices te rogamus (In humble prayer we ask you, almighty God)*. The same kind of bow is made by the Deacon when he asks for a blessing before the proclamation of the Gospel. In addition, the Priest bows slightly as he pronounces the words of the Lord at the Consecration.

276. Thurification or incensation is an expression of reverence and of prayer, as is signified in Sacred Scripture (cf. Ps 140 [141]:2; Rev 8:3).

Incense may be used optionally in any form of Mass:

a) during the Entrance Procession;

b) at the beginning of Mass, to incense the cross and the altar;

c) at the procession before the Gospel and the proclamation of the Gospel itself;

d) after the bread and the chalice have been placed on the altar, to incense the offerings, the cross, and the altar, as well as the Priest and the people;

e) at the elevation of the host and the chalice after the Consecration.

277. The Priest, having put incense into the thurible, blesses it with the Sign of the Cross, without saying anything.

Before and after an incensation, a profound bow is made to the person or object that is incensed, except for the altar and the offerings for the Sacrifice of the Mass.

Three swings of the thurible are used to incense: the Most Blessed Sacrament, a relic of the Holy Cross and images of the Lord exposed for public veneration, the offerings for the Sacrifice of the Mass, the altar cross, the *Book of the Gospels*, the paschal candle, the Priest, and the people.

Two swings of the thurible are used to incense relics and images of the Saints exposed for public veneration; this should be done, however, only at the beginning of the celebration, following the incensation of the altar.

The altar is incensed with single swings of the thurible in this way:

a) if the altar is freestanding with respect to the wall, the Priest incenses walking around it;

b) if the altar is not freestanding, the Priest incenses it while walking first to the right hand side, then to the left.

The cross, if situated on the altar or near it, is incensed by the Priest before he incenses the altar; otherwise, he incenses it when he passes in front of it.

The Priest incenses the offerings with three swings of the thurible or by making the Sign of the Cross over the offerings with the thurible before going on to incense the cross and the altar.

THE PURIFICATION

278. Whenever a fragment of the host adheres to his fingers, especially after the fraction or after the Communion of the faithful, the Priest should wipe his fingers over the paten or, if necessary, wash them. Likewise, he should also gather any fragments that may have fallen outside the paten.

279. The sacred vessels are purified by the Priest, the Deacon, or an instituted acolyte after Communion or after Mass, in so far as possible at the credence table. The purification of the chalice is done with water alone or with wine and water, which is then consumed by whoever does the purification. The paten is wiped clean as usual with the purificator.

Care is to be taken that whatever may remain of the Blood of Christ after the distribution of Communion is consumed immediately and completely at the altar.

280. If a host or any particle should fall, it is to be picked up reverently; and if any of the Precious Blood is spilled, the area where the spill occurred should be washed with water, and this water should then be poured into the *sacrarium* in the sacristy.

COMMUNION UNDER BOTH KINDS

281. Holy Communion has a fuller form as a sign when it takes place under both kinds. For in this form the sign of the Eucharistic banquet is more clearly evident and clearer expression is given to the divine will by which the new and eternal Covenant is ratified in the Blood of the Lord, as also the connection between the Eucharistic banquet and the eschatological banquet in the Kingdom of the Father.[104]

282. Sacred pastors should take care to ensure that the faithful who participate in the rite or are present at it, are made aware by the most suitable means possible of the Catholic teaching on the form of Holy Communion as laid down by the Ecumenical Council of Trent. Above all, they should instruct the Christian faithful that the Catholic faith teaches that Christ, whole and entire, and the true Sacrament, is received even under only one species, and hence that as regards the resulting fruits, those who receive under only one species are not deprived of any grace that is necessary for salvation.[105]

Furthermore, they should teach that the Church, in her administration of the Sacraments, has the power to lay down or alter whatever provisions, apart from the substance of the Sacraments, that she judges to be more readily conducive to reverence for the Sacraments and the good of the recipients, in view of changing conditions, times, and places.[106] However, at the same time the faithful should be instructed to participate more readily in this sacred rite, by which the sign of the Eucharistic banquet is made more fully evident.

283. In addition to those cases given in the ritual books, Communion under both kinds is permitted for:

a) Priests who are not able to celebrate or concelebrate Mass;

b) the Deacon and others who perform some duty at the Mass;

c) members of communities at the Conventual Mass or the "community" Mass, along with seminarians, and all those engaged in a retreat or taking part in a spiritual or pastoral gathering.

---

104. Cf. Sacred Congregation of Rites, Instruction, *Eucharisticum mysterium*, May 25, 1967, no. 32: *Acta Apostolicae Sedis* 59 (1967), p. 558.

105. Cf. Ecumenical Council of Trent, Session XXI, *Doctrina de communione sub utraque specie et parvulorum*, July 16, 1562, chapters 1–3: Denzinger-Schönmetzer, nos. 1725–1729.

106. Cf. *ibidem*, chapter 2: Denzinger-Schönmetzer, no. 1728.

The Diocesan Bishop may establish norms for Communion under both kinds for his own diocese, which are also to be observed in churches of religious and at celebrations with small groups. The Diocesan Bishop is also given the faculty to permit Communion under both kinds whenever it may seem appropriate to the Priest to whom a community has been entrusted as its own shepherd, provided that the faithful have been well instructed and that there is no danger of profanation of the Sacrament or of the rite's becoming difficult because of the large number of participants or for some other cause.

In all that pertains to Communion under both kinds, the *Norms for the Distribution and Reception of Holy Communion under Both Kinds in the Dioceses of the United States of America* are to be followed (particularly nos. 27–54).

284. When Communion is distributed under both kinds:

a) the chalice is usually administered by a Deacon or, in the absence of a Deacon, by a Priest, or even by a duly instituted acolyte or another extraordinary minister of Holy Communion, or by one of the faithful who, in a case of necessity, has been entrusted with this duty for a single occasion;

b) whatever may remain of the Blood of Christ is consumed at the altar by the Priest or the Deacon or the duly instituted acolyte who ministered the chalice. The same then purifies, wipes, and arranges the sacred vessels in the usual way.

Any of the faithful who wish to receive Holy Communion under the species of bread alone should be given Communion in this form.

285. For Communion under both kinds the following should be prepared:

a) If Communion from the chalice is done by drinking directly from the chalice, a chalice of a sufficiently large size or several chalices are prepared. However, care should be taken lest beyond what is needed of the Blood of Christ remains to be consumed at the end of the celebration.

b) If Communion from the chalice is done by intinction, the hosts should be neither too thin nor too small, but rather a little thicker than usual, so that after being intincted partly into the Blood of Christ they can still be easily distributed.

286. If Communion of the Blood of Christ is carried out by communicants' drinking from the chalice, each communicant, after receiving the Body of Christ, moves to the minister of the chalice and stands facing him. The minister says, *The Blood of Christ,* the communicant replies, *Amen,* and the minister hands over the chalice, which the communicant raises to his or her mouth. Each communicant drinks a little from the chalice, hands it back to the minister, and then withdraws; the minister wipes the rim of the chalice with the purificator.

287. If Communion from the chalice is carried out by intinction, each communicant, holding a Communion-plate under the mouth, approaches the Priest who holds a vessel with the sacred particles, with a minister standing at his side and holding the chalice. The Priest takes a host, intincts it partly in the chalice

and, showing it, says, *The Body and Blood of Christ*. The communicant replies, *Amen*, receives the Sacrament in the mouth from the Priest, and then withdraws.

CHAPTER V
THE ARRANGEMENT AND ORNAMENTATION OF CHURCHES FOR THE CELEBRATION OF THE EUCHARIST

I. GENERAL PRINCIPLES

288. For the celebration of the Eucharist, the People of God are normally gathered together in a church or, if there is no church or if it is too small, then in another respectable place that is nonetheless worthy of so great a mystery. Therefore, churches or other places should be suitable for carrying out the sacred action and for ensuring the active participation of the faithful. Moreover, sacred buildings and requisites for divine worship should be truly worthy and beautiful and be signs and symbols of heavenly realities.[107]

289. Consequently, the Church constantly seeks the noble assistance of the arts and admits the artistic expressions of all peoples and regions.[108] In fact, just as she is intent on preserving the works of art and the artistic treasures handed down from past centuries[109] and, in so far as necessary, on adapting them to new needs, so also she strives to promote new works of art that are in harmony with the character of each successive age.[110]

On account of this, in appointing artists and choosing works of art to be admitted into a church, what should be looked for is that true excellence in art which nourishes faith and devotion and accords authentically with both the meaning and the purpose for which it is intended.[111]

290. All churches should be dedicated or at least blessed. Cathedrals and parish churches, however, are to be dedicated with a solemn rite.

291. For the proper construction, restoration, and arrangement of sacred buildings, all those involved should consult the diocesan commission for the Sacred

---

107. Cf. Second Ecumenical Council of the Vatican, Constitution on the Sacred Liturgy, *Sacrosanctum Concilium*, nos. 122–124; Decree on the Ministry and Life of Priests, *Presbyterorum ordinis*, no. 5; Sacred Congregation of Rites, Instruction, *Inter Oecumenici*, September 26, 1964, no. 90: *Acta Apostolicae Sedis* 56 (1964), p. 897; Instruction, *Eucharisticum mysterium*, May 25, 1967, no. 24: *Acta Apostolicae Sedis* 59 (1967), p. 554; *Code of Canon Law*, can. 932 §1.
108. Cf. Second Ecumenical Council of the Vatican, Constitution on the Sacred Liturgy, *Sacrosanctum Concilium*, no. 123.
109. Cf. Sacred Congregation of Rites, Instruction, *Eucharisticum mysterium*, May 25, 1967, no. 24: *Acta Apostolicae Sedis* 59 (1967), p. 554.
110. Cf. Second Ecumenical Council of the Vatican, Constitution on the Sacred Liturgy, *Sacrosanctum Concilium*, nos. 123, 129; Sacred Congregation of Rites, Instruction, *Inter Oecumenici*, September 26, 1964, no. 13c: *Acta Apostolicae Sedis* 56 (1964), p. 880.
111. Cf. Second Ecumenical Council of the Vatican, Constitution on the Sacred Liturgy, *Sacrosanctum Concilium*, no. 123.

Liturgy and sacred art. Moreover, the Diocesan Bishop should employ the counsel and help of this commission whenever it comes to laying down norms on this matter, approving plans for new buildings, and making decisions on the more important matters.[112]

292. The ornamentation of a church should contribute toward its noble simplicity rather than to ostentation. Moreover, in the choice of elements attention should be paid to authenticity and there should be the intention of fostering the instruction of the faithful and the dignity of the entire sacred place.

293. The suitable arrangement of a church, and of what goes with it, in such a way as to meet appropriately the needs of our own age requires not only that care be taken as regards whatever pertains more immediately to the celebration of sacred actions but also that the faithful be provided with whatever is conducive to their appropriate comfort and is normally provided in places where people habitually gather.

294. The People of God which is gathered for Mass is coherently and hierarchically ordered, and this finds its expression in the variety of ministries and the variety of actions according to the different parts of the celebration. Hence the general arrangement of the sacred building must be such that in some way it conveys the image of the assembled congregation and allows the appropriate ordering of all the participants, as well as facilitating each in the proper carrying out of his function.

The faithful and the *schola cantorum* (choir) shall have a place that facilitates their active participation.[113]

The Priest Celebrant, the Deacon, and the other ministers have places in the sanctuary. There, also, should be prepared seats for concelebrants, but if their number is great, seats should be arranged in another part of the church, though near the altar.

All these elements, even though they must express the hierarchical structure and the diversity of functions, should nevertheless bring about a close and coherent unity that is clearly expressive of the unity of the entire holy people. Indeed, the nature and beauty of the place and all its furnishings should foster devotion and express visually the holiness of the mysteries celebrated there.

II. ARRANGEMENT OF THE SANCTUARY
FOR THE SACRED SYNAXIS

295. The sanctuary is the place where the altar stands, the Word of God is proclaimed, and the Priest, the Deacon, and the other ministers exercise their functions. It should be appropriately marked off from the body of the church either by its being somewhat elevated or by a particular structure and ornamentation.

---

112. Cf. *ibidem*, no. 126; Sacred Congregation of Rites, Instruction, *Inter Oecumenici*, September 26, 1964, no. 91: *Acta Apostolicae Sedis* 56 (1964), p. 898.

113. Cf. Sacred Congregation of Rites, Instruction, *Inter Oecumenici*, September 26, 1964, nos. 97–98: *Acta Apostolicae Sedis* 56 (1964), p. 899.

It should, moreover, be large enough to allow the Eucharist to be easily celebrated and seen.[114]

THE ALTAR AND ITS ORNAMENTATION

296. The altar, on which is effected the Sacrifice of the Cross made present under sacramental signs, is also the table of the Lord to which the People of God is convoked to participate in the Mass, and it is also the center of the thanksgiving that is accomplished through the Eucharist.

297. The celebration of the Eucharist in a sacred place is to take place on an altar; however, outside a sacred place, it may take place on a suitable table, always with the use of a cloth, a corporal, a cross, and candles.

298. It is desirable that in every church there be a fixed altar, since this more clearly and permanently signifies Christ Jesus, the Living Stone (1 Pt 2:4; cf. Eph 2:20). In other places set aside for sacred celebrations, the altar may be movable.

An altar is said to be fixed if it is so constructed as to be attached to the floor and not removable; it is said to be movable if it can be displaced.

299. The altar should be built separate from the wall, in such a way that it is possible to walk around it easily and that Mass can be celebrated at it facing the people, which is desirable wherever possible. Moreover, the altar should occupy a place where it is truly the center toward which the attention of the whole congregation of the faithful naturally turns.[115] The altar should usually be fixed and dedicated.

300. An altar, whether fixed or movable, should be dedicated according to the rite prescribed in the Roman Pontifical; but it is permissible for a movable altar simply to be blessed.

301. In keeping with the Church's traditional practice and with what the altar signifies, the table of a fixed altar should be of stone and indeed of natural stone. In the Dioceses of the United States of America, wood which is dignified, solid, and well-crafted may be used, provided that the altar is structurally immobile. As to the supports or base for supporting the table, these may be made of any material, provided it is dignified and solid.

A movable altar may be constructed of any noble and solid material suited to liturgical use, according to the traditions and usages of the different regions.

302. The practice of the deposition of relics of Saints, even those not Martyrs, under the altar to be dedicated is fittingly retained. However, care should be taken to ensure the authenticity of such relics.

---

114. Cf. *ibidem*, no. 91: p. 898.
115. Cf. *ibidem*.

303. In building new churches, it is preferable for a single altar to be erected, one that in the gathering of the faithful will signify the one Christ and the one Eucharist of the Church.

In already existing churches, however, when the old altar is so positioned that it makes the people's participation difficult but cannot be moved without damage to artistic value, another fixed altar, skillfully made and properly dedicated, should be erected and the sacred rites celebrated on it alone. In order that the attention of the faithful not be distracted from the new altar, the old altar should not be decorated in any special way.

304. Out of reverence for the celebration of the memorial of the Lord and for the banquet in which the Body and Blood of the Lord are offered, there should be, on an altar where this is celebrated, at least one cloth, white in color, whose shape, size, and decoration are in keeping with the altar's structure. When, in the Dioceses of the United States of America, other cloths are used in addition to the altar cloth, then those cloths may be of other colors possessing Christian honorific or festive significance according to longstanding local usage, provided that the uppermost cloth covering the mensa (i.e., the altar cloth itself) is always white in color.

305. Moderation should be observed in the decoration of the altar.

During Advent the floral decoration of the altar should be marked by a moderation suited to the character of this time of year, without expressing in anticipation the full joy of the Nativity of the Lord. During Lent it is forbidden for the altar to be decorated with flowers. Exceptions, however, are *Laetare* Sunday (Fourth Sunday of Lent), Solemnities, and Feasts.

Floral decoration should always show moderation and be arranged around the altar rather than on the altar table.

306. For only what is required for the celebration of the Mass may be placed on the altar table: namely, from the beginning of the celebration until the proclamation of the Gospel, the *Book of the Gospels*; then from the Presentation of the Gifts until the purification of the vessels, the chalice with the paten, a ciborium, if necessary, and, finally, the corporal, the purificator, the pall, and the Missal.

In addition, arranged discreetly, there should be whatever may be needed to amplify the Priest's voice.

307. The candlesticks required for the different liturgical services for reasons of reverence or the festive character of the celebration (cf. no. 117) should be appropriately placed either on the altar or around it, according to the design of the altar and the sanctuary, so that the whole may be harmonious and the faithful may not be impeded from a clear view of what takes place at the altar or what is placed upon it.

308. Likewise, either on the altar or near it, there is to be a cross, with the figure of Christ crucified upon it, a cross clearly visible to the assembled people. It is

desirable that such a cross should remain near the altar even outside of liturgical celebrations, so as to call to mind for the faithful the saving Passion of the Lord.

THE AMBO

309. The dignity of the Word of God requires that in the church there be a suitable place from which it may be proclaimed and toward which the attention of the faithful naturally turns during the Liturgy of the Word.[116]

It is appropriate that generally this place be a stationary ambo and not simply a movable lectern. The ambo must be located in keeping with the design of each church in such a way that the ordained ministers and readers may be clearly seen and heard by the faithful.

From the ambo only the readings, the Responsorial Psalm, and the Easter Proclamation (*Exsultet*) are to be proclaimed; likewise it may be used for giving the Homily and for announcing the intentions of the Universal Prayer. The dignity of the ambo requires that only a minister of the word should stand at it.

It is appropriate that before being put into liturgical use a new ambo be blessed according to the rite described in the Roman Ritual.[117]

THE CHAIR FOR THE PRIEST CELEBRANT AND OTHER SEATS

310. The chair of the Priest Celebrant must signify his function of presiding over the gathering and of directing the prayer. Thus the more suitable place for the chair is facing the people at the head of the sanctuary, unless the design of the building or other features prevent this: as, for example, if on account of too great a distance, communication between the Priest and the congregation would be difficult, or if the tabernacle were to be positioned in the center behind the altar. In any case, any appearance of a throne is to be avoided.[118] It is appropriate that before being put into liturgical use, the chair be blessed according to the rite described in the Roman Ritual.[119]

Likewise, seats should be arranged in the sanctuary for concelebrating Priests as well as for Priests who are present at the celebration in choir dress but without concelebrating.

The seat for the Deacon should be placed near that of the celebrant. For the other ministers seats should be arranged so that they are clearly distinguishable from seats for the clergy and so that the ministers are easily able to carry out the function entrusted to them.[120]

---

116. Cf. Sacred Congregation of Rites, Instruction, *Inter Oecumenici*, September 26, 1964, no. 92: *Acta Apostolicae Sedis* 56 (1964), p. 899.

117. Cf. Rituale Romanum, *De Benedictionibus*, editio typica, 1984, *Ordo benedictionis occasione data auspicandi novum ambonem*, nos. 900–918.

118. Cf. Sacred Congregation of Rites, Instruction, *Inter Oecumenici*, September 26, 1964, no. 92: *Acta Apostolicae Sedis* 56 (1964), p. 898.

119. Cf. Rituale Romanum, *De Benedictionibus*, editio typica, 1984, *Ordo benedictionis occasione data auspicandi novam cathedram seu sedem praesidentiae*, nos. 880–899.

120. Cf. Sacred Congregation of Rites, Instruction, *Inter Oecumenici*, September 26, 1964, no. 92: *Acta Apostolicae Sedis* 56 (1964), p. 898.

III. THE ARRANGEMENT OF THE CHURCH

THE PLACES FOR THE FAITHFUL

311. Places for the faithful should be arranged with appropriate care so that they are able to participate in the sacred celebrations, duly following them with their eyes and their attention. It is desirable that benches or seating usually should be provided for their use. However, the custom of reserving seats for private persons is to be reprobated.[121] Moreover, benches or seating should be so arranged, especially in newly built churches, that the faithful can easily take up the bodily postures required for the different parts of the celebration and can have easy access for the reception of Holy Communion.

Care should be taken to ensure that the faithful be able not only to see the Priest, the Deacon, and the readers but also, with the aid of modern technical means, to hear them without difficulty.

THE PLACE FOR THE *SCHOLA CANTORUM* AND THE MUSICAL INSTRUMENTS

312. The *schola cantorum* (choir) should be so positioned with respect to the arrangement of each church that its nature may be clearly evident, namely as part of the assembled community of the faithful undertaking a specific function. The positioning should also help the choir to exercise this function more easily and allow each choir member full sacramental participation in the Mass in a convenient manner.[122]

313. The organ and other lawfully approved musical instruments should be placed in a suitable place so that they can sustain the singing of both the choir and the people and be heard with ease by everybody if they are played alone. It is appropriate that before being put into liturgical use, the organ be blessed according to the rite described in the Roman Ritual.[123]

In Advent the use of the organ and other musical instruments should be marked by a moderation suited to the character of this time of year, without expressing in anticipation the full joy of the Nativity of the Lord.

In Lent the playing of the organ and musical instruments is allowed only in order to support the singing. Exceptions, however, are *Laetare* Sunday (Fourth Sunday of Lent), Solemnities, and Feasts.

THE PLACE FOR THE RESERVATION OF THE MOST HOLY EUCHARIST

314. In accordance with the structure of each church and legitimate local customs, the Most Blessed Sacrament should be reserved in a tabernacle in a part

---

121. Cf. Second Ecumenical Council of the Vatican, Constitution on the Sacred Liturgy, *Sacrosanctum Concilium*, no. 32.
122. Cf. Sacred Congregation of Rites, Instruction, *Musicam sacram*, March 5, 1967, no. 23: *Acta Apostolicae Sedis* 59 (1967), p. 307.
123. Cf. Rituale Romanum, *De Benedictionibus*, editio typica, 1984, *Ordo benedictionis organi*, nos. 1052–1067.

of the church that is truly noble, prominent, conspicuous, worthily decorated, and suitable for prayer.[124]

The tabernacle should usually be the only one, be irremovable, be made of solid and inviolable material that is not transparent, and be locked in such a way that the danger of profanation is prevented to the greatest extent possible.[125] Moreover, it is appropriate that before it is put into liturgical use, the tabernacle be blessed according to the rite described in the Roman Ritual.[126]

315. It is more appropriate as a sign that on an altar on which Mass is celebrated there not be a tabernacle in which the Most Holy Eucharist is reserved.[127]

Consequently, it is preferable that the tabernacle be located, according to the judgment of the Diocesan Bishop:

a) either in the sanctuary, apart from the altar of celebration, in a appropriate form and place, not excluding its being positioned on an old altar no longer used for celebration (cf. no. 303);

b) or even in some chapel suitable for the private adoration and prayer of the faithful[128] and organically connected to the church and readily noticeable by the Christian faithful.

316. In accordance with traditional custom, near the tabernacle a special lamp, fueled by oil or wax, should shine permanently to indicate the presence of Christ and honor it.[129]

317. In no way should any of the other things be forgotten which are prescribed by law concerning the reservation of the Most Holy Eucharist.[130]

---

124. Cf. Sacred Congregation of Rites, Instruction, *Eucharisticum mysterium*, May 25, 1967, no. 54: *Acta Apostolicae Sedis* 59 (1967), p. 568; cf. also Instruction, *Inter Oecumenici*, September 26, 1964, no. 95: *Acta Apostolicae Sedis* 56 (1964), p. 898.

125. Cf. Sacred Congregation of Rites, Instruction, *Eucharisticum mysterium*, May 25, 1967. no. 52: *Acta Apostolicae Sedis* 59 (1967), p. 568; Sacred Congregation of Rites, Instruction, *Inter Oecumenici*, September 26, 1964, no. 95: *Acta Apostolicae Sedis* 56 (1964), p. 898; Sacred Congregation for the Sacraments, Instruction, *Nullo umquam tempore*, May 28, 1938, no. 4: *Acta Apostolicae Sedis* 30 (1938), pp. 199–200; Rituale Romanum, *De sacra Communione et de cultu mysterii eucharistici extra Missam*, editio typica, 1973, nos. 10–11; *Code of Canon Law*, can. 938 §3.

126. Cf. Rituale Romanum, *De Benedictionibus*, editio typica,1984, *Ordo benedictionis occasione data auspicandi novum tabernaculum eucharisticum*, nos. 919–929.

127. Cf. Sacred Congregation of Rites, Instruction, *Eucharisticum mysterium*, May 25, 1967, no. 55: *Acta Apostolicae Sedis* 59 (1967), p. 569.

128. Cf. Sacred Congregation of Rites, Instruction, *Eucharisticum mysterium*, May 25, 1967, no. 53: *Acta Apostolicae Sedis* 59 (1967), p. 568; Rituale Romanum, *De sacra Communione et de cultu mysterii eucharistici extra Missam*, editio typica, 1973, no. 9; *Code of Canon Law*, can. 938 §2; John Paul II, Apostolic Letter, *Dominicae Cenae*, February 24, 1980, no. 3: *Acta Apostolicae Sedis* (1980), pp. 117–119.

129. Cf. *Code of Canon Law*, can. 940; Sacred Congregation of Rites, Instruction, *Eucharisticum mysterium*, May 25, 1967, no. 57: *Acta Apostolicae Sedis* 59 (1967), p. 569; Rituale Romanum, *De sacra Communione et de cultu mysterii eucharistici extra Missam*, editio typica, 1973, no. 11.

130. Cf. particularly in Sacred Congregation for the Sacraments, Instruction, *Nullo umquam tempore*, May 28, 1938: *Acta Apostolicae Sedis* 30 (1938), pp. 198–207; *Code of Canon Law*, cc. 934–944.

318. In the earthly Liturgy, the Church participates, by a foretaste, in that heavenly Liturgy which is celebrated in the holy city of Jerusalem, toward which she journeys as a pilgrim, and where Christ is seated at the right hand of God; and by venerating the memory of the Saints, she hopes one day to have some share and fellowship with them.[131]

Thus, in sacred buildings images of the Lord, of the Blessed Virgin Mary, and of the Saints, in accordance with most ancient tradition of the Church, should be displayed for veneration by the faithful[132] and should be so arranged so as to lead the faithful toward the mysteries of faith celebrated there. Care should, therefore, be taken that their number not be increased indiscriminately, and moreover that they be arranged in proper order so as not to draw the attention of the faithful to themselves and away from the celebration itself.[133] There should usually be only one image of any given Saint. Generally speaking, in the ornamentation and arrangement of a church, as far as images are concerned, provision should be made for the devotion of the entire community as well as for the beauty and dignity of the images.

CHAPTER VI
THE REQUISITES FOR THE CELEBRATION OF MASS

I. THE BREAD AND WINE FOR CELEBRATING THE EUCHARIST

319. Following the example of Christ, the Church has always used bread and wine with water to celebrate the Lord's Supper.

320. The bread for celebrating the Eucharist must be made only from wheat, must be recently made, and, according to the ancient tradition of the Latin Church, must be unleavened.

321. By reason of the sign, it is required that the material for the Eucharistic Celebration truly have the appearance of food. Therefore, it is desirable that the Eucharistic Bread, even though unleavened and made in the traditional form, be fashioned in such a way that the Priest at Mass with the people is truly able to break it into parts and distribute these to at least some of the faithful. However, small hosts are not at all excluded when the large number of those receiving Holy Communion or other pastoral reasons call for them. Moreover, the gesture of the fraction or breaking of bread, which was quite simply the term by which the Eucharist was known in apostolic times, will bring out more clearly the force and importance of the sign of the unity of all in the one bread, and of the

---

131. Cf. Second Ecumenical Council of the Vatican, Constitution on the Sacred Liturgy, *Sacrosanctum Concilium*, no. 8.

132. Cf. Pontificale Romanum, *Ordo Dedicationis ecclesiae et altaris*, editio typica, 1977, chapter IV, no. 10; Rituale Romanum, *De Benedictionibus*, editio typica, 1984, *Ordo ad benedicendas imagines quae fidelium venerationi publicae exhibentur*, nos. 984–1031.

133. Cf. Second Ecumenical Council of the Vatican, Constitution on the Sacred Liturgy, *Sacrosanctum Concilium*, no. 125.

sign of charity by the fact that the one bread is distributed among the brothers and sisters.

322. The wine for the celebration of the Eucharist must be from the fruit of the vine (cf. Lk 22:18), natural, and unadulterated, that is, without admixture of extraneous substances.

323. Diligent care should be taken to ensure that the bread and wine intended for the Eucharist are kept in a perfect state of conservation: that is, that the wine does not turn to vinegar nor the bread spoil or become too hard to be broken easily.

324. If after the Consecration or as he receives Communion, the Priest notices that not wine but only water was poured into the chalice, he pours the water into some container, pours wine with water into the chalice and consecrates it, saying the part of narrative relating to the Consecration of the chalice, without being obliged to consecrate the bread again.

II. SACRED FURNISHINGS IN GENERAL

325. As in the case of the building of churches, so also regarding all sacred furnishings, the Church admits the manner of art of each individual region and accepts those adaptations that are in keeping with the culture and traditions of the individual nations, provided that all are suited to the purpose for which the sacred furnishings are intended.[134]

In this matter as well, that noble simplicity should be ensured which is the best accompaniment of genuine art.

326. In choosing materials for sacred furnishings, besides those which are traditional, others are admissible that, according to the mentality of our own age, are considered to be noble and are durable, and well suited for sacred use. In the Dioceses of the United States of America these materials may include wood, stone, or metal which are solid and appropriate to the purpose for which they are employed.

III. SACRED VESSELS

327. Among the requisites for the celebration of Mass, the sacred vessels are held in special honor, and among these especially the chalice and paten, in which the bread and wine are offered and consecrated and from which they are consumed.

328. Sacred vessels should be made from precious metal. If they are made from metal that rusts or from a metal less precious than gold, they should generally be gilded on the inside.

---

134. Cf. Second Ecumenical Council of the Vatican, Constitution on the Sacred Liturgy, *Sacrosanctum Concilium*, no. 128.

329. In the Dioceses of the United States of America, sacred vessels may also be made from other solid materials which in the common estimation in each region are considered precious or noble, for example, ebony or other harder woods, provided that such materials are suitable for sacred use. In this case, preference is always to be given to materials that do not easily break or deteriorate. This applies to all vessels that are intended to hold the hosts, such as the paten, the ciborium, the pyx, the monstrance, and others of this kind.

330. As regards chalices and other vessels that are intended to serve as receptacles for the Blood of the Lord, they are to have a bowl of material that does not absorb liquids. The base, on the other hand, may be made of other solid and worthy materials.

331. For the Consecration of hosts, a large paten may fittingly be used, on which is placed the bread both for the Priest and the Deacon and also for the other ministers and for the faithful.

332. As regards the form of the sacred vessels, it is for the artist to fashion them in a manner that is more particularly in keeping with the customs of each region, provided the individual vessels are suitable for their intended liturgical use and are clearly distinguishable from vessels intended for everyday use.

333. As for the blessing of sacred vessels, the rites prescribed in the liturgical books should be followed.[135]

334. The practice should be kept of building in the sacristy a *sacrarium* into which is poured the water from the washing of sacred vessels and linens (cf. no. 280).

IV. SACRED VESTMENTS

335. In the Church, which is the Body of Christ, not all members have the same function. This diversity of offices is shown outwardly in the celebration of the Eucharist by the diversity of sacred vestments, which must therefore be a sign of the function proper to each minister. Moreover, these same sacred vestments should also contribute to the decoration of the sacred action itself. The vestments worn by Priests and Deacons, as well as the attire worn by lay ministers, are blessed before being put into liturgical use according to the rite described in the Roman Ritual.[136]

336. The sacred garment common to all ordained and instituted ministers of any rank is the alb, to be tied at the waist with a cincture unless it is made so as to fit even without such. Before the alb is put on, should this not completely cover the ordinary clothing at the neck, an amice should be used. The alb may not be exchanged for a surplice, not even over a cassock, on occasions when

---

135. Cf. Pontificale Romanum, *Ordo Dedicationis ecclesiae et altaris*, editio typica, 1977, *Ordo benedictionis calicis et patenae;* Rituale Romanum, *De Benedictionibus*, editio typica, 1984, *Ordo benedictionis rerum quæ in liturgicis celebrationibus usurpantur*, nos. 1068–1084.
136. Cf. Rituale Romanum, *De Benedictionibus*, editio typica, 1984, *Ordo benedictionis rerum quae in liturgicis celebrationibus usurpantur*, no. 1070.

a chasuble or dalmatic is to be worn or when, according to the norms, only a stole is worn without a chasuble or dalmatic.

337. The vestment proper to the Priest Celebrant at Mass and during other sacred actions directly connected with Mass is the chasuble worn, unless otherwise indicated, over the alb and stole.

338. The vestment proper to the Deacon is the dalmatic, worn over the alb and stole; however, the dalmatic may be omitted out of necessity or on account of a lesser degree of solemnity.

339. In the Dioceses of the United States of America, acolytes, altar servers, readers, and other lay ministers may wear the alb or other appropriate and dignified clothing.

340. The stole is worn by the Priest around his neck and hanging down in front of his chest, while it is worn by the Deacon over his left shoulder and drawn diagonally across the chest to the right side, where it is fastened.

341. The cope is worn by the Priest in processions and during other sacred actions, in accordance with the rubrics proper to the individual rites.

342. As regards the form of sacred vestments, Conferences of Bishops may determine and propose to the Apostolic See adaptations that correspond to the needs and the usages of the individual regions.[137]

343. For making sacred vestments, in addition to traditional materials, natural fabrics proper to each region may be used, and also artificial fabrics that are in keeping with the dignity of the sacred action and the sacred person. The Conference of Bishops will be the judge of this matter.[138]

344. It is fitting that the beauty and nobility of each vestment not be sought in an abundance of overlaid ornamentation, but rather in the material used and in the design. Ornamentation on vestments should, moreover, consist of figures, that is, of images or symbols, that denote sacred use, avoiding anything unbecoming to this.

345. Diversity of color in the sacred vestments has as its purpose to give more effective expression even outwardly whether to the specific character of the mysteries of faith to be celebrated or to a sense of Christian life's passage through the course of the liturgical year.

346. As regards the color of sacred vestments, traditional usage should be observed, namely:

   a) The color white is used in the Offices and Masses during Easter Time and Christmas Time; on the Solemnity of the Most Holy Trinity; and

---

137. Cf. Second Ecumenical Council of the Vatican, Constitution on the Sacred Liturgy, *Sacrosanctum Concilium*, no. 128.
138. Cf. *ibidem*.

furthermore on celebrations of the Lord other than of his Passion, celebrations of the Blessed Virgin Mary, of the Holy Angels, and of Saints who were not Martyrs; on the Solemnities of All Saints (November 1) and of the Nativity of St. John the Baptist (June 24); and on the Feasts of St. John the Evangelist (December 27), of the Chair of St. Peter (February 22), and of the Conversion of St. Paul (January 25).

b) The color red is used on Palm Sunday of the Lord's Passion and on Friday of Holy Week (Good Friday), on Pentecost Sunday, on celebrations of the Lord's Passion, on the "birthday" feast days of Apostles and Evangelists, and on celebrations of Martyr Saints.

c) The color green is used in the Offices and Masses of Ordinary Time.

d) The color violet or purple is used in Advent and Lent. It may also be worn in Offices and Masses for the Dead.

e) Besides the color violet, the colors white or black may be used at funeral services and at other Offices and Masses for the Dead in the Dioceses of the United States of America.

f) The color rose may be used, where it is the practice, on *Gaudete* Sunday (Third Sunday of Advent) and on *Laetare* Sunday (Fourth Sunday of Lent).

g) On more solemn days, festive, that is, more precious, sacred vestments may be used even if not of the color of the day.

h) The colors gold or silver may be worn on more solemn occasions in the Dioceses of the United States of America.

347. Ritual Masses are celebrated in their proper color, in white, or in a festive color; Masses for Various Needs, on the other hand, are celebrated in the color proper to the day or the time of year or in violet if they have a penitential character, for example, nos. 31, 33, or 38; Votive Masses are celebrated in the color suited to the Mass itself or even in the color proper to the day or the time of the year.

V. OTHER THINGS INTENDED FOR CHURCH USE

348. Besides the sacred vessels and the sacred vestments, for which some particular material is prescribed, other furnishings that either are intended for direct liturgical use[139] or are in any other way admitted into a church should be worthy and in keeping with their particular intended purpose.

349. Special care must be taken to ensure that the liturgical books, particularly the *Book of the Gospels* and the Lectionary, which are intended for the proclamation of the Word of God and hence receive special veneration, are to be in a liturgical action truly signs and symbols of higher realities and hence should be truly worthy, dignified, and beautiful.

---

139. For blessing objects that are intended for liturgical use in churches, cf. Rituale Romanum, *De Benedictionibus*, editio typica, 1984, part III.

350. Furthermore, every care is to be taken with respect to those things directly associated with the altar and the celebration of the Eucharist, for example, the altar cross and the cross carried in procession.

351. Every effort should be made, even in minor matters, to observe appropriately the requirements of art and to ensure that a noble simplicity is combined with elegance.

CHAPTER VII
THE CHOICE OF THE MASS AND ITS PARTS

352. The pastoral effectiveness of a celebration will be greatly increased if the texts of the readings, the prayers, and the liturgical chants correspond as aptly as possible to the needs, the preparation, and the culture of the participants. This will be achieved by appropriate use of the many possibilities of choice described below.

Hence in arranging the celebration of Mass, the Priest should be attentive rather to the common spiritual good of the People of God than to his own inclinations. He should also remember that choices of this kind are to be made in harmony with those who exercise some part in the celebration, including the faithful, as regards the parts that more directly pertain to them.

Since, indeed, many possibilities are provided for choosing the different parts of the Mass, it is necessary for the Deacon, the readers, the psalmist, the cantor, the commentator, and the choir to know properly before the celebration the texts that concern each and that are to be used, and it is necessary that nothing be in any sense improvised. For harmonious ordering and carrying out of the rites will greatly help in disposing the faithful for participation in the Eucharist.

I. THE CHOICE OF MASS

353. On Solemnities the Priest is obliged to follow the Calendar of the church where he is celebrating.

354. On Sundays, on the weekdays during Advent, Christmas Time, Lent, and Easter Time, on Feasts, and on Obligatory Memorials:

a) If Mass is celebrated with the people, the Priest should follow the Calendar of the church where he is celebrating;

b) If Mass is celebrated with the participation of one minister only, the Priest may choose either the Calendar of the church or his proper Calendar.

355. On Optional Memorials,

a) On the weekdays of Advent from December 17 to December 24, on days within the Octave of the Nativity of the Lord, and on the weekdays of Lent, except Ash Wednesday and during Holy Week, the Mass texts for the current liturgical day are used; but the Collect may be taken from a Memorial which happens to be inscribed in the General Calendar for that day, except on Ash Wednesday and during Holy Week. On weekdays of Easter Time, Memorials of Saints may rightly be celebrated in full.

b) On weekdays of Advent before December 17, on weekdays of Christmas Time from January 2, and on weekdays of Easter Time, one of the following may be chosen: either the Mass of the weekday, or the Mass of the Saint or of one of the Saints whose Memorial is observed, or the Mass of any Saint inscribed in the *Martyrology* for that day.

c) On weekdays in Ordinary Time, there may be chosen either the Mass of the weekday, or the Mass of an Optional Memorial which happens to occur on that day, or the Mass of any Saint inscribed in the *Martyrology* for that day, or a Mass for Various Needs, or a Votive Mass.

If he celebrates with the people, the Priest will take care not to omit too frequently and without sufficient reason the readings assigned each day in the Lectionary to the weekdays, for the Church desires that a richer portion at the table of God's Word should be spread before the people.[140]

For the same reason he should choose Masses for the Dead in moderation, for every Mass is offered for both the living and the dead, and there is a commemoration of the dead in the Eucharistic Prayer.

Where, however, the Optional Memorials of the Blessed Virgin Mary or of the Saints are dear to the faithful, the legitimate devotion of the latter should be satisfied.

Moreover, as regards the option of choosing between a Memorial inscribed in the General Calendar and one inserted in a diocesan or religious Calendar, preference should be given, all else being equal and in keeping with tradition, to the Memorial in the particular Calendar.

II. THE CHOICE OF TEXTS FOR THE MASS

356. In choosing texts for the different parts of the Mass, whether for the time of the year or for Saints, the norms that follow should be observed.

THE READINGS

357. Sundays and Solemnities have assigned to them three readings, that is, from a Prophet, an Apostle, and a Gospel, by which the Christian people are instructed in the continuity of the work of salvation according to God's wonderful design. These readings should be followed strictly. In Easter Time, according to the tradition of the Church, instead of being from the Old Testament, the reading is taken from the Acts of the Apostles.

---

140. Cf. Second Ecumenical Council of the Vatican, Constitution on the Sacred Liturgy, *Sacrosanctum Concilium*, no. 51.

For Feasts, two readings are assigned. If, however, according to the norms a Feast is raised to the rank of a Solemnity, a third reading is added, and this is taken from the Common.

For Memorials of Saints, unless proper readings are given, the readings assigned for the weekday are normally used. In certain cases, particularized readings are provided, that is to say, readings which highlight some particular aspect of the spiritual life or activity of the Saint. The use of such readings is not to be insisted upon, unless a pastoral reason truly suggests it.

358. In the Lectionary for weekdays, readings are provided for each day of every week throughout the entire course of the year; hence, these readings will in general be used on the days to which they are assigned, unless there occurs a Solemnity, a Feast, or Memorial that has its own New Testament readings, that is to say, readings in which mention is made of the Saint being celebrated.

Should, however, the continuous reading during the week from time to time be interrupted, on account of some Solemnity or Feast, or some particular celebration, then the Priest shall be permitted, bearing in mind the scheme of readings for the entire week, either to combine parts omitted with other readings or to decide which readings are to be given preference over others.

In Masses for special groups, the Priest shall be allowed to choose texts more particularly suited to the particular celebration, provided they are taken from the texts of an approved Lectionary.

359. In addition, in the Lectionary a special selection of texts from Sacred Scripture is given for Ritual Masses into which certain Sacraments or Sacramentals are incorporated, or for Masses that are celebrated for certain needs.

Sets of readings of this kind have been so prescribed so that through a more apt hearing of the Word of God the faithful may be led to a fuller understanding of the mystery in which they are participating, and may be educated to a more ardent love of the Word of God.

Therefore, the texts proclaimed in the celebration are to be chosen keeping in mind both an appropriate pastoral reason and the options allowed in this matter.

360. At times, a longer and shorter form of the same text is given. In choosing between these two forms, a pastoral criterion should be kept in mind. On such an occasion, attention should be paid to the capacity of the faithful to listen with fruit to a reading of greater or lesser length, and to their capacity to hear a more complete text, which is then explained in the Homily.[141]

361. When a possibility is given of choosing between one or other text laid down, or suggested as optional, attention shall be paid to the good of participants, whether, that is to say, it is a matter of using an easier text or one more appropriate for a given gathering, or of repeating or setting aside a text that is assigned

---

141. Missale Romanum, *Ordo lectionum Missae*, editio typica altera, 1981, Praenotanda, no. 80.

as proper to some particular celebration while being optional for another,[142] just as pastoral advantage may suggest.

Such a situation may arise either when the same text would have to be read again within a few days, as, for example, on a Sunday and on a subsequent weekday, or when it is feared that a certain text might give rise to some difficulties for a particular group of the Christian faithful. However, care should be taken that, when choosing scriptural passages, parts of Sacred Scripture are not permanently excluded.

362. The adaptations to the *Ordo Lectionum Missae* as contained in the Lectionary for Mass for use in the Dioceses of the United States of America should be carefully observed.

THE ORATIONS

363. In any Mass the orations proper to that Mass are used, unless otherwise noted.

On Memorials of Saints, the proper Collect is said or, if this is lacking, one from an appropriate Common. As to the Prayer over the Offerings and the Prayer after Communion, unless these are proper, they may be taken either from the Common or from the weekday of the current time of year.

On the weekdays in Ordinary Time, however, besides the orations from the previous Sunday, orations from another Sunday in Ordinary Time may be used, or one of the Prayers for Various Needs provided in the Missal. However, it shall always be permissible to use from these Masses the Collect alone.

In this way a richer collection of texts is provided, by which the prayer life of the faithful is more abundantly nourished.

However, during the more important times of the year, provision has already been made for this by means of the orations proper to these times of the year that exist for each weekday in the Missal.

THE EUCHARISTIC PRAYER

364. The numerous Prefaces with which the *Roman Missal* is endowed have as their purpose to bring out more fully the motives for thanksgiving within the Eucharistic Prayer and to set out more clearly the different facets of the mystery of salvation.

365. The choice between the Eucharistic Prayers found in the Order of Mass is suitably guided by the following norms:

   a) Eucharistic Prayer I, or the Roman Canon, which may always be used, is especially suited for use on days to which a proper text for the *Communicantes (In communion with those whose memory we venerate)* is assigned or in Masses endowed with a proper form of the *Hanc igitur (Therefore, Lord, we pray)* and also in the celebrations of the Apostles

---

142. *Ibidem*, no. 81.

and of the Saints mentioned in the Prayer itself; likewise it is especially suited for use on Sundays, unless for pastoral reasons Eucharistic Prayer III is preferred.

b) Eucharistic Prayer II, on account of its particular features, is more appropriately used on weekdays or in special circumstances. Although it is provided with its own Preface, it may also be used with other Prefaces, especially those that sum up the mystery of salvation, for example, the Common Prefaces. When Mass is celebrated for a particular deceased person, the special formula given may be used at the proper point, namely, before the part *Remember also our brothers and sisters.*

c) Eucharistic Prayer III may be said with any Preface. Its use should be preferred on Sundays and festive days. If, however, this Eucharistic Prayer is used in Masses for the Dead, the special formula for a deceased person may be used, to be included at the proper place, namely after the words: *in your compassion, O merciful Father, gather to yourself all your children scattered throughout the world.*

d) Eucharistic Prayer IV has an invariable Preface and gives a fuller summary of salvation history. It may be used when a Mass has no Preface of its own and on Sundays in Ordinary Time. On account of its structure, no special formula for a deceased person may be inserted into this prayer.

THE CHANTS

366. It is not permitted to substitute other chants for those found in the Order of Mass, for example, at the *Agnus Dei (Lamb of God).*

367. In choosing the chants between the readings, as well as the chants at the Entrance, at the Offertory, and at Communion, the norms laid down in their proper places are to be observed (cf. nos. 40–41, 47–48, 61–64, 74, 86–88).

CHAPTER VIII
MASSES AND PRAYERS FOR VARIOUS NEEDS AND OCCASIONS AND MASSES FOR THE DEAD

I. MASSES AND PRAYERS FOR VARIOUS NEEDS AND OCCASIONS

368. Since the liturgy of the Sacraments and Sacramentals has as its effect that for the faithful who are properly disposed almost every event in life is sanctified by the divine grace that flows from the Paschal Mystery,[143] and because the Eucharist is the Sacrament of Sacraments, the Missal provides examples of Mass formularies and orations that may be used in the various occasions of Christian life for the needs of the whole world or for the needs of the Church, whether universal or local.

---

143. Cf. Second Ecumenical Council of the Vatican, Constitution on the Sacred Liturgy, *Sacrosanctum Concilium,* no. 61.

369. In view of the rather broad possibilities of choice among the readings and orations, it is desirable that Masses for Various Needs and Occasions be used in moderation, that is, when truly required.

370. In all the Masses for Various Needs and Occasions, unless expressly indicated otherwise, it is permissible to use the weekday readings and also the chants between them, if they are suited to the celebration.

371. Among Masses of this kind are included Ritual Masses, Masses for Various Needs and Occasions, and Votive Masses.

372. Ritual Masses are connected to the celebration of certain Sacraments or Sacramentals. They are prohibited on Sundays of Advent, Lent, and Easter, on Solemnities, on the days within the Octave of Easter, on the Commemoration of All the Faithful Departed (All Souls' Day), on Ash Wednesday, and during Holy Week, and furthermore due regard is to be had for the norms set out in the ritual books or in the Masses themselves.

373. Masses for Various Needs and Occasions are used in certain situations either as occasion arises or at fixed times.

Days or periods of prayer for the fruits of the earth, prayer for human rights and equality, prayer for world justice and peace, and penitential observances outside Lent are to be observed in the Dioceses of the United States of America at times to be designated by the Diocesan Bishop.

In all the Dioceses of the United States of America, January 22 (or January 23, when January 22 falls on a Sunday) shall be observed as a particular day of prayer for the full restoration of the legal guarantee of the right to life and of penance for violations to the dignity of the human person committed through acts of abortion. The liturgical celebrations for this day may be the Mass "For Giving Thanks to God for the Gift of Human Life" (no. 48/1 of the Masses and Prayers for Various Needs and Occasions), celebrated with white vestments, or the Mass "For the Preservation of Peace and Justice" (no. 30 of the Masses and Prayers for Various Needs and Occasions), celebrated with violet vestments.

374. If any case of a graver need or of pastoral advantage should arise, at the direction of the Diocesan Bishop or with his permission, an appropriate Mass may be celebrated on any day except Solemnities, the Sundays of Advent, Lent, and Easter, days within the Octave of Easter, the Commemoration of All the Faithful Departed (All Souls' Day), Ash Wednesday, and the days of Holy Week.

375. Votive Masses of the mysteries of the Lord or in honor of the Blessed Virgin Mary or of the Angels or of any given Saint or of all the Saints may be said in response to the devotion of the faithful on weekdays in Ordinary Time, even if an Optional Memorial occurs. However, it is not permitted to celebrate as Votive Masses those that refer to mysteries related to events in the life of the Lord or of the Blessed Virgin Mary, with the exception of the Mass of the Immaculate Conception, since their celebration is an integral part of the course of the liturgical year.

376. On days when there occurs an Obligatory Memorial or on a weekday of Advent up to and including December 16, of Christmas Time from January 2, and of Easter Time after the Octave of Easter, Masses for Various Needs and Occasions and Votive Masses are in principle forbidden. If, however, some real necessity or pastoral advantage calls for it, in the estimation of the rector of the church or the Priest Celebrant himself, a Mass appropriate to the same may be used in a celebration with the people.

377. On weekdays in Ordinary Time when an Optional Memorial occurs or when the Office is of the weekday, it is permissible to celebrate any Mass for Various Needs and Occasions, or use any prayer for the same, but to the exclusion of Ritual Masses.

378. Particularly recommended is the Saturday commemoration of the Blessed Virgin Mary, because it is to the Mother of the Redeemer that in the Liturgy of the Church firstly and before all the Saints veneration is given.[144]

II. MASSES FOR THE DEAD

379. The Church offers the Eucharistic Sacrifice of Christ's Pasch for the dead so that, since all the members of Christ's Body are in communion with one another, what implores spiritual help for some, may bring comforting hope to others.

380. Among the Masses for the Dead, the Funeral Mass holds first place. It may be celebrated on any day except for Solemnities that are Holydays of Obligation, Thursday of Holy Week (Holy Thursday), the Paschal Triduum, and the Sundays of Advent, Lent, and Easter, with due regard also for all the other requirements of the norm of the law.[145]

381. A Mass for the Dead, on receiving the news of a death, for the final burial, or the first anniversary, may be celebrated even on days within the Octave of the Nativity of the Lord, on days when an Obligatory Memorial occurs, and on weekdays other than Ash Wednesday or the weekdays of Holy Week.

Other Masses for the Dead or "daily" Masses, may be celebrated on weekdays in Ordinary Time on which Optional Memorials occur or when the Office is of the weekday, provided such Masses are actually applied for the dead.

382. At Funeral Masses there should usually be a short Homily, but to the exclusion of a funeral eulogy of any kind.

383. The faithful, and especially those of the deceased's family, should be urged to participate in the Eucharistic Sacrifice offered for the deceased person, also by receiving Holy Communion.

---

144. Cf. Second Ecumenical Council of the Vatican, Dogmatic Constitution on the Church, *Lumen gentium*, no. 54; Paul VI, Apostolic Exhortation, *Marialis cultus*, February 2, 1974, no. 9: *Acta Apostolicae Sedis* 66 (1974), pp. 122–123.

145. Cf. particularly *Code of Canon Law*, cc. 1176–1185; Rituale Romanum, *Ordo Exsequiarum*, editio typica, 1969.

384. If the Funeral Mass is directly joined to the rite of burial, once the Prayer after Communion has been said and omitting the Concluding Rites, there takes place the Rite of Final Commendation or Farewell. This rite is celebrated only if the body is present.

385. In the arranging and choosing of the variable parts of the Mass for the Dead, especially the Funeral Mass (for example, orations, readings, and the Universal Prayer), pastoral considerations bearing upon the deceased, the family, and those attending should be kept in mind.

Moreover, pastors should take into special account those who are present at a liturgical celebration or who hear the Gospel on the occasion of the funeral and who may be non-Catholics or Catholics who never or hardly ever participate in the Eucharist or who seem even to have lost the faith. For Priests are ministers of Christ's Gospel for all.

CHAPTER IX
ADAPTATIONS WITHIN THE COMPETENCE OF BISHOPS AND BISHOPS' CONFERENCES

386. The renewal of the *Roman Missal* carried out in our time in accordance with the decrees of the Second Vatican Ecumenical Council has taken great care that all the faithful may display in the celebration of the Eucharist that full, conscious, and active participation that is required by the very nature of the Liturgy and to which the faithful, in virtue of their status as such, have a right and duty.[146]

However, in order that such a celebration may correspond all the more fully to the norms and the spirit of the Sacred Liturgy, certain further adaptations are set out in this Instruction and in the Order of Mass and entrusted to the judgment either of the Diocesan Bishop or of the Conferences of Bishops.

387. The Diocesan Bishop, who is to be regarded as the High Priest of his flock, from whom the life in Christ of his faithful in some sense derives and upon whom it depends,[147] must promote, regulate, and be vigilant over the liturgical life in his diocese. It is to him that in this Instruction is entrusted the regulating of the discipline of concelebration (cf. nos. 202, 374) and the establishing of norms regarding the function of serving the Priest at the altar (cf. no. 107), the distribution of Holy Communion under both kinds (cf. no. 283), and the construction and ordering of churches (cf. no. 291). It is above all for him, moreover, to nourish the spirit of the Sacred Liturgy in the Priests, Deacons, and faithful.

388. Those adaptations spoken of below that necessitate a wider degree of coordination are to be decided, in accord with the norm of law, in the Conference of Bishops.

---

146. Cf. Second Ecumenical Council of the Vatican, Constitution on the Sacred Liturgy, *Sacrosanctum Concilium*, no. 14.

147. Cf. *ibidem*, no. 41.

389. It is the competence, in the first place, of the Conferences of Bishops to prepare and approve an edition of this *Roman Missal* in the authorized vernacular languages, so that, once their decisions have been accorded the *recognitio* of the Apostolic See, the edition may be used in the regions to which it pertains.[148]

The *Roman Missal,* whether in Latin or in legitimately approved vernacular translations, is to be published in its entirety.

390. It is for the Conferences of Bishops to formulate the adaptations indicated in this *General Instruction* and in the Order of Mass and, once their decisions have been accorded the *recognitio* of the Apostolic See, to introduce them into the Missal itself. They are such as these:

- the gestures and bodily posture of the faithful (cf. no. 43);
- the gestures of veneration toward the altar and the *Book of the Gospels* (cf. no. 273);
- the texts of the chants at the Entrance, at the Presentation of the Gifts, and at Communion (cf. nos. 48, 74, 87);
- the readings from Sacred Scripture to be used in special circumstances (cf. no. 362);
- the form of the gesture of peace (cf. no. 82);
- the manner of receiving Holy Communion (cf. nos. 160, 283);
- the materials for the altar and sacred furnishings, especially the sacred vessels, and also the materials, form, and color of the liturgical vestments (cf. nos. 301, 326, 329, 339, 342–346).

It shall be permissible for Directories or pastoral Instructions that the Conferences of Bishops judge useful to be included, with the prior *recognitio* of the Apostolic See, in the *Roman Missal* at an appropriate place.

391. It is for the same Conferences of Bishops to attend to the translations of the biblical texts that are used in the celebration of Mass, exercising special care in this. For it is out of the Sacred Scripture that the readings are read and are explained in the Homily and that Psalms are sung, and it is by the influence of Sacred Scripture and at its prompting that prayers, orations, and liturgical chants are fashioned in such a way that it is from Sacred Scripture that actions and signs derive their meaning.[149]

Language should be used that corresponds to the capacity for understanding of the faithful and is suitable for public proclamation, while maintaining those characteristics that are proper to the different ways of speaking used in the biblical books.

---

148. Cf. *Code of Canon Law,* can. 838 §3.
149. Cf. Second Ecumenical Council of the Vatican, Constitution on the Sacred Liturgy, *Sacrosanctum Concilium,* no. 24.

392. It shall also be for Conferences of Bishops to prepare with care a translation of the other texts, so that, even though the character of each language is respected, the meaning of the original Latin text is fully and faithfully rendered. In accomplishing this task, it is desirable that the different literary genres used at Mass be taken into account, such as the presidential prayers, the antiphons, the acclamations, the responses, the litanies of supplication, and so on.

It should be borne in mind that the primary purpose of the translation of the texts is not for meditation, but rather for their proclamation or singing during an actual celebration.

Language should be used that is accommodated to the faithful of the region, but is noble and marked by literary quality, even though there will always be a necessity for some catechesis on the biblical and Christian meaning of certain words and expressions.

Moreover, it is preferable that in regions that share the same language, the same translation be used in so far as possible for liturgical texts, especially for biblical texts and for the Order of Mass.[150]

393. Bearing in mind the important place that singing has in a celebration as a necessary or integral part of the Liturgy,[151] all musical settings for the texts of the Ordinary of Mass, for the people's responses and acclamations, and for the special rites that occur in the course of the liturgical year must be submitted to the Secretariat of Divine Worship of the United States Conference of Catholic Bishops for review and approval prior to publication.

While the organ is to be accorded pride of place, other wind, stringed, or percussion instruments may be admitted into divine worship in the Dioceses of the United States of America, according to longstanding local usage, in so far as these are truly suitable for sacred use, or can be made suitable.

394. Each diocese should have its own Calendar and Proper of Masses. For its part, the Conference of Bishops should draw up a proper Calendar for the nation or, together with other Conferences, a Calendar for a wider territory, to be approved by the Apostolic See.[152]

In carrying out this task, to the greatest extent possible the Lord's Day is to be preserved and safeguarded, as the primordial feast day, and hence other celebrations, unless they are truly of the greatest importance, should not have precedence over it.[153] Care should likewise be taken that the liturgical year as revised by decree of the Second Vatican Council not be obscured by secondary elements.

---

150. Cf. *ibidem*, no. 36 §3.

151. Cf. *ibidem*, no. 112.

152. Cf. *Universal Norms on the Liturgical Year and the Calendar*, nos. 48–51, infra, p. 99; Sacred Congregation for Divine Worship, Instruction, *Calendaria particularia*, June 24, 1970, nos. 4, 8: *Acta Apostolicae Sedis* 62 (1970), pp. 652–653.

153. Cf. Second Ecumenical Council of the Vatican, Constitution on the Sacred Liturgy, *Sacrosanctum Concilium*, no. 106.

In the drawing up of the Calendar of a nation, the Rogation Days and Ember Days should be indicated (cf. no. 373), as well as the forms and texts for their celebration,[154] and other special measures should also be kept in mind.

It is appropriate that in publishing the Missal, celebrations proper to an entire nation or territory be inserted at the proper place among the celebrations of the General Calendar, while those proper to a region or diocese should have a place in a special appendix.

395. Finally, if the participation of the faithful and their spiritual welfare require variations and profounder adaptations in order for the sacred celebration to correspond with the culture and traditions of the different nations, then Conferences of Bishops may propose these to the Apostolic See in accordance with article 40 of the Constitution on the Sacred Liturgy for introduction with the Apostolic See's consent, especially in the case of nations to whom the Gospel has been more recently proclaimed.[155] The special norms handed down by means of the *Instruction on the Roman Liturgy and Inculturation*[156] should be attentively observed.

As regards the procedures in this matter, these should be observed:

Firstly, a detailed preliminary proposal should be set before the Apostolic See, so that, after the necessary faculty has been granted, the detailed working out of the individual points of adaptation may proceed.

Once these proposals have been duly approved by the Apostolic See, experiments should be carried out for specified periods and at specified places. When the period of experimentation is concluded, the Conference of Bishops shall decide, if the case requires, upon pursuing the adaptations and shall submit a mature formulation of the matter to the judgment of the Apostolic See.[157]

396. However, before proceeding to new adaptations, especially profounder ones, great care shall be taken to promote due instruction of the clergy and the faithful in a wise and orderly manner, so as to take advantage of the faculties already foreseen and to apply fully the pastoral norms in keeping with the spirit of the celebration.

397. The principle shall moreover be respected, according to which each particular Church must be in accord with the universal Church not only regarding the doctrine of the faith and sacramental signs, but also as to the usages universally received from apostolic and unbroken tradition. These are to be kept not only so that errors may be avoided, but also so that the faith may be handed on

---

154. Cf. *Universal Norms on the Liturgical Year and the Calendar*, nos. 48–51, infra, p. 99; Sacred Congregation for Divine Worship, Instruction, *Calendaria particularia*, June 24, 1970, no. 38: *Acta Apostolicae Sedis* 62 (1970), p. 660.

155. Cf. Second Ecumenical Council of the Vatican, Constitution on the Sacred Liturgy, *Sacrosanctum Concilium*, nos. 37–40.

156. Cf. Congregation for Divine Worship and the Discipline of the Sacraments, Instruction, *Varietates legitimae*, January 25, 1994, nos. 54, 62–69: *Acta Apostolicae Sedis* 87 (1995), pp. 308–309, 311–313.

157. Cf. *ibidem*, nos. 66–68: *Acta Apostolicae Sedis* 87 (1995), p. 313.

in its integrity, since the Church's rule of prayer (*lex orandi*) corresponds to her rule of faith (*lex credendi*).[158]

The Roman Rite constitutes a notable and precious part of the liturgical treasure and patrimony of the Catholic Church; its riches are conducive to the good of the universal Church, so that their loss would gravely harm her.

This Rite has in the course of the centuries not only preserved the liturgical usages that arose in the city of Rome, but has also in a deep, organic, and harmonious way integrated into itself certain other usages derived from the customs and culture of different peoples and of various particular Churches whether of the West or the East, so acquiring a certain supra-regional character. As to our own times, the identity and unitary expression of this Rite is found in the typical editions of the liturgical books promulgated by authority of the Supreme Pontiff, and in the liturgical books corresponding to them approved for their territories by the Conferences of Bishops and endowed with the *recognitio* of the Apostolic See.[159]

398. The norm established by the Second Vatican Council, namely that in the liturgical renewal innovations should not be made unless required by true and certain usefulness to the Church, nor without exercising caution to ensure that new forms grow in some sense organically from forms already existing,[160] must also be applied to implementation of the inculturation of the Roman Rite as such.[161] Inculturation, moreover, requires a necessary length of time, lest the authentic liturgical tradition suffer hasty and incautious contamination.

Finally, the pursuit of inculturation does not have as its purpose in any way the creation of new families of rites, but aims rather at meeting the needs of a particular culture, though in such a way that adaptations introduced either into the Missal or coordinated with other liturgical books are not at variance with the proper character of the Roman Rite.[162]

399. And so, the *Roman Missal*, though in a diversity of languages and with some variety of customs,[163] must in the future be safeguarded as an instrument and an outstanding sign of the integrity and unity of the Roman Rite.[164]

---

158. Cf. *ibidem*, nos. 26–27: *Acta Apostolicae Sedis* 87 (1995), pp. 298–299.

159. Cf. John Paul II, Apostolic Letter, *Vicesimus quintus annus*, December 4, 1988, no. 16: *Acta Apostolicae Sedis* 81 (1989), p. 912; Congregation for Divine Worship and the Discipline of the Sacraments, Instruction, *Varietates legitimae*, January 25, 1994, nos. 2, 36: *Acta Apostolicae Sedis* 87 (1995), pp. 288, 302.

160. Cf. Second Ecumenical Council of the Vatican, Constitution on the Sacred Liturgy, *Sacrosanctum Concilium*, no. 23.

161. Cf. Congregation for Divine Worship and the Discipline of the Sacraments, Instruction, *Varietates legitimae*, January 25, 1994, no. 46: *Acta Apostolicae Sedis* 87 (1995), p. 306.

162. Cf. *ibidem*, no. 36: *Acta Apostolicae Sedis* 87 (1995), p. 302.

163. Cf. *ibidem*, no. 54: *Acta Apostolicae Sedis* 87 (1995), pp. 308–309.

164. Cf. Second Ecumenical Council of the Vatican, Constitution on the Sacred Liturgy, *Sacrosanctum Concilium*, no. 38; Paul VI, Apostolic Constitution, *Missale Romanum*, above, p. 13.

NORMS FOR
THE DISTRIBUTION
AND RECEPTION OF
HOLY COMMUNION
UNDER BOTH KINDS IN THE DIOCESES
OF THE UNITED STATES OF AMERICA

APPROVED BY THE UNITED STATES CONFERENCE
OF CATHOLIC BISHOPS
JUNE 14, 2001

APPROVED BY THE CONGREGATION FOR DIVINE WORSHIP
AND DISCIPLINE OF THE SACRAMENTS
MARCH 22, 2002

PROMULGATED FOR USE IN THE DIOCESES OF
THE UNITED STATES OF AMERICA
APRIL 7, 2002

OVERVIEW OF *NORMS FOR THE DISTRIBUTION AND RECEPTION OF HOLY COMMUNION UNDER BOTH KINDS IN THE DIOCESES OF THE UNITED STATES OF AMERICA*

Rev. Msgr. Joseph DeGrocco

Norms for the Distribution and Reception of Holy Communion Under Both Kinds in the Dioceses of the United States of America (NDRHC) is a document of the United States Conference of Catholic Bishops (USCCB). It received the *recognitio* from the Congregation for Divine Worship and the Discipline of the Sacraments (CDWDS) on March 22, 2002, and is therefore considered to be particular law for all Latin celebrations of the Eucharist in the dioceses of the United States of America as of its effective date of April 7, 2002. The *recognitio* from the CDWDS directs that the document is to be included in all future editions of *The Roman Missal* published in English for the dioceses of the United States, and so it can be found in the newly published editions of the third typical edition of *The Roman Missal*.

As with *The General Instruction of the Roman Missal* (GIRM), this document contains a wealth of theological insight beyond just norms and instructions. The text is divided into two main parts: Part I, "Holy Communion: The Body and Blood of the Lord Jesus," gives broad theological foundations for the celebration of the Eucharist and reception of Holy Communion; Part II, "Norms for the Distribution of Holy Communion Under Both Kinds," gives more specific and detailed norms for how Holy Communion under both kinds is to be carried out.

It is unfortunate that there is a tendency in certain circles today to downplay the importance of distributing Holy Communion under both kinds. This document clearly endorses the practice, and one might argue that the document supports a certain preference for its practice based on a full understanding of liturgical theology rooted in the importance of the use of perceptible signs in the liturgy. Sacred realities are conveyed through the use of perceptible signs; the sanctification of men and women who participate in liturgy occurs through signs perceptible to the senses. The Real Presence of the Lord is conveyed through the signs of bread and wine that have been transformed into his Body and Blood. It is by participation in those signs as we take and share in the Eucharistic bread and chalice "that we obey the Lord's command and grow in the likeness of the Lord whose Body and Blood they both signify and contain."[1] Therefore, as the document notes, the Church, in her wisdom, makes provision for receiving Holy

---

1. *Norms for the Distribution and Reception of Holy Communion Under Both Kinds in the Dioceses of the United States of America* (NDRHC), 2.

Communion under both forms precisely because "sharing in both Eucharistic species reflects more fully the sacred realities that the Liturgy signifies."[2]

It is instructive to note how the document, in discussing "the ineffable depths of the mystery that is the Holy Eucharist,"[3] uses a preponderance of action words. This underscores an appropriate liturgical theology that understands the Eucharist as an action that is celebrated and a mystery in which participants are engaged, rather than as an object to be received passively. Images such as "Eucharistic assemnly (synaxis), action of thanksgiving, breaking of the bread, memorial, holy sacrifice, Lord's Supper, holy and divine Liturgy, Holy Communion, and Holy Mass"[4] are used to underscore the point that for the Church the Eucharist is "union with Christ from whom she came, through whom she lives, and towards whom she directs her life."[5] Thus, the meaning of participation in the Eucharistic mystery as engaging in actions that express and signify union with Christ is affirmed.

The culmination of union with Christ through participation in the Eucharistic mystery is to be found in Holy Communion. We must make sure our Eucharistic theology maintains this important point, and not allow a misplaced devotionalism centered exclusively on the act of consecration to overshadow this. The document notes that while the Eucharistic Prayer, during which the consecration of the elements takes place, is rightly the "heart of the celebration," its "consummation"[6] is found in Holy Communion. It is the action of the assembly's eating and drinking (a communal action) that is seen as the high point of the celebration of the Eucharistic mystery to its fulfillment. The document describes the action of Holy Communion as the action "whereby the people purchased for the Father by his beloved Son eat and drink the Body and Blood of Christ. They are thereby joined together as members of Christ's mystical Body, sharing the one life of the Spirit. In the great sacrament of the altar, they are joined to Christ Jesus and to one another."[7] One might note a particular emphasis on the inclusion of drinking as well as eating, with both actions together being the fullest liturgical expression of the sacramental mystery presented to us under the sign of a sacrificial banquet.

It must be clarified that the emphasis the document places on reception of Holy Communion under both kinds is in no way meant to diminish the Church's traditional teaching concerning concomitance (that is, the teaching that the entire Christ is contained under even only one species): the consecrated bread is both the Body and Blood of Christ, and the consecrated wine is also both the Body and Blood of Christ.[8] The Real Presence of Christ is not "divided" or "split up" in any way. Consequently, receiving under only one form cannot be considered in any way theologically incomplete, or as though Christ were not fully present, or as though the communicant were being denied a full reception of the Body and Blood of the Lord. However, while Communion under only one species is not lacking in any way theologically, there is a fullness to the sign

---

2. Ibid., 11.

3. Ibid., 4.

4. Ibid.

5. Ibid.

6. Ibid., 5.

7. Ibid.

8. See ibid., 8–11.

value that is lost, and therefore there is a diminishment in the outward expression of the sacred realities. Thus, while it is theologically correct to say that the whole and entire Christ is present under one species, this "should not diminish in any way the fuller sign value of reception of Holy Communion under both kinds."[9] The value of this practice is promoted not only in this document, but is also enshrined in *The General Instruction of the Roman Missal* (GIRM).[10]

Part II of the document spells out the norms for distribution of Holy Communion under both kinds. The norms ensure a reverent and careful distribution of Holy Communion under both kinds.

The third typical edition of *The Roman Missal* considerably expands the occasions when Holy Communion may be offered to the faithful under both species. Individual ritual books describe various opportunities for Communion under both kinds, and the GIRM lists instances as well. Of particular note, this document cites article 283 in the GIRM,[11] which gives permission for the diocesan bishop to establish norms for Holy Communion under both kinds for his diocese, including allowing a priest in charge of a parish to permit Communion under both kinds whenever he deems it appropriate—as long as the faithful have been well instructed on the practice and that there is no danger of profanation of the sacrament or of the rite becoming cumbersome for some reason. Thus, there is the possibility of widespread adoption of this important practice. Instruction of the faithful should include areas such as the Eucharist as the memorial of Christ's sacrifice, his Death and Resurrection; the Real Presence of Christ in the Eucharistic elements, including the whole Christ as present in each element of consecrated bread and wine; the reverence due the sacrament; and the role of ordinary and extraordinary ministers.[12]

Concerning the role of ordinary and extraordinary ministers, the document notes that the distinction between ordinary ministers of Holy Communion (bishops, priests, and deacons) and extraordinary ministers of Holy Communion (laypeople) should not be blurred. One important component of this is that the extraordinary ministers of Holy Communion should never act in a way that mimics the actions of concelebrating priests. Thus, for example, extraordinary

---

9. Ibid., 16.

10. See GIRM, 281–287.

11. "In addition to those cases given in the ritual books, Communion under both kinds is permitted for:

    a) Priests who are not able to celebrate or concelebrate Mass;

    b) the Deacon and others who perform some duty at the Mass;

    c) members of communities at the Conventual Mass or the 'community' Mass, along with seminarians, and all those engaged in a retreat or taking part in a spiritual or pastoral gathering.

"The Diocesan bishop may establish norms for Communion under both kinds for his own diocese, which are also to be observed in churches of religious and at celebrations with small groups. The Diocesan Bishop is also given the faculty to permit Communion under both kinds whenever it may seem appropriate to the Priest to whom a community has been entrusted as its own shepherd, provided that the faithful have been well instructed and that there is no danger of profanation of the Sacrament or of the rite's becoming difficult because of the large number of participants or for some other cause.

"In all that pertains to Communion under both kinds, the *Norms for the Distribution and Reception of Holy Communion Under Both Kinds in the Dioceses of the United States of America* are to be followed (particularly nos. 27–54)" [GIRM, 283].

12. See NDRHC, 25e.

ministers do not assist in breaking the Eucharistic bread or in apportioning hosts from one large vessel into smaller ones. In fact, they only approach the altar after the priest has received Communion (although the document does not say anything about extraordinary ministers not being allowed at all in the sanctuary, only that they "not approach the altar,"[13] so as not to be confused with concelebrating priests). Also, lay ministers never receive Holy Communion in the manner of a concelebrating priest: they do not self-communicate or pass the vessels from one to another down the line. Finally, it is clarified that lay ministers are handed the vessels they will administer by the priest or deacon; they do not take the vessels off the altar themselves.[14]

Also specified is the deacon's role as a minister of the chalice.[15] It is presumed that, whenever possible, the deacon is a minister of the chalice, distributing the Precious Blood. This is in keeping with the role of the deacon at Mass as one who essentially has custody of the chalice: he prepares it during the preparation rites, he elevates it at the doxology, and therefore he administers it during Holy Communion.

The document describes how careful preparation must be a part of celebrations that include distribution of Holy Communion under both kinds. The presumption that Holy Communion is given from hosts consecrated at the same Mass, and not from those reserved in the tabernacle, is reiterated. Additionally, it is suggested that there be two ministers of the Precious Blood for every one minister of the Body of Christ; this is to ensure a smooth flow to the procession and to avoid having the "celebration be unduly prolonged."[16] The norms for the actual distribution of the Body and Blood of the Lord to the faithful are reiterated, including the famous teaching of Saint Cyril of Jerusalem about the proper manner for receiving the Body of Christ in the hand.[17] Parishes will no doubt find the words of Saint Cyril most useful in their own catechesis of their parishioners. Worthy of note is the specific mention in the document that children should be encouraged to receive Holy Communion under both kinds, as long as they have been properly instructed and that they are old enough to properly receive from the chalice.[18] In the mind of the Church, age alone is no reason for children to be denied receiving the Precious Blood, and parishes should inform their parishioners accordingly, allowing the decision of whether or not children receive from the chalice to be a family decision, not a parish one.

The importance of sign value is again affirmed in a suggestion that it is preferable to use on the altar one single chalice and one large paten for all the bread, so that the Eucharistic meaning of being gathered into one Body by the Holy Spirit can be expressed through the signs themselves. Where this is not possible, "care should be taken that the number of vessels should not exceed the need."[19]

The document also notes how extraordinary ministers of Holy Communion are allowed, with the permission of the bishop, to consume what remains of the

---

13. Ibid., 38.
14. See ibid., 37–40.
15. See ibid., 26.
16. Ibid., 30.
17. See ibid., 41.
18. See ibid., 47.
19. Ibid., 32.

Precious Blood from their chalice. Also specified is that purification of the vessels, either immediately after Communion or after Mass, is reserved to priests, deacons, and instituted acolytes; extraordinary ministers may not purify the vessels.[20] Although it is not explicitly stated, extraordinary ministers may, of course, if it is the parish custom to do so, assist in the cleansing of the vessels for purposes of washing and good hygiene, after they have been purified.

Parishes will no doubt find the NDRHC a useful resource both for instruction of liturgical ministers and for the liturgical formation of their parishioners. Members of the parish liturgy committee and other liturgical leaders should be thoroughly familiar with its contents.

---

20. See ibid., 51–55.

OUTLINE

NORMS FOR THE DISTRIBUTION AND RECEPTION OF HOLY COMMUNION UNDER BOTH KINDS IN THE DIOCESES OF THE UNITED STATES

PART I
HOLY COMMUNION:
THE BODY AND BLOOD OF THE LORD JESUS

THE MYSTERY OF THE HOLY EUCHARIST

1.   On the night before he died, Christ gathered his Apostles in the upper room to celebrate the Last Supper and to give us the inestimable gift of his Body and Blood. "He did this in order to perpetuate the sacrifice of the Cross throughout the centuries until He should come again, and so to entrust to His beloved spouse, the Church, a memorial of His death and resurrection. . . ."[1] Thus, in the eucharistic Liturgy we are joined with Christ on the altar of the cross and at the table of the upper room in "the sacrificial memorial in which the sacrifice of the cross is perpetuated and [in] the sacred banquet of communion with the Lord's body and blood."[2]

2.   Like all acts of the sacred Liturgy, the Eucharist uses signs to convey sacred realities. *Sacrosanctum Concilium: Constitution on the Sacred Liturgy* reminds us that "the sanctification of man is manifested by signs perceptible to the senses, and is effected in a way which is proper to each of these signs."[3] In a preeminent way the eucharistic Liturgy uses the signs of bread and wine in obedience to the Lord's command and after their transformation gives them to us as the Body and Blood of Christ in the act of communion. It is by taking and sharing the eucharistic bread and chalice—"signs perceptible to the senses"—that we obey the Lord's command and grow in the likeness of the Lord whose Body and Blood they both signify and contain.

---

1. Second Ecumenical Council of the Vatican, Constitution on the Sacred Liturgy, *Sacrosanctum Concilium*, no. 47. (All Vatican II citations here refer to the following edition: Walter M. Abbott, ed., *The Documents of Vatican II* [New York: Guild Press, 1966].)

2. United States Catholic Conference–Libreria Editrice Vaticana, *Catechism of the Catholic Church* [CCC] (2000), no. 1382.

3. Second Ecumenical Council of the Vatican, Constitution on the Sacred Liturgy, *Sacrosanctum Concilium*, no. 7.

3.   The Eucharist constitutes "the Church's entire spiritual wealth, that is, Christ Himself, our Passover and living bread."[4] It is the "Sacrament of Sacraments."[5] Through it "the work of our redemption is accomplished."[6] He who is the "living bread that came down from heaven" (Jn 6:51) assures us, "Whoever eats my flesh and drinks my blood has eternal life, and I will raise him on the last day. For my flesh is true food, and my blood is true drink" (Jn 6:54–55).

4.   The eyes of faith enable the believer to recognize the ineffable depths of the mystery that is the Holy Eucharist. The *Catechism of the Catholic Church* offers us a number of images from our tradition to refer to this most sacred reality: Eucharistic assembly (*synaxis*), action of thanksgiving, breaking of the bread, memorial, holy sacrifice, Lord's Supper, holy and divine Liturgy, Holy Communion, and Holy Mass.[7] The eucharistic species of bread and wine derive from the work of human hands. In the action of the Eucharist this bread and this wine are transformed and become our spiritual food and drink. It is Christ, the true vine, who gives life to the branches (cf. Jn 15:1–6). As bread from heaven (cf. Jn 6:41), bread of angels, the chalice of salvation, and the medicine of immortality,[8] the Eucharist is the promise of eternal life to all who eat and drink it (cf. Jn 6:50–51). The Eucharist is a sacred meal, "a sacrament of love, a sign of unity, a bond of charity"[9] in which Christ calls us as his friends to share in the banquet of the kingdom of heaven (cf. Jn 15:15). This bread and chalice were given to his disciples at the Last Supper. This spiritual food has been the daily bread and sustenance for his disciples throughout the ages. The bread and wine of the Lord's Supper—his Body and Blood—as broken and poured out constitute the irreplaceable food for the journey of the "pilgrim church on earth."[10] The Eucharist perpetuates the sacrifice of Christ, offered once and for all for us and for our salvation, making present the victory and triumph of Christ's death and resurrection.[11] It is strength for those who journey in hope through this life and who desire to dwell with God in the life to come. Our final sharing in the Eucharist is *viaticum*, the food for the final journey of the believer to heaven itself. Through these many images, the Church helps us to see the Eucharist as union with Christ from whom she came, through whom she lives, and towards whom she directs her life.[12]

---

4. Second Vatican Council, *Presbyterorum Ordinis: Decree on the Ministry and Life of Priests* [PO] (December 7, 1965), no. 5.

5. Congregation for Divine Worship and the Discipline of the Sacraments, *General Instruction of the Roman Missal* [GIRM] (2000), no. 368.

6. *The Roman Missal*, Prayer over the Offerings, Holy Thursday Mass of the Lord's Supper, p. 303.

7. CCC, nos. 1328–1332.

8. Cf. St. Ignatius of Antioch, *Ad. Eph.*, 20, 2.

9. Second Ecumenical Council of the Vatican, Constitution on the Sacred Liturgy, *Sacrosanctum Concilium*, no. 47.

10. *The Roman Missal*, Eucharistic Prayer III, p. 654.

11. Second Ecumenical Council of the Vatican, Constitution on the Sacred Liturgy, *Sacrosanctum Concilium*, no. 6.

12. Cf. Second Vatican Council, *Lumen Gentium: Dogmatic Constitution on the Church* (November 21, 1964), no. 3.

5.   While the heart of the celebration of the Eucharist is the Eucharistic Prayer, the consummation of the Mass is found in Holy Communion, whereby the people purchased for the Father by his beloved Son eat and drink the Body and Blood of Christ. They are thereby joined together as members of Christ's mystical Body, sharing the one life of the Spirit. In the great sacrament of the altar, they are joined to Christ Jesus and to one another.

It was also Christ's will that this sacrament be received as the soul's spiritual food to sustain and build up those who live with his life, as he said, "He who eats me, he also shall live because of me" (Jn 6:57). This sacrament is also to be a remedy to free us from our daily defects and to keep us from mortal sin. It was Christ's will, moreover, that this sacrament be a pledge of our future glory and our everlasting happiness and, likewise, a symbol of that one body of which he is the head (cf. Lk 22:19 and 1 Cor 11:3). He willed that we, as members of this body should be united to it by firm bonds of faith, hope, and love, so that we might all say the same thing, and that there might be no dissensions among us (cf. 1 Cor 1:10).[13]

As Catholics, we fully participate in the celebration of the Eucharist when we receive Holy Communion. We are encouraged to receive Communion devoutly and frequently. In order to be properly disposed to receive Communion, participants should not be conscious of grave sin and normally should have fasted for one hour. A person who is conscious of grave sin is not to receive the Body and Blood of the Lord without prior sacramental confession except for a grave reason where there is no opportunity for confession. In this case, the person is to be mindful of the obligation to make an act of perfect contrition, including the intention of confessing as soon as possible (canon 916). A frequent reception of the Sacrament of Penance is encouraged for all.[14]

UNION WITH CHRIST

6.   The Lord himself gave us the Eucharist at the Last Supper. The eucharistic sacrifice "is wholly directed toward the intimate union of the faithful with Christ through communion."[15] It is Christ himself who is received in Holy Communion, who said to his disciples, "Take and eat, this is my body." Giving thanks, he then took the chalice and said: "Take and drink, this is the cup of my blood. Do this in remembrance of me" (Mt 26:26–27; 1 Cor 11:25).

7.   Bread and wine are presented by the faithful and placed upon the altar by the Priest. These are simple gifts, but they were foreshadowed in the Old Testament and chosen by Christ himself for the Eucharistic sacrifice. When

---

13. Council of Trent, Session xiii (October 11, 1551), *De ratione institutionis ss. huius sacramenti.* (Latin text in Henricus Denzinger and Adolfus Schönmetzer, eds., *Enchiridion Symbolorum: Definitionum et Declarationum de Rebus Fidei et Morum* [DS] [Barcinone: Herder, 1976], 1638. English text in John F. Clarkson et al., *The Church Teaches* [TCT] [St. Louis, MO: B. Herder, 1955], 720.)

14. National Conference of Catholic Bishops, *Guidelines for the Reception of Communion* (Washington, D.C., 1996).

15. CCC, no. 1382.

these gifts of bread and wine are offered by the Priest in the name of the Church to the Father in the great Eucharistic Prayer of thanksgiving, they are transformed by the Holy Spirit into the Body and Blood of the only-begotten Son of the Father. Finally, when the one bread is broken, the unity of the faithful is expressed and through Communion they "receive from the one bread the Lord's Body and from the one chalice the Lord's Blood in the same way that the Apostles received them from the hands of Christ himself."[16] Hence the import of the words of the hymn adapted from the *Didache*:

> As grain once scattered on the hillsides
> was in this broken bread made one
> so from all lands your church be gathered
> into your kingdom by your Son.[17]

CHRIST HIMSELF IS PRESENT IN THE EUCHARISTIC SPECIES

8.   Christ is "truly, really, and substantially contained"[18] in Holy Communion. His presence is not momentary nor simply signified, but wholly and permanently real under each of the consecrated species of bread and wine.[19]

9.   The Council of Trent teaches that "the true body and blood of our Lord, together with his soul and divinity, exist under the species of bread and wine. His body exists under the species of bread and his blood under the species of wine, according to the import of his words."[20]

10.   The Church also teaches and believes that "immediately after the consecration the true body of our Lord and his true blood exist along with his soul and divinity under the form of bread and wine. The body is present under the form of bread and the blood under the form of wine, by virtue of the words [of Christ]. The same body, however, is under the form of wine and the blood under the form of bread, and the soul under either form, by virtue of the natural link and concomitance by which the parts of Christ the Lord, who has now risen from the dead and will die no more, are mutually united."[21]

---

16. GIRM, no. 72(c).

17. F. Bland Tucker, trans., "Father, We Thank Thee, Who Hast Planted," a hymn adapted from the *Didache*, c. 110 (The Church Pension Fund, 1940).

18. Council of Trent, Session xiii (October 11, 1551), *Canones de ss. Eucharistiae sacramento*, can. 1 (DS 1651; TCT 728).

19. Cf. Council of Trent, Session xiii (October 11, 1551), *Decretum de ss. Eucharistiae sacramento*, cap. IV, *De transubstantione* (DS 1642; TCT 722): "Because Christ our Redeemer said that it was truly his body that he was offering under the species of bread (see Matthew 26:26ff.; Mark 14:22ff.; Luke 22:19ff.; 1 Corinthians 11:24ff.), it has always been the conviction of the Church, and this holy council now again declares it that, by the consecration of the bread and wine a change takes place in which the whole substance of bread is changed into the substance of the Body of Christ our Lord and the whole substance of the wine into the substance of his blood. This change the holy Catholic Church fittingly and properly names transubstantiation."

20. Council of Trent, Session xiii (October 11, 1551), *Decretum de ss. Eucharistiae sacramento*, cap. III, *De excellentia ss. Eucharistiae super reliqua sacramenta* (DS 1640; TCT 721).

21. *Ibid.* (DS 1640; Norman P. Tanner, ed., *Decrees of the Ecumenical Councils*, Vol. 2: *Trent to Vatican II* [London: Sheed & Ward, 1990], 695.)

11.   Since, however, by reason of the sign value, sharing in both Eucharistic species reflects more fully the sacred realities that the Liturgy signifies, the Church in her wisdom has made provisions in recent years so that more frequent eucharistic participation from both the sacred host and the chalice of salvation might be made possible for the laity in the Latin Church.

HOLY COMMUNION AS AN ACT OF FAITH

12.   Christ's presence in the Eucharist challenges human understanding, logic, and ultimately reason. His presence cannot be known by the senses, but only through faith[22]—a faith that is continually deepened through that communion which takes place between the Lord and his faithful in the very act of the celebration of the Eucharist. Thus the Fathers frequently warned the faithful that by relying solely on their senses they would see only bread and wine. Rather, they exhorted the members of the Church to recall the word of Christ by whose power the bread and wine have been transformed into his own Body and Blood.[23]

13.   The teaching of St. Cyril of Jerusalem assists the Church even today in understanding this great mystery:

> We have been instructed in these matters and filled with an unshakable faith that what seems to be bread is not bread, though it tastes like it, but the Body of Christ, and that what seems to be wine is not wine, though it tastes like it, but the Blood of Christ.[24]

14.   The act of Communion, therefore, is also an act of faith. For when the minister says, "The Body of Christ" or "The Blood of Christ," the communicant's "Amen" is a profession in the presence of the saving Christ, body and blood, soul and divinity, who now gives life to the believer.

15.   The communicant makes this act of faith in the total presence of the Lord Jesus Christ whether in Communion under one form or in Communion under both kinds. It should never be construed, therefore, that Communion under the form of bread alone or Communion under the form of wine alone is somehow an incomplete act or that Christ is not fully present to the communicant. The Church's unchanging teaching from the time of the Fathers through the ages— notably in the ecumenical councils of Lateran IV, Constance, Florence, Trent, and Vatican II—has witnessed to a constant unity of faith in the presence of Christ in both elements.[25] Clearly there are some pastoral circumstances that require eucharistic sharing in one species only, such as when Communion is brought to the sick or when one is unable to receive either the Body of the Lord or the Precious Blood due to an illness. Even in the earliest days of the Church's life, when Communion under both species was the norm, there were always

---

22. Cf. CCC, no. 1381.

23. Cf. Paul VI, *Mysterium Fidei: On the Doctrine and Worship of the Eucharist* (September 3, 1965), no. 47 (in International Committee on English in the Liturgy, *Documents on the Liturgy, 1963–1979: Conciliar, Papal, and Curial Texts* [DOL] [1982] 176, no. 1192).

24. *Ibid.*, no. 48 (DOL 176, no. 1193).

25. Cf. GIRM, no. 281.

instances when the Eucharist was received under only the form of bread or wine. Those who received Holy Communion at home or who were sick would usually receive under only one species, as would the whole Church during the Good Friday Liturgy.[26] Thus, the Church has always taught the doctrine of concomitance, by which we know that under each species alone, the whole Christ is sacramentally present and we "receive all the fruit of Eucharistic grace."[27]

16.   At the same time an appreciation for reception of "the whole Christ" through one species should not diminish in any way the fuller sign value of reception of Holy Communion under both kinds. For just as Christ offered his whole self, body and blood, as a sacrifice for our sins, so too is our reception of his Body and Blood under both kinds an especially fitting participation in his memorial of eternal life.

HOLY COMMUNION UNDER BOTH KINDS

17.   From the first days of the Church's celebration of the Eucharist, Holy Communion consisted of the reception of both species in fulfillment of the Lord's command to "take and eat . . . take and drink." The distribution of Holy Communion to the faithful under both kinds was thus the norm for more than a millennium of Catholic liturgical practice.

18.   The practice of Holy Communion under both kinds at Mass continued until the late eleventh century, when the custom of distributing the Eucharist to the faithful under the form of bread alone began to grow. By the twelfth century theologians such as Peter Cantor speak of Communion under one kind as a "custom" of the Church.[28] This practice spread until the Council of Constance in 1415 decreed that Holy Communion under the form of bread alone would be distributed to the faithful.

19.   In 1963, the Fathers of the Second Vatican Council authorized the extension of the faculty for Holy Communion under both kinds in *Sacrosanctum Concilium*:

> The dogmatic principles which were laid down by the Council of Trent remaining intact, Communion under both kinds may be granted when the bishops think fit, not only to clerics and religious, but also to the laity, in cases to be determined by the Apostolic See. . . .[29]

20.   The Council's decision to restore Holy Communion under both kinds at the bishop's discretion took expression in the first edition of the *Missale Romanum* and enjoys an even more generous application in the third typical edition of the *Missale Romanum*:

---

26. Cf. St. Cyprian, *De Lapsis*, 25, on Communion of infants and children; on Communion of the sick and dying, cf. *Statuta ecclesiae antiqua*, can. 76.

27. CCC, no. 1390.

28. Cf. Petrus Cantor, *Summa de Sacramentis et Animae Consiliis*, ed. J.-A. Dugauquier, *Analecta Medievalis Namurcensia*, vol. 4 (Louvain/Lille, 1954), I, 144.

29. Second Ecumenical Council of the Vatican, Constitution on the Sacred Liturgy, *Sacrosanctum Concilium*, no. 55.

Holy Communion has a fuller form as a sign when it takes place under both kinds. For in this form the sign of the Eucharistic banquet is more clearly evident and clearer expression is given to the divine will by which the new and eternal Covenant is ratified in the Blood of the Lord, as also the connection between the Eucharistic banquet and the eschatological banquet in the Kingdom of the Father.[30]

The *General Instruction* further states that "at the same time the faithful should be instructed to participate more readily in this sacred rite, by which the sign of the Eucharistic banquet is made more fully evident."[31]

21.   The extension of the faculty for the distribution of Holy Communion under both kinds does not represent a change in the Church's immemorial beliefs concerning the Holy Eucharist. Rather, today the Church finds it salutary to restore a practice, when appropriate, that for various reasons was not opportune when the Council of Trent was convened in 1545.[32] But with the passing of time, and under the guidance of the Holy Spirit, the reform of the Second Vatican Council has resulted in the restoration of a practice by which the faithful are again able to experience "a fuller sign of the Eucharistic banquet."[33]

PART II
NORMS FOR THE DISTRIBUTION OF
HOLY COMMUNION UNDER BOTH KINDS

THE PURPOSE OF THESE NORMS

22.   In response to a provision of the *General Instruction of the Roman Missal*, the United States Conference of Catholic Bishops herein describes the methods of distributing Holy Communion to the faithful under both kinds and approves the following norms, with the proper *recognitio* of the Apostolic See.[34] The purpose of these norms is to ensure the reverent and careful distribution of Holy Communion under both kinds.

---

30. GIRM, no. 281. The GIRM goes on to say, "The faithful who participate in the rite or are present at it, are made aware by the most suitable means possible of the Catholic teaching on the form of Holy Communion as laid down by the Ecumenical Council of Trent. Above all, they should instruct the Christian faithful that the Catholic faith teaches that Christ, whole and entire, and the true Sacrament, is received even under only one species, and hence that as regards the resulting fruits, those who receive under only one species are not deprived of any grace that is necessary for salvation.

"Furthermore, they should teach that the Church, in her administration of the Sacraments, has the power to lay down or alter whatever provisions, apart from the substance of the Sacraments, that she judges to be more readily conducive to reverence for the Sacraments and the good of the recipients, in view of changing conditions, times, and places" (no. 282).

31. *Ibid.*, no. 282.

32. Cf. Council of Trent, Session xxi (July 16, 1562), *De doctrina de communione sub utraque specie et parvulorum* (DS 1725–1734; TCT 739–745).

33. *Ibid.*

34. Cf. GIRM, no. 283. The text before approval of Adaptations for the Dioceses of the United States of America read, "As to the manner of distributing Holy Communion under both kinds to the faithful and the extent of the faculty for doing so, the Conferences of Bishops may publish norms, once their decisions have received the *recognitio* of the Apostolic See."

23.   The revised *Missale Romanum*, third typical edition, significantly expands those opportunities when Holy Communion may be offered under both kinds. In addition to those instances specified by individual ritual books, the *General Instruction* states that Communion under both kinds may be permitted as follows:

a. for Priests who are not able to celebrate or concelebrate

b. for the Deacon and others who perform some duty at Mass

c. members of communities at the Conventual Mass or the "community" Mass, along with seminarians, and all those engaged in a retreat or taking part in a spiritual or pastoral gathering[35]

24.   The *General Instruction* then indicates that the Diocesan Bishop may lay down norms for the distribution of Communion under both kinds for his own diocese, which must be observed. . . . The Diocesan Bishop also has the faculty to allow Communion under both kinds, whenever it seems appropriate to the Priest to whom charge of a given community has been entrusted as [its] own pastor, provided that the faithful have been well instructed and there is no danger of the profanation of the Sacrament or that the rite would be difficult to carry out on account of the number of participants or for some other reason.[36]

In practice, the need to avoid obscuring the role of the Priest and the Deacon as the ordinary ministers of Holy Communion by an excessive use of extraordinary minister might in some circumstances constitute a reason either for limiting the distribution of Holy Communion under both species or for using intinction instead of distributing the Precious Blood from the chalice.

Norms established by the Diocesan Bishop must be observed wherever the Eucharist is celebrated in the diocese, "which are also to be observed in churches of religious and at celebrations with small groups."[37]

CATECHESIS FOR RECEIVING THE BODY AND BLOOD OF THE LORD

25.   When Communion under both kinds is first introduced by the Diocesan Bishop and also whenever the opportunity for instruction is present, the faithful should be properly catechized on the following matters in the light of the teaching and directives of the *General Instruction*:

a. the ecclesial nature of the Eucharist as the common possession of the whole Church;

b. the Eucharist as the memorial of Christ's sacrifice, his death and resurrection, and as the sacred banquet;

c. the real presence of Christ in the eucharistic elements, whole and entire—in each element of consecrated bread and wine (the doctrine of concomitance);

---

35. *Ibid.*

36. *Ibid.*

37. *Ibid.*

d. the kinds of reverence due at all times to the sacrament, whether within the eucharistic Liturgy or outside the celebration;[38] and

e. the role that ordinary and, if necessary, extraordinary ministers of the Eucharist are assigned in the eucharistic assembly.

THE MINISTER OF HOLY COMMUNION

26. By virtue of his sacred ordination, the bishop or Priest offers the sacrifice in the person of Christ, the Head of the Church. He receives gifts of bread and wine from the faithful, offers the sacrifice to God, and returns to them the very Body and Blood of Christ, as from the hands of Christ himself.[39] Thus bishops and Priests are considered the ordinary ministers of Holy Communion. In addition the Deacon who assists the bishop or Priest in distributing Communion is an ordinary minister of Holy Communion. When the Eucharist is distributed under both forms, "the Deacon himself administers the chalice."[40]

27. In every celebration of the Eucharist there should be a sufficient number of ministers for Holy Communion so that it can be distributed in an orderly and reverent manner. Bishops, Priests, and Deacons distribute Holy Communion by virtue of their office as ordinary ministers of the Body and Blood of the Lord.[41]

EXTRAORDINARY MINISTERS OF HOLY COMMUNION

28. When the size of the congregation or the incapacity of the bishop, Priest, or Deacon requires it, the celebrant may be assisted by other bishops, Priests, or Deacons.[42] If such ordinary ministers of Holy Communion are not present, "the Priest may call upon extraordinary ministers to assist him, that is, duly instituted acolytes or even other faithful who have been duly deputed for this purpose. In case of necessity, the Priest may depute suitable faithful for this single occasion."[43] Extraordinary ministers of Holy Communion should receive sufficient spiritual, theological, and practical preparation to fulfill their role with knowledge and reverence. When recourse is had to Extraordinary Minister of Holy Communion, especially in the distribution of Holy Communion under both kinds, their number should not be increased beyond what is required for the orderly and reverent distribution of the Body and Blood of the Lord. In all matters such Extraordinary Ministers of Holy Communion should follow the guidance of the Diocesan Bishop.

---

38. Cf. Congregation of Rites, *Eucharisticum Mysterium: On Worship of the Eucharist* [EM] (May 25, 1967), part I, "General Principles to Be Given Prominence in Catechizing the People on the Eucharistic Mystery" (DOL 179, nos. 1234–1244).

39. Cf. GIRM, no. 93.

40. GIRM, no. 182.

41. Cf. GIRM, no. 108.

42. Cf. GIRM, no. 162.

43. GIRM, no. 162. Cf. also Sacred Congregation for the Discipline of the Sacraments, *Immensae Caritatis: Instruction on Facilitating Reception of Communion in Certain Circumstances*, section 1.I.c (DOL 264, no. 2075).

29.   All ministers of Holy Communion should show the greatest reverence for the Most Holy Eucharist by their demeanor, their attire, and the manner in which they handle the consecrated bread or wine. Should there be any mishap—as when, for example, the consecrated wine is spilled from the chalice—then the affected "area . . . should be washed with water, and this water should be then poured into the sacrarium."[44]

PLANNING

30.   When Holy Communion is to be distributed under both species, careful planning should be undertaken so that:

- enough bread and wine are made ready for the communication of the faithful at each Mass.[45] As a general rule, Holy Communion is given from hosts consecrated at the same Mass and not from those reserved in the tabernacle. Precious Blood may not be reserved at one Mass for use at another;[46] and

- a suitable number of ministers of Holy Communion are provided at each Mass. For Communion from the chalice, it is desirable that there be generally two ministers of the Precious Blood for each minister of the Body of Christ, lest the liturgical celebration be unduly prolonged.

31.   Even when Communion will be ministered in the form of bread alone to the congregation, care should be taken that sufficient amounts of the elements are consecrated so that the Precious Blood may be distributed to all concelebrating Priests.

PREPARATIONS

32.   Before Mass begins, wine and hosts should be provided in vessels of appropriate size and number. The presence on the altar of a single chalice and one large paten can signify the one bread and one chalice by which we are gathered "into one Body by the Holy Spirit . . . [and] may truly become a living sacrifice in Christ."[47] When this is not possible, care should be taken that the number of vessels should not exceed the need.

---

44. GIRM, no. 280.

45. Cf. EM, no. 31 (DOL 179, no. 1260): "The faithful share more fully in the celebration of the eucharist through sacramental communion. It is strongly recommended that they should receive it as a rule in the Mass itself and at that point in the celebration which is prescribed by the rite, that is, right after the communion of the Priest celebrant.

"In order that the communion may stand out more clearly even through signs as a participation in the sacrifice actually being celebrated, steps should be taken that enable the faithful to receive hosts consecrated at that Mass."

46. Cf. GIRM, no. 284b: "Whatever may remain of the Blood of Christ [after the distribution of Holy Communion] is consumed at the altar by the Priest or the Deacon or the duly instituted acolyte who ministered the chalice."

47. *The Roman Missal*, Eucharistic Prayer IV, p. 660.

33.   The unity of all in the one bread will be better expressed when the bread to be broken is of sufficient size that at least some of the faithful are able to receive a piece broken from it. When the number of the faithful is great, however, a single large bread may be used for the breaking of the bread with small breads provided for the rest of the faithful.[48]

34.   Sacred vessels, which "hold a place of honor," should be of noble materials, appropriate to their use, and in conformity to the requirements of liturgical law, as specified in the *General Instruction of the Roman Missal*, nos. 327–332.

35.   Before being used, vessels for the celebration must be blessed by the bishop or Priest according to the *Rite of Blessing a Chalice and Paten*.[49]

AT THE PREPARATION OF THE GIFTS

36.   The altar is prepared with corporal, purificator, Missal, and chalice (unless the chalice is prepared at a side table) by the Deacon and the servers. The gifts of bread and wine are brought forward by the faithful and received by the Priest or Deacon or at a convenient place.[50] If one chalice is not sufficient for Holy Communion to be distributed under both kinds to the Priest concelebrants or Christ's faithful, several chalices are placed on a corporal on the altar in an appropriate place, filled with wine. It is praiseworthy that the main chalice be larger than the other chalices prepared for distribution.[51]

AT THE BREAKING OF THE BREAD

37.   As the *Agnus Dei* or *Lamb of God* is begun, the Bishop or Priest alone, or with the assistance of the Deacon, and if necessary of concelebrating Priests, breaks the eucharistic bread. Other empty ciboria or patens are then brought to the altar if this is necessary. The Deacon or Priest places the consecrated bread in several ciboria or patens, if necessary, as required for the distribution of Holy Communion. If it is not possible to accomplish this distribution in a reasonable time, the celebrant may call upon the assistance of other Deacons or concelebrating Priests.

38.   If extraordinary ministers of Holy Communion are required by pastoral need, they should not approach the altar before the Priest has received Communion. After the Priest has concluded his own Communion, he distributes Communion to the extraordinary ministers, assisted by the Deacon, and then hands the sacred vessels to them for distribution of Holy Communion to the people.

---

48. Cf. GIRM, no. 321.

49. Cf. GIRM, no. 333.

50. Cf. *ibid.*, no. 73.

51. Cf. Congregation for Divine Worship and the Discipline of the Sacraments, Instruction, *Redemptionis Sacramentum* (2004), nos. 105–106. These sentences were added to correspond to this Instruction.

39.   All receive Holy Communion in the manner described by the *General Instruction of the Roman Missal*, whether Priest concelebrants (cf. GIRM, nos. 159, 242, 243, 246), Deacons (cf. GIRM, nos. 182, 244, 246), or extraordinary ministers of Holy Communion (cf. GIRM, no. 284). Neither Deacons nor lay ministers may ever receive Holy Communion in the manner of a concelebrating Priest. The practice of extraordinary ministers of Holy Communion waiting to receive Holy Communion until after the distribution of Holy Communion is not in accord with liturgical law.

40.   After all eucharistic ministers have received Communion, the bishop or Priest celebrant reverently hands vessels containing the Body or the Blood of the Lord to the Deacons or extraordinary ministers who will assist with the distribution of Holy Communion. The Deacon may assist the Priest in handing the vessels containing the Body and Blood of the Lord to the extraordinary ministers of Holy Communion.

DISTRIBUTION OF THE BODY AND BLOOD OF THE LORD

41.   Holy Communion under the form of bread is offered to the communicant with the words "The Body of Christ." The communicant may choose whether to receive the Body of Christ in the hand or on the tongue. When receiving in the hand, the communicant should be guided by the words of St. Cyril of Jerusalem: "When you approach, take care not to do so with your hand stretched out and your fingers open or apart, but rather place your left hand as a throne beneath your right, as befits one who is about to receive the King. Then receive him, taking care that nothing is lost."[52]

42.   Among the ways of ministering the Precious Blood as prescribed by the *General Instruction of the Roman Missal*, Communion from the chalice is generally the preferred form in the Latin Church, provided that it can be carried out properly according to the norms and without any risk of even apparent irreverence toward the Blood of Christ.[53]

43.   The chalice is offered to the communicant with the words "The Blood of Christ," to which the communicant responds, "Amen."

44.   The chalice may never be left on the altar or another place to be picked up by the communicant for self-communication (except in the case of concelebrating bishops or Priests), nor may the chalice be passed from one communicant to another. There shall always be a minister of the chalice.

45.   After each communicant has received the Blood of Christ, the minister carefully wipes both sides of the rim of the chalice with a purificator. This action is a matter of both reverence and hygiene. For the same reason, the minister turns the chalice slightly after each communicant has received the Precious Blood.

---

52. Cat. Myst. V, 21–22.

53. Cf. Sacred Congregation for Divine Worship, *Sacramentali Communione: Instruction Extending the Practice of Communion Under Both Kinds* (June 29, 1970), no. 6 (DOL 270, no. 2115).

46.   It is the choice of the communicant, not the minister, to receive from the chalice.

47.   Children are encouraged to receive Communion under both kinds provided that they are properly instructed and that they are old enough to receive from the chalice.

OTHER FORMS OF DISTRIBUTION OF THE PRECIOUS BLOOD

48.   Distribution of the Precious Blood by a spoon or through a straw is not customary in the Latin dioceses of the United States of America.

49.   Holy Communion may be distributed by intinction in the following manner: "Each communicant, while holding a Communion-plate under the mouth, approaches the Priest who holds a vessel with the sacred particles, with a minister standing at his side and holding the chalice. The Priest takes a host, intincts it partly in the chalice and, showing it, says: 'The Body and Blood of Christ.' The communicant replies, 'Amen,' receives the Sacrament in the mouth from the Priest, and then withdraws."[54]

50.   The communicant, including the extraordinary minister, is never allowed to self-communicate, even by means of intinction. Communion under either form, bread or wine, must always be given by an ordinary or extraordinary minister of Holy Communion.

PURIFICATION OF SACRED VESSELS

51.   After Communion the consecrated bread that remains is to be reserved in the tabernacle. Care should be taken with any fragments remaining on the corporal or in the sacred vessels. The Deacon returns to the altar with the Priest and collects and consumes any remaining fragments.

52.   When more of the Precious Blood remains than was necessary for Communion, and if not consumed by the bishop or Priest celebrant, the Deacon, standing at the altar, "immediately and reverently consumes all of the Blood of Christ that remains, assisted, if the case requires, by other Deacons and Priests."[55] When there are extraordinary ministers of Holy Communion, they may consume what remains of the Precious Blood from their chalice of distribution with permission of the Diocesan Bishop.

53.   The sacred vessels are to be purified by the Priest, the Deacon or an instituted acolyte.[56] The chalice and other vessels may be taken to a side table, where they are cleansed and arranged in the usual way. Other sacred vessels that held the Precious Blood are purified in the same way as chalices. Provided the remaining consecrated bread has been consumed or reserved and the remaining Precious Blood has been consumed, "it is also permitted to leave vessels needing to be

---

54. GIRM, no. 287.
55. GIRM, no. 182.
56. Cf. GIRM, no. 279.

purified on a corporal, suitably covered, on the credence table, and to purify them immediately after Mass, following the Dismissal of the people."[57]

54.   The Precious Blood may not be reserved, except for giving Communion to someone who is sick. Only sick people who are unable to receive Communion under the form of bread may receive it under the form of wine alone at the discretion of the Priest. If not consecrated at a Mass in the presence of the sick person, the Blood of the Lord is kept in a properly covered vessel and is placed in the tabernacle after Communion. The Precious Blood should be carried to the sick in a vessel that is closed in such a way as to eliminate all danger of spilling. If some of the Precious Blood remains after the sick person has received Communion, it should be consumed by the minister, who should also see to it that the vessel is properly purified.

55.   The reverence due to the Precious Blood of the Lord demands that it be fully consumed after Communion is completed and never be poured into the ground or the sacrarium.

CONCLUSION

56.   The norms and directives established by the Church for the celebration of any liturgical rite always have as their immediate goal the proper and careful celebration of those rites. However, such directives also have as their purpose the fostering of celebrations that glorify God and deepen the faith, hope, and charity of the participants in liturgical worship. The ordered preparation and celebration of the Mass, and of Holy Communion in particular, should always profoundly affect the faith of communicants in all its aspects and dimensions. In the case of the distribution of Holy Communion under both kinds, Christian faith in the real presence of Christ in the Holy Eucharist can only be renewed and deepened in the life of the faithful by this esteemed practice.

57.   In all other matters pertaining to the Rite of Communion under both kinds, the directives of the *General Instruction*, nos. 281–287, are to be consulted.

---

57. GIRM, no. 183.

UNIVERSAL NORMS
ON THE
LITURGICAL YEAR
AND THE
GENERAL ROMAN CALENDAR

CONGREGATION FOR DIVINE WORSHIP AND DISCIPLINE
OF THE SACRAMENTS

CURRENT LATIN EDITION
MARCH 17, 2002

CURRENT ENGLISH TRANSLATION APPROVED
MARCH 26, 2010

CURRENT ENGLISH TRANSLATION PROMULGATED FOR USE IN
THE DIOCESE OF THE UNITED STATES OF AMERICA
NOVEMBER 27, 2011

AN OVERVIEW OF *UNIVERSAL NORMS ON THE LITURGICAL YEAR AND THE GENERAL ROMAN CALENDAR*

Jason J. McFarland

Christians live within one great Sunday. This principle sums up the thrust of the reform of the liturgical year called for by the *Constitution on the Sacred Liturgy* (CSL) of the Second Vatican Council and articulated in the *Universal Norms on the Liturgical Year and the General Roman Calendar* (UNLY). Our weekly celebration of Jesus' Resurrection on Sunday is the "primordial feast day."[1] The Church unpacks this original feast, however, through the annual commemoration of the "entire mystery of Christ and . . . the birthdays of the Saints."[2] In the course of the year the entire Paschal Mystery is celebrated: Jesus' saving Incarnation, Life, Death, Resurrection, Ascension, and giving of the Spirit, as well as Christ's eternal reign at the right hand of the Father in the unity of the Holy Spirit.

The continuous weekly cycle, then, is overlapped by an annual cycle, and this overlapping reveals something profound about the Catholic Christian understanding of salvation. Salvation is "already" in that we participate truly, but still sacramentally, in the saving work of Christ. This understanding relates to the Sunday celebration, the "Eighth Day," the day of salvation. As Blessed John Paul II wrote in his apostolic letter, *Dies Domini* (DD): "Springing from the resurrection, [Sunday] cuts through human time, the months, the years, the centuries, like a directional arrow that points them towards their target: Christ's Second Coming. Sunday foreshadows the last day, the day of the *Parousia*, which in a way is already anticipated by Christ's glory in the event of the resurrection."[3]

Salvation, paradoxically, is also "not yet," in that we still await this final culmination of creation in Christ's second coming, when sacraments will cease. The annual cycle of commemoration presses us ever closer to the end of time. Indeed, as Pope John Paul II says, "The paschal mystery of Christ is the full revelation of the mystery of the world's origin, the climax of the history of salvation and the anticipation of the eschatological fulfillment of the world."[4] The result is a twofold cycle in which we glory in the Resurrection yet still commemorate year by year the saving Christ-events. The entire arc of time, both its fulfillment and its annual progression, is now seen through the lens of Christ.

---

1. *Universal Norms on the Liturgical Year and the General Roman Caledar* (UNLY) , 4; see also the *Constitution on the Sacred Liturgy* (CSL), 106.

2. UNLY, 1.

3. *Dies Domini* (DD), 75.

4. Ibid., 18.

From a historical perspective, the weekly Sunday cycle predates the annual cycle, but by at least the second century there was an annual celebration of Easter, and then, by at least the fourth century, Christmas, Epiphany, and Pentecost. Periods of preparation for the great commemorations developed over time. The gradual expansion of this preparatory period is most evident for Easter. At first, the period was just a few days, then the entire week (Holy Week), and eventually several weeks (Lent). The development of Advent—the period of "devout and expectant delight"[5] for both the commemoration of the Lord's first coming in the Incarnation and Second Coming at the end of time—came later, but it is another example of this backward expansion of a commemoration. Indeed, this seems a natural development given the ancient practice of fasting prior to the weekly Sunday celebration.

The great commemorations were not only expanded backward with preparatory periods, but also forward with periods of rejoicing. In the current structure of the liturgical year, the ongoing nature of the great solemnities are "extended over eight days,"[6] giving us the Octaves of the Nativity of the Lord and Easter. These solemnities are further extended into Christmas Time (up to and including the Sunday after Epiphany, or after January 6) and Easter Time (fifty days culminating in Pentecost Sunday). Saints' days were also part of the calendar from very early on, and over time became standardized.

We might say that Ordinary Time is a remnant or recovery of the earliest weekly cycle in which "no particular aspect of the mystery of Christ is celebrated, but rather the mystery of Christ itself is honored in its fullness."[7] The Collect for the Fourteenth Sunday in Ordinary Time, for example, alludes to no particular mystery, but focuses upon the Paschal Mystery in general:

> O God, who in the abasement of your Son
> have raised up a fallen world,
> fill your faithful with holy joy,
> for on those you have rescued from slavery to sin
> you bestow eternal gladness.
> Through our Lord Jesus Christ, your Son,
> who lives and reigns with you in the unity of the Holy Spirit,
> one God, for ever and ever.

PRIMARY THEMES

The UNLY, issued by the Sacred Congregation of Rites and promulgated by Pope Paul VI on February 14, 1969, for use starting January 1, 1970, is universally authoritative for all Catholics that celebrate the Roman Rite.[8] The foundations for these norms can be seen in efforts at reform by Paul VI's predecessors, particularly in the restoration of the Paschal Triduum[9] and assertion that the liturgical year "possesses a distinct sacramental power and efficacy to strengthen

---

5. UNLY, 39.

6. Ibid., 12.

7. Ibid., 43.

8. See ibid., 2. General norms are to be applied also to other rites in communion with Rome, but many of the particular norms in the document relate only to the Roman Rite.

9. Sacred Congregation of Rites, Decree, *Dominicae resurrectionis*, February 9, 1951.

the Christian life"[10] during the pontificate of Pius XII. Saint Pius X, Pius XII, and Blessed John XXIII also called for some reform of the liturgical year, even if they were unable to bring such reform to fruition. The Consilium for the implementation of CSL began reform of the liturgical year in 1964. A draft of the revised liturgical calendar was approved during the seventh plenary session of the Second Vatican Council on October 12, 1966, and was subsequently submitted to Pope Paul VI by the Consilium on April 17, 1967.[11]

The completion of the reform of the liturgical year and calendar was mandated by CSL.[12] As Paul VI notes in his apostolic letter *motu proprio, Paschal Mystery,* that promulgated the norms, the reform was to allow that the "Paschal Mystery of Christ be placed in clearer light. . . . For in fact, with the passage of centuries, it has happened that, partly from the increase in the number of vigils, religious festivals and their extension over an octave, and partly from the gradual introduction of new elements into the liturgical year, the Christian faithful had come not rarely to practice particular pious exercises in such a way that their minds seemed to have become somewhat distracted from the principal mysteries of divine redemption."[13] In order to remedy this problem, the norms have a twofold focus: the restoration of the Proper of Time—both the weekly and annual cycles—to its rightful prominence, and the revision of the Proper of Saints.

The restoration of the Proper of Time means, first, that the weekly celebration of Sunday takes precedence in the liturgical year and gives way to solemnities and feasts only by way of exception: the Feast of the Holy Family of Jesus, Mary, and Joseph; the Feast of the Baptism of the Lord; the Solemnity of the Most Holy Trinity; and the Solemnity of Our Lord Jesus Christ, King of the Universe.[14] The prominence of Sunday is muted in territories where certain solemnities are not observed as Holydays of Obligation, and are thus transferred to a Sunday (for example, the Solemnity of the Epiphany of the Lord, the Solemnity of the Ascension of the Lord, and the Solemnity of the Most Holy Body and Blood of Christ).[15] There is a tension evident in this deviation from the principle that "Sunday excludes . . . the permanent assigning of any other celebration."[16] The nature of civil calendars in many territories, however, makes it difficult for the faithful to observe Holydays of Obligation that fall on weekdays. The judgment was made, therefore, that a compromise was preferable to what in effect would be a permanent removal of these important solemnities from the liturgical experience of

---

10. Sacred Congregation of Rites, General Decree, *Maxima redemptionis nostrae mysteria,* November 16, 1955.

11. See Consilium for the Implementation of the Constitution on the Sacred Liturgy, "Commentary on the General Norms for the Liturgical Year and the Calendar," trans. International Commission on English in the Liturgy (1975), in *Norms Governing Liturgical Calendars,* Liturgy Documentary Series 6 (Washington, DC: United States Catholic Conference, 1984), 62.

12. See CSL, 102–111.

13. Please note that this apostolic letter is found in the third edition of *The Roman Missal.* It precedes UNLY.

14. See UNLY, 6.

15. Ibid., 7.

16. UNLYGRC, 6.

the majority of Catholics.[17] In any case, the prominence of Sunday is maintained for much of the year and "the Sundays of Advent, Lent, and Easter have precedence over all Feasts of the Lord and over all Solemnities."[18]

The reform of the Proper of Time was not accomplished merely through revised norms or rubrics. In fact, it required a profound revision and expansion of the liturgical texts of the Roman Rite. Collects (Opening Prayers) specific to each Sunday and certain weekdays were now required, and the Lectionary had to be completely revised. The new Collects[19] (along with other proper Mass texts) and readings help to express more clearly the mysteries of the Lord throughout the year and are the primary means of the liturgical "education of the faithful."[20] In addition, the clearer expression of Sunday and the major annual commemorations required the removal of certain celebrations that had previously been part of the liturgical year. Vigils were retained (and in a few cases added) only for the most important liturgical days; others were removed from the calendar. The Octave of Pentecost was suppressed so that the nature of Pentecost as the culmination of the fifty days of Easter would be more evident. Septuagesima—the period anticipating Lent—and Passiontide were also suppressed so that the unity and meaning of Lent could be more clearly expressed.[21]

To be sure, the celebration of the saints, and in particular of the Blessed Virgin Mary, is integral to the Roman Rite. By the time of the Second Vatican Council, however, the number of saints' days and devotional feasts on the General Roman Calendar had become excessive, reaching 338 celebrations of varying rank.[22] Many Sundays and weekdays of the Proper of Time had been completely eclipsed.

Revising the Proper of Saints involved four primary changes. First, the number of feasts on the General Roman Calendar was greatly decreased, "lest the feasts of the saints take precedence over the feasts commemorating the very mysteries of salvation. . . ."[23] Second, the feasts in the revised Proper of Saints are ranked in order of importance as solemnities, feasts, and memorials. Memorials are further distinguished as obligatory or optional. Third, a saint's feast day is assigned, whenever possible, to his or her "birthday"[24] into eternal life. Finally, the calendar was made more relevant to the universal Church: first, by including only those saints of "universal significance";[25] and second, by revising the list of saints on the General Roman Calendar so that it represents a broader swath of eras, geographical regions, and cultural groups.[26]

---

17. See ibid., 58.

18. Ibid., 5.

19. The prayers were either newly composed, drawn from ancient liturgical sources, or reassigned from those feasts that were suppressed in the liturgical reform.

20. UNLY, 1.

21. See "Commentary on the General Norms," 64, 66.

22. See ibid., 72.

23. CSL, 111.

24. UNLY, 56.

25. CSL, 111.

26. See ibid., 77; Paul VI, *Paschal Mystery.*

THE IMPORTANCE OF READING THE DOCUMENT
AND ITS IMPLICATIONS FOR LITURGICAL PREPARATION

While the content of the UNLY has not changed since its promulgation, it is important to read the document again at this point in the history of the English-speaking Church because the norms have been newly translated as they appear in this collection and within the third typical edition of *The Roman Missal*. With a new translation comes a fresh reading, and perhaps new insights.

Knowledge of the norms is essential for those responsible for planning liturgical celebrations throughout the year because they establish the principles that determine when each celebration takes place. The last part of the document entitled "Table of Liturgical Days" summarizes the requirements of the rest of the document in this regard. The table shows, in essence, how the weekly and annual cycles are reconciled.

The norms should not be read in isolation. It is important to read them together with the *General Instruction of the Roman Missal* (GIRM) and of the *Liturgy of the Hours* (GILOH), for example, because the norms pertain both to the celebration of the Mass and of the Hours.[27] The rubrics that introduce the different sections of the Missal are also important, in that they provide guidance as to the days on which particular sacraments and rites are appropriately celebrated, and which texts should be used.

Every episcopal conference is responsible for developing each year a calendar for its territory, following the requirements of the norms. Because the application of the norms can be a complex task, those who prepare the liturgy would do well to follow the calendar as prepared by their conference or diocese. It is also the task of each conference to develop a particular calendar for its territory "combined organically with the general cycle,"[28] which incorporates celebrations of local saints and commemorations. Given the requirements of the norms, a particular calendar should not overburden the General Roman Calendar, nor should it eclipse the Proper of Time.[29] The responsibility for a particular calendar also pertains to religious orders, dioceses, and even local churches.[30]

THE DOCUMENT'S IMPACT ON THE LIFE OF THE CHURCH

The impact of UNLY on the life of the Church was and continues to be profound. As Pope Paul VI says in *Paschal Mystery*, "The purpose of the revision of the liturgical year and of the norms accomplishing its reform, is nothing other than that through faith, hope, and charity the faithful may share more deeply in 'the whole mystery of Christ, unfolded through the cycle of the year.'"[31] The weekly cycle has been restored to its original primacy and the annual cycle celebrating the Paschal Mystery can now shine forth with greater clarity for the benefit of the faithful. The Sanctoral Cycle has been simplified and allows "clear examples

---

27. See UNLY, 14.
28. Ibid. 49.
29. See ibid. 50, 53.
30. See ibid., 52.
31. Pope Paul VI, *Paschal Mystery*, quoting CSL, 102.

of holiness"[32] to be more effectively "put before the whole People of God."[33] Finally, it is of no small significance that the General Roman Calendar now reflects more faithfully the diversity of the Church's saints. This reform is an example of liturgical inculturation at its best.

THE ONGOING LITURGICAL REFORM: UNRESOLVED ISSUES
IN THE POST-CONCILIAR LITURGICAL YEAR

As with the liturgical reform as a whole, that of the liturgical year and calendar is never finished. Local adaptations will continue, and over time the saints and celebrations of the universal calendar will slowly evolve "in keeping with the spiritual attitudes and sentiments of [the] times."[34] Many episcopal conferences have yet to take seriously the recommendation that Rogation and Ember days be celebrated regularly.[35] Such celebrations seem especially appropriate today—an age of crisis both in terms of the environment and human labor. The centuries-old goal of a common Easter date for all Christian Churches is another aim of the reform yet to be accomplished.[36] Achieving such a goal will take time paired with ecumenical conversation and charity. As a final point, the Church, both local and universal, must be ever-vigilant about maintaining a noble simplicity in the Calendar. On the one hand, the simplification of the universal calendar could be even more thoroughly accomplished. Indeed, many saints have been added to the General Roman Calendar since these norms were promulgated in 1969, and it can be difficult to find appropriate dates for local celebrations. On the other hand, there will be a continuous need for the addition of local and universal saints to the calendar. Additions should be done with care, and might even require the removal of other less universally significant saints for the sake of a clear liturgical expression of Sunday and of the Paschal Mystery.

---

32. Pope Paul VI, *Paschal Mystery*.
33. Ibid.
34. Ibid.
35. See UNLY, 45–47.
36. See "Commentary on the General Norms," 71.

OUTLINE

UNIVERSAL NORMS ON THE LITURGICAL YEAR AND THE GENERAL ROMAN CALENDAR

CHAPTER I
THE LITURGICAL YEAR

1. Holy Church celebrates the saving work of Christ on prescribed days in the course of the year with sacred remembrance. Each week, on the day called the Lord's Day, she commemorates the Resurrection of the Lord, which she also celebrates once a year in the great Paschal Solemnity, together with his blessed Passion. In fact, throughout the course of the year the Church unfolds the entire mystery of Christ and observes the birthdays of the Saints. ⟶ Death day

During the different periods of the liturgical year, in accord with traditional discipline, the Church completes the education of the faithful by means of both spiritual and bodily devotional practices, instruction, prayer, works of penance, and works of mercy.[1]

2. The principles that follow can and must be applied both to the Roman Rite and all other Rites; however, the practical norms are to be understood as applying solely to the Roman Rite, except in the case of those that by their very nature also affect the other Rites.[2]

TITLE I—THE LITURGICAL DAYS

I. The Liturgical Day in General

3. Each and every day is sanctified by the liturgical celebrations of the People of God, especially by the Eucharistic Sacrifice and the Divine Office.

The liturgical day runs from midnight to midnight. However, the celebration of Sunday and of Solemnities begins already on the evening of the previous day.

II. Sunday

4. On the first day of each week, which is known as the Day of the Lord or the Lord's Day, the Church, by an apostolic tradition that draws its origin from the very day of the Resurrection of Christ, celebrates the Paschal Mystery. Hence, Sunday must be considered the primordial feast day.[3]

---

1. Cf. Second Vatican Council, Constitution on the Sacred Liturgy, *Sacrosanctum Concilium*, nos. 102–105.

2. Cf. *ibidem*, no. 3.

3. Cf. *ibidem*, no. 106.

5.   Because of its special importance, the celebration of Sunday gives way only to Solemnities and Feasts of the Lord; indeed, the Sundays of Advent, Lent, and Easter have precedence over all Feasts of the Lord and over all Solemnities. In fact, Solemnities occurring on these Sundays are transferred to the following Monday unless they occur on Palm Sunday or on Sunday of the Lord's Resurrection.

6.   Sunday excludes in principle the permanent assigning of any other celebration. However:

a) the Sunday within the Octave of the Nativity is the Feast of the Holy Family;

b) the Sunday following January 6 is the Feast of the Baptism of the Lord;

c) the Sunday after Pentecost is the Solemnity of the Most Holy Trinity;

d) the Last Sunday in Ordinary Time is the Solemnity of Our Lord Jesus Christ, King of the Universe.

7.   Where the Solemnities of the Epiphany, the Ascension and the Most Holy Body and Blood of Christ are not observed as Holydays of Obligation, they should be assigned to a Sunday as their proper day in this manner:

a) the Epiphany is assigned to the Sunday that falls between January 2 and January 8;

b) the Ascension to the Seventh Sunday of Easter;

c) the Solemnity of the Most Holy Body and Blood of Christ to the Sunday after Trinity Sunday.

III. Solemnities, Feasts, and Memorials

8.   In the cycle of the year, as she celebrates the mystery of Christ, the Church also venerates with a particular love the Blessed Mother of God, Mary, and proposes to the devotion of the faithful the Memorials of the Martyrs and other Saints.[4]

9.   The Saints who have universal importance are celebrated in an obligatory way throughout the whole Church; other Saints are either inscribed in the calendar, but for optional celebration, or are left to be honored by a particular Church, or nation, or religious family.[5]

10.   Celebrations, according to the importance assigned to them, are hence distinguished one from another and termed: Solemnity, Feast, Memorial.

11.   Solemnities are counted among the most important days, whose celebration begins with First Vespers (Evening Prayer I) on the preceding day. Some Solemnities are also endowed with their own Vigil Mass, which is to be used on the evening of the preceding day, if an evening Mass is celebrated.

---

4. Cf. *ibidem*, nos. 103–104.
5. Cf. *ibidem*, no. 111.

12.   The celebration of the two greatest Solemnities, Easter and the Nativity, is extended over eight days. Each Octave is governed by its own rules.

13.   Feasts are celebrated within the limits of the natural day; accordingly they have no First Vespers (Evening Prayer I), except in the case of Feasts of the Lord that fall on a Sunday in Ordinary Time or in Christmas Time and which replace the Sunday Office.

14.   Memorials are either obligatory or optional; their observance is integrated into the celebration of the occurring weekday in accordance with the norms set forth in the *General Instruction of the Roman Missal* and of the Liturgy of the Hours.

Obligatory Memorials which fall on weekdays of Lent may only be celebrated as Optional Memorials.

If several Optional Memorials are inscribed in the Calendar on the same day, only one may be celebrated, the others being omitted.

15.   On Saturdays in Ordinary Time when no Obligatory Memorial occurs, an Optional Memorial of the Blessed Virgin Mary may be celebrated.

IV. Weekdays

16.   The days of the week that follow Sunday are called weekdays; however, they are celebrated differently according to the importance of each.

   a) Ash Wednesday and the weekdays of Holy Week, from Monday up to and including Thursday, take precedence over all other celebrations.

   b) The weekdays of Advent from December 17 up to and including December 24 and all the weekdays of Lent have precedence over Obligatory Memorials.

   c) Other weekdays give way to all Solemnities and Feasts and are combined with Memorials.

TITLE II—THE CYCLE OF THE YEAR

17.   Over the course of the year the Church celebrates the whole mystery of Christ, from the Incarnation to Pentecost Day and the days of waiting for the Advent of the Lord.[6]

I. The Paschal Triduum

18.   Since Christ accomplished his work of human redemption and of the perfect glorification of God principally through his Paschal Mystery, in which by dying he has destroyed our death, and by rising restored our life, the sacred Paschal Triduum of the Passion and Resurrection of the Lord shines forth as the

---

6. Cf. *ibidem*, no. 102.

high point of the entire liturgical year.[7] Therefore the preeminence that Sunday has in the week, the Solemnity of Easter has in the liturgical year.[8]

19.   The Paschal Triduum of the Passion and Resurrection of the Lord begins with the evening Mass of the Lord's Supper, has its center in the Easter Vigil, and closes with Vespers (Evening Prayer) of the Sunday of the Resurrection.

20.   On Friday of the Passion of the Lord[9] (Good Friday) and, if appropriate, also on Holy Saturday until the Easter Vigil,[10] the sacred Paschal Fast is everywhere observed.

21.   The Easter Vigil, in the holy night when the Lord rose again, is considered the "mother of all holy Vigils,"[11] in which the Church, keeping watch, awaits the Resurrection of Christ and celebrates it in the Sacraments. Therefore, the entire celebration of this sacred Vigil must take place at night, so that it both begins after nightfall and ends before the dawn on the Sunday.

II. Easter Time

22.   The fifty days from the Sunday of the Resurrection to Pentecost Sunday are celebrated in joy and exultation as one feast day, indeed as one "great Sunday."[12]

These are the days above all others in which the *Alleluia* is sung.

23.   The Sundays of this time of year are considered to be Sundays of Easter and are called, after Easter Sunday itself, the Second, Third, Fourth, Fifth, Sixth, and Seventh Sundays of Easter. This sacred period of fifty days concludes with Pentecost Sunday.

24.   The first eight days of Easter Time constitute the Octave of Easter and are celebrated as Solemnities of the Lord.

25.   On the fortieth day after Easter the Ascension of the Lord is celebrated, except where, not being observed as a Holyday of Obligation, it has been assigned to the Seventh Sunday of Easter (cf. no. 7).

26.   The weekdays from the Ascension up to and including the Saturday before Pentecost prepare for the coming of the Holy Spirit, the Paraclete.

III. Lent

27.   Lent is ordered to preparing for the celebration of Easter, since the Lenten liturgy prepares for celebration of the Paschal Mystery both catechumens, by

---

7. Cf. *ibidem*, no. 5.

8. Cf. *ibidem*, no. 106.

9. Cf. Paul VI, Apostolic Constitution, *Paenitemini*, February 17, 1966, II §3: *Acta Apostolicae Sedis* 58 (1966), p. 184.

10. Cf. Second Vatican Council, Constitution on the Sacred Liturgy, *Sacrosanctum Concilium*, no. 110.

11. St. Augustine, *Sermo* 219: PL 38, 1088.

12. St. Athanasius, *Epistula festalis*: PG 26, 1366.

the various stages of Christian Initiation, and the faithful, who recall their own Baptism and do penance.[13]

28.   The forty days of Lent run from Ash Wednesday up to but excluding the Mass of the Lord's Supper exclusive.

From the beginning of Lent until the Paschal Vigil, the *Alleluia* is not said.

29.   On Ash Wednesday, the beginning of Lent, which is observed everywhere as a fast day,[14] ashes are distributed.

30.   The Sundays of this time of year are called the First, Second, Third, Fourth, and Fifth Sundays of Lent. The Sixth Sunday, on which Holy Week begins, is called, "Palm Sunday of the Passion of the Lord."

31.   Holy Week is ordered to the commemoration of Christ's Passion, beginning with his Messianic entrance into Jerusalem.

On Thursday of Holy Week, in the morning, the Bishop concelebrates Mass with his presbyterate and blesses the holy oils and consecrates the chrism.

IV. Christmas Time

32.   After the annual celebration of the Paschal Mystery, the Church has no more ancient custom than celebrating the memorial of the Nativity of the Lord and of his first manifestations, and this takes place in Christmas Time.

33.   Christmas Time runs from First Vespers (Evening Prayer I) of the Nativity of the Lord up to and including the Sunday after Epiphany or after January 6.

34.   The Vigil Mass of the Nativity is used on the evening of December 24, either before or after First Vespers (Evening Prayer I).

On the day of the Nativity of the Lord, following ancient Roman tradition, Mass may be celebrated three times, that is, in the night, at dawn, and during the day.

35.   The Nativity of the Lord has its own Octave, arranged thus:

    a) Sunday within the Octave or, if there is no Sunday, December 30, is the Feast of the Holy Family of Jesus, Mary, and Joseph;

    b) December 26 is the Feast of Saint Stephen, the First Martyr;

    c) December 27 is the Feast of Saint John, Apostle and Evangelist;

    d) December 28 is the Feast of the Holy Innocents;

    e) December 29, 30, and 31 are days within the Octave;

---

13. Cf. Second Vatican Council, Constitution on the Sacred Liturgy, *Sacrosanctum Concilium*, no. 109.

14. Cf. Paul VI, Apostolic Constitution, *Paenitemini*, February 17, 1966, II §3: *Acta Apostolicae Sedis* 58 (1966), p. 184.

f) January 1, the Octave Day of the Nativity of the Lord, is the Solemnity of Mary, the Holy Mother of God, and also the commemoration of the conferral of the Most Holy Name of Jesus.

36.   The Sunday falling between January 2 and January 5 is the Second Sunday after the Nativity.

37.   The Epiphany of the Lord is celebrated on January 6, unless, where it is not observed as a Holyday of Obligation, it has been assigned to the Sunday occurring between January 2 and 8 (cf. no. 7).

38.   The Sunday falling after January 6 is the Feast of the Baptism of the Lord.

V. Advent

39.   Advent has a twofold character, for it is a time of preparation for the Solemnities of Christmas, in which the First Coming of the Son of God to humanity is remembered, and likewise a time when, by remembrance of this, minds and hearts are led to look forward to Christ's Second Coming at the end of time. For these two reasons, Advent is a period of devout and expectant delight.

40.   Advent begins with First Vespers (Evening Prayer I) of the Sunday that falls on or closest to November 30 and it ends before First Vespers (Evening Prayer I) of Christmas.

41.   The Sundays of this time of year are named the First, Second, Third, and Fourth Sundays of Advent.

42.   The weekdays from December 17 up to and including December 24 are ordered in a more direct way to preparing for the Nativity of the Lord.

VI. Ordinary Time

43.   Besides the times of year that have their own distinctive character, there remain in the yearly cycle thirty-three or thirty-four weeks in which no particular aspect of the mystery of Christ is celebrated, but rather the mystery of Christ itself is honored in its fullness, especially on Sundays. This period is known as Ordinary Time.

44.   Ordinary Time begins on the Monday which follows the Sunday occurring after January 6 and extends up to and including the Tuesday before the beginning of Lent; it begins again on the Monday after Pentecost Sunday and ends before First Vespers (Evening Prayer I) of the First Sunday of Advent.

During these times of the year there is used the series of formularies given for the Sundays and weekdays of this time both in the Missal and in the Liturgy of the Hours (Vol. III–IV).

45.   On Rogation and Ember Days the Church is accustomed to entreat the Lord for the various needs of humanity, especially for the fruits of the earth and for human labor, and to give thanks to him publicly.

46.   In order that the Rogation Days and Ember Days may be adapted to the different regions and different needs of the faithful, the Conferences of Bishops should arrange the time and manner in which they are held.

Consequently, concerning their duration, whether they are to last one or more days, or be repeated in the course of the year, norms are to be established by the competent authority, taking into consideration local needs.

47.   The Mass for each day of these celebrations should be chosen from among the Masses for Various Needs, and should be one which is more particularly appropriate to the purpose of the supplications.

CHAPTER II
THE CALENDAR

TITLE I—THE CALENDAR AND
CELEBRATIONS TO BE INSCRIBED IN IT

48.   The ordering of the celebration of the liturgical year is governed by a calendar, which is either general or particular, depending on whether it has been laid down for the use of the entire Roman Rite, or for the use of a Particular Church or religious family.

49.   In the General Calendar is inscribed both the entire cycle of celebrations of the mystery of salvation in the Proper of Time, and that of those Saints who have universal significance and therefore are obligatorily celebrated by everyone, and of other Saints who demonstrate the universality and continuity of sainthood within the People of God.

Particular calendars, on the other hand, contain celebrations of a more proper character, appropriately combined organically with the general cycle.[15] For individual Churches or religious families show special honor to those Saints who are proper to them for some particular reason.

Particular calendars, however, are to be drawn up by the competent authority and approved by the Apostolic See.

50.   In drawing up a particular calendar, attention should be paid to the following:

   a) The Proper of Time, that is, the cycle of Times, Solemnities, and Feasts by which the mystery of redemption is unfolded and honored during the

---

15. Cf. Sacred Congregation for Divine Worship, Instruction, *Calendaria particularia*, June 24,1970: *Acta Apostolicae Sedis* 62 (1970), pp. 651–663.

liturgical year, must always be kept intact and enjoy its rightful pre-eminence over particular celebrations.

b) Proper celebrations must be combined organically with universal celebrations, with attention to the rank and precedence indicated for each in the Table of Liturgical Days. So that particular calendars may not be overburdened, individual Saints should have only one celebration in the course of the liturgical year, although, where pastoral reasons recommend it, there may be another celebration in the form of an Optional Memorial marking the *translatio* or *inventio* of the bodies of Patron Saints or Founders of Churches or of religious families.

c) Celebrations granted by indult should not duplicate other celebrations already occurring in the cycle of the mystery of salvation, nor should their number be increased out of proportion.

51.   Although it is appropriate for each diocese to have its own Calendar and Proper for the Office and Mass, there is nevertheless nothing to prevent entire provinces, regions, nations, or even larger areas, having Calendars and Propers in common, prepared by cooperation among all concerned.

This principle may also be similarly observed in the case of religious calendars for several provinces under the same civil jurisdiction.

52.   A particular calendar is prepared by the insertion in the General Calendar of proper Solemnities, Feasts and Memorials, that is:

a) in a diocesan calendar, besides celebrations of Patrons and of the dedication of the cathedral church, the Saints and Blessed who have special connections with the diocese, e.g., by their birth, residence over a long period, or their death;

b) in a religious calendar, besides celebrations of the Title, the Founder and the Patron, those Saints and Blessed who were members of that religious family or had a special relationship with it;

c) in calendars for individual churches, besides the proper celebrations of the diocese or religious family, celebrations proper to the church that are listed in the Table of Liturgical Days, and Saints whose body is kept in the church. Members of religious families, too, join the community of the local Church in celebrating the anniversary of the dedication of the cathedral church and the principal Patrons of the place and of the wider region where they live.

53.   When a diocese or religious family has the distinction of having many Saints and Blessed, care must be taken so that the calendar of the entire diocese or entire institute does not become overburdened. Consequently:

a) A common celebration can, first of all, be held of all the Saints and Blessed of a diocese or religious family, or of some category among them.

b) Only the Saints and Blessed of particular significance for the entire diocese or the entire religious family should be inscribed in the calendar
as an individual celebration.

c) The other Saints or Blessed should be celebrated only in those places
with which they have closer ties or where their bodies are kept.

54.   Proper celebrations should be inscribed in the Calendar as Obligatory or
Optional Memorials, unless other provisions have been made for them in the
Table of Liturgical Days, or there are special historical or pastoral reasons. There
is no reason, however, why some celebrations may not be observed in certain
places with greater solemnity than in the rest of the diocese or religious family.

55.   Celebrations inscribed in a particular calendar must be observed by all
who are bound to follow that calendar and may only be removed from the calendar or changed in rank with the approval of the Apostolic See.

TITLE II—THE PROPER DAY FOR CELEBRATIONS

56.   The Church's practice has been to celebrate the Saints on their "birthday,"
a practice that it is appropriate to follow when proper celebrations are inscribed
in particular calendars.

However, even though proper celebrations have special importance for
individual particular Churches or individual religious families, it is greatly
expedient that there be as much unity as possible in the celebration of Solemnities,
Feasts and Obligatory Memorials inscribed in the General Calendar.

Consequently in inscribing proper celebrations in a particular calendar,
the following should be observed:

a) Celebrations that are also listed in the General Calendar are to be inscribed
on the same date in a particular calendar, with a change if necessary in
the rank of celebration.
     The same must be observed with regard to a diocesan or religious
calendar for the inscription of celebrations proper to a single church.

b) Celebrations of Saints not found in the General Calendar should be
assigned to their "birthday." If this is not known, the celebrations should
be assigned to a date proper to the Saint for some other reason, e.g., the
date of ordination or of the *inventio* or *translatio* of the Saint's body;
otherwise to a day that is free from other celebrations in the particular
Calendar.

c) If, on the other hand, the "birthday" or other proper day is impeded by
another obligatory celebration, even of lower rank, in the General Calendar
or in a particular calendar, the celebration should be assigned to the
closest date not so impeded.

d) However, if it is a question of celebrations that for pastoral reasons cannot be transferred to another date, the impeding celebration must itself
be transferred.

e) Other celebrations, termed celebrations by indult, should be inscribed on a date more pastorally appropriate.

f) In order that the cycle of the liturgical year shine forth in all its clarity, but that the celebration of the Saints not be permanently impeded, dates that usually fall during Lent and the Octave of Easter, as well as the weekdays from December 17 to December 31, should remain free of any particular celebration, unless it is a question of Obligatory Memorials, of Feasts found in the Table of Liturgical Days under no. 8: a, b, c, d, or of Solemnities that cannot be transferred to another time of the year.

The Solemnity of Saint Joseph, where it is observed as a Holyday of Obligation, should it fall on Palm Sunday of the Lord's Passion, is anticipated on the preceding Saturday, March 18. Where, on the other hand, it is not observed as a Holyday of Obligation, it may be transferred by the Conference of Bishops to another day outside Lent.

57. If any Saints or Blessed are inscribed together in the Calendar, they are always celebrated together, whenever their celebrations are of equal rank, even though one or more of them may be more proper. If, however, the celebration of one or more of these Saints or Blessed is of a higher rank, the Office of this or those Saints or Blessed alone is celebrated and the celebration of the others is omitted, unless it is appropriate to assign them to another date in the form of an Obligatory Memorial.

58. For the pastoral good of the faithful, it is permitted to observe on Sundays in Ordinary Time those celebrations that fall during the week and that are agreeable to the devotion of the faithful, provided the celebrations rank above that Sunday in the Table of Liturgical Days. The Mass of such celebrations may be used at all the celebrations of Mass at which the people are present.

59. Precedence among liturgical days, as regards their celebration, is governed solely by the following Table.

TABLE OF LITURGICAL DAYS
ACCORDING TO THEIR ORDER OF PRECEDENCE

I

1. The Paschal Triduum of the Passion and Resurrection of the Lord.

2. The Nativity of the Lord, the Epiphany, the Ascension, and Pentecost.
   Sundays of Advent, Lent, and Easter.
   Ash Wednesday.
   Weekdays of Holy Week from Monday up to and including Thursday.
   Days within the Octave of Easter.

3. Solemnities inscribed in the General Calendar, whether of the Lord, of the Blessed Virgin Mary, or of Saints.

   The Commemoration of All the Faithful Departed.

4. Proper Solemnities, namely:

   a) The Solemnity of the principal Patron of the place, city, or state.

   b) The Solemnity of the dedication and of the anniversary of the dedication of one's own church.

   c) The Solemnity of the Title of one's own church.

   d) The Solemnity either of the Title

   or of the Founder

   or of the principal Patron of an Order
   or Congregation.

II

5. Feasts of the Lord inscribed in the General Calendar.

6. Sundays of Christmas Time and the Sundays in Ordinary Time.

7. Feasts of the Blessed Virgin Mary and of the Saints in the General Calendar.

8. Proper Feasts, namely:

   a) The Feast of the principal Patron of the diocese.

   b) The Feast of the anniversary of the dedication of the cathedral church.

   c) The Feast of the principal Patron of a region or province, or a country, or of a wider territory.

   d) The Feast of the Title, Founder, or principal Patron of an Order or Congregation and of a religious province, without prejudice to the prescriptions given under no. 4.

   e) Other Feasts proper to an individual church.

   f) Other Feasts inscribed in the Calendar of each diocese or Order or Congregation.

9. Weekdays of Advent from December 17 up to and including December 24.

   Days within the Octave of Christmas.

   Weekdays of Lent.

10.   Obligatory Memorials in the General Calendar.

11.   Proper Obligatory Memorials, namely:

    a) The Memorial of a secondary Patron of the place, diocese, region, or religious province.

    b) Other Obligatory Memorials inscribed in the Calendar of each diocese, or Order or Congregation.

12.   Optional Memorials, which, however, may be celebrated, in the special manner described in the *General Instruction of the Roman Missal* and of the Liturgy of the Hours, even on the days listed in no. 9.

    In the same manner Obligatory Memorials may be celebrated as Optional Memorials if they happen to fall on Lenten weekdays.

13.   Weekdays of Advent up to and including December 16.

    Weekdays of Christmas Time from January 2 until the Saturday after the Epiphany.

    Weekdays of the Easter Time from Monday after the Octave of Easter up to and including the Saturday before Pentecost.

    Weekdays in Ordinary Time.

---

60.   If several celebrations fall on the same day, the one that holds the highest rank according to the Table of Liturgical Days is observed. However, a Solemnity impeded by a liturgical day that takes precedence over it should be transferred to the closest day not listed under nos. 1–8 in the Table of Precedence, provided that what is laid down in no. 5 is observed. As to the Solemnity of the Annunciation of the Lord, whenever it falls on any day of Holy Week, it shall always be transferred to the Monday after the Second Sunday of Easter.

    Other celebrations are omitted in that year.

61.   Should on the other hand, Vespers (Evening Prayer) of the current day's Office and First Vespers (Evening Prayer I) of the following day be assigned for celebration on the same day, then Vespers (Evening Prayer) of the celebration with the higher rank in the Table of Liturgical Days takes precedence; in cases of equal rank, Vespers (Evening Prayer) of the current day takes precedence.

ECCLESIA DE EUCHARISTIA
ON THE EUCHARIST IN
ITS RELATIONSHIP TO THE CHURCH

POPE JOHN PAUL II
ENCYCLICAL LETTER
APRIL 17, 2003

AN OVERVIEW OF *ECCLESIA DE EUCHARISTIA: ON THE EUCHARIST IN ITS RELATIONSHIP TO THE CHURCH*

Christopher Carstens

WHAT DOES CHRIST LOOK LIKE?

Polls tell us that many Catholics have difficulty seeing Christ—Body, Blood, soul, and divinity—in the Eucharist. And while the percentage of believers in the Real Presence is directly related to whether those believers practice their faith and, in particular, attend Mass on a regular basis, Catholics of all kinds are not impervious to the challenges of an increasingly secular age. It is against this background that Pope John Paul II forcefully proclaims the Eucharist as the foundation of the Christian life and of the Church herself.

Ecclesia de Eucharistia: On the Eucharist In Its Relationship to the Church, grounds all things in the mystery of the Eucharist and, through it, to Christ and his saving work in the Paschal Mystery. Citing the Second Vatican Council, the Holy Father calls the Eucharistic sacrifice "the source and summit of the Christian life,"[1] for it contains "the Church's entire spiritual wealth: Christ himself, our passover and living bread."[2]

That a papal encyclical, an expression of the ordinary magisterium of the Church, would call the Church to attend to her founder, Christ, and his work—both of which the Eucharist makes present—is no surprise. That he should do so in a way that men and women of our age can find personal and intimate is novel. Pope John Paul II, both in the present encyclical and the last years of his papacy, sought not simply to increase the percentage of Catholics who would believe in the Real Presence, but he sought to teach us to recognize the true and beautiful face of Christ alive in the Eucharist.

CONTEMPLATING THE FACE OF CHRIST

Ecclesia de Eucharistia, which is John Paul II's 14th and last encyclical, reveals something of the pope and the direction of his papacy at the beginning of the Third Christian Millennium. Like *Redemptor hominis*, his first encyclical, the Holy Father's last encyclical focuses our eyes on Christ, but it does so now by meditating on his presence in the Eucharist.

The pope admits in the encyclical, given on Holy Thursday 2003, that he cannot let the occasion pass "without halting before the 'Eucharistic face' of Christ and pointing out with new force to the Church the centrality of the Eucharist."[3] Contemplating the "'face' of Christ"[4] was one theme that dominated Pope John

---

1. *Ecclesia de Eucharistia (EE)*, 1, quoting *Lumen gentium* (LG), 11.
2. Ibid., 1.
3. Ibid., 7.
4. Ibid.

Paul's papacy. For example, the pope described the Jubilee Year of 2000 as a year when the Church "devoted herself to contemplating the face of her Bridegroom and Lord."[5] During the Year of the Rosary, celebrated October 2002 through October 2003, the pope reminded us that "to recite the Rosary is nothing other than *to contemplate with Mary the face of Christ*."[6] And the Year of the Eucharist—to begin eighteen months after the writing of *Ecclesia de Eucharistia*—would be "rooted in the theme of Christ and the contemplation of his face."[7]

THE FACE OF CHRIST AND THE NEW EVANGELIZATION

The contemplation of Christ's face establishes another major theme of the encyclical and of Pope John Paul II's papacy: the New Evangelization. All evangelization—whether new or old—follows the model given by that "very first and greatest evangelizer,"[8] Christ himself.

As many Gospel narratives relate—such as that of Zacchaeus the tax collector, the Samaritan woman at the well, or the disciples on the road to Emmaus—evangelization always begins with a personal encounter with Christ, is usually followed by a conversion of heart, and leads the converted to proclaim the Good News that began with that personal and life-changing encounter with Christ. Note that first and most important element of Christ's evangelization is the personal encounter: the first and most important element of the *New* Evangelization is the new encounter with the face of Christ.

In the context of the New Evangelization, *Ecclesia de Eucharistia* shows its significance, for to the eyes of John Paul II, the "Eucharist is the outstanding moment of encounter with the living Christ,"[9] "the deepest and most effective answer to this yearning for the encounter with God."[10] The encyclical is a meditation on learning to see, to encounter, and to contemplate the face of the Eucharistic Christ.

THE FACE OF CHRIST IS THE FACE OF THE CHURCH

After the encounter with Christ and the New Evangelization, a third important theme is the role of the Church in manifesting the face of Christ to us. We know, after Saint Paul, that the Church is the Body of Christ: he is the head, we are his members. The Church thinks, loves, and acts as Christ does, and always with the same goal in mind: the glory of God and the salvation of souls. Christ and his Church belong together—and are inseparable—just as head and body exist together. An encounter with the Eucharistic face of Christ, therefore, takes place within the body of the Church.

The relationship between the Church and the Eucharist is more profound than it may at first appear. It is true enough to say that the Church "makes" the Eucharist: the priest confects the Sacrament of the Eucharist and the assembly participates in the offering. But in another and perhaps truer sense, the Eucharist

---

5. *Novo millennio ineunte* (NMI), 1.

6. *Rosarium virginis mariae* (RVM), 3.

7. *Mane nobiscum domine* (MND), 10.

8. *Evangelii nuntiandi* (EN), 7.

9. *Ecclesia in America* (EA), 35.

10. *Spiritus et sponsa* (SS), 12.

makes the Church, for in the Eucharist is contained the founding of the Church: the Paschal Mystery of Christ. At every Eucharistic celebration, then, the moment of the Church's birth is relived.

The Church's birth through the Eucharist is the meaning of the work's Latin title—*Ecclesia de Eucharistia.* Many English translations of the title don't capture this profound mystery which, ironically, is one of the central themes—if not *the* central theme—of the work. In some instances *Ecclesia de Eucharistia* is rendered simply as "On the Eucharist." But it is not until the first lines of the work that we gather the true import: "The Church draws her life from the Eucharist." The Pope continues: "This truth does not simply express a daily experience of faith, but recapitulates *the heart of the mystery of the Church.*"[11]

These themes—the Eucharistic face of Christ, the New Evangelization, and the mystery of the Church—unfold themselves in the six chapters that make up the Encyclical.

THE EUCHARISTIC FACE OF CHRIST

Following the consecration of the wine at Mass, those present acclaim "the mystery of faith" with words inspired by Saint Paul: "We proclaim your Death, O Lord, / and profess your Resurrection, / until you come again."[12] Christ's Death, Resurrection, and Second Coming structure Chapter One of the encyclical, which is also called "The Mystery of Faith."

The Church now joins Christ's gift of himself to the Father, and this gift is made sacramentally—which is to say *really*—present in the Mass. "What is repeated is its *memorial* celebration," John Paul writes, "which makes Christ's one, definitive redemptive sacrifice always present in time. The sacrificial nature of the Eucharistic mystery cannot therefore be understood as something separate, independent of the Cross."[13]

Christ's sacrifice is "crowned"[14] by his Resurrection, which the Eucharist also makes present. Made possible by the power of the Holy Spirit—who, along with the Sacrament, is also eaten by the communicant[15]—the change of elements, or transubstantiation, presents the entire Christ to us.

The mystery of faith also looks forward to the pledge of heaven.[16] The Holy Father says, "With the Eucharist we digest, as it were, the 'secret' of the resurrection."[17] But this heavenly anticipation is not simply futuristic, for it entails today a renewed commitment to Eucharistic living,[18] serving not only the world but especially the most powerless within it.

"The Eucharist Builds the Church": this is not only the essence of the encyclical but the title of Chapter Two. *"A causal influence of the Eucharist"*[19] exists in the Church's growth. The Apostles, who are the foundations of the

---

11. EE, 1.
12. The third edition of *The Roman Missal*; see also 1 Corinthians 11:26.
13. EE, 12 (emphasis added).
14. Ibid., 14.
15. See ibid., 17.
16. See ibid., 18–19.
17. Ibid., 18.
18. See ibid., 20.
19. Ibid., 21.

Church, were involved by Jesus in his Paschal work, which they continued to recall in the Eucharist. Today, too, after the example of the Apostles, the Church in the Eucharist recalls her founding from Christ's work.[20] Communion in this sacrament builds up the Church, incorporating members into her body, uniting them with Christ and each other.[21]

Mindful of the New Evangelization, the Holy Father goes on to say: "The Eucharist thus appears as both *the source* and *the summit* of all evangelization, since its goal is the communion of mankind with Christ and in him with the Father and the Holy Spirit."[22]

The pope examines the "apostolicity" of both Church and Eucharist in Chapter Three. First, both are founded upon the Apostles and were entrusted by Jesus to them.[23] Second, both the deposit of the Church's faith and celebration of her Eucharist are in conformity with the Apostles' faith.[24] Third, the Church and the Eucharist continue to exist and thrive through the Apostles' successors, the bishops and, with them, the Church's priests.[25]

Related to the apostolicity of the Eucharist is the Holy Father's teaching on "The Eucharist and Ecclesial Communion" in Chapter 4. Eucharistic communion and ecclesial communion go hand in hand. Not only must an "invisible communion"[26] exist—a communion of grace with God, free from sin, and a life of virtue—but a visible communion[27] with the external structures of the Church—with the bishop and pope, for example—must also be present for Eucharistic communion.

Chapter five, "The Dignity of the Eucharistic Celebration," has special interest to those who assist in the preparation of the liturgy. Reminding us of the Jewish and early Christian roots of today's Eucharistic celebrations, the Holy Father says that "*the Church has feared no 'extravagance,'* devoting the best of her resources to expressing her wonder and adoration before the *unsurpassable gift of the Eucharist.*"[28] Church art, architecture, and music not only serve worship but shape cultures themselves.[29]

The regulations safeguarding the outward forms of the Eucharistic celebration express and foster the unity of the Church and demonstrate our love for the Church born of the Eucharist. "No one is permitted," the pope says, "to undervalue the mystery entrusted to our hands: it is too great for anyone to feel free to treat it lightly and with disregard for its sacredness and its universality."[30]

A final chapter devoted to Mary, the "Woman of the Eucharist," gives the Church her model of Eucharistic faith and life. At Mary's school the Mother of

---

20. See ibid., 21.
21. See ibid., 22.
22. Ibid., 22.
23. See ibid., 27.
24. See ibid., 28.
25. Ibid.
26. Ibid., 36.
27. See ibid., 38.
28. Ibid., 48.
29. See ibid., 51.
30. Ibid., 52.

God teaches us to contemplate her Son's face.[31] What better teacher could there be? Mary embodied the same Christ that comes to us in the Sacrament. Her *fiat*, "Let it be done," is imitated by our "Amen" when receiving the Eucharistic Lord.[32] We become, like Mary, living tabernacles, taking the incarnate Christ into the world.[33]

A LITURGICAL MASTERPIECE: THE EUCHARISTIC FACE OF CHRIST

In recent years, liturgical celebration has been described as *ars celebrandi*, an "art of celebrating," and the Holy Spirit called "artisan of 'God's masterpieces,'"[34] the sacraments. This work of art is nothing other than the face of a person, "Christ himself, who is to be known, loved and imitated."[35]

What does the face of Jesus look like? While we may see only dimly at times, we are not the first to struggle. There were once two disciples on a road to Emmaus, and even though Jesus himself walked alongside them, they did not recognize him. But as he accompanied them on the road, a personal intimacy developed between them so that when they stopped, the disciples' eyes were opened and they recognized him "in the breaking of the bread."[36]

Pope John Paul's *Ecclesia de Eucharistia* helps us in the Church today to recognize that same Eucharistic face of the Risen Lord.

---

31. See ibid., 53.
32. See ibid., 55.
33. Ibid.
34. *Catechism of the Catholic Church* (CCC), 1091.
35. NMI, 29.
36. Luke 24:35.

OUTLINE

ECCLESIA DE EUCHARISTIA

ON THE EUCHARIST IN ITS RELATIONSHIP TO THE CHURCH

INTRODUCTION

1.   The Church draws her life from the Eucharist. This truth does not simply express a daily experience of faith, but recapitulates *the heart of the mystery of the Church*. In a variety of ways she joyfully experiences the constant fulfillment of the promise: "Lo, I am with you always, to the close of the age" (Matthew 28:20), but in the Holy Eucharist, through the changing of bread and wine into the body and blood of the Lord, she rejoices in this presence with unique intensity. Ever since Pentecost, when the Church, the People of the New Covenant, began her pilgrim journey towards her heavenly homeland, the Divine Sacrament has continued to mark the passing of her days, filling them with confident hope.

The Second Vatican Council rightly proclaimed that the Eucharistic sacrifice is "the source and summit of the Christian life."[1] "For the most holy Eucharist contains the Church's entire spiritual wealth: Christ himself, our passover and living bread. Through his own flesh, now made living and life-giving by the Holy Spirit, he offers life to men."[2] Consequently the gaze of the Church is constantly turned to her Lord, present in the Sacrament of the Altar, in which she discovers the full manifestation of his boundless love.

2.   During the Great Jubilee of the Year 2000 I had an opportunity to celebrate the Eucharist in the Cenacle of Jerusalem where, according to tradition, it was first celebrated by Jesus himself. *The Upper Room was where this most holy Sacrament was instituted.* It is there that Christ took bread, broke it and gave it to his disciples, saying: "Take this, all of you, and eat it: this is my body which will be given up for you" (cf. Mark 26:26; Luke 22:19; 1 Corinthians 11:24). Then he took the cup of wine and said to them: "Take this, all of you and drink from it: this is the cup of my blood, the blood of the new and everlasting covenant. It will be shed for you and for all, so that sins may be forgiven" (cf. Matthew 14:24; Luke 22:20; 1 Corinthians 11:25). I am grateful to the Lord Jesus for allowing me to repeat in that same place, in obedience to his command: "Do this in memory of me" (Luke 22:19), the words which he spoke two thousand years ago.

---

1. Second Vatican Ecumenical Council, Dogmatic Constitution on the Church *Lumen Gentium*, 11.

2. Second Vatican Ecumenical Council, Decree on the Ministry and Life of Priests *Presbyterorum Ordinis*, 5.

Did the Apostles who took part in the Last Supper understand the meaning of the words spoken by Christ? Perhaps not. Those words would only be fully clear at the end of the *Triduum sacrum*, the time from Thursday evening to Sunday morning. Those days embrace the *mysterium paschale*; they also embrace the *mysterium eucharisticum*.

3.   The Church was born of the paschal mystery. For this very reason the Eucharist, which is in an outstanding way the sacrament of the paschal mystery, *stands at the center of the Church's life*. This is already clear from the earliest images of the Church found in the Acts of the Apostles: "They devoted themselves to the Apostles' teaching and fellowship, to the breaking of bread and the prayers" (2:42). The "breaking of the bread" refers to the Eucharist. Two thousand years later, we continue to relive that primordial image of the Church. At every celebration of the Eucharist, we are spiritually brought back to the paschal Triduum: to the events of the evening of Holy Thursday, to the Last Supper and to what followed it. The institution of the Eucharist sacramentally anticipated the events which were about to take place, beginning with the agony in Gethsemane. Once again we see Jesus as he leaves the Upper Room, descends with his disciples to the Kidron valley and goes to the Garden of Olives. Even today that Garden shelters some very ancient olive trees. Perhaps they witnessed what happened beneath their shade that evening, when Christ in prayer was filled with anguish "and his sweat became like drops of blood falling down upon the ground" (cf. Luke 22:44). The blood which shortly before he had given to the Church as the drink of salvation in the sacrament of the Eucharist, *began to be shed*; its outpouring would then be completed on Golgotha to become the means of our redemption: "Christ . . . as high priest of the good things to come . . . entered once for all into the Holy Place, taking not the blood of goats and calves but his own blood, thus securing an eternal redemption" (Hebrews 9:11–12).

4.   *The hour of our redemption.* Although deeply troubled, Jesus does not flee before his "hour." "And what shall I say? 'Father, save me from this hour?' No, for this purpose I have come to this hour" (John 12:27). He wanted his disciples to keep him company, yet he had to experience loneliness and abandonment: "So, could you not watch with me one hour? Watch and pray that you may not enter into temptation" (Matthew 26:40–41). Only John would remain at the foot of the Cross, at the side of Mary and the faithful women. The agony in Gethsemane was the introduction to the agony of the Cross on Good Friday. *The holy hour,* the hour of the redemption of the world. Whenever the Eucharist is celebrated at the tomb of Jesus in Jerusalem, there is an almost tangible return to his "hour," the hour of his Cross and glorification. Every priest who celebrates Holy Mass, together with the Christian community which takes part in it, is led back in spirit to that place and that hour.

"*He was crucified, he suffered death and was buried; he descended to the dead; on the third day he rose again.*" The words of the profession of faith are echoed by the words of contemplation and proclamation: "*This is the wood of the Cross, on which hung the Savior of the world. Come, let us worship.*" This is the invitation which the Church extends to all in the afternoon hours of Good

Friday. She then takes up her song during the Easter season in order to proclaim: *"The Lord is risen from the tomb; for our sake he hung on the Cross, Alleluia."*

5.   *"Mysterium fidei!—The Mystery of Faith!"* When the priest recites or chants these words, all present acclaim: "We announce your death, O Lord, and we proclaim your resurrection, until you come in glory."

In these or similar words the Church, while pointing to Christ in the mystery of his passion, *also reveals her own mystery: Ecclesia de Eucharistia.* By the gift of the Holy Spirit at Pentecost the Church was born and set out upon the pathways of the world, yet a decisive moment in her taking shape was certainly the institution of the Eucharist in the Upper Room. Her foundation and wellspring is the whole *Triduum paschale,* but this is as it were gathered up, foreshadowed and "concentrated" for ever in the gift of the Eucharist. In this gift Jesus Christ entrusted to his Church the perennial making present of the paschal mystery. With it he brought about a mysterious "oneness in time" between that *Triduum* and the passage of the centuries.

The thought of this leads us to profound amazement and gratitude. In the paschal event and the Eucharist which makes it present throughout the centuries, there is a truly enormous "capacity" which embraces all of history as the recipient of the grace of the redemption. This amazement should always fill the Church assembled for the celebration of the Eucharist. But in a special way it should fill the minister of the Eucharist. For it is he who, by the authority given him in the sacrament of priestly ordination, effects the consecration. It is he who says with the power coming to him from Christ in the Upper Room: "This is my body which will be given up for you This is the cup of my blood, poured out for you . . . ." The priest says these words, or rather *he puts his voice at the disposal of the One who spoke these words in the Upper Room* and who desires that they should be repeated in every generation by all those who in the Church ministerially share in his priesthood.

6.   I would like to rekindle this Eucharistic "amazement" by the present Encyclical Letter, in continuity with the Jubilee heritage which I have left to the Church in the Apostolic Letter *Novo Millennio Ineunte* and its Marian crowning, *Rosarium Virginis Mariae.* To contemplate the face of Christ, and to contemplate it with Mary, is the "program" which I have set before the Church at the dawn of the third millennium, summoning her to put out into the deep on the sea of history with the enthusiasm of the new evangelization. To contemplate Christ involves being able to recognize him wherever he manifests himself, in his many forms of presence, but above all in the living sacrament of his body and his blood. *The Church draws her life from Christ in the Eucharist;* by him she is fed and by him she is enlightened. The Eucharist is both a mystery of faith and a "mystery of light."[3] Whenever the Church celebrates the Eucharist, the faithful can in some way relive the experience of the two disciples on the road to Emmaus: "their eyes were opened and they recognized him" (Luke 24:31).

---

3. Cf. John Paul II, Apostolic Letter *Rosarium Virginis Mariae* (16 October 2002), 21: AAS 95 (2003), 19.

7.   From the time I began my ministry as the Successor of Peter, I have always marked Holy Thursday, the day of the Eucharist and of the priesthood, by sending a letter to all the priests of the world. This year, the twenty-fifth of my Pontificate, I wish to involve the whole Church more fully in this Eucharistic reflection, also as a way of thanking the Lord for the gift of the Eucharist and the priesthood: "Gift and Mystery."[4] By proclaiming the Year of the Rosary, I wish to put this, my twenty-fifth anniversary, *under the aegis of the contemplation of Christ at the school of Mary.* Consequently, I cannot let this Holy Thursday 2003 pass without halting before the "Eucharistic face" of Christ and pointing out with new force to the Church the centrality of the Eucharist.

From it the Church draws her life. From this "living bread" she draws her nourishment. How could I not feel the need to urge everyone to experience it ever anew?

8.   When I think of the Eucharist, and look at my life as a priest, as a Bishop and as the Successor of Peter, I naturally recall the many times and places in which I was able to celebrate it. I remember the parish church of Niegowi, where I had my first pastoral assignment, the collegiate church of Saint Florian in Krakow, Wawel Cathedral, Saint Peter's Basilica and so many basilicas and churches in Rome and throughout the world. I have been able to celebrate Holy Mass in chapels built along mountain paths, on lakeshores and seacoasts; I have celebrated it on altars built in stadiums and in city squares . . . This varied scenario of celebrations of the Eucharist has given me a powerful experience of its universal and, so to speak, cosmic character. Yes, cosmic! Because even when it is celebrated on the humble altar of a country church, the Eucharist is always in some way celebrated *on the altar of the world.* It unites heaven and earth. It embraces and permeates all creation. The Son of God became man in order to restore all creation, in one supreme act of praise, to the One who made it from nothing. He, the Eternal High Priest who by the blood of his Cross entered the eternal sanctuary, thus gives back to the Creator and Father all creation redeemed. He does so through the priestly ministry of the Church, to the glory of the Most Holy Trinity. Truly this is the *mysterium fidei* which is accomplished in the Eucharist: the world which came forth from the hands of God the Creator now returns to him redeemed by Christ.

9.   The Eucharist, as Christ's saving presence in the community of the faithful and its spiritual food, is the most precious possession which the Church can have in her journey through history. This explains the *lively concern* which she has always shown for the Eucharistic mystery, a concern which finds authoritative expression in the work of the Councils and the Popes. How can we not admire the doctrinal expositions of the Decrees on the Most Holy Eucharist and on the Holy Sacrifice of the Mass promulgated by the Council of Trent? For centuries those Decrees guided theology and catechesis, and they are still a dogmatic reference-point for the continual renewal and growth of God's People in faith and in love for the Eucharist. In times closer to our own, three Encyclical

---

4. This is the title which I gave to an autobiographical testimony issued for my fiftieth anniversary of priestly ordination.

Letters should be mentioned: the Encyclical *Mirae Caritatis* of Leo XIII (28 May 1902),[5] the Encyclical *Mediator Dei* of Pius XII (20 November 1947)[6] and the Encyclical *Mysterium Fidei* of Paul VI (3 September 1965).[7]

The Second Vatican Council, while not issuing a specific document on the Eucharistic mystery, considered its various aspects throughout its documents, especially the Dogmatic Constitution on the Church *Lumen Gentium* and the Constitution on the Sacred Liturgy *Sacrosanctum Concilium*.

I myself, in the first years of my apostolic ministry in the Chair of Peter, wrote the Apostolic Letter *Dominicae Cenae* (24 February 1980),[8] in which I discussed some aspects of the Eucharistic mystery and its importance for the life of those who are its ministers. Today I take up anew the thread of that argument, with even greater emotion and gratitude in my heart, echoing as it were the word of the Psalmist: "What shall I render to the Lord for all his bounty to me? I will lift up the cup of salvation and call on the name of the Lord" (Psalm 116:12–13).

10.   The Magisterium's commitment to proclaiming the Eucharistic mystery has been matched by interior growth within the Christian community. Certainly *the liturgical reform inaugurated by the Council* has greatly contributed to a more conscious, active and fruitful participation in the Holy Sacrifice of the Altar on the part of the faithful. In many places, *adoration of the Blessed Sacrament* is also an important daily practice and becomes an inexhaustible source of holiness. The devout participation of the faithful in the Eucharistic procession on the Solemnity of the Body and Blood of Christ is a grace from the Lord which yearly brings joy to those who take part in it.

Other positive signs of Eucharistic faith and love might also be mentioned.

Unfortunately, alongside these lights, *there are also shadows*. In some places the practice of Eucharistic adoration has been almost completely abandoned. In various parts of the Church abuses have occurred, leading to confusion with regard to sound faith and Catholic doctrine concerning this wonderful sacrament. At times one encounters an extremely reductive understanding of the Eucharistic mystery. Stripped of its sacrificial meaning, it is celebrated as if it were simply a fraternal banquet. Furthermore, the necessity of the ministerial priesthood, grounded in apostolic succession, is at times obscured and the sacramental nature of the Eucharist is reduced to its mere effectiveness as a form of proclamation. This has led here and there to ecumenical initiatives which, albeit well-intentioned, indulge in Eucharistic practices contrary to the discipline by which the Church expresses her faith. How can we not express profound grief at all this? The Eucharist is too great a gift to tolerate ambiguity and depreciation.

It is my hope that the present Encyclical Letter will effectively help to banish the dark clouds of unacceptable doctrine and practice, so that the Eucharist will continue to shine forth in all its radiant mystery.

---

5. *Leonis XIII P.M. Acta*, XXII (1903), 115–136.

6. AAS 39 (1947), 521–595.

7. AAS 57 (1965), 753–774.

8. AAS 72 (1980), 113–148.

CHAPTER I
THE MYSTERY OF FAITH

11.   "The Lord Jesus on the night he was betrayed" (1 Corinthians 11:23) instituted the Eucharistic Sacrifice of his body and his blood. The words of the Apostle Paul bring us back to the dramatic setting in which the Eucharist was born. The Eucharist is indelibly marked by the event of the Lord's passion and death, of which it is not only a reminder but the sacramental re-presentation. It is the sacrifice of the Cross perpetuated down the ages.[9] This truth is well expressed by the words with which the assembly in the Latin rite responds to the priest's proclamation of the "Mystery of Faith": *We announce your death, O Lord.*"

The Church has received the Eucharist from Christ her Lord not as one gift—however precious—among so many others, but as *the gift par excellence*, for it is the gift of himself, of his person in his sacred humanity, as well as the gift of his saving work. Nor does it remain confined to the past, since "all that Christ is—all that he did and suffered for all men—participates in the divine eternity, and so transcends all times."[10]

When the Church celebrates the Eucharist, the memorial of her Lord's death and resurrection, this central event of salvation becomes really present and "the work of our redemption is carried out."[11] This sacrifice is so decisive for the salvation of the human race that Jesus Christ offered it and returned to the Father only *after he had left us a means of sharing in it* as if we had been present there. Each member of the faithful can thus take part in it and inexhaustibly gain its fruits. This is the faith from which generations of Christians down the ages have lived. The Church's Magisterium has constantly reaffirmed this faith with joyful gratitude for its inestimable gift.[12] I wish once more to recall this truth and to join you, my dear brothers and sisters, in adoration before this mystery: a great mystery, a mystery of mercy. What more could Jesus have done for us? Truly, in the Eucharist, he shows us a love which goes "to the end" (cf. John 13:1), a love which knows no measure.

12.   This aspect of the universal charity of the Eucharistic Sacrifice is based on the words of the Savior himself. In instituting it, he did not merely say: "This is my body," "this is my blood," but went on to add: "which is given for you," "which is poured out for you" (Luke 22:19–20). Jesus did not simply state that what he was giving them to eat and drink was his body and his blood; he also expressed *its sacrificial meaning* and made sacramentally present his sacrifice which would soon be offered on the Cross for the salvation of all. "The Mass is

---

9. Cf. Second Vatican Ecumenical Council, Constitution *Sacrosanctum Concilium*, 47: " . . . our Savior instituted the Eucharistic Sacrifice of his body and blood, in order to perpetuate the sacrifice of the Cross throughout time, until he should return."

10. Catechism of the Catholic Church, 1085.

11. Second Vatican Ecumenical Council, Dogmatic Constitution on the Church *Lumen Gentium*, 3.

12. Cf. Paul VI, *Solemn Profession of Faith*, 30 June 1968, 24: AAS 60 (1968), 442; John Paul II, Apostolic Letter *Dominicae Cenae* (24 February 1980), 12: AAS 72 (1980), 142.

at the same time, and inseparably, the sacrificial memorial in which the sacrifice of the Cross is perpetuated and the sacred banquet of communion with the Lord's body and blood."[13]

The Church constantly draws her life from the redeeming sacrifice; she approaches it not only through faith-filled remembrance, but also through a real contact, since *this sacrifice is made present ever anew*, sacramentally perpetuated, in every community which offers it at the hands of the consecrated minister. The Eucharist thus applies to men and women today the reconciliation won once for all by Christ for mankind in every age. "The sacrifice of Christ and the sacrifice of the Eucharist are *one single sacrifice*."[14] Saint John Chrysostom put it well: "We always offer the same Lamb, not one today and another tomorrow, but always the same one. For this reason the sacrifice is always only one . . . Even now we offer that victim who was once offered and who will never be consumed."[15]

The Mass makes present the sacrifice of the Cross; it does not add to that sacrifice nor does it multiply it.[16] What is repeated is its memorial celebration, its "commemorative representation" (*memorialis demonstratio*),[17] which makes Christ's one, definitive redemptive sacrifice always present in time. The sacrificial nature of the Eucharistic mystery cannot therefore be understood as something separate, independent of the Cross or only indirectly referring to the sacrifice of Calvary.

13.   By virtue of its close relationship to the sacrifice of Golgotha, the Eucharist is *a sacrifice in the strict sense*, and not only in a general way, as if it were simply a matter of Christ's offering himself to the faithful as their spiritual food. The gift of his love and obedience to the point of giving his life (cf. John 10:17–18) is in the first place a gift to his Father. Certainly it is a gift given for our sake, and indeed that of all humanity (cf. Matthew 26:28; Mark 14:24; Luke 22:20; John 10:15), yet it is *first and foremost a gift to the Father*: "a sacrifice that the Father accepted, giving, in return for this total self-giving by his Son, who 'became obedient unto death' (Philippians 2:8), his own paternal gift, that is to say the grant of new immortal life in the resurrection."[18]

In giving his sacrifice to the Church, Christ has also made his own the spiritual sacrifice of the Church, which is called to offer herself in union with the sacrifice of Christ. This is the teaching of the Second Vatican Council concerning all the faithful: "Taking part in the Eucharistic Sacrifice, which is the source and summit of the whole Christian life, they offer the divine victim to God, and offer themselves along with it."[19]

---

13. *Catechism of the Catholic Church*, 1382.
14. *Catechism of the Catholic Church*, 1367.
15. *In Epistolam ad Hebraeos Homiliae, Hom.* 17,3: PG 63, 131.
16. Cf. Ecumenical Council of Trent, Session XXII, *Doctrina de ss. Missae Sacrificio*, Chapter 2: DS 1743: "It is one and the same victim here offering himself by the ministry of his priests, who then offered himself on the Cross; it is only the manner of offering that is different."
17. Pius XII, Encyclical Letter *Mediator Dei* (20 November 1947): AAS 39 (1947), 548.
18. John Paul II, Encyclical Letter *Redemptor Hominis* (15 March 1979), 20: AAS 71 (1979), 310.
19. Dogmatic Constitution on the Church *Lumen Gentium*, 11.

14.   Christ's passover includes not only his passion and death, but also his resurrection. This is recalled by the assembly's acclamation following the consecration: *"We proclaim your resurrection."* The Eucharistic Sacrifice makes present not only the mystery of the Savior's passion and death, but also the mystery of the resurrection which crowned his sacrifice. It is as the living and risen One that Christ can become in the Eucharist the "bread of life" (John 6:35, 48), the "living bread" (John 6:51). Saint Ambrose reminded the newly-initiated that the Eucharist applies the event of the resurrection to their lives: "Today Christ is yours, yet each day he rises again for you."[20] Saint Cyril of Alexandria also makes clear that sharing in the sacred mysteries "is a true confession and a remembrance that the Lord died and returned to life for us and on our behalf."[21]

15.   The sacramental re-presentation of Christ's sacrifice, crowned by the resurrection, in the Mass involves a most special presence which—in the words of Paul VI—"is called 'real' not as a way of excluding all other types of presence as if they were 'not real,' but because it is a presence in the fullest sense: a substantial presence whereby Christ, the God-Man, is wholly and entirely present."[22] This sets forth once more the perennially valid teaching of the Council of Trent: "the consecration of the bread and wine effects the change of the whole substance of the bread into the substance of the body of Christ our Lord, and of the whole substance of the wine into the substance of his blood. And the holy Catholic Church has fittingly and properly called this change transubstantiation."[23] Truly the Eucharist is a *mysterium fidei*, a mystery which surpasses our understanding and can only be received in faith, as is often brought out in the catechesis of the Church Fathers regarding this divine sacrament: "Do not see—Saint Cyril of Jerusalem exhorts—in the bread and wine merely natural elements, because the Lord has expressly said that they are his body and his blood: faith assures you of this, though your senses suggest otherwise."[24]

Adoro te devote, latens Deitas, we shall continue to sing with the Angelic Doctor. Before this mystery of love, human reason fully experiences its limitations. One understands how, down the centuries, this truth has stimulated theology to strive to understand it ever more deeply.

These are praiseworthy efforts, which are all the more helpful and insightful to the extent that they are able to join critical thinking to the "living faith" of the Church, as grasped especially by the Magisterium's "sure charism of truth" and the "intimate sense of spiritual realities"[25] which is attained above all by the saints. There remains the boundary indicated by Paul VI: "Every theological explanation which seeks some understanding of this mystery, in order to be in accord with Catholic faith, must firmly maintain that in objective reality, independently of our mind, the bread and wine have ceased to exist after the

20. *De Sacramentis*, V, 4, 26: CSEL 73, 70.

21. *In Ioannis Evangelium*, XII, 20: PG 74, 726.

22. Encyclical Letter *Mysterium Fidei* (3 September 1965): AAS 57 (1965), 764.

23. Session XIII, *Decretum de ss. Eucharistia*, Chapter 4: DS 1642.

24. *Mystagogical Catecheses*, IV, 6: SCh 126, 138.

25. Second Vatican Ecumenical Council, Dogmatic Constitution on Divine Revelation *Dei Verbum*, 8.

consecration, so that the adorable body and blood of the Lord Jesus from that moment on are really before us under the sacramental species of bread and wine."[26]

16.   The saving efficacy of the sacrifice is fully realized when the Lord's body and blood are received in communion. The Eucharistic Sacrifice is intrinsically directed to the inward union of the faithful with Christ through communion; we receive the very One who offered himself for us, we receive his body which he gave up for us on the Cross and his blood which he "poured out for many for the forgiveness of sins" (Matthew 26:28). We are reminded of his words: "As the living Father sent me, and I live because of the Father, so he who eats me will live because of me" (John 6:57). Jesus himself reassures us that this union, which he compares to that of the life of the Trinity, is truly realized. *The Eucharist is a true banquet,* in which Christ offers himself as our nourishment. When for the first time Jesus spoke of this food, his listeners were astonished and bewildered, which forced the Master to emphasize the objective truth of his words: "Truly, truly, I say to you, unless you eat the flesh of the Son of Man and drink his blood, you have no life within you" (John 6:53). This is no metaphorical food: "My flesh is food indeed, and my blood is drink indeed" (John 6:55).

17.   Through our communion in his body and blood, Christ also grants us his Spirit. Saint Ephrem writes: "He called the bread his living body and he filled it with himself and his Spirit . . . .

He who eats it with faith, eats Fire and Spirit . . . . Take and eat this, all of you, and eat with it the Holy Spirit. For it is truly my body and whoever eats it will have eternal life."[27] The Church implores this divine Gift, the source of every other gift, in the Eucharistic epiclesis. In the *Divine Liturgy* of Saint John Chrysostom, for example, we find the prayer: "We beseech, implore and beg you: send your Holy Spirit upon us all and upon these gifts . . . that those who partake of them may be purified in soul, receive the forgiveness of their sins, and share in the Holy Spirit."[28] And in the *Roman Missal* the celebrant prays: "grant that we who are nourished by his body and blood may be filled with his Holy Spirit, and become one body, one spirit in Christ."[29] Thus by the gift of his body and blood Christ increases within us the gift of his Spirit, already poured out in Baptism and bestowed as a "seal" in the sacrament of Confirmation.

18.   The acclamation of the assembly following the consecration appropriately ends by expressing the eschatological thrust which marks the celebration of the Eucharist (cf. 1 Corinthians 11:26): *"until you come in glory."* The Eucharist is a straining towards the goal, a foretaste of the fullness of joy promised by Christ (cf. John 15:11); it is in some way the anticipation of heaven, the "pledge of future glory."[30] In the Eucharist, everything speaks of confident waiting "in joyful hope for the coming of our Savior, Jesus Christ."[31] Those who feed on Christ in the

---

26. *Solemn Profession of Faith,* 30 June 1968, 25: AAS 60 (1968), 442–443.

27. *Sermo IV in Hebdomadam Sanctam:* CSCO 413/Syr. 182, 55.

28. Anaphora.

29. Eucharistic Prayer III.

30. Solemnity of the Body and Blood of Christ, Second Vespers, Antiphon to the *Magnificat.*

31. *Missale Romanum,* Embolism following the Lord's Prayer.

Eucharist need not wait until the hereafter to receive eternal life: *they already possess it on earth,* as the first-fruits of a future fullness which will embrace man in his totality. For in the Eucharist we also receive the pledge of our bodily resurrection at the end of the world: "He who eats my flesh and drinks my blood has eternal life, and I will raise him up at the last day" (John 6:54). This pledge of the future resurrection comes from the fact that the flesh of the Son of Man, given as food, is his body in its glorious state after the resurrection. With the Eucharist we digest, as it were, the "secret" of the resurrection. For this reason Saint Ignatius of Antioch rightly defined the Eucharistic Bread as "a medicine of immortality, an antidote to death."[32]

19.   The eschatological tension kindled by the Eucharist *expresses and reinforces our communion with the Church in heaven.* It is not by chance that the Eastern Anaphoras and the Latin Eucharistic Prayers honor Mary, the ever-Virgin Mother of Jesus Christ our Lord and God, the angels, the holy apostles, the glorious martyrs and all the saints. This is an aspect of the Eucharist which merits greater attention: in celebrating the sacrifice of the Lamb, we are united to the heavenly "liturgy" and become part of that great multitude which cries out: "Salvation belongs to our God who sits upon the throne, and to the Lamb!" (Revelation 7:10). The Eucharist is truly a glimpse of heaven appearing on earth. It is a glorious ray of the heavenly Jerusalem which pierces the clouds of our history and lights up our journey.

20.   A significant consequence of the eschatological tension inherent in the Eucharist is also the fact that it spurs us on our journey through history and plants a seed of living hope in our daily commitment to the work before us. Certainly the Christian vision leads to the expectation of "new heavens" and "a new earth" (Revelation 21:1), but this increases, rather than lessens, *our sense of responsibility for the world today.*[33] I wish to reaffirm this forcefully at the beginning of the new millennium, so that Christians will feel more obliged than ever not to neglect their duties as citizens in this world. Theirs is the task of contributing with the light of the Gospel to the building of a more human world, a world fully in harmony with God's plan.

Many problems darken the horizon of our time. We need but think of the urgent need to work for peace, to base relationships between peoples on solid premises of justice and solidarity, and to defend human life from conception to its natural end. And what should we say of the thousand inconsistencies of a "globalized" world where the weakest, the most powerless and the poorest appear to have so little hope! It is in this world that Christian hope must shine forth! For this reason too, the Lord wished to remain with us in the Eucharist, making his presence in meal and sacrifice the promise of a humanity renewed by his love. Significantly, in their account of the Last Supper, the Synoptics recount the institution of the Eucharist, while the Gospel of John relates, as a way of bringing out its profound meaning, the account of the "washing of the feet," in which Jesus appears as the teacher of communion and of service (cf. John 13:1–20).

---

32. *Ad Ephesios,* 20: PG 5, 661.
33. Cf. Second Vatican Ecumenical Council, Pastoral Constitution on the Church in the Modern World *Gaudium et Spes,* 39.

The Apostle Paul, for his part, says that it is "unworthy" of a Christian community to partake of the Lord's Supper amid division and indifference towards the poor (cf. 1 Corinthians 11:17–22, 27–34).[34]

Proclaiming the death of the Lord "until he comes" (1 Corinthians 11:26) entails that all who take part in the Eucharist be committed to changing their lives and making them in a certain way completely "Eucharistic." It is this fruit of a transfigured existence and a commitment to transforming the world in accordance with the Gospel which splendidly illustrates the eschatological tension inherent in the celebration of the Eucharist and in the Christian life as a whole: "Come, Lord Jesus!" (Revelation 22:20).

CHAPTER II
THE EUCHARIST BUILDS THE CHURCH

21.   The Second Vatican Council teaches that the celebration of the Eucharist is at the center of the process of the Church's growth. After stating that "the Church, as the Kingdom of Christ already present in mystery, grows visibly in the world through the power of God."[35] Then, as if in answer to the question: "How does the Church grow?," the Council adds: "as often as the sacrifice of the Cross by which 'Christ our pasch is sacrificed' (1 Corinthians 5:7) is celebrated on the altar, the work of our redemption is carried out. At the same time in the sacrament of the Eucharistic bread, the unity of the faithful, who form one body in Christ (cf. 1 Corinthians 10:17), is both expressed and brought about."[36]

A causal influence of the Eucharist is present at the Church's very origins. The Evangelists specify that it was the Twelve, the Apostles, who gathered with Jesus at the Last Supper (cf. Matthew 26:20; Mark 14:17; Luke 22:14). This is a detail of notable importance, for the Apostles "were both the seeds of the new Israel and the beginning of the sacred hierarchy."[37] By offering them his body and his blood as food, Christ mysteriously involved them in the sacrifice which would be completed later on Calvary. By analogy with the Covenant of Mount Sinai, sealed by sacrifice and the sprinkling of blood,[38] the actions and words of Jesus at the Last Supper laid the foundations of the new messianic community, the People of the New Covenant.

---

34. "Do you wish to honor the body of Christ? Do not ignore him when he is naked. Do not pay him homage in the temple clad in silk, only then to neglect him outside where he is cold and ill-clad. He who said: 'This is my body' is the same who said: 'You saw me hungry and you gave me no food,' and 'Whatever you did to the least of my brothers you did also to me'. . . . What good is it if the Eucharistic table is overloaded with golden chalices when your brother is dying of hunger. Start by satisfying his hunger and then with what is left you may adorn the altar as well": Saint John Chrysostom, *In Evangelium S. Matthaei*, hom. 50:3–4: PG 58, 508–509; cf. John Paul II, Encyclical Letter *Sollicitudo Rei Socialis* (30 December 1987), 31: AAS 80 (1988), 553–556.

35. Dogmatic Constitution *Lumen Gentium*, 3.

36. *Ibid.*

37. Second Vatican Ecumenical Council, Decree on the Missionary Activity of the Church *Ad Gentes*, 5.

38. "Moses took the blood and threw it upon the people, and said: 'Behold the blood of the Covenant which the Lord has made with you in accordance with all these words'" (Exodus 24:8).

The Apostles, by accepting in the Upper Room Jesus' invitation: "Take, eat," "Drink of it, all of you" (Matthew 26:26–27), entered for the first time into sacramental communion with him. From that time forward, until the end of the age, the Church is built up through sacramental communion with the Son of God who was sacrificed for our sake: "Do this is remembrance of me . . . . Do this, as often as you drink it, in remembrance of me" (1 Corinthians 11:24–25; cf. Luke 22:19).

22.   Incorporation into Christ, which is brought about by Baptism, is constantly renewed and consolidated by sharing in the Eucharistic Sacrifice, especially by that full sharing which takes place in sacramental communion. We can say not only that *each of us receives Christ*, but also that *Christ receives each of us*. He enters into friendship with us: "You are my friends" (John 15:14). Indeed, it is because of him that we have life: "He who eats me will live because of me" (John 6:57). Eucharistic communion brings about in a sublime way the mutual "abiding" of Christ and each of his followers: "Abide in me, and I in you" (John 15:4).

By its union with Christ, the People of the New Covenant, far from closing in upon itself, becomes a "sacrament" for humanity,[39] a sign and instrument of the salvation achieved by Christ, the light of the world and the salt of the earth (cf. Matthew 5:13–16), for the redemption of all.[40] The Church's mission stands in continuity with the mission of Christ: "As the Father has sent me, even so I send you" (John 20:21). From the perpetuation of the sacrifice of the Cross and her communion with the body and blood of Christ in the Eucharist, the Church draws the spiritual power needed to carry out her mission. The Eucharist thus appears as both *the source* and *the summit* of all evangelization, since its goal is the communion of mankind with Christ and in him with the Father and the Holy Spirit.[41]

23.   Eucharistic communion also confirms the Church in her unity as the body of Christ. Saint Paul refers to this *unifying power* of participation in the banquet of the Eucharist when he writes to the Corinthians: "The bread which we break, is it not a communion in the body of Christ? Because there is one bread, we who are many are one body, for we all partake of the one bread" (1 Corinthians 10:16–17). Saint John Chrysostom's commentary on these words is profound and perceptive: "For what is the bread? It is the body of Christ. And what do those who receive it become? The Body of Christ—not many bodies but one body. For as bread is completely one, though made of up many grains of wheat, and these, albeit unseen, remain nonetheless present, in such a way that their difference is not apparent since they have been made a perfect whole, so too are we mutually joined to one another and together united with Christ."[42] The argument is

---

39. Cf. Second Vatican Ecumenical Council, Dogmatic Constitution on the Church *Lumen Gentium*, 1.

40. Cf. *ibid.*, 9.

41. Cf. Second Vatican Ecumenical Council, Decree on the Life and Ministry of Priests *Presbyterorum Ordinis*, 5. The same Decree, in No. 6, says: "No Christian community can be built up which does not grow from and hinge on the celebration of the most holy Eucharist."

42. *In Epistolam I ad Corinthios Homiliae*, 24, 2: PG 61, 200; cf. *Didache*, IX, 4: F.X. Funk, I, 22; Saint Cyprian, *Ep.* LXIII, 13: PL 4, 384.

compelling: our union with Christ, which is a gift and grace for each of us, makes it possible for us, in him, to share in the unity of his body which is the Church. The Eucharist reinforces the incorporation into Christ which took place in Baptism though the gift of the Spirit (cf. 1 Corinthians 12:13, 27).

The joint and inseparable activity of the Son and of the Holy Spirit, which is at the origin of the Church, of her consolidation and her continued life, is at work in the Eucharist. This was clearly evident to the author of the *Liturgy of Saint James:* in the epiclesis of the Anaphora, God the Father is asked to send the Holy Spirit upon the faithful and upon the offerings, so that the body and blood of Christ "may be a help to all those who partake of it . . . for the sanctification of their souls and bodies."[43] The Church is fortified by the divine Paraclete through the sanctification of the faithful in the Eucharist.

24. The gift of Christ and his Spirit which we receive in Eucharistic communion superabundantly fulfils the yearning for fraternal unity deeply rooted in the human heart; at the same time it elevates the experience of fraternity already present in our common sharing at the same Eucharistic table to a degree which far surpasses that of the simple human experience of sharing a meal. Through her communion with the body of Christ the Church comes to be ever more profoundly "in Christ in the nature of a sacrament, that is, a sign and instrument of intimate unity with God and of the unity of the whole human race."[44]

The seeds of disunity, which daily experience shows to be so deeply rooted in humanity as a result of sin, are countered by *the unifying power* of the body of Christ. The Eucharist, precisely by building up the Church, creates human community.

25. The *worship of the Eucharist outside of the Mass* is of inestimable value for the life of the Church. This worship is strictly linked to the celebration of the Eucharistic Sacrifice. The presence of Christ under the sacred species reserved after Mass—a presence which lasts as long as the species of bread and of wine remain[45]—derives from the celebration of the sacrifice and is directed towards communion, both sacramental and spiritual.[46] It is the responsibility of Pastors to encourage, also by their personal witness, the practice of Eucharistic adoration, and exposition of the Blessed Sacrament in particular, as well as prayer of adoration before Christ present under the Eucharistic species.[47]

It is pleasant to spend time with him, to lie close to his breast like the Beloved Disciple (cf. John 13:25) and to feel the infinite love present in his heart.

---

43. PO 26, 206.

44. Second Vatican Ecumenical Council, Dogmatic Constitution on the Church *Lumen Gentium,* 1.

45. Cf. Ecumenical Council of Trent, Session XIII, *Decretum de ss. Eucharistia,* Canon 4: DS 1654.

46. Cf. *Rituale Romanum: De sacra communione et de cultu mysterii eucharistici extra Missam,* 36 (No. 80).

47. Cf. *ibid.,* 38–39 (Nos. 86–90).

If in our time Christians must be distinguished above all by the "art of prayer,"[48] how can we not feel a renewed need to spend time in spiritual converse, in silent adoration, in heartfelt love before Christ present in the Most Holy Sacrament? How often, dear brother and sisters, have I experienced this, and drawn from it strength, consolation and support!

This practice, repeatedly praised and recommended by the Magisterium,[49] is supported by the example of many saints. Particularly outstanding in this regard was Saint Alphonsus Liguori, who wrote: "Of all devotions, that of adoring Jesus in the Blessed Sacrament is the greatest after the sacraments, the one dearest to God and the one most helpful to us."[50] The Eucharist is a priceless treasure: by not only celebrating it but also by praying before it outside of Mass we are enabled to make contact with the very wellspring of grace. A Christian community desirous of contemplating the face of Christ in the spirit which I proposed in the Apostolic Letters *Novo Millennio Ineunte* and *Rosarium Virginis Mariae* cannot fail also to develop this aspect of Eucharistic worship, which prolongs and increases the fruits of our communion in the body and blood of the Lord.

CHAPTER III
THE APOSTOLICITY OF
THE EUCHARIST AND OF THE CHURCH

26.   If, as I have said, the Eucharist builds the Church and the Church makes the Eucharist, it follows that there is a profound relationship between the two, so much so that we can apply to the Eucharistic mystery the very words with which, in the Nicene-Constantinopolitan Creed, we profess the Church to be "one, holy, catholic and apostolic." The Eucharist too is one and catholic. It is also holy, indeed, the Most Holy Sacrament. But it is above all its apostolicity that we must now consider.

27.   The Catechism of the Catholic Church, in explaining how the Church is apostolic—founded on the Apostles—sees *three meanings* in this expression. First, "she was and remains built on 'the foundation of the Apostles' (Ephesians 2:20), the witnesses chosen and sent on mission by Christ himself."[51] The Eucharist too has its foundation in the Apostles, not in the sense that it did not originate in Christ himself, but because it was entrusted by Jesus to the Apostles and has been handed down to us by them and by their successors. It is in continuity with the practice of the Apostles, in obedience to the Lord's command, that the Church has celebrated the Eucharist down the centuries.

---

48. John Paul II, Apostolic Letter *Novo Millennio Ineunte* (6 January 2001), 32: AAS 93 (2001), 288.

49. "In the course of the day the faithful should not omit visiting the Blessed Sacrament, which in accordance with liturgical law must be reserved in churches with great reverence in a prominent place. Such visits are a sign of gratitude, an expression of love and an acknowledgment of the Lord's presence": Paul VI, Encyclical Letter *Mysterium Fidei* (3 September 1965): AAS 57 (1965), 771.

50. *Visite al SS. Sacramento e a Maria Santissima,* Introduction: Opere Ascetiche, Avellino, 2000, 295.

51. No. 857.

The second sense in which the Church is apostolic, as the *Catechism* points out, is that "with the help of the Spirit dwelling in her, the Church keeps and hands on the teaching, the 'good deposit,' the salutary words she has heard from the Apostles."[52] Here too the Eucharist is apostolic, for it is celebrated in conformity with the faith of the Apostles. At various times in the two-thousand-year history of the People of the New Covenant, the Church's Magisterium has more precisely defined her teaching on the Eucharist, including its proper terminology, precisely in order to safeguard the apostolic faith with regard to this sublime mystery. This faith remains unchanged and it is essential for the Church that it remain unchanged.

28. Lastly, the Church is apostolic in the sense that she "continues to be taught, sanctified and guided by the Apostles until Christ's return, through their successors in pastoral office: the college of Bishops assisted by priests, in union with the Successor of Peter, the Church's supreme pastor."[53] Succession to the Apostles in the pastoral mission necessarily entails the sacrament of Holy Orders, that is, the uninterrupted sequence, from the very beginning, of valid episcopal ordinations.[54] This succession is essential for the Church to exist in a proper and full sense.

The Eucharist also expresses this sense of apostolicity. As the Second Vatican Council teaches, "the faithful join in the offering of the Eucharist by virtue of their royal priesthood,"[55] yet it is the ordained priest who, "acting in the person of Christ, brings about the Eucharistic Sacrifice and offers it to God in the name of all the people."[56] For this reason, the *Roman Missal* prescribes that only the priest should recite the Eucharistic Prayer, while the people participate in faith and in silence.[57]

29. The expression repeatedly employed by the Second Vatican Council, according to which "the ministerial priest, acting in the person of Christ, brings about the Eucharistic Sacrifice."[58] was already firmly rooted in papal teaching.[59] As I have pointed out on other occasions, the phrase *in persona Christi* "means more than offering 'in the name of' or 'in the place of' Christ. *In persona* means in specific sacramental identification with the eternal High Priest who is the author and principal subject of this sacrifice of his, a sacrifice in which, in truth,

---

52. *Ibid.*

53. *Ibid.*

54. Cf. Congregation for the Doctrine of the Faith, Letter *Sacerdotium Ministeriale* (6 August 1983), III.2: AAS 75 (1983), 1005.

55. Second Vatican Ecumenical Council, Dogmatic Constitution on the Church *Lumen Gentium*, 10.

56. *Ibid.*

57. Cf. *Institutio Generalis:* Editio typica tertia, No. 147.

58. Cf. Dogmatic Constitution on the Church *Lumen Gentium*, 10 and 28; Decree on the Ministry and Life of Priests *Presbyterorum Ordinis*, 2.

59. "The minister of the altar acts in the person of Christ inasmuch as he is head, making an offering in the name of all the members": Pius XII, Encyclical Letter *Mediator Dei* (20 November 1947): AAS 39 (1947), 556; cf. Pius X, Apostolic Exhortation *Haerent Animo* (4 August 1908): *Acta Pii X*, IV, 16; Pius XI, Encyclical Letter *Ad Catholici Sacerdotii* (20 December 1935): AAS 28 (1936), 20.

nobody can take his place."[60] The ministry of priests who have received the sacrament of Holy Orders, in the economy of salvation chosen by Christ, makes clear that the Eucharist which they celebrate is *a gift which radically transcends the power of the assembly* and is in any event essential for validly linking the Eucharistic consecration to the sacrifice of the Cross and to the Last Supper. The assembly gathered together for the celebration of the Eucharist, if it is to be a truly Eucharistic assembly, absolutely requires the presence of an ordained priest as its president. On the other hand, the community is by itself incapable of providing an ordained minister. This minister is a gift which the assembly *receives through episcopal succession going back to the Apostles.* It is the Bishop who, through the Sacrament of Holy Orders, makes a new presbyter by conferring upon him the power to consecrate the Eucharist. Consequently, "the Eucharistic mystery cannot be celebrated in any community except by an ordained priest, as the Fourth Lateran Council expressly taught."[61]

30.   The Catholic Church's teaching on the relationship between priestly ministry and the Eucharist and her teaching on the Eucharistic Sacrifice have both been the subject in recent decades of a fruitful dialogue *in the area of ecumenism.* We must give thanks to the Blessed Trinity for the significant progress and convergence achieved in this regard, which lead us to hope one day for a full sharing of faith. Nonetheless, the observations of the Council concerning the Ecclesial Communities which arose in the West from the sixteenth century onwards and are separated from the Catholic Church remain fully pertinent: "The Ecclesial Communities separated from us lack that fullness of unity with us which should flow from Baptism, and we believe that especially because of the lack of the sacrament of Orders they have not preserved the genuine and total reality of the Eucharistic mystery. Nevertheless, when they commemorate the Lord's death and resurrection in the Holy Supper, they profess that it signifies life in communion with Christ and they await his coming in glory."[62]

The Catholic faithful, therefore, while respecting the religious convictions of these separated brethren, must refrain from receiving the communion distributed in their celebrations, so as not to condone an ambiguity about the nature of the Eucharist and, consequently, to fail in their duty to bear clear witness to the truth. This would result in slowing the progress being made towards full visible unity. Similarly, it is unthinkable to substitute for Sunday Mass ecumenical celebrations of the word or services of common prayer with Christians from the aforementioned Ecclesial Communities, or even participation in their own liturgical services. Such celebrations and services, however praiseworthy in certain situations, prepare for the goal of full communion, including Eucharistic communion, but they cannot replace it.

The fact that the power of consecrating the Eucharist has been entrusted only to Bishops and priests does not represent any kind of belittlement of the

---

60. Apostolic Letter *Dominicae Cenae* (24 February 1980), 8: AAS 72 (1980), 128–129.

61. Congregation for the Doctrine of the Faith, Letter *Sacerdotium Ministeriale* (6 August 1983), III.4: AAS 75 (1983), 1006; cf. Fourth Lateran Ecumenical Council, Chapter 1, Constitution on the Catholic Faith *Firmiter Credimus:* DS 802.

62. Second Vatican Ecumenical Council, Decree on Ecumenism *Unitatis Redintegratio*, 22.

rest of the People of God, for in the communion of the one body of Christ which is the Church this gift redounds to the benefit of all.

31.   If the Eucharist is the center and summit of the Church's life, it is likewise the center and summit of priestly ministry. For this reason, with a heart filled with gratitude to our Lord Jesus Christ, I repeat that the Eucharist "is the principal and central *raison d'être* of the sacrament of priesthood, which effectively came into being at the moment of the institution of the Eucharist."[63]

Priests are engaged in a wide variety of pastoral activities. If we also consider the social and cultural conditions of the modern world it is easy to understand how priests face the very real *risk of losing their focus* amid such a great number of different tasks. The Second Vatican Council saw in pastoral charity the bond which gives unity to the priest's life and work. This, the Council adds, "flows mainly from the Eucharistic Sacrifice, which is therefore the center and root of the whole priestly life."[64] We can understand, then, how important it is for the spiritual life of the priest, as well as for the good of the Church and the world, that priests follow the Council's recommendation to celebrate the Eucharist daily: "for even if the faithful are unable to be present, it is an act of Christ and the Church."[65] In this way priests will be able to counteract the daily tensions which lead to a lack of focus and they will find in the Eucharistic Sacrifice—the true center of their lives and ministry—the spiritual strength needed to deal with their different pastoral responsibilities. Their daily activity will thus become truly Eucharistic.

The centrality of the Eucharist in the life and ministry of priests is the basis of its centrality in the *pastoral promotion of priestly vocations*. It is in the Eucharist that prayer for vocations is most closely united to the prayer of Christ the Eternal High Priest. At the same time the diligence of priests in carrying out their Eucharistic ministry, together with the conscious, active and fruitful participation of the faithful in the Eucharist, provides young men with a powerful example and incentive for responding generously to God's call. Often it is the example of a priest's fervent pastoral charity which the Lord uses to sow and to bring to fruition in a young man's heart the seed of a priestly calling.

32.   All of this shows how distressing and irregular is the situation of a Christian community which, despite having sufficient numbers and variety of faithful to form a parish, does not have a priest to lead it. Parishes are communities of the baptized who express and affirm their identity above all through the celebration of the Eucharistic Sacrifice. But this requires the presence of a presbyter, who alone is qualified to offer the Eucharist *in persona Christi*. When a community lacks a priest, attempts are rightly made somehow to remedy the situation so that it can continue its Sunday celebrations, and those religious and laity who lead their brothers and sisters in prayer exercise in a praiseworthy way the common priesthood of all the faithful based on the grace of Baptism. But such solutions must be considered merely temporary, while the community awaits a priest.

---

63. Apostolic Letter *Dominicae Cenae* (24 February 1980), 2: AAS 72 (1980), 115.

64. Decree on the Life and Ministry of Priests *Presbyterorum Ordinis*, 14.

65. Ibid., 13; cf. *Code of Canon Law*, Canon 904; *Code of Canons of the Eastern Churches*, Canon 378.

The sacramental incompleteness of these celebrations should above all inspire the whole community to pray with greater fervor that the Lord will send laborers into his harvest (cf. Matthew 9:38). It should also be an incentive to mobilize all the resources needed for an adequate pastoral promotion of vocations, without yielding to the temptation to seek solutions which lower the moral and formative standards demanded of candidates for the priesthood.

33.   When, due to the scarcity of priests, non-ordained members of the faithful are entrusted with a share in the pastoral care of a parish, they should bear in mind that—as the Second Vatican Council teaches—"no Christian community can be built up unless it has its basis and center in the celebration of the most Holy Eucharist."[66] They have a responsibility, therefore, to keep alive in the community a genuine "hunger" for the Eucharist, so that no opportunity for the celebration of Mass will ever be missed, also taking advantage of the occasional presence of a priest who is not impeded by Church law from celebrating Mass.

CHAPTER IV
THE EUCHARIST AND ECCLESIAL COMMUNION

34.   The Extraordinary Assembly of the Synod of Bishops in 1985 saw in the concept of an "ecclesiology of communion" the central and fundamental idea of the documents of the Second Vatican Council.[67] The Church is called during her earthly pilgrimage to maintain and promote communion with the Triune God and communion among the faithful. For this purpose she possesses the word and the sacraments, particularly the Eucharist, by which she "constantly lives and grows"[68] and in which she expresses her very nature. It is not by chance that the term *communion* has become one of the names given to this sublime sacrament.

The Eucharist thus appears as the culmination of all the sacraments in perfecting our communion with God the Father by identification with his only-begotten Son through the working of the Holy Spirit. With discerning faith a distinguished writer of the Byzantine tradition voiced this truth: in the Eucharist "unlike any other sacrament, the mystery [of communion] is so perfect that it brings us to the heights of every good thing: here is the ultimate goal of every human desire, because here we attain God and God joins himself to us in the most perfect union."[69] Precisely for this reason it is good to *cultivate in our hearts a constant desire for the sacrament of the Eucharist.* This was the origin of the practice of "spiritual communion," which has happily been established in the Church for centuries and recommended by saints who were masters of the spiritual life. Saint Teresa of Jesus wrote: "When you do not receive communion and you do not attend Mass, you can make a spiritual communion, which is a most beneficial practice; by it the love of God will be greatly impressed on you."[70]

---

66. Decree on the Ministry and Life of Priests *Presbyterorum Ordinis*, 6.

67. Cf. Final Report, II.C.1: *L'Osservatore Romano*, 10 December 1985, 7.

68. Second Vatican Ecumenical Council, Dogmatic Constitution on the Church *Lumen Gentium*, 26.

69. Nicolas Cabasilas, *Life in Christ*, IV, 10: SCh 355, 270.

70. *Camino de Perfección*, Chapter 35.

35.   The celebration of the Eucharist, however, cannot be the starting-point for communion; it presupposes that communion already exists, a communion which it seeks to consolidate and bring to perfection. The sacrament is an expression of this bond of communion both in its *invisible* dimension, which, in Christ and through the working of the Holy Spirit, unites us to the Father and among ourselves, and in its *visible* dimension, which entails communion in the teaching of the Apostles, in the sacraments and in the Church's hierarchical order. The profound relationship between the invisible and the visible elements of ecclesial communion is constitutive of the Church as the sacrament of salvation.[71] Only in this context can there be a legitimate celebration of the Eucharist and true participation in it. Consequently it is an intrinsic requirement of the Eucharist that it should be celebrated in communion, and specifically maintaining the various bonds of that communion intact.

36.   Invisible communion, though by its nature always growing, presupposes the life of grace, by which we become "partakers of the divine nature" (2 Peter 1:4), and the practice of the virtues of faith, hope and love. Only in this way do we have true communion with the Father, the Son and the Holy Spirit. Nor is faith sufficient; we must persevere in sanctifying grace and love, remaining within the Church "bodily" as well as "in our heart";[72] what is required, in the words of Saint Paul, is "faith working through love" (Galatians 5:6).

Keeping these invisible bonds intact is a specific moral duty incumbent upon Christians who wish to participate fully in the Eucharist by receiving the body and blood of Christ. The Apostle Paul appeals to this duty when he warns: "Let a man examine himself, and so eat of the bread and drink of the cup" (1 Corinthians 11:28). Saint John Chrysostom, with his stirring eloquence, exhorted the faithful: "I too raise my voice, I beseech, beg and implore that no one draw near to this sacred table with a sullied and corrupt conscience. Such an act, in fact, can never be called 'communion,' not even were we to touch the Lord's body a thousand times over, but 'condemnation,' 'torment' and 'increase of punishment.'"[73]

Along these same lines, the Catechism of the Catholic Church rightly stipulates that "anyone conscious of a grave sin must receive the sacrament of Reconciliation before coming to communion."[74] I therefore desire to reaffirm that in the Church there remains in force, now and in the future, the rule by which the Council of Trent gave concrete expression to the Apostle Paul's stern warning when it affirmed that, in order to receive the Eucharist in a worthy manner, "one must first confess one's sins, when one is aware of mortal sin."[75]

---

71. Cf. Congregation for the Doctrine of the Faith, Letter to the Bishops of the Catholic Church on Some Aspects of the Church Understood as Communion *Communionis Notio* (28 May 1992), 4: AAS 85 (1993), 839–840.

72. Cf. Second Vatican Ecumenical Council, Dogmatic Constitution on the Church *Lumen Gentium*, 14.

73. *Homiliae in Isaiam*, 6, 3: PG 56, 139.

74. No. 1385; cf. *Code of Canon Law*, Canon 916; *Code of Canons of the Eastern Churches*, Canon 711.

75. Address to the Members of the Sacred Apostolic Penitentiary and the Penitentiaries of the Patriarchal Basilicas of Rome (30 January 1981): AAS 73 (1981), 203. Cf. Ecumenical Council of Trent, Sess. XIII, *Decretum de ss. Eucharistia*, Chapter 7 and Canon 11: DS 1647, 1661.

37.   The two sacraments of the Eucharist and Penance are very closely connected. Because the Eucharist makes present the redeeming sacrifice of the Cross, perpetuating it sacramentally, it naturally gives rise to a continuous need for conversion, for a personal response to the appeal made by Saint Paul to the Christians of Corinth: "We beseech you on behalf of Christ, be reconciled to God" (2 Corinthians 5:20). If a Christian's conscience is burdened by serious sin, then the path of penance through the sacrament of Reconciliation becomes necessary for full participation in the Eucharistic Sacrifice.

The judgment of one's state of grace obviously belongs only to the person involved, since it is a question of examining one's conscience. However, in cases of outward conduct which is seriously, clearly and steadfastly contrary to the moral norm, the Church, in her pastoral concern for the good order of the community and out of respect for the sacrament, cannot fail to feel directly involved. The *Code of Canon Law* refers to this situation of a manifest lack of proper moral disposition when it states that those who "obstinately persist in manifest grave sin" are not to be admitted to Eucharistic communion.[76]

38.   Ecclesial communion, as I have said, is likewise *visible*, and finds expression in the series of "bonds" listed by the Council when it teaches: "They are fully incorporated into the society of the Church who, possessing the Spirit of Christ, accept her whole structure and all the means of salvation established within her, and within her visible framework are united to Christ, who governs her through the Supreme Pontiff and the Bishops, by the bonds of profession of faith, the sacraments, ecclesiastical government and communion."[77]

The Eucharist, as the supreme sacramental manifestation of communion in the Church, demands to be celebrated in *a context where the outward bonds of communion are also intact*. In a special way, since the Eucharist is "as it were the summit of the spiritual life and the goal of all the sacraments,"[78] it requires that the bonds of communion in the sacraments, particularly in Baptism and in priestly Orders, be real. It is not possible to give communion to a person who is not baptized or to one who rejects the full truth of the faith regarding the Eucharistic mystery. Christ is the truth and he bears witness to the truth (cf. John 14:6; 18:37); the sacrament of his body and blood does not permit duplicity.

39.   Furthermore, given the very nature of ecclesial communion and its relation to the sacrament of the Eucharist, it must be recalled that "the Eucharistic Sacrifice, while always offered in a particular community, is never a celebration of that community alone. In fact, the community, in receiving the Eucharistic presence of the Lord, receives the entire gift of salvation and shows, even in its lasting visible particular form, that it is the image and true presence of the one, holy, catholic and apostolic Church."[79] From this it follows that a truly

---

76. Canon 915; *Code of Canons of the Eastern Churches*, Canon 712.

77. Dogmatic Constitution on the Church *Lumen Gentium*, 14.

78. Saint Thomas Aquinas, *Summa Theologiae*, III, q. 73, a. 3c.

79. Congregation for the Doctrine of the Faith, Letter to the Bishops of the Catholic Church on Some Aspects of the Church Understood as Communion *Communionis Notio* (28 May 1992), 11: AAS 85 (1993), 844.

Eucharistic community cannot be closed in upon itself, as though it were somehow self-sufficient; rather it must persevere in harmony with every other Catholic community.

The ecclesial communion of the Eucharistic assembly is a communion with its own *Bishop* and with the *Roman Pontiff*. The Bishop, in effect, is the *visible* principle and the foundation of unity within his particular Church.[80] It would therefore be a great contradiction if the sacrament *par excellence* of the Church's unity were celebrated without true communion with the Bishop. As Saint Ignatius of Antioch wrote: "That Eucharist which is celebrated under the Bishop, or under one to whom the Bishop has given this charge, may be considered certain."[81] Likewise, since "the Roman Pontiff, as the successor of Peter, is the perpetual and visible source and foundation of the unity of the Bishops and of the multitude of the faithful,"[82] communion with him is intrinsically required for the celebration of the Eucharistic Sacrifice. Hence the great truth expressed which the Liturgy expresses in a variety of ways: "Every celebration of the Eucharist is performed in union not only with the proper Bishop, but also with the Pope, with the episcopal order, with all the clergy, and with the entire people. Every valid celebration of the Eucharist expresses this universal communion with Peter and with the whole Church, or objectively calls for it, as in the case of the Christian Churches separated from Rome."[83]

40.   The Eucharist *creates communion* and *fosters communion*. Saint Paul wrote to the faithful of Corinth explaining how their divisions, reflected in their Eucharistic gatherings, contradicted what they were celebrating, the Lord's Supper. The Apostle then urged them to reflect on the true reality of the Eucharist in order to return to the spirit of fraternal communion (cf. 1 Corinthians 11:17–34). Saint Augustine effectively echoed this call when, in recalling the Apostle's words: "You are the body of Christ and individually members of it" (1 Corinthians 12:27), he went on to say: "If you are his body and members of him, then you will find set on the Lord's table your own mystery. Yes, you receive your own mystery."[84] And from this observation he concludes: "Christ the Lord . . . hallowed at his table the mystery of our peace and unity. Whoever receives the mystery of unity without preserving the bonds of peace receives not a mystery for his benefit but evidence against himself."[85]

41.   The Eucharist's particular effectiveness in promoting communion is one of the reasons for the importance of Sunday Mass. I have already dwelt on this and on the other reasons which make Sunday Mass fundamental for the life of

---

80. Cf. Second Vatican Ecumenical Council, Dogmatic Constitution on the Church *Lumen Gentium*, 23.

81. *Ad Smyrnaeos*, 8: PG 5, 713.

82. Second Vatican Ecumenical Council, Dogmatic Constitution on the Church *Lumen Gentium*, 23.

83. Congregation for the Doctrine of the Faith, Letter to the Bishops of the Catholic Church on Some Aspects of the Church Understood as Communion *Communionis Notio* (28 May 1992), 14: AAS 85 (1993), 847.

84. *Sermo* 272: PL 38, 1247.

85. *Ibid.*, 1248.

the Church and of individual believers in my Apostolic Letter on the sanctification of Sunday *Dies Domini*,[86] There I recalled that the faithful have the obligation to attend Mass, unless they are seriously impeded, and that Pastors have the corresponding duty to see that it is practical and possible for all to fulfill this precept.[87] More recently, in my Apostolic Letter *Novo Millennio Ineunte*, in setting forth the pastoral path which the Church must take at the beginning of the third millennium, I drew particular attention to the Sunday Eucharist, emphasizing its effectiveness for building communion. "It is"—I wrote—"the privileged place where communion is ceaselessly proclaimed and nurtured. Precisely through sharing in the Eucharist, *the Lord's Day* also becomes *the Day of the Church*, when she can effectively exercise her role as the sacrament of unity."[88]

42. The safeguarding and promotion of ecclesial communion is a task of each member of the faithful, who finds in the Eucharist, as the sacrament of the Church's unity, an area of special concern. More specifically, this task is the particular responsibility of the Church's Pastors, each according to his rank and ecclesiastical office. For this reason the Church has drawn up norms aimed both at fostering the frequent and fruitful access of the faithful to the Eucharistic table and at determining the objective conditions under which communion may not be given. The care shown in promoting the faithful observance of these norms becomes a practical means of showing love for the Eucharist and for the Church.

43. In considering the Eucharist as the sacrament of ecclesial communion, there is one subject which, due to its importance, must not be overlooked: I am referring to the *relationship of the Eucharist to ecumenical activity*. We should all give thanks to the Blessed Trinity for the many members of the faithful throughout the world who in recent decades have felt an ardent desire for unity among all Christians. The Second Vatican Council, at the beginning of its Decree on Ecumenism, sees this as a special gift of God.[89] It was an efficacious grace which inspired us, the sons and daughters of the Catholic Church and our brothers and sisters from other Churches and Ecclesial Communities, to set forth on the path of ecumenism.

Our longing for the goal of unity prompts us to turn to the Eucharist, which is the supreme sacrament of the unity of the People of God, in as much as it is the apt expression and the unsurpassable source of that unity.[90] In the celebration of the Eucharistic Sacrifice the Church prays that God, the Father of mercies, will grant his children the fullness of the Holy Spirit so that they may become one body and one spirit in Christ.[91] In raising this prayer to the Father of lights, from whom comes every good endowment and every perfect gift (cf. James 1:17), the Church believes that she will be heard, for she prays in union

---

86. Cf. Nos. 31-51: AAS 90 (1998), 731–746.

87. Cf. *ibid.*, Nos. 48–49: AAS 90 (1998), 744.

88. No. 36: AAS 93 (2001), 291–292.

89. Cf. Decree on Ecumenism *Unitatis Redintegratio*, 1.

90. Cf. Dogmatic Constitution on the Church *Lumen Gentium*, 11.

91. "Join all of us, who share the one bread and the one cup, to one another in the communion of the one Holy Spirit": *Anaphora of the Liturgy of Saint Basil*.

with Christ her Head and Spouse, who takes up this plea of his Bride and joins it to that of his own redemptive sacrifice.

44.   Precisely because the Church's unity, which the Eucharist brings about through the Lord's sacrifice and by communion in his body and blood, absolutely requires full communion in the bonds of the profession of faith, the sacraments and ecclesiastical governance, it is not possible to celebrate together the same Eucharistic liturgy until those bonds are fully re-established. Any such concelebration would not be a valid means, and might well prove instead to be *an obstacle, to the attainment of full communion,* by weakening the sense of how far we remain from this goal and by introducing or exacerbating ambiguities with regard to one or another truth of the faith. The path towards full unity can only be undertaken in truth. In this area, the prohibitions of Church law leave no room for uncertainty,[92] in fidelity to the moral norm laid down by the Second Vatican Council.[93]

I would like nonetheless to reaffirm what I said in my Encyclical Letter *Ut Unum Sint* after having acknowledged the impossibility of Eucharistic sharing: "And yet we do have a burning desire to join in celebrating the one Eucharist of the Lord, and this desire itself is already a common prayer of praise, a single supplication. Together we speak to the Father and increasingly we do so 'with one heart.'"[94]

45.   While it is never legitimate to concelebrate in the absence of full communion, the same is not true with respect to the administration of the Eucharist *under special circumstances, to individual persons* belonging to Churches or Ecclesial Communities not in full communion with the Catholic Church. In this case, in fact, the intention is to meet a grave spiritual need for the eternal salvation of an individual believer, not to bring about an *intercommunion* which remains impossible until the visible bonds of ecclesial communion are fully re-established.

This was the approach taken by the Second Vatican Council when it gave guidelines for responding to Eastern Christians separated in good faith from the Catholic Church, who spontaneously ask to receive the Eucharist from a Catholic minister and are properly disposed.[95] This approach was then ratified by both Codes, which also consider—with necessary modifications—the case of other non-Eastern Christians who are not in full communion with the Catholic Church.[96]

---

92. Cf. *Code of Canon Law,* Canon 908; *Code of Canons of the Eastern Churches,* Canon 702; Pontifical Council for the Promotion of Christian Unity, *Ecumenical Directory,* 25 March 1993, 122–125, 129–131: AAS 85 (1993), 1086–1089; Congregation for the Doctrine of the Faith, Letter *Ad Exsequendam,* 18 May 2001: AAS 93 (2001), 786.

93. "Divine law forbids any common worship which would damage the unity of the Church, or involve formal acceptance of falsehood or the danger of deviation in the faith, of scandal, or of indifferentism": Decree on the Eastern Catholic Churches *Orientalium Ecclesiarum,* 26.

94. No. 45: AAS 87 (1995), 948.

95. Decree on the Eastern Catholic Churches *Orientalium Ecclesiarum,* 27.

96. Cf. *Code of Canon Law,* Canon 844 §§ 3–4; *Code of Canons of the Eastern Churches,* Canon 671 §§ 3–4.

46.   In my Encyclical *Ut Unum Sint* I expressed my own appreciation of these norms, which make it possible to provide for the salvation of souls with proper discernment: "It is a source of joy to note that Catholic ministers are able, in certain particular cases, to administer the sacraments of the Eucharist, Penance and Anointing of the Sick to Christians who are not in full communion with the Catholic Church but who greatly desire to receive these sacraments, freely request them and manifest the faith which the Catholic Church professes with regard to these sacraments. Conversely, in specific cases and in particular circumstances, Catholics too can request these same sacraments from ministers of Churches in which these sacraments are valid."[97]

These conditions, from which no dispensation can be given, must be carefully respected, even though they deal with specific individual cases, because the denial of one or more truths of the faith regarding these sacraments and, among these, the truth regarding the need of the ministerial priesthood for their validity, renders the person asking improperly disposed to legitimately receiving them. And the opposite is also true: Catholics may not receive communion in those communities which lack a valid sacrament of Orders.[98]

The faithful observance of the body of norms established in this area[99] is a manifestation and, at the same time, a guarantee of our love for Jesus Christ in the Blessed Sacrament, for our brothers and sisters of different Christian confessions—who have a right to our witness to the truth—and for the cause itself of the promotion of unity.

CHAPTER V
THE DIGNITY OF THE EUCHARISTIC CELEBRATION

47.   Reading the account of the institution of the Eucharist in the Synoptic Gospels, we are struck by the simplicity and the "solemnity" with which Jesus, on the evening of the Last Supper, instituted this great sacrament. There is an episode which in some way serves as its prelude: *the anointing at Bethany*. A woman, whom John identifies as Mary the sister of Lazarus, pours a flask of *costly ointment* over Jesus' head, which provokes from the disciples—and from Judas in particular (cf. Matthew 26:8; Mark 14:4; John 12:4)—an indignant response, as if this act, in light of the needs of the poor, represented an intolerable "waste." But Jesus' own reaction is completely different. While in no way detracting from the duty of charity towards the needy, for whom the disciples must always show special care—"the poor you will always have with you" (Matthew 26, 11; Mark 14:7; cf. John 12:8)—he looks towards his imminent death and burial, and sees this act of anointing as an anticipation of the honor which his body will continue to merit even after his death, indissolubly bound as it is to the mystery of his person.

The account continues, in the Synoptic Gospels, with Jesus' charge to the disciples to *prepare carefully the "large upper room"* needed for the Passover meal (cf. Mark 14:15; Luke 22:12) and with the narration of the institution of the

---

97. No. 46: AAS 87 (1995), 948.

98. Cf. Second Vatican Ecumenical Council, Decree on Ecumenism *Unitatis Redintegratio*, 22.

99. *Code of Canon Law*, Canon 844; *Code of Canons of the Eastern Churches*, Canon 671.

Eucharist. Reflecting at least in part the *Jewish rites* of the Passover meal leading up to the singing of the Hallel (cf. Matthew 26:30; Mark 14:26), the story presents with sobriety and solemnity, even in the variants of the different traditions, the words spoken by Christ over the bread and wine, which he made into concrete expressions of the handing over of his body and the shedding of his blood. All these details are recorded by the Evangelists in the light of a praxis of the "breaking of the bread" already well-established in the early Church. But certainly from the time of Jesus on, the event of Holy Thursday has shown visible traces of a liturgical "sensibility" shaped by Old Testament tradition and open to being reshaped in Christian celebrations in a way consonant with the new content of Easter.

48.   Like the woman who anointed Jesus in Bethany, *the Church has feared no "extravagance,"* devoting the best of her resources to expressing her wonder and adoration before the *unsurpassable gift of the Eucharist.* No less than the first disciples charged with preparing the "large upper room," she has felt the need, down the centuries and in her encounters with different cultures, to celebrate the Eucharist in a setting worthy of so great a mystery. In the wake of Jesus' own words and actions, and building upon the ritual heritage of Judaism, the *Christian liturgy was born.* Could there ever be an adequate means of expressing the acceptance of that self-gift which the divine Bridegroom continually makes to his Bride, the Church, by bringing the Sacrifice offered once and for all on the Cross to successive generations of believers and thus becoming nourishment for all the faithful? Though the idea of a "banquet" naturally suggests familiarity, the Church has never yielded to the temptation to trivialize this "intimacy" with her Spouse by forgetting that he is also her Lord and that the "banquet" always remains a sacrificial banquet marked by the blood shed on Golgotha. *The Eucharistic Banquet is truly a "sacred" banquet,* in which the simplicity of the signs conceals the unfathomable holiness of God: *O sacrum convivium, in quo Christus sumitur!* The bread which is broken on our altars, offered to us as wayfarers along the paths of the world, is *panis angelorum,* the bread of angels, which cannot be approached except with the humility of the centurion in the Gospel: "Lord, I am not worthy to have you come under my roof" (Matthew 8:8; Luke 7:6).

49.   With this heightened sense of mystery, we understand how the faith of the Church in the mystery of the Eucharist has found historical expression not only in the demand for an interior disposition of devotion, but also *in outward forms* meant to evoke and emphasize the grandeur of the event being celebrated. This led progressively to the development of *a particular form of regulating the Eucharistic liturgy,* with due respect for the various legitimately constituted ecclesial traditions. On this foundation *a rich artistic heritage* also developed. Architecture, sculpture, painting and music, moved by the Christian mystery, have found in the Eucharist, both directly and indirectly, a source of great inspiration.

Such was the case, for example, with architecture, which witnessed the transition, once the historical situation made it possible, from the first places of Eucharistic celebration in the *domus* or "homes" of Christian families to the solemn *basilicas* of the early centuries, to the imposing *cathedrals* of the Middle

Ages, and to the *churches*, large and small, which gradually sprang up throughout the lands touched by Christianity. The designs of altars and tabernacles within Church interiors were often not simply motivated by artistic inspiration but also by a clear understanding of the mystery. The same could be said for *sacred music*, if we but think of the inspired Gregorian melodies and the many, often great, composers who sought to do justice to the liturgical texts of the Mass. Similarly, can we overlook the enormous quantity of *artistic production*, ranging from fine craftsmanship to authentic works of art, in the area of Church furnishings and vestments used for the celebration of the Eucharist?

It can be said that the Eucharist, while shaping the Church and her spirituality, has also powerfully affected "culture," and the arts in particular.

50. In this effort to adore the mystery grasped in its ritual and aesthetic dimensions, a certain "competition" has taken place between Christians of the West and the East. How could we not give particular thanks to the Lord for the contributions to Christian art made by the great architectural and artistic works of the Greco-Byzantine tradition and of the whole geographical area marked by Slav culture? In the East, sacred art has preserved a remarkably powerful sense of mystery, which leads artists to see their efforts at creating beauty not simply as an expression of their own talents, but also as *a genuine service to the faith*. Passing well beyond mere technical skill, they have shown themselves docile and open to the inspiration of the Holy Spirit.

The architectural and mosaic splendors of the Christian East and West are a patrimony belonging to all believers; they contain a hope, and even a pledge, of the desired fullness of communion in faith and in celebration. This would presuppose and demand, as in Rublëv's famous depiction of the Trinity, *a profoundly Eucharistic Church* in which the presence of the mystery of Christ in the broken bread is as it were immersed in the ineffable unity of the three divine Persons, making of the Church herself an "icon" of the Trinity.

Within this context of an art aimed at expressing, in all its elements, the meaning of the Eucharist in accordance with the Church's teaching, attention needs to be given to the norms regulating *the construction and decor of sacred buildings*. As history shows and as I emphasized in my Letter to Artists,[100] the Church has always left ample room for the creativity of artists. But sacred art must be outstanding for its ability to express adequately the mystery grasped in the fullness of the Church's faith and in accordance with the pastoral guidelines appropriately laid down by competent Authority. This holds true both for the figurative arts and for sacred music.

51. The development of sacred art and liturgical discipline which took place in lands of ancient Christian heritage is also taking place *on continents where Christianity is younger*. This was precisely the approach supported by the Second Vatican Council on the need for sound and proper "inculturation." In my numerous Pastoral Visits I have seen, throughout the world, the great vitality which the celebration of the Eucharist can have when marked by the forms, styles and

---

100. Cf. AAS 91 (1999), 1155–1172.

sensibilities of different cultures. By adaptation to the changing conditions of time and place, the Eucharist offers sustenance not only to individuals but to entire peoples, and it shapes cultures inspired by Christianity.

It is necessary, however, that this important work of adaptation be carried out with a constant awareness of the ineffable mystery against which every generation is called to measure itself. The "treasure" is too important and precious to risk impoverishment or compromise through forms of experimentation or practices introduced without a careful review on the part of the competent ecclesiastical authorities. Furthermore, the centrality of the Eucharistic mystery demands that any such review must be undertaken in close association with the Holy See. As I wrote in my Post-Synodal Apostolic Exhortation Ecclesia in Asia, "such cooperation is essential because the Sacred Liturgy expresses and celebrates the one faith professed by all and, being the heritage of the whole Church, cannot be determined by local Churches in isolation from the universal Church."[101]

52.   All of this makes clear the great responsibility which belongs to priests in particular for the celebration of the Eucharist. It is their responsibility to preside at the Eucharist *in persona Christi* and to provide a witness to and a service of communion not only for the community directly taking part in the celebration, but also for the universal Church, which is a part of every Eucharist. It must be lamented that, especially in the years following the post-conciliar liturgical reform, as a result of a misguided sense of creativity and adaptation there have been a number of *abuses* which have been a source of suffering for many. A certain reaction against "formalism" has led some, especially in certain regions, to consider the "forms" chosen by the Church's great liturgical tradition and her Magisterium as non-binding and to introduce unauthorized innovations which are often completely inappropriate.

I consider it my duty, therefore to appeal urgently that the liturgical norms for the celebration of the Eucharist be observed with great fidelity. These norms are a concrete expression of the authentically ecclesial nature of the Eucharist; this is their deepest meaning. Liturgy is never anyone's private property, be it of the celebrant or of the community in which the mysteries are celebrated. The Apostle Paul had to address fiery words to the community of Corinth because of grave shortcomings in their celebration of the Eucharist resulting in divisions (*schismata*) and the emergence of factions (*haireseis*) (cf. 1 Corinthians 11:17–34). Our time, too, calls for a renewed awareness and appreciation of liturgical norms as a reflection of, and a witness to, the one universal Church made present in every celebration of the Eucharist. Priests who faithfully celebrate Mass according to the liturgical norms, and communities which conform to those norms, quietly but eloquently demonstrate their love for the Church. Precisely to bring out more clearly this deeper meaning of liturgical norms, I have asked the competent offices of the Roman Curia to prepare a more specific document, including prescriptions of a juridical nature, on this very important subject. No one is permitted to undervalue the mystery entrusted to our hands: it is too great for anyone to feel free to treat it lightly and with disregard for its sacredness and its universality.

---

101. No. 22: AAS 92 (2000), 485.

CHAPTER VI
AT THE SCHOOL OF MARY, "WOMAN OF THE EUCHARIST"

53.   If we wish to rediscover in all its richness the profound relationship between the Church and the Eucharist, we cannot neglect Mary, Mother and model of the Church. In my Apostolic Letter *Rosarium Virginis Mariae*, I pointed to the Blessed Virgin Mary as our teacher in contemplating Christ's face, and among the mysteries of light I included *the institution of the Eucharist*.[102] Mary can guide us towards this most holy sacrament, because she herself has a profound relationship with it.

At first glance, the Gospel is silent on this subject. The account of the institution of the Eucharist on the night of Holy Thursday makes no mention of Mary. Yet we know that she was present among the Apostles who prayed "with one accord" (cf. Acts 1:14) *in the first community which gathered after the Ascension in expectation of Pentecost*. Certainly Mary must have been present at the Eucharistic celebrations of the first generation of Christians, who were devoted to "the breaking of bread" (Acts 2:42).

But in addition to her sharing in the Eucharistic banquet, an indirect picture of Mary's relationship with the Eucharist can be had, beginning with her interior disposition. *Mary is a "woman of the Eucharist" in her whole life.* The Church, which looks to Mary as a model, is also called to imitate her in her relationship with this most holy mystery.

54.   *Mysterium fidei!* If the Eucharist is a mystery of faith which so greatly transcends our understanding as to call for sheer abandonment to the word of God, then there can be no one like Mary to act as our support and guide in acquiring this disposition. In repeating what Christ did at the Last Supper in obedience to his command: "Do this in memory of me!" we also accept Mary's invitation to obey him without hesitation: "Do whatever he tells you" (John 2:5). With the same maternal concern which she showed at the wedding feast of Cana, Mary seems to say to us: "Do not waver; trust in the words of my Son. If he was able to change water into wine, he can also turn bread and wine into his body and blood, and through this mystery bestow on believers the living memorial of his passover, thus becoming the 'bread of life.'"

55.   In a certain sense Mary lived her *Eucharistic faith* even before the institution of the Eucharist, by the very fact that *she offered her virginal womb for the Incarnation of God's Word*. The Eucharist, while commemorating the passion and resurrection, is also in continuity with the incarnation. At the Annunciation Mary conceived the Son of God in the physical reality of his body and blood, thus anticipating within herself what to some degree happens sacramentally in every believer who receives, under the signs of bread and wine, the Lord's body and blood.

As a result, there is a profound analogy between the *Fiat* which Mary said in reply to the angel, and the *Amen* which every believer says when receiving the body of the Lord. Mary was asked to believe that the One whom she conceived

---

102. Cf. No. 21: AAS 95 (2003), 20.

"through the Holy Spirit" was "the Son of God" (Luke 1:30–35). In continuity with the Virgin's faith, in the Eucharistic mystery we are asked to believe that the same Jesus Christ, Son of God and Son of Mary, becomes present in his full humanity and divinity under the signs of bread and wine.

"Blessed is she who believed" (Luke 1:45). Mary also anticipated, in the mystery of the incarnation, the Church's Eucharistic faith. When, at the Visitation, she bore in her womb the Word made flesh, she became in some way a "tabernacle"—the first "tabernacle" in history—in which the Son of God, still invisible to our human gaze, allowed himself to be adored by Elizabeth, radiating his light as it were through the eyes and the voice of Mary. And is not the enraptured gaze of Mary as she contemplated the face of the newborn Christ and cradled him in her arms that unparalleled model of love which should inspire us every time we receive Eucharistic communion?

56. Mary, throughout her life at Christ's side and not only on Calvary, made her own *the sacrificial dimension of the Eucharist*. When she brought the child Jesus to the Temple in Jerusalem "to present him to the Lord" (Luke 2:22), she heard the aged Simeon announce that the child would be a "sign of contradiction" and that a sword would also pierce her own heart (cf. Luke 2:34–35). The tragedy of her Son's crucifixion was thus foretold, and in some sense Mary's *Stabat Mater* at the foot of the Cross was foreshadowed. In her daily preparation for Calvary, Mary experienced a kind of "anticipated Eucharist"—one might say a "spiritual communion"—of desire and of oblation, which would culminate in her union with her Son in his passion, and then find expression after Easter by her partaking in the Eucharist which the Apostles celebrated as the memorial of that passion.

What must Mary have felt as she heard from the mouth of Peter, John, James and the other Apostles the words spoken at the Last Supper: "This is my body which is given for you" (Luke 22:19)? The body given up for us and made present under sacramental signs was the same body which she had conceived in her womb! For Mary, receiving the Eucharist must have somehow meant welcoming once more into her womb that heart which had beat in unison with hers and reliving what she had experienced at the foot of the Cross.

57. "Do this in remembrance of me" (Luke 22:19). In the "memorial" of Calvary all that Christ accomplished by his passion and his death is present. Consequently *all that Christ did with regard to his Mother* for our sake is also present. To her he gave the beloved disciple and, in him, each of us: "Behold, your Son!" To each of us he also says: "Behold your mother!" (cf. John 19:26–27).

Experiencing the memorial of Christ's death in the Eucharist also means continually receiving this gift. It means accepting—like John—the one who is given to us anew as our Mother. It also means taking on a commitment to be conformed to Christ, putting ourselves at the school of his Mother and allowing her to accompany us. Mary is present, with the Church and as the Mother of the Church, at each of our celebrations of the Eucharist. If the Church and the Eucharist are inseparably united, the same ought to be said of Mary and the Eucharist. This is one reason why, since ancient times, the commemoration of

Mary has always been part of the Eucharistic celebrations of the Churches of East and West.

58. In the Eucharist the Church is completely united to Christ and his sacrifice, and makes her own the spirit of Mary. This truth can be understood more deeply by *re-reading the Magnificat* in a Eucharistic key. The Eucharist, like the Canticle of Mary, is first and foremost praise and thanksgiving. When Mary exclaims: "My soul magnifies the Lord and my spirit rejoices in God my Savior," she already bears Jesus in her womb. She praises God "through" Jesus, but she also praises him "in" Jesus and "with" Jesus. This is itself the true "Eucharistic attitude."

At the same time Mary recalls the wonders worked by God in salvation history in fulfillment of the promise once made to the fathers (cf. Luke 1:55), and proclaims the wonder that surpasses them all, the redemptive incarnation. Lastly, the *Magnificat* reflects the eschatological tension of the Eucharist. Every time the Son of God comes again to us in the "poverty" of the sacramental signs of bread and wine, the seeds of that new history wherein the mighty are "put down from their thrones" and "those of low degree are exalted" (cf. Luke 1:52), take root in the world. Mary sings of the "new heavens" and the "new earth" which find in the Eucharist their anticipation and in some sense their program and plan. The *Magnificat* expresses Mary's spirituality, and there is nothing greater than this spirituality for helping us to experience the mystery of the Eucharist. The Eucharist has been given to us so that our life, like that of Mary, may become completely a *Magnificat*!

CONCLUSION

59. *Ave, verum corpus natum de Maria Virgine!* Several years ago I celebrated the fiftieth anniversary of my priesthood. Today I have the grace of offering the Church this Encyclical on the Eucharist on the Holy Thursday which falls *during the twenty-fifth year of my Petrine ministry*. As I do so, my heart is filled with gratitude. For over a half century, every day, beginning on 2 November 1946, when I celebrated my first Mass in the Crypt of Saint Leonard in Wawel Cathedral in Krakow, my eyes have gazed in recollection upon the host and the chalice, where time and space in some way "merge" and the drama of Golgotha is re-presented in a living way, thus revealing its mysterious "contemporaneity." Each day my faith has been able to recognize in the consecrated bread and wine the divine Wayfarer who joined the two disciples on the road to Emmaus and opened their eyes to the light and their hearts to new hope (cf. Luke 24:13–35).

Allow me, dear brothers and sisters, to share with deep emotion, as a means of accompanying and strengthening your faith, my own testimony of faith in the Most Holy Eucharist. *Ave verum corpus natum de Maria Virgine, vere passum, immolatum, in cruce pro homine!* Here is the Church's treasure, the heart of the world, the pledge of the fulfillment for which each man and woman, even unconsciously, yearns. A great and transcendent mystery, indeed, and one that taxes our mind's ability to pass beyond appearances. Here our senses fail us: *visus, tactus, gustus in te fallitur*, in the words of the hymn *Adoro Te Devote*; yet faith alone, rooted in the word of Christ handed down to us by the Apostles, is sufficient for us. Allow me, like Peter at the end of the Eucharistic discourse in John's Gospel, to say once more to Christ, in the name of the whole Church and in the name of each of you: "Lord to whom shall we go? You have the words of eternal life" (John 6:68).

60.   At the dawn of this third millennium, we, the children of the Church, are called to undertake with renewed enthusiasm the journey of Christian living. As I wrote in my Apostolic Letter *Novo Millennio Ineunte*, "it is not a matter of inventing a 'new program.' The program already exists: it is the plan found in the Gospel and in the living Tradition; it is the same as ever. Ultimately, it has its center in Christ himself, who is to be known, loved and imitated, so that in him we may live the life of the Trinity, and with him transform history until its fulfillment in the heavenly Jerusalem."[103] The implementation of this program of a renewed impetus in Christian living passes through the Eucharist.

Every commitment to holiness, every activity aimed at carrying out the Church's mission, every work of pastoral planning, must draw the strength it needs from the Eucharistic mystery and in turn be directed to that mystery as its culmination. In the Eucharist we have Jesus, we have his redemptive sacrifice, we have his resurrection, we have the gift of the Holy Spirit, we have adoration, obedience and love of the Father. Were we to disregard the Eucharist, how could we overcome our own deficiency?

61.   The mystery of the Eucharist—sacrifice, presence, banquet—*does not allow for reduction or exploitation*; it must be experienced and lived in its integrity, both in its celebration and in the intimate converse with Jesus which takes place after receiving communion or in a prayerful moment of Eucharistic adoration apart from Mass. These are times when the Church is firmly built up and it becomes clear what she truly is: one, holy, catholic and apostolic; the people, temple and family of God; the body and bride of Christ, enlivened by the Holy Spirit; the universal sacrament of salvation and a hierarchically structured communion.

The path taken by the Church in these first years of the third millennium is also a *path of renewed ecumenical commitment*. The final decades of the second millennium, culminating in the Great Jubilee, have spurred us along this path and called for all the baptized to respond to the prayer of Jesus *"ut unum sint"* (John 17:11). The path itself is long and strewn with obstacles greater than our human resources alone can overcome, yet we have the Eucharist, and in its presence we can hear in the depths of our hearts, as if they were addressed to us, the same words heard by the Prophet Elijah: "Arise and eat, else the journey will be too great for you" (1 Kings 19:7). The treasure of the Eucharist, which the Lord places before us, impels us towards the goal of full sharing with all our brothers and sisters to whom we are joined by our common Baptism. But if this treasure is not to be squandered, we need to respect the demands which derive from its being the sacrament of communion in faith and in apostolic succession.

By giving the Eucharist the prominence it deserves, and by being careful not to diminish any of its dimensions or demands, we show that we are truly

---

103. No. 29: AAS 93 (2001), 285.

conscious of the greatness of this gift. We are urged to do so by an uninterrupted tradition, which from the first centuries on has found the Christian community ever vigilant in guarding this "treasure." Inspired by love, the Church is anxious to hand on to future generations of Christians, without loss, her faith and teaching with regard to the mystery of the Eucharist. There can be no danger of excess in our care for this mystery, for "in this sacrament is recapitulated the whole mystery of our salvation."[104]

62.   Let us take our place, dear brothers and sisters, *at the school of the saints*, who are the great interpreters of true Eucharistic piety. In them the theology of the Eucharist takes on all the splendor of a lived reality; it becomes "contagious" and, in a manner of speaking, it "warms our hearts." Above all, let us *listen to Mary Most Holy*, in whom the mystery of the Eucharist appears, more than in anyone else, as *a mystery of light*. Gazing upon Mary, we come to *know the transforming power present in the Eucharist*. In her we see the world renewed in love. Contemplating her, assumed body and soul into heaven, we see opening up before us those "new heavens" and that "new earth" which will appear at the second coming of Christ. Here below, the Eucharist represents their pledge, and in a certain way, their anticipation: *"Veni, Domine Iesu!"* (Revelation 22:20).

In the humble signs of bread and wine, changed into his body and blood, Christ walks beside us as our strength and our food for the journey, and he enables us to become, for everyone, witnesses of hope. If, in the presence of this mystery, reason experiences its limits, the heart, enlightened by the grace of the Holy Spirit, clearly sees the response that is demanded, and bows low in adoration and unbounded love.

Let us make our own the words of Saint Thomas Aquinas, an eminent theologian and an impassioned poet of Christ in the Eucharist, and turn in hope to the contemplation of that goal to which our hearts aspire in their thirst for joy and peace:

> *Bone pastor, panis vere,*
> *Iesu, nostri Miserere . . .*
>
> *Come then, good Shepherd, bread divine,*
> *Still show to us thy mercy sign;*
> *Oh, feed us, still keep us thine;*
> *So we may see thy glories shine*
> *in fields of immortality.*
>
> *O thou, the wisest, mightiest, best,*
> *Our present food, our future rest,*
> *Come, make us each thy chosen guest,*
> *Co-heirs of thine, and comrades blest*
> *With saints whose dwelling is with thee.*

Given in Rome, at Saint Peter's, on 17 April, Holy Thursday, in the year 2003, the twenty-fifth of my Pontificate, the Year of the Rosary.

Ioannes Paulus II

---

104. Saint Thomas Aquinas, *Summa Theologiae*, III, q. 83, a. 4c.

REDEMPTIONIS SACRAMENTUM

ON CERTAIN MATTERS TO BE OBSERVED
OR TO BE AVOIDED REGARDING
THE MOST HOLY EUCHARIST

CONGREGATION FOR DIVINE WORSHIP AND
THE DISCIPLINE OF THE SACRAMENTS

INSTRUCTION
MARCH 19, 2004

AN OVERVIEW OF *REDEMPTIONIS SACRAMENTUM: ON CERTAIN MATTERS TO BE OBSERVED OR TO BE AVOIDED REGARDING THE MOST HOLY EUCHARIST*

Rev. Daniel J. Merz

On Holy Thursday, 2003, Pope John Paul II signed his fourteenth encyclical, *Ecclesia de Eucharistia* (EE), which included a paragraph calling upon the appropriate Roman Congregations to prepare and publish an instruction, "including prescriptions of a juridical nature" explaining the "deeper meaning of liturgical norms" in the light of liturgical abuses in violation of those same norms.[1] Less than a year later, on March 19, 2004, the Congregation for Divine Worship and the Discipline of the Sacraments (CDWDS), after significant consultation with the Congregation for the Doctrine of the Faith (CDF), published the instruction, *Redemptionis sacramentum* (RS).

The title for the instruction is taken from the Prayer over the Offerings in the Votive Mass for "The Mercy of God" as found in the third edition of *The Roman Missal*.

> Receive in your kindness, O Lord,
> the offerings of your servants
> and transform them into the **Sacrament of redemption. . . .**[2]

LEVEL OF AUTHORITY

An instruction seeks to "clarify the prescripts of laws and elaborate on and determine the methods to be observed in fulfilling them."[3] Issued in *forma commune* (as opposed to in *forma specifica*), it remains a document of the Congregation and not of the Holy Father himself. This means that *Redemptionis sacramentum* should be understood as binding norms for interpreting and carrying out the liturgical laws, which themselves are found in *The General Instruction of the Roman Missal* (GIRM) and the *praenotanda* of the liturgical books, as well as the rubrics within those books. The instruction makes no change in already existing liturgical law.

IS IT WORTHWHILE?

The instruction is intended to be read as a companion to the pope's encyclical letter, *Ecclesia de Eucharistia* (EE), in which John Paul II sought "to banish the dark clouds of unacceptable doctrine and practice, so that the Eucharist will

---

1. *Ecclesia de Eucharistia* (EE), 52.
2. Emphasis added.
3. *Code of Canon Law* (CIC), §34.1.

continue to shine forth in all its radiant mystery."[4] *Redemptionis sacramentum*, then, is the practical follow-up to the more theological encyclical. The positive vision for the sacred mysteries is given in the *praenotanda* of the liturgical books, and so the instruction limits itself primarily to an exhortation against abuses, calling for fidelity to the liturgical norms and the tradition of the Church. It often reads as the Congregation's response to an accumulated list of reported liturgical irregularities. In the course of its pages, however, the positive vision of the liturgy is never far away. It is less a warning document than a call to care for the Eucharist with love, and to respect its form and shape as determined by the Magisterium. Both the encyclical and the instruction presume that the majority of liturgical abuses are not ill-intentioned, but rather manifestations of misconceptions or personal tastes or beliefs that differ from the norms. In that light, the goal of the instruction is to move pastors and the faithful beyond personal desires. The model is the self-offering of Christ, who gave himself wholeheartedly to the will of his Father. Members of the Church should similarly strive to celebrate the liturgy wholeheartedly, as it has been handed on by the Magisterium.

This is not to say that there is only "one way" of celebrating the Roman Rite. Indeed, what is unique about the Roman Rite is the extraordinary number of adaptations that can be made for the sake of different circumstances, customs, and cultures. Being Roman, however, also means that it is Rome who has final judgment regarding the extent and variety of such adaptations. If someone in the Church has serious concerns regarding the sufficiency of current liturgical norms, the instruction does point to a process for seeking an indult, or permission for change. Article 27 in RS states that while "individual Bishops and their Conferences do not have the faculty to permit experimentation with liturgical texts or the other matters that are prescribed in the liturgical books," at the same time, an avenue of approach remains: "In order to carry out experimentation of this kind in the future, the permission of the Congregation for Divine Worship and the Discipline of the Sacraments is required."[5] In addition, a bishop or conference has the right to request an indult for particular customs or uses.

HOW DOES THIS INSTRUCTION AFFECT LITURGICAL PREPARATION?

Any public event, be it a relationship, an athletic event, or even a game of chess, depends on a common understanding of the "rules of the game" to enable participation with comfort and with complete heart and mind. Liturgically, one could call this "full, conscious, and active participation."[6] The focus of the instruction on fidelity to the rubrics is intended to enable such participation by all and not just by some. In the familiarity of a ritual ceremony, true freedom to worship may be experienced. This is why "preparation" rather than "planning" better describes the work leading to the liturgical celebration.

The instruction is aware that participation is more than mere rubrics. A certain level of understanding should also be fostered. For example, article 38 states, "The constant teaching of the Church on the nature of the Eucharist not only as a meal, but also and pre-eminently as a Sacrifice, is therefore rightly

---

4. EE, 10.

5. *Redemptionis sacramentum* (RS), 27.

6. *Constitution on the Sacred Liturgy* (CSL), 14.

understood to be one of the principal keys to the full participation of all the faithful in so great a sacrament."

Liturgical preparation should always bear in mind such basic catechesis as the twofold dimension of Eucharist as meal and sacrifice. In article 39, the instruction highlights the interior dimension of participation as necessary: "It should be remembered that the power of the liturgical celebrations does not consist in frequently altering the rites, but in probing more deeply the word of God and the mystery being celebrated." Full participation in the liturgy, then, includes regular prayer and study of the Scriptures. Article 41 highlights how the Church seeks to encourage this kind of praying: "For encouraging, promoting and nourishing this interior understanding of liturgical participation, the continuous and widespread celebration of the Liturgy of the Hours, the use of the sacramentals and exercises of Christian popular piety are extremely helpful." The Liturgy of the Hours, while growing among the faithful, remains an underutilized resource for fostering not only regular prayer, but also scriptural meditation, precisely the enrichment that fosters authentic liturgical participation.

Although the primacy of liturgical participation rests with interior preparation ("A merely external observation of norms would obviously be contrary to the nature of the sacred Liturgy . . . "[7]), the exterior means of engaging likewise serves to deepen one's spiritual involvement ("external action must be illuminated by faith and charity . . ."[8]). In several places the instruction highlights the latitude of the Roman Rite regarding these external means of participation. Article 39, for example, provides a kind of *tour de force* of the extraordinary level of adaptation available within the Roman liturgy:

> [T]he Council fostered acclamations of the people, responses, psalmody, antiphons, and canticles, as well as actions or movements and gestures, and called for sacred silence to be maintained at the proper times, while providing rubrics for the parts of the faithful as well. In addition, ample flexibility is given for appropriate creativity aimed at allowing each celebration to be adapted to the needs of the participants, to their comprehension, their interior preparation and their gifts, according to the established liturgical norms. In the songs, the melodies, the choice of prayers and readings, the giving of the homily, the preparation of the prayer of the faithful, the occasional explanatory remarks, and the decoration of the Church building according to the various seasons, there is ample possibility for introducing into each celebration a certain variety by which the riches of the liturgical tradition will also be more clearly evident, and so, in keeping with pastoral requirements, the celebration will be carefully imbued with those particular features that will foster the recollection of the participants.

---

7. RS, 5.
8. Ibid.

The instruction has an introduction, eight chapters, and a conclusion.

The first chapter focuses on the responsibilities of the hierarchy, especially the bishop, who is not only to regulate the liturgy but also to foster its development, especially through music and art.[9] The bishop is encouraged to make use of all the means available to him (the document explicitly names commissions, councils and committees, "all these sorts of bodies and other entities"[10]) for the promotion and development of the liturgy. He is also instructed to "take care not to allow the removal of that liberty foreseen by the norms of the liturgical books so that the celebration may be adapted in an intelligent manner to the Church building, or to the group of the faithful who are present, or to particular pastoral circumstances in such a way that the universal sacred rite is truly accommodated to human understanding."[11]

For priests and deacons, the bishop is charged, among other tasks, with "promoting meetings and other projects . . . so that they may have the opportunity to consider the nature of the homily more precisely and find help in its preparation."[12] Given the growing importance that the faithful place on the homily, this particular injunction to provide a variety of resources to aid more effective preaching is a welcome exhortation.

The second chapter concerns the rights and responsibilities of the lay faithful in the liturgy. All liturgical participation is based on Baptism.[13] The instruction stresses the importance of all playing their proper role, neither clericalizing the laity nor laicizing the clergy.[14] The key to full, conscious, and active participation is given as interior engagement above exterior activity. Thus, the instruction asks that silent contemplation ("wonder") not be forgotten or denigrated, but promoted as integral.[15] The majority of the chapter treats of ordinary ministerial roles for the laity in the liturgical celebration.

Chapters 3, 4, and 5 address specific issues, often of liturgical abuse, that come to the Congregation's attention regarding Holy Mass. The responses of the dicastery are firm but pastoral, simply pointing to the appropriate liturgical norms and calling for greater fidelity.

Chapter 6 treats worship of the Holy Eucharist outside Mass, dealing with due respect for the tabernacle, visits to the Blessed Sacrament, instructions regarding a perpetual adoration chapel, and Eucharistic processions and congresses.

Chapter 7 concerns the extraordinary offices that are available to the lay faithful, such as those of extraordinary ministers of Holy Communion, and instructors or leaders of prayer services in the absence of a priest.[16] Chapter 2 dealt with the ordinary participation of the lay faithful, but there are also occasions when the laity are needed to supplement the ordinary ministry of clerics,

---

9. See ibid., 25.

10. Ibid., 25.

11. Ibid., 21.

12. Ibid., 68.

13. See ibid., 36–37.

14. See ibid., 42, 45.

15. See ibid., 40–41.

16. See ibid., 146–167.

due to absence, infirmity, or insufficient numbers. The concern is always to avoid confusion of the distinct roles of clergy and laity, while affirming all legitimate possibilities.

The final chapter provides canonical remedies and recourse for treating abuses against the Holy Eucharist. It gives a clear reminder that all the faithful have the duty to address abuses in a clear and charitable way.[17] The instruction places great weight, as always, on proper formation and instruction, showing the Congregation's deeply held belief that most abuses are not malicious. Indeed, the implication seems to be that with authentic dialogue and appropriate teaching, the truth and beauty of the liturgy will "shine forth in all its radiant mystery."[18]

---

17. See ibid., 183–184.
18. EE, 10.

OUTLINE

INSTRUCTION
REDEMPTIONIS SACRAMENTUM

PREAMBLE

1.   In the Most Holy Eucharist, Mother Church with steadfast faith acknowledges the *Sacrament of redemption*,[1] joyfully takes it to herself, celebrates it and reveres it in adoration, proclaiming the death of Christ Jesus and confessing his Resurrection until he comes in glory[2] to hand over, as unconquered Lord and Ruler, eternal Priest and King of the Universe, a kingdom of truth and life to the immense majesty of the Almighty Father.[3]

2.   The Church's doctrine regarding the Most Holy Eucharist, in which the whole spiritual wealth of the Church is contained—namely Christ, our Paschal Lamb[4]—the Eucharist which is the source and summit of the whole of Christian life,[5] and which lies as a causative force behind the very origins of the Church,[6] has been expounded with thoughtful care and with great authority over the course of the centuries in the writings of the Councils and the Supreme Pontiffs. Most recently, in fact, the Supreme Pontiff John Paul II, in the Encyclical Letter *Ecclesia de Eucharistia*, set forth afresh certain elements of great importance on this subject in view of the ecclesial circumstances of our times.[7]

In order that especially in the celebration of the Sacred Liturgy the Church might duly safeguard so great a mystery in our own time as well, the Supreme Pontiff has mandated that this Congregation for Divine Worship and the Discipline of the Sacraments,[8] in collaboration with the Congregation for the Doctrine of

---

1. Cf. *Missale Romanum*, ex decreto sacrosancti Oecumenici Concilii Vaticani II instauratum, auctoritate Pauli Pp. VI promulgatum, Ioannis Pauli Pp. II cura recognitum, editio typica tertia, diei 20 aprilis 2000, Typis Vaticanis, 2002, Missa votiva de Dei misericordia, oratio super oblata, p. 1159.

2. Cf. 1 Corinthians 11, 26; *Missale Romanum*, Prex Eucharistica, acclamatio post consecrationem, p. 576; John Paul II, Encyclical Letter, *Ecclesia de Eucharistia*, 17 April 2003, nn. 5, 11, 14, 18: AAS 95 (2003) pp. 436, 440–441, 442, 445.

3. Cf. Isaiah 10: 33; 51, 22; *Missale Romanum*, In sollemnitate Domini nostri Iesu Christi, universorum Regis, Praefatio, p. 499.

4. Cf.1 Corinthians 5: 7; Second Vatican Ecumenical Council, Decree on the Ministry and Life of Priests, *Presbyterorum ordinis*, 7 December 1965, n. 5; John Paul II, Apostolic Exhortation., *Ecclesia in Europa*, n. 75: AAS 95 (2003) pp. 649–719, here p. 693.

5. Cf. Second Vatican Ecumenical Council, Dogmatic Constitution on the Church, *Lumen gentium*, 21 November 1964, n. 11.

6. Cf. John Paul II, Encyclical Letter *Ecclesia de Eucharistia*, 17 April 2003, n. 21: AAS 95 (2003) p. 447.

7. Ibidem: AAS 95 (2003) pp. 433–475.

8. Ibidem, n. 52: AAS 95 (2003) p. 468.

the Faith, should prepare this Instruction treating of certain matters pertaining to the discipline of the Sacrament of the Eucharist. Those things found in this Instruction are therefore to be read in the continuity with the above-mentioned Encyclical Letter, *Ecclesia de Eucharistia*.

It is not at all the intention here to prepare a compendium of the norms regarding the Most Holy Eucharist, but rather, to take up within this Instruction some elements of liturgical norms that have been previously expounded or laid down and even today remain in force in order to assure a deeper appreciation of the liturgical norms;[9] to establish certain norms by which those earlier ones are explained and complemented; and also to set forth for Bishops, as well as for Priests, Deacons and all the lay Christian faithful, how each should carry them out in accordance with his own responsibilities and the means at his disposal.

3.   The norms contained in the present Instruction are to be understood as pertaining to liturgical matters in the Roman Rite, and, *mutatis mutandis*, in the other Rites of the Latin Church that are duly acknowledged by law.

4.   "Certainly the liturgical reform inaugurated by the Council has greatly contributed to a more conscious, active and fruitful participation in the Holy Sacrifice of the Altar on the part of the faithful."[10] Even so, "shadows are not lacking."[11] In this regard it is not possible to be silent about the abuses, even quite grave ones, against the nature of the Liturgy and the Sacraments as well as the tradition and the authority of the Church, which in our day not infrequently plague liturgical celebrations in one ecclesial environment or another. In some places the perpetration of liturgical abuses has become almost habitual, a fact which obviously cannot be allowed and must cease.

5.   The observance of the norms published by the authority of the Church requires conformity of thought and of word, of external action and of the application of the heart. A merely external observation of norms would obviously be contrary to the nature of the Sacred Liturgy, in which Christ himself wishes to gather his Church, so that together with himself she will be "one body and one spirit."[12] For this reason, external action must be illuminated by faith and charity, which unite us with Christ and with one another and engender love for the poor and the abandoned. The liturgical words and rites, moreover, are a faithful expression, matured over the centuries, of the understanding of Christ, and they teach us to think as he himself does;[13] by conforming our minds to these words, we raise our hearts to the Lord. All that is said in this Instruction is directed toward such a conformity of our own understanding with that of Christ, as expressed in the words and the rites of the Liturgy.

---

9. Ibidem.

10. Ibidem, n. 10: AAS 95 (2003) p. 439.

11. Ibidem; cf. John Paul II, Apostolic Letter, *Vicesimus quintus annus*, 4 December 1988, nn. 12–13: AAS 81 (1989) pp. 909–910; cf. also Second Vatican Ecumenical Council, Constitution on the Sacred Liturgy, *Sacrosanctum Concilium*, 4 December 1963 n. 48.

12. *Missale Romanum*, Prex Eucharistica III, p. 588; cf. 1 Corinthians 12:12–13; Ephesians 4:4.

13. Cf. Philippians 2:5.

6.   For abuses "contribute to the obscuring of the Catholic faith and doctrine concerning this wonderful sacrament."[14] Thus, they also hinder the faithful from "re-living in a certain way the experience of the two disciples of Emmaus: 'and their eyes were opened, and they recognized him.'"[15] For in the presence of God's power and divinity[16] and the splendour of his goodness, made manifest especially in the Sacrament of the Eucharist, it is fitting that all the faithful should have and put into practice that power of acknowledging God's majesty that they have received through the saving Passion of the Only-Begotten Son.[17]

7.   Not infrequently, abuses are rooted in a false understanding of liberty. Yet God has not granted us in Christ an illusory liberty by which we may do what we wish, but a liberty by which we may do that which is fitting and right.[18] This is true not only of precepts coming directly from God, but also of laws promulgated by the Church, with appropriate regard for the nature of each norm. For this reason, all should conform to the ordinances set forth by legitimate ecclesiastical authority.

8.   It is therefore to be noted with great sadness that "ecumenical initiatives which are well-intentioned, nevertheless indulge at times in Eucharistic practices contrary to the discipline by which the Church expresses her faith." Yet the Eucharist "is too great a gift to tolerate ambiguity or depreciation." It is therefore necessary that some things be corrected or more clearly delineated so that in this respect as well "the Eucharist will continue to shine forth in all its radiant mystery."[19]

9.   Finally, abuses are often based on ignorance, in that they involve a rejection of those elements whose deeper meaning is not understood and whose antiquity is not recognized. For "the liturgical prayers, orations and songs are pervaded by the inspiration and impulse" of the Sacred Scriptures themselves, "and it is from these that the actions and signs receive their meaning."[20] As for the visible signs "which the Sacred Liturgy uses in order to signify the invisible divine realities, they have been chosen by Christ or by the Church."[21] Finally, the structures and forms of the sacred celebrations according to each of the Rites of both East and West are in harmony with the practice of the universal Church also as regards

---

14. John Paul II, Encyclical Letter *Ecclesia de Eucharistia*, n. 10: AAS 95 (2003), p. 439.

15. Ibidem, n. 6: AAS 95 (2003) p. 437; cf. Luke 24:31.

16. Cf. Romans 1:20.

17. Cf. *Missale Romanum*, Praefatio I de Passione Domini, p. 528.

18. Cf. John Paul II, Encyclical Letter *Veritatis splendor*, 6 August 1993, n. 35: AAS 85 (1993) pp. 1161–1162; Homily given at Camden Yards, 9 October 1995, n. 7: *Insegnamenti di Giovanni Paolo II, XVII, 2 (1995)*, Libreria Editrice Vaticana, 1998, p. 788.

19. Cf. John Paul II, Encyclical Letter *Ecclesia de Eucharistia*, n. 10: AAS 95 (2003) p. 439.

20. Second Vatican Ecumenical Council, Constitution on the Sacred Liturgy, *Sacrosanctum Concilium*, n. 24; cf. Congregation for Divine Worship and the Discipline of the Sacraments, Instruction *Varietates legitimae*, 25 January 1994, nn. 19 and 23: AAS 87 (1995) pp. 295–296, 297.

21. Second Vatican Ecumenical Council, Constitution on the Sacred Liturgy, *Sacrosanctum Concilium*, n. 33.

practices received universally from apostolic and unbroken tradition,[22] which it is the Church's task to transmit faithfully and carefully to future generations. All these things are wisely safeguarded and protected by the liturgical norms.

10.   The Church herself has no power over those things which were established by Christ himself and which constitute an unchangeable part of the Liturgy.[23] Indeed, if the bond were to be broken which the Sacraments have with Christ himself who instituted them, and with the events of the Church's founding,[24] it would not be beneficial to the faithful but rather would do them grave harm. For the Sacred Liturgy is quite intimately connected with principles of doctrine,[25] so that the use of unapproved texts and rites necessarily leads either to the attenuation or to the disappearance of that necessary link between the *lex orandi* and the *lex credendi*.[26]

11.   The Mystery of the Eucharist "is too great for anyone to permit himself to treat it according to his own whim, so that its sacredness and its universal ordering would be obscured."[27] On the contrary, anyone who acts thus by giving free reign to his own inclinations, even if he is a Priest, injures the substantial unity of the Roman Rite, which ought to be vigorously preserved,[28] and becomes responsible for actions that are in no way consistent with the hunger and thirst for the living God that is experienced by the people today. Nor do such actions serve authentic pastoral care or proper liturgical renewal; instead, they deprive Christ's faithful of their patrimony and their heritage. For arbitrary actions are not conducive to true renewal,[29] but are detrimental to the right of Christ's faithful to a liturgical celebration that is an expression of the Church's life in accordance

---

22. Cf. St Irenaeus, *Adversus Haereses*, III, 2: SCh., 211, 24–31; St Augustine, *Epistula ad Ianuarium:* 54,I: PL 33,200: "Illa autem quae non scripta, sed tradita custodimus, quae quidem toto terrarum orbe servantur, datur intellegi vel ab ipsis Apostolis, vel plenariis conciliis, quorum est Ecclesia saluberrima auctoritas, commendata atque statuta retineri"; John Paul II, Encyclical Letter *Redemptoris missio*, 7 December 1990, nn. 53–54: AAS 83 (1991) pp. 300–302; Congregation for the Doctrine of the Faith, Letter to the Bishops of the Catholic Church on Certain Aspects of the Church as Communion, *Communionis notio*, 28 May 1992, nn. 7–10: AAS 85 (1993) pp. 842–844; Congregation for Divine Worship and the Discipline of the Sacraments, Instruction *Varietates legitimae*, n. 26: AAS 87 (1995) pp. 298–299.

23. Cf. Second Vatican Ecumenical Council, Constitution on the Sacred Liturgy, *Sacrosanctum Concilium*, n. 21.

24. Cf. Pius XII, Apostolic Constitution *Sacramentum Ordinis*, 30 November 1947: AAS 40 (1948) p. 5; Congregation for the Doctrine of the Faith, Declaration *Inter insigniores*, 15 October 1976, part IV: AAS 69 (1977) pp. 107–108; Congregation for Divine Worship and the Discipline of the Sacraments, Instruction *Varietates legitimae*, n. 25: AAS 87 (1995) p. 298.

25. Cf. Pius XII, Encyclical Letter *Mediator Dei*, 20 November 1947: AAS 39 (1947) p. 540.

26. Cf. Sacred Congregation for the Sacraments and Divine Worship, Instruction *Inaestimabile donum*, 3 April 1980: AAS 72 (1980) p. 333.

27. John Paul II, Encyclical Letter *Ecclesia de Eucharistia*, n. 52: AAS 95 (2003), p. 468.

28. Second Vatican Ecumenical Council, Constitution on the Sacred Liturgy, *Sacrosanctum Concilium*, nn. 4, 38; Decree on the Catholic Eastern Churches, *Orientalium Ecclesiarum*, 21 November 1964, nn. 1,2,6; Paul VI, Apostolic Constitution *Missale Romanum:* AAS 61 (1969) pp. 217–222; *Missale Romanum*, Institutio Generalis, n. 399; Congregation for Divine Worship and the Discipline of the Sacraments, Instruction *Liturgiam authenticam*, 28 March 2001, n. 4: AAS 93 (2001) pp. 685–726, here p. 686.

29. Cf. John Paul II, Apostolic Exhortation *Ecclesia in Europa*, n. 72: AAS 95 (2003) p. 692.

with her tradition and discipline. In the end, they introduce elements of distortion and disharmony into the very celebration of the Eucharist, which is oriented in its own lofty way and by its very nature to signifying and wondrously bringing about the communion of divine life and the unity of the People of God.[30] The result is uncertainty in matters of doctrine, perplexity and scandal on the part of the People of God, and, almost as a necessary consequence, vigorous opposition, all of which greatly confuse and sadden many of Christ's faithful in this age of ours when Christian life is often particularly difficult on account of the inroads of "secularization" as well.[31]

12.   On the contrary, it is the right of all of Christ's faithful that the Liturgy, and in particular the celebration of Holy Mass, should truly be as the Church wishes, according to her stipulations as prescribed in the liturgical books and in the other laws and norms. Likewise, the Catholic people have the right that the Sacrifice of the Holy Mass should be celebrated for them in an integral manner, according to the entire doctrine of the Church's Magisterium. Finally, it is the Catholic community's right that the celebration of the Most Holy Eucharist should be carried out for it in such a manner that it truly stands out as a sacrament of unity, to the exclusion of all blemishes and actions that might engender divisions and factions in the Church.[32]

13.   All of the norms and exhortations set forth in this Instruction are connected, albeit in various ways, with the mission of the Church, whose task it is to be vigilant concerning the correct and worthy celebration of so great a mystery. The last chapter of the present Instruction will treat of the varying degrees to which the individual norms are bound up with the supreme norm of all ecclesiastical law, namely concern for the salvation of souls.[33]

CHAPTER I
THE REGULATION OF THE SACRED LITURGY

14.   "The regulation of the Sacred Liturgy depends solely on the authority of the Church, which rests specifically with the Apostolic See and, according to the norms of law, with the Bishop."[34]

15.   The Roman Pontiff, "the Vicar of Christ and the Pastor of the universal Church on earth, by virtue of his supreme office enjoys full, immediate and

---

30. Cf. John Paul II, Encyclical Letter *Ecclesia de Eucharistia*, n. 23: AAS 95 (2003) pp. 448–449; S. Congregation of Rites, Instruction *Eucharisticum mysterium*, 25 May 1967, n. 6: AAS 59 (1967) p. 545.

31. Sacred Congregation for the Sacraments and Divine Worship, Instruction *Inaestimabile donum*: AAS 72 (1980) pp. 332–333.

32. Cf. 1 Corinthians 11:17–34; John Paul II, Encyclical Letter, *Ecclesia de Eucharistia*, n. 52: AAS 95 (2003) pp. 467–468.

33. Cf. *Code of Canon Law*, 25 January 1983, canon 1752.

34. Second Vatican Ecumenical Council, Constitution on the Sacred Liturgy, *Sacrosanctum Concilium*, n. 22 §1; cf. *Code of Canon Law*, canon 838 §1.

universal ordinary power, which he may always freely exercise,"[35] also by means of communication with the pastors and with the members of the flock.

16. "It pertains to the Apostolic See to regulate the Sacred Liturgy of the universal Church, to publish the liturgical books and to grant the *recognitio* for their translation into vernacular languages, as well as to ensure that the liturgical regulations, especially those governing the celebration of the most exalted celebration of the Sacrifice of the Mass, are everywhere faithfully observed."[36]

17. "The Congregation for Divine Worship and the Discipline of the Sacraments attends to those matters that pertain to the Apostolic See as regards the regulation and promotion of the Sacred Liturgy, and especially the Sacraments, with due regard for the competence of the Congregation for the Doctrine of the Faith. It fosters and enforces sacramental discipline, especially as regards their validity and their licit celebration." Finally, it "carefully seeks to ensure that the liturgical regulations are observed with precision, and that abuses are prevented or eliminated whenever they are detected."[37] In this regard, according to the tradition of the universal Church, pre-eminent solicitude is accorded the celebration of Holy Mass, and also to the worship that is given to the Holy Eucharist even outside Mass.

18. Christ's faithful have the right that ecclesiastical authority should fully and efficaciously regulate the Sacred Liturgy lest it should ever seem to be "anyone's private property, whether of the celebrant or of the community in which the mysteries are celebrated."[38]

1. THE DIOCESAN BISHOP, HIGH PRIEST OF HIS FLOCK

19. The diocesan Bishop, the first steward of the mysteries of God in the particular Church entrusted to him, is the moderator, promoter and guardian of her whole liturgical life.[39] For "the Bishop, endowed with the fullness of the Sacrament of Order, is 'the steward of the grace of the high Priesthood,'[40] especially in the Eucharist which he either himself offers or causes to be offered,[41] by which the Church continually lives and grows."[42]

---

35. *Code of Canon Law*, canon 331; cf. Second Vatican Ecumenical Council, Dogmatic Constitution on the Church, *Lumen gentium*, n. 22.

36. *Code of Canon Law*, canon 838 §2.

37. Cf. John Paul II, Apostolic Constitution, *Pastor bonus*, 28 June 1988: AAS 80 (1988) pp. 841–924, here articles 62, 63, and 66, pp. 876–877.

38. Cf. John Paul II, Encyclical Letter, *Ecclesia de Eucharistia*, n. 52: AAS 95 (2003) p. 468.

39. Cf. Second Vatican Ecumenical Council, Decree on the Pastoral Office of Bishops, *Christus Dominus*, 28 October 1965, n. 15; cf. also the Constitution on the Sacred Liturgy, *Sacrosanctum Concilium*, n. 41; *Code of Canon Law*, canon 387.

40. Prayer for the Consecration of a Bishop in the Byzantine Rite: *Euchologion to mega*, Rome, 1873, p. 139.

41. Cf. St. Ignatius of Antioch, *Ad Smyrn.* 8,1: ed. F. X. Funk, I, p. 282.

42. Second Vatican Ecumenical Council, Dogmatic Constitution on the Church, *Lumen gentium*, n. 26; cf. Sacred Congregation of Rites, Instruction, *Eucharisticum mysterium*, n. 7: AAS 59 (1967) p. 545; cf. also John Paul II, Apostolic Exhortation, *Pastores gregis*, 16 October 2003, nn. 32–41: *L'Osservatore Romano*, 17 October 2003, pp. 6–8.

20.   Indeed, the pre-eminent manifestation of the Church is found whenever the rites of Mass are celebrated, especially in the Cathedral Church, "with the full and active participation of the entire holy People of God, joined in one act of prayer, at one altar at which the Bishop presides," surrounded by his presbyterate with the Deacons and ministers.[43] Furthermore, "every lawful celebration of the Eucharist is directed by the Bishop, to whom is entrusted the office of presenting the worship of the Christian religion to the Divine Majesty and ordering it according to the precepts of the Lord and the laws of the Church, further specified by his own particular judgement for the Diocese."[44]

21.   It pertains to the diocesan Bishop, then, "within the limits of his competence, to set forth liturgical norms in his Diocese, by which all are bound."[45] Still, the Bishop must take care not to allow the removal of that liberty foreseen by the norms of the liturgical books so that the celebration may be adapted in an intelligent manner to the Church building, or to the group of the faithful who are present, or to particular pastoral circumstances in such a way that the universal sacred rite is truly accommodated to human understanding.[46]

22.   The Bishop governs the particular Church entrusted to him,[47] and it is his task to regulate, to direct, to encourage, and sometimes also to reprove;[48] this is a sacred task that he has received through episcopal Ordination,[49] which he fulfils in order to build up his flock in truth and holiness.[50] He should elucidate the inherent meaning of the rites and the liturgical texts, and nourish the spirit of the Liturgy in the Priests, Deacons and lay faithful[51] so that they are all led to the active and fruitful celebration of the Eucharist,[52] and in like manner he should take care to ensure that the whole body of the Church is able to grow in the same understanding, in the unity of charity, in the diocese, in the nation and in the world.[53]

---

43. Cf. Second Vatican Ecumenical Council, Constitution on the Sacred Liturgy, *Sacrosanctum Concilium*, n. 41; cf. St. Ignatius of Antioch, *Ad Magn.* 7, *Ad Philad.* 4, *Ad Smyrn.* 8: ed. F. X. Funk, I, pp. 236, 266, 281; *Missale Romanum*, Institutio Generalis, n. 22; cf. also *Code of Canon Law*, canon 389.

44. Second Vatican Ecumenical Council, Constitution on the Sacred Liturgy, *Lumen gentium*, n. 26.

45. *Code of Canon Law*, canon 838 §4.

46. Cf. Consilium for Implementing the Constitution on the Liturgy, Dubium: *Notitiae* 1 (1965) p. 254.

47. Cf. Acts 20,28; Second Vatican Ecumenical Council, Dogmatic Constitution on the Church, *Lumen gentium*, nn. 21 and 27; Decree on the Pastoral Office of Bishops in the Church, *Christus Dominus*, n. 3.

48. Cf. S. Congregation for Divine Worship, Instruction, *Liturgicae instaurationes*, 5 September 1970: AAS 62 (1970) p. 694.

49. Cf. Second Vatican Ecumenical Council, Dogmatic Constitution on the Church, *Lumen gentium*, n. 21; Decree on the Pastoral Office of Bishops in the Church, *Christus Dominus*, n. 3.

50. Cf. Caeremoniale Episcoporum ex decreto sacrosancti Oecumenici Concilii Vaticani II instauratum, auctoritate Ioannis Pauli Pp. II promulgatum, editio typica, 14 September 1984, Vatican Polyglot Press, 1985, n. 10.

51. Cf. *Missale Romanum*, Institutio Generalis, n. 387.

52. Cf. ibidem, n. 22.

53. Cf. Sacred Congregation for Divine Worship, Instruction, *Liturgicae instaurationes:* AAS 62 (1970) p. 694.

23.   The faithful "should cling to the Bishop as the Church does to Jesus Christ, and as Jesus Christ does to the Father, so that all may be in harmonious unity, and that they may abound to the glory of God."[54] All, including members of Institutes of consecrated life and Societies of apostolic life as well as those of all ecclesial associations and movements of any kind, are subject to the authority of the diocesan Bishop in all liturgical matters,[55] apart from rights that have been legitimately conceded. To the diocesan Bishop therefore falls the right and duty of overseeing and attending to Churches and oratories in his territory in regard to liturgical matters, and this is true also of those which are founded by members of the above-mentioned institutes or under their direction, provided that the faithful are accustomed to frequent them.[56]

24.   It is the right of the Christian people themselves that their diocesan Bishop should take care to prevent the occurrence of abuses in ecclesiastical discipline, especially as regards the ministry of the word, the celebration of the sacraments and sacramentals, the worship of God and devotion to the Saints.[57]

25.   Commissions as well as councils or committees established by the Bishop to handle "the promotion of the Liturgy, sacred music and art in his diocese" should act in accordance with the intentions and the norms of the Bishop; they must rely on his authority and his approval so that they may carry out their office in a suitable manner[58] and so that the effective governance of the Bishop in his diocese will be preserved. As regards all these sorts of bodies and other entities and all undertakings in liturgical matters, there has long been the need for the Bishops to consider whether their working has been fruitful thus far,[59] and to consider carefully which changes or improvements should be made in their composition and activity[60] so that they might find new vigour. It should be borne in mind that the experts are to be chosen from among those whose soundness in the Catholic faith and knowledge of theological and cultural matters are evident.

2. THE CONFERENCE OF BISHOPS

26.   The same holds for those commissions of this kind which have been established by the Conference of Bishops in accordance with the will of the Council,[61] commissions whose members consist of Bishops who are clearly distinguished

---

54. Second Vatican Ecumenical Council, Dogmatic Constitution on the Church, *Lumen gentium*, n. 27; cf. 2 Corinthians 4:15.

55. Cf. *Code of Canon Law*, canons 397 §1; 678 §1.

56. Cf. ibidem, canon 683 §1.

57. Ibidem, canon 392.

58. Cf. John Paul II, Apostolic Letter *Vicesimus quintus annus*, n. 21: AAS 81 (1989) p. 917; Second Vatican Ecumenical Council, Constitution on the Sacred Liturgy, *Sacrosanctum Concilium*, nn. 45–46; Pius XII, Encyclical Letter *Mediator Dei:* AAS 39 (1947) p. 562.

59. Cf. John Paul II, Apostolic Letter *Vicesimus quintus annus*, n. 20: AAS 81 (1989) p. 916.

60. Cf. ibidem.

61. Cf. Second Vatican Ecumenical Council, Constitution on the Sacred Liturgy, *Sacrosanctum Concilium*, n. 44; Congregation for Bishops, Letter sent to the Presidents of the Conferences of Bishops together with the Congregation for the Evangelization of Peoples, 21 June 1999, n. 9: AAS 91 (1999) p. 999.

from their expert helpers. Where the number of members of a Conference of Bishops is not sufficient for the effective establishment of a liturgical commission from among their own number, then a council or group of experts should be named, always under the presidency of a Bishop, which is to fulfil the same role insofar as possible, albeit without the name of "liturgical commission."

27.   As early as the year 1970, the Apostolic See announced the cessation of all experimentation as regards the celebration of Holy Mass[62] and reiterated the same in 1988.[63] Accordingly, individual Bishops and their Conferences do not have the faculty to permit experimentation with liturgical texts or the other matters that are prescribed in the liturgical books. In order to carry out experimentation of this kind in the future, the permission of the Congregation for Divine Worship and the Discipline of the Sacraments is required. It must be in writing, and it is to be requested by the Conference of Bishops. In fact, it will not be granted without serious reason. As regards projects of inculturation in liturgical matters, the particular norms that have been established are strictly and comprehensively to be observed.[64]

28.   All liturgical norms that a Conference of Bishops will have established for its territory in accordance with the law are to be submitted to the Congregation for Divine Worship and the Discipline of the Sacraments for the *recognitio*, without which they lack any binding force.[65]

3. PRIESTS

29. Priests, as capable, prudent and indispensable co-workers of the order of Bishops,[66] called to the service of the People of God, constitute one presbyterate with their Bishop,[67] though charged with differing offices. "In each local congregation of the faithful, in a certain way, they make present the Bishop with whom they are associated in trust and in generosity of heart; according to their rank, they take upon themselves his duties and his solicitude, and they carry these out in their daily work." And "because of this participation in the Priesthood

---

62. Cf. Congregation for Divine Worship, Instruction *Liturgicae instaurationis*, n. 12: AAS 62 (1970) pp. 692–704; cf., here p. 703.

63. Cf. Congregation For Divine Worship, *Declaration on Eucharistic Prayers and liturgical experimentation*, 21 March 1988: *Notitiae* 24 (1988) pp. 234–236.

64. Cf. Congregation for Divine Worship and the Discipline of the Sacraments, Instruction *Varietates legitimae*: AAS 87 (1995) pp. 288–314.

65. Cf. *Code of Canon Law*, canon 838 § 3; S. Congregation of Rites, Instruction *Inter Oecumenici*, 26 September 1964, n. 31: AAS 56 (1964) p. 883; Congregation for Divine Worship and the Discipline of the Sacraments, Instruction *Liturgiam authenticam*, nn. 79–80: AAS 93 (2001) pp. 711–713.

66. Cf. Second Vatican Ecumenical Council, Decree on the Ministry and Life of Priests, *Presbyterorum ordinis*, 7 December 1965, n. 7; Pontificale Romanum, ed. 1962: Ordo consecrationis sacerdotalis, in Praefatione; Pontificale Romanum *ex decreto sacrosancti Oecumenici Concilii Vaticani II renovatum, auctoritate Pauli Pp. VI editum, Ioannis Pauli Pp. II cura recognitum:* De Ordinatione Episcopi, presbyterorum et diaconorum, editio typica altera, 29 June 1989, Typis Polyglottis Vaticanis, 1990, cap. II: De Ordin. presbyterorum, Praenotanda, n. 101.

67. St. Ignatius of Antioch, *Ad Philad.*, 4: ed. F. X. Funk, I, p. 266; St. Cornelius I, cited by St. Cyprian, Letter 48,2: ed. G. Hartel, III,2, p. 610.

and mission, Priests should recognize the Bishop as truly their father and obey him reverently."[68] Furthermore, "ever intent upon the good of God's children, they should seek to contribute to the pastoral mission of the whole diocese, and indeed of the whole Church."[69]

30.   The office "that belongs to Priests in particular in the celebration of the Eucharist" is a great one, "for it is their responsibility to preside at the Eucharist *in persona Christi* and to provide a witness to and a service of communion not only for the community directly taking part in the celebration, but also for the universal Church, which is always brought into play within the context of the Eucharist. It must be lamented that, especially in the years following the post-Conciliar liturgical reform, as a result of a misguided sense of creativity and adaptation, there have been a number of abuses which have been a source of suffering for many."[70]

31.   In keeping with the solemn promises that they have made in the rite of Sacred Ordination and renewed each year in the Mass of the Chrism, let Priests celebrate "devoutly and faithfully the mysteries of Christ for the praise of God and the sanctification of the Christian people, according to the tradition of the Church, especially in the Eucharistic Sacrifice and in the Sacrament of Reconciliation."[71] They ought not to detract from the profound meaning of their own ministry by corrupting the liturgical celebration either through alteration or omission, or through arbitrary additions.[72] For as St. Ambrose said, "It is not in herself . . . but in us that the Church is injured. Let us take care so that our own failure may not cause injury to the Church."[73] Let the Church of God not be injured, then, by Priests who have so solemnly dedicated themselves to the ministry. Indeed, under the Bishop's authority let them faithfully seek to prevent others as well from committing this type of distortion.

32.   "Let the Parish Priest strive so that the Most Holy Eucharist will be the center of the parish congregation of the faithful; let him work to ensure that Christ's faithful are nourished through the devout celebration of the Sacraments, and in particular, that they frequently approach the Most Holy Eucharist and the Sacrament of Penance; let him strive, furthermore, to ensure that the faithful are encouraged to offer prayers in their families as well, and to participate consciously and actively in the Sacred Liturgy, which the Parish Priest, under

68. Second Vatican Ecumenical Council, Dogmatic Constitution on the Church, *Lumen gentium*, n. 28.

69. Cf. *ibidem*.

70. John Paul II, Encyclical Letter *Ecclesia de Eucharistia*, n. 52; cf. n. 29: AAS 95 (2003) pp. 467–468, 452–435.

71. *Pontificale Romanum, De Ordinatione Episcopi, presbyterorum et diaconorum*, editio typica altera: *De Ordinatione Presbyterorum*, n. 124; cf. *Missale Romanum*, Feria V in Hebdomada Sancta: Ad Missam chrismatis, Renovatio promissionum sacerdotalium, p. 292.

72. Cf. Ecumenical Council of Trent, Session VII, 3 March 1547, Decree on the Sacraments, canon 13, DS 1613; Second Vatican Ecumenical Council, Constitution on the Sacred Liturgy, *Sacrosanctum Concilium*, n. 22; Pius XII, Encyclical Letter *Mediator Dei*: AAS 39 (1947) pp. 544, 546–547, 562; *Codex Iuris Canonici*, canon 846, § 1; *Missale Romanum*, Institutio Generalis, n. 24.

73. St. Ambrose, *De Virginitate*, n. 48: PL 16, 278.

the authority of the diocesan Bishop, is bound to regulate and supervise in his parish lest abuses occur."[74] Although it is appropriate that he should be assisted in the effective preparation of the liturgical celebrations by various members of Christ's faithful, he nevertheless must not cede to them in any way those things that are proper to his own office.

33.   Finally, all "Priests should go to the trouble of properly cultivating their liturgical knowledge and ability, so that through their liturgical ministry, God the Father, Son and Holy Spirit will be praised in an ever more excellent manner by the Christian communities entrusted to them."[75] Above all, let them be filled with that wonder and amazement that the Paschal Mystery, in being celebrated, instills in the hearts of the faithful.[76]

4. DEACONS

34.   Deacons "upon whom hands are imposed not for the Priesthood but for the ministry,"[77] as men of good repute,[78] must act in such a way that with the help of God they may be recognized as the true disciples[79] of him "who came not to be served but to serve,"[80] and who was among his disciples "as one who serves."[81] Strengthened by the gift of the Holy Spirit through the laying on of hands, they are in service to the People of God, in communion with the Bishop and his presbyterate.[82] They should therefore consider the Bishop as a father, and give assistance to him and to the Priests "in the ministry of the word, of the altar, and of charity."[83]

35.   Let them never fail, "as the Apostle says, to hold the mystery of faith with a clear conscience,[84] and to proclaim this faith by word and deed according to the Gospel and the tradition of the Church,"[85] in wholehearted, faithful and humble service to the Sacred Liturgy as the source and summit of ecclesial life, "so that all, made children of God through faith and Baptism, may come together as one, praising God in the midst of the Church, to participate in the Sacrifice

---

74. *Code of Canon Law*, canon 528 § 2.

75. Second Vatican Ecumenical Council, Decree on the Ministry and Life of Priests, *Presbyterorum Ordinis*, n. 5.

76. Cf. John Paul II, Encyclical Letter *Ecclesia de Eucharistia*, n. 5: AAS 95 (2003) p. 436.

77. Second Vatican Ecumenical Council, Dogmatic Constitution on the Church, *Lumen gentium*, n. 29; cf. *Constitutiones Ecclesiae Aegypticae*, III, 2: ed. F. X. Funk, *Didascalia*, II, p. 103; *Statuta Ecclesiae Ant.*, 37–41: ed. D. Mansi 3, 954.

78. Cf. Acts 6:3.

79. John 13:35.

80. Matthew 20:28.

81. Cf. Luke 22:27.

82. Cf. *Caeremoniale Episcoporum*, nn. 9, 23. Cf. Second Vatican Ecumenical Council, Dogmatic Constitution on the Church, *Lumen gentium*, n. 29.

83. Cf. *Pontificale Romanum, De Ordinatione Episcopi, presbyterorum et diaconorum*, editio typica altera, cap. III, *De Ordin. diaconorum*, n. 199.

84. Cf. 1 Timothy 3:9.

85. Cf. *Pontificale Romanum, De Ordinatione Episcopi, presbyterorum et diaconorum*, editio typica altera, cap. III, *De Ordin. diaconorum*, n. 200.

and to eat the Lord's Supper."[86] Let all Deacons, then, do their part so that the Sacred Liturgy will be celebrated according to the norms of the duly approved liturgical books.

CHAPTER II
THE PARTICIPATION OF THE LAY CHRISTIAN FAITHFUL IN THE EUCHARISTIC CELEBRATION

1. ACTIVE AND CONSCIOUS PARTICIPATION

36.   The celebration of the Mass, as the action of Christ and of the Church, is the center of the whole Christian life for the universal as well as the particular Church, and also for the individual faithful,[87] who are involved "in differing ways according to the diversity of orders, ministries, and active participation.[88] In this way the Christian people, "a chosen race, a royal priesthood, a holy people, a people God has made his own,"[89] manifests its coherent and hierarchical ordering."[90] "For the common priesthood of the faithful and the ministerial or hierarchical Priesthood, though they differ in essence and not only in degree, are ordered to one another, for both partake, each in its own way, of the one Priesthood of Christ."[91]

37.   All of Christ's faithful, freed from their sins and incorporated into the Church through Baptism, are deputed by means of a sacramental character for the worship of the Christian religion,[92] so that by virtue of their royal priesthood,[93] persevering in prayer and praising God,[94] they may offer themselves as a living and holy sacrifice pleasing to God and attested to others by their works,[95] giving witness to Christ throughout the earth and providing an answer to those who ask concerning their hope of eternal life that is in them.[96] Thus the participation

---

86. Second Vatican Ecumenical Council, Constitution on the Sacred Liturgy, *Sacrosanctum Concilium*, n. 10.

87. Cf. ibidem, n. 41; Second Vatican Ecumenical Council, Dogmatic Constitution on the Church, *Lumen gentium*, n. 11; Decree on the Ministry and Life of Priests, *Presbyterorum ordinis*, nn. 2, 5, 6; Decree on the Pastoral Office of Bishops, *Christus Dominus*, n. 30, Decree on Ecumenism, *Unitatis redintegratio*, 21 November 1964, n. 15; Sacred Congregation of Rites, Instruction *Eucharisticum mysterium*, nn. 3e, 6: AAS 59 (1967) pp. 542, 544–545; *Missale Romanum*, Institutio Generalis, n. 16.

88. Cf. Second Vatican Ecumenical Council, Constitution on the Sacred Liturgy, *Sacrosanctum Concilium*, n. 26; *Missale Romanum*, Institutio Generalis, n. 91.

89. 1 Peter 2:9; cf. 2:4–5.

90. *Missale Romanum*, Institutio Generalis, n. 91; cf. Second Vatican Ecumenical Council, Constitution on the Sacred Liturgy, *Sacrosanctum Concilium*, n. 41.

91. Second Vatican Ecumenical Council, Dogmatic Constitution on the Church, *Lumen gentium*, n. 10.

92. Cf. St. Thomas Aquinas, *Summa Theologica*, III, q. 63, a. 2.

93. Second Vatican Ecumenical Council, Dogmatic Constitution on the Church, *Lumen gentium*, n. 10; cf. John Paul II, Encyclical Letter *Ecclesia de Eucharistia*, n. 28: AAS 95 (2003) p. 452.

94. Cf. Acts 2:42–47.

95. Cf. Romans 12:1.

96. Cf. 1 Peter 3:15; 2:4–10.

of the lay faithful too in the Eucharist and in the other celebrations of the Church's rites cannot be equated with mere presence, and still less with a passive one, but is rather to be regarded as a true exercise of faith and of the baptismal dignity.

38.   The constant teaching of the Church on the nature of the Eucharist not only as a meal, but also and pre-eminently as a Sacrifice, is therefore rightly understood to be one of the principal keys to the full participation of all the faithful in so great a Sacrament.[97] For when "stripped of its sacrificial meaning, the mystery is understood as if its meaning and importance were simply that of a fraternal banquet."[98]

39.   For promoting and elucidating active participation, the recent renewal of the liturgical books according to the mind of the Council fostered acclamations of the people, responses, psalmody, antiphons, and canticles, as well as actions or movements and gestures, and called for sacred silence to be maintained at the proper times, while providing rubrics for the parts of the faithful as well.[99] In addition, ample flexibility is given for appropriate creativity aimed at allowing each celebration to be adapted to the needs of the participants, to their comprehension, their interior preparation and their gifts, according to the established liturgical norms. In the songs, the melodies, the choice of prayers and readings, the giving of the homily, the preparation of the prayer of the faithful, the occasional explanatory remarks, and the decoration of the Church building according to the various seasons, there is ample possibility for introducing into each celebration a certain variety by which the riches of the liturgical tradition will also be more clearly evident, and so, in keeping with pastoral requirements, the celebration will be carefully imbued with those particular features that will foster the recollection of the participants. Still, it should be remembered that the power of the liturgical celebrations does not consist in frequently altering the rites, but in probing more deeply the word of God and the mystery being celebrated.[100]

40.   Nevertheless, from the fact that the liturgical celebration obviously entails activity, it does not follow that everyone must necessarily have something concrete to do beyond the actions and gestures, as if a certain specific liturgical ministry must necessarily be given to the individuals to be carried out by them. Instead, catechetical instruction should strive diligently to correct those widespread superficial notions and practices often seen in recent years in this regard, and ever to instill anew in all of Christ's faithful that sense of deep wonder before the greatness of the mystery of faith that is the Eucharist, in whose celebration the Church is forever passing from what is obsolete into newness of life: "*in novitatem a vetustate.*"[101] For in the celebration of the Eucharist, as in the

97. Cf. John Paul II, Encyclical Letter *Ecclesia de Eucharistia*, nn. 12–18: AAS 95 (2003) pp. 441–445; Letter *Dominicae Cenae*, 24 February 1980, n. 9: AAS 72 (1980) pp. 129–133.

98. John Paul II, Encyclical Letter *Ecclesia de Eucharistia*, n. 10: AAS 95 (2003) p. 439.

99. Cf. Second Vatican Ecumenical Council, Constitution on the Sacred Liturgy, *Sacrosanctum Concilium*, nn. 30–31.

100. Cf. Sacred Congregation for Divine Worship, Instruction *Liturgicae instaurationes*, n. 1: AAS 62 (1970) p. 695.

101. Cf. *Missale Romanum*, Feria secunda post Dominica V in Quadragesima, Collecta, p. 258.

whole Christian life which draws its power from it and leads toward it, the Church, after the manner of Saint Thomas the Apostle, prostrates herself in adoration before the Lord who was crucified, suffered and died, was buried and arose, and perpetually exclaims to him who is clothed in the fullness of his divine splendour: "My Lord and my God!"[102]

41.   For encouraging, promoting and nourishing this interior understanding of liturgical participation, the continuous and widespread celebration of the Liturgy of the Hours, the use of the sacramentals and exercises of Christian popular piety are extremely helpful. These latter exercises—which "while not belonging to the Liturgy in the strict sense, possess nonetheless a particular importance and dignity"—are to be regarded as having a certain connection with the liturgical context, especially when they have been lauded and attested by the Magisterium itself,[103] as is the case especially of the Marian Rosary.[104] Furthermore, since these practices of piety lead the Christian people both to the reception of the sacraments—especially the Eucharist—and "to meditation on the mysteries of our Redemption and the imitation of the excellent heavenly examples of the Saints, they are therefore not without salutary effects for our participation in liturgical worship."[105]

42.   It must be acknowledged that the Church has not come together by human volition; rather, she has been called together by God in the Holy Spirit, and she responds through faith to his free calling (thus the word *ekklesia* is related to *klesis*, or "calling").[106] Nor is the Eucharistic Sacrifice to be considered a "concelebration," in the univocal sense, of the Priest along with the people who are present.[107] On the contrary, the Eucharist celebrated by the Priests "is a gift which radically transcends the power of the community . . . .The community that gathers for the celebration of the Eucharist absolutely requires an ordained Priest, who presides over it so that it may truly be a eucharistic convocation. On the other hand, the community is by itself incapable of providing an ordained minister."[108] There is pressing need of a concerted will to avoid all ambiguity in this matter and to remedy the difficulties of recent years. Accordingly, terms such as "celebrating community" or "celebrating assembly" (in other languages

---

102. Cf. John Paul II, Apostolic Letter *Novo Millennio ineunte*, 6 January 2001, n. 21: AAS 93 (2001) p. 280; cf. John 20:28.

103. Cf. Pius XII, Encyclical Letter *Mediator Dei:* AAS 39 (1947) p. 586; cf. also Second Vatican Ecumenical Council, Dogmatic Constitution on the Church, *Lumen gentium*, n. 67; Paul VI, Apostolic Exhortation *Marialis cultus*, 11 February 1974, n. 24: AAS 66 (1974) pp. 113–168, here p. 134; Congregation for Divine Worship and the Discipline of the Sacraments, *Direttorio su pietà popolare e Liturgia*, 17 December 2001.

104. John Paul II, Apostolic Letter, *Rosarium Virginis Mariae*, 16 October 2002: AAS 95 (2003) pp. 5–36.

105. Cf. Pius XII, Encyclical Letter *Mediator Dei:* AAS 39 (1947) pp. 586–587.

106. Cf. Congregation for Divine Worship and the Discipline of the Sacraments, Instruction, *Varietates legitimae*, n. 22: AAS 87 (1995) p. 297.

107. Cf. Pius XII, Encyclical Letter, *Mediator Dei:* AAS 39 (1947) p. 553.

108. John Paul II, Encyclical Letter, *Ecclesia de Eucharistia*, n. 29: AAS 95 (2003) p. 453; cf. Fourth Lateran Ecumenical Council, 11–30 November 1215, Chapter I: DS 802; Ecumenical Council of Trent, Session XXIII, 15 July 1563, Doctrine and Canons on Sacred Order, Chapter 4: DS 1767–1770; Pius XII, Encyclical Letter, *Mediator Dei:* AAS 39 (1947) p. 553.

"asamblea celebrante," "assemblée célébrante," assemblea celebrante") and similar terms should not be used injudiciously.

2. THE MINISTRIES OF THE LAY CHRISTIAN FAITHFUL IN THE CELEBRATION OF HOLY MASS

43.   For the good of the community and of the whole Church of God, some of the lay faithful according to tradition have rightly and laudably exercised ministries in the celebration of the Sacred Liturgy.[109] It is appropriate that a number of persons distribute among themselves and exercise various ministries or different parts of the same ministry.[110]

44.   Apart from the duly instituted ministries of acolyte and lector,[111] the most important of these ministries are those of acolyte[112] and lector[113] by temporary deputation. In addition to these are the other functions that are described in the Roman Missal,[114] as well as the functions of preparing the hosts, washing the liturgical linens, and the like. All, "whether ordained ministers or lay faithful, in exercising their own office or ministry should do exclusively and fully that which pertains to them."[115] In the liturgical celebration itself as well as in its preparation, they should do what is necessary so that the Church's Liturgy will be carried out worthily and appropriately.

45.   To be avoided is the danger of obscuring the complementary relationship between the action of clerics and that of laypersons, in such a way that the ministry of laypersons undergoes what might be called a certain "clericalization," while the sacred ministers inappropriately assume those things that are proper to the life and activity of the lay faithful.[116]

---

109. Cf. *Code of Canon Law*, canon 230 § 2; cf. also the *Missale Romanum*, Institutio Generalis, n. 97.

110. Cf. *Missale Romanum*, General Instruction, n. 109.

111. Cf. Paul VI, Apostolic Letter (Motu Proprio) *Ministeria quaedam*, 15 August 1972, nn. VI–XII; *Pontificale Romanum* ex decreto sacrosancti oecumenici Concilii Vaticani II instauratum, auctoritate Pauli Pp. VI promulgatum, *De institutione lectorum et acolythorum, de admissione inter candidatos ad diaconatum et presbyteratum, de sacro caelibatu amplectendo*, editio typica, 3 December 1972, Typis Polyglottis Vaticanis, 1973, p. 10: AAS 64 (1972) pp. 529–534, here pp. 532–533; *Code of Canon Law*, canon 230 §1; *Missale Romanum*, Institutio Generalis, nn. 98–99, 187–193.

112. Cf. *Missale Romanum*, Institutio Generalis, nn. 187–190, 193; *Code of Canon Law*, canon 230 §2–3.

113. Cf. Second Vatican Ecumenical Council, Constitution on the Sacred Liturgy, *Sacrosanctum Concilium*, n. 24; Sacred Congregation for the Sacraments and Divine Worship, Instruction, *Inaestimabile donum*, nn. 2 and 18: AAS 72 (1980) pp. 334, 338; *Missale Romanum*, Institutio Generalis, nn. 101, 194–198; *Code of Canon Law*, canon 230 §2–3.

114. Cf. *Missale Romanum*, Institutio Generalis, nn. 100–107.

115. Ibidem, n. 91; cf. Second Vatican Ecumenical Council, Constitution on the Sacred Liturgy, *Sacrosanctum Concilium*, n. 28.

116. Cf. John Paul II, Allocution to the Conference of Bishops of the Antilles, 7 May 2002, n. 2: AAS 94 (2002) pp. 575–577; Post-Synodal Apostolic Exhortation, *Christifideles laici*, 30 December 1988, n. 23: AAS 81 (1989) pp. 393–521, here pp. 429–431; Congregation for the Clergy et al., Instruction, *Ecclesiae de mysterio*, 15 August 1997, Theological Principles, n. 4: AAS 89 (1997) pp. 860–861.

46.   The lay Christian faithful called to give assistance at liturgical celebrations should be well instructed and must be those whose Christian life, morals and fidelity to the Church's Magisterium recommend them. It is fitting that such a one should have received a liturgical formation in accordance with his or her age, condition, state of life, and religious culture.[117] No one should be selected whose designation could cause consternation for the faithful.[118]

47.   It is altogether laudable to maintain the noble custom by which boys or youths, customarily termed servers, provide service of the altar after the manner of acolytes, and receive catechesis regarding their function in accordance with their power of comprehension.[119] Nor should it be forgotten that a great number of sacred ministers over the course of the centuries have come from among boys such as these.[120] Associations for them, including also the participation and assistance of their parents, should be established or promoted, and in such a way greater pastoral care will be provided for the ministers. Whenever such associations are international in nature, it pertains to the competence of the Congregation for Divine Worship and the Discipline of the Sacraments to establish them or to approve and revise their statutes.[121] Girls or women may also be admitted to this service of the altar, at the discretion of the diocesan Bishop and in observance of the established norms.[122]

CHAPTER III
THE PROPER CELEBRATION OF MASS

1. THE MATTER OF THE MOST HOLY EUCHARIST

48.   The bread used in the celebration of the Most Holy Eucharistic Sacrifice must be unleavened, purely of wheat, and recently made so that there is no danger of decomposition.[123] It follows therefore that bread made from another substance, even if it is grain, or if it is mixed with another substance different from wheat to such an extent that it would not commonly be considered wheat bread, does not constitute valid matter for confecting the Sacrifice and the Eucharistic

---

117. Cf. Second Vatican Ecumenical Council, Constitution on the Sacred Liturgy, *Sacrosanctum Concilium*, n. 19.
118. Sacred Congregation for Divine Worship, Instruction, *Immensae caritatis*, 29 January 1973: AAS 65 (1973) p. 266.
119. Cf. Sacred Congregation of Rites, Instruction, *De Musica sacra*, 3 September 1958, n. 93c: AAS 50 (1958) p. 656.
120. Cf. Pontifical Council for the Interpretation of Legislative Texts, Response to dubium, 11 July 1992: AAS 86 (1994) pp. 541–542; Congregation for Divine Worship and the Discipline of the Sacraments, Letter to the Presidents of Conferences of Bishops on the liturgical service of laypersons, 15 March 1994: *Notitiae* 30 (1994) pp. 333–335, 347–348.
121. Cf. John Paul II, Apostolic Constitution, *Pastor Bonus*, article 65: AAS 80 (1988) p. 877.
122. Cf. Pontifical Council for the Interpretation of Legislative Texts, Response to dubium, 11 July 1992: AAS 86 (1994) pp. 541–542; Congregation for Divine Worship and the Discipline of the Sacraments, Letter to the Presidents of the Conferences of Bishops concerning the liturgical service of laypersons, 15 March 1994: *Notitiae* 30 (1994) pp. 333–335, 347–348; Letter to a Bishop, 27 July 2001: *Notitiae* 38 (2002) 46–54.
123. Cf. *Code of Canon Law*, can. 924 §2; *Missale Romanum*, Institutio Generalis, n. 320.

Sacrament.[124] It is a grave abuse to introduce other substances, such as fruit or sugar or honey, into the bread for confecting the Eucharist. Hosts should obviously be made by those who are not only distinguished by their integrity, but also skilled in making them and furnished with suitable tools.[125]

49.   By reason of the sign, it is appropriate that at least some parts of the Eucharistic Bread coming from the fraction should be distributed to at least some of the faithful in Communion. "Small hosts are, however, in no way ruled out when the number of those receiving Holy Communion or other pastoral needs require it,"[126] and indeed small hosts requiring no further fraction ought customarily to be used for the most part.

50.   The wine that is used in the most sacred celebration of the Eucharistic Sacrifice must be natural, from the fruit of the grape, pure and incorrupt, not mixed with other substances.[127] During the celebration itself, a small quantity of water is to be mixed with it. Great care should be taken so that the wine intended for the celebration of the Eucharist is well conserved and has not soured.[128] It is altogether forbidden to use wine of doubtful authenticity or provenance, for the Church requires certainty regarding the conditions necessary for the validity of the sacraments. Nor are other drinks of any kind to be admitted for any reason, as they do not constitute valid matter.

2. THE EUCHARISTIC PRAYER

51.   Only those Eucharistic Prayers are to be used which are found in the Roman Missal or are legitimately approved by the Apostolic See, and according to the manner and the terms set forth by it. "It is not to be tolerated that some Priests take upon themselves the right to compose their own Eucharistic Prayers"[129] or to change the same texts approved by the Church, or to introduce others composed by private individuals.[130]

52.   The proclamation of the Eucharistic Prayer, which by its very nature is the climax of the whole celebration, is proper to the Priest by virtue of his Ordination. It is therefore an abuse to proffer it in such a way that some parts of the Eucharistic Prayer are recited by a Deacon, a lay minister, or by an individual member of the faithful, or by all members of the faithful together. The Eucharistic Prayer, then, is to be recited by the Priest alone in full.[131]

---

124. Cf. Sacred Congregation for the Discipline of the Sacraments, Instruction,
Dominus Salvator noster, 26 March 1929, n. 1: AAS 21 (1929) pp. 631–642, here p. 632.

125. Cf. ibidem, n. II: AAS 21 (1929) p. 635.

126. Cf. *Missale Romanum*, Institutio Generalis, n. 321.

127. Cf. Luke 22:18; *Code of Canon Law*, canon 924 §§ 1, 3; *Missale Romanum*,
Institutio Generalis, n. 322.

128. Cf. *Missale Romanum*, Institutio Generalis, n. 323.

129. John Paul II, Apostolic Letter, *Vicesimus quintus annus*, n. 13, AAS 81 (1989).

130. Sacred Congregation for the Sacraments and Divine Worship, Instruction,
Inaestimabile donum, n. 5: AAS 72 (1980) p. 335.

131. Cf. John Paul II, Encyclical Letter, *Ecclesia de Eucharistia*, n. 28: AAS 95 (2003) p. 452;
Missale Romanum, Institutio Generalis, n. 147; Sacred Congregation for Divine Worship,

53.   While the Priest proclaims the Eucharistic Prayer "there should be no other prayers or singing, and the organ or other musical instruments should be silent,"[132] except for the people's acclamations that have been duly approved, as described below.

54.   The people, however, are always involved actively and never merely passively: for they "silently join themselves with the Priest in faith, as well as in their interventions during the course of the Eucharistic Prayer as prescribed, namely in the responses in the Preface dialogue, the *Sanctus*, the acclamation after the consecration and the *"Amen"* after the final doxology, and in other acclamations approved by the Conference of Bishops with the *recognitio* of the Holy See."[133]

55.   In some places there has existed an abuse by which the Priest breaks the host at the time of the consecration in the Holy Mass. This abuse is contrary to the tradition of the Church. It is reprobated and is to be corrected with haste.

56.   The mention of the name of the Supreme Pontiff and the diocesan Bishop in the Eucharistic Prayer is not to be omitted, since this is a most ancient tradition to be maintained, and a manifestation of ecclesial communion. For "the coming together of the eucharistic community is at the same time a joining in union with its own Bishop and with the Roman Pontiff."[134]

3. THE OTHER PARTS OF THE MASS

57.   It is the right of the community of Christ's faithful that especially in the Sunday celebration there should customarily be true and suitable sacred music, and that there should always be an altar, vestments and sacred linens that are dignified, proper, and clean, in accordance with the norms.

58.   All of Christ's faithful likewise have the right to a celebration of the Eucharist that has been so carefully prepared in all its parts that the word of God is properly and efficaciously proclaimed and explained in it; that the faculty for selecting the liturgical texts and rites is carried out with care according to the norms; and that their faith is duly safeguarded and nourished by the words that are sung in the celebration of the Liturgy.

59.   The reprobated practice by which Priests, Deacons or the faithful here and there alter or vary at will the texts of the Sacred Liturgy that they are charged to pronounce, must cease. For in doing thus, they render the celebration of the Sacred Liturgy unstable, and not infrequently distort the authentic meaning of the Liturgy.

Instruction, *Liturgicae instaurationes*, n. 4: AAS 62 (1970) p. 698; Sacred Congregation for the Sacraments and Divine Worship, Instruction, *Inaestimabile donum*, n. 4: AAS 72 (1980) p. 334.
132. *Missale Romanum*, Institutio Generalis, n. 32.
133. Ibidem, n. 147; cf. John Paul II, Encyclical Letter, *Ecclesia de Eucharistia*, n. 28: AAS 95 (2003) p. 452; cf. also Congregation for the Sacraments and Divine Worship, Instruction, *Inaestimabile donum*, n. 4: AAS 72 (1980) pp. 334–335.
134. John Paul II, Encyclical Letter, *Ecclesia de Eucharistia*, n. 39: AAS 95 (2003) p. 459.

60.   In the celebration of Mass, the Liturgy of the Word and the Liturgy of the Eucharist are intimately connected to one another, and form one single act of worship. For this reason it is not licit to separate one of these parts from the other and celebrate them at different times or places.[135] Nor is it licit to carry out the individual parts of Holy Mass at different times of the same day.

61.   In selecting the biblical readings for proclamation in the celebration of Mass, the norms found in the liturgical books are to be followed,[136] so that indeed "a richer table of the word of God will be prepared for the faithful, and the biblical treasures opened up for them."[137]

62.   It is also illicit to omit or to substitute the prescribed biblical readings on one's own initiative, and especially "to substitute other, non-biblical texts for the readings and responsorial Psalm, which contain the word of God."[138]

63.   "Within the celebration of the Sacred Liturgy, the reading of the Gospel, which is "the high point of the Liturgy of the Word,"[139] is reserved by the Church's tradition to an ordained minister.[140] Thus it is not permitted for a layperson, even a religious, to proclaim the Gospel reading in the celebration of Holy Mass, nor in other cases in which the norms do not explicitly permit it.[141]

64.   The homily, which is given in the course of the celebration of Holy Mass and is a part of the Liturgy itself,[142] "should ordinarily be given by the Priest celebrant himself. He may entrust it to a concelebrating Priest or occasionally, according to circumstances, to a Deacon, but never to a layperson.[143] In particular cases and for a just cause, the homily may even be given by a Bishop or a Priest who is present at the celebration but cannot concelebrate."[144]

---

135. Cf. Sacred Congregation for Divine Worship, Instruction, *Liturgicae instaurationes*, n. 2b: AAS 62 (1970) p. 696.

136. Cf. *Missale Romanum*, Institutio Generalis, nn. 356–362.

137. Cf. Second Vatican Ecumenical Council, Constitution on the Sacred Liturgy, *Sacrosanctum Concilium*, n. 51.

138. *Missale Romanum*, Institutio Generalis, n. 57; cf. John Paul II, Apostolic Letter, *Vicesimus quintus annus*, n. 13: AAS 81 (1989) p. 910; Congregation for the Doctrine of the Faith, Declaration, *Dominus Iesus*, on the unicity and salvific universality of Jesus Christ and the Church, 6 August 2000: AAS 92 (2000) pp. 742–765.

139. *Missale Romanum*, General Instruction, n. 60.

140. Cf. ibidem, nn. 59–60.

141. Cf., e.g., *Rituale Romanum*, ex decreto sacrosancti Oecumenici Concilii Vaticani II renovatum, auctoritate Pauli Pp. VI editum Ioannis Pauli Pp. II cura recognitum: *Ordo celebrandi Matrimonium*, editio typica altera, 19 March 1990, Typis Polyglottis Vaticanis 1991, n. 125; *Roman Ritual*, renewed by decree of the Second Vatican Ecumenical Council and promulgated by authority of Pope Paul VI: Order for Anointing of the Sick and for their Pastoral Care, *editio typica*, 7 December 1972, Vatican Polyglot Press, 1972, n. 72.

142. Cf. *Code of Canon Law*, canon 767 §1.

143. Cf. *Missale Romanum*, Institutio Generalis, n. 66; cf. also the *Code of Canon Law*, canon 6, §1, 2; also canon 767 §1, regarding which other noteworthy prescriptions may be found in Congregation for the Clergy et al., Instruction, *Ecclesiae de mysterio*, Practical Provisions, article 3 § 1: AAS 89 (1997) p. 865.

144. *Missale Romanum*, Institutio Generalis, n. 66; cf. also the *Code of Canon Law*, canon 767 §1.

65.   It should be borne in mind that any previous norm that may have admitted non-ordained faithful to give the homily during the eucharistic celebration is to be considered abrogated by the norm of canon 767 §1.[145] This practice is reprobated, so that it cannot be permitted to attain the force of custom.

66.   The prohibition of the admission of laypersons to preach within the Mass applies also to seminarians, students of theological disciplines, and those who have assumed the function of those known as "pastoral assistants"; nor is there to be any exception for any other kind of layperson, or group, or community, or association.[146]

67.   Particular care is to be taken so that the homily is firmly based upon the mysteries of salvation, expounding the mysteries of the Faith and the norms of Christian life from the biblical readings and liturgical texts throughout the course of the liturgical year and providing commentary on the texts of the Ordinary or the Proper of the Mass, or of some other rite of the Church.[147] It is clear that all interpretations of Sacred Scripture are to be referred back to Christ himself as the one upon whom the entire economy of salvation hinges, though this should be done in light of the specific context of the liturgical celebration. In the homily to be given, care is to be taken so that the light of Christ may shine upon life's events. Even so, this is to be done so as not to obscure the true and unadulterated word of God: for instance, treating only of politics or profane subjects, or drawing upon notions derived from contemporary pseudo-religious currents as a source.[148]

68.   The diocesan Bishop must diligently oversee the preaching of the homily,[149] also publishing norms and distributing guidelines and auxiliary tools to the sacred ministers, and promoting meetings and other projects for this purpose so that they may have the opportunity to consider the nature of the homily more precisely and find help in its preparation.

69.   In Holy Mass as well as in other celebrations of the Sacred Liturgy, no Creed or Profession of Faith is to be introduced which is not found in the duly approved liturgical books.

70.   The offerings that Christ's faithful are accustomed to present for the Liturgy of the Eucharist in Holy Mass are not necessarily limited to bread and wine for the eucharistic celebration, but may also include gifts given by the faithful in

---

145. Cf. Congregation for the Clergy et al., Instruction, *Ecclesiae de mysterio*, Practical Provisions, article 3 §1: AAS 89 (1997) p. 865; cf. also the *Code of Canon Law*, canon 6 §1, 2; Pontifical Commission for the Authentic Interpretation of the Code of Canon Law, Response to dubium, 20 June 1987: AAS 79 (1987) p. 1249.
146. Cf. Congregation for the Clergy et al., Instruction, *Ecclesiae de mysterio*, Practical Provisions, article 3 § 1: AAS 89 (1997) pp. 864–865.
147. Cf. Ecumenical Council of Trent, Session XXII, 17 September 1562, on the Most Holy Sacrifice of the Mass, Chapter 8: DS 1749; *Missale Romanum*, Institutio Generalis, n. 65.
148. Cf. John Paul II, Allocution to a number of Bishops from the United States of America who had come to Rome for a visit "ad Limina Apostolorum," 28 May 1993, n. 2: AAS 86 (1994) p. 330.
149. Cf. *Code of Canon Law*, canon 386 §1.

the form of money or other things for the sake of charity toward the poor. Moreover, external gifts must always be a visible expression of that true gift that God expects from us: a contrite heart, the love of God and neighbour by which we are conformed to the sacrifice of Christ, who offered himself for us. For in the Eucharist, there shines forth most brilliantly that mystery of charity that Jesus brought forth at the Last Supper by washing the feet of the disciples. In order to preserve the dignity of the Sacred Liturgy, in any event, the external offerings should be brought forward in an appropriate manner. Money, therefore, just as other contributions for the poor, should be placed in an appropriate place which should be away from the eucharistic table.[150] Except for money and occasionally a minimal symbolic portion of other gifts, it is preferable that such offerings be made outside the celebration of Mass.

71.   The practice of the Roman Rite is to be maintained according to which the peace is extended shortly before Holy Communion. For according to the tradition of the Roman Rite, this practice does not have the connotation either of reconciliation or of a remission of sins, but instead signifies peace, communion and charity before the reception of the Most Holy Eucharist.[151] It is rather the Penitential Act to be carried out at the beginning of Mass (especially in its first form) which has the character of reconciliation among brothers and sisters.

72.   It is appropriate "that each one give the sign of peace only to those who are nearest and in a sober manner." "The Priest may give the sign of peace to the ministers but always remains within the sanctuary, so as not to disturb the celebration. He does likewise if for a just reason he wishes to extend the sign of peace to some few of the faithful." "As regards the sign to be exchanged, the manner is to be established by the Conference of Bishops in accordance with the dispositions and customs of the people," and their acts are subject to the *recognitio* of the Apostolic See.[152]

73.   In the celebration of Holy Mass the breaking of the Eucharistic Bread—done only by the Priest celebrant, if necessary with the help of a Deacon or of a concelebrant—begins after the exchange of peace, while the *Agnus Dei* is being recited. For the gesture of breaking bread "carried out by Christ at the Last Supper, which in apostolic times gave the whole eucharistic action its name, signifies that the faithful, though they are many, are made one Body in the communion of the one Bread of Life who is Christ, who died and rose for the world's salvation" (cf. 1 Corinthian 10:17).[153] For this reason the rite must be carried out with great reverence.[154] Even so, it should be brief. The abuse that has prevailed in some places, by which this rite is unnecessarily prolonged and given undue emphasis, with laypersons also helping in contradiction to the norms, should be corrected with all haste.[155]

---

150. Cf. *Missale Romanum*, Institutio Generalis, n. 73.

151. Cf. ibidem, n. 154.

152. Cf. ibidem, nn. 82, 154.

153. Cf. ibidem, n. 83.

154. Cf. Sacred Congregation for Divine Worship, Instruction, *Liturgicae instaurationes*, n. 5: AAS 62 (1970) p. 699.

155. Cf. *Missale Romanum*, Institutio Generalis, nn. 83, 240, 321.

74.   If the need arises for the gathered faithful to be given instruction or testimony by a layperson in a Church concerning the Christian life, it is altogether preferable that this be done outside Mass. Nevertheless, for serious reasons it is permissible that this type of instruction or testimony be given after the Priest has proclaimed the Prayer after Communion. This should not become a regular practice, however. Furthermore, these instructions and testimony should not be of such a nature that they could be confused with the homily,[156] nor is it permissible to dispense with the homily on their account.

4. ON THE JOINING OF VARIOUS RITES WITH THE CELEBRATION OF MASS

75.   On account of the theological significance inherent in a particular rite and the Eucharistic Celebration, the liturgical books sometimes prescribe or permit the celebration of Holy Mass to be joined with another rite, especially one of those pertaining to the Sacraments.[157] The Church does not permit such a conjoining in other cases, however, especially when it is a question of trivial matters.

76.   Furthermore, according to a most ancient tradition of the Roman Church, it is not permissible to unite the Sacrament of Penance to the Mass in such a way that they become a single liturgical celebration. This does not exclude, however, that Priests other than those celebrating or concelebrating the Mass might hear the confessions of the faithful who so desire, even in the same place where Mass is being celebrated, in order to meet the needs of those faithful.[158] This should nevertheless be done in an appropriate manner.

77.   The celebration of Holy Mass is not to be inserted in any way into the setting of a common meal, nor joined with this kind of banquet. Mass is not to be celebrated without grave necessity on a dinner table[159] nor in a dining room or banquet hall, nor in a room where food is present, nor in a place where the participants during the celebration itself are seated at tables. If out of grave necessity Mass must be celebrated in the same place where eating will later take place, there is to be a clear interval of time between the conclusion of Mass and the beginning of the meal, and ordinary food is not to be set before the faithful during the celebration of Mass.

---

156. Cf. Congregation For the Clergy et al., Instruction, *Ecclesiae de mysterio*, Practical Provisions, article 3 §2: AAS 89 (1997) p. 865.

157. Cf. especially the General Instruction of the Liturgy of the Hours, nn. 93–98; *Roman Ritual*, revised by decree of the Second Vatican Ecumenical Council and published by authority of Pope John Paul II: *Book of Blessings*, editio typica, 31 May 1984, General Introduction, n. 28; Order of Crowning an Image of the Blessed Virgin Mary, editio typica, 25 March 1981, nn. 10 and 14; S. Congregation for Divine Worship, Instruction, on Masses with Particular Groups, *Actio pastoralis*, 15 May 1969: AAS 61 (1969) pp. 806–811; Directory for Masses with Children, Pueros baptizatos, 1 November 1973: AAS 66 (1974) pp. 30–46; *Missale Romanum*, Institutio Generalis, n. 21.

158. Cf. John Paul II, Apostolic Letter (Motu Proprio), *Misericordia Dei*, 7 April 2002, n. 2: AAS 94 (2002) p. 455; Cf. Congregation for Divine Worship and the Discipline of the Sacraments, Response to Dubium: *Notitiae* 37 (2001) pp. 259–260.

159. Cf. Sacred Congregation for Divine Worship, Instruction, *Liturgicae instaurationes*, n. 9: AAS 62 (1970) p. 702.

78.   It is not permissible to link the celebration of Mass to political or secular events, nor to situations that are not fully consistent with the Magisterium of the Catholic Church. Furthermore, it is altogether to be avoided that the celebration of Mass should be carried out merely out of a desire for show, or in the manner of other ceremonies including profane ones, lest the Eucharist should be emptied of its authentic meaning.

79.   Finally, it is strictly to be considered an abuse to introduce into the celebration of Holy Mass elements that are contrary to the prescriptions of the liturgical books and taken from the rites of other religions.

CHAPTER IV
HOLY COMMUNION

1. DISPOSITIONS FOR THE RECEPTION OF HOLY COMMUNION

80.   The Eucharist is to be offered to the faithful, among other reasons, "as an antidote, by which we are freed from daily faults and preserved from mortal sins,"[160] as is brought to light in various parts of the Mass. As for the Penitential Act placed at the beginning of Mass, it has the purpose of preparing all to be ready to celebrate the sacred mysteries;[161] even so, "it lacks the efficacy of the Sacrament of Penance,"[162] and cannot be regarded as a substitute for the Sacrament of Penance in remission of graver sins. Pastors of souls should take care to ensure diligent catechetical instruction, so that Christian doctrine is handed on to Christ's faithful in this matter.

81.   The Church's custom shows that it is necessary for each person to examine himself at depth,[163] and that anyone who is conscious of grave sin should not celebrate or receive the Body of the Lord without prior sacramental confession, except for grave reason when the possibility of confession is lacking; in this case he will remember that he is bound by the obligation of making an act of perfect contrition, which includes the intention to confess as soon as possible."[164]

82.   Moreover, "the Church has drawn up norms aimed at fostering the frequent and fruitful access of the faithful to the Eucharistic table and at determining the objective conditions under which Communion may not be given."[165]

---

160. Ecumenical Council of Trent, Session XIII, 11 October 1551, Decree on the Most Holy Eucharist, Chapter 2: DS 1638; cf. Session XXII, 17 September 1562, On the Most Holy Sacrifice of the Mass, Chapters 1–2: DS 1740, 1743; Sacred Congregation of Rites, Instruction, *Eucharisticum mysterium*, n. 35: AAS 59 (1967) p. 560.
161. Cf. *Missale Romanum*, Ordo Missae, n. 4, p. 505.
162. *Missale Romanum*, Institutio Generalis, n. 51.
163. Cf. 1 Corinthians 11:28.
164. Cf. *Code of Canon Law*, canon 916; cf. Ecumenical Council of Trent, Session XIII, 11 October 1551, Decree on the Most Holy Eucharist, Chapter 7: DS 1646–1647; John Paul II, Encyclical Letter, *Ecclesia de Eucharistia*, n. 36: AAS 95 (2003) pp. 457–458; Sacred Congregation of Rites, Instruction, *Eucharisticum mysterium*, n. 35: AAS 59 (1967) p. 561.
165. Cf. John Paul II, Encyclical Letter, *Ecclesia de Eucharistia*, n. 42: AAS 95 (2003) p. 461.

83.   It is certainly best that all who are participating in the celebration of Holy Mass with the necessary dispositions should receive Communion. Nevertheless, it sometimes happens that Christ's faithful approach the altar as a group indiscriminately. It pertains to the Pastors prudently and firmly to correct such an abuse.

84.   Furthermore when Holy Mass is celebrated for a large crowd—for example, in large cities—care should be taken lest out of ignorance non-Catholics or even non-Christians come forward for Holy Communion, without taking into account the Church's Magisterium in matters pertaining to doctrine and discipline. It is the duty of Pastors at an opportune moment to inform those present of the authenticity and the discipline that are strictly to be observed.

85.   Catholic ministers licitly administer the Sacraments only to the Catholic faithful, who likewise receive them licitly only from Catholic ministers, except for those situations for which provision is made in canon 844 §§ 2, 3, and 4, and canon 861 § 2.[166] In addition, the conditions comprising canon 844 § 4, from which no dispensation can be given,[167] cannot be separated; thus, it is necessary that all of these conditions be present together.

86.   The faithful should be led insistently to the practice whereby they approach the Sacrament of Penance outside the celebration of Mass, especially at the scheduled times, so that the Sacrament may be administered in a manner that is tranquil and truly beneficial to them, so as not to be prevented from active participation at Mass. Those who are accustomed to receiving Communion often or daily should be instructed that they should approach the Sacrament of Penance at appropriate intervals, in accordance with the condition of each.[168]

87.   The First Communion of children must always be preceded by sacramental confession and absolution.[169] Moreover First Communion should always be administered by a Priest and never outside the celebration of Mass. Apart from exceptional cases, it is not particularly appropriate for First Communion to be administered on Holy Thursday of the Lord's Supper. Another day should be chosen instead, such as a Sunday between the Second and the Sixth Sunday of Easter, or the Solemnity of the Body and Blood of Christ, or the Sundays of

---

166. Cf. *Code of Canon Law*, n. 844 § 1; John Paul II, Encyclical Letter *Ecclesia de Eucharistia*, nn. 45–46: AAS 95 (2003) pp. 463–464; cf. also Pontifical Council for the Promotion of Christian Unity, Directory for the application of the principles and norms on ecumenism, *La recherche de l'unité*, nn. 130–131: AAS 85 (1993) 1039–1119, here p. 1089.

167. Cf. John Paul II, Encyclical Letter *Ecclesia de Eucharistia*, n. 46: AAS 95 (2003) pp. 463–464.

168. Cf. Sacred Congregation of Rites, Instruction, *Eucharisticum mysterium*, n. 35: AAS 59 (1967) p. 561.

169. Cf. *Code of Canon Law*, can. 914; Sacred Congregation for the Discipline of the Sacraments, Declaration, *Sanctus Pontifex*, diei 24 maii 1973: AAS 65 (1973) p. 410; Sacred Congregation for the Sacraments and Divine Worship and Sacred Congregation for the Clergy, Letter to the Presidents of the Bishops' Conferences. Episcoporum, *In quibusdam*, 31 March 1977: *Enchiridion Documentorum Instaurationis Liturgicae*, II, pp. 142–144; Sacred Congregation for the Sacraments and Divine Worship and S. Congregation for the Clergy, Response to dubium, 20 May 1977: AAS 69 (1977) p. 427.

Ordinary Time, since Sunday is rightly regarded as the day of the Eucharist.[170] "Children who have not attained the age of reason, or those whom" the Parish Priest "has determined to be insufficiently prepared" should not come forward to receive the Holy Eucharist.[171] Where it happens, however, that a child who is exceptionally mature for his age is judged to be ready for receiving the Sacrament, the child must not be denied First Communion provided he has received sufficient instruction.

2. THE DISTRIBUTION OF HOLY COMMUNION

88.   The faithful should normally receive sacramental Communion of the Eucharist during Mass itself, at the moment laid down by the rite of celebration, that is to say, just after the Priest celebrant's Communion.[172] It is the Priest celebrant's responsibility to minister Communion, perhaps assisted by other Priests or Deacons; and he should not resume the Mass until after the Communion of the faithful is concluded. Only when there is a necessity may extraordinary ministers assist the Priest celebrant in accordance with the norm of law.[173]

89.   "So that even by means of the signs Communion may stand out more clearly as a participation in the Sacrifice being celebrated,"[174] it is preferable that the faithful be able to receive hosts consecrated in the same Mass.[175]

90.   "The faithful should receive Communion kneeling or standing, as the Conference of Bishops will have determined," with its acts having received the *recognitio* of the Apostolic See. "However, if they receive Communion standing, it is recommended that they give due reverence before the reception of the Sacrament, as set forth in the same norms."[176]

91.   In distributing Holy Communion it is to be remembered that "sacred ministers may not deny the sacraments to those who seek them in a reasonable manner, are rightly disposed, and are not prohibited by law from receiving them."[177] Hence any baptized Catholic who is not prevented by law must be admitted to Holy Communion. Therefore, it is not licit to deny Holy Communion to any of Christ's faithful solely on the grounds, for example, that the person wishes to receive the Eucharist kneeling or standing.

---

170. Cf. John Paul II, Apostolic Letter, *Dies Domini*, 31 May 1998, nn. 31–34: AAS 90 (1998) pp. 713–766, here pp. 731–734.

171. Cf. *Code of Canon Law*, canon 914.

172. Cf. Second Vatican Ecumenical Council, Constitution on the Sacred Liturgy, *Sacrosanctum Concilium*, n. 55.

173. Cf. Sacred Congregation of Rites, Instruction, *Eucharisticum mysterium*, n. 31: AAS 59 (1967) p. 558; Pontifical Commission for the Authentic Interpretation of the Code of Canon Law, Response to dubium, 1 June 1988: AAS 80 (1988) p. 1373.

174. *Missale Romanum*, Institutio Generalis, n. 85.

175. Cf. Second Vatican Ecumenical Council, Constitution on the Sacred Liturgy, *Sacrosanctum Concilium*, n. 55; Sacred Congregation of Rites, Instruction, *Eucharisticum mysterium*, n. 31: AAS 59 (1967) p. 558; *Missale Romanum*, Institutio Generalis, nn. 85, 157, 243.

176. Cf. *Missale Romanum*, Institutio Generalis, n. 160.

177. *Code of Canon Law*, canon 843 § 1; cf. canon 915.

92. Although each of the faithful always has the right to receive Holy Communion on the tongue, at his choice,[178] if any communicant should wish to receive the Sacrament in the hand, in areas where the Bishops' Conference with the *recognitio* of the Apostolic See has given permission, the sacred host is to be administered to him or her. However, special care should be taken to ensure that the host is consumed by the communicant in the presence of the minister, so that no one goes away carrying the Eucharistic species in his hand. If there is a risk of profanation, then Holy Communion should not be given in the hand to the faithful.[179]

93. The Communion-plate for the Communion of the faithful should be retained, so as to avoid the danger of the sacred host or some fragment of it falling.[180]

94. It is not licit for the faithful "to take . . . by themselves . . . and, still less, to hand . . . from one to another" the sacred host or the sacred chalice.[181] Moreover, in this regard, the abuse is to be set aside whereby spouses administer Holy Communion to each other at a Nuptial Mass.

95. A lay member of Christ's faithful "who has already received the Most Holy Eucharist may receive it again on the same day only within a Eucharistic Celebration in which he or she is participating, with due regard for the prescriptions of canon 921 § 2."[182]

96. The practice is reprobated whereby either unconsecrated hosts or other edible or inedible things are distributed during the celebration of Holy Mass or beforehand after the manner of Communion, contrary to the prescriptions of the liturgical books. For such a practice in no way accords with the tradition of the Roman Rite, and carries with it the danger of causing confusion among Christ's faithful concerning the Eucharistic doctrine of the Church. Where there exists in certain places by concession a particular custom of blessing bread after Mass for distribution, proper catechesis should very carefully be given concerning this action. In fact, no other similar practices should be introduced, nor should unconsecrated hosts ever be used for this purpose.

3. THE COMMUNION OF PRIESTS

97. A Priest must communicate at the altar at the moment laid down by the Missal each time he celebrates Holy Mass, and the concelebrants must communicate before they proceed with the distribution of Holy Communion. The Priest celebrant or a concelebrant is never to wait until the people's Communion is concluded before receiving Communion himself.[183]

---

178. Cf. *Missale Romanum*, Institutio Generalis, n. 161.

179. Congregation for Divine Worship and the Discipline of the Sacraments, Dubium: *Notitiae* 35 (1999) pp. 160–161.

180. Cf. *Missale Romanum*, Institutio Generalis, n. 118.

181. Ibidem, n.160.

182. Cf. *Code of Canon Law*, can. 917; Pontifical Commission for the Authentic Interpretation of the Code of Canon Law, Response to Dubium, 11 July 1984: AAS 76 (1984) p. 746.

183. Cf. Second Vatican Ecumenical Council, Constitution on the Sacred Liturgy, *Sacrosanctum Concilium*, n. 55; *Missale Romanum*, General Instruction, nn. 158–160, 243–244, 246.

98. The Communion of Priest concelebrants should proceed according to the norms prescribed in the liturgical books, always using hosts consecrated at the same Mass[184] and always with Communion under both kinds being received by all of the concelebrants. It is to be noted that if the Priest or Deacon hands the sacred host or chalice to the concelebrants, he says nothing; that is to say, he does not pronounce the words "The Body of Christ" or "The Blood of Christ."

99. Communion under both kinds is always permitted "to Priests who are not able to celebrate or concelebrate Mass."[185]

4. COMMUNION UNDER BOTH KINDS

100. So that the fullness of the sign may be made more clearly evident to the faithful in the course of the Eucharistic banquet, lay members of Christ's faithful, too, are admitted to Communion under both kinds, in the cases set forth in the liturgical books, preceded and continually accompanied by proper catechesis regarding the dogmatic principles on this matter laid down by the Ecumenical Council of Trent.[186]

101. In order for Holy Communion under both kinds to be administered to the lay members of Christ's faithful, due consideration should be given to the circumstances, as judged first of all by the diocesan Bishop. It is to be completely excluded where even a small danger exists of the sacred species being profaned.[187] With a view to wider co-ordination, the Bishops' Conferences should issue norms, once their decisions have received the *recognitio* of the Apostolic See through the Congregation for Divine Worship and the Discipline of the Sacraments, especially as regards "the manner of distributing Holy Communion to the faithful under both kinds, and the faculty for its extension."[188]

102. The chalice should not be ministered to lay members of Christ's faithful where there is such a large number of communicants[189] that it is difficult to gauge the amount of wine for the Eucharist and there is a danger that "more than a reasonable quantity of the Blood of Christ remain to be consumed at the end of the celebration."[190] The same is true wherever access to the chalice would be difficult to arrange, or where such a large amount of wine would be required that its certain provenance and quality could only be known with difficulty, or wherever there is not an adequate number of sacred ministers or extraordinary

---

184. Cf. *Missale Romanum*, Institutio Generalis, nn. 237–249; cf. also nn. 85, 157.

185. Cf. ibidem, n. 283a.

186. Cf. Ecumenical Council of Trent, Session XXI, 16 July 1562, Decree on Eucharistic Communion, Chapters 1–3: DS 1725–1729; Second Vatican Ecumenical Council, Constitution on the Sacred Liturgy, *Sacrosanctum Concilium*, n. 55; *Missale Romanum*, Institutio Generalis, nn. 282–283.

187. Cf. *Missale Romanum*, Institutio Generalis, n. 283.

188. Cf. ibidem.

189. Cf. Sacred Congregation for Divine Worship, Instruction, *Sacramentali Communione*, 29 June 1970: AAS 62 (1970) p. 665; Instruction, *Liturgicae instaurationes*, n. 6a: AAS 62 (1970) p. 699.

190. *Missale Romanum*, Institutio Generalis, n. 285a.

ministers of Holy Communion with proper formation, or where a notable part of the people continues to prefer not to approach the chalice for various reasons, so that the sign of unity would in some sense be negated.

103. The norms of the Roman Missal admit the principle that in cases where Communion is administered under both kinds, "the Blood of the Lord may be received either by drinking from the chalice directly, or by intinction, or by means of a tube or a spoon."[191] As regards the administering of Communion to lay members of Christ's faithful, the Bishops may exclude Communion with the tube or the spoon where this is not the local custom, though the option of administering Communion by intinction always remains. If this modality is employed, however, hosts should be used which are neither too thin nor too small, and the communicant should receive the Sacrament from the Priest only on the tongue.[192]

104. The communicant must not be permitted to intinct the host himself in the chalice, nor to receive the intincted host in the hand. As for the host to be used for the intinction, it should be made of valid matter, also consecrated; it is altogether forbidden to use non-consecrated bread or other matter.

105. If one chalice is not sufficient for Communion to be distributed under both kinds to the Priest concelebrants or Christ's faithful, there is no reason why the Priest celebrant should not use several chalices.[193] For it is to be remembered that all Priests in celebrating Holy Mass are bound to receive Communion under both kinds. It is praiseworthy, by reason of the sign value, to use a main chalice of larger dimensions, together with smaller chalices.

106. However, the pouring of the Blood of Christ after the consecration from one vessel to another is completely to be avoided, lest anything should happen that would be to the detriment of so great a mystery. Never to be used for containing the Blood of the Lord are flagons, bowls, or other vessels that are not fully in accord with the established norms.

107. In accordance with what is laid down by the canons, "one who throws away the consecrated species or takes them away or keeps them for a sacrilegious purpose, incurs a *latae sententiae* excommunication reserved to the Apostolic See; a cleric, moreover, may be punished by another penalty, not excluding dismissal from the clerical state."[194] To be regarded as pertaining to this case is any action that is voluntarily and gravely disrespectful of the sacred species. Anyone, therefore, who acts contrary to these norms, for example casting the sacred species into the sacrarium or in an unworthy place or on the ground, incurs the penalties laid down.[195] Furthermore all will remember that once the distribution of Holy Communion during the celebration of Mass has been completed,

---

191. Ibidem, n. 245.
192. Cf. ibidem, nn. 285b and 287.
193. Cf. ibidem, nn. 207 and 285a.
194. Cf. *Code of Canon Law*, canon 1367.
195. Cf. Pontifical Council for the Interpretation of Legislative Texts, Response to dubium, 3 July 1999: AAS 91 (1999) p. 918.

the prescriptions of the Roman Missal are to be observed, and in particular, whatever may remain of the Blood of Christ must be entirely and immediately consumed by the Priest or by another minister, according to the norms, while the consecrated hosts that are left are to be consumed by the Priest at the altar or carried to the place for the reservation of the Eucharist.[196]

CHAPTER V
CERTAIN OTHER MATTERS CONCERNING
THE EUCHARIST

1. THE PLACE FOR THE CELEBRATION OF HOLY MASS

108. "The celebration of the Eucharist is to be carried out in a sacred place, unless in a particular case necessity requires otherwise. In this case the celebration must be in a decent place."[197] The diocesan Bishop shall be the judge for his diocese concerning this necessity, on a case-by-case basis.

109. It is never lawful for a Priest to celebrate in a temple or sacred place of any non-Christian religion.

2. VARIOUS CIRCUMSTANCES RELATING TO THE MASS

110. "Remembering always that in the mystery of the Eucharistic Sacrifice the work of redemption is constantly being carried out, Priests should celebrate frequently. Indeed, daily celebration is earnestly recommended, because, even if it should not be possible to have the faithful present, the celebration is an act of Christ and of the Church, and in carrying it out, Priests fulfil their principal role."[198]

111. A Priest is to be permitted to celebrate or concelebrate the Eucharist "even if he is not known to the rector of the church, provided he presents commendatory letters" (i.e., a *celebret*) not more than a year old from the Holy See or his Ordinary or Superior "or unless it can be prudently judged that he is not impeded from celebrating."[199] Let the Bishops take measures to put a stop to any contrary practice.

---

196. Cf. *Missale Romanum*, Institutio Generalis, nn. 163, 284.

197. *Code of Canon Law*, canon 932 § 1; Sacred Congregation for Divine Worship, Instruction, *Liturgicae instaurationes*, n. 9: AAS 62 (1970) p. 701.

198. *Code of Canon Law*, canon 904; cf. Second Vatican Ecumenical Council, Dogmatic Constitution on the Church, *Lumen gentium*, n. 3; Decree on the Ministry and Life of Priests, *Presbyterorum ordinis*, n. 13; cf. also Ecumenical Council of Trent, Session XXII, 17 September 1562, On the Most Holy Sacrifice of the Mass, Chapter 6: DS 1747; Paul Pp. VI, Encyclical Letter *Mysterium fidei*, 3 September 1965: AAS 57 (1965) pp. 753–774, here pp. 761–762; cf. John Paul II, Encyclical Letter, *Ecclesia de Eucharistia*, n. 11: AAS 95 (2003) pp. 440–441; Sacred Congregation of Rites, Instruction, *Eucharisticum mysterium*, n. 44: AAS 59 (1967) p. 564; *Missale Romanum*, Institutio Generalis, n. 19.

199. Cf. *Code of Canon Law*, canon 903; *Missale Romanum*, Institutio Generalis, n. 200.

112. Mass is celebrated either in Latin or in another language, provided that liturgical texts are used which have been approved according to the norm of law. Except in the case of celebrations of the Mass that are scheduled by the ecclesiastical authorities to take place in the language of the people, Priests are always and everywhere permitted to celebrate Mass in Latin.[200]

113. When Mass is concelebrated by several Priests, a language known both to all the concelebrating Priests and to the gathered people should be used in the recitation of the Eucharist Prayer. Where it happens that some of the Priests who are present do not know the language of the celebration and therefore are not capable of pronouncing the parts of the Eucharistic Prayer proper to them, they should not concelebrate, but instead should attend the celebration in choral dress in accordance with the norms.[201]

114. "At Sunday Masses in parishes, insofar as parishes are 'Eucharistic communities,' it is customary to find different groups, movements, associations, and even the smaller religious communities present in the parish."[202] While it is permissible that Mass should be celebrated for particular groups according to the norm of law,[203] these groups are nevertheless not exempt from the faithful observance of the liturgical norms.

115. The abuse is reprobated by which the celebration of Holy Mass for the people is suspended in an arbitrary manner contrary to the norms of the Roman Missal and the healthy tradition of the Roman Rite, on the pretext of promoting a "fast from the Eucharist."

116. Masses are not to be multiplied contrary to the norm of law, and as regards Mass stipends, all those things are to be observed which are otherwise laid down by law.[204]

3. SACRED VESSELS

117. Sacred vessels for containing the Body and Blood of the Lord must be made in strict conformity with the norms of tradition and of the liturgical books.[205] The Bishops' Conferences have the faculty to decide whether it is appropriate, once their decisions have been given the *recognitio* by the Apostolic See, for sacred vessels to be made of other solid materials as well. It is strictly required, however, that such materials be truly noble in the common estimation within

---

200. Cf. Second Vatican Ecumenical Council, Constitution on the Sacred Liturgy, *Sacrosanctum Concilium*, n. 36 § 1; *Code of Canon Law*, canon 928.

201. Cf. *Missale Romanum*, Institutio Generalis, n. 114.

202. John Paul II, Apostolic Letter *Dies Domini*, n. 36: AAS 90 (1998) p. 735; cf. also Sacred Congregation of Rites, Instruction *Eucharisticum mysterium*, n. 27: AAS 59 (1967) p. 556.

203. Cf. John Paul II, Apostolic Letter *Dies Domini*, esp. n. 36: AAS 90 (1998) pp. 713–766, here pp. 735–736; Sacred Congregation for Divine Worship, Instruction *Actio pastoralis:* AAS 61 (1969) pp. 806–811.

204. Cf. *Code of Canon Law*, canon 905, 945–958; cf. Congregation for the Clergy, Decree, *Mos iugiter*, 22 February 1991: AAS 83 (1991), pp. 443–446.

205. Cf. *Missale Romanum*, Institutio Generalis, nn. 327–333.

a given region,[206] so that honour will be given to the Lord by their use, and all risk of diminishing the doctrine of the Real Presence of Christ in the Eucharistic species in the eyes of the faithful will be avoided. Reprobated, therefore, is any practice of using for the celebration of Mass common vessels, or others lacking in quality, or devoid of all artistic merit or which are mere containers, as also other vessels made from glass, earthenware, clay, or other materials that break easily. This norm is to be applied even as regards metals and other materials that easily rust or deteriorate.[207]

118. Before they are used, sacred vessels are to be blessed by a Priest according to the rites laid down in the liturgical books.[208] It is praiseworthy for the blessing to be given by the diocesan Bishop, who will judge whether the vessels are worthy of the use to which they are destined.

119. The Priest, once he has returned to the altar after the distribution of Communion, standing at the altar or at the credence table, purifies the paten or ciborium over the chalice, then purifies the chalice in accordance with the prescriptions of the Missal and wipes the chalice with the purificator. Where a Deacon is present, he returns with the Priest to the altar and purifies the vessels. It is permissible, however, especially if there are several vessels to be purified, to leave them, covered as may be appropriate, on a corporal on the altar or on the credence table, and for them to be purified by the Priest or Deacon immediately after Mass once the people have been dismissed. Moreover a duly instituted acolyte assists the Priest or Deacon in purifying and arranging the sacred vessels either at the altar or the credence table. In the absence of a Deacon, a duly instituted acolyte carries the sacred vessels to the credence table and there purifies, wipes and arranges them in the usual way.[209]

120. Let Pastors take care that the linens for the sacred table, especially those which will receive the sacred species, are always kept clean and that they are washed in the traditional way. It is praiseworthy for this to be done by pouring the water from the first washing, done by hand, into the church's sacrarium or into the ground in a suitable place. After this a second washing can be done in the usual way.

4. LITURGICAL VESTURE

121. "The purpose of a variety of colour of the sacred vestments is to give effective expression even outwardly to the specific character of the mysteries of faith being celebrated and to a sense of Christian life's passage through the course of

---

206. Cf. ibidem, n. 332.

207. Cf. ibidem, n. 332; Congregation for Divine Worship and the Discipline of the Sacraments, Instruction, *Inaestimabile donum*, n. 16: AAS 72 (1980) p. 338.

208. Cf. *Missale Romanum*, Institutio Generalis, n. 333; Appendix IV. *Ordo benedictionis calicis et patenae intra Missam adhibendus*, pp. 1255–1257; *Pontificale Romanum* ex decreto sacrosancti Oecumenici Concilii Vaticani II instauratum, auctoritate Pauli Pp. VI promulgatum, *Ordo Dedicationis ecclesiae et altaris*, editio typica, diei 29 maii 1977, Typis Polyglottis Vaticanis, 1977, cap. VII, pp. 125–132.

209. Cf. *Missale Romanum*, Institutio Generalis, nn. 163, 183, 192.

the liturgical year."[210] On the other hand, the variety "of offices in the celebration of the Eucharist is shown outwardly by the diversity of sacred vestments. In fact, these "sacred vestments should also contribute to the beauty of the sacred action itself."[211]

122. "The alb" is "to be tied at the waist with a cincture unless it is made so as to fit even without a cincture. Before the alb is put on, if it does not completely cover the ordinary clothing at the neck, an amice should be put on."[212]

123. "The vestment proper to the Priest celebrant at Mass, and in other sacred actions directly connected with Mass unless otherwise indicated, is the chasuble, worn over the alb and stole."[213] Likewise the Priest, in putting on the chasuble according to the rubrics, is not to omit the stole. All Ordinaries should be vigilant in order that all usage to the contrary be eradicated.

124. A faculty is given in the Roman Missal for the Priest concelebrants at Mass other than the principal concelebrant (who should always put on a chasuble of the prescribed colour), for a just reason such as a large number of concelebrants or a lack of vestments, to omit "the chasuble, using the stole over the alb."[214] Where a need of this kind can be foreseen, however, provision should be made for it insofar as possible. Out of necessity the concelebrants other than the principal celebrant may even put on white chasubles. For the rest, the norms of the liturgical books are to be observed.

125. The proper vestment of the Deacon is the dalmatic, to be worn over an alb and stole. In order that the beautiful tradition of the Church may be preserved, it is praiseworthy to refrain from exercising the option of omitting the dalmatic.[215]

126. The abuse is reprobated whereby the sacred ministers celebrate Holy Mass or other rites without sacred vestments or with only a stole over the monastic cowl or the common habit of religious or ordinary clothes, contrary to the prescriptions of the liturgical books, even when there is only one minister participating.[216] In order that such abuses be corrected as quickly as possible, Ordinaries should take care that in all churches and oratories subject to their jurisdiction there is present an adequate supply of liturgical vestments made in accordance with the norms.

127. A special faculty is given in the liturgical books for using sacred vestments that are festive or more noble on more solemn occasions, even if they are not of the colour of the day.[217] However, this faculty, which is specifically intended in

---

210. Ibidem, n. 345.
211. Ibidem, n. 335.
212. Cf. ibidem, n. 336.
213. Cf. ibidem, n. 337.
214. Cf. ibidem, n. 209.
215. Cf. ibidem, n. 338.
216. Cf. Sacred Congregation for Divine Worship, Instruction, *Liturgicae Instaurationes*, n. 8c: AAS 62 (1970) p. 701.
217. Cf. *Missale Romanum*, Institutio Generalis, n. 346g.

reference to vestments made many years ago, with a view to preserving the Church's patrimony, is improperly extended to innovations by which forms and colours are adopted according to the inclination of private individuals, with disregard for traditional practice, while the real sense of this norm is lost to the detriment of the tradition. On the occasion of a feastday, sacred vestments of a gold or silver colour can be substituted as appropriate for others of various colours, but not for purple or black.

128. Holy Mass and other liturgical celebrations, which are acts of Christ and of the people of God hierarchically constituted, are ordered in such a way that the sacred ministers and the lay faithful manifestly take part in them each according to his own condition. It is preferable therefore that "Priests who are present at a Eucharistic Celebration, unless excused for a good reason, should as a rule exercise the office proper to their Order and thus take part as concelebrants, wearing the sacred vestments. Otherwise, they wear their proper choir dress or a surplice over a cassock."[218] It is not fitting, except in rare and exceptional cases and with reasonable cause, for them to participate at Mass, as regards to externals, in the manner of the lay faithful.

CHAPTER VI
THE RESERVATION OF THE MOST HOLY EUCHARIST AND EUCHARISTIC WORSHIP OUTSIDE MASS

1. THE RESERVATION OF THE MOST HOLY EUCHARIST

129. "The celebration of the Eucharist in the Sacrifice of the Mass is truly the origin and end of the worship given to the Eucharist outside the Mass. Furthermore the sacred species are reserved after Mass principally so that the faithful who cannot be present at Mass, above all the sick and those advanced in age, may be united by sacramental Communion to Christ and his Sacrifice which is offered in the Mass."[219] In addition, this reservation also permits the practice of adoring this great Sacrament and offering it the worship due to God. Accordingly, forms of adoration that are not only private but also public and communitarian in nature, as established or approved by the Church herself, must be greatly promoted.[220]

130. "According to the structure of each church building and in accordance with legitimate local customs, the Most Holy Sacrament is to be reserved in a tabernacle in a part of the church that is noble, prominent, readily visible, and adorned in a dignified manner" and furthermore "suitable for prayer" by reason of the quietness of the location, the space available in front of the tabernacle,

---

218. *Ibidem*, n. 114 cf. nn. 16–17.
219. Sacred Congregation for Divine Worship, Decree, *Eucharistiae sacramentum*, 21 June 1973: AAS 65 (1973) 610.
220. Cf. ibidem.

and also the supply of benches or seats and kneelers.[221] In addition, diligent attention should be paid to all the prescriptions of the liturgical books and to the norm of law,[222] especially as regards the avoidance of the danger of profanation.[223]

131. Apart from the prescriptions of canon 934 § 1, it is forbidden to reserve the Blessed Sacrament in a place that is not subject in a secure way to the authority of the diocesan Bishop, or where there is a danger of profanation. Where such is the case, the diocesan Bishop should immediately revoke any permission for reservation of the Eucharist that may already have been granted.[224]

132. No one may carry the Most Holy Eucharist to his or her home, or to any other place contrary to the norm of law. It should also be borne in mind that removing or retaining the consecrated species for a sacrilegious purpose or casting them away are *graviora delicta*, the absolution of which is reserved to the Congregation for the Doctrine of the Faith.[225]

133. A Priest or Deacon, or an extraordinary minister who takes the Most Holy Eucharist when an ordained minister is absent or impeded in order to administer it as Communion for a sick person, should go insofar as possible directly from the place where the Sacrament is reserved to the sick person's home, leaving aside any profane business so that any danger of profanation may be avoided and the greatest reverence for the Body of Christ may be ensured. Furthermore the Rite for the administration of Communion to the sick, as prescribed in the Roman Ritual, is always to be used.[226]

2. CERTAIN FORMS OF WORSHIP OF THE MOST HOLY EUCHARIST OUTSIDE MASS

134. "The worship of the Eucharist outside the Sacrifice of the Mass is a tribute of inestimable value in the life of the Church. Such worship is closely linked to the celebration of the Eucharistic Sacrifice."[227] Therefore both public and private devotion to the Most Holy Eucharist even outside Mass should be vigorously promoted, for by means of it the faithful give adoration to Christ, truly and really

---

221. Cf. Sacred Congregation of Rites, Instruction, *Eucharisticum mysterium*, n. 54: AAS 59 (1967) p. 568; Instruction, *Inter Oecumenici*, 26 September 1964, n. 95: AAS 56 (1964) pp. 877–900, here p. 898; *Missale Romanum*, Institutio Generalis, n. 314.
222. Cf. John Paul II, Letter, *Dominicae Cenae*, n. 3: AAS 72 (1980) pp. 117–119; Sacred Congregation of Rites, Instruction, *Eucharisticum mysterium*, n. 53: AAS 59 (1967) p. 568; *Code of Canon Law*, canon 938 § 2; *Roman Ritual, Holy Communion and Worship of the Eucharist Outside Mass*, Introduction, n. 9; *Missale Romanum*, Institutio Generalis, nn. 314–317.
223. Cf. *Code of Canon Law*, canon 938 §§ 3–5.
224. Sacred Congregation for the Discipline of the Sacraments, Instruction, Nullo unquam, diei 26 maii 1938, n. 10d: AAS 30 (1938), pp. 198–207, here p. 206.
225. Cf. John Paul II, Apostolic Letter (Motu Proprio), *Sacramentorum sanctitatis tutela*, 30 April 2001: AAS 93 (2001) pp. 737–739; Congregation for the Doctrine of the Faith, Ep. ad totius Catholicae Ecclesiae Episcopos aliosque Ordinarios et Hierarchas quorum interest: de delictis gravioribus eidem Congregationi pro Doctrina Fidei reservatis: AAS 93 (2001) p. 786.
226. Cf. *Roman Ritual, Holy Communion and Worship of the Eucharist Outside Mass*, nn. 26–78.
227. John Paul II, Encyclical Letter, *Ecclesia de Eucharistia*, n. 25: AAS 95 (2003) pp. 449–450.

present,[228] the "High Priest of the good things to come"[229] and Redeemer of the whole world. "It is the responsibility of sacred Pastors, even by the witness of their life, to support the practice of Eucharistic worship and especially exposition of the Most Holy Sacrament, as well as prayer of adoration before Christ present under the eucharistic species."[230]

135.   The faithful "should not omit making visits during the day to the Most Holy Sacrament, as a proof of gratitude, a pledge of love, and a debt of the adoration due to Christ the Lord who is present in it."[231] For the contemplation of Jesus present in the Most Holy Sacrament, as a communion of desire, powerfully joins the faithful to Christ, as is splendidly evident in the example of so many Saints.[232] "Unless there is a grave reason to the contrary, a church in which the Most Holy Eucharist is reserved should be open to the faithful for at least some hours each day, so that they can spend time in prayer before the Most Holy Sacrament."[233]

136.   The Ordinary should diligently foster Eucharistic adoration, whether brief or prolonged or almost continuous, with the participation of the people. For in recent years in so many places "adoration of the Most Holy Sacrament is also an important daily practice and becomes an inexhaustible source of holiness," although there are also places "where there is evident almost a total lack of regard for worship in the form of eucharistic adoration."[234]

137.   Exposition of the Most Holy Eucharist must always be carried out in accordance with the prescriptions of the liturgical books.[235] Before the Most Holy Sacrament either reserved or exposed, the praying of the Rosary, which is admirable "in its simplicity and even its profundity," is not to be excluded either.[236] Even so, especially if there is Exposition, the character of this kind of prayer as a contemplation of the mystery of the life of Christ the Redeemer and the

228. Cf. Ecumenical Council of Trent, Session XIII, 11 October 1551, Decree on the Most Holy Eucharist, Chapter 5: DS 1643; Pius Pp. XII, Encyclical Letter *Mediator Dei:* AAS 39 (1947) p. 569; Paul Pp. VI, Encyclical Letter *Mysterium Fidei*, 3 September 1965: AAS 57 (1965) pp. 751–774, here 769–770; S. Congregation of Rites, Instruction, *Eucharisticum mysterium*, n. 3f: AAS 59 (1967) p. 543; Sacred Congregation for the Sacraments and Divine Worship, Instruction, *Inaestimabile donum*, n. 20: AAS 72 (1980) p. 339; John Paul II, Encyclical Letter, *Ecclesia de Eucharistia*, n. 25: AAS 95 (2003) pp. 449–450.
229. Cf. Hebrews 9:11; John Paul II, Encyclical Letter, *Ecclesia de Eucharistia*, n. 3: AAS 95 (2003) p. 435.
230. John Paul II, Encyclical Letter, *Ecclesia de Eucharistia*, n. 25: AAS 95 (2003) p. 450.
231. Paul. VI, Encyclical Letter *Mysterium fidei:* AAS 57 (1965) p. 771.
232. Cf. John Paul II, Encyclical Letter, *Ecclesia de Eucharistia*, n. 25: AAS 95 (2003) pp. 449–450.
233. *Code of Canon Law*, canon 937.
234. John Paul II, Encyclical Letter, *Ecclesia de Eucharistia*, n. 10: AAS 95 (2003) p. 439.
235. Cf. *Roman Ritual, Holy Communion and Worship of the Eucharist Outside Mass*, nn. 82–100; *Missale Romanum*, Institutio Generalis, n. 317; *Code of Canon Law*, canon 941 § 2.
236. John Paul II, Apostolic Letter, *Rosarium Virginis Mariae*, diei 16 octobris 2002: AAS 95 (2003) pp. 5–36; here n. 2, p. 6.

Almighty Father's design of salvation should be emphasized, especially by making use of readings taken from Sacred Scripture.[237]

138. Still, the Most Holy Sacrament, when exposed, must never be left unattended even for the briefest space of time. It should therefore be arranged that at least some of the faithful always be present at fixed times, even if they take alternating turns.

139. Where the diocesan Bishop has sacred ministers or others whom he can assign to this purpose, the faithful have a right to visit the Most Holy Sacrament of the Eucharist frequently for adoration, and to take part in adoration before the Most Holy Eucharist exposed at least at some time in the course of any given year.

140. It is highly recommended that at least in the cities and the larger towns the diocesan Bishop should designate a church building for perpetual adoration; in it, however, Holy Mass should be celebrated frequently, even daily if possible, while the Exposition should rigorously be interrupted while Mass is being celebrated.[238] It is fitting that the host to be exposed for adoration should be consecrated in the Mass immediately preceding the time of adoration, and that it should be placed in the monstrance upon the altar after Communion.[239]

141. The diocesan Bishop should acknowledge and foster insofar as possible the right of the various groups of Christ's faithful to form guilds or associations for the carrying out of adoration, even almost continuous adoration. Whenever such associations assume an international character, it pertains to the Congregation for Divine Worship and the Discipline of the Sacraments to erect them and to approve their statutes.[240]

3. EUCHARISTIC CONGRESSES AND EUCHARISTIC PROCESSIONS

142. "It is for the diocesan Bishop to establish regulations about processions in order to provide for participation in them and for their being carried out in a dignified way"[241] and to promote adoration by the faithful.

143. "Wherever it is possible in the judgement of the diocesan Bishop, a procession through the public streets should be held, especially on the Solemnity of the Body and Blood of Christ as a public witness of reverence for the Most Holy

---

237. Cf. Congregation for Divine Worship and the Discipline of the Sacraments, Letter of the Congregation, 15 January 1997: *Notitiae* 34 (1998) pp. 506–510; Apostolic Penitentiary, Letter to a Priest, 8 March 1996: *Notitiae* 34 (1998) p. 511.
238. Cf. Sacred Congregation of Rites, Instruction, *Eucharisticum mysterium*, n. 61: AAS 59 (1967) p. 571; *Roman Ritual, Holy Communion and Worship of the Eucharist Outside Mass*, n. 83; *Missale Romanum*, Institutio Generalis, n. 317; *Code of Canon Law*, canon 941 § 2.
239. Cf. *Roman Ritual, Holy Communion and Worship of the Eucharist Outside Mass*, n. 94.
240. Cf. John Paul II, Apostolic Constitution, *Pastor bonus*, article 65: AAS 80 (1988) p. 877.
241. *Code of Canon Law*, canon 944 § 2; cf. *Roman Ritual, Holy Communion and Worship of the Eucharist Outside Mass*, Introduction, n. 102; *Missale Romanum*, Institutio Generalis, n. 317.

Sacrament,"[242] for the "devout participation of the faithful in the eucharistic procession on the Solemnity of the Body and Blood of Christ is a grace from the Lord which yearly fills with joy those who take part in it."[243]

144. Although this cannot be done in some places, the tradition of holding eucharistic processions should not be allowed to be lost. Instead, new ways should be sought of holding them in today's conditions: for example, at shrines, or in public gardens if the civil authority agrees.

145. The pastoral value of Eucharistic Congresses should be highly esteemed, and they "should be a genuine sign of faith and charity."[244] Let them be diligently prepared and carried out in accordance with what has been laid down,[245] so that Christ's faithful may have the occasion to worship the sacred mysteries of the Body and Blood of the Son of God in a worthy manner, and that they may continually experience within themselves the fruits of the Redemption.[246]

CHAPTER VII
EXTRAORDINARY FUNCTIONS OF LAY FAITHFUL

146. There can be no substitute whatsoever for the ministerial Priesthood. For if a Priest is lacking in the community, then the community lacks the exercise and sacramental function of Christ the Head and Shepherd, which belongs to the essence of its very life.[247] For "the only minister who can confect the sacrament of the Eucharist *in persona Christi* is a validly ordained Priest."[248]

147. When the Church's needs require it, however, if sacred ministers are lacking, lay members of Christ's faithful may supply for certain liturgical offices according to the norm of law.[249] Such faithful are called and appointed to carry out certain functions, whether of greater or lesser weight, sustained by the Lord's grace. Many of the lay Christian faithful have already contributed eagerly to

242. *Code of Canon Law*, canon 944 § 1; cf. *Roman Ritual, Holy Communion and Worship of the Eucharist Outside Mass*, Introduction, nn. 101–102; *Missale Romanum*, Institutio Generalis, n. 317.
243. John Paul II, Encyclical Letter, *Ecclesia de Eucharistia*, n. 10: AAS 95 (2003) p. 439.
244. Cf. *Roman Ritual, Holy Communion and Worship of the Eucharist Outside Mass*, Introduction, n. 109.
245. Cf. *ibidem*, nn. 109–112.
246. Cf. *Missale Romanum*, In sollemnitate sanctissimi Corporis et Sanguinis Christi, Collecta, p. 489.
247. Cf. Congregation for the Clergy, and others, Instruction, *Ecclesiae de mysterio*, Theological Principles, n. 3: AAS 89 (1997) p. 859.
248. Cf. *Code of Canon Law*, can. 900 § 1; cf. Fourth Lateran Ecumenical Council, 11–30 November 1215, Chapter 1: DS802; Clement VI, Letter to Mekhitar, Catholicos of the Armenians, *Super quibusdam*, 29 September 1351: DS 1084; Ecumenical Council of Trent, Session XXIII, 15 July 1563, Doctrine and Canons on Sacred Orders, Chapter 4: DS 1767–1770; Pius XII, Encyclical Letter, *Mediator Dei:* AAS 39 (1947) p. 553.
249. Cf. *Code of Canon Law*, canon 230 § 3; John Paul II, Allocution during a Symposium concerning the collaboration of laypersons in the pastoral ministry of Priests, 22 April 1994, n. 2: *L'Osservatore Romano*, 23 April 1994; Congregation for the Clergy et al., Instruction, *Ecclesiae de mysterio*, Prooemium: AAS 89 (1997) pp. 852–856.

this service and still do so, especially in missionary areas where the Church is still of small dimensions or is experiencing conditions of persecution,[250] but also in areas affected by a shortage of Priests and Deacons.

148. Particular importance is to be attached to the training of catechists, who by means of great labours have given and still give outstanding and altogether necessary help in the spreading of the faith and of the Church.[251]

149. More recently, in some dioceses long since evangelized, members of Christ's lay faithful have been appointed as "pastoral assistants," and among them many have undoubtedly served the good of the Church by providing assistance to the Bishop, Priests and Deacons in the carrying out of their pastoral activity. Let care be taken, however, lest the delineation of this function be assimilated too closely to the form of pastoral ministry that belongs to clerics. That is to say, attention should be paid to ensuring that "pastoral assistants" do not take upon themselves what is proper to the ministry of the sacred ministers.

150. The activity of a pastoral assistant should be directed to facilitating the ministry of Priests and Deacons, to ensuring that vocations to the Priesthood and Diaconate are awakened and that lay members of Christ's faithful in each community are carefully trained for the various liturgical functions, in keeping with the variety of charisms and in accordance with the norm of law.

151. Only out of true necessity is there to be recourse to the assistance of extraordinary ministers in the celebration of the Liturgy. Such recourse is not intended for the sake of a fuller participation of the laity but rather, by its very nature, is supplementary and provisional.[252] Furthermore, when recourse is had out of necessity to the functions of extraordinary ministers, special urgent prayers of intercession should be multiplied that the Lord may soon send a Priest for the service of the community and raise up an abundance of vocations to sacred Orders.[253]

152. These purely supplementary functions must not be an occasion for disfiguring the very ministry of Priests, in such a way that the latter neglect the celebration of Holy Mass for the people for whom they are responsible, or their personal care of the sick, or the baptism of children, or assistance at weddings or the celebration of Christian funerals, matters which pertain in the first place to Priests assisted by Deacons. It must therefore never be the case that in parishes Priests alternate indiscriminately in shifts of pastoral service with Deacons or laypersons, thus confusing what is specific to each.

---

250. Cf. John Paul II, Encyclical Letter, *Redemptoris missio*, nn. 53–54: AAS 83 (1991) pp. 300–302; Congregation for the Clergy et al., Instruction, *Ecclesiae de mysterio*, Prooemium: AAS 89 (1997) pp. 852–856.
251. Cf. Second Vatican Ecumenical Council, Decree on the Missionary Activity of the Church, *Ad gentes*, 7 December 1965, n. 17; John Paul II, Encyclical Letter *Redemptoris missio*, n. 73: AAS 83 (1991) p. 321.
252. Cf. Congregation for the Clergy et al., Instruction, *Ecclesiae de mysterio*, Practical Provisions, article 8 § 2: AAS 89 (1997) p. 872.
253. Cf. John Paul II, Encyclical Letter, *Ecclesia de Eucharistia*, n. 32: AAS 95 (2003) p. 455.

153. Furthermore, it is never licit for laypersons to assume the role or the vesture of a Priest or a Deacon or other clothing similar to such vesture.

1. THE EXTRAORDINARY MINISTER OF HOLY COMMUNION

154. As has already been recalled, "the only minister who can confect the Sacrament of the Eucharist *in persona Christi* is a validly ordained Priest."[254] Hence the name "minister of the Eucharist" belongs properly to the Priest alone. Moreover, also by reason of their sacred Ordination, the ordinary ministers of Holy Communion are the Bishop, the Priest and the Deacon,[255] to whom it belongs therefore to administer Holy Communion to the lay members of Christ's faithful during the celebration of Mass. In this way their ministerial office in the Church is fully and accurately brought to light, and the sign value of the Sacrament is made complete.

155. In addition to the ordinary ministers there is the formally instituted acolyte, who by virtue of his institution is an extraordinary minister of Holy Communion even outside the celebration of Mass. If, moreover, reasons of real necessity prompt it, another lay member of Christ's faithful may also be delegated by the diocesan Bishop, in accordance with the norm of law,[256] for one occasion or for a specified time, and an appropriate formula of blessing may be used for the occasion. This act of appointment, however, does not necessarily take a liturgical form, nor, if it does take a liturgical form, should it resemble sacred Ordination in any way. Finally, in special cases of an unforeseen nature, permission can be given for a single occasion by the Priest who presides at the celebration of the Eucharist.[257]

156. This function is to be understood strictly according to the name by which it is known, that is to say, that of extraordinary minister of Holy Communion, and not "special minister of Holy Communion" nor "extraordinary minister of the Eucharist" nor "special minister of the Eucharist," by which names the meaning of this function is unnecessarily and improperly broadened.

157. If there is usually present a sufficient number of sacred ministers for the distribution of Holy Communion, extraordinary ministers of Holy Communion may not be appointed. Indeed, in such circumstances, those who may have already been appointed to this ministry should not exercise it. The practice of those

---

254. Cf. *Code of Canon Law*, canon 900 § 1.
255. Cf. *ibidem*, canon 910 § 1; cf. also John Paul II, Letter, *Dominicae Cenae*, n. 11: AAS 72 (1980) p. 142; Congregation for the Clergy et al., Instruction, *Ecclesiae de mysterio*, Practical Provisions, article 8 § 1: AAS 89 (1997) pp. 870–871.
256. Cf. *Code of Canon Law*, canon 230 § 3.
257. Cf. Sacred Congregation for the Discipline of the Sacraments, Instruction, *Immensae caritatis*, prooemium: AAS 65 (1973) p. 264; Paul VI, Apostolic Letter (Motu Proprio), *Ministeria quaedam*, 15 August 1972: AAS 64 (1972) p. 532; *Missale Romanum*, Appendix III: Ritus ad deputandum ministrum sacrae Communionis ad actum distribuendae, p. 1253; Congregation for the Clergy et al., Instruction, *Ecclesiae de mysterio*, Practical Provisions, article 8 § 1: AAS 89 (1997) p. 871.

Priests is reprobated who, even though present at the celebration, abstain from distributing Communion and hand this function over to laypersons.[258]

158. Indeed, the extraordinary minister of Holy Communion may administer Communion only when the Priest and Deacon are lacking, when the Priest is prevented by weakness or advanced age or some other genuine reason, or when the number of faithful coming to Communion is so great that the very celebration of Mass would be unduly prolonged.[259] This, however, is to be understood in such a way that a brief prolongation, considering the circumstances and culture of the place, is not at all a sufficient reason.

159. It is never allowed for the extraordinary minister of Holy Communion to delegate anyone else to administer the Eucharist, as for example a parent or spouse or child of the sick person who is the communicant.

160. Let the diocesan Bishop give renewed consideration to the practice in recent years regarding this matter, and if circumstances call for it, let him correct it or define it more precisely. Where such extraordinary ministers are appointed in a widespread manner out of true necessity, the diocesan Bishop should issue special norms by which he determines the manner in which this function is to be carried out in accordance with the law, bearing in mind the tradition of the Church.

2. PREACHING

161. As was already noted above, the homily on account of its importance and its nature is reserved to the Priest or Deacon during Mass.[260] As regards other forms of preaching, if necessity demands it in particular circumstances, or if usefulness suggests it in special cases, lay members of Christ's faithful may be allowed to preach in a church or in an oratory outside Mass in accordance with the norm of law.[261] This may be done only on account of a scarcity of sacred ministers in certain places, in order to meet the need, and it may not be transformed from an exceptional measure into an ordinary practice, nor may it be understood as an authentic form of the advancement of the laity.[262] All must remember besides that the faculty for giving such permission belongs to the local Ordinary, and this as regards individual instances; this permission is not the competence of anyone else, even if they are Priests or Deacons.

---

258. Sacred Congregation for the Sacraments and Divine Worship, Instruction, *Inaestimabile donum*, n. 10: AAS 72 (1980) p. 336; Pontifical Commission for the Authentic Interpretation of the Code of Canon Law, Response to dubium, 11 July 1984: AAS 76 (1984) p. 746.

259. Cf. Sacred Congregation for the Discipline of the Sacraments, Instruction, *Immensae caritatis*, n. 1: AAS 65 (1973) pp. 264–271, here pp. 265–266; Pontifical Commission for the Authentic Interpretation of the Code of Canon Law, Responsio ad propositum dubium, 1 June 1988: AAS 80 (1988) p. 1373; Congregation for the Clergy et al., Instruction, *Ecclesiae de mysterio*, Practical Provisions, article 8 § 2: AAS 89 (1997) p. 871.

260. Cf. *Code of Canon Law*, canon 767 § 1.

261. Cf. ibidem, canon 766.

262. Cf. Congregation for the Clergy et al., Instruction, *Ecclesiae de mysterio*, Practical Provisions, article 2 §§ 3–4: AAS 89 (1997) p. 865.

3. PARTICULAR CELEBRATIONS CARRIED OUT IN THE ABSENCE OF A PRIEST

162. On the day known as the Lord's Day, the Church faithful gathers together to commemorate the Lord's Resurrection and the whole Paschal Mystery, especially by the celebration of Mass.[263] For "no Christian community is built up unless it is rooted in and hinges upon the celebration of the Most Holy Eucharist."[264] Hence it is the Christian people's right to have the Eucharist celebrated for them on Sunday, and whenever holydays of obligation or other major feasts occur, and even daily insofar as this is possible. Therefore when it is difficult to have the celebration of Mass on a Sunday in a parish church or in another community of Christ's faithful, the diocesan Bishop together with his Priests should consider appropriate remedies.[265] Among such solutions will be that other Priests be called upon for this purpose, or that the faithful transfer to a church in a nearby place so as to participate in the Eucharistic mystery there.[266]

163. All Priests, to whom the Priesthood and the Eucharist are entrusted *for the sake of* others,[267] should remember that they are enjoined to provide the faithful with the opportunity to satisfy the obligation of participating at Mass on Sundays.[268] For their part, the lay faithful have the right, barring a case of real impossibility, that no Priest should ever refuse either to celebrate Mass for the people or to have it celebrated by another Priest if the people otherwise would not be able to satisfy the obligation of participating at Mass on Sunday or the other days of precept.

164. "If participation at the celebration of the Eucharist is impossible on account of the absence of a sacred minister or for some other grave cause,"[269] then it is the Christian people's right that the diocesan Bishop should provide as far as he is able for some celebration to be held on Sundays for that community under his authority and according to the Church's norms. Sunday celebrations of this specific kind, however, are to be considered altogether extraordinary. All Deacons or lay members of Christ's faithful who are assigned a part in such celebrations

---

263. Cf. John Paul II, Apostolic Letter, *Dies Domini*, esp. nn. 31–51: AAS 90 (1998) pp. 713–766, here pp. 731–746; Pope John Paul II, Apostolic Letter, *Novo Millennio ineunte*, diei 6 ianuarii 2001, nn. 35–36: AAS 93 (2001) pp. 290–292; John Paul II, Encyclical Letter, *Ecclesia de Eucharistia*, n. 41: AAS 95 (2003) pp. 460–461.

264. Second Vatican Ecumenical Council, Decree on the Ministry and Life of Priests, *Presbyterorum ordinis*, n. 6; cf. John Paul II, Encyclical Letter, *Ecclesia de Eucharistia*, nn. 22, 33: AAS 95 (2003) pp. 448, 455–456.

265. Cf. Sacred Congregation of Rites, Instruction, *Eucharisticum mysterium*, n. 26: AAS 59 (1967) pp. 555–556; Congregation for Divine Worship, Directory for Sunday Celebrations in the Absence of a Priest, *Christi Ecclesia*, 2 June 1988, nn. 5 and 25: *Notitiae* 24 (1988) pp. 366–378, here pp. 367, 372.

266. Cf. Congregation for Divine Worship, Directory for Sunday Celebrations in the Absence of a Priest, *Christi Ecclesia*, n. 18: *Notitiae* 24 (1988) p. 370.

267. Cf. John Paul II, Letter, *Dominicae Cenae*, n. 2: AAS 72 (1980) p. 116.

268. Cf. John Paul II, Apostolic Letter, *Dies Domini*, n. 49: AAS 90 (1998) p. 744; Encyclical Letter, *Ecclesia de Eucharistia*, n. 41: AAS 95 (2003) pp. 460–461; *Code of Canon Law*, canon 1246–1247.

269. Cf. *Code of Canon Law*, canon 1248 § 2; Congregation for Divine Worship, Directory for Sunday Celebrations in the Absence of a Priest, *Christi Ecclesia*, nn. 1–2: *Notitiae* 24 (1988) p. 366.

by the diocesan Bishop should strive "to keep alive in the community a genuine 'hunger' for the Eucharist, so that no opportunity for the celebration of Mass will ever be missed, also taking advantage of the occasional presence of a Priest who is not impeded by Church law from celebrating Mass."[270]

165. It is necessary to avoid any sort of confusion between this type of gathering and the celebration of the Eucharist.[271] The diocesan Bishops, therefore, should prudently discern whether Holy Communion ought to be distributed in these gatherings. The matter would appropriately be determined in view of a more ample co-ordination in the Bishops' Conference, to be put into effect after the *recognitio* of the acts by the Apostolic See through the Congregation for Divine Worship and the Discipline of the Sacraments. It will be preferable, moreover, when both a Priest and a Deacon are absent, that the various parts be distributed among several faithful rather than having a single lay member of the faithful direct the whole celebration alone. Nor is it ever appropriate to refer to any member of the lay faithful as "presiding" over the celebration.

166. Likewise, especially if Holy Communion is distributed during such celebrations, the diocesan Bishop, to whose exclusive competence this matter pertains, must not easily grant permission for such celebrations to be held on weekdays, especially in places where it was possible or would be possible to have the celebration of Mass on the preceding or the following Sunday. Priests are therefore earnestly requested to celebrate Mass daily for the people in one of the churches entrusted to their care.

167. "Similarly, it is unthinkable on the Lord's Day to substitute for Holy Mass either ecumenical celebrations of the word or services of common prayer with Christians from the . . . Ecclesial Communities, or even participation in these Communities' liturgical services."[272] Should the diocesan Bishop out of necessity authorize the participation of Catholics for a single occasion, let pastors take care lest confusion arise among the Catholic faithful concerning the necessity of taking part at Mass at another hour of the day even in such circumstances, on account of the obligation.[273]

---

270. John Paul II, Encyclical Letter, *Ecclesia de Eucharistia*, n. 33: AAS 95 (2003) pp. 455–456.

271. Cf. Congregation for Divine Worship, Directory for Sunday Celebrations in the Absence of a Priest, *Christi Ecclesia*, n. 22: *Notitiae* 24 (1988) p. 371.

272. John Paul II, Encyclical Letter, *Ecclesia de Eucharistia*, n. 30: AAS 95 (2003) pp. 453–454; cf. also Pontifical Council for the Promotion of Christian Unity, Directory for the application of the principles and norms on ecumenism, *La recherche de l'unité*, 25 March 1993, n. 115: AAS 85 (1993) pp. 1039–1119, here p. 1085.

273. Cf. Pontifical Council for the Promotion of Christian Unity, Directory for the application of the principles and norms on ecumenism, *La recherche de l'unité*, n. 115: AAS 85 (1993) p. 1085.

4. THOSE WHO HAVE LEFT THE CLERICAL STATE

168. "A cleric who loses the clerical state in accordance with the law . . . is prohibited from exercising the power of order."[274] It is therefore not licit for him to celebrate the sacraments under any pretext whatsoever save in the exceptional case set forth by law,[275] nor is it licit for Christ's faithful to have recourse to him for the celebration, since there is no reason which would permit this according to canon 1335.[276] Moreover, these men should neither give the homily[277] nor ever undertake any office or duty in the celebration of the sacred Liturgy, lest confusion arise among Christ's faithful and the truth be obscured.

CHAPTER VIII
REMEDIES

169. Whenever an abuse is committed in the celebration of the sacred Liturgy, it is to be seen as a real falsification of Catholic Liturgy. St Thomas wrote, "the vice of falsehood is perpetrated by anyone who offers worship to God on behalf of the Church in a manner contrary to that which is established by the Church with divine authority, and to which the Church is accustomed."[278]

170. In order that a remedy may be applied to such abuses, "there is a pressing need for the biblical and liturgical formation of the people of God, both pastors and faithful,"[279] so that the Church's faith and discipline concerning the sacred Liturgy may be accurately presented and understood. Where abuses persist, however, proceedings should be undertaken for safeguarding the spiritual patrimony and rights of the Church in accordance with the law, employing all legitimate means.

171. Among the various abuses there are some which are objectively *graviora delicta* or otherwise constitute grave matters, as well as others which are nonetheless to be carefully avoided and corrected. Bearing in mind everything that is treated especially in Chapter I of this Instruction, attention should be paid to what follows.

---

274. Cf. *Code of Canon Law*, can. 292; Pontifical Council for the Interpretation of Legislative Texts, Declaration de recta interpretatione canon 1335, secundae partis, C.I.C., 15 May 1997, n. 3: AAS 90 (1998) p. 64.

275. Cf. *Code of Canon Law*, canon 976; 986 § 2.

276. Cf. Pontifical Council for the Interpretation of Legislative Texts, Declaratio de recta interpretatione can. 1335, secundae partis, C.I.C., 15 May 1997, nn. 1–2: AAS 90 (1998) pp. 63–64.

277. As regards Priests who have obtained the dispensation from celibacy, cf. Sacred Congregation for the Doctrine of the Faith, Normae de dispensatione a sacerdotali caelibatu ad instantiam partis, *Normae substantiales*, 14 October 1980, article 5; cf. also Congregation for the Clergy et al., Instruction, *Ecclesiae de mysterio*, Practical Provisions, article 3 § 5: AAS 89 (1997) p. 865.

278. St. Thomas Aquinas, *Summa Theologica.*, II, 2, q. 93, a. 1.

279. Cf. John Paul II, Apostolic Letter, *Vicesimus quintus annus*, n. 15: AAS 81 (1989) p. 911; cf. also Second Vatican Ecumenical Council, Constitution on the Sacred Liturgy, *Sacrosanctum Concilium*, nn. 15–19.

1. GRAVIORA DELICTA

172. *Graviora delicta* against the sanctity of the Most August Sacrifice and Sacrament of the Eucharist are to be handled in accordance with the "Norms concerning *graviora delicta* reserved to the Congregation for the Doctrine of the Faith,"[280] namely:

a) taking away or retaining the consecrated species for sacrilegious ends, or the throwing them away;[281]

b) the attempted celebration of the liturgical action of the Eucharistic Sacrifice or the simulation of the same;[282]

c) the forbidden concelebration of the Eucharistic Sacrifice with ministers of Ecclesial Communities that do not have the apostolic succession nor acknowledge the sacramental dignity of priestly Ordination;[283]

d) the consecration for sacrilegious ends of one matter without the other in the celebration of the Eucharist or even of both outside the celebration of the Eucharist.[284]

2. GRAVE MATTERS

173. Although the gravity of a matter is to be judged in accordance with the common teaching of the Church and the norms established by her, objectively to be considered among grave matters is anything that puts at risk the validity and dignity of the Most Holy Eucharist: namely, anything that contravenes what is set out above in nn. 48–52, 56, 76–77, 79, 91–92, 94, 96, 101–102, 104, 106, 109, 111, 115, 117, 126, 131–133, 138, 153 and 168. Moreover, attention should be given to the other prescriptions of the Code of Canon Law, and especially what is laid down by canons 1364, 1369, 1373, 1376, 1380, 1384, 1385, 1386, and 1398.

---

280. Cf. John Paul II, Apostolic Letter (Motu Proprio), *Sacramentorum sanctitatis tutela:* AAS 93 (2001) pp. 737–739; Congregation for the Doctrine of the Faith, Ep. ad totius Catholicae Ecclesiae Episcopos aliosque Ordinarios et Hierarchas quorum interest: de delictis gravioribus eidem Congregationi pro Doctrina Fidei reservatis: AAS 93 (2001) p. 786.

281. Cf. *Code of Canon Law,* can. 1367; Pontifical Council for the Interpretation of Legislative Texts, Responsio ad propositum dubium, 3 July 1999: AAS 91 (1999) p. 918; Congregation for the Doctrine of the Faith, Ep. ad totius Catholicae Ecclesiae Episcopos aliosque Ordinarios et Hierarchas quorum interest: de delictis gravioribus eidem Congregationi pro Doctrina Fidei reservatis: AAS 93 (2001) p. 786.

282. Cf. *Code of Canon Law,* canon 1378 § 2 n. 1 et 1379; Congregation for the Doctrine of the Faith, Ep. ad totius Catholicae Ecclesiae Episcopos aliosque Ordinarios et Hierarchas quorum interest: de delictis gravioribus eidem Congregationi pro Doctrina Fidei reservatis: AAS 93 (2001) p. 786.

283. Cf. *Code of Canon Law,* canon 908 et 1365; Congregation for the Doctrine of the Faith, Ep. ad totius Catholicae Ecclesiae Episcopos aliosque Ordinarios et Hierarchas quorum interest: de delictis gravioribus eidem Congregationi pro Doctrina Fidei reservatis: AAS 93 (2001) p. 786.

284. Cf. *Code of Canon Law,* canon 927; Congregation for the Doctrine of the Faith, Ep. ad totius Catholicae Ecclesiae Episcopos aliosque Ordinarios et Hierarchas quorum interest: de delictis gravioribus eidem Congregationi pro Doctrina Fidei reservatis: AAS 93 (2001) p. 786.

3. OTHER ABUSES

174. Furthermore, those actions that are brought about which are contrary to the other matters treated elsewhere in this Instruction or in the norms established by law are not to be considered of little account, but are to be numbered among the other abuses to be carefully avoided and corrected.

175. The things set forth in this Instruction obviously do not encompass all the violations against the Church and its discipline that are defined in the canons, in the liturgical laws and in other norms of the Church for the sake of the teaching of the Magisterium or sound tradition. Where something wrong has been committed, it is to be corrected according to the norm of law.

4. THE DIOCESAN BISHOP

176. The diocesan Bishop, "since he is the principal dispenser of the mysteries of God, is to strive constantly so that Christ's faithful entrusted to his care may grow in grace through the celebration of the sacraments, and that they may know and live the Paschal Mystery."[285] It is his responsibility, "within the limits of his competence, to issue norms on liturgical matters by which all are bound."[286]

177. "Since he must safeguard the unity of the universal Church, the Bishop is bound to promote the discipline common to the entire Church and therefore to insist upon the observance of all ecclesiastical laws. He is to be watchful lest abuses encroach upon ecclesiastical discipline, especially as regards the ministry of the Word, the celebration of the Sacraments and sacramentals, the worship of God and the veneration of the Saints."[287]

178. Hence whenever a local Ordinary or the Ordinary of a religious Institute or of a Society of apostolic life receives at least a plausible notice of a delict or abuse concerning the Most Holy Eucharist, let him carefully investigate, either personally or by means of another worthy cleric, concerning the facts and the circumstances as well as the imputability.

179. Delicts against the faith as well as *graviora delicta* committed in the celebration of the Eucharist and the other Sacraments are to be referred without delay to the Congregation for the Doctrine of the Faith, which "examines [them] and, if necessary, proceeds to the declaration or imposition of canonical sanctions according to the norm of common or proper law."[288]

180. Otherwise the Ordinary should proceed according the norms of the sacred canons, imposing canonical penalties if necessary, and bearing in mind in particular that which is laid down by canon 1326. If the matter is serious, let him inform the Congregation for Divine Worship and the Discipline of the Sacraments.

---

285. *Code of Canon Law*, canon 387.
286. *Ibidem*, canon 838 § 4.
287. *Ibidem*, canon 392.
288. Cf. John Paul II, Apostolic Constitution, *Pastor bonus*, article 52: AAS 80 (1988) p. 874.

5. THE APOSTOLIC SEE

181. Whenever the Congregation for Divine Worship and the Discipline of the Sacraments receives at least a plausible notice of a delict or an abuse concerning the Most Holy Eucharist, it informs the Ordinary so that he may investigate the matter. When the matter turns out to be serious, the Ordinary should send to the same Dicastery as quickly as possible a copy of the acts of the inquiry that has been undertaken, and where necessary, the penalty imposed.

182. In more difficult cases the Ordinary, for the sake of the good of the universal Church in the care for which he too has a part by virtue of his sacred Ordination, should not fail to handle the matter, having previously taken advice from the Congregation for Divine Worship and the Discipline of the Sacraments. For its part, this Congregation, on the strength of the faculties given to it by the Roman Pontiff, according to the nature of the case, will assist the Ordinary, granting him the necessary dispensations[289] or giving him instructions or prescriptions, which he is to follow diligently.

6. COMPLAINTS REGARDING ABUSES IN LITURGICAL MATTERS

183. In an altogether particular manner, let everyone do all that is in their power to ensure that the Most Holy Sacrament of the Eucharist will be protected from any and every irreverence or distortion and that all abuses be thoroughly corrected. This is a most serious duty incumbent upon each and every one, and all are bound to carry it out without any favoritism.

184. Any Catholic, whether Priest or Deacon or lay member of Christ's faithful, has the right to lodge a complaint regarding a liturgical abuse to the diocesan Bishop or the competent Ordinary equivalent to him in law, or to the Apostolic See on account of the primacy of the Roman Pontiff.[290] It is fitting, however, insofar as possible, that the report or complaint be submitted first to the diocesan Bishop. This is naturally to be done in truth and charity.

CONCLUSION

185. "Against the seeds of discord which daily experience shows to be so deeply ingrained in human nature as a result of sin, there stands the creative power of the unity of Christ's body. For it is precisely by building up the Church that the Eucharist establishes fellowship among men."[291] It is therefore the hope of this Congregation for Divine Worship and the Discipline of the Sacraments that also, by the diligent application of those things that are recalled in this Instruction, human weakness may come to pose less of an obstacle to the action of the Most Holy Sacrament of the Eucharist, and that with all distortion set aside and every

---

289. Cf. *ibidem*, n. 63: AAS 80 (1988) p. 876.

290. Cf. ibidem, canon 1417 § 1.

291. John Paul II, Encyclical Letter, *Ecclesia de Eucharistia*, n. 24: AAS 95 (2003) p. 449.

reprobated practice removed,[292] through the intercession of the Blessed Virgin Mary, "Woman of the Eucharist," the saving presence of Christ in the Sacrament of his Body and Blood may shine brightly upon all people.

186. Let all Christ's faithful participate in the Most Holy Eucharist as fully, consciously and actively as they can,[293] honouring it lovingly by their devotion and the manner of their life. Let Bishops, Priests and Deacons, in the exercise of the sacred ministry, examine their consciences as regards the authenticity and fidelity of the actions they have performed in the name of Christ and the Church in the celebration of the Sacred Liturgy. Let each one of the sacred ministers ask himself, even with severity, whether he has respected the rights of the lay members of Christ's faithful, who confidently entrust themselves and their children to him, relying on him to fulfil for the faithful those sacred functions that the Church intends to carry out in celebrating the sacred Liturgy at Christ's command.[294] For each one should always remember that he is a servant of the Sacred Liturgy.[295]

All things to the contrary notwithstanding.

This Instruction, prepared by the Congregation for Divine Worship and the Discipline of the Sacraments by mandate of the Supreme Pontiff John Paul II in collaboration with the Congregation for the Doctrine of the Faith, was approved by the same Pontiff on the Solemnity of St. Joseph, 19 March 2004, and he ordered it to be published and to be observed immediately by all concerned.

From the offices of the Congregation for Divine Worship and the Discipline of the Sacraments, Rome, on the Solemnity of the Annunciation of the Lord, 25 March 2004.

Francis Cardinal Arinze
Prefect

Domenico Sorrentino
Archbishop Secretary

---

292. Cf. *ibidem*, nn. 53–58: AAS 95 (2003) pp. 469–472.
293. Cf. Second Vatican Ecumenical Council, Constitution on the Sacred Liturgy, *Sacrosanctum Concilium*, n. 14; cf. also nn. 11, 41, et 48.
294. Cf. S. Thomas Aquinas, *Summa Theologica.*, III, q. 64, a. 9 ad 1.
295. Cf. *Missale Romanum*, Institutio Generalis, n. 24.

LECTIONARY FOR MASS
INTRODUCTION

CONGREGATION FOR DIVINE WORSHIP AND
THE DISCIPLINE OF THE SACRAMENTS

CURRENT LATIN EDITION
JANUARY 21, 1981

CURRENT ENGLISH TRANSLATION APPROVED
OCTOBER 6, 1997

CURRENT ENGLISH TRANSLATION PROMULGATED FOR USE
IN THE DIOCESES OF THE UNITED STATES OF AMERICA
JUNE 19, 1998

OVERVIEW OF THE *LECTIONARY FOR MASS: INTRODUCTION*

Mary Elizabeth Sperry

The Holy See issued the second edition of the "Introduction" to the *Lectionary for Mass* (LM) in 1981, accompanying the revised *Ordo Lectionum Missae* (Order of Readings for Mass). In accord with canon 2 of the *Code of Canon Law* (CIC), the "Introduction" is liturgical law governing the Liturgy of the Word. The rubrics do not address the use of the Word in celebrations outside of Mass, including Penance and the Liturgy of the Hours.

The "Introduction" has three sections: a brief preamble and two larger parts. The preamble provides an overview of the role that the Word of God plays in the life and mission of the Church. The first part looks more closely at the role of the Word of God in Mass. The second part offers a detailed look at the contents and organization of the Order of Readings.

The primary theme of the preamble is the intrinsic connection between Scripture and the liturgy. Both Scripture and the Eucharist draw the faithful into the life of the Trinity. All Scripture—the Old Testament and the New Testament—proclaims Christ, tells of the Father's love, and receives its power from the Holy Spirit. The faithful's response to the Word proclaimed leads them to a closer relationship with Christ, allowing them to enter more deeply into Christ's Paschal Mystery celebrated in the Eucharist. Similarly, the more the faithful understand the liturgy, the more they appreciate the importance of Scripture. In the celebration of the Mass, the Liturgy of the Word and the Liturgy of the Eucharist form a single act of worship, both deserving of reverence and both nourishing the Church to fulfill the mission entrusted to it by Christ.

The first part of the "Introduction" addresses the structure of the Liturgy of the Word and the offices and ministries involved. Each element of the Liturgy of the Word is discussed, and rubrics are provided for its appropriate celebration. The "Introduction" emphasizes that the biblical readings that form the backbone of the Liturgy of the Word may never be replaced by nonbiblical readings. The Liturgy of the Word reaches its climax in the proclamation of the Gospel, greeted with its own acclamation.

Those charged with preparing liturgies will do well to note the significant role that silence plays in the Liturgy of the Word. Silence fosters meditation and offers the listeners an opportunity to take the Word to heart. Similarly, the singing of the Responsorial Psalm allows the faithful to respond to the Word and to pray the Psalms with the heart of the Church. Catechesis on praying with the Psalms may be of benefit.

The Homily provides an explanation of the readings, helping the faithful to view their lives through the prism of Scripture, and calling them to conversion and a renewed commitment to life in Christ, a commitment that will be strengthened through reception of the Eucharist. Since the publication of the

"Introduction," both *Redemptionis sacramentum* (RS) and *Verbum domini* (VD) have given extensive attention to the importance of good preaching.

The Creed allows the faithful to give assent to the Word. In the Prayer of the Faithful (or Universal Prayer), the people respond to the Word of God by presenting the needs of the Church and the world to God.

Reverence for Scripture is embodied by the use of worthy liturgical books and by the reservation of the ambo for its proclamation. Those responsible for liturgy should ensure that the books are not replaced by worship leaflets or scripts and that the ambo is not used to lead song or make announcements.

The first part of the "Introduction" concludes by examining the offices and ministries in the Liturgy of the Word. The priest celebrant at the liturgy bears primary responsibility for the celebration of the Liturgy of the Word. He should ensure that the Word is proclaimed well. To do so, he should have a thorough knowledge of the structure of the order of readings and the options contained therein so that he can make choices for the spiritual benefit of the faithful. Through his teaching in the Homily, he leads people to a deeper knowledge of and relationship with Christ, encouraging them to the fruitful reception of Holy Communion.

The faithful have an important office in the Liturgy of the Word. As the "Introduction" states, "Christ's word gathers the people of God as one and increases and sustains them."[1] The faithful hear the Word and respond to it, growing in the spiritual life and being drawn ever more deeply into the Paschal Mystery. Hearing the Word of God proclaimed in the liturgy makes the faithful aware of the presence of Christ in Scripture and arouses in them a living faith. Thus, it is essential for the faithful to be present for both the Liturgy of the Word and the Liturgy of the Eucharist.

The "Introduction" explains the roles of the other ministers involved in the Liturgy of the Word—namely, the deacon, the lector or reader, and the psalmist. Those responsible for training liturgical ministers should give special attention to the discussion of the appropriate formation for those charged with proclaiming the Word of God. In addition to being able to proclaim the Word well with the assistance of amplification, all should strive for a deep and abiding love of Scripture, interpreted with the mind of the Church.

The second part of the "Introduction" describes the structure of the order of readings. The guiding principle behind the order of readings is pastoral. The readings were selected to give the faithful a sense of the scope of God's Word and to make sure that they hear the principal stories in salvation history. The goal of the reading selection is to encourage a deeper faith among the listeners. While the primary purpose of the Liturgy of the Word is worship, not catechesis, it does contain elements of teaching, drawing people into an ever-closer relationship with Christ and his Church.

In addition, the order of readings gives evidence of the unity of the Church, as all churches that follow the ordinary form of the Roman liturgy use the same readings, with some provision for pastors to make use of options. Since the publication of *Summorum pontificorum*, communities that celebrate the extraordinary form of the Roman liturgy use the order of readings found in the 1962

---

1. *Lectionary for Mass: Introduction*, 44.

edition of the *Missale Romanum*. This order of readings differs from the order described in the 1981 "Introduction" in both structure and content.

Two general principles guide the selection of readings for Sundays: harmony and semicontinuous reading. As a rule, the Gospel is read in a semicontinuous fashion throughout the year. The synoptic Gospel accounts (Matthew, Mark, and Luke) are read almost in their entirety in Years A, B, and C of the Sunday cycle, respectively. Throughout Ordinary Time, each Sunday's Gospel picks up at approximately the chapter and verse where the preceding Sunday's Gospel concluded. The Old Testament reading is selected to harmonize with the Gospel reading. The Old Testament reading may be quoted in the Gospel reading, or it may share an underlying theme. The Psalm reflects on the theme of the Old Testament reading. For the second readings, the New Testament Letters are read semi-continuously, with the most important parts of each letter selected.

For major feast days and for the Sundays of the liturgical times of Advent, Christmas Time, Lent, and Easter Time, all three readings for each Sunday reflect the key themes of the celebration. This principle also guides the selection of readings for the weekdays of Advent, Christmas Time, Lent, and Easter Time. All of the First Readings in Advent and Lent come from the Old Testament. The First Readings in Christmas Time come from the First Letter of John. In Easter Time, Acts of the Apostles is read semicontinuously.

In Ordinary Time, the weekday synoptic Gospel accounts are read semi-continuously beginning with Mark, followed by Matthew and Luke. Two sets of First Readings and Responsorial Psalms are provided so that the faithful who attend daily Mass may feast more richly from the banquet of Scripture. The Year I readings are used in odd-numbered years and the Year II readings are used in even-numbered years. In both years, books are read semicontinuously, with the most important parts selected. The books of both the Old and New Testament are read, though a larger percentage of the New Testament is read, due to the greater length of the Old Testament.

The Lectionary provides two sets of readings for the celebrations of the saints. The Proper of Saints gives the proper reading selected for a particular saint or identifies a reading from the Common of Saints that is most appropriate for a specific celebration. The Common of Saints provides readings from the Old Testament, New Testament, and the Gospel accounts, as well as Responsorial Psalms and Gospel Acclamations for various groups of saints, such as martyrs, pastors, and Doctors of the Church. Readings for a given saint's observance may always be selected from the commons.

Finally, the Lectionary gives readings for Ritual Masses, Masses for Various Needs and Intentions, Votive Masses, and Masses for the Dead. These readings are organized as in the Common of Saints and reflect appropriate themes for the given celebrations.

The "Introduction" goes on to explain the criteria used for choosing the various readings. These include the tradition of reserving certain books to specific seasons and concern for the length of readings. Biblical passages that present pastoral difficulties are typically not selected for Sunday liturgies. When such difficult readings do appear, the priest celebrant should take care to explain the readings with pastoral care and in the context of the other readings. In some cases, certain verses have been omitted from readings, often because of length or because a few verses present grave difficulties for understanding that cannot be addressed appropriately in the liturgical assembly.

The priest and others charged with preparing the liturgy should have an excellent knowledge of the options available for any given celebration, for example, choosing the longer or shorter form of a reading, or replacing the Responsorial Psalm prescribed with a seasonal Psalm. They should choose among these options for the spiritual benefit of the faithful.

The "Introduction" then provides a detailed description of the readings for each season. This description is an excellent complement to the descriptions in the *Universal Norms on the Liturgical Year and the General Roman Calendar* (UNLY). These resources will help those charged with liturgical preparation to develop a better understanding of themes and images that receive particular attention in the various liturgical times.

Finally, the "Introduction" describes the layout of each reading. Readers, as well as deacons and priests, should have a clear understanding of this layout to ensure that they read each reading properly.

As the "Introduction" to the *Lectionary for Mass* presents the essential role of the Word of God in the life and mission of the Church, as well as a complete overview of the Liturgy of the Word, this text should provide the basis for training those who proclaim the Word in the liturgical assembly. By developing a love of Scripture and a thorough knowledge of its use in the liturgy, they will undertake their ministry with ever-greater care and devotion. Those who prepare and preside at liturgy should refer to the "Introduction" to ensure that the Liturgy of the Word is prepared and celebrated with due reverence.

OUTLINE

SECOND PART: THE STRUCTURE OF THE ORDER OF THE READINGS FOR MASS

CHAPTER IV: The General Arrangement of Readings for Mass

CHAPTER V: Description of the Order of Readings

LECTIONARY FOR MASS
INTRODUCTION

PREAMBLE

CHAPTER I
GENERAL PRINCIPLES FOR THE LITURGICAL CELEBRATION
OF THE WORD OF GOD

1. Certain Preliminaries

A) THE IMPORTANCE OF THE WORD OF GOD IN LITURGICAL CELEBRATION

1.　The Second Vatican Council,[1] the magisterium of the Popes,[2] and various documents promulgated after the Council by the organisms of the Holy See[3] have already had many excellent things to say about the importance of the word of God and about reestablishing the use of Sacred Scripture in every celebration of the Liturgy. The Introduction to the 1969 edition of the Order of Readings for Mass has clearly stated and briefly explained some of the more important principles.[4]

On the occasion of this new edition of the Order of Readings for Mass, requests have come from many quarters for a more detailed exposition of the same principles. Hence, this expanded and more suitable arrangement of the Introduction first gives a general statement on the essential bond between the word of God and the liturgical celebration,[5] then deals in greater detail with the word of God in the celebration of Mass, and, finally explains the precise structure of the Order of Readings for Mass.

B) TERMS USED TO REFER TO THE WORD OF GOD

2.　For the sake of clear and precise language on this topic, a definition of terms might well be expected as a prerequisite. Nevertheless this Introduction will simply use the same terms employed in conciliar and postconciliar documents. Furthermore it will use "Sacred Scripture" and "word of God" interchangeably

---

1. See SC, 7, 24, 33, 35, 48, 51, 52, 56; DV, 21, 25, 26; AG, 6; PO, 18.

2. See Paul VI, *motu proprio Ministeria quaedam*, V; apostolic exhortation *Evangelii nuntiandi* (EN), 28, 43, 47; apostolic exhortation *Marialis cultus* (MC), 12; John Paul II, apostolic constitution *Scripturarum thesaurus*, p. v–viii; apostolic exhortation *Catechesi tradendae* (CT), 23, 27, 48; letter *Dominicae cenae* (DC), 10.

3. See EM, 10; CDW, instruction *Liturgicae instaurationes* (LI) 2; GCD, 10–12, 25; GIRM, 9, 11, 24, 33, 60, 62, 316, 320; SDW, instruction *Inaestimabile donum*, (ID), 1, 2, 3.

4. See LMIn (1969), nos. 1–7; decree of promulgation: AAS 61 (1969) 548–549.

5. See SC, 35, 56; EN, 28, 47; DC, 10, 11, 12.

throughout when referring to the books written under the inspiration of the Holy Spirit, thus avoiding any confusion of language or meaning.[6]

c) THE SIGNIFICANCE OF THE WORD OF GOD IN THE LITURGY

3.   The many riches contained in the one word of God are admirably brought out in the different kinds of liturgical celebration and in the different gatherings of the faithful who take part in those celebrations. This takes place as the unfolding mystery of Christ is recalled during the course of the liturgical year, as the Church's sacraments and sacramentals are celebrated, or as the faithful respond individually to the Holy Spirit working within them.[7] For then the liturgical celebration, founded primarily on the word of God and sustained by it, becomes a new event and enriches the word itself with new meaning and power. Thus in the Liturgy the Church faithfully adheres to the way Christ himself read and explained the Sacred Scriptures, beginning with the "today" of his coming forward in the synagogue and urging all to search the Scriptures.[8]

2. Liturgical Celebration of the Word of God

A) THE PROPER CHARACTER OF THE WORD OF GOD IN THE LITURGICAL CELEBRATION

4.   In the celebration of the Liturgy the word of God is not announced in only one way[9] nor does it always stir the hearts of the hearers with the same efficacy. Always, however, Christ is present in his word,[10] as he carries out the mystery of salvation, he sanctifies humanity and offers the Father perfect worship.[11]

Moreover, the word of God unceasingly calls to mind and extends the economy of salvation, which achieves its fullest expression in the Liturgy. The liturgical celebration becomes therefore the continuing, complete, and effective presentation of God's word.

The word of God constantly proclaimed in the Liturgy is always, then, a living and effective word[12] through the power of the Holy Spirit. It expresses the Father's love that never fails in its effectiveness toward us.

---

6. CDW, instruction *Liturgicae instaurantiones* (LI) 2, for example, the terms, *word of God, sacred Scripture, Old* and *New Testament, reading(s) of the word of God, reading(s) from sacred scripture, celebration(s) of the word of God,* etc.

7. Thus the same text may be read or used for various reasons on various occasions and celebrations of the church's liturgical year. This is to be recalled in the homily, in pastoral exegesis, and in catechesis.

8. See Luke 4:16–21; 24:25–35 and 44–49.

9. Thus, for example, in the celebration of the Mass there is proclamation, reading, etc. (see GIRM, 21, 23, 95, 131, 146, 234, 235). There are also other celebrations of the word of God in the Roman Pontifical, Ritual and Liturgy of the Hours as restored by decree of the Second Vatican Council.

10. See SC, 7, 33; Mark 16:19–20; Matthew 28:20.

11. See SC, 7.

12. See Hebrews 4:12.

5.   When in celebrating the Liturgy the Church proclaims both the Old and New Testament, it is proclaiming one and the same mystery of Christ.

The New Testament lies hidden in the Old; the Old Testament comes fully to light in the New.[13] Christ himself is the center and fullness of the whole of Scripture, just as he is of all liturgical celebration.[14] Thus the Scriptures are the living waters from which all who seek life and salvation must drink.

The more profound our understanding of the celebration of the liturgy, the higher our appreciation of the importance of God's word. Whatever we say of the one, we can in turn say of the other, because each recalls the mystery of Christ and each in its own way causes the mystery to be carried forward.

c) THE WORD OF GOD IN THE LITURGICAL PARTICIPATION OF THE FAITHFUL

6.   In celebrating the Liturgy the Church faithfully echoes the "Amen" that Christ, the mediator between God and men and women, uttered once for all as he shed his blood to seal God's new covenant in the Holy Spirit.[15]

When God communicates his word, he expects a response, one that is, of listening and adoring "in Spirit and in truth" (John 4:23). The Holy Spirit makes that response effective, so that what is heard in the celebration of the Liturgy may be carried out in a way of life: "Be doers of the word and not hearers only" (James 1:22).

The liturgical celebration and the participation of the faithful receive outward expression in actions, gestures, and words. These derive their full meaning not simply from their origin in human experience but from the word of God and the economy of salvation, to which they refer. Accordingly, the participation of the faithful in the Liturgy increases to the degree that, as they listen to the word of God proclaimed in the Liturgy, they strive harder to commit themselves to the Word of God incarnate in Christ. Thus, they endeavor to conform their way of life to what they celebrate in the Liturgy, and then in turn to bring to the celebration of the Liturgy all that they do in life.[16]

3. The Word of God in the Life of the People of the Covenant

a) THE WORD OF GOD IN THE LIFE OF THE CHURCH

7.   In the hearing of God's word the Church is built up and grows, and in the signs of the liturgical celebration God's wonderful, past works in the history of salvation are presented anew as mysterious realities. God in turn makes use of

---

13. See Augustine, *Quaestionum in Heptateuchum*, book 2; DV, 16.

14. See Jerome, "If, as St. Paul says (1 Cor 1:24), Christ is the power of God and the wisdom of God, anyone who does not know the Scriptures does not know the power of God or his wisdom. For not to know the Scriptures is not to know Christ" (*Commentarii in Isaiam prophetam*, prologue); DV, 25.

15. See 2 Corinthians 1:20–22.

16. See SC, 10.

the congregation of the faithful that celebrates the Liturgy in order that his word may speed on and be glorified and that his name be exalted among the nations.[17]

Whenever, therefore, the Church, gathered by the Holy Spirit for liturgical celebration,[18] announces and proclaims the word of God, she is aware of being a new people in whom the covenant made in the past is perfected and fulfilled. Baptism and confirmation in the Spirit have made all Christ's faithful into messengers of God's word because of the grace of hearing they have received. They must therefore be the bearers of the same word in the Church and in the world, at least by the witness of their lives.

The word of God proclaimed in the celebration of God's mysteries does not only address present conditions but looks back to past events and forward to what is yet to come. Thus God's word shows us what we should hope for with such a longing that in this changing world our hearts will be set on the place where our true joys lie.[19]

B) THE CHURCH'S EXPLANATION OF THE WORD OF GOD

8.   By Christ's own will there is a marvelous diversity of members in the new people of God and each has different duties and responsibilities with respect to the word of God. Accordingly, the faithful listen to God's word and meditate on it, but only those who have the office of teaching by virtue of sacred ordination or who have been entrusted with exercising that ministry expound the word of God.

This is how in doctrine, life, and worship the Church keeps alive and passes on to every generation all that she is, all that she believes. Thus with the passage of the centuries, the Church is ever to advance toward the fullness of divine truth until God's word is wholly accomplished in her.[20]

C) THE CONNECTION BETWEEN THE WORD OF GOD PROCLAIMED AND THE WORKING OF THE HOLY SPIRIT

9.   The working of the Holy Spirit is needed if the word of God is to make what we hear outwardly have its effect inwardly. Because of the Holy Spirit's inspiration and support, the word of God becomes the foundation of the liturgical celebration and the rule and support of all our life.

The working of the Holy Spirit precedes, accompanies, and brings to completion the whole celebration of the Liturgy. But the Spirit also brings home[21] to each person individually everything that in the proclamation of the word of God is spoken for the good of the whole gathering of the faithful. In strengthening the unity of all, the Holy Spirit at the same time fosters a diversity of gifts and furthers their multiform operation.

---

17. See 2 Thessalonians 3:1.
18. See RomM, opening prayers A, B and C in Mass for the Universal Church.
19. See RomM, opening prayer for the Twenty-first Sunday in Ordinary Time.
20. See DV, 8.
21. See John 14:15–17, 25–26; 15:26—16:15.

D) THE ESSENTIAL BOND BETWEEN THE WORD OF GOD
AND THE MYSTERY OF THE EUCHARIST

10.   The Church has honored the word of God and the Eucharistic mystery with the same reverence, although not with the same worship, and has always and everywhere insisted upon and sanctioned such honor. Moved by the example of its Founder, the Church has never ceased to celebrate his paschal mystery by coming together to read "what referred to him in all the Scriptures" (Luke 24:27) and to carry out the work of salvation through the celebration of the memorial of the Lord and through the sacraments. "The preaching of the word is necessary for the ministry of the sacraments, for these are sacraments of faith, which is born and nourished from the word."[22]

The Church is nourished spiritually at the twofold table of God's word and of the Eucharist:[23] from the one it grows in wisdom and from the other in holiness. In the word of God the divine covenant is announced; in the Eucharist the new and everlasting covenant is renewed. On the one hand the history of salvation is brought to mind by means of human sounds; on the other it is made manifest in the sacramental signs of the Liturgy.

It can never be forgotten, therefore, that the divine word read and proclaimed by the Church in the Liturgy has as its one purpose the sacrifice of the New Covenant and the banquet of grace, that is, the Eucharist. The celebration of Mass in which the word is heard and the Eucharist is offered and received forms but one single act of divine worship.[24] That act offers the sacrifice of praise to God and makes available to God's creatures the fullness of redemption.

FIRST PART
THE WORD OF GOD IN THE CELEBRATION OF MASS

CHAPTER II
THE CELEBRATION OF THE LITURGY OF THE WORD AT MASS

1. The Elements of the Liturgy of the Word and their Rites

11.   "Readings from Sacred Scripture and the chants between the readings form the main part of the liturgy of the word. The homily, the profession of faith, and the universal prayer or prayer of the faithful carry it forward and conclude it."[25]

A) THE BIBLICAL READINGS

12.   In the celebration of Mass the biblical readings with their accompanying chants from the Sacred Scriptures may not be omitted, shortened, or, worse still, replaced by nonbiblical readings.[26] For it is out of the word of God handed down

---

22. See PO, 4.
23. See SC, 51; PO, 18; DV, 21; AG, 6; GIRM, 8.
24. SC, 56.
25. GIRM, 33.
26. See LI, 2; DC, 10; ID, 1.

in writing that even now "God speaks to his people"[27] and it is from the continued use of Sacred Scripture that the people of God, docile to the Holy Spirit under the light of faith, is enabled to bear witness to Christ before the world by its manner of life.

13.　The reading of the Gospel is the high point of the liturgy of the word. For this the other readings, in their established sequence from the Old to the New Testament, prepare the assembly.

14.　A speaking style on the part of the readers that is audible, clear, and intelligent is the first means of transmitting the word of God properly to the congregation. The readings, taken from the approved editions,[28] may be sung in a way suited to different languages. This singing, however, must serve to bring out the sense of the words, not obscure them. On occasions when the readings are in Latin, the manner given in the *Ordo cantus Missae* is to be maintained.[29]

15.　There may be concise introductions before the readings, especially the first. The style proper to such comments must be respected, that is, they must be simple, faithful to the text, brief, well prepared, and properly varied to suit the text they introduce.[30]

16.　In a Mass with the people the readings are always to be proclaimed at the ambo.[31]

17.　Of all the rites connected with the liturgy of the word, the reverence due to the Gospel reading must receive special attention.[32] Where there is an Evangeliary or Book of Gospels that has been carried in by the deacon or reader during the entry procession,[33] it is most fitting that the deacon or a priest, when there is no deacon, take the book from the altar[34] and carry it to the ambo. He is preceded by servers with candles and incense or other symbols of reverence that may be customary. As the faithful stand and acclaim the Lord, they show honor to the Book of Gospels. The deacon who is to read the Gospel, bowing in front of the one presiding, asks and receives the blessing. When no deacon is present, the priest, bowing before the altar, prays inaudibly, *Almighty God, cleanse my heart . . . .*[35]

At the ambo the one who proclaims the Gospel greets the people, who are standing, and announces the reading as he makes the sign of the cross on forehead, mouth, and breast. If incense is used, he next incenses the book, then reads the Gospel. When finished, he kisses the book, saying the appointed words inaudibly.

----

27. SC, 33.
28. See LMIn, 111.
29. See RomM, *Ordo cantus Missae* (ed. typ., 1972), Praenotanda, 4, 6, 10.
30. See GIRM, 11.
31. See GIRM, 272; LMIn, 32–34.
32. See GIRM, 35, 95.
33. See GIRM, 82–84.
34. See GIRM, 94, 131.
35. See RomM, Order of Mass, "Liturgy of the Word: The Gospel."

Even if the Gospel itself is not sung, it is appropriate for the greeting *The Lord be with you*, and *A reading from the holy Gospel according to . . .* , and at the end *The Gospel of the Lord* to be sung, in order that the congregation may also sing its acclamations. This is a way both of bringing out the importance of the Gospel reading and of stirring up the faith of those who hear it.

18.   At the conclusion of the other readings, *The word of the Lord* may be sung, even by someone other than the reader; all respond with the acclamation. In this way the assembled congregation pays reverence to the word of God it has listened to in faith and gratitude.

B) THE RESPONSORIAL PSALM

19.   The responsorial psalm, also called the gradual, has great liturgical and pastoral significance because it is an "integral part of the liturgy of the word."[36] Accordingly, the faithful must be continually instructed on the way to perceive the word of God speaking in the psalms and to turn these psalms into the prayer of the Church. This, of course, "will be achieved more readily if a deeper understanding of the psalms, according to the meaning with which they are sung in the sacred Liturgy, is more diligently promoted among the clergy and communicated to all the faithful by means of appropriate catechesis."[37]

Brief remarks about the choice of the psalm and response as well as their correspondence to the readings may be helpful.

20.   As a rule the responsorial psalm should be sung. There are two established ways of singing the psalm after the first reading: responsorially and directly. In responsorial singing, which, as far as possible, is to be given preference, the psalmist, or cantor of the psalm, sings the psalm verse and the whole congregation joins in by singing the response. In direct singing of the psalm there is no intervening response by the community; either the psalmist, or cantor of the psalm, sings the psalm alone as the community listens or else all sing it together.

21.   The singing of the psalm, or even of the response alone, is a great help toward understanding and meditating on the psalm's spiritual meaning.

To foster the congregation's singing, every means available in each individual culture is to be employed. In particular, use is to be made of all the relevant options provided in the Order of Readings for Mass[38] regarding responses corresponding to the different liturgical seasons.

22.   When not sung, the psalm after the reading is to be recited in a manner conducive to meditation on the word of God.[39]

---

36. See GIRM, 36.

37. Paul VI, apostolic constitution *Laudis canticum*, in *The Liturgy of the Hours*; see also SC, 24, 90; CR, instruction *Musicam Sacram* (MS) 39.

38. See LMIn, 89–90.

39. See GIRM, 18, 39.

The responsorial psalm is sung or recited by the psalmist or cantor at the ambo.[40]

c) THE ACCLAMATION BEFORE THE READING OF THE GOSPEL

23. The *Alleluia* or, as the liturgical season requires, the verse before the Gospel, is also a "rite or act standing by itself."[41] It serves as the greeting of welcome of the assembled faithful to the Lord who is about to speak to them and as an expression of their faith through song.

The *Alleluia* or the verse before the Gospel must be sung and during it all stand. It is not to be sung only by the cantor who intones it or by the choir, but by the whole of the people together.[42]

d) THE HOMILY

24. Through the course of the liturgical year the homily sets forth the mysteries of faith and the standards of the Christian life on the basis of the sacred text. Beginning with the Constitution on the Liturgy, the homily as part of the liturgy of the word[43] has been repeatedly and strongly recommended and in some cases it is obligatory. As a rule it is to be given by the one presiding.[44] The purpose of the homily at Mass is that the spoken word of God and the liturgy of the Eucharist may together become "a proclamation of God's wonderful works in the history of salvation, the mystery of Christ."[45] Through the readings and homily Christ's paschal mystery is proclaimed; through the sacrifice of the Mass it becomes present.[46] Moreover Christ himself is always present and active in the preaching of his Church.[47]

Whether the homily explains the text of the Sacred Scriptures proclaimed in the readings or some other text of the Liturgy,[48] it must always lead the community of the faithful to celebrate the Eucharist actively, "so that they may hold fast in their lives to what they have grasped by faith."[49] From this living explanation, the word of God proclaimed in the readings and the Church's celebration of the day's Liturgy will have greater impact. But this demands that the homily be truly the fruit of meditation, carefully prepared, neither too long nor too short, and suited to all those present, even children and the uneducated.[50]

---

40. See GIRM, 272; LMIn, 32ff.
41. See GIRM, 39.
42. See GIRM, 37—39; RomM, *Ordo cantus Missae*, Praenotanda, 7–9; *Graduale Romanum* (1974), Praenotanda, 7, *Graduale Simple* (2d ed. typ., 1975); Praenotanda, 16.
43. See SC, 52; CR, instruction *Inter oecumenici* (IOe) 54.
44. See GIRM, 42.
45. See SC, 35, 2.
46. See SC, 6, 47.
47. See Paul vi, encyclical, *Mysterium fidei*, 3 Sept 1965; AG, 9; EN, 43.
48. See SC, 35, 2; GIRM, 41.
49. SC, 10.
50. See CT, 48.

At a concelebration, the celebrant or one of the concelebrants as a rule gives the homily.[51]

25.   On the prescribed days, that is, Sundays and holydays of obligation, there must be a homily in all Masses celebrated with a congregation, even Masses on the preceding evening; the homily may not be omitted without a serious reason.[52] There is also to be a homily in Masses with children and with special groups[53]

A homily is strongly recommended on the weekdays of Advent, Lent, and the Easter season for the sake of the faithful who regularly take part in the celebration of Mass; also on other feasts and occasions when a large congregation is present.[54]

26.   The priest celebrant gives the homily, standing either at the chair or at the ambo.[55]

27.   Any necessary announcements are to be kept completely separate from the homily; they must take place following the prayer after Communion.[56]

E) SILENCE

28.   The liturgy of the word must be celebrated in a way that fosters meditation; clearly, any sort of haste that hinders recollection must be avoided. The dialogue between God and his people taking place through the Holy Spirit demands short intervals of silence, suited to the assembled congregation, as an opportunity to take the word of God to heart and to prepare a response to it in prayer.

Proper times for silence during the liturgy of the word are, for example, before this liturgy begins, after the first and the second reading, after the homily.[57]

F) THE PROFESSION OF FAITH

29.   The symbol, creed or profession of faith, said when the rubrics require, has as its purpose in the celebration of Mass that the assembled congregation may respond and give assent to the word of God heard in the readings and through the homily, and that before beginning to celebrate in the Eucharist the mystery of faith it may call to mind the rule of faith in a formulary approved by the Church.[58]

G) THE UNIVERSAL PRAYER OR PRAYER OF THE FAITHFUL

30.   In the light of God's word and in a sense in response to it, the congregation of the faithful prays in the universal prayer as a rule for the needs of the universal Church and the local community, for the salvation of the world and those oppressed by any burden, and for special categories of people.

---

51. See GIRM, 165.
52. See GIRM, 42; EM, 28.
53. See AP, 6g; DMC, 48.
54. See GIRM, 42, 338; *Rite of Marriage* (1969), 22, 42, 57 and *Rite of Funerals* (1969), 41, 64.
55. See GIRM, 97.
56. See GIRM, 139.
57. See GIRM, 23.
58. See GIRM, 43.

The celebrant introduces the prayer; a deacon, another minister, or some of the faithful may propose intentions that are short and phrased with a measure of freedom. In these petitions "the people, exercising its priestly function, makes intercession for all men and women,"[59] with the result that, as the liturgy of the word has its full effects in the faithful, they are better prepared to proceed to the liturgy of the Eucharist.

31. For the prayer of the faithful the celebrant presides at the chair and the intentions are announced at the ambo.[60]

The assembled congregation takes part in the prayer of the faithful while standing and by saying or singing a common response after each intention or by silent prayer.[61]

2. Aids to the Proper Celebration of the Liturgy of the Word

A) THE PLACE FOR THE PROCLAMATION OF THE WORD OF GOD

32. There must be a place in the church that is somewhat elevated, fixed, and of a suitable design and nobility. It should reflect the dignity of God's word and be a clear reminder to the people that in the Mass the table of God's word and of Christ's body is placed before them.[62] The place for the readings must also truly help the people's listening and attention during the liturgy of the word. Great pains must therefore be taken, in keeping with the design of each church, over the harmonious and close relationship of the ambo with the altar.

33. Either permanently or at least on occasions of greater solemnity, the ambo should be decorated simply and in keeping with its design.

Since the ambo is the place from which the word of God is proclaimed by the ministers, it must of its nature be reserved for the readings, the responsorial psalm, and the Easter Proclamation (the *Exsultet*). The ambo may rightly be used for the homily and the prayer of the faithful, however, because of their close connection with the entire liturgy of the word. It is better for the commentator, cantor, or director of singing, for example, not to use the ambo.[63]

34. In order that the ambo may properly serve its liturgical purpose, it is to be rather large, since on occasion several ministers must use it at the same time. Provision must also be made for the readers to have enough light to read the text and, as required, to have modern sound equipment enabling the faithful to hear them without difficulty.

B) THE BOOKS FOR PROCLAMATION OF THE WORD OF GOD IN THE LITURGY

35. Along with the ministers, the actions, the allocated places, and other elements, the books containing the readings of the word of God remind the hearers

---

59. See GIRM, 45.
60. See GIRM, 99.
61. See GIRM, 47.
62. See LMIn, note 23.
63. See GIRM, 272.

of the presence of God speaking to his people. Since in liturgical celebrations the books too serve as signs and symbols of the higher realities, care must be taken to ensure that they truly are worthy, dignified and beautiful.[64]

36.   The proclamation of the Gospel always stands as the high point of the liturgy of the word. Thus the liturgical tradition of both West and East has consistently made a certain distinction between the books for the readings. The Book of Gospels was always fabricated and decorated with the utmost care and shown greater respect than any of the other books of readings. In our times also, then, it is very desirable that cathedrals and at least the larger, more populous parishes and the churches with a larger attendance possess a beautifully designed Book of Gospels, separate from any other book of readings. For good reason it is the Book of Gospels that is presented to a deacon at his ordination and that at an ordination to the episcopate is laid upon the head of the bishop-elect and held there.[65]

37.   Because of the dignity of the word of God, the books of readings used in the celebration are not to be replaced by other pastoral aids, for example, by leaflets printed for the preparation of the readings by the faithful or for their personal meditation.

CHAPTER III
OFFICES AND MINISTRIES IN THE CELEBRATION
OF THE LITURGY OF THE WORD WITHIN MASS

1. The Function of the President at the Liturgy of the Word

38.   The one presiding at the liturgy of the word communicates the spiritual nourishment it contains to those present, especially in the homily. Even if he too is a listener to the word of God proclaimed by others, the duty of proclaiming it has been entrusted above all to him. Personally or through others he sees to it that the word of God is properly proclaimed. He then as a rule reserves to himself the tasks of composing comments to help the people listen more attentively and of preaching a homily that fosters in them a richer understanding of the word of God.

39.   The first requirement for one who is to preside over the celebration is a thorough knowledge of the structure of the Order of Readings, so that he will know how to work a fruitful effect in the hearts of the faithful. Through study and prayer he must also develop a full understanding of the coordination and connection of the various texts in the liturgy of the word, so that the Order of Readings will become the source of a sound understanding of the mystery of Christ and his saving work.

40.   The one presiding is to make ready use of the various options provided in the Lectionary regarding readings, responses, responsorial psalms, and Gospel

---

64. See SC, 122.

65. See Roman Pontifical, *Ordination of Deacons, Priests and Bishops* (1968): of deacons, 24; of deacons and priests, 21; of a deacon, 24; of a bishop, 25; of bishops, 25.

acclamations;[66] but he is to do so in harmony[67] with all concerned and after listening to the opinions of the faithful in what concerns them.[68]

41.   The one presiding exercises his proper office and the ministry of the word of God also as he preaches the homily.[69] In this way he leads his brothers and sisters to an affective knowledge of Scripture. He opens their minds to thanksgiving for the wonderful works of God. He strengthens the faith of those present in the word that in the celebration becomes sacrament through the Holy Spirit. Finally, he prepares them for a fruitful reception of Communion and invites them to take upon themselves the demands of the Christian life.

42.   The president is responsible for preparing the faithful for the liturgy of the word on occasion by means of introductions before the readings.[70] These comments can help the assembled congregation toward a better hearing of the word of God, because they stir up an attitude of faith and good will. He may also carry out this responsibility through others, a deacon, for example, or a commentator.[71]

43.   As he directs the prayer of the faithful and through their introduction and conclusion connects them, if possible, with the day's readings and the homily, the president leads the faithful toward the liturgy of the Eucharist.[72]

2. The Role of the Faithful in the Liturgy of the Word

44.   Christ's word gathers the people of God as one and increases and sustains them. "This applies above all to the liturgy of the word in the celebration of Mass, where there are inseparably united the proclamation of the death of the Lord, the response of the people listening, and the very offering through which Christ has confirmed the New Covenant in his Blood, and in which the people share by their intentions and by reception of the sacrament."[73] For "not only when things are read 'that were written for our instruction' (Romans 15:4), but also when the Church prays or sings or acts, the faith of those taking part is nourished and their minds are raised to God, so that they may offer him rightful worship and receive his grace more abundantly."[74]

45.   In the liturgy of the word, the congregation of Christ's faithful even today receives from God the word of his covenant through the faith that comes by hearing, and must respond to that word in faith, so that they may become more and more truly the people of the New Covenant.

---

66. See LMIn, 78–91.
67. See GIRM, 318–320; 324–325.
68. See GIRM, 313.
69. See GIRM, 42; ID, 3.
70. See GIRM, 11.
71. See GIRM, 68.
72. See GIRM, 33, 47.
73. PO, 4.
74. SC, 33.

The people of God have a spiritual right to receive abundantly from the treasury of God's word. Its riches are presented to them through use of the Order of Readings, the homily, and pastoral efforts.

For their part, the faithful at the celebration of Mass are to listen to the word of God with an inward and outward reverence that will bring them continuous growth in the spiritual life and draw them more deeply into the mystery which is celebrated.[75]

46.   As a help toward celebrating the memorial of the Lord with eager devotion, the faithful should be keenly aware of the one presence of Christ in both the word of God—it is he himself "who speaks when the Sacred Scriptures are read in the Church"—and "above all under the Eucharistic species."[76]

47.   To be received and integrated into the life of Christ's faithful, the word of God demands a living faith.[77] Hearing the word of God unceasingly proclaimed arouses that faith.

The Sacred Scriptures, above all in their liturgical proclamation, are the source of life and strength. As the Apostle Paul attests, the Gospel is the saving power of God for everyone who believes.[78] Love of the Scriptures is therefore a force reinvigorating and renewing the entire people of God.[79] All the faithful without exception must therefore always be ready to listen gladly to God's word.[80] When this word is proclaimed in the Church and put into living practice, it enlightens the faithful through the working of the Holy Spirit and draws them into the entire mystery of the Lord as a reality to be lived.[81] The word of God reverently received moves the heart and its desires toward conversion and toward a life resplendent with both individual and community faith,[82] since God's word is the food of Christian life and the source of the prayer of the whole Church.[83]

48.   The intimate connection between the liturgy of the word and the liturgy of the Eucharist in the Mass should prompt the faithful to be present right from the beginning of the celebration,[84] to take part attentively, and to prepare themselves in so far as possible to hear the word, especially by learning beforehand more about Sacred Scripture. That same connection should also awaken in them a desire for a liturgical understanding of the texts read and a readiness to respond through singing.[85]

---

75. See GIRM, 9.
76. See SC, 7.
77. See SC, 9.
78. See Romans 1:16.
79. See DV, 21.
80. Ibid.
81. See John 14:15–26; 15:26—16:4, 5–15.
82. See AG, 6, 15; DV, 26.
83. See SC, 24; GCD, 25.
84. See SC, 56; ID, 1.
85. See SC, 24, 35.

When they hear the word of God and reflect deeply on it, Christ's faithful are enabled to respond to it actively with full faith, hope, and charity through prayer and self-giving, and not only during Mass but in their entire Christian life.

3. Ministries in the Liturgy of the Word

49.   Liturgical tradition assigns responsibility for the biblical readings in the celebration of Mass to ministers: to readers and the deacon. But when there is no deacon or no other priest present, the priest celebrant is to read the Gospel[86] and when there is no reader present, all the readings.[87]

50.   It pertains to the deacon in the liturgy of the word at Mass to proclaim the Gospel, sometimes to give the homily, as occasion suggests, and to propose to the people the intentions of the prayer of the faithful.[88]

51.   "The reader has his own proper function in the Eucharistic celebration and should exercise this even though ministers of a higher rank may be present."[89] The ministry of reader, conferred through a liturgical rite, must be held in respect. When there are instituted readers available, they are to carry out their office at least on Sundays and festive days, especially at the principal Mass of the day. These readers may also be given responsibility for assisting in the arrangement of the liturgy of the word, and, to the extent necessary, of seeing to the preparation of others of the faithful who may be appointed on a given occasion to read at Mass.[90]

52.   The liturgical assembly truly requires readers, even those not instituted. Proper measures must therefore be taken to ensure that there are certain suitable laypeople who have been trained to carry out this ministry.[91] Whenever there is more than one reading, it is better to assign the readings to different readers, if available.

53.   In Masses without a deacon, the function of announcing the intentions for the prayer of the faithful is to be assigned to the cantor, particularly when they are to be sung, to a reader, or to someone else.[92]

54.   During the celebration of Mass with a congregation a second priest, a deacon, and an instituted reader must wear the distinctive vestment of their office when they go up to the ambo to read the word of God. Those who carry out the ministry of reader just for the occasion or even regularly but without institution may go to the ambo in ordinary attire, but this should be in keeping with the customs of the different regions.

---

86. See GIRM, 34.
87. See GIRM, 96.
88. See GIRM, 47, 61, 132; ID 3.
89. GIRM, 66.
90. See MQ, no. V.
91. See ID, 2, 18; DMC, 22, 24, 27.
92. See GIRM, 47, 66, 151.

55. "It is necessary that those who exercise the ministry of reader, even if they have not received institution, be truly suited and carefully prepared, so that the faithful may develop a warm and living love for Sacred Scripture from listening to the sacred readings."[93]

Their preparation must above all be spiritual, but what may be called a technical preparation is also needed. The spiritual preparation presupposes at least a biblical and liturgical formation. The purpose of their biblical formation is to give readers the ability to understand the readings in context and to perceive by the light of faith the central point of the revealed message. The liturgical formation ought to equip the readers to have some grasp of the meaning and structure of the liturgy of the word and of the significance of its connection with the liturgy of the Eucharist. The technical preparation should make the readers more skilled in the art of reading publicly, either with the power of their own voice or with the help of sound equipment.

56. The psalmist, or cantor of the psalm, is responsible for singing, responsorially or directly, the chants between the readings—the psalm or other biblical canticle, the gradual and *Alleluia,* or other chant. The psalmist may, as occasion requires, intone the *Alleluia* and verse.[94]

For carrying out the function of psalmist it is advantageous to have in each ecclesial community laypeople with the ability to sing and read with correct diction. The points made about the formation of readers apply to cantors as well.

57. The commentator also fulfills a genuine liturgical ministry, which consists in presenting to the congregation of the faithful, from a suitable place, relevant explanations and comments that are clear, of marked sobriety, meticulously prepared, and as a rule written out and approved beforehand by the celebrant.[95]

SECOND PART
THE STRUCTURE OF THE ORDER OF READINGS FOR MASS

CHAPTER IV
THE GENERAL ARRANGEMENT OF READINGS FOR MASS

1. The Pastoral Purpose of the Order of Readings for Mass

58. On the basis of the intention of the Second Vatican Council, the Order of Readings provided by the Lectionary of the Roman Missal has been composed above all for a pastoral purpose. To achieve this aim, not only the principles underlying this new Order of Readings but also the lists of texts that it provides have been discussed and revised over and over again, with the cooperation of a great many experts in exegetical, liturgical, catechetical, and pastoral studies from all parts of the world. The Order of Readings is the fruit of this combined effort.

---

93. GIRM, 66.
94. See GIRM, 37a, 67.
95. See GIRM, 68.

The prolonged use of this Order of Readings to proclaim and explain Sacred Scripture in the Eucharistic celebration will, it is hoped, prove to be an effective step toward achieving the objective stated repeatedly by the Second Vatican Council.[96]

59.   The decision on revising the Lectionary for Mass was to draw up and edit a single, rich, and full Order of Readings that would be in complete accord with the intent and prescriptions of the Second Vatican Council.[97] At the same time, however, the Order was meant to be of a kind that would meet the requirements and usages of particular Churches and celebrating congregations. For this reason, those responsible for the revision took pains to safeguard the liturgical tradition of the Roman Rite, but valued highly the merits of all the systems of selecting, arranging, and using the biblical readings in other liturgical families and in certain particular Churches. The revisers made use of those elements that experience has confirmed, but with an effort to avoid certain shortcomings found in the preceding form of the tradition.

60.   The present Order of Readings for Mass, then, is an arrangement of biblical readings that provides the faithful with a knowledge of the whole of God's word, in a pattern suited to the purpose. Throughout the liturgical year, but above all during the seasons of Easter, Lent, and Advent, the choice and sequence of readings are aimed at giving Christ's faithful an ever-deepening perception of the faith they profess and of the history of salvation.[98] Accordingly, the Order of Readings corresponds to the requirements and interests of the Christian people.

61.   The celebration of the Liturgy is not in itself simply a form of catechesis, but it does contain an element of teaching. The Lectionary of the Roman Missal brings this out[99] and therefore deserves to be regarded as a pedagogical resource aiding catechesis.

This is so because the Order of Readings for Mass aptly presents from Sacred Scripture the principal deeds and words belonging to the history of salvation. As its many phases and events are recalled in the liturgy of the word, it will become clear to the faithful that the history of salvation is continued here and now in the representation of Christ's paschal mystery celebrated through the Eucharist.

62.   The pastoral advantage of having in the Roman Rite a single Order of Readings for the Lectionary is obvious on other grounds. All the faithful, particularly those who for various reasons do not always take part in Mass with the same assembly, will everywhere be able to hear the same readings on any given day or in any liturgical season and to meditate on the application of these readings to their own concrete circumstances. This is the case even in places that have

---

96. See Paul VI, apostolic constitution, *Missale Romanum.*

97. See SC, 35, 51.

98. See Paul VI, apostolic constitution, *Missale Romanum:* "This is meant to provide a fuller exposition of the continuing process of the mystery of salvation as shown in the words of divine revelation."

99. See SC, 9, 33; IOe, 7; CT, 23.

no priest and where a deacon or someone else deputed by the bishop conducts a celebration of the word of God.[100]

63.　Pastors may wish to respond specifically from the word of God to the concerns of their own congregations. Although they must be mindful that they are above all to be heralds of the entire mystery of Christ and of the Gospel, they may rightfully use the options provided in the Order of Readings for Mass. This applies particularly to the celebration of a ritual or votive Mass, a Mass in honor of the Saints, or one of the Masses for various needs and occasions. With due regard for the general norms, special faculties are granted concerning the readings in Masses celebrated for particular groups.[101]

2. The Principles of Composition of the Order of Readings for Mass

64.　To achieve the purpose of the Order of Readings for Mass, the parts have been selected and arranged in such a way as to take into account the sequence of the liturgical seasons and the hermeneutical principles whose understanding and definition have been facilitated by modern biblical research.

It was judged helpful to state here the principles guiding the composition of the Order of Readings for Mass.

A) THE CHOICE OF TEXTS

65.　The course of readings in the Proper of Seasons is arranged as follows. Sundays and festive days present the more important biblical passages. In this way the more significant parts of God's revealed word can be read to the assembled faithful within an appropriate period of time. Weekdays present a second series of texts from Sacred Scripture and in a sense these complement the message of salvation explained on festive days. But neither series in these main parts of the Order of Readings—the series for Sundays and festive days and that for weekdays—is dependent on the other. The Order of Readings for Sundays and festive days extends over three years; for weekdays, over two. Thus each runs its course independently of the other.

The sequence of readings in other parts of the Order of Readings is governed by its own rules. This applies to the series of readings for celebrations of the Saints, ritual Masses, Masses for various needs and occasions, votive Masses, or Masses for the dead.

B) THE ARRANGEMENT OF THE READINGS FOR SUNDAYS AND FESTIVE DAYS

66.　The following are features proper to the readings for Sundays and festive days:

1. Each Mass has three readings: the first from the Old Testament, the second from an Apostle (that is, either from a Letter or from the Book of Revelation, depending on the season), and the third from the Gospels. This

---

100. See SC, 35,4; IOe, 37–38.
101. See AP, 6; DMC, 41–47; MC, 12.

arrangement brings out the unity of the Old and New Testaments and of the history of salvation, in which Christ is the central figure, commemorated in his paschal mystery.

2. A more varied and richer reading of Sacred Scripture on Sundays and festive days results from the three-year cycle provided for these days, in that the same texts are read only every fourth year.[102]

3. The principles governing the Order of Reading for Sundays and festive days are called the principles of "harmony" and of "semicontinuous reading." One or the other applies according to the different seasons of the year and the distinctive character of the particular liturgical season.

67. The best instance of harmony between the Old and New Testament readings occurs when it is one that Scripture itself suggests. This is the case when the doctrine and events recounted in texts of the New Testament bear a more or less explicit relationship to the doctrine and events of the Old Testament. The present Order of Readings selects Old Testament texts mainly because of their correlation with New Testament texts read in the same Mass, and particularly with the Gospel text.

Harmony of another kind exists between texts of the readings for each Mass during Advent, Lent, and Easter, the seasons that have a distinctive importance or character.

In contrast, the Sundays in Ordinary Time do not have a distinctive character. Thus the text of both the apostolic and Gospel readings are arranged in order of semicontinuous reading, whereas the Old Testament reading is harmonized with the Gospel.

68. The decision was made not to extend to Sundays the arrangement suited to the liturgical seasons mentioned, that is, not to have an organic harmony of themes devised with a view to facilitating homiletic instruction. Such an arrangement would be in conflict with the genuine conception of liturgical celebration, which is always the celebration of the mystery of Christ and which by its own tradition makes use of the word of God not only at the prompting of logical or extrinsic concerns but spurred by the desire to proclaim the Gospel and to lead those who believe to the fullness of truth.

---

102. Each of the years is designated by the letter A, B or C. The following is the procedure to determine which year is A, B, or C. The letter C designates a year whose number is divisible into three equal parts, as though the cycle had taken its beginning from the first year of the Christian era. Thus the year 1 would have been Year A; year 2, Year B; year 3, Year C (as would years 6, 9 and 12). [Thus, year 1998 was Year C; 1999, Year A; 2000, Year B; and 2001, Year C again.] And so forth. Obviously, each cycle runs in accord with the plan of the liturgical year, that is, it begins with the first week of Advent, which falls in the preceding year of the civil calendar.

The years in each cycle [are] marked in a sense by the principal charadcteristic of the synoptic gospel (Matthew, Mark or Luke) used for the semicontinuous reading of Ordinary Time. Thus the first Year of the cycle is the Year for the reading of the Gospel of Matthew and is so named; the second and third Years are the Year of Mark and the Year of Luke.

69.   The weekday readings have been arranged in the following way.

1. Each Mass has two readings: the first is from the Old Testament or from an Apostle (that is, either from a Letter or from the Book of Revelation), and during the Easter season from the Acts of the Apostles; the second, from the Gospels.

2. The yearly cycle for Lent has its own principles of arrangement, which take into account the baptismal and penitential character of this season.

3. The cycle for the weekdays of Advent, the Christmas season, and the Easter season is also yearly and the readings thus remain the same each year.

4. For the thirty-four weeks of Ordinary Time, the weekday Gospel readings are arranged in a single cycle, repeated each year. But the first reading is arranged in a two-year cycle and is thus read every other year. Year I is used during odd-numbered years; Year II, during even-numbered years.

Like the Order for Sundays and festive days, then, the weekday Order of Readings is governed by similar application of the principles of harmony and of semicontinuous reading, especially in the case of seasons with their own distinctive character.

D) THE READINGS FOR CELEBRATIONS OF THE SAINTS

70.   Two series of readings are provided for celebrations of the Saints.

1. The Proper of Saints provides the first series, for solemnities, feasts, or memorials and particularly when there are proper texts for one or other such celebration. Sometimes in the Proper, however, there is a reference to the most appropriate among the texts in the Commons as the one to be given preference.

2. The Commons of Saints provide the second, more extensive group of readings. There are, first, appropriate texts for the different classes of Saints (martyrs, pastors, virgins, etc.), then numerous texts that deal with holiness in general. These may be freely chosen whenever the Commons are indicated as the source for the choice of readings.

71.   As to their sequence, all the texts in this part of the Order of Readings appear in the order in which they are to be read at Mass. Thus the Old Testament texts are first, then the texts from the Apostles, followed by the psalms and verses between the readings, and finally the texts from the Gospels. The rationale of this arrangement is that, unless otherwise noted, the celebrant may choose at will from such texts, in view of the pastoral needs of the congregation taking part in the celebration.

E) READINGS FOR RITUAL MASSES, MASSES FOR VARIOUS NEEDS AND OCCASIONS, VOTIVE MASSES, AND MASSES FOR THE DEAD

72.   For ritual Masses, Masses for various needs and occasions, votive Masses, and Masses for the dead, the texts for the readings are arranged as just described,

that is, numerous texts are grouped together in the order of their use, as in the Commons of Saints.

73. In addition to the guiding principles already given for the arrangement of readings in the individual parts of the Order of Readings, others of a more general nature follow.

1) The Reservation of Some Books to Particular Liturgical Seasons

74. In this Order of Readings, some biblical books are set aside for particular liturgical seasons on the basis both of the intrinsic importance of subject matter and of liturgical tradition. For example, the Western (Ambrosian and Hispanic) and Eastern tradition of reading the Acts of the Apostles during the Easter season is maintained. This usage results in a clear presentation of how the Church's entire life derives its beginning from the paschal mystery. The tradition of both West and East is also retained, namely the reading of the Gospel of John in the latter weeks of Lent and in the Easter season.

Tradition assigns the reading of Isaiah, especially the first part, to Advent. Some texts of this book, however, are read during the Christmas season, to which the First Letter of John is also assigned.

2) The Length of the Texts

75. A *middle way* is followed in regard to the length of texts. A distinction has been made between narratives, which require reading a fairly long passage but which usually hold the attention of the faithful, and texts that should not be lengthy because of the profundity of their doctrine.

In the case of certain rather lengthy texts, longer and shorter versions are provided to suit different situations. The editing of the shorter version has been carried out with great caution.

3) Difficult Texts

76. In readings for Sundays and solemnities, texts that present real difficulties are avoided for pastoral reasons. The difficulties may be objective, in that the texts themselves raise profound literary, critical, or exegetical problems; or the difficulties may lie, at least to a certain extent, in the ability of the faithful to understand the texts. But there could be no justification for concealing from the faithful the spiritual riches of certain texts on the grounds of difficulty if the problem arises from the inadequacy either of the religious education that every Christian should have or of the biblical formation that every pastor of souls should have. Often a difficult reading is clarified by its correlation with another in the same Mass.

4) The Omission of Certain Verses

77. The omission of verses in readings from Scripture has at times been the tradition of many liturgies, including the Roman liturgy. Admittedly such omissions may not be made lightly, for fear of distorting the meaning of the text or

the intent and style of Scripture. Yet on pastoral grounds it was decided to continue the traditional practice in the present Order of Readings, but at the same time to ensure that the essential meaning of the text remained intact. One reason for the decision is that otherwise some texts would have been unduly long. It would also have been necessary to omit completely certain readings of high spiritual value for the faithful because those readings include some verse that is pastorally less useful or that involves truly difficult questions.

3. Principles to be Followed in the Use of the Order of Readings

A) THE FREEDOM OF CHOICE REGARDING SOME TEXTS

78.   The Order of Readings sometimes leaves it to the celebrant to choose between alternative texts or to choose one from the several listed together for the same reading. The option seldom exists on Sundays, solemnities, or feasts, in order not to obscure the character proper to the particular liturgical season or needlessly interrupt the semicontinuous reading of some biblical book. On the other hand, the option is given readily in celebrations of the Saints, in ritual Masses, Masses for various needs and occasions, votive Masses, and Masses for the dead.

These options, together with those indicated in the General Instruction of the Roman Missal and the *Ordo cantus Missae*,[103] have a pastoral purpose. In arranging the liturgy of the word, then, the priest should "consider the general spiritual good of the congregation rather than his personal outlook. He should be mindful that the choice of texts is to be made in harmony with the ministers and others who have any role in the celebration and should listen to the opinions of the faithful in what concerns them more directly."[104]

1) The Two Readings before the Gospel

79.   In Masses to which three readings are assigned, all three are to be used. If, however, for pastoral reasons the Conference of Bishops has given permission for two readings only to be used,[105] the choice between the two first readings is to be made in such a way as to safeguard the Church's intent to instruct the faithful more completely in the mystery of salvation. Thus, unless the contrary is indicated in the text of the Lectionary, the reading to be chosen as the first reading is the one that is more closely in harmony with the Gospel, or, in accord with the intent just mentioned, the one that is more helpful toward a coherent catechesis over an extended period, or that preserves the semicontinuous reading of some biblical book.[106]

---

103. See GIRM, 36–40.

104. GIRM, 313.

105. See GIRM, 318; ID, 1.

106. For example: in Lent the continuity of the Old Testament readings corresponds to the unfolding of the history of salvation; the Sundays in Ordinary Time provide the semicontinuous reading of one of the letters of the apostles. In these cases it is right that the pastor of souls choose one or other of the readings in a systematic way over a series of Sundays, so that he may establish a coherent plan for catechesis. It is not right to read indiscriminately on one day from the Old Testament, on another from the letter of an apostle, without any orderly plan for the texts that follow.

80.   A pastoral criterion must also guide the choice between the longer and shorter forms of the same text. The main consideration must be the capacity of the hearers to listen profitably either to the longer or to the shorter reading; or to listen to a more complete text that will be explained through the homily.

3) When Two Texts Are Provided

81.   When a choice is allowed between alternative texts, whether they are fixed or optional, the first consideration must be the best interest of those taking part. It may be a matter of using the easier texts or the one more relevant to the assembled congregation or, as pastoral advantage may suggest, of repeating or replacing a text that is assigned as proper to one celebration and optional to another.

The issue may arise when it is feared that some text will create difficulties for a particular congregation or when the same text would have to be repeated within a few days, as on a Sunday and on a day during the week following.

4) The Weekday Readings

82.   The arrangement of weekday readings provides texts for every day of the week throughout the year. In most cases, therefore, these readings are to be used on their assigned days, unless a solemnity, a feast, or else a memorial with proper readings occurs.[107]

In using the Order of Readings for weekdays attention must be paid to whether one reading or another from the same biblical book will have to be omitted because of some celebration occurring during the week. With the arrangement of readings for the entire week in mind, the priest in that case arranges to omit the less significant passages or combines in the most appropriate manner them with other readings, if they contribute to an integral view of a particular theme.

5) The Celebrations of the Saints

83.   When they exist, proper readings are given for celebrations of the Saints, that is, biblical passages about the Saint or the mystery that the Mass is celebrating. Even in the case of a memorial these readings must take the place of the weekday readings for the same day. This Order of Readings makes explicit note of every case of proper readings on a memorial.

In some cases there are accommodated readings, those, namely, that bring out some particular aspect of a Saint's spiritual life or work. Use of such readings does not seem binding, except for compelling pastoral reasons. For the most part references are given to readings in the Commons in order to facilitate choice. But these are merely suggestions: in place of an accommodated reading or the particular reading proposed from a Common, any other reading from the Commons referred to may be selected.

The first concern of a priest celebrating with a congregation is the spiritual benefit of the faithful and he will be careful not to impose his personal preference on them. Above all he will make sure not to omit too often or without sufficient

---

107. See GIRM, 319.

cause the readings assigned for each day in the weekday Lectionary: the Church's desire is that a more lavish table of the word of God be spread before the faithful.[108]

There are also common readings, that is, those placed in the Commons either for some determined class of Saints (martyrs, virgins, pastors) or for the Saints in general. Because in these cases several texts are listed for the same reading, it will be up to the priest to choose the one best suited to those listening.

In all celebrations of Saints the readings may be taken not only from the Commons to which the references are given in each case, but also from the Common of Men and Women Saints, whenever there is special reason for doing so.

84.   For celebrations of the Saints the following should be observed:

1. On solemnities and feasts the readings must be those that are given in the Proper or in the Commons. For solemnities and feasts of the General Roman Calendar proper readings are always assigned.

2. On solemnities inscribed in particular calendars, three readings are to be assigned, unless the Conference of Bishops has decreed that there are to be only two readings.[109] The first reading is from the Old Testament (but during the Easter season, from the Acts of the Apostles or the Book of Revelation); the second, from an Apostle; the third, from the Gospels.

3. On feasts and memorials, which have only two readings, the first reading can be chosen from either the Old Testament or from an Apostle; the second is from the Gospels. Following the Church's traditional practice, however, the first reading during the Easter season is to be taken from an Apostle, the second, as far as possible, from the Gospel of John.

6) Other Parts of the Order of Readings

85.   In the Order of Readings for ritual Masses the references given are to the texts already published for the individual rites. This obviously does not include the texts belonging to celebrations that must not be integrated with Mass.[110]

86.   The Order of Readings for Masses for various needs and occasions, votive Masses, and Masses for the dead provides many texts that can be of assistance in adapting such celebrations to the situation, circumstances, and concerns of the particular groups taking part.[111]

87.   In ritual Masses, Masses for various needs and occasions, votive Masses, and Masses for the dead, since many texts are given for the same reading, the choice of readings follows the criteria already indicated for the choice of readings from the Common of Saints.

---

108. See GIRM, 316c; SC, 51.
109. See GIRM, 318.
110. See *Rite of Penance* (1974), introduction, no. 13.
111. See GIRM, 320.

88.   On a day when some ritual Mass is not permitted and when the norms in the individual rite allow the choice of one reading from those provided for ritual Masses, the general spiritual welfare of the participants must be considered.[112]

B) THE RESPONSORIAL PSALM AND THE ACCLAMATION
BEFORE THE GOSPEL READING

89.   Among the chants between the readings, the psalm which follows the first reading is of great importance. As a rule the psalm to be used is the one assigned to the reading. But in the case of readings for the Common of Saints, ritual Masses, Masses for various needs and occasions, votive Masses, and Masses for the dead the choice is left up to the priest celebrating. He will base his choice on the principle of the pastoral benefit of those present.

But to make it easier for the people to join in the response to the psalm, the Order of Readings lists certain other texts of psalms and responses that have been chosen according to the various seasons or classes of Saints. Whenever the psalm is sung, these texts may replace the text corresponding to the reading.[113]

90.   The chant between the second reading and the Gospel is either specified in each Mass and correlated with the Gospel or else it is left as a choice to be made from those in the series given for a liturgical season or one of the Commons.

91.   During Lent one of the acclamations from those given in the Order of Readings may be used, depending on the occasion.[114] This acclamation precedes and follows the verse before the Gospel.

CHAPTER V
DESCRIPTION OF THE ORDER OF READINGS

92.   It seems useful to provide here a brief description of the Order of Readings, at least for the principal celebrations and the different seasons of the liturgical year. With these in mind, readings were selected on the basis of the rules already stated. This description is meant to assist pastors of souls to understand the structure of the Order of Readings, so that their use of it will become more perceptive and the Order of Readings a source of good for Christ's faithful.

I. Advent

A) THE SUNDAYS

93.   Each Gospel reading has a distinctive theme: the Lord's coming at the end of time (First Sunday of Advent), John the Baptist (Second and Third Sunday), and the events that prepared immediately for the Lord's birth (Fourth Sunday).

The Old Testament readings are prophecies about the Messiah and the Messianic age, especially from the Book of Isaiah.

---

112. See GIRM, 313.
113. See Lectionary for Mass, nos. 173–174.
114. See Lectionary for Mass, no. 223.

The readings from an Apostle contain exhortations and proclamations, in keeping with the different themes of Advent.

94.   There are two series of readings: one to be used from the beginning of Advent until 16 December; the other from 17 to 24 December.

In the first part of Advent there are readings from the Book of Isaiah, distributed in accord with the sequence of the book itself and including the more important texts that are also read on the Sundays. For the choice of the weekday Gospel the first reading has been taken into consideration.

On Thursday of the second week the readings from the Gospel concerning John the Baptist begin. The first reading is either a continuation of Isaiah or a text chosen in view of the Gospel.

In the last week before Christmas the events that immediately prepared for the Lord's birth are presented from the Gospel of Matthew (chapter 1) and Luke (chapter 1). The texts in the first reading, chosen in view of the Gospel reading, are from different Old Testament books and include important Messianic prophecies.

2. The Christmas Season

A) THE SOLEMNITIES, FEASTS, AND SUNDAYS

95.   For the vigil and the three Masses of Christmas both the prophetic readings and the others have been chosen from the Roman tradition.

The Gospel on the Sunday within the Octave of Christmas, Feast of the Holy Family, is about Jesus' childhood and the other readings are about the virtues of family life.

On the Octave Day of Christmas, Solemnity of the Blessed Virgin Mary, the Mother of God, the readings are about the Virgin Mother of God and the giving of the holy Name of Jesus.

On the second Sunday after Christmas, the readings are about the mystery of the Incarnation.

On the Epiphany of the Lord, the Old Testament reading and the Gospel continue the Roman tradition; the text for the reading from the Letters of the Apostles is about the calling of the nations to salvation.

On the Feast of the Baptism of the Lord, the texts chosen are about this mystery.

B) THE WEEKDAYS

96.   From 29 December on, there is a continuous reading of the whole of the First Letter of John, which actually begins earlier, on 27 December, the Feast of St. John the Evangelist, and on 28 December, the Feast of the Holy Innocents.

The Gospels relate manifestations of the Lord: events of Jesus' childhood from the Gospel of Luke (29–30 December); passages from the first chapter of the Gospel of John (31 December–5 January); other manifestations of the Lord from the four Gospels (7–12 January).

3. *Lent*

97.　The Gospel readings are arranged as follows:

The first and second Sundays maintain the accounts of the Temptation and Transfiguration of the Lord, with readings, however, from all three Synoptics.

On the next three Sundays, the Gospels about the Samaritan woman, the man born blind, and the raising of Lazarus have been restored in Year A. Because these Gospels are of major importance in regard to Christian initiation, they may also be read in Year B and Year C, especially in places where there are catechumens.

Other texts, however, are provided for Year B and Year C: for Year B, a text from John about Christ's coming glorification through his Cross and Resurrection and for Year C, a text from Luke about conversion.

On Palm Sunday of the Lord's Passion the texts for the procession are selections from the Synoptic Gospels concerning the Lord's solemn entry into Jerusalem. For the Mass the reading is the account of the Lord's Passion.

The Old Testament readings are about the history of salvation, which is one of the themes proper to the catechesis of Lent. The series of texts for each Year presents the main elements of salvation history from its beginning until the promise of the New Covenant.

The readings from the Letters of the Apostles have been selected to fit the Gospel and the Old Testament readings and, to the extent possible, to provide a connection between them.

B) THE WEEKDAYS

98.　The readings from the Gospels and the Old Testament were selected because they are related to each other. They treat various themes of the Lenten catechesis that are suited to the spiritual significance of this season. Beginning with Monday of the Fourth week of Lent, there is a semicontinuous reading of the Gospel of John, made up of texts that correspond more closely to the themes proper to Lent.

Because the readings about the Samaritan woman, the man born blind, and the raising of Lazarus are now assigned to Sundays, but only for Year A (in Year B and Year C they are optional), provision has been made for their use on weekdays. Thus at the beginning of the Third, Fourth, and Fifth Weeks of Lent optional Masses with these texts for the Gospel have been inserted and may be used in place of the readings of the day on any weekday of the respective week.

In the first days of Holy Week the readings are about the mystery of Christ's passion. For the Chrism Mass the readings bring out both Christ's Messianic mission and its continuation in the Church by means of the sacraments.

4. The Sacred Triduum and the Easter Season

A) THE SACRED EASTER TRIDUUM

99.   On Holy Thursday at the evening Mass the remembrance of the meal preceding the Exodus casts its own special light because of the Christ's example in washing the feet of his disciples and Paul's account of the institution of the Christian Passover in the Eucharist.

On Good Friday the liturgical service has as its center John's narrative of the Passion of he who was proclaimed in Isaiah as the Servant of the Lord and who became the one High Priest by offering himself to the Father.

At the Vigil on the holy night of Easter there are seven Old Testament readings which recall the wonderful works of God in the history of salvation. There are two New Testament readings, the announcement of the Resurrection according to one of the Synoptic Gospels and a reading from St. Paul on Christian baptism as the sacrament of Christ's Resurrection.

The Gospel reading for the Mass on Easter day is from John on the finding of the empty tomb. There is also, however, the option to use the Gospel texts from the Easter Vigil or, when there is an evening Mass on Easter Sunday, to use the account in Luke of the Lord's appearance to the disciples on the road to Emmaus. The first reading is from the Acts of the Apostles, which throughout the Easter season replaces the Old Testament reading. The reading from the Apostle Paul concerns the living out of the paschal mystery in the Church.

B) THE SUNDAYS

100. The Gospel readings for the first three Sundays recount the appearances of the risen Christ. The readings about the Good Shepherd are assigned to the Fourth Sunday. On the Fifth, Sixth, and Seventh Sundays, there are excerpts from the Lord's discourse and prayer at the end of the Last Supper.

The first reading is from the Acts of the Apostles, in a three-year cycle of parallel and progressive selections: material is presented on the life of the early Church, its witness, and its growth.

For the reading from the Apostles, the First Letter of Peter is in Year A, the First Letter of John in Year B, the Book of Revelation in Year C. These are the texts that seem to fit in especially well with the spirit of joyous faith and sure hope proper to this season.

C) THE WEEKDAYS

101. As on the Sundays, the first reading is a semicontinuous reading from the Acts of the Apostles. The Gospel readings during the Easter octave are accounts of the Lord's appearances. After that there is a semicontinuous reading of the Gospel of John, but with texts that have a paschal character, in order to complete the reading from John during Lent. This paschal reading is made up in large part of the Lord's discourse and prayer at the end of the Last Supper.

102. For the first reading the Solemnity of the Ascension retains the account of the Ascension according to the Acts of the Apostles. This text is complemented by the second reading from the Apostle on Christ in exaltation at the right hand of the Father. For the Gospel reading, each of the three Years has its own text in accord with the differences in the Synoptic Gospels.

In the evening Mass celebrated on the Vigil of Pentecost four Old Testament texts are provided; any one of them may be used, in order to bring out the many aspects of Pentecost. The reading from the Apostles shows the actual working of the Holy Spirit in the Church. The Gospel reading recalls the promise of the Spirit made by Christ before his own glorification.

For the Mass on Pentecost day itself, in accord with received usage, the account in the Acts of the Apostles of the great occurrence on Pentecost day is taken as the first reading. The texts from the Apostle Paul bring out the effect of the action of the Spirit in the life of the Church. The Gospel reading is a remembrance of Jesus bestowing his Spirit on the disciples on the evening of Easter day; other optional texts describe the action of the Spirit on the disciples and on the Church.

5. Ordinary Time

A) THE ARRANGEMENT AND CHOICE OF TEXTS

103. Ordinary Time begins on the Monday after the Sunday following 6 January; it lasts until the Tuesday before Lent inclusive. It begins again on the Monday after Pentecost Sunday and finishes before evening prayer I of the First Sunday of Advent.

The Order of Readings provides readings for thirty-four Sundays and the weeks following them. In some years, however, there are only thirty-three weeks of Ordinary Time. Further, some Sundays either belong to another season (the Sunday on which the Feast of the Baptism of the Lord falls and Pentecost Sunday) or else are impeded by a solemnity that coincides with that Sunday (e.g. The Most Holy Trinity or Christ the King).

104. For the correct arrangement in the use of the readings for Ordinary Time, the following are to be respected.

1. The Sunday on which the Feast of the Baptism of the Lord falls replaces the First Sunday in Ordinary Time. Therefore the readings of the First Week in Ordinary Time begin on the Monday after the Sunday following 6 January. When the Feast of the Baptism of the Lord is celebrated on Monday because the Epiphany has been celebrated on the Sunday, the readings of the First Week begin on Tuesday.

2. The Sunday following the Feast of the Baptism of the Lord is the Second Sunday of Ordinary Time. The remaining Sundays are numbered consecutively up to the Sunday preceding the beginning of Lent. The readings for

the week in which Ash Wednesday falls are interrupted after the Tuesday readings.

3. For the resumption of the readings of Ordinary Time after Pentecost Sunday:

—when there are thirty-four Sundays in Ordinary Time, the week to be used is the one that immediately follows the last week used before Lent;[115]

—when there are thirty-three Sundays in Ordinary Time, the first week that would have been used after Pentecost is omitted, in order to reserve for the end of the year the eschatological texts that are assigned to the last two weeks.[116]

B) THE SUNDAY READINGS

1) The Gospel Readings

105. On the Second Sunday in Ordinary Time the Gospel continues to center on the manifestation of the Lord, which is celebrated on the Solemnity of the Epiphany, through the traditional passage about the wedding feast at Cana and two other passages from the Gospel of John.

Beginning with the Third Sunday, there is a semicontinuous reading of the Synoptic Gospels. This reading is arranged in such a way that as the Lord's life and preaching unfold the doctrine proper to each of these Gospels is presented.

This distribution also provides a certain coordination between the meaning of each Gospel and the progress of the liturgical year. Thus after Epiphany the readings are on the beginning of the Lord's preaching and they fit in well with Christ's baptism and the first events in which he manifests himself. The liturgical year leads quite naturally to a conclusion in the eschatological theme proper to the last Sundays, since the chapters of the Synoptics that precede the account of the Passion treat this eschatological theme rather extensively.

After the Sixteenth Sunday in Year B, five readings are incorporated from John chapter 6 (the discourse on the bread of life). This is the natural place for these readings because the multiplication of the loaves from the Gospel of John takes the place of the same account in Mark. In the semicontinuous reading of Luke for Year C, the introduction of this Gospel has been prefixed to the first text (that is, on the Third Sunday). This passage expresses the author's intention very beautifully and there seemed to be no better place for it.

2) The Old Testament Readings

106. These readings have been chosen to correspond to the Gospel passages in order to avoid an excessive diversity between the readings of different Masses and above all to bring out the unity between the Old and the New Testament.

---

115. So, for example, when there are six weeks before Lent, the seventh week begins on the Monday after Pentecost. The solemnity of the Most Holy Trinity replaces the Sunday of Ordinary Time.

116. When there are, for example, five weeks before Lent, the Monday after Pentecost begins with the Seventh Week of Ordinary Time and the Sixth Week is omitted.

The connection between the readings of the same Mass is shown by a precise choice of the readings prefixed to the individual readings.

To the degree possible, the readings were chosen in such a way that they would be short and easy to grasp. But care has been taken to ensure that many Old Testament texts of major significance would be read on Sundays. Such readings are distributed not according to a logical order but on the basis of what the Gospel reading requires. Still, the treasury of the word of God will be opened up in such a way that nearly all the principal pages of the Old Testament will become familiar to those taking part in the Mass on Sundays.

3) The Readings from the Apostles

107. There is a semicontinuous reading of the Letters of Paul and James (the Letters of Peter and John being read during the Easter and Christmas seasons).

Because it is quite long and deals with such diverse issues, the First Letter to the Corinthians has been spread over the three years of the cycle at the beginning of Ordinary Time. It also was thought best to divide the Letter to the Hebrews into two parts; the first part is read in Year B and the second in Year C.

Only readings that are short and readily grasped by the people have been chosen.

Table II at the end of this Introduction[117] indicates the distribution of Letters of the Apostles over the three-year cycle of the Sundays of Ordinary Time.

C) THE READINGS FOR SOLEMNITIES OF THE LORD DURING ORDINARY TIME

108. On the solemnities of Holy Trinity, Corpus Christi, and the Sacred Heart, the texts chosen correspond to the principal themes of these celebrations.

The readings of the Thirty-Fourth and last Sunday in Ordinary Time celebrate Christ the universal King. He was prefigured by David and proclaimed as king amid the humiliations of his Passion and Cross; he reigns in the Church and will come again at the end of time.

D) THE WEEKDAY READINGS

109. The *Gospels* are so arranged that Mark is read first (First to Ninth Week), then Matthew (Tenth to Twenty-First Week), then Luke (Twenty-Second to Thirty-Fourth Week). Mark chapters 1–12 are read in their entirety, with the exception only of the two passages of Mark chapter 6 that are read on weekdays in other seasons. From Matthew and Luke the readings comprise all the material not contained in Mark. All the passages that either are distinctively presented in each Gospel or are needed for a proper understanding of its progression are read two or three times. Jesus' eschatological discourse as contained in its entirety in Luke is read at the end of the liturgical year.

---

117. See LMIn, Table II.

110. The *first reading* is taken in periods of several weeks at a time first from one then from the other Testament; the number of weeks depends on the length of the biblical books read.

Rather large sections are read from the New Testament books in order to give the substance, as it were, of each of the Letters.

From the Old Testament there is room only for select passages that, as far as possible, bring out the character of the individual books. The historical texts have been chosen in such a way as to provide an overall view of the history of salvation before the Incarnation of the Lord. But lengthy narratives could hardly be presented; sometimes verses have been selected that make for a reading of moderate length. In addition, the religious significance of the historical events is sometimes brought out by means of certain texts from the wisdom books that are placed as prologues or conclusions to a series of historical readings.

Nearly all the Old Testament books have found a place in the Order of Readings for weekdays in the Proper of Seasons. The only omissions are the shortest of the prophetic books (Obadiah and Zephaniah) and a poetic book (the Song of Songs). Of those narratives of edification requiring a lengthy reading if they are to be understood, Tobit and Ruth are included, but the others (Esther and Judith) are omitted. Texts from these latter two books are assigned, however, to Sundays and weekdays at other times of the year.

Table III at the end of this Introduction[118] lists the way the books of the Old and the New Testament are distributed over the weekdays in Ordinary Time in the course of two years.

At the end of the liturgical year the readings are from the books that correspond to the eschatological character of this period, Daniel and the Book of Revelation.

CHAPTER VI
ADAPTATIONS, TRANSLATIONS AND FORMAT
OF THE ORDER OF READINGS

1. Adaptations and Translations

111. In the liturgical assembly the word of God must always be read either from the Latin texts prepared by the Holy See or from vernacular translations approved for liturgical use by the Conferences of Bishops, according to existing norms.[119]

112. The Lectionary for Mass must be translated integrally in all its parts, including the Introduction. If the Conference of Bishops has judged it necessary and useful to add certain adaptations, these are to be incorporated after their confirmation by the Holy See.[120]

---

118. See LMIn, Table III.
119. See Consilium, instruction *De Popularibus interpretationibus conficiendis*, 25 Jan 1969: Notitiae 5 (1969) 3–12; CDW, *Epistola ad Praesides Conferentiarum Episcoporum de linguis vulgaribus in S. Liturgiam inducendis:* Notitiae 12 (1976) 300–302.
120. See LI, 11; GIRM, 325.

113. The size of the Lectionary will necessitate editions in more than one volume; no particular division of the volumes is prescribed. But each volume is to contain the explanatory texts on the structure and purpose of the section it contains.

The ancient custom is recommended of having separate books, one for the Gospels and the other for the other readings for the Old and New Testament.

It may also be useful to publish separately a Sunday lectionary (which could also contain selected excerpts from the sanctoral cycle), and a weekday lectionary. A practical basis for dividing the Sunday lectionary is the three-year cycle, so that all the readings for each year are presented in sequence.

But there is freedom to adopt other arrangements that may be devised and seem to have pastoral advantages.

114. The texts for the chants are always to be adjoined to the readings, but separate books containing the chants alone are permitted. It is recommended that the texts be printed with divisions into stanzas.

115. Whenever a text consists of different parts, the typography must make this structure of the text clear. It is likewise recommended that even non-poetic texts be printed with division into sense lines to assist the proclamation of the readings.

116. Where there are longer and shorter forms of a text, they are to be printed separately, so that each can be read with ease. But if such a separation does not seem feasible, a way is to be found to ensure that each text can be proclaimed without mistakes.

117. In vernacular editions the texts are not to be printed without headings prefixed. If it seems advisable, an introductory note on the general meaning of the passage may be added to the heading. This note is to carry some distinctive symbol or is to be set in different type to show clearly that it is an optional text.[121]

118. It would be useful for every volume to have an index of the passages of the Bible, modeled on the biblical index of the present volume.[122] This will provide ready access to texts of the lectionaries for Mass that may be needed or helpful for specific occasions.

---

121. See GIRM, 11, 29, 68a, 139.
122. See Lectionary for Mass, index of readings.

2. The Format of Individual Readings

For each reading the present volume carries the textual reference, the headings, and the *incipit*.

A) THE BIBLICAL REFERENCES

119. The text reference (that is, to chapter and verses) is always given according to the Neo-Vulgate edition for the psalms.[123] But a second reference according to the original text (Hebrew, Aramaic, or Greek) has been added wherever there is a discrepancy. Depending on the decrees of the competent Authorities for the individual languages, vernacular versions may retain the enumeration corresponding to the version of the Bible approved for liturgical use by the same Authorities. Exact references to chapter and verses, however, must always appear and may be given in the text or in the margin.

120. These references provide liturgical books with the basis of the "announcement" of the text that must be read in the celebration, but which is not printed in this volume. This "announcement" of the text will observe the following norms, but they may be altered by decree of the competent authorities on the basis of what is customary and useful for different places and languages.

121. The formula to be used is always: "A *reading* from the Book of . . . ," "A *reading* from the Letter of . . . ," or "A *reading* from the holy Gospel according to . . . ," and not: "The *beginning* of . . . ," (unless this seems advisable in particular instances) nor: "The *continuation* of . . . ."

122. The traditionally accepted titles for books are to be retained with the following exceptions.

1. Where there are two books with the same name, the title is to be: The first Book, The second Book (for example, of Kings, of Maccabees) or The first Letter, The second Letter.

2. The title more common in current usage is to be accepted for the following books:

—I and II Samuel instead of I and II Kings;

—I and II Kings instead of III and IV Kings;

—I and II Chronicles instead of I and II Paralipomenon;

—The Books of Ezra and Nehemiah instead of I and II Ezra.

3. The distinguishing titles for the wisdom books are: The Book of Job, Book of Proverbs, Book of Ecclesiastes, the Song of Songs, the Book of Wisdom, and the Book of Sirach.

4. For all the books that are included among the prophets in the Neo-Vulgate, the formula is to be: "A reading from the Book of the prophet Isaiah, or of

---

123. The references for the psalms follow the order of the *Liber Psalmorum*, Pontifical Commission for the Neo-Vulgate.

the prophet Jeremiah or of the prophet Baruch" and: "A reading from the Book of the prophet Ezekiel, of the prophet Daniel, of the prophet Hosea, of the prophet Malachi," even in the case of books not regarded by some as being in actual fact prophetic.

5. The title is to be book of Lamentations and letter to the Hebrews, with no mention of Jeremiah or Paul.

b) THE HEADING

123. There is a *heading* prefixed to each text, chosen carefully (usually from the words of the text itself) in order to point out the main theme of the reading and, when necessary, to make the connection between the readings of the same Mass clear.

c) THE "INCIPIT"

124. In this Order of Readings the first element of the *incipit* is the customary introductory phrase: "At that time," "In those days," "Brothers and Sisters," "Beloved," "Dearly Beloved," "Dearest Brothers and Sisters," or "Thus says the Lord", "Thus says the Lord God." These words are not given when the text itself provides sufficient indication of the time or the persons involved or where such phrases would not fit in with the very nature of the text. For the individual languages, such phrases may be changed or omitted by decree of the competent Authorities.

After the first words of the *incipit* the Order of Readings gives the proper beginning of the reading, with some words deleted or supplied for intelligibility, inasmuch as the text is separated from its context. When the text for a reading is made up of non-consecutive verses and this has required changes in wording, these are appropriately indicated.

d) THE FINAL ACCLAMATION

125. In order to facilitate the congregation's acclamation, the words for the reader *The word of the Lord,* or similar words suited to local custom, are to be printed at the end of the reading for use by the reader.

TABLES

TABLE I

Principal Celebrations of the Liturgical Year

YEAR	SUNDAY CYCLE	WEEKDAY CYCLE	ASH WEDNESDAY	EASTER	ASCENSION THURSDAY	PENTECOST
2013	C	I	13 Feb.	31 March	9 May	19 May
2014	A	II	5 March	20 April	29 May	8 June
2015	B	I	18 Feb.	5 April	14 May	24 May
2016	C	II	10 Feb.	27 March	5 May	15 May
2017	A	I	1 March	16 April	25 May	4 June
2018	B	II	14 Feb.	1 April	10 May	20 May
2019	C	I	6 March	21 April	30 May	9 June
2020	A	II	26 Feb.	12 April	21 May	31 May
2021	B	I	17 Feb.	4 April	13 May	23 May
2022	C	II	2 March	17 April	26 May	5 June
2023	A	I	22 Feb.	9 April	18 May	28 May
2024	B	II	14 Feb.	31 March	9 May	19 May
2025	C	I	5 March	20 April	29 May	8 June
2026	A	II	18 Feb.	5 April	14 May	24 May
2027	B	I	10 Feb.	28 March	6 May	16 May

| WEEKS IN ORDINARY TIME | | | | |
| BEFORE LENT | | AFTER EASTER SEASON | | |
ENDING	IN WEEK NO.	BEGINNING	IN WEEK NO.	1ST SUNDAY OF ADVENT
12 Feb.	5	20 May	7	1 Dec.
4 March	8	9 June	9	30 Nov.
17 Feb.	6	25 May	7	29 Nov.
9 Feb.	5	16 May	6	27 Nov.
28 Feb.	8	5 June	9	3 Dec.
13 Feb.	5	21 May	7	2 Dec.
5 March	8	10 June	10	1 Dec.
25 Feb.	7	1 June	9	29 Nov.
16 Feb.	6	24 May	7	28 Nov.
1 March	8	6 June	9	27 Nov.
21 Feb.	6	29 May	8	3 Dec.
13 Feb.	5	20 May	7	1 Dec.
4 March	8	9 June	9	30 Nov.
17 Feb.	6	25 May	7	29 Nov.
9 Feb.	5	17 May	6	28 Nov.

TABLE II

Order of the Second Reading on the Sundays of Ordinary Time

SUNDAY	YEAR A	YEAR B	YEAR C
2	1 Corinthians 1–4	1 Corinthians 6–11	1 Corinthians 12–15
3	"	"	"
4	"	"	"
5	"	"	"
6	"	"	"
7	"	2 Corinthians	"
8	"	"	"
9	Romans	"	Galatians
10	"	"	"
11	"	"	"
12	"	"	"
13	"	"	"
14	"	"	"
15	"	Ephesians	Colossians
16	"	"	"
17	"	"	"
18	"	"	"
19	"	"	Hebrews 11–12
20	"	"	"
21	"	"	"
22	"	James	"
23	"	"	Philemon
24	"	"	1 Timothy
25	Philippians	"	"
26	"	"	"
27	"	Hebrews 2–10	2 Timothy
28	"	"	"
29	1 Thessalonians	"	"
30	"	"	"
31	"	"	2 Thessalonians
32	"	"	"
33	"	"	"

TABLE III

Order of the First Reading on the Weekdays of Ordinary Time

WEEK	YEAR I	YEAR II
1	Hebrews	1 Samuel
2	"	"
3	"	2 Samuel
4	"	2 Samuel; 1 Kings 1–16
5	Genesis 1–11	1 Kings 1–16
6	"	James
7	Sirach (Ecclesiasticus)	"
8	"	1 Peter; Jude
9	Tobit	2 Peter; 2 Timothy
10	2 Corinthians	1 Kings 17–22
11	"	1 Kings 17–22; 2 Kings
12	Genesis 12–50	2 Kings; Lamentations
13	"	Amos
14	"	Hosea; Isaiah
15	Exodus	Isaiah; Micah
16	"	Micah; Jeremiah
17	Exodus; Leviticus	Jeremiah
18	Numbers; Deuteronomy	Jeremiah; Nahum; Habakkuk
19	Deuteronomy; Joshua	Ezekiel
20	Judges; Ruth	"
21	1 Thessalonians	2 Thessalonians; 1 Corinthians
22	1 Thessalonians; Colossians	1 Corinthians
23	Colossians; 1 Timothy	"
24	1 Timothy	"
25	Ezra; Haggai; Zechariah	Proverbs, Qoheleth (Ecclesiastes)
26	Zechariah; Nehemiah; Baruch	Job
27	Jonah; Malachi; Joel	Galatians
28	Romans	Galatians; Ephesians
29	"	Ephesians
30	"	"
31	"	Ephesians; Philippians
32	Wisdom	Titus; Philemon; 2 and 3 John
33	1 and 2 Maccabees	Revelation
34	Daniel	"

BOOK OF THE GOSPELS
INTRODUCTION

APPROVED BY THE NATIONAL CONFERENCE OF CATHOLIC BISHOPS
NOVEMBER 16, 1999

APPROVED BY THE CONGREGATION FOR DIVINE WORSHIP
AND THE DISCIPLINE OF THE SACRAMENTS
MAY 23, 2000

PROMULGATED FOR USE IN THE DIOCESES OF
THE UNITED STATES OF AMERICA
DECEMBER 3, 2000

OVERVIEW OF THE *BOOK OF THE GOSPELS: INTRODUCTION*

Corinna Laughlin

Like the introductions to the other liturgical books of the Roman Rite, the "Introduction" to the *Book of the Gospels* (BG) complements *The General Instruction of the Roman Missal* (GIRM), and is binding on the universal Church wherever the *Book of the Gospels* is used. It should be noted, however, that the *Book of the Gospels* continues to be optional except for certain rites, like the Ordination of Bishops and Deacons.

Beginning in the fifth and sixth centuries, there was a proliferation of liturgical books, ranging from Lectionaries to Antiphonaries and Sacramentaries. At about this time, "Evangeliaries" (or "Books of the Gospels") began to emerge as well. These were often richly decorated inside and out, with covers made of precious metals and set with jewels. The Irish *Book of Kells*, which dates from around 800, is one of the most famous examples. These books typically contained the complete text of the four Gospel accounts.

With the development of *The Roman Missal*, which included both the readings and the prayers of the Mass, the use of other liturgical books declined. The *Book of the Gospels* continued to have a special role in the liturgy, however. From the time of the *Apostolic Constitutions* (c. 400), the *Book of the Gospels* has figured in the Rite for the Ordination of a Bishop, and it has been enthroned at every Ecumenical Council since about 800.

Following the Second Vatican Council, the use of the *Book of the Gospels* was restored to the liturgy. While the reformers envisioned that the *Book of the Gospels* would be used in "cathedrals and at least the larger, more populous parishes,"[1] the *Book of the Gospels* has become a treasured and indeed essential aspect of the celebration of Mass in churches large and small. Even communities with quite limited resources have made acquiring the *Book of the Gospels* a priority.

The brief "Introduction" to the *Book of the Gospels* consists of two sections, focusing on the centrality of the Gospel itself in the life of the Church, and on the proclamation of the Gospel at Mass.

The first part cites, in quick succession, the *Constitution on the Sacred Liturgy* (CSL), the Council of Trent, and the *Lectionary for Mass* (LM) on the importance of the Scriptures and especially of the Gospel accounts, which are the "foundation of every liturgical celebration" and "the rule and support of all our life" as Church.[2] From the earliest times, the Gospel accounts have been singled out for special reverence: "While the whole corpus of the Scriptures is venerated by the Church as the word of God, the Gospels have always been proclaimed as the very voice of her Bridegroom."[3] And while a reading from the

---

1. *Lectionary for Mass: Introduction* (LM), 36.
2. *Book of the Gospels* (BG), 3; quoting LM, 9.
3. Ibid., 4.

Gospel is proclaimed at every Mass, Sunday stands out as the day when "the Church proclaims the Gospel passages which are at the heart of her faith."[4]

The book containing the Gospel accounts is a sign of the presence of Christ, and is to be designed and handled accordingly. In the liturgy, it is treated like the other signs of Christ: carried between lighted candles like the cross, kissed like the altar. It is handled by a special minister, the deacon (or by a lector or reader when no deacon is present). The "Introduction" highlights its special liturgical role at the Ordination of Bishops, when it is a sign of the new bishop's teaching office, and at the Ordination of Deacons, when it is a symbol of the deacon's responsibility to proclaim and preach the Gospel. The "Introduction" also notes that when the *Book of the Gospels* is enthroned at a synod or council, it acts as "a sign of the presence of Christ himself as teacher and guide."[5]

The second part of the "Introduction" brings together the rubrics around the proclamation of the Gospel from the GIRM, the *Lectionary for Mass*, and the *Ceremonial of Bishops* (CB). It clarifies the place of the *Book of the Gospels* in the Entrance Procession, and summarizes the rites around the proclamation of the Gospel by the deacon or priest. There are some interesting notes that explain not only what is done, but why it is done. The people stand and sing an acclamation before the Gospel reading, "to welcome and acclaim the Word made flesh and to honor the *Book of the Gospels*, which is a sign of his presence."[6] They sign their foreheads, lips, and hearts so "that the Word may enlighten their minds, cleanse their hearts and open their lips to proclaim the praise of the Lord."[7] The dialogues preceding and following the Gospel, and the Gospel itself, may be sung "in order to stir the hearts of the faithful and convey the importance of the Gospel."[8]

It should be noted that the *Book of the Gospels* we have today is not only for Sundays: it includes Gospel readings for all solemnities, feasts of the Lord, and Ritual Masses. It does have its limitations, in that it does not include readings for other days when parishes may wish to heighten the solemnity of the Mass or give special honor to the Word: for example, Ash Wednesday, a patronal feast day, or a large parish or school gathering on a ferial day. Perhaps as the use of the *Book of the Gospels* becomes ever more widespread, additional readings will be included. In the meantime, the *Book of the Gospels*, along with the Lectionary, can fairly be called one of the great successes of the liturgical reforms of the Second Vatican Council.[9]

---

4. Ibid.
5. Ibid., 7.
6. Ibid., 11.
7. Ibid., 18.
8. Ibid., 19.
9. Please note that the "Introduction" reprints texts from the previous translation of *The Sacramentary*. While at Mass, the texts must come from the third edition of *The Roman Missal*.

OUTLINE

BOOK OF THE GOSPELS

INTRODUCTION

I. THE CENTRALITY OF THE GOSPEL
IN THE LIFE OF THE CHURCH AND HER LITURGY

1.   In the fullness of time, God "sent His Son, the Word made flesh, anointed by the Holy Spirit, to preach the Gospel to the poor, to heal the contrite of heart, to be a bodily and spiritual medicine, the Mediator between God and man . . . "[1] Entrusted by the Lord to his Apostles, this Gospel was set down by the Holy Evangelists in written form so that the events fulfilled in Jesus might be known and believed, and that through this belief every person in every time might "have life in his name."[2]

2.   Thus, the Church has received the Gospel from the Apostles to whom the Lord explained the Holy Scriptures.[3] From that time onwards the Church has never failed to come together to read "what referred to him in all the Scriptures"[4] and to celebrate the paschal mystery wherein "the victory and triumph of his death are again made present."[5]

3.   By the power of the Holy Spirit, the word of God proclaimed is the foundation of every liturgical celebration and "the rule and support of all our life. The working of the Holy Spirit precedes, accompanies, and brings to completion the whole celebration of the Liturgy. But the Spirit also brings home to each person individually everything that in the proclamation of the word of God is spoken for the good of the whole gathering of the faithful. In strengthening the unity of all, the Holy Spirit at the same time fosters a diversity of gifts and furthers their multiform operation."[6]

4.   From the time of the Apostolic Fathers, the Church has consistently read the Sacred Scriptures, especially the Gospels, as an integral part of the celebration of the Eucharist which helps to prepare the congregation for the Liturgy of

---

1. Second Vatican Council, Constitution on the Sacred Liturgy, *Sacrosanctum Concilium*, no. 5.

2. John 20:31; cf. Luke 1:1–4, Acts 1:1–2.

3. See Acts 8:30–31; Saint Irenaeus, *Adversus Haereses*, III, 2, 2 and 3.

4. Luke 24:27.

5. See Council of Trent, sess. 13, 11 October 1551, *Decr. De ss. Eucharist.* cap. 5; see also Second Vatican Council, Constitution on the Sacred Liturgy, *Sacrosanctum Concilium*, no. 6.

6. Lectionary for Mass for Use in the Dioceses of the United States of America, *(editio typica altera, 1998)*, no. 9.

the Eucharist itself. While the whole corpus of the Scriptures is venerated by the Church as the word of God, the Gospels have always been proclaimed as the very voice of her Bridegroom. Especially on Sunday, "the day of the Resurrection . . . the day of Christians . . . our day,"[7] the Church proclaims the Gospel passages which are at the heart of her faith.[8]

THE BOOK OF THE GOSPELS

5.   Formal liturgical books containing readings from Sacred Scripture have been common in the Church from the time of Saint Gregory the Great.[9] In our own day every effort is made to assure that the Scriptures are bound in books which are "worthy, dignified, and beautiful."[10]

6.   This is particularly true of the *Book of the Gospels* which is venerated above all the books of readings by Churches of both East and West.[11] So clearly is the *Book of the Gospels* a sign of Christ present in the liturgy, that it is revered with the same holy kiss given to the altar. For this reason it is desirable that "cathedrals and at least the larger, more populous parishes and the churches with a larger attendance possess a beautifully designed *Book of the Gospels*, separate from any other book of readings."[12]

7.   Thus the *Book of the Gospels* as a sign of the presence of Christ in his word proclaimed is always accorded a place of honor in the Church's liturgy. It is borne by the deacon in solemn procession for the veneration of the entire congregation and accompanied by candles and incense at Mass. The imposition and presentation of the *Book of the Gospels* to a newly ordained Bishop illustrate that the faithful preaching of the word of God[13] is among his principle duties. The presentation of the *Book of the Gospels* to the newly ordained deacon "symbolizes the office of the deacon to proclaim the Gospel in liturgical celebrations and to preach the faith of the Church in word and deed."[14] Finally, the enshrinement of the *Book of the Gospels* whenever the Church gathers in a council or synod is a sign of the presence of Christ himself as teacher and guide.[15]

II. THE PROCLAMATION OF THE GOSPEL AT MASS

8.   Every time the Church unites herself with Christ in the celebration of the Holy Eucharist, the Body of the Lord and the eternal Word of divine truth are

---

7. Saint Jerome, *In die dominica Paschae*, II, 52; Cf. John Paul II, Apostolic Letter *Dies Domini*, 2.

8. *Lectionary for Mass*, no. 65.

9. Saint Gregory the Great, *Homilia in evangelia*, 14, 1.

10. *Lectionary for Mass*, no. 35.

11. Ibid., no. 36.

12. Ibid.

13. See *De Ordinatione Episcopi, Presbyterorum et Diaconorum (editio typica altera*, 1989), no. 26; see also Second Vatican Council, Decree on the Pastoral Office of Bishops in the Church, *Christus Dominus*, no. 12.

14. Ibid., no. 188.

15. *Cæremoniale Episcoporum, (editio typica*, 1984), no. 1172.

received as from a twofold table, as a participation in the one sacrifice of praise.[16] While opening up a vast treasury of Sacred Scripture in the Liturgy of the Word, the Church nonetheless acknowledges the preeminent place of the Gospels[17] by according "special marks of honor" to their proclamation.[18] The proclamation of the Gospel is reserved to the deacon, if he is present, or to a priest. It can be preceded by a procession which marks the coming of Christ, present in the words of life he unfailingly addresses to his followers whenever, as members of the Church, they gather in his name. The procession may be accompanied by particular marks of reverence, above all, the use of incense and lighted candles. To the proclamation and the accompanying manifestations of reverence, all the faithful present respond in faith, receiving the message of the Gospel into their hearts and praying that it may purify and transform their lives, building up the Body of Christ which is the Church.

ENTRANCE PROCESSION

9.   In the Entrance Procession the vested deacon reverently carries the *Book of the Gospels* before him so that it may be seen by the faithful.[19] With the priest he makes the proper reverence and goes up to the altar, placing the *Book of the Gospels* on it. The deacon then kisses the altar at the same time as the priest.[20] In the absence of a deacon, the reader reverently carries the *Book of the Gospels* in procession. The reader follows the acolytes and other ministers in procession. The reader places the *Book of the Gospels* on the altar, but the reader does not kiss the altar.

PREPARATION FOR THE GOSPEL PROCESSION

10.   After a brief silent reflection on the last reading from the *Lectionary*, or as the occasion dictates, after the Responsorial Psalm, the reader removes the *Lectionary*. The candle bearers go to the altar where the *Book of the Gospels* has been placed.

11.   The faithful stand to welcome and acclaim the Word made flesh and to honor the *Book of the Gospels*, which is a sign of his presence. All sing the Gospel Acclamation which ends when the deacon reaches the ambo.[21]

12.   The deacon, accompanied by the thurifer, goes to the priest celebrant. As the congregation begins to sing the Gospel Acclamation, the deacon assists the priest who puts incense into the thurible.[22]

---

16. *Lectionary for Mass*, no. 10.

17. Ibid., no. 17.

18. *Institutio Generalis Missalis Romani*, nos. 60, 175.

19. Ibid., no. 172.

20. Ibid., no. 173.

21. Ibid., nos. 132, 175; *Lectionary for Mass*, no. 17; *Cæremoniale Episcoporum*, no. 140.

22. *Institutio Generalis Missalis Romani*, nos. 91, 131; *Cæremoniale Episcoporum*, no. 140.

13.   After the preparation of the incense, the deacon bows before the priest and asks for the blessing.[23] The priest blesses him with the words, *The Lord be in your heart* . . . The deacon answers, *Amen.*

IN THE ABSENCE OF A DEACON

14.   When no deacon is present, a concelebrating priest may proclaim the Gospel.[24] When no concelebrant is present, the priest celebrant proclaims the Gospel. Unless the celebrant is a Bishop, the concelebrant bows before the altar, praying inaudibly, *Almighty God, cleanse my heart* . . .[25]

15.   When the celebrant is the Bishop, the priest asks for the blessing in the same manner as the deacon.[26] Everything else is carried out by the concelebrating priest in the same manner as the deacon.

PROCESSION

16.   After receiving the blessing, the deacon, preceded by the thurifer and acolytes with lighted candles or other symbols of reverence that may be customary, takes the *Book of the Gospels* from the altar and carries it to the ambo, accompanied by the Gospel Acclamation.[27]

PROCLAMATION

17.   Once he has reached the ambo and placed the *Book of the Gospels* on it, with hands joined, he greets the faithful. Acolytes with candles may position themselves on either side of the deacon at the ambo as he proclaims the Gospel.

18.   Then the deacon announces the reading while making the sign of the cross with his thumb, first on the book at the beginning of the Gospel passage he is about to read, then on his forehead, lips and breast. Together with the deacon who proclaims the Gospel, the faithful sign themselves similarly that the Word may enlighten their minds, cleanse their hearts and open their lips to proclaim the praise of the Lord.[28] All present respond with the words: *Glory to you, Lord.* The deacon then incenses the book three times, to the center, left and right.[29] The Gospel is then proclaimed in a clear voice.

---

23. *Institutio Generalis Missalis Romani*, no. 175; *Lectionary for Mass*, no. 17; *Cæremoniale Episcoporum*, no. 140.

24. *Lectionary for Mass*, no. 49.

25. Ibid., no. 17.

26. *Cæremoniale Episcoporum*, no. 74.

27. *Institutio Generalis Missalis Romani*, no. 175; *Lectionary for Mass*, no. 17; *Cæremoniale Episcoporum*, nos. 74, 140.

28. *Cæremoniale Episcoporum*, nos. 74, 141.

29. *Institutio Generalis Missalis Romani*, no. 175; *Cæremoniale Episcoporum*, no. 74.

19.   In order to stir the hearts of the faithful and convey the importance of the Gospel itself, the greeting, the announcement of the reading, the concluding acclamation and even the entire Gospel may be sung.[30] Musical settings should be easily understood and enhance rather than obscure the meaning of the sacred text.[31]

ACCLAMATION AT THE END OF THE GOSPEL

20.   At the end of the Gospel, the deacon proclaims *The Gospel of the Lord* without raising the book from the stand. All present respond with the words: *Praise to you, Lord Jesus Christ.*[32]

21.   Then the deacon kisses the book, saying in a low voice: *"Through the words of the Gospel . . . ."*[33] If the celebrant is a Bishop, the deacon either may bring the *Book of the Gospels* to the Bishop, who reverences it with a kiss, or he may kiss the book himself. The *Book of the Gospels* is then reverently taken to some other suitable place.[34]

22.   The *Book of the Gospels* is not carried in the procession at the end of Mass.

30. *Lectionary for Mass*, no. 17.
31. Ibid., no. 14.
32. *Institutio Generalis Missalis Romani*, no. 134; *Lectionary for Mass*, no. 17.
33. Ibid.
34. *Cæremoniale Episcoporum*, no. 74.

SING TO THE LORD

MUSIC IN DIVINE WORSHIP

UNITED STATES CONFERENCE OF CATHOLIC BISHOPS
NOVEMBER 14, 2007

UPDATED IN 2013 TO REFLECT
THE ROMAN MISSAL, THIRD EDITION

OVERVIEW OF *SING TO THE LORD: MUSIC IN DIVINE WORSHIP*

Steven R. Janco

Sing to the Lord: Music in Divine Worship (STL), approved on November 14, 2007 and updated in 2013 to reflect *The Roman Missal*, is the first document on liturgical music issued by the United States Conference of Catholic Bishops (USCCB). Two earlier and influential statements, *Music in Catholic Worship* (MCW), issued in 1972 and revised slightly in 1983, and *Liturgical Music Today* (LMT), issued in 1982, were approved by the Bishops' Committee on the Liturgy (now Committee on Divine Worship). *Sing to the Lord* presents itself as a revision of MCW[1] rather than a completely new document—an acknowledgement of the influence of the earlier statements and a signal of continuity of thought and practice rather than a completely new direction. At 259 articles, however, STL is a significantly more substantial and ambitious document than the earlier two statements, which together contain a total of 158 articles.

STL is "designed to provide direction to those preparing for the celebration of the Sacred Liturgy according to the current liturgical books (in the ordinary form of celebration)."[2] Though issued as guidelines, STL incorporates directives on liturgical music from *The General Instruction of the Roman Missal* (GIRM) and nearly every other approved ritual book, and offers guidance in the interpretation and pastoral application of the principles, requirements, and options set forth in those books. STL also draws insight from the Scriptures and a wide variety of ecclesiastical sources, including the *Catechism of the Catholic Church* (CCC), papal and Vatican statements, and three documents issued by the USCCB.[3] STL provides a comprehensive overview of the integral role of music in the liturgical life of the Church; describes the roles of the assembly and the ministers of liturgical music; discusses the evaluation and selection of liturgical music; and surveys the musical needs of specific rites. It provides clear affirmation that music is integral to liturgical celebration and that stewardship of the Church's treasured tradition of liturgical song requires competent ministers with a broad and long-range vision that sees beyond the immediate task of preparing for upcoming liturgies.

STL serves as a reminder that the implementation of the Second Vatican Council's liturgical reform is an ongoing challenge. The document calls attention to the role of music in several rites that have been in use since the 1970s, some of which have received inadequate attention over the years as parish leaders focused their energy and resources on the celebration of Sunday Mass. For example, the *Rite of Baptism for Children* provides numerous opportunities for

---

1. Pastoral Liturgy Series Edition, *Sing to the Lord: Music in Divine Worship*, p. x.

2. Ibid.

3. These documents include *Built of Living Stones* (2000), *Welcoming the Stranger: Unity in Diversity* (2000), and *Co-Workers in the Vineyard of the Lord: A Resource for Guiding the Development of Lay Ecclesial Ministry* (2005).

singing, including a Psalm or hymn at the beginning, the conclusion, and during each procession; the Litany of Saints; and an acclamation after each Baptism.[4] Liturgical music also "has an integral role in the funeral rites,"[5] including the Vigil for the Deceased and the Rite of Committal as well as the Funeral Liturgy.[6]

Recognizing the ongoing pastoral challenges involved in wedding liturgies, STL devotes nine articles to issues concerning music for the *Rite of Marriage*. The document takes a pastoral approach, viewing the preparation and celebration of each wedding liturgy as an opportunity for catechesis and good pastoral care. Pastors and musicians "should make every effort to assist couples to understand and share in the planning of their marriage Liturgy."[7] Each diocese or parish should have a "definite but flexible policy that provides clear guidance and also allows for pastoral sensitivity regarding wedding music."[8] In addition, "local custom and the culture of the families"[9] should be taken into account.

This pastoral approach to wedding liturgies offers one glimpse of an assumption that informs much of STL. Though liturgy is an action of the universal Church, every liturgy is celebrated locally. Liturgy comes to life only when a particular group of the faithful gathers to worship at a particular time and place. Hence all who are responsible for liturgical preparation and celebration at the local level must be equipped with the liturgical background, musical skills, spiritual formation, familiarity with cultural traditions, and pastoral sensibility necessary to serve the local Church well—be they priests, deacons, directors of music ministry, singers, instrumentalists, or planners. The document indicates that dioceses and parishes should encourage ministers to participate in ongoing formation opportunities that support competent leadership in liturgical music—and should provide financial support when needed.[10] In addition, the musical formation of the assembly "must be a continuing concern in order to foster full, conscious and active participation."[11]

In its discussion of the ministers of liturgical music (choir, psalmist, cantor, organist, and other instrumentalists) STL notes that each exercises a "genuine liturgical ministry."[12] While it outlines the specific responsibilities of each ministry, STL also calls for a certain modesty on the part of all music ministers. The choir "must not minimize the musical participation of the faithful"[13] and, when not exercising its particular role, should join, but not "lead" the congregation in singing.[14] The cantor "should not be heard above the congregation" and should use gestures "sparingly."[15] The organist and other instrumentalists should

---

4. See STL, 207–210.
5. Ibid., 246.
6. See ibid., 244–257.
7. Ibid., 218.
8. Ibid., 219.
9. Ibid., 222.
10. See ibid., 50–51.
11. Ibid., 26.
12. Ibid., 50; see also CSL, 29.
13. Ibid., 28.
14. Ibid., 31.
15. Ibid., 38.

lead the singing "without dominating or overpowering [the assembly]."[16] Amplified choirs and ensembles, demonstrative cantors singing directly into microphones, and forceful instrumentalists, while perhaps at one point in time considered helpful to promote assembly singing, may now simply be intrusive—distracting or even discouraging members of the assembly rather than fostering their participation. In its call for modesty for music ministers, STL acknowledges that congregational singing in the United States has come a long way.

One significant point of continuity with MCW is STL's retention of the "three judgments" to be employed in the evaluation of liturgical music. STL changes the order of the judgments from musical/liturgical/pastoral to liturgical/pastoral/musical and describes the three judgments as aspects of "one evaluation" that needs to be made with "cooperation, consultation, collaboration, and mutual respect."[17] Within its discussion of the musical judgment, STL retains another oft-cited principle of MCW: the distinction between "sufficiency of artistic expression" and "musical style."[18] The document notes that, "in recent times, the Church has consistently recognized and freely welcomed the use of various styles of music as an aid to worship."[19]

STL brings renewed attention to the singing of Gregorian chant. Echoing the *Constitution on the Sacred Liturgy* (CSL, 1963) 54, *Musicam sacram* (1967) 47, *Iubilate deo* (1974), the *General Instruction of the Roman Missal* (1974) 19, the *General Instruction of the Roman Missal (2003)* 41, and *Sacramentum caritatis* (Benedict XVI, 2007) 62, STL indicates that all worshiping communities, including all age groups and ethnic groups, should be able to sing some parts of the Mass in Latin. Catholics should, "at a minimum, learn *Kyrie XVI, Sanctus XVIII*, and *Agnus Dei XVIII*, all of which are typically included in congregational worship aids."[20] Recognizing that the singing of chant will be new for some communities, the document calls for "prudence, pastoral sensitivity, and reasonable time for progress."[21] STL cites as the foundation of its call for the use of Latin chant in vernacular liturgy, CSL, which indicates that "'other things being equal,'" [Gregorian chant] should be given "pride of place" in the liturgy.[22] STL does not cite two more recent documents, *Musicam sacram* and John Paul II's 2003 "Chirograph on the Centenary of the *Motu Proprio 'Tra le sollecitudini,'*" which specify that this section of the CSL is referring to the use of chant in "liturgies celebrated in Latin."[23]

The rationale STL provides for the singing of chant is interesting and helpful. Here the document engages in some mystagogical reflection. Gregorian chant is:

- uniquely the Church's own music
- a living connection with our forebears in the faith

---

16. Ibid., 41.
17. Ibid., 126.
18. Ibid., 136.
19. Ibid.
20. Ibid., 75.
21. Ibid., 74.
22. STL, 72; see also CSL, 116.
23. *Musicam sacram* 50, "Chirograph," 7.

- the traditional music of the Roman rite
- a sign of communion with the universal Church
- a bond of unity across cultures
- a means for diverse communities to participate together in song
- a summons to contemplative participation in the Liturgy.[24]

This kind of reflection would be useful to bring out the significance and formative impact of singing other kinds of music in Catholic worship:

- music common to Catholic and Protestant Christians
- music of diverse cultures
- psalmody
- music sung in dialogue in contrast with music sung together by all
- music written in contemporary genres and styles

While comprehensive in scope, STL does not address every pastoral issue facing liturgical musicians today. For example, the threefold evaluation does not discuss the need to evaluate the texts of hymns and songs from theological, scriptural, or poetic perspectives. Nor does the document discuss the need for a diverse and well-rounded parish repertory that as a whole reflects the breadth of Catholic theology and tradition. The document provides helpful guidance concerning liturgical music in Catholic schools, but does not address the needs of religious education programs.

When it comes to liturgy in multicultural communities, STL echoes the pastoral experience of many and discusses diversity as both a gift and a challenge. But while attempting to strike a balance between creativity and caution in the four articles devoted to this topic,[25] STL sends contradictory messages that together offer little practical guidance to pastoral practitioners. Given the ever-growing significance of this issue, I'd like to call attention to two examples of conflicting signals in STL.

The first example concerns the frequency of multicultural celebrations. The document encourages local communities to celebrate bicultural or multicultural liturgies "from time to time," but then suggests that communities need to move beyond celebrations that "merely highlight" multicultural differences to celebrations that "better reflect the intercultural relationships of the assembly."[26] Celebrating multicultural liturgies infrequently—perhaps during different seasons—does not afford the repetition and consistency necessary for a group to become familiar and comfortable with the kind of relatively stable musical repertory that's needed in order to promote confident participation and foster authentic unity-in-diversity in multicultural liturgical celebrations.

The second example concerns the place of music of particular ethnic traditions in the repertory of the wider Church. STL echoes a section of LMT that

---

24. STL, 72 (bulleted list is author's style for emphasis).
25. See ibid., 57–60.
26. Ibid., 59.

was prophetic in 1982: "The valuable musical gifts of the diverse cultural and ethnic communities should enrich the whole Church in the United States . . . ."[27] But STL later indicates that planners need to avoid musical choices "that could be misconstrued as tokenism."[28] While such a caution aims at pastoral sensitivity, STL provides no suggestions as to how appropriate choices might actually be made.

For years, *Music in Catholic Worship* and *Liturgical Music Today* were used widely in seminaries, colleges, diocesan liturgical formation programs, and workshops. They were cited frequently in books, articles, and documents on liturgical music of both Catholic and Protestant authorship. The level of acceptance and the status of authority they achieved were not the result of their legal weight as ecclesiastical documents. Their *gravitas* was earned over time by the helpfulness of their insight and by the pastoral fruitfulness that resulted when pastoral ministers put their principles and recommendations into practice. As of this writing, STL is still a young document. But even at this point there is every indication that its foundational principles and pastoral approach will influence the formation of music ministers and the practice of liturgical music in the United States for years to come.

---

27. Ibid.
28. Ibid., 60.

OUTLINE

SING TO THE LORD
MUSIC IN DIVINE WORSHIP

FOREWORD

Greetings from the bishops of the United States to priests, deacons, liturgists, music directors, composers, cantors, choirs, congregations, and faith communities throughout the United States. "Grace to you and peace from God our Father and the Lord Jesus Christ."[1] It is our duty and our joy as shepherds of the Church to guide and oversee liturgical song in each particular Church. Liturgy is the source of the Church's prayer and action, and the summit by which our lives and all our ministries ascend to the Father. We pray that this document will draw all who worship the Lord into the fullness of liturgical, musical prayer.

I. WHY WE SING

1.   God has bestowed upon his people the gift of song. God dwells within each human person, in the place where music takes its source. Indeed, God, the giver of song, is present whenever his people sing his praises.[2]

2.   A cry from deep within our being, music is a way for God to lead us to the realm of higher things.[3] As St. Augustine says, "Singing is for the one who loves."[4] Music is therefore a sign of God's love for us and of our love for him. In this sense, it is very personal. But unless music sounds, it is not music, and whenever it sounds, it is accessible to others. By its very nature song has both an individual and a communal dimension. Thus, it is no wonder that singing together in church expresses so well the sacramental presence of God to his people.

3.   Our ancestors reveled in this gift, sometimes with God's urging. "Write out this song, then, for yourselves," God said to Moses. "Teach it to the Israelites and have them recite it, so that this song may be a witness for me."[5] The Chosen

---

1. Eph 1:1.

2. "Do you not know that you are the temple of God, and that the Spirit of God dwells in you? If anyone destroys God's temple, God will destroy that person; for the temple of God, which you are, is holy" (1 Cor 3:16–17).

3. See St. Augustine, Epis. 161, *De origine animae hominis*, 1, 2; PL XXXIII, 725, as quoted in Pope Pius XII, Encyclical *On Sacred Music (Musicae Sacrae Disciplina)* (MSD), no. 5, www.vatican.va/holy_father/pius_xii/encyclicals/documents/hf_p-xii_enc_25121955_musicae-sacrae_en.html.

4. St. Augustine, *Sermo 336*, 1 (PL 1844–1855, 38, 1472).

5. Dt 31:19.

People, after they passed through the Red Sea, sang as one to the Lord.[6] Deborah, a judge of Israel, sang to the Lord with Barak after God gave them victory.[7] David and the Israelites "made merry before the Lord with all their strength, with singing and with citharas, harps, tambourines, sistrums and cymbals."[8]

4.　　Jesus and his apostles sang a hymn before their journey to the Mount of Olives.[9] St. Paul instructed the Ephesians to "[address] one another in psalms and hymns and spiritual songs, singing and playing to the Lord in your hearts."[10] He sang with Silas in captivity.[11] The letter of St. James asks, "Is anyone among you suffering? He should pray. Is anyone in good spirits? He should sing praise."[12]

5.　　Obedient to Christ and to the Church, we gather in liturgical assembly, week after week. As our predecessors did, we find ourselves "singing psalms, hymns and spiritual songs with gratitude in [our] hearts to God."[13] This common, sung expression of faith within liturgical celebrations strengthens our faith when it grows weak and draws us into the divinely inspired voice of the Church at prayer. Faith grows when it is well expressed in celebration. Good celebrations can foster and nourish faith. Poor celebrations may weaken it. Good music "make[s] the liturgical prayers of the Christian community more alive and fervent so that everyone can praise and beseech the Triune God more powerfully, more intently and more effectively."[14]

6.　　"In human life, signs and symbols occupy an important place. As a being at once body and spirit, man expresses and perceives spiritual realities through physical signs and symbols. . . . Inasmuch as they are creatures, these perceptible realities can become means of expressing the action of God who sanctifies men, and the action of men who offer worship to God."[15] This sacramental principle is the consistent belief of the Church throughout history. In Liturgy, we use words, gestures, signs, and symbols to proclaim Christ's presence and to reply with our worship and praise.

7.　　The primordial song of the Liturgy is the canticle of victory over sin and death. It is the song of the saints, standing beside "the sea of glass": "They were holding God's harps, and they sang the song of Moses, the servant of God, and the song of the Lamb."[16] "Liturgical singing is established in the midst of this

---

6. Ex 15:1–18, 21.

7. Jgs 4:4–5:31.

8. 2 Sm 6:5.

9. See Mt 26:30; Mk 14:26.

10. Eph 5:18–19.

11. "About midnight . . . Paul and Silas were praying and singing hymns to God, as the other prisoners listened" (Acts 16:25).

12. Jas 5:13.

13. Col 3:16; see *General Instruction of the Roman Missal* (GIRM), no. 39 (Washington, DC: United States Conference of Catholic Bishops [USCCB], 2003). See Eph 5:19.

14. MSD, no. 31; see no. 33.

15. *Catechism of the Catholic Church* (CCC), 2nd ed., nos. 1146, 1148 (Washington, DC: Libreria Editrice Vaticana–USCCB, 2000).

16. Rev 15:3.

great historical tension. For Israel, the event of salvation in the Red Sea will always be the main reason for praising God, the basic theme of the songs it sings before God. For Christians, the Resurrection of Christ is the true Exodus. . . . The definitively new song has been intoned. . . ."[17]

8.   The Paschal hymn, of course, does not cease when a liturgical celebration ends. Christ, whose praises we have sung, remains with us and leads us through church doors to the whole world, with its joys and hopes, griefs and anxieties.[18] The words Jesus chose from the book of Isaiah at the beginning of his ministry become the song of the Body of Christ. "The Spirit of the Lord is upon me, / because he has anointed me / to bring glad tidings to the poor. / He has sent me to proclaim liberty to / captives and recovery of sight to the blind, / to let the oppressed go free, / and to proclaim a year acceptable to the Lord."[19]

9.   Charity, justice, and evangelization are thus the normal consequences of liturgical celebration. Particularly inspired by sung participation, the body of the Word Incarnate goes forth to spread the Gospel with full force and compassion. In this way, the Church leads men and women "to the faith, freedom and peace of Christ by the example of its life and teaching, by the sacraments and other means of grace. Its aim is to open up for all men a free and sure path to full participation in the mystery of Christ."[20]

PARTICIPATION

10.   Holy Mother Church clearly affirms the role within worship of the entire liturgical assembly (bishop, priest, deacon, acolytes, ministers of the Word, music leaders, choir, extraordinary ministers of Holy Communion, and the congregation). Through grace, the liturgical assembly partakes in the life of the Blessed Trinity, which is itself a communion of love. In a perfect way, the Persons of the Trinity remain themselves even as they share all that they are. For our part, "we, though many, are one body in Christ and individually parts of one another."[21] The Church urges all members of the liturgical assembly to receive this divine gift and to participate fully "depending on their orders [and] their role in the liturgical services."[22]

11.   Within the gathered assembly, the role of the congregation is especially important. "The full and active participation by all the people is the aim to be

---

17. Cardinal Joseph Ratzinger, *The Spirit of the Liturgy* (Ignatius Press, 2000), 137–138.

18. See Second Vatican Council, *Gaudium et Spes (Pastoral Constitution on the Church in the Modern World)* (GS), no. 1, in *Vatican Council II: The Conciliar and Post Conciliar Documents*, new revised edition, ed. Austin Flannery, OP (Northport, NY: Costello Publishing, 1996). All subsequent Second Vatican Council passages come from the Flannery edition.

19. Lk 4:18; see Is 61:1–2, 58:6.

20. Second Vatican Council, *Ad Gentes Divinitus (Decree on the Church's Missionary Activity)* (AG), no. 5.

21. Rom 12:5–6.

22. Second Vatican Council, *Sacrosanctum Concilium (Constitution on the Sacred Liturgy)* (SC), no. 26.

considered before all else, for it is the primary and indispensable source from which the faithful are to derive the true Christian spirit."[23]

12. Participation in the Sacred Liturgy must be "internal, in the sense that by it the faithful join their mind to what they pronounce or hear, and cooperate with heavenly grace."[24] Even when listening to the various prayers and readings of the Liturgy or to the singing of the choir, the assembly continues to participate actively as they "unite themselves interiorly to what the ministers or choir sing, so that by listening to them they may raise their minds to God."[25] "In a culture which neither favors nor fosters meditative quiet, the art of interior listening is learned only with difficulty. Here we see how the liturgy, though it must always be properly inculturated, must also be counter-cultural."[26]

13. Participation must also be external, so that internal participation can be expressed and reinforced by actions, gestures, and bodily attitudes, and by the acclamations, responses, and singing.[27] The quality of our participation in such sung praise comes less from our vocal ability than from the desire of our hearts to sing together of our love for God. Participation in the Sacred Liturgy both expresses and strengthens the faith that is in us.

14. Our participation in the Liturgy is challenging. Sometimes, our voices do not correspond to the convictions of our hearts. At other times, we are distracted or preoccupied by the cares of the world. Christ always invites us, however, to enter into song, to rise above our own preoccupations, and to give our entire selves to the hymn of his Paschal Sacrifice for the honor and glory of the Most Blessed Trinity.

II. THE CHURCH AT PRAYER

15. The Church is always at prayer in her ministers and her people, and that prayer takes various forms in her life. Authentic sacred music supports the Church's prayer by enriching its elements. What follows below are the principal persons and elements that should guide both the development and the use of sacred music in the Liturgy.

A. THE BISHOP

16. In his capacity as "the prime steward of the mysteries of God in the particular Church entrusted to his care,"[28] the diocesan bishop is particularly concerned with the promotion of the dignity of liturgical celebrations, "the beauty

---

23. SC, no. 14.

24. Sacred Congregation for Rites, *Musicam Sacram (Instruction on Music in the Liturgy)* (MS), no. 15, in Flannery, *Vatican Council II*; see SC, no. 11.

25. MS, no. 15.

26. Pope John Paul II, Address to Bishops of the Northwest Provinces of the USCCB, in *Ad Limina Addresses: The Addresses of His Holiness Pope John Paul II to the Bishops of the United States, February 1998–October 1998* (Washington, DC: USCCB, 1998), no. 3.

27. See SC, no. 30.

28. GIRM, no. 22.

of the sacred place, of the music, and of art."[29] He carries out this duty through the example of his own celebration of the Sacred Liturgy, encouraging sung participation by his own example; by his attention to the practice of liturgical music in the parishes and communities of his diocese, especially in his own cathedral church; by his promotion of the continuing musical education and formation of clergy and musicians; and by his careful attention to the musical training of future priests and deacons.

17.　The bishop is assisted in this role by his staff in the diocesan Office of Worship and/or the diocesan music or liturgical commission, which provides "valuable assistance in promoting sacred music together with pastoral liturgical action in the diocese."[30]

B. THE PRIEST

18.　No other single factor affects the Liturgy as much as the attitude, style, and bearing of the priest celebrant, who "expresses prayers in the name of the Church and of the assembled community."[31] "When he celebrates the Eucharist, . . . [the priest] must serve God and the people with dignity and humility, and by his bearing and by the way he pronounces the divine words he must convey to the faithful the living presence of Christ."[32]

19.　The importance of the priest's participation in the Liturgy, especially by singing, cannot be overemphasized. The priest sings the presidential prayers and dialogues of the Liturgy according to his capabilities,[33] and he encourages sung participation in the Liturgy by his own example, joining in the congregational song. "If, however . . . the priest or minister does not possess a voice suitable for the proper execution of the singing, he can render without singing one or more of the more difficult parts which concern him, reciting them in a loud and distinct voice. However, this must not be done merely for the convenience of the priest or minister."[34]

20.　Seminaries and other programs of priestly formation should train priests to sing with confidence and to chant those parts of the Mass assigned to them. Those priests who are capable should be trained in the practice of chanting the Gospel on more solemn occasions when a deacon may not be present. At the very least, all priests should be comfortable singing those parts of the Eucharistic

---

29. GIRM, no. 22.

30. MS, no. 68.

31. GIRM, no. 33.

32. GIRM, no. 93.

33. The documents of the post-conciliar liturgical renewal repeatedly commend the ideal of a sung Liturgy with sung dialogues between priest and people, such as *The Lord be with you*, the acclamation at the end of the Gospel, and the introductory dialogue to the Eucharistic Prayer. See MS, nos. 29–31; *Lectionary for Mass (Second Typical Edition): Introduction* (LFM) (Washington, DC: USCCB, 1998), no. 17; GIRM, no. 40.

34. MS, no. 8.

Prayer that are assigned to them for which musical notation is provided in the *Roman Missal.*[35]

21.   The priest joins with the congregation in singing the acclamations, chants, hymns, and songs of the Liturgy. However, the priest does not join in the singing of the Memorial Acclamation or the Great Amen. To the greatest extent possible, he should use a congregational worship aid during the processions and other rituals of the Liturgy and should be attentive to the cantor and Psalmist as they lead the gathered assembly in song. In order to promote the corporate voice of the assembly when it sings, the priest's own voice should not be heard above the congregation, nor should he sing the congregational response of the dialogues. While the assembly sings, the priest should step back from a microphone, or, if he is using a wireless microphone, he should turn it off.

C. THE DEACON

22.   After the priest, the deacon is first among the liturgical ministers, and he should provide an example by actively participating in the song of the gathered assembly.[36]

23.   In accord with their abilities, deacons should be prepared to sing those parts of the Liturgy that belong to them. Deacons should receive training in singing the dialogues between deacon and people, such as those at the Gospel and at the dismissal. They should also learn to sing various invitations in the rites, the *Exsultet,* the third form of the Penitential Act, and the Universal Prayer (Prayer of the Faithful). If they are capable, deacons should be trained in the practice of chanting the Gospel on more solemn occasions. Programs of diaconal formation should include major and compulsory courses in the chant and song of the Liturgy.

D. THE GATHERED LITURGICAL ASSEMBLY

24.   "In the celebration of Mass the faithful form a holy people, a people of God's own possession and a royal Priesthood, so that they may give thanks to God and offer the unblemished sacrificial Victim not only by means of the hands of the Priest but also together with him and so that they may learn to offer their very selves."[37] This is the basis for the "full, conscious and active participation" of the faithful demanded by the very nature of the Liturgy.[38]

25.   Because the gathered liturgical assembly forms one body, each of its members must shun "any appearance of singularity or division, keeping in mind that they have only one Father in heaven and that hence are all brothers or sisters one to the other."[39]

---

35. See GIRM, no. 147.
36. See GIRM, no. 94.
37. GIRM, no. 95.
38. See SC, no. 14.
39. GIRM, no. 95.

26. Singing is one of the primary ways that the assembly of the faithful participates actively in the Liturgy. The people are encouraged "to take part by means of acclamations, responses, psalms, antiphons [and] hymns. . . ."[40] The musical formation of the assembly must be a continuing concern in order to foster full, conscious, and active participation.

27. So that the holy people may sing with one voice, the music must be within its members' capability. Some congregations are able to learn more quickly and will desire more variety. Others will be more comfortable with a stable number of songs so that they can be at ease when they sing. Familiarity with a stable repertoire of liturgical songs rich in theological content can deepen the faith of the community through repetition and memorization. A pastoral judgment must be made in all cases.

E. MINISTERS OF LITURGICAL MUSIC

The Choir

28. The Second Vatican Council stated emphatically that choirs must be diligently promoted while ensuring that "the whole body of the faithful may be able to contribute that active participation which is rightly theirs. . . ."[41] The choir must not minimize the musical participation of the faithful. The congregation commonly sings unison melodies, which are more suitable for generally unrehearsed community singing. This is the primary song of the Liturgy. Choirs and ensembles, on the other hand, comprise persons drawn from the community who possess the requisite musical skills and a commitment to the established schedule of rehearsals and liturgies. Thus, they are able to enrich the celebration by adding musical elements beyond the capabilities of the congregation alone.

29. Choirs (and ensembles—another form of choir that commonly includes a combination of singers and instrumentalists) exercise their ministry in various ways. An important ministerial role of the choir or ensemble is to sing various parts of the Mass in dialogue or alternation with the congregation. Some parts of the Mass that have the character of a litany, such as the *Kyrie* and the *Agnus Dei*, are clearly intended to be sung in this manner. Other Mass parts may also be sung in dialogue or alternation, especially the *Gloria*, the Creed, and the three processional songs: the Entrance, the Preparation of the Gifts, and Communion. This approach often takes the form of a congregational refrain with verses sung by the choir. Choirs may also enrich congregational singing by adding harmonies and descants.

30. At times, the choir performs its ministry by singing alone. The choir may draw on the treasury of sacred music, singing compositions by composers of various periods and in various musical styles, as well as music that expresses the faith of the various cultures that enrich the Church. Appropriate times when

---

40. SC, no. 30.
41. SC, no. 114.

the choir might commonly sing alone include a prelude before Mass, the Entrance chant, the Preparation of the Gifts, during the Communion procession or after the reception of Communion, and the recessional. Other appropriate examples are given in the section of this document entitled "Music and the Structure of the Mass" (nos. 137–199). The music of the choir must always be appropriate to the Liturgy, either by being a proper liturgical text or by expressing themes appropriate to the Liturgy.

31.   When the choir is not exercising its particular role, it joins the congregation in song. The choir's role in this case is not to lead congregational singing, but to sing with the congregation, which sings on its own or under the leadership of the organ or other instruments.

32.   Choir members, like all liturgical ministers, should exercise their ministry with evident faith and should participate in the entire liturgical celebration, recognizing that they are servants of the Liturgy and members of the gathered assembly.

33.   Choir and ensemble members may dress in albs or choir robes, but always in clean, presentable, and modest clothing. Cassock and surplice, being clerical attire, are not recommended as choir vesture.

The Psalmist

34.   The psalmist, or "cantor of the Psalm," proclaims the Psalm after the first reading and leads the gathered assembly in singing the refrain.[42] The psalmist may also, when necessary, intone the Gospel Acclamation and verse.[43] Although this ministry is distinct from the role of the cantor, the two ministries are often entrusted to the same person.

35.   Persons designated for the ministry of psalmist should "be accomplished in the art of singing Psalms and have a facility in public speaking and elocution."[44] As one who proclaims the Word, the psalmist should be able to proclaim the text of the Psalm with clarity, conviction, and sensitivity to the text, the musical setting, and those who are listening.

36.   The psalmist sings the verses of the Responsorial Psalm from the ambo or another suitable place.[45] The psalmist may dress in an alb or choir robe, but always wears clean, presentable, and modest clothing. Cassock and surplice, being clerical attire, are not recommended as vesture for the psalmist.

The Cantor

37.   The cantor is both a singer and a leader of congregational song. Especially when no choir is present, the cantor may sing in alternation or dialogue with

---

42. LFM, no. 56.
43. See LFM, no. 56.
44. GIRM, no. 102. See LFM, no. 56.
45. See GIRM, no. 61.

the assembly. For example, the cantor may sing the invocations of the *Kyrie*, intone the *Gloria*, lead the short acclamations at the end of the Scripture readings, intone and sing the verse of the Gospel Acclamation, sing the invocations of the Universal Prayer (Prayer of the Faithful), and lead the singing of the *Agnus Dei*. The cantor may also sing the verses of the Psalm or song that accompany the Entrance, Preparation of the Gifts, and Communion. Finally, the cantor may serve as psalmist, leading and proclaiming the verses of the Responsorial Psalm.

38.   As a leader of congregational song, the cantor should take part in singing with the entire gathered assembly. In order to promote the singing of the liturgical assembly, the cantor's voice should not be heard above the congregation. As a transitional practice, the voice of the cantor might need to be amplified to stimulate and lead congregational singing when this is still weak. However, as the congregation finds its voice and sings with increasing confidence, the cantor's voice should correspondingly recede. At times, it may be appropriate to use a modest gesture that invites participation and clearly indicates when the congregation is to begin, but gestures should be used sparingly and only when genuinely needed.

39.   Cantors should lead the assembly from a place where they can be seen by all without drawing attention from the liturgical action. When, however, a congregation is singing very familiar responses, acclamations, or songs that do not include verses for the cantor alone, the cantor need not be visible.

40.   The cantor exercises his or her ministry from a conveniently located stand, but not from the ambo.[46] The cantor may dress in an alb or choir robe, but always in clean, presentable, and modest clothing. Cassock and surplice, being clerical attire, are not recommended as vesture for the cantor.

The Organist and the Other Instrumentalists

41.   The primary role of the organist, other instrumentalists, or instrumental ensemble is to lead and sustain the singing of the assembly and of the choir, cantor, and psalmist, without dominating or overpowering them.

42.   The many voices of the organ and of instrumental ensembles, with their great range of expression, add varied and colorful dimensions to the song of the assembly, especially with the addition of harmonization.

43.   Those with the requisite talent and training should be encouraged to continue the musical tradition of improvisation. The liturgical action may call for improvisation, for example, when a congregational hymn or choral piece concludes before the ritual action is completed. The art of improvisation requires its own special talent and training. More than mere background sound is called for. When worthy improvisation is not possible, it is recommended that musicians play quality published literature, which is available at all levels of difficulty.

---

46. See LFM, no. 33.

44.   There are also times when the organ or other instruments may be played alone, such as a prelude before the Mass, an instrumental piece during the Preparation of the Gifts, a recessional if there is no closing song, or a postlude following a closing song.

The Director of Music Ministries

45.   A professional director of music ministries, or music director, provides a major service by working with the bishop or pastor to oversee the planning, coordination, and ministries of the parish or diocesan liturgical music program. The director of music ministries fosters the active participation of the liturgical assembly in singing; coordinates the preparation of music to be sung at various liturgical celebrations; and promotes the ministries of choirs, psalmists, cantors, organists, and all who play instruments that serve the Liturgy. In the present day, many potential directors of music are not of our faith tradition. It is significant as we go forward that directors of music are properly trained to express our faith traditions effectively and with pastoral sensitivity.

46.   Since every ministry is rooted in the Sacraments of Initiation, which form the People of God into "a community of disciples formed by and for the mission of Christ,"[47] the director of music ministries has a role that "finds its place within the communion of the Church and serves the mission of Christ in the Spirit."[48]

47.   Directors of music ministries and other lay ecclesial ministers exercise their role in relation both to the ordained and to the community of the faithful. Directors are collaborators with bishops, priests, and deacons, who exercise a pastoral ministry based on the Sacrament of Holy Orders, which configures them to Christ the Head and consecrates them for a role that is unique and necessary for the communion of the Church.[49] At the same time, lay ecclesial ministers are members of the lay faithful, "sharing in the common priesthood of all the baptized" and "called to discipleship."[50]

F. LEADERSHIP AND FORMATION

48.   The whole assembly is actively involved in the music of the Liturgy. Some members of the community, however, are recognized for the special gifts they exhibit in leading the musical praise and thanksgiving of Christian assemblies. These are the liturgical musicians, as described in section E, above, and their ministry is especially cherished by the Church.

49.   Liturgical musicians are first of all disciples, and only then are they ministers. Joined to Christ through the Sacraments of Initiation, musicians belong to the assembly of the baptized faithful; they are worshipers above all else. Like

---

47. USCCB, *Co-Workers in the Vineyard of the Lord: A Resource for Guiding the Development of Lay Ecclesial Ministry* (CVL) (Washington, DC: USCCB, 2005), 21.

48. CVL, 17.

49. See CVL, 21ff.; CCC, no. 1581.

50. CVL, 25.

other baptized members of the assembly, pastoral musicians need to hear the Gospel, experience conversion, profess faith in Christ, and so proclaim the praise of God. Thus, musicians who serve the Church at prayer are not merely employees or volunteers. They are ministers who share the faith, serve the community, and express the love of God and neighbor through music.

50. All pastoral musicians—professional or volunteer, full-time or part-time, director or choir member, cantor or instrumentalist—exercise a genuine liturgical ministry.[51] The community of the faithful has a right to expect that this service will be provided competently. Pastoral musicians should receive appropriate formation that is based on their baptismal call to discipleship; that grounds them in a love for and knowledge of Scripture, Catholic teaching, Liturgy, and music; and that equips them with the musical, liturgical, and pastoral skills to serve the Church at prayer.

51. Preparation for music ministry should include appropriate human formation, spiritual formation, intellectual formation, and pastoral formation.[52] Bishops and pastors should encourage liturgical musicians to take part in ministerial formation opportunities offered by universities, colleges, seminaries, ministry formation programs, dioceses, and national ministry associations. Parishes and dioceses should provide the financial support needed to ensure competent liturgical musical leadership.

52. The service of pastoral musicians should be recognized as a valued and integral part of the overall pastoral ministry of the parish or diocese; provision should be made for just compensation. Professional directors of music ministries and part-time pastoral music ministers should each receive appropriate wages and benefits that affirm the dignity of their work.[53]

53. Liturgical music ministers should be provided with the proper resources to carry out their administrative functions in a professional manner.

G. MUSIC IN CATHOLIC SCHOOLS

54. Catholic educational institutions have a special obligation toward music and the Sacred Liturgy. Catholic schools are called to foster the joy of singing and making music, to cultivate the repertoire of sacred music inherited from the past, to engage the creative efforts of contemporary composers and the diverse repertoires of various cultures, and to celebrate the Sacred Liturgy worthily.

55. Catholic grade schools and high schools, which sometimes have students from several parishes and a variety of faith traditions, should at a minimum help all of their students to become singers. Singing should be a regular part of the school day, e.g., in homeroom, in music classes, and at school assemblies. School Liturgies, while appropriate to the age level of the participants, should

---

51. See SC, no. 29.
52. CVL, 33–53.
53. CVL, 63.

follow the prescriptions of nos. 110–114 in this document, and the other relevant guidelines on sacred music. Choirs should be promoted, and their ministry should be employed regularly at school Liturgies in accord with nos. 28–33. A variety of musical styles is recommended at school Liturgies, while care should be taken to include selections from the repertoire typically sung by the wider Church at Sunday Liturgies. In this way, students will be introduced to music they will sing throughout their life, and they will be better prepared for their eventual role as adult members of the worshiping assembly.

56.　Catholic colleges and universities show that they come "from the heart of the Church"[54] especially in their worthy celebration of the Church's Liturgy, which should be a priority at every Catholic school. Catholic institutions of higher education should cultivate a high level of musical skill and a broad range of repertoire at campus Liturgies, and they should strive to make use of the talents of the entire academic community, especially music students and faculty, while taking care to include selections from the repertoire typically sung by the wider Church at Sunday Liturgies.

H. DIVERSE CULTURES AND LANGUAGES

57.　Even as the liturgical music of the Western European tradition is to be remembered, cherished, and used, the rich cultural and ethnic heritage of the many peoples of our country must also be recognized, fostered, and celebrated. Cultural pluralism has been the common heritage of all Americans, and "the Catholic community is rapidly re-encountering itself as an immigrant Church."[55] "The cultural gifts of the new immigrants" are "taking their place alongside those of older generations of immigrants,"[56] and this calls for interaction and collaboration between peoples who speak various languages and celebrate their faith in the songs and musical styles of their cultural, ethnic, and racial roots. In order to do so effectively, music publishers need to be encouraged to offer multilingual options for use which would be more expressive of our unity amidst such great diversity.

58.　Liturgical music must always be chosen and sung "with due consideration for the culture of peoples and abilities of each liturgical assembly."[57] Immigrants should be welcomed and should be provided with the resources they need to worship in their own language. "Religious singing by the faithful is to be intelligently fostered so that in devotions and sacred exercises as well as in liturgical services, the voices of the faithful may be heard, in conformity with the norms and requirements of the rubrics."[58] However, as the second generation of an immigrant group comes to maturity in the worshiping assembly, bilingual (native

---

54. See John Paul II, Apostolic Constitution *Ex Corde Ecclesiae (On Catholic Colleges and Universities)* (1990).

55. USCCB, *Welcoming the Stranger: Unity in Diversity* (Washington, DC: USCCB, 2000), 7.

56. *Welcoming the Stranger*, 16.

57. GIRM, no. 40.

58. SC, no. 118.

language and English) resources and songs are needed to promote participation of the multicultural and multigenerational assembly.

59.   As dioceses, parishes, and neighborhoods become increasingly diverse, the different cultural groups strive for some expression of unity. In a spirit of hospitality, local worshiping communities are encouraged to develop bicultural or multicultural celebrations from time to time that reflect the changing face of the Church in America. When prepared with an attitude of mutual reciprocity, local communities might eventually expand from those celebrations that merely highlight their multicultural differences to celebrations that better reflect the intercultural relationships of the assembly and the unity that is shared in Christ. Likewise, the valuable musical gifts of the diverse cultural and ethnic communities should enrich the whole Church in the United States by contributing to the repertory of liturgical song and to the growing richness of Christian faith.

60.   Liturgical music today must reflect the multicultural diversity and intercultural relationships of the members of the gathered liturgical assembly. The varied use of musical forms such as ostinato refrains, call and response, song translations, and bilingual or multilingual repertoire can assist in weaving the diverse languages and ethnicities of the liturgical assembly into a tapestry of sung praise. Liturgical leaders and musicians should encourage not only the use of traditional music of other languages and peoples, but also the incorporation of newly composed liturgical music appropriate to various cultural expressions in harmony with the theological meaning of the rites. Care should be taken, however, to choose appropriate hymns in other languages so as to avoid an expression that could be misconstrued as tokenism.

I. LATIN IN THE LITURGY

61.   The use of the vernacular is the norm in most liturgical celebrations in the dioceses of the United States "so that the people may more fully understand the mystery which is celebrated."[59] However, care should be taken to foster the role of Latin in the Liturgy, particularly in liturgical song. Pastors should ensure "that the faithful may also be able to say or to sing together in Latin those parts of the Ordinary of the Mass which pertain to them."[60] They should be able to sing these parts of the Mass proper to them, at least according to the simpler melodies.

62.   At international and multicultural gatherings of different language groups, it is most appropriate to celebrate the Liturgy in Latin, "with the exception of the readings, the homily and the prayer of the faithful."[61] In addition, "selections of Gregorian chant should be sung" at such gatherings, whenever possible.[62]

---

59. GIRM, no. 12.

60. SC, no. 54; see MS, no. 47; Sacred Congregation for Rites, *Inter Oecumenici (Instruction on the Proper Implementation of the Constitution on the Sacred Liturgy)*, no. 59, in Flannery, Vatican Council II.

61. Pope Benedict XVI, Post-Synodal Apostolic Exhortation *Sacramentum Caritatis (The Sacrament of Charity)* (SacCar) (Washington, DC: USCCB, 2007), no. 62.

62. SacCar, no. 62.

63.   To facilitate the singing of texts in Latin, the singers should be trained in its correct pronunciation and understand its meaning. To the greatest extent possible and applicable, singers and choir directors are encouraged to deepen their familiarity with the Latin language.

64.   Whenever the Latin language poses an obstacle to singers, even after sufficient training has been provided—for example, in pronunciation, understanding of the text, or confident rendition of a piece—it would be more prudent to employ a vernacular language in the Liturgy.

65.   Seminarians should "receive the preparation needed to understand and to celebrate Mass in Latin, and also to use Latin texts and execute Gregorian chant."[63]

66.   In promoting the use of Latin in the Liturgy, pastors should always "employ that form of participation which best matches the capabilities of each congregation."[64]

III. THE MUSIC OF CATHOLIC WORSHIP

A. DIFFERENT KINDS OF MUSIC FOR THE LITURGY

Music for the Sacred Liturgy

67.   "Sacred music is to be considered the more holy the more closely connected it is with the liturgical action, whether making prayer more pleasing, promoting unity of minds, or conferring greater solemnity upon the sacred rites."[65] This holiness involves *ritual* and *spiritual* dimensions, both of which must be considered within *cultural* context.

68.   The *ritual dimension* of sacred music refers to those ways in which it is "connected with the liturgical action" so that it accords with the structure of the Liturgy and expresses the shape of the rite. The musical setting must allow the rite to unfold with the proper participation of the assembly and its ministers, without overshadowing the words and actions of the Liturgy.

69.   The *spiritual dimension* of sacred music refers to its inner qualities that enable it to add greater depth to prayer, unity to the assembly, or dignity to the ritual. Sacred music is holy when it mediates the holiness of God and forms the Holy People of God more fully into communion with him and with each other in Christ.

70.   The *cultural context* refers to the setting in which the ritual and spiritual dimensions come into play. Factors such as the age, spiritual heritage, and cultural and ethnic background of a given liturgical assembly must be considered. The choice of individual compositions for congregational participation will often

---

63. SacCar, no. 62.
64. MS, no. 47.
65. SC, no. 112.

depend on those ways in which a particular group finds it best to join their hearts and minds to the liturgical action.

71.   With gratitude to the Creator for giving humanity such a rich diversity of musical styles, the Church seeks to employ only that which, in a given style, meets the ritual-spiritual demands of the Liturgy. In discerning the sacred quality of liturgical music, liturgical musicians will find guidance in music from the Church's treasury of sacred music, which is of inestimable value and which past generations have found suitable for worship.[66] They also should strive to promote a fruitful dialogue between the Church and the modern world.[67]

Gregorian Chant

72.   "The Church recognizes Gregorian chant as being specially suited to the Roman Liturgy. Therefore, other things being equal, it should be given pride of place in liturgical services."[68] Gregorian chant is uniquely the Church's own music. Chant is a living connection with our forebears in the faith, the traditional music of the Roman rite, a sign of communion with the universal Church, a bond of unity across cultures, a means for diverse communities to participate together in song, and a summons to contemplative participation in the Liturgy.

73.   The "pride of place" given to Gregorian chant by the Second Vatican Council is modified by the important phrase "other things being equal."[69] These "other things" are the important liturgical and pastoral concerns facing every bishop, pastor, and liturgical musician. In considering the use of the treasures of chant, pastors and liturgical musicians should take care that the congregation is able to participate in the Liturgy with song. They should be sensitive to the cultural and spiritual milieu of their communities, in order to build up the Church in unity and peace.

74.   The Second Vatican Council directed that the faithful be able to sing parts of the Ordinary of the Mass together in Latin.[70] In many worshiping communities in the United States, fulfilling this directive will mean introducing Latin chant to worshipers who perhaps have not sung it before. While prudence, pastoral sensitivity, and reasonable time for progress are encouraged to achieve this end, every effort in this regard is laudable and highly encouraged.

75.   Each worshiping community in the United States, including all age groups and all ethnic groups, should, at a minimum, learn *Kyrie XVI, Sanctus XVIII,*

---

66. See SC, no. 112.

67. "New art forms adapted to our times and in keeping with the characteristics of different nations and regions should be acknowledged by the Church. They may also be brought into the sanctuary whenever they raise the mind up to God with suitable forms of expression and in conformity with liturgical requirements" (GS, no. 62).

68. SC, no. 116.

69. MS, no. 50a, further specifies that chant has pride of place "in sung liturgical services celebrated in Latin."

70. "Steps should be taken enabling the faithful to say or to sing together in Latin those parts of the Ordinary of the Mass belonging to them" (SC, no. 54).

and *Agnus Dei XVIII*, all of which are typically included in congregational worship aids. More difficult chants, such as *Gloria VIII* and settings of the *Credo* and *Pater Noster*, might be learned after the easier chants have been mastered.[71]

76.   "The assembly of the faithful should participate in singing the Proper of the Mass as much as possible, especially through simple responses and other suitable settings."[72] When the congregation does not sing an antiphon or hymn, proper chants from the *Graduale Romanum* might be sung by a choir that is able to render these challenging pieces well. As an easier alternative, chants of the *Graduale Simplex* are recommended. Whenever a choir sings in Latin, it is helpful to provide the congregation with a vernacular translation so that they are able to "unite themselves interiorly" to what the choir sings.[73]

77.   The Entrance and Communion antiphons are found in their proper place in the *Roman Missal*. Composers seeking to create musical arrangements of the appointed antiphons and Psalms may also draw from the *Graduale Romanum*, either in their entirety or in shortened refrains for the congregation or choir.

78.   Gregorian chant draws its life from the sacred text it expresses, and recent official chant editions employ revised notation suggesting natural speech rhythm rather than independent melodic principles.[74] Singers are encouraged to adopt a manner of singing sensitive to the Latin text.

79.   Missals in various languages provide vernacular chants inspired by Latin chant, or other melodies, for sung responses between ministers and people. For the sake of unity across the Church, musicians should not take it upon themselves to adjust or alter these melodies locally.

80.   Whenever strophic chant hymns are published with Latin or vernacular texts, their melodies should be drawn from the *Liber Hymnarius*.

The Composer and Music of Our Day

81.   The Church needs artists, and artists need the Church. In every age, the Church has called upon creative artists to give new voice to praise and prayer. Throughout history, God has continued to breathe forth his creative Spirit, making noble the work of musicians' hearts and hands. The forms of expression have been many and varied.

82.   The Church has safeguarded and celebrated these expressions for centuries. In our own day, she continues to desire to bring forth the new with the old.

---

71. See GIRM, no. 41. Further resources for congregational Latin chant are *Iubilate Deo* (Vatican City: Libreria Editrice Vaticana, 1986) and *Liber Cantualis* (Sablesur-Sarthe, France: Abbaye Saint-Pierre de Solesmes, 1983).

72. MS, no. 33.

73. MS, no. 15.

74. The Praenotanda to the 1983 *Liber Hymnarius* explains the flexible rhythms intended by the revised notation.

The Church joyfully urges composers and text writers to draw upon their special genius so that she can continue to augment the treasure house of sacred musical art.[75]

83.   The Church never ceases to find new ways to sing her love for God each new day. The Sacred Liturgy itself, in its actions and prayers, best makes known the forms in which compositions will continue to evolve. Composers find their inspiration in Sacred Scripture, and especially in the texts of the Sacred Liturgy, so that their works flow from the Liturgy itself.[76] Moreover, "to be suitable for use in the Liturgy, a sung text must not only be doctrinally correct, but must in itself be an expression of the Catholic faith." Therefore, "liturgical songs must never be permitted to make statements about faith which are untrue."[77] Only within this scriptural, liturgical, and creedal context is the composer who is aware of the Church's long journey through human history and "who is profoundly steeped in the *sensus Ecclesiae*" properly equipped "to perceive and express in melody the truth of the Mystery that is celebrated in the Liturgy."[78] No matter what the genre of music, liturgical beauty emanates directly from that mystery and is passed through the talents of composers to emerge in music of the assembled People of God.

84.   In the years immediately following the liturgical reforms of the Second Vatican Council, especially because of the introduction of vernacular language, composers and publishers worked to provide a new repertoire of music for indigenous language(s). In subsequent decades, this effort has matured, and a body of worthy vernacular liturgical music continues to develop, even though much of the early music has fallen into disuse. Today, as they continue to serve the Church at prayer, composers are encouraged to concentrate on craftsmanship and artistic excellence in all musical genres.

85.   The Church awaits an ever richer song of her entire gathered people. "The faith of countless believers has been nourished by melodies flowing from the hearts of other believers, either introduced into the Liturgy or used as an aid to dignified worship. In song, faith is experienced as vibrant joy, love, and confident expectation of the saving intervention of God."[79]

---

75. "Then every scribe who has been instructed in the kingdom of heaven is like the head of a household who brings from his storeroom both the new and the old" (Mt 13:52); see USCCB, *Directory on Music and the Liturgy*, awaiting confirmation from the Holy See.

76. Pope John Paul II voiced the charism and praised the work of creative artists in his 1999 *Letter to Artists* (LTA): "None can sense more deeply than you artists, ingenious creators of beauty that you are, something of the pathos with which God at the dawn of creation looked upon the work of his hands. A glimmer of that feeling has shone so often in your eyes when—like the artists of every age—. . . you have admired the work of your inspiration, sensing in it some echo of the mystery of creation with which God, the sole creator of all things, has wished in some way to associate you" (no. 1, *www.vatican.va/holy_father/john_paul_ii/letters/documents/hf_jp-ii_let_23041999_artists_en.html*).

77. USCCB, *Directory on Music and the Liturgy* (2006), awaiting confirmation from the Holy See.

78. Pope John Paul II, Chirograph of the Supreme Pontiff John Paul II for the Centenary of the Motu Proprio *Tra le Sollecitudini (On Sacred Music)*, no. 12, *www.vatican.va/holy_father/john_paul_ii/letters/2003/documents/hf_jp-ii_let_20031203_ musica-sacra_en.html*.

79. LTA, no. 12.

B. INSTRUMENTS

The Human Voice

86.   Of all the sounds of which human beings, created in the image and likeness of God, are capable, voice is the most privileged and fundamental. Musical instruments in the Liturgy are best understood as an extension of and support for the primary liturgical instrument, which is the human voice.

Musical Instruments

87.   Among all other instruments which are suitable for divine worship, the organ is "accorded pride of place"[80] because of its capacity to sustain the singing of a large gathered assembly, due to both its size and its ability to give "resonance to the fullness of human sentiments, from joy to sadness, from praise to lamentation." Likewise, "the manifold possibilities of the organ in some way remind us of the immensity and the magnificence of God."[81]

88.   In addition to its ability to lead and sustain congregational singing, the sound of the pipe organ is most suited for solo playing of sacred music in the Liturgy at appropriate moments. Pipe organs also play an important evangelical role in the Church's outreach to the wider community in sacred concerts, music series, and other musical and cultural programs. For all of these reasons, the place of the organ should be taken into account from the outset in the planning process for the building or renovation of churches.

89.   However, from the days when the Ark of the Covenant was accompanied in procession by cymbals, harps, lyres, and trumpets, God's people have, in various periods, used a variety of musical instruments to sing his praise.[82] Each of these instruments, born of the culture and the traditions of a particular people, has given voice to a wide variety of forms and styles through which Christ's faithful continue to join their voices to his perfect song of praise upon the Cross.

90.   Many other instruments also enrich the celebration of the Liturgy, such as wind, stringed, or percussion instruments "according to longstanding local usage, in so far as these are truly suitable for sacred use, or can be made suitable."[83]

Instrumental Music

91.   Although instruments are used in Christian worship primarily to lead and sustain the singing of assembly, choir, psalmist, and cantor, they may also, when appropriate, be played by themselves. Such instrumental music can assist the gathering assembly in preparing for worship in the form of a prelude. It may give

---

80. GIRM, no. 393.

81. Pope Benedict XVI, Greeting of the Holy Father on the Occasion of Blessing of the New Organ at Regensburg's Alte Kapelle, Regensburg, Germany (September 13, 2006), *www.vatican .va/holy_father/benedict_xvi/speeches/2006/september/documents/hf_ben-xvi_spe_20060913 _alte-kapelle-regensburg_en.html.*

82. 1 Chr 15:20–21.

83. GIRM, no. 393.

voice to the sentiments of the human heart through pieces played during the Liturgy and postludes after the Liturgy. Instrumentalists are to remember that the Liturgy calls for significant periods of silent reflection. Silence need not always be filled.

92.   Instrumentalists are encouraged to play pieces from the treasury of sacred music by composers of various eras and cultures. In addition, those with the requisite talent and training are encouraged to improvise, as described in no. 43.

Recorded Music

93.   Recorded music lacks the authenticity provided by a living liturgical assembly gathered for the Sacred Liturgy. While recorded music might be used advantageously outside the Liturgy as an aid in the teaching of new music, it should not, as a general norm, be used within the Liturgy.

94.   Some exceptions to this principle should be noted. Recorded music may be used to accompany the community's song during a procession outside and, when used carefully, in Masses with children. Occasionally, it might be used as an aid to prayer, for example, during long periods of silence in a communal celebration of reconciliation. However, recorded music should never become a substitute for the community's singing.

C. LOCATION OF MUSICIANS AND THEIR INSTRUMENTS

95.   Musicians and musical instruments should be located so as to enable proper interaction with the liturgical action, with the rest of the assembly, and among the various musicians. Ideally, ministers of music are located so as to enable their own full participation by being able to see and hear the Liturgy. In most cases, it will work best if musicians are in close proximity with each other—for example, by placing the organ console or keyboard close to the choir and to the cantor's stand.

96.   When not engaged in the direct exercise of their particular role, music ministers, like all ministers of the Liturgy, remain attentive members of the gathered assembly and should never constitute a distraction.

97.   The cantor should generally be located in front of the congregation to lead the singing. When a congregation is able to sing on its own, either in response to the priest or ministers or through instrumental leadership, the cantor does not need to be visible. The Responsorial Psalm is usually proclaimed from the ambo or another location that is visible to the assembly. The psalmist, therefore, should sit in a place where the ambo is easily accessible.

98.   The placement of the choir should show the choir members' presence as a part of the worshiping community, yet serving in a unique way. Acoustical considerations will also play a role in determining the best location for the choir.

99.   Placement of the organ console and pipes, speakers of amplified instruments, and acoustic instruments such as the piano is determined both by visual considerations, so that there is no distraction from the liturgical action, and by acoustical considerations, so that the sound can support the congregation and so that the instrumentalist is readily able to accompany cantors, psalmists, and choirs.

100. If the space occupied by the choir and instruments is visible to the assembly, it must reflect the sacredness of the music ministry. Any appearance of clutter or disorganization must be avoided. Just as no one would tolerate stacks of books and papers in the sanctuary, the music ministry space should be free from clutter.

D. ACOUSTICS

101. Acoustics refers to the quality of a space for sustaining sound, especially its generation, transmission, and reception. While individual ministers of the Liturgy, ensembles, and even choirs can be sound-enhanced through amplification methods, the only amplification of the singing assembly comes from the room itself. Given the primacy of the assembly's song among all musical elements of the Liturgy, the acoustical properties of the worship space are critical. For this reason, specialists in acoustics should be consulted when building or modifying liturgical space.

102. If each member of the assembly senses his or her voice joined to the entire community in a swell of collective sound, the acoustics are well suited to the purpose of a gathered community engaged in sung prayer. If, on the other hand, each person hears primarily only his or her own voice, the acoustics of the space are fundamentally deficient.

103. Sound-absorbing building materials include carpet, porous ceiling tiles, soft wood, untreated soft stone, cast concrete or cinder block, and padded seating. Avoiding excessive use of such materials makes it easier to achieve the ideal of many voices united in song.[84]

104. The acoustics of a church or chapel should be resonant so that there is no need for excessive amplification of musical sound in order to fill the space and support the assembly's song. When the acoustics of the building naturally support sound, acoustic instruments and choirs generally need no amplification. An acoustically dead space precipitates a high cost of sound reinforcement, even for the organ.

E. COPYRIGHTS AND PARTICIPATION AIDS

105. Many published works are protected by national and international copyright laws, which are intended to ensure that composers, text writers, publishers, and their employees receive a fair return for their work. Churches and other

---

84. See USCCB, *Built of Living Stones: Art, Architecture, and Worship* (BLS) (Washington, DC: USCCB, 2000), no. 200.

institutions have a legal and moral obligation to seek proper permissions and to pay for reprinting of published works when required, even if copies are intended only for the use of the congregation.

106. Many publishers provide licenses and other convenient ways for obtaining permission for reprinting texts and music for the use of a liturgical assembly. Pastors, directors of music ministries, and other pastoral musicians need to be informed about the legal requirements for copying printed and recorded music, and they should act with a sense of justice.

107. The United States Conference of Catholic Bishops has delegated to the Committee on Divine Worship the responsibility of overseeing the publication of liturgical books that describe and guide the reformed rites developed in the years since the Second Vatican Council. In light of this responsibility, *Guidelines for the Publication of Participation Aids* has been developed for publishers of popular participation materials.

108. Hymns, songs, and acclamations written for the liturgical assembly are approved for use in the Liturgy by the bishop of the diocese wherein they are published, in order to ensure that these texts truly express the faith of the Church with theological accuracy and are appropriate to the liturgical context.

109. Composers who set liturgical texts to musical settings must respect the integrity of the approved text. Only with the approval of the USCCB Secretariat of Divine Worship may minor adaptations be made to approved liturgical texts.[85]

IV. PREPARING MUSIC FOR CATHOLIC WORSHIP

A. WHAT PARTS DO WE SING?

The Principle of Progressive Solemnity

110. Music should be considered a normal and ordinary part of the Church's liturgical life. However, the use of music in the Liturgy is always governed by the principle of progressive solemnity.

111. Progressive solemnity means that "between the solemn, fuller form of liturgical celebration, in which everything that demands singing is in fact sung, and the simplest form, in which singing is not used, there can be various degrees according to the greater or lesser place allotted to singing."[86]

112. Progressive solemnity includes not only the nature and style of the music, but how many and which parts of the rite are to be sung. For example, greater feasts such as Easter Sunday or Pentecost might suggest a chanted Gospel, but

---

85. See Bishops' Committee on the Liturgy (BCL), *Policy for Approval of Sung Settings of Liturgical Texts*, in *Thirty-Five Years of the BCL Newsletter* (Washington, DC: USCCB, 2004), 1527–1528.

86. MS, no. 7. See *General Instruction of the Liturgy of the Hours* (GILH) (Washington, DC: USCCB, 2002), nos. 271–273.

a recited Gospel might be more appropriate for Ordinary Time. Musical selections and the use of additional instruments reflect the season of the liturgical year or feast that is being celebrated.

113. Solemnities and feasts invite more solemnity. Certain musical selections are more capable of expressing this solemnity, adding an extraordinary richness to these special celebrations. Such solemnity, however, should never be allowed to devolve to an empty display of ceremony.[87] The most solemn musical expressions retain their primary responsibility of engaging human hearts in the mystery of Christ that is being celebrated on a particular occasion by the Church.

114. At other times, the liturgical season calls for a certain musical restraint. In Advent, for example, musical instruments should be used with moderation and should not anticipate the full joy of the Nativity of the Lord. In Lent, musical instruments should be used only to support the singing of the gathered assembly.[88]

The Parts to Be Sung

115. Singing by the gathered assembly and ministers is important at all celebrations. Not every part that can be sung should necessarily be sung at every celebration; rather "preference is to be given to those [parts] that are of greater importance."[89]

a.   *Dialogues and Acclamations*

Among the parts to be sung, preference should be given "especially to those which are to be sung by the Priest or the Deacon or a reader, with the people replying, or by the Priest and people together."[90] This includes dialogues such as *God, come to my assistance. Lord make haste to help me* in the Office, or *The Lord be with you. And with your spirit* in the Mass. The dialogues of the Liturgy are fundamental because they "are not simply outward signs of communal celebration but foster and bring about communion between Priest and people."[91] By their nature, they are short and uncomplicated and easily invite active participation by the entire assembly. Every effort should therefore be made to introduce or strengthen as a normative practice the singing of the dialogues between the priest, deacon, or lector and the people. Even the priest with very limited singing ability is capable of chanting *The Lord be with you* on a single pitch.

The acclamations of the Eucharistic Liturgy and other rites arise from the whole gathered assembly as assents to God's Word and action. The Eucharistic acclamations include the Gospel Acclamation, the *Sanctus,*

---

87. "It should be borne in mind that the true solemnity of liturgical worship depends less on a more ornate form of singing and a more magnificent ceremonial than on its worthy and religious celebration, which takes into account the integrity of the liturgical celebration itself, and the performance of each of its parts according to their own particular nature" (MS, no. 11).

88. See GIRM, no. 313. Exceptions are *Laetare* Sunday, solemnities, and feasts, when a more abundant use of musical instruments is usually appropriate.

89. GIRM, no. 40.

90. GIRM, no. 40; MS, nos. 7 and 16.

91. GIRM, no. 34.

the Memorial Acclamation, and the Great Amen. They are appropriately sung at any Mass, including daily Mass and any Mass with a smaller congregation. Ideally, the people should know the acclamations by heart and should be able to sing them readily, even without accompaniment.

b. *Antiphons and Psalms*

The Psalms are poems of praise that are meant, whenever possible, to be sung.[92] The Psalter is the basic songbook of the Liturgy. Tertullian witnesses to this when he says that in the assemblies of the Christians, "the Scriptures are read, the psalms are sung, sermons are preached."[93] Psalms have a prominent place in every Office of the Liturgy of the Hours.[94]

The Responsorial Psalm in the Liturgy of the Word of the Mass and of other rites "has great liturgical and pastoral importance, since it fosters meditation on the Word of God."[95] The Entrance and Communion chants with their Psalm verses serve to accompany the two most important processions of the Mass: the entrance procession, by which the Mass begins, and the Communion procession, by which the faithful approach the altar to receive Holy Communion. Participation in song on the part of the assembly is commended during both of these important processions, as the People of God gather at the beginning of Mass and as the faithful approach the holy altar to receive the Body and Blood of the Lord.

c. *Refrains and Repeated Responses*

The Liturgy also has texts of a litanic character that may be sung as appropriate. These include the *Kyrie* and *Agnus Dei* of the Mass, the response to the Prayer of the Faithful at Mass or the intercessions at Morning Prayer and Evening Prayer, and the Litany of the Saints in various rites.

d. *Hymns*

A hymn is sung at each Office of the Liturgy of the Hours, which is the original place for strophic hymnody in the Liturgy. At Mass, in addition to the *Gloria* and a small number of strophic hymns in the *Roman Missal* and *Graduale Romanum*, congregational hymns of a particular nation or group that have been judged appropriate by the competent authorities mentioned in the GIRM, nos. 48, 74, and 87, may be admitted to the Sacred Liturgy. Church legislation today permits as an option the use of vernacular hymns at the Entrance, Preparation of the Gifts, Communion, and Recessional. Because these popular hymns are fulfilling a properly liturgical role, it is especially important that they be appropriate to the liturgical action. In accord with an uninterrupted history of nearly five centuries,

---

92. See GIRM, no. 61.

93. MSD, no. 10; Tertullian, *De anima*, ch. 9; PL II, 701; and Apol. 39; PL I, 540.

94. "In the liturgy of the hours the Church in large measure prays through the magnificent songs that the Old Testament authors composed under the inspiration of the Holy Spirit. The origin of these verses gives them great power to raise the mind to God, to inspire devotion, to evoke gratitude in times of favor, and to bring consolation and courage in times of trial" (GILH, no. 100).

95. GIRM, no. 61.

nothing prevents the use of some congregational hymns coming from other Christian traditions, provided that their texts are in conformity with Catholic teaching and they are appropriate to the Catholic Liturgy.

116. At daily Mass, the above priorities should be followed as much as possible, in this order: dialogues and acclamations (Gospel Acclamation, *Sanctus*, Memorial Acclamation, Amen); litanies (*Kyrie, Agnus Dei*); Responsorial Psalm, perhaps in a simple chanted setting; and finally, a hymn or even two on more important days. Even when musical accompaniment is not possible, every attempt should be made to sing the acclamations and dialogues.

117. Proper antiphons from the liturgical books are to be esteemed and used especially because they are the very voice of God speaking to us in the Scriptures. Here, "the Father who is in heaven comes lovingly to meet his children, and talks with them. And such is the force and power of the Word of God that it can serve the Church as her support and vigor, and the children of the Church as strength for their faith, food for the soul, and a pure and lasting fount of spiritual life."[96] The Christian faithful are to be led to an ever deeper appreciation of the Psalms as the voice of Christ and the voice of his Church at prayer.[97]

Sacred Silence

118. Music arises out of silence and returns to silence. God is revealed both in the beauty of song and in the power of silence. The Sacred Liturgy has its rhythm of texts, actions, songs, and silence. Silence in the Liturgy allows the community to reflect on what it has heard and experienced, and to open its heart to the mystery celebrated. Ministers and pastoral musicians should take care that the rites unfold with the proper ebb and flow of sound and silence.[98] The importance of silence in the Liturgy cannot be overemphasized.

B. WHO PREPARES THE MUSIC FOR THE LITURGY?

119. Preparation for the celebration of the Sacred Liturgy, and particularly for the selection of what is to be sung at the Liturgy, is ultimately the responsibility of the pastor and of the priest who will celebrate the Mass.[99] At the same time, "in arranging the celebration of Mass, the Priest should be attentive rather to the common spiritual good of the People of God than to his own inclinations."[100]

120. In order that there "be harmony and diligence among all those involved in the effective preparation of each liturgical celebration in accordance with the

---

96. Second Vatican Council, *Dei Verbum (Dogmatic Constitution on Divine Revelation)* (DV) (1965), no. 21.

97. "The praying of the psalms . . . must be grasped with new warmth by the people of God. This will be achieved more readily if a deeper understanding of the psalms, in the meaning in which they are used in the liturgy, is more diligently promoted among the clergy and communicated to all the faithful by means of appropriate catechesis" (Paul VI, Apostolic Constitution *Laudis Canticum* [1970], no. 8).

98. See nos. 91, 94, 151, 176, 199, 209, 215, 243, and 249.

99. See GIRM, no. 111.

100. GIRM, no. 352.

Missal and other liturgical books,"[101] the pastor may designate that the director of music or a Liturgy or music committee meet regularly to make the preparations necessary for a good use of the available liturgical and musical options.

121. When a Liturgy or music committee is chosen to prepare music for the Liturgy, it should include persons with the knowledge and artistic skills needed in celebration: men and women trained in Catholic theology, Liturgy, and liturgical music and familiar with current resources in these areas. It is always good to include as consultants some members of the worshiping assembly so that their perspective is represented.

C. CARE IN THE CHOICE OF MUSIC FOR THE LITURGY

122. Music for the Liturgy must be carefully chosen and prepared. Such preparation should be characterized by "harmony and diligence . . . under the direction of the rector [or pastor] of the Church and after consultation with the faithful in things that directly pertain to them."[102] Effective preparation of liturgical song that fosters the maximum participation of the gathered assembly is a cooperative venture that respects the essential role of a variety of persons with mutual competencies.

123. Each particular liturgical celebration is composed of many variable verbal and non-verbal elements: proper prayers, scriptural readings, the liturgical season, the time of day, processional movement, sacred objects and actions, the socio-economic context in which the particular community is set, or even particular events impacting the life of the Christian faithful. Every effort should be made to lend such disparate elements a certain unity by the skillful and sensitive selection and preparation of texts, music, homily, movement, vesture, color, environment, and sacred objects and actions. This kind of ritual art requires that those who prepare the Liturgy approach it with artistic sensitivity and pastoral perspective.

124. Music does what words alone cannot do. It is capable of expressing a dimension of meaning and feeling that words alone cannot convey. While this dimension of an individual musical composition is often difficult to describe, its affective power should be carefully considered along with its textual component.

125. The role of music is to serve the needs of the Liturgy and not to dominate it, seek to entertain, or draw attention to itself or the musicians. However, there are instances when the praise and adoration of God leads to music taking on a far greater dimension. At other times, simplicity is the most appropriate response. The primary role of music in the Liturgy is to help the members of the gathered assembly to join themselves with the action of Christ and to give voice to the gift of faith.

---

101. GIRM, no. 111.
102. GIRM, no. 111.

D. JUDGING THE QUALITIES OF MUSIC FOR THE LITURGY

The Three Judgments: One Evaluation

126. In judging the appropriateness of music for the Liturgy, one will examine its liturgical, pastoral, and musical qualities. Ultimately, however, these three judgments are but aspects of one evaluation, which answers the question: "Is this particular piece of music appropriate for this use in this particular Liturgy?" All three judgments must be considered together, and no individual judgment can be applied in isolation from the other two. This evaluation requires cooperation, consultation, collaboration, and mutual respect among those who are skilled in any of the three judgments, be they pastors, musicians, liturgists, or planners.

The Liturgical Judgment

127. The question asked by this judgment may be stated as follows: Is this composition capable of meeting the structural and textual requirements set forth by the liturgical books for this particular rite?

128. Structural considerations depend on the demands of the rite itself to guide the choice of parts to be sung, taking into account the principle of progressive solemnity (see nos. 110ff. in this document). A certain balance among the various elements of the Liturgy should be sought, so that less important elements do not overshadow more important ones. Textual elements include the ability of a musical setting to support the liturgical text and to convey meaning faithful to the teaching of the Church.

129. A brief introduction to the aspects of music and the various liturgical rites is provided below in nos. 137ff. Pastoral musicians should develop a working familiarity with the requirements of each rite through a study of the liturgical books themselves.

The Pastoral Judgment

130. The pastoral judgment takes into consideration the actual community gathered to celebrate in a particular place at a particular time. Does a musical composition promote the sanctification of the members of the liturgical assembly by drawing them closer to the holy mysteries being celebrated? Does it strengthen their formation in faith by opening their hearts to the mystery being celebrated on this occasion or in this season? Is it capable of expressing the faith that God has planted in their hearts and summoned them to celebrate?

131. In the dioceses of the United States of America today, liturgical assemblies are composed of people of many different nations. Such peoples often "have their own musical tradition, and this plays a great part in their religious and social life. For this reason their music should be held in proper esteem and a suitable place is to be given to it, not only in forming their religious sense but also in adapting worship to their native genius. . . ."[103]

---

103. SC, no. 119.

132. Other factors—such as the age, culture, language, and education of a given liturgical assembly—must also be considered. Particular musical forms and the choice of individual compositions for congregational participation will often depend on those ways in which a particular group finds it easiest to join their hearts and minds to the liturgical action. Similarly, the musical experience of a given liturgical assembly is to be carefully considered, lest forms of musical expression that are alien to their way of worshiping be introduced precipitously. On the other hand, one should never underestimate the ability of persons of all ages, cultures, languages, and levels of education to learn something new and to understand things that are properly and thoroughly introduced.

133. The pastoral question, finally, is always the same: Will this composition draw this particular people closer to the mystery of Christ, which is at the heart of this liturgical celebration?

The Musical Judgment

134. The musical judgment asks whether this composition has the necessary aesthetic qualities that can bear the weight of the mysteries celebrated in the Liturgy. It asks the question: Is this composition technically, aesthetically, and expressively worthy?

135. This judgment requires musical competence. Only artistically sound music will be effective and endure over time. To admit to the Liturgy the cheap, the trite, or the musical cliché often found in secular popular songs is to cheapen the Liturgy, to expose it to ridicule, and to invite failure.

136. Sufficiency of artistic expression, however, is not the same as musical style, for "the Church has not adopted any particular style of art as her own. She has admitted styles from every period, in keeping with the natural characteristics and conditions of peoples and the needs of the various rites."[104] Thus, in recent times, the Church has consistently recognized and freely welcomed the use of various styles of music as an aid to liturgical worship.

V. THE MUSICAL STRUCTURE OF CATHOLIC WORSHIP

A. MUSIC AND THE STRUCTURE OF THE MASS

137.   Those responsible for preparing music for the celebration of the Eucharist in accord with the three preceding judgments must have a clear understanding of the structure of the Liturgy. They must be aware of what is of primary importance. They should know the nature of each of the parts of the Mass and the relationship of each part to the overall rhythm of the liturgical action.

138. The Mass is made up of the Liturgy of the Word and the Liturgy of the Eucharist. Although each has its own distinctive character, these two parts are so closely connected as to form one act of worship. "The Church is nourished

---

104. SC, no. 123.

spiritually at the twofold table of God's word and of the Eucharist:[105] from the one it grows in wisdom and from the other in holiness."[106] In addition, the Mass has introductory and concluding rites.

The Introductory Rites

139. The first part of the Mass consists of rites that "have the character of a beginning, an introduction, and a preparation."[107] They include an Entrance chant or song, the reverencing of the altar, a greeting of the people, Penitential Act and the *Kyrie* (or the Sprinkling Rite), *Gloria*, and Collect.

140. These rites are designed "to ensure that the faithful, who come together as one, establish communion and dispose themselves properly to listen to the Word of God and to celebrate the Eucharist worthily."[108] So that the people might come together as one, it is appropriate that they always sing at least one piece as a congregation in the introductory rites—Entrance song or chant, *Kyrie*, or *Gloria*—apart from the sung dialogues of the Liturgy.

141. On certain occasions, such as Palm Sunday, or when the other sacraments or rites are celebrated at Mass, some of these rites are omitted or celebrated in a particular manner that requires variations in the choice of music. Those responsible for the musical preparation of the Liturgy must be aware of these variations in practice.

THE ENTRANCE CHANT OR SONG

142. After the entire liturgical assembly has been gathered, an Entrance chant or song is sung as the procession with the priest, deacon, and ministers enters the church. The purpose of this chant "is to open the celebration, foster the unity of those who have been gathered, introduce their thoughts to the mystery of the liturgical time or festivity, and accompany the procession of the Priest and ministers."[109]

143. Care must be taken in the treatment of the texts of Psalms, hymns, and songs in the Liturgy. Verses and stanzas should not be omitted arbitrarily in ways that risk distorting their content. While not all musical pieces require that all verses or stanzas be sung, verses should be omitted only if the text to be sung forms a coherent whole.

144. The text and music for the Entrance song may be drawn from a number of sources.

> a. The singing of an antiphon and Psalm during the entrance procession has been a long-standing tradition in the Roman Liturgy. Antiphons and

---

105. See SC, no. 51; Second Vatican Council, *Presbyterorum Ordinis (Decree on the Ministry and Life of Priests)* (1965), no. 18; DV, no. 21; AG, no. 6; GIRM, no. 8.

106. LFM, no. 10.

107. GIRM, no. 46.

108. GIRM, no. 46.

109. GIRM, no. 47.

Psalms may be drawn from the official liturgical books—the *Graduale Romanum*, or the *Graduale Simplex*—or from other collections of antiphons and Psalms.

b. Other hymns and songs may also be sung at the Entrance, providing that they are in keeping with the purpose of the Entrance chant or song. The texts of antiphons, Psalms, hymns, and songs for the Liturgy must have been approved either by the United States Conference of Catholic Bishops or by the local diocesan bishop.[110]

THE PENITENTIAL ACT

145. After the greeting, the Penitential Act follows as the entire assembly prays a formula of general confession.[111] When the third form of the Penitential Act is sung (e.g., "You were sent to heal the contrite of heart: Lord, have mercy . . .") variable invocations of Christ's mercy may be chosen.[112]

THE *KYRIE ELEISON*

146. The ancient invocation *Kyrie* is a "chant by which the faithful acclaim the Lord and implore his mercy."[113] If the *Kyrie* is not included in the Penitential Act, it is sung or said immediately afterwards. It is usually sung in dialogue by the entire liturgical assembly with the choir or cantor.

THE BLESSING AND SPRINKLING OF WATER

147. "From time to time on Sundays, especially in Easter Time, instead of the customary Penitential Act, the blessing and sprinkling of water may take place as a reminder of Baptism."[114] The blessing of the water may be sung. The song accompanying the sprinkling with blessed water should have an explicitly baptismal character.

THE *GLORIA IN EXCELSIS*

148. "The *Gloria in excelsis (Glory to God in the highest)* is a most ancient and venerable hymn by which the Church, gathered in the Holy Spirit, glorifies and entreats God the Father and the Lamb. The text of this hymn may not be replaced by any other. . . . It is sung or said on Sundays outside Advent and Lent,

---

110. "This chant is sung alternately by the choir and the people or similarly by a cantor and the people, or entirely by the people, or by the choir alone. In the Dioceses of the United States of America, there are four options for the Entrance Chant: (1) the antiphon from the Missal or the antiphon with its Psalm from the *Graduale Romanum*, as set to music there or in another setting; (2) the antiphon and Psalm of the *Graduale Simplex* for the liturgical time; (3) a chant from another collection of Psalms and antiphons, approved by the Conference of Bishops or the Diocesan Bishop, including Psalms arranged in responsorial or metrical forms; (4) another liturgical chant that is suited to the sacred action, the day, or the time of year, similarly approved by the Conference of Bishops or the Diocesan Bishop" (GIRM, no. 48).

111. See GIRM, no. 51.

112. See GIRM, no. 52; see *The Roman Missal*, Appendix VI.

113. GIRM, no. 52.

114. GIRM, no. 51; see *The Roman Missal*, Appendix II.

and also on Solemnities and Feasts, and at particular celebrations of a more solemn character."[115]

149. The priest, or the cantor or choir, intones the *Gloria*. It is sung by all, by the people alternately with the choir or cantor, or by the choir alone. If not sung, it is recited either by all together or by two parts of the congregation in alternation. While through-composed settings of the *Gloria* give clearest expression to the text, the addition of refrains is permitted, provided the refrains encourage congregational participation.[116]

150. The *Gloria* may not be moved to a different part of the Mass than the one assigned by the *Roman Missal*. It may not, for example, be used in place of the Entrance chant or song, or during the sprinkling with blessed water.

THE COLLECT

151. The priest then invites all to pray and, after a brief silence, sings or says the Collect.[117] Even when the Collect is not sung, the conclusion to the prayer may be sung, along with the response by the people.

The Liturgy of the Word

152. The Liturgy of the Word consists of readings and responses from Sacred Scripture.[118] In receiving the Word of God with their hearts and minds, and in responding to it in song, "the people make this divine word their own."[119]

THE READINGS FROM SACRED SCRIPTURE

153. While the readings are ordinarily read in a clear, audible, and intelligent way,[120] they may also be sung. "This singing, however, must serve to bring out the sense of the words, not obscure them."[121]

154. Even if the readings are not sung, the concluding acclamation *The Word of the Lord* may be sung, even by someone other than the reader; all respond with the acclamation *Thanks be to God*. "In this way the assembled congregation pays reverence to the word of God it has listened to in faith and gratitude."[122]

THE RESPONSORIAL PSALM

155. The Responsorial Psalm follows the first reading. Because it is an integral part of the Liturgy of the Word, and is in effect a reading from Scripture, it has

---

115. GIRM, no. 53.
116. BCL, *Policy for the Approval of Sung Settings of Liturgical Texts*.
117. See GIRM, no. 54.
118. See GIRM, no. 55.
119. GIRM, no. 55.
120. See LFM, no. 14.
121. "On occasions when the readings are in Latin, the manner of singing given in the *Ordo cantus Missae* is to be maintained" (LFM, no. 14).
122. LFM, no. 18.

great liturgical and pastoral significance.[123] Corresponding to the reading that it follows, the Responsorial Psalm is intended to foster meditation on the Word of God. Its musical setting should aid in this, being careful to not overshadow the other readings.[124]

156. "As a rule the Responsorial Psalm should be sung."[125] Preferably, the Psalm is sung responsorially: "the psalmist, or cantor of the psalm, sings the psalm verses and the whole congregation joins in by singing the response."[126] If this is not possible, the Psalm is sung completely without an intervening response by the community.

157. The proper or seasonal Responsorial Psalm from the *Lectionary for Mass*, with the congregation singing the response, is to be preferred to the gradual from the *Graduale Romanum*.[127] When the Latin gradual is sung *in directum* (straight through) by choir alone, the congregation should be given a vernacular translation.

158. Because the Psalm is properly a form of sung prayer, "every means available in each individual culture is to be employed"[128] in fostering the singing of the Psalm at Mass, including the extraordinary options provided by the *Lectionary for Mass*. In addition to the proper or seasonal Psalm in the *Lectionary*, the Responsorial Psalm may also be taken from the *Graduale Romanum* or the *Graduale Simplex*, or it may be an antiphon and Psalm from another collection of the Psalms and antiphons, including Psalms arranged in paraphrase or in metrical form, providing that they have been approved by the United States Conference of Catholic Bishops or the diocesan bishop.

159. Songs or hymns that do not at least paraphrase a Psalm may never be used in place of the Responsorial Psalm.[129]

160. If it is not possible for the Psalm to be sung, the response alone may be sung, while the lector reads the intervening verses of the Psalm "in a manner conducive to meditation on the word of God."[130]

THE ACCLAMATION BEFORE THE GOSPEL

161. In the Gospel Acclamation, the assembled faithful welcome "the Lord who is about to speak to them."[131] The cantor may intone the Acclamation, which is repeated by the whole assembly. After the cantor or choir sings the verse, the

---

123. LFM, nos. 19–22; see GIRM, no. 61.
124. See LFM, no. 19.
125. LFM, no. 20.
126. LFM, no. 20.
127. "The Responsorial Psalm should correspond to each reading and should usually be taken from the Lectionary" (GIRM, no. 61; see LFM, nos. 20, 89).
128. LFM, no. 21.
129. See GIRM, no. 61.
130. LFM, no. 22; see LFM, no. 21.
131. LFM, no. 23.

entire assembly again sings the Acclamation. If there is a Gospel procession, the Acclamation may be repeated as often as necessary to accompany the Gospel procession. The verses are as a rule taken from the *Lectionary for Mass*.

162. The Gregorian settings of the Gospel Acclamation are most appropriate for use in those communities which are able to sing the response communally.[132]

163. During most of the church year, the *Alleluia* with the proper verse serves as the Gospel Acclamation. During the season of Lent, alternate acclamations with their proper verse are used, as found in *the Lectionary for Mass* (or, when there is only one reading before the Gospel, the Psalm alone may be used). The Gospel Acclamation may be omitted when it is not sung.

164. When there is only one reading before the Gospel, the Gospel Acclamation may be omitted; if it is a season in which the *Alleluia* is said, the *Alleluia* may be used as the response of the Psalm, or the Psalm with its proper response may be used followed by the *Alleluia* with its verse. The Gospel Acclamation may be omitted when it is not sung.[133]

THE SEQUENCE

165. The Sequence is a liturgical hymn that is sung before the Gospel Acclamation on certain days. On Easter Sunday (*Victimae paschali laudes*) and Pentecost Day (*Veni Sancte Spiritus*), the Sequence is required.[134] On the Solemnity of the Most Holy Body and Blood of the Lord (*Lauda Sion Salvatorem*) and Our Lady of Sorrows (*Stabat Mater*), the Sequence is optional.

166. The Sequence may be sung by all together, or in alternation between the congregation and choir and cantor, or by the choir or cantor alone. The text from the *Lectionary for Mass* may be used, or a metrical paraphrase may be sung, provided that it is found in an approved collection of liturgical songs.

THE GOSPEL

167. "Of all the rites connected with the Liturgy of the Word, the reverence due to the Gospel reading must receive special attention."[135]

168. While the Gospel is ordinarily proclaimed in a clear, audible, and intelligent way,[136] it may also be sung.[137] "This singing, however, must serve to bring out the sense of the words, not obscure them."[138]

---

132. GIRM, no. 62, "[The Gospel Acclamation] is sung by everybody, standing."
133. See GIRM, no. 63.
134. GIRM, no. 64.
135. LFM, no. 17.
136. LFM, no. 14.
137. On occasions when the Gospel is in Latin, the manner of singing given in the *Ordo cantus Missae* is to be maintained. (See LFM, no. 14.)
138. LFM, no. 14.

169. "Even if the Gospel itself is not sung, it is appropriate for the greeting *The Lord be with you*, and *A reading from the holy Gospel according to* . . . , and at the end *The Gospel of the Lord* to be sung, in order that the congregation may also sing its acclamations. This is a way both of bringing out the importance of the Gospel reading and of stirring up the faith of those who hear it."[139]

THE PROFESSION OF FAITH

170. The Creed or Profession of Faith is said by the entire assembly. Because it is an expression of faith by "the whole gathered people,"[140] the participation of all present should be carefully safeguarded, whether it is said or sung. "If it is sung, it is intoned by the Priest or, if appropriate, by a cantor or by the choir. It is then sung either by everybody together or by the people alternating with the choir."[141] The use of a congregational refrain may be helpful in this regard.

THE UNIVERSAL PRAYER

171. The Universal Prayer, or Prayer of the Faithful, consists of intercessions by which "the people respond in some sense to the Word of God which they have received in faith and, exercising the office of their baptismal Priesthood, offer prayers to God for the salvation of all."[142] Because it has the structure of a litany, and provided that it can be understood when sung, it is appropriate to sing the Prayer of the Faithful, or just the invitation and response, or even the response only.

The Liturgy of the Eucharist

172. The Liturgy of the Eucharist is made up of three main parts: the Preparation of the Gifts, the Eucharistic Prayer, and the Communion Rite.[143]

THE PREPARATION OF THE GIFTS: OFFERTORY PROCESSION

173. After the altar has been prepared, gifts of bread and wine are brought to the priest or deacon by members of the liturgical assembly. This procession is accompanied by an Offertory chant or song,[144] "which continues at least until the gifts have been placed on the altar."[145] The norms on the manner of singing are the same as for the Entrance chant (see nos. 142ff. in this document).

174. Even when there is no procession with the gifts, singing may still accompany the rites at the Offertory.[146] Instrumental music is also appropriate.

---

139. LFM, no. 17.
140. GIRM, no. 67.
141. GIRM, no. 68.
142. GIRM, no. 69. See LFM, nos. 31 and 53.
143. See GIRM, no. 72.
144. See GIRM, nos. 37b, 111.
145. GIRM, no. 74.
146. See GIRM, no. 74.

175. The priest then prays the Prayer over the Offerings. Even when the prayer is not sung, the conclusion to the prayer may be sung, along with the response by the people.

176. The Eucharistic Prayer is the center and summit of the entire celebration. Joining the people with himself, the priest prays the Eucharistic Prayer in the name of the entire assembly "to God the Father through Jesus Christ in the Holy Spirit."[147] Through the Eucharistic Prayer "the whole congregation of the faithful joins with Christ in confessing the great deeds of God and in the offering of Sacrifice. The Eucharistic Prayer requires that everybody listens to it with reverence and in silence,"[148] giving voice to their interior participation by joining in the Eucharistic acclamations.

177. The Eucharistic Prayer is a single liturgical act, consisting of several parts: an introductory dialogue, the thanksgiving or preface, the *Sanctus*, the calling down of the Holy Spirit (*epiclesis*), the institution narrative, the Memorial Acclamation, the anamnesis, the offering, the intercessions, and the doxology with its Amen.[149]

178. In order to make clear the ritual unity of the Eucharistic Prayer, it is recommended that there be a stylistic unity to the musical elements of the prayer, especially the *Sanctus*, the Memorial Acclamation, and the Great Amen. As much as possible, elements such as the preface dialogue and preface should be chanted at a pitch that best relates them to the key and modality of the other sung elements of the Eucharistic Prayer.

179. The Eucharistic Prayer begins with a dialogue between the priest and the people that expresses their communion with one another in offering the Eucharistic sacrifice. The faithful "give thanks to God and offer the unblemished sacrificial Victim not only by means of the hands of the Priest but also together with him."[150] Because the preface dialogue is among the most important dialogues of the Mass, it is very appropriate that it be sung, especially on Sundays and other solemn occasions.[151]

180. The people take part in the Eucharistic Prayer by listening attentively to the words sung or spoken by the priest and joining their hearts and minds to the actions of the prayer. Their voices should be joined together in the acclamations of the Eucharistic Prayer, including the *Sanctus*, the great cosmic acclamation of praise; the Memorial Acclamation, by which the faithful participate in keeping the memory of Christ's Paschal Mystery; and the Amen that follows the

---

147. GIRM, no. 78.
148. GIRM, no. 78.
149. See GIRM, no. 79.
150. GIRM, no. 95.
151. See GIRM, no. 40.

concluding doxology, by which they give assent to the entire prayer. These acclamations should be sung, especially on Sundays and solemnities.[152]

181. Because the Eucharistic Prayer is the central action of the entire celebration, priests should, if possible, sing at least those parts for which musical notation is provided in the *Roman Missal*, at least on Sundays and on more solemn occasions. These parts include the opening dialogue and the Preface, the invitation to the Memorial Acclamation, and the concluding doxology. It is not permitted to recite the Eucharistic Prayer inaudibly while the *Sanctus* is sung.

182. It is likewise appropriate for priests to sing the entire Eucharistic Prayer, especially on solemn occasions. The chant setting provided in the *Roman Missal* or another composition approved by the United States Conference of Catholic Bishops may be used. "While the Priest proclaims the Eucharistic Prayer 'there should be no other prayers or singing, and the organ or other musical instruments should be silent,' except for the people's acclamations."[153]

183. "It is a praiseworthy practice for the parts that are to be said by all the concelebrants together and for which musical notation is provided in the Missal to be sung."[154]

The Communion Rite

184. The high point of the Communion Rite is the reception of Holy Communion. This is preceded by rites that prepare the faithful to receive the Lord's Body and Blood as spiritual food.[155]

185. The Lord's Prayer and the Rite of Peace are followed by the Breaking of the Bread, "which in apostolic times gave the entire Eucharistic Action its name" and which "signifies that the many faithful are made one body (1 Cor 10:17) by receiving Communion from the one Bread of Life, which is Christ, who for the salvation of the world died and rose."[156] This Fraction Rite, accompanied by the *Agnus Dei* chant, is followed by the *Ecce Agnus Dei* and the reception of Holy Communion. The Communion Rite concludes with the Prayer after Communion.

THE LORD'S PRAYER

186. The rites of preparation for the reception of Holy Communion begin with the Lord's Prayer. When the Lord's Prayer is sung, the doxology should also be sung by all. If possible, the invitation and embolism should also be sung by the priest.

---

152. See GIRM, no. 40.
153. Congregation for Divine Worship and the Discipline of the Sacraments, *Redemptionis Sacramentum (Instruction on the Eucharist)*, no. 53 (Washington, DC: USCCB, 2004).
154. GIRM, no. 218.
155. See GIRM, no. 80.
156. GIRM, no. 83.

187.   The brief period of time needed for the exchange of the Rite of Peace must not be protracted by the singing of a song.

THE FRACTION OF THE BREAD AND THE *AGNUS DEI*

188.   The supplicatory chant *Agnus Dei* accompanies the Fraction Rite. It is "usually sung by the choir or cantor with the congregation replying; or at least recited aloud. This invocation accompanies the fraction of the bread and, for this reason, may be repeated as many times as necessary until the rite has been completed. The final time it concludes with the words *grant us peace*."[157] The *Agnus Dei* should not be prolonged unnecessarily (see GIRM, no. 83), nor may other texts be added to the chant.

THE COMMUNION CHANT OR SONG

189.   "While the Priest is receiving the Sacrament, the Communion Chant [or song] is begun, its purpose being to express the spiritual union of the communicants by means of the unity of their voices, to show gladness of heart, and to bring out more clearly the 'communitarian' character of the procession to receive the Eucharist."[158] The singing begins immediately and continues "for as long as the Sacrament is being administered to the faithful."[159] The Communion chant or song may be sung by the people with choir or cantor, or by the choir alone. Because the Communion chant expresses the unity of those processing and receiving the Holy Sacrament, communal singing is commendable. The singing of the people should be preeminent.

190.   There are several options for the Communion song or chant,[160] including the proper antiphon from the *Graduale Romanum*, a seasonal antiphon from the *Graduale Simplex*[161], an antiphon and Psalm from a collection approved for liturgical use, or another appropriate liturgical song.[162]

191.   In selecting a Communion song suitable for the Eucharistic banquet in which God's blessings are bestowed so abundantly, one should look for texts that have themes of joy, wonder, unity, gratitude, and praise. Following ancient Roman liturgical tradition, the Communion song might reflect themes of the

---

157. GIRM, no. 83.

158. GIRM, no. 86.

159. GIRM, no. 86.

160. "In the Dioceses of the United States of America, there are four options for singing at Communion: (1) the antiphon from the Missal or the antiphon with its Psalm from the *Graduale Romanum*, as set to music there or in another musical setting; (2) the antiphon with Psalm from the *Graduale Simplex* of the liturgical time; (3) a chant from another collection of Psalms and antiphons, approved by the Conference of Bishops or the Diocesan Bishop, including Psalms arranged in responsorial or metrical forms; (4) some other suitable liturgical chant (cf. no. 86) approved by the Conference of Bishops or the Diocesan Bishop. This is sung either by the choir alone or by the choir or a cantor with the people" (GIRM, no. 87).

161. Antiphons from the *Graduale Romanum* or *Graduale Simplex* might be sung in Latin or vernacular.

162. See GIRM, no. 87.

Gospel reading of the day. It is also appropriate to select a Communion processional song that reflects the liturgical action, i.e., eating and drinking the Body and Blood of Christ.

192. As a processional piece, the Communion chant or song presents particular challenges. The faithful are encouraged to grasp ever more deeply the essentially communitarian nature of the Communion procession. In order to foster participation of the faithful with "unity of voices," it is recommended that Psalms sung in the responsorial style, or songs with easily memorized refrains, be used. The refrains will generally need to be limited in number and repeated often, especially at the outset, so that they become familiar to the faithful.

193. When the Communion procession is lengthy, more than one piece of music might be desirable. In this case, there may be a combination of pieces for congregation and pieces for choir alone. Choirs with the requisite ability may sing the proper Communion chant from the *Graduale Romanum*, either in Gregorian chant or in a polyphonic setting, or other suitable choral pieces. Instrumental music may also be used to foster a spirit of unity and joy. If there is a hymn or song after Communion, the Communion music should be ended "in a timely manner."[163] A period of silent reflection for the entire congregation after the reception of Communion is also appropriate.

194. During the various seasons of the year, the Psalm or song during Communion should be chosen with the spirit of that season in mind. On most Sundays and other days, it would be appropriate to sing one of the Psalms that have long been associated with participation in the Eucharistic banquet, such as Psalms 23, 34, and 147. There is also a substantial repertory of liturgical songs that give expression to the joy and wonder of sharing in the Lord's Supper.

195. Care should be taken to ensure that the musicians (singers and instrumentalists), too, "can receive Communion with ease."[164] Since the Communion song begins while the priest is receiving the Sacrament, the singers and other musicians may receive Communion at or near the end of the procession.

SONG AFTER COMMUNION

196. "When the distribution of Communion is over, if appropriate, the Priest and faithful pray quietly for some time. If desired, a Psalm or other canticle of praise or a hymn may also be sung by the whole congregation."[165] The song after Communion should focus the assembly on the mystery of the Holy Communion in which it participates, and it should never draw undue attention to the choir or other musicians. The congregation may stand for the song after Communion if the nature of the music seems to call for it.

---

163. GIRM, no. 86.
164. GIRM, no. 86.
165. GIRM, no. 88.

197. The priest may sing the Prayer After Communion, or even just the concluding formula. At the conclusion of the prayer, the entire assembly sings the Amen as a sign of assent.

The Concluding Rites

198. Especially on Sundays and other solemn occasions, the blessing may be sung by the priest with the assembly singing the Amen, and the dismissal may be sung by the deacon or priest with the assembly singing *Thanks be to God*.

199. Although it is not necessary to sing a recessional hymn,[166] when it is a custom, all may join in a hymn or song after the dismissal. When a closing song is used, the procession of ministers should be arranged in such a way that it finishes during the final stanza. At times, e.g., if there has been a song after Communion, it may be appropriate to choose an option other than congregational song for the recessional. Other options include a choral or instrumental piece or, particularly during Lent, silence.

B. MUSIC AND THE OTHER SACRAMENTS

200. The liturgical books for the various rites offer suggested texts for many of the instances in which a song is suggested. While not mandatory, these suggested texts offer compositional opportunities for composers and, at the very least, indicate the nature of texts appropriate for specific moments in the rite.

The Sacraments of Initiation

201. "In the sacraments of Christian initiation we are freed from the power of darkness and joined to Christ's death, burial, and resurrection. We receive the Spirit of filial adoption and are part of the entire people of God in the celebration of the memorial of the Lord's death and resurrection."[167]

The Initiation of Adults

202. The Rite of Christian Initiation of Adults (RCIA) includes several major ritual celebrations that presuppose the presence and participation of the local community, given that "the initiation of adults is the responsibility of all the baptized."[168] Since singing is one of the most important forms of active participation in the Liturgy, it is important to choose sung responses, acclamations, antiphons, Psalms, and other songs that will enable the whole community to participate at the appropriate times.

203. In the Rite of Acceptance into the Order of Catechumens, often celebrated during Sunday Mass, the assembly may join in a Psalm or song while candidates, sponsors, ministers, and the community gather outside the church. The rite

---

166. See GIRM, no. 90.
167. "Christian Initiation: General Introduction," no. 1, in *Rite of Christian Initiation of Adults* (RCIA) (Washington, DC: USCCB, 1988); see AG, no. 14.
168. RCIA, no. 9.

indicates a sung acclamation as the candidates are signed with the cross, and then a Psalm or song as all enter the church for the Liturgy of the Word.

204. During the Rite of Election, ordinarily celebrated on the First Sunday of Lent, an appropriate Psalm or song may be sung during the enrollment of names, as catechumens sign the Book of the Elect.

205. The Scrutinies are ordinarily celebrated during the Sunday Masses of the Third, Fourth, and Fifth Sundays of Lent. The texts for these Masses are always drawn from Year A of the *Lectionary*. At the conclusion of the exorcism rite, all may join in singing an appropriate Psalm or song.

206. During the Easter Vigil, the three Sacraments of Initiation—Baptism, Confirmation, and the Eucharist—are ordinarily celebrated. The assembly should join in singing responses and acclamations during the Litany of the Saints, the acclamations for and at the conclusion of the blessing prayer over the baptismal water, and the acclamations following each Baptism. There may be a song between the celebration of Baptism and Confirmation, especially if the neophytes need to change into dry clothing or if there is a procession from the font to the sanctuary. A song may also be sung during Confirmation as the neophytes are anointed with chrism, especially if a large number of persons are being confirmed.

The Baptism of Children

207. It is important to recall the unique circumstances that often accompany the Baptism of children, along with the importance of singing envisioned by these rites. For this and certain other sacraments, cantors and other ministers will often need to develop the skill of leading unaccompanied singing.

208. In the beginning of the rite, "the people may sing a psalm or hymn suitable for the occasion" as the celebrating priest or deacon, accompanied by the ministers, "goes to the entrance of the church or the part of the church where the parents and godparents are waiting with those who are to be baptized."[169] After questioning the parents and godparents and signing the forehead of the children, the celebrant invites all those present to take part in the Liturgy of the Word. Then "there is a procession to the place where this will be celebrated, during which a song is sung, e.g., Psalm 85:7, 8, 9ab."[170]

209. After the homily or, if there is no homily, after the litany invoking the intercession of the saints, "it is desirable to have a period of silence while all pray at the invitation of the celebrant. If convenient, a suitable song follows."[171] After the prayer of exorcism and the anointing before Baptism, if the baptistery is located outside the church or is not in view of the congregation, all should

---

169. *Rite of Baptism for Children* (RBC), in *The Rites*, no. 35 (New York: Pueblo Publishing, 1976); see RBC, nos. 74, 107.
170. RBC, no. 42; see no. 80.
171. RBC, no. 46; see no. 83.

process to the baptistery while an appropriate song is sung, for example, Psalm 23.[172] The Rite of Baptism also allows for the possibility that the Profession of Faith may be followed by a suitable song "by which the community expresses its faith with a single voice."[173] Furthermore, after each Baptism, the rite indicates that "it is appropriate for the people to sing a short acclamation."[174]

210. Following the celebration of the sacrament, those who have been baptized are clothed in a white garment and given a candle, which has been lit from the Easter candle. If there is an exceptionally large number of children, the people may sing a song until each child has a candle.[175] Once this has been done, everyone processes to the altar while singing a "baptismal song."[176] Following the Lord's Prayer, the blessing, and the dismissal, "all may sing a hymn which suitably expresses thanksgiving and Easter joy, or they may sing the song of the Blessed Virgin Mary, the Magnificat."[177] Chapter VII in the *Rite of Baptism for Children* offers numerous acclamations and hymns that may be used during the Liturgy.[178]

The Baptism of Children During Sunday Mass

211. Baptism may be celebrated during Mass on Sunday, "so that the entire community may be present and the relationship between baptism and Eucharist may be clearly seen; but this should not be done too often."[179]

212. When the Rite of Baptism of Children is celebrated at Mass, music for the rite should be included. Among the parts that may be sung are an opening antiphon or processional song during the Introductory Rites; the intercessions and Litany of the Saints following the homily; and an acclamation following the Profession of Faith. Furthermore, after each child is baptized, the people may sing a short acclamation.

The Sacrament of Confirmation

213. Given this sacrament's importance, the *Rite of Confirmation* urges that "attention should be paid to the festive and solemn character of the liturgical service and its significance for the local church."[180] Since, as a rule, the celebration of Confirmation takes place within Mass, music during the Liturgy of Confirmation should follow the guidelines already mentioned above in nos. 137–199.[181]

---

172. See RBC, no. 52.
173. RBC, no. 59; see no. 96.
174. RBC, no. 60; see nos. 97, 125.
175. See RBC, no. 127.
176. RBC, no. 67; see no. 102.
177. RBC, no. 71; see nos. 106, 131.
178. See RBC, nos. 225–245.
179. RBC, no. 9.
180. *Rite of Confirmation* (RC) (Washington, DC: USCCB, 2006), no. 4.
181. See RC, no. 13.

214. Additionally, the *Rite of Confirmation* suggests that the Profession of Faith may be followed by a suitable song in which "the community may express its faith."[182] Likewise, one or more songs may be sung while the bishop anoints those to be confirmed, such as *Veni Creator Spiritus*.[183]

215. If the Sacrament of Confirmation is being celebrated outside Mass, in addition to the moments mentioned above, "all may sing a psalm or appropriate song" while the bishop goes to the sanctuary with the other ministers.[184] During the Liturgy of the Word, two or three readings are used following the traditional order (a reading from the Old Testament or the Acts of the Apostles [during the Easter season], an epistle from the New Testament, and a Gospel). "After the first and second reading there should be a psalm or song, or a period of silence may be observed."[185]

The Rite of Marriage

216. The lifelong bond established by the marriage covenant between a man and a woman derives its force from creation. Jesus Christ has raised this natural covenant to a higher dignity as a sacrament of the new and eternal covenant.[186] Above all else, the "grace of Christian marriage is a fruit of Christ's cross, the source of all Christian life."[187]

217. "According to the Latin tradition, the spouses as ministers of Christ's grace mutually confer upon each other the Sacrament of Matrimony by expressing their consent before the Church."[188] Therefore, while the celebration of marriage concerns the spouses and their families, it is not only a private matter. Since their consent is given in the presence of the Church, the celebration of marriage is governed by the appropriate liturgical norms. The Church desires that a person's wedding day be filled with joy and grace. When preparing the Liturgy, pastors should address any concerns with the couple with due pastoral sensitivity and sound judgment.

218. The preparation of the Liturgy must concern not only those involved but also the norms of the ritual itself.[189] The marriage Liturgy presents particular challenges and opportunities to planners. Both musicians and pastors should make every effort to assist couples to understand and share in the planning of their marriage Liturgy. Since oftentimes the only music familiar to the couple

---

182. RC, no. 23; see no. 40.

183. See RC, nos. 29, 46.

184. RC, no. 34.

185. RC, no. 37.

186. See *Code of Canon Law: Latin-English Edition: New English Translation* (*Codex Iuris Canonici*) (CIC) (Washington, DC: Canon Law Society of America, 1998), can. 1055, §1; GS, no. 48, §1.

187. CCC, no. 1615.

188. CCC, no. 1623.

189. See *Rite of Marriage* (RM), nos. 28–32, from the *Ordo Celebrandi Matrimonium*, editio typica altera (Typis Polyglottis Vaticanis, 1990). While this second edition of the *Rite of Marriage* has not yet been published in an English edition, the rubrics of the Latin edition are current liturgical law.

is not necessarily suitable to the sacrament, the pastoral musician will make an effort to demonstrate a wide range of music appropriate for the Liturgy.

219. It is helpful for a diocese or a parish to have a definite but flexible policy that provides clear guidance and also allows for pastoral sensitivity regarding wedding music. This policy should be communicated early to couples as a normal part of their preparation in order to avoid last-minute crises and misunderstandings.

220. Particular decisions about choice and placement of wedding music should be based on the three judgments proposed above (see nos. 126ff.): the liturgical judgment, the pastoral judgment, and the musical judgment. As indicated previously, all three of these judgments must be taken into account, since they are aspects of a single judgment. Additionally, music should reflect the truth that all the sacraments celebrate the Paschal Mystery of Christ.[190] Secular music, even though it may emphasize the love of the spouses for one another, is not appropriate for the Sacred Liturgy. Songs that are chosen for the Liturgy should be appropriate for the celebration and express the faith of the Church.[191]

221. If vocal soloists are to be employed in the celebration of the sacrament, they should be instructed on the nature of the Liturgy and trained in the unique aspects of singing in a liturgical context. Either the soloist should be trained to carry out the ministry of psalmist and cantor, or else another singer should be secured for this liturgically important role. In all cases, soloists should be aware that their talents are offered at the service of the Liturgy. Vocalists may sing alone during the Preparation of the Gifts or after Communion, provided the music and their manner of singing does not call attention to themselves but rather assists in the contemplation of the sacred mysteries being celebrated. Soloists should not usurp parts of the Mass designated for congregational participation.

222. If the Rite of Marriage is celebrated within Mass, the norms for music within Mass as described in nos. 137–199 of this document apply. The entrance procession—consisting of the ministers, attendants, witnesses, bride, and groom—is accompanied by a suitable song or instrumental music. If instrumental music is played, the assembly may join in a song once all have taken their places. The Liturgy of the Word proceeds as usual with a Responsorial Psalm, which may be sung. Following the homily, the sacrament is celebrated with the exchange of consent and the Church's reception of consent. After the blessing and exchanging of rings, a song or hymn of praise may be sung.[192] Depending on the local custom and the culture of the families, after the exchange of rings, the veiling of the bride and groom and other customary actions may be added, during which an appropriate Psalm or song may be sung.

---

190. See SC, no. 61; CCC, no. 1621.
191. See RM, no. 30; SC, nos. 118, 121.
192. See RM, no. 68.

223. When, for pastoral reasons, the sacrament is celebrated outside of Mass, the Liturgy should begin with an entrance song or instrumental piece.[193] If instrumental music is played, the assembly may join in a song once all have taken their places. The Liturgy of the Word takes place in the usual manner, with the possibility of singing a Responsorial Psalm.[194] Following the homily, the sacrament is celebrated with the exchange of consent and the Church's reception of consent. After the blessing and exchanging of rings, a song or hymn of praise may be sung.[195] When the sacrament is celebrated outside of Mass but Communion is distributed, a chant or song may accompany the distribution of the sacrament, as well as the period of thanksgiving after Communion is distributed.[196]

224. Since the celebration of marriage is a communal celebration, participation aids should be provided to the congregation so that they might follow the ritual with understanding. This, in turn, allows them to have full and active participation in the celebration. Participation aids should include especially those elements of the Liturgy unique to the marriage rite, as well as translations of any songs not sung in the vernacular. Such participation aids should also include proper copyright notices for permission to use copyrighted music in the program.

The Rites of Ordination

225. For the ordination of bishops, priests, or deacons, an "entrance antiphon with its psalm or another suitable liturgical song is sung" at the beginning of the Liturgy.[197] Once the bishop receives the promises of those elected to orders, the Litany of Supplication is sung as the elect prostrate themselves.[198]

226. As the newly ordained are clothed in the vestments of their order, an antiphon is sung with its proper Psalm as indicated in the rite.[199] Otherwise, "another appropriate liturgical song of the same kind with suitable antiphon may be sung."[200] This is especially appropriate if the Psalm indicated in the rite has already been used during the Liturgy of the Word.[201] The *Rites of Ordination* suggests that a second antiphon and a second Psalm be sung during the kiss of peace.[202] Here, too, another appropriate liturgical song may be substituted.[203] Finally, "a liturgical song of thanksgiving may be sung after the distribution of Communion."[204]

---

193. See RM, no. 81.
194. See RM, no. 90.
195. See RM, no. 102.
196. See RM, nos. 113, 114.
197. *Rites of Ordination of a Bishop, of Priests, and of Deacons* (ORD) (Washington, DC: USCCB, 2003), no. 118; see ORD, no. 193.
198. See ORD, nos. 127, 203.
199. See ORD, nos. 134, 209.
200. See ORD, nos. 134, 209.
201. See ORD, nos. 134, 209.
202. See ORD, nos. 137, 212.
203. See ORD, nos. 137, 212.
204. ORD, no. 142; see no. 217.

227. When the Sacrament of Anointing of the Sick takes place within a large congregation, "the full participation of those present must be fostered by every means, especially through the use of appropriate songs, so that the celebration manifest[s] the Easter joy which is proper to this Sacrament."[205]

228. "When the condition of the sick person permits, and especially when communion is to be received, the Sacrament of Anointing may be celebrated within Mass."[206] Music for the Mass should be selected in accordance with the norms set forth above and with sensitivity to the nature and locale of the celebration. Musical settings for the litany may be developed. Additionally, if large numbers of sick persons are present, instrumental music may be played as the priest anoints each of them.

The Sacrament of Penance

229. The Rite for Reconciliation of Several Penitents with Individual Confession and Absolution normally requires an entrance song or song of gathering; a Responsorial Psalm and a Gospel Acclamation during the Liturgy of the Word; an optional hymn after the homily; and a hymn of praise for God's mercy following the absolution. The litany within the General Confession of Sins (alternating between the deacon or cantor and the assembly) or another appropriate song may also be sung, as well as the Lord's Prayer. Singing or soft instrumental music may be used during the time of individual confessions, especially when a large number of people is present for the celebration.

C. MUSIC AND THE LITURGY OF THE HOURS

230. The public celebration of the Liturgy of the Hours, especially Morning and Evening Prayer, sanctifies time and participates in the prayer of Christ and his Church. Such celebrations should foster "the active participation of all according to their individual circumstances through acclamations, dialogues, alternating psalmody and other things of this kind, and takes into account various forms of expression. . . . In this way the wish of the Apostle is fulfilled: 'Let the word of Christ dwell in you richly, as in all wisdom you teach and admonish one another, singing Psalms, hymns, and spiritual songs with gratitude in your hearts to God.'"[207]

231. As much as possible, communal celebration of the Liturgy of the Hours with singing is to be preferred to private recitation.[208] Those bound to the Office are reminded that private recitation is commended only when communal celebration is not possible. The hours are not to be anticipated but are to be celebrated at their proper times.[209]

---

205. *Pastoral Care of the Sick* (PCS), no. 108, in *The Rites*.
206. PCS, no. 131.
207. Col 3:16; see Eph 5:19–20; GILH, no. 33.
208. See SC, nos. 99, 100, 101.
209. See SC, no. 94.

232. The Psalms and canticles should be sung whenever possible. The *General Instruction of the Liturgy of the Hours* lists several ways in which the Psalms may be sung: responsorially, antiphonally, or straight through (*in directum*). Music may be of the formula type (e.g., Psalm tones) or through-composed for each Psalm or canticle.

Responsorial

233. The responsorial form of Psalm singing appears to have been the original style for congregational use and still remains an excellent method for engaging the congregation in the singing of Psalms. In this model, the psalmist or choir sings the verses of the Psalm, and the assembly responds with a brief antiphon (refrain). For pastoral or musical reasons, the *General Instruction* permits the substitution of other approved texts for these refrains.

Antiphonal

234. In the antiphonal style, the praying assembly is divided into two groups. The text of the Psalm is shared between them; generally the same musical configuration (e.g., a Psalm tone) is used by both. A refrain is ordinarily sung before and after the Psalm by the whole body. This method of singing has its roots in the choir and monastic traditions. Today, where it is used by the congregation, care must be taken that the people can be at ease with this form of sung prayer.

Through-Composed

235. In a through-composed setting (*in directum*), the musical material is ordinarily not repeated, unless the Psalm calls for it. The music may be for soloist, soloist and choir, or choir alone (e.g., an anthem). Only rarely will this form be found in settings designed for congregational use. The purpose of the *in directum* setting should be to complement the literary structure of the Psalm and to capture its emotions.

Metrical Psalms

236. A metrical Psalm is a Psalm text that has been transformed into a strophic hymn with a recurring metrical structure, such that its stanzas can be sung to a hymn melody. Metrical psalmody has been a part of Protestant and Catholic practice ever since the sixteenth century. Due to its four-hundred-year tradition, a large and important repertoire of metrical Psalms in English is available today. Poets and composers continue to add to this resource of Psalm settings. In order to foster the sung rendition of Psalms, metrical psalmody may be used in the Liturgy of the Hours, provided that the metrical text is faithful to the sacred text of the original Psalm.

Formula Tones

237. Formula tones (newly written Psalm tones, Anglican chants, fauxbourdons) are readily available and well suited for vernacular texts. Care should be taken when setting vernacular texts so that the verbal accent pattern is not distorted by the musical cadence. Gregorian chant tones are suited to the Latin language,

which does not, for the most part, have accents on the final syllable of a line. For this reason, Gregorian tones should generally not be used for those vernacular languages that have final accents, or else the Gregorian cadences should be adapted to fit the accentuation of the vernacular language.

238. Where formula tones are employed for the hours of the Divine Office, especially with a parish congregation, variety should be sought in the use of other forms of sung prayer, particularly the responsorial style. The Old Testament Canticle in Morning Prayer and the New Testament Canticle in Evening Prayer are especially suitable for this latter method of singing.

Other Elements

239. The principle mentioned earlier concerning the mixing of different musical idioms has special application in a sung celebration of the Liturgy of the Hours. Psalms may be sung in the manners discussed above. Certain Psalms, however, might be sung by a choir alone. A few might lend themselves to recitation. The nature and literary form of the Psalm itself should suggest the way it is to be prayed. Likewise, in the same Office, some parts may be rendered unaccompanied, while others are accompanied by organ, piano, guitar, or other instruments.

240. In accord with their nature, the hymns in the Liturgy of the Hours should be sung. The responsories also lend themselves to singing. The readings are not usually chanted. The introductory versicles and greetings can be easily learned and sung. The Lord's Prayer and the intercessions at Morning and Evening Prayer—either in the form of a litany with a fixed response (by far the easiest and most effective method for praying the intercessions) or as versicles and responses—are suited to singing.

D. OTHER LITURGICAL RITES

Sunday Celebrations in the Absence of a Priest

241. In exceptional circumstances, the rites contained in the ritual edition of *Sunday Celebrations in the Absence of a Priest* will constitute the liturgical commemoration of the Lord's Day for a given parish or community. These rites consist of the celebration either of a Liturgy of the Word or of the Liturgy of the Hours, with or without the distribution of Holy Communion. While the individual elements of these ritual patterns are described in nos. 137–199 in this document, it is important that singing normally be included in these celebrations.

Worship of the Eucharist Outside Mass

242. A distinction should be made between adoration of the reserved Blessed Sacrament and exposition of the Blessed Sacrament. Eucharistic adoration of the reserved Blessed Sacrament is a devotional act. Eucharistic exposition is a liturgical action, by which the Blessed Sacrament is displayed outside the tabernacle in a monstrance or ciborium for public veneration by the faithful. It is a public celebration that enables the faithful to perceive more clearly the relationship

between the reserved Sacrament and the "sacrifice of the Mass [which] is the origin and consummation of the worship shown to the Eucharist outside Mass."[210] Since it is a liturgical act, adoration of the Blessed Sacrament exposed in either a monstrance or a ciborium is governed by the liturgical book *Holy Communion and Worship of the Eucharist Outside Mass.*

243. While the Blessed Sacrament is exposed, and the ciborium or monstrance is placed upon the altar, it is fitting that a song be sung by those gathered. For the period of adoration, "there should be prayers, songs, and readings to direct the attention of the faithful to the worship of Christ the Lord."[211] A homily or brief exhortation is also appropriate, as are extended periods of silence. If benediction follows a period of exposition, the priest or deacon goes to the altar, genuflects, and kneels. Then a hymn or other Eucharistic song is sung, especially songs particularly appropriate for the adoration of the Blessed Sacrament, rather than those more suited to accompany the procession to receive Holy Communion at Mass. While more traditional songs like *O Salutaris* or *Tantum Ergo* are appropriate, other songs of adoration should not be excluded. "Meanwhile the minister, while kneeling, incenses the Sacrament if the exposition has taken place with the monstrance."[212] After the prayer and Eucharistic blessing, the Blessed Sacrament is placed in the tabernacle. The minister genuflects and leaves. "Meanwhile, the people may sing or say an acclamation."[213]

Order of Christian Funerals

THE IMPORTANCE OF MUSIC IN THE ORDER OF CHRISTIAN FUNERALS

244. The Church's funeral rites offer thanksgiving to God for the gift of life that has been returned to him. Following ancient custom, the funeral rites consist of three stages or stations that are joined by two processions. In Christian Rome, "Christians accompanied the body on its last journey. From the home of the deceased the Christian community proceeded to the church singing psalms. When the service in the church concluded, the body was carried in solemn procession to the grave or tomb."[214] Throughout the liturgies, the ancient Christians sang Psalms and antiphons praising God's mercy and entrusting the deceased to the angels and the saints.[215]

245. The Psalms are given pride of place in the funeral rites because "they powerfully express the suffering and pain, the hope and trust of people of every age and culture. Above all the psalms sing of faith in God, of revelation and

---

210. Sacred Congregation for Rites, *Eucharisticum Mysterium* (*Instruction on the Worship of the Eucharistic Mystery*), no. 3e, in Flannery, *Vatican Council II.*
211. *Holy Communion and Worship of the Eucharist Outside Mass* (HCWEOM), no. 95, in *The Rites.*
212. HCWEOM, no. 97.
213. HCWEOM, no. 100.
214. *Order of Christian Funerals* (OCF) (New York: Catholic Book Publishing Co., 1989), no. 42.
215. See OCF, no. 42.

redemption."[216] Effective catechesis will allow communities to understand the significance of the Psalms used in the funeral rites.

246. Sacred music has an integral role in the funeral rites, since it can console and uplift mourners while, at the same time, uniting the assembly in faith and love.[217] Funeral music should express the Paschal Mystery and the Christian's share in it.[218] Since music can evoke strong feelings, it should be chosen with care. It should console the participants and "help to create in them a spirit of hope in Christ's victory over death and in the Christian's share in that victory."[219] Secular music, even though it may reflect on the background, character, interests, or personal preferences of the deceased or mourners, is not appropriate for the Sacred Liturgy.

247. Music should be provided for the vigil and funeral Mass. Whenever possible, music should accompany the funeral processions and the rite of committal.[220] For the processions, preference should be given to "settings of psalms and songs that are responsorial or litanic in style and that allow the people to respond to the verses with an invariable refrain."[221]

248. Music should never be used to memorialize the deceased, but rather to give praise to the Lord, whose Paschal Sacrifice has freed us from the bonds of death.

THE VIGIL FOR THE DECEASED

249. If the Vigil for the Deceased is celebrated with the body's reception at the church, a special rite is used.[222] The minister, with the assisting ministers, meets the coffin at the door of the church; and the coffin is sprinkled with holy water and the pall is placed, the entrance procession begins and proceeds to the place the coffin will occupy. "During the procession a psalm, song, or responsory is sung."[223] The Vigil for the Deceased then proceeds as usual and may conclude with silence or a song.[224]

250. After the minister greets those present, the Vigil for the Deceased begins with a song.[225] Following the opening prayer, the Liturgy of the Word begins. For the Responsorial Psalm, "Psalm 27 is sung or said or another psalm or song."[226] Silence or a song may conclude the vigil.[227]

---

216. OCF, no. 25.
217. See OCF, no. 30.
218. See OCF, no. 30.
219. OCF, no. 31.
220. See OCF, nos. 32, 41.
221. OCF, no. 41.
222. See OCF, nos. 82–97.
223. OCF, no. 85.
224. See OCF, no. 97.
225. See OCF, no. 70.
226. OCF, no. 75.
227. See OCF, no. 81.

251. The rite for the transfer of the body to the church or to the place of committal includes an invitation to prayer, a brief reading of Scripture, a litany, the Lord's Prayer, and a concluding prayer. Following the concluding prayer, the minister invites those present to join the procession to the church or the place of committal. "During the procession, psalms and other suitable songs may be sung. If this is not possible, a psalm is sung or recited either before or after the procession." The rite specifically suggests Psalm 122 with its provided antiphon.[228]

THE FUNERAL LITURGY

252. If the body has not yet been received at the church, the priest, with the assisting ministers, meets the coffin at the door of the church; and after the coffin is sprinkled with holy water and the pall is placed, the entrance procession begins moving to the place the coffin will occupy. "During the procession a psalm, song, or responsory is sung" while the priest and ministers take their place in the sanctuary.[229]

253. Unless it is to be celebrated at the place of committal, the final commendation follows the Prayer After Communion. After the invitation to prayer, the song of farewell is sung.[230]

254. "The song of farewell, which should affirm hope and trust in the paschal mystery, is the climax of the rite of final commendation. It should be sung to a melody simple enough for all to sing. It may take the form of a responsory or even a hymn."[231] If the song of farewell is sung, it is not recited.

255. Following the prayer of commendation, the deacon or priest invites those present to join the procession to the place of committal. One or more of the Psalms provided by the rite may be sung during the procession to the entrance of the church. If convenient, singing may continue during the journey to the place of committal. The Psalms particularly appropriate for this procession are Psalms 25, 42, 93, 116, 118, and 119.[232]

RITE OF COMMITTAL

256. The rite of committal is the conclusion of the funeral rite and is celebrated at the grave, tomb, mausoleum, or crematorium. It may also be used for burial at sea.[233] The rite begins with an invitation to prayer and is followed by a Scripture verse, a prayer over the place of committal, intercessions, the Lord's Prayer, a concluding prayer, and finally a prayer over the people. A song may conclude the rite.[234]

---

228. OCF, no. 127.
229. OCF, no. 162.
230. See OCF, no. 174.
231. OCF, no. 147.
232. See OCF, no. 176.
233. See OCF, nos. 204ff., 316.
234. See OCF, no. 326.

257. The practice of developing funeral choirs within parish communities should be encouraged. The funeral choir is commonly made up of individuals who tend to be available on weekday mornings and who gather to lend their collective voice in support of the assembly song at the funeral Mass.

E. DEVOTIONS

258. "Sacred music is also very effective in fostering the devotion of the faithful in celebrations of the word of God, and in popular devotions. . . . In all popular devotions the psalms will be especially useful, and also works of sacred music drawn from both the old and the more recent heritage of sacred music, popular religious songs, and the playing of the organ, or of other instruments characteristic of a particular people. Moreover, in these same popular devotions, and especially in celebrations of the word of God, it is excellent to include as well some of those musical works which, although they no longer have a place in the liturgy, can nevertheless foster a religious spirit and encourage meditation on the sacred mystery."[235]

VI. CONCLUSION

259. As the Church in the United States continues its journey of liturgical renewal and spiritual growth, we hope that this document will be a further encouragement in our progress along that course. The words of St. Augustine remind us of our pilgrimage: "You should sing as wayfarers do—sing but continue your journey. Do not grow tired, but sing with joy!"[236]

---

235. MS, no. 46.
236. St. Augustine, *Sermo* 256, 1.2.3 (PL 38, 1191–1193).

BUILT OF LIVING STONES
ART, ARCHITECTURE, AND WORSHIP

GUIDELINES OF THE UNITED STATES CONFERENCE
OF CATHOLIC BISHOPS
NOVEMBER 16, 2000

OVERVIEW OF *BUILT OF LIVING STONES:*
ART, ARCHITECTURE, AND WORSHIP
GUIDELINES OF THE NATIONAL CONFERENCE OF CATHOLIC BISHOPS
Rev. J. Philip Horrigan

INTRODUCTION

In the experience of building or renovating its place of worship, a faith community engages in a conversation that can not only shape a space for liturgy but also renew the faith life of the local Church. This conversation has four essential partners: (1) the local faith community understanding what it means to be Church; (2) a thorough knowledge of and appreciation for the liturgical practices and traditions of the Catholic Church; (3) the architectural design and the relationships of the liturgical areas within the existing or the proposed new church building; and (4) the meaning that is attached to and embedded in these respective partners of this overarching conversation. This exciting, and sometimes complex, dialogue raises many other questions in the course of a building or renovation project. It can challenge the parish to reflect on and to restate its self-understanding as Church, its desire for a vibrant liturgical practice, its appreciation for good artistic expression, and its commitment to a Gospel-based mission. The document *Built of Living Stones: Art, Architecture, and Worship* (BLS) is intended to serve as a significant resource for this conversation.

The United States Conference of Catholic Bishops (USCCB) published BLS in November 2000. This document was designed to assist the faithful involved in the building or renovation of churches, chapels, and oratories of the Latin Church in the United States. It was intended for use by architects, liturgical consultants and artists, contractors, and other professionals engaged in the design and/or the construction of these places of worship.[1]

In 1978 the Bishops' Committee on the Liturgy (BCL)[2] published *Environment and Art in Catholic Worship* (EACW) as a resource for parishes engaged in the building and renovation of churches following the changes brought about by the *Constitution on the Sacred Liturgy* (CSL). The preface to BLS points out that this document "builds on and replaces"[3] EACW and addresses the needs of the next generation of parishes engaged in building or renovating churches. Some of the needs and issues that BLS addresses—and which were not dealt with in EACW—include accessibility; the aspects of a renovation project that differ from those of a new church construction project; the importance of the involvement of the whole parish community in a renovation or new building project; the spiritual nature of the arts in worship; the theology of liturgical space; and a wide variety of practical considerations.

---

1. See *Built of Living Stones: Art, Architecture, and Worship* (BLS), 3.
2. The BCL is now called the Bishops' Committee on Divine Worship (BCDW).
3. BLS, 9.

The subtitle of BLS offers the first insight into the nature of the document: *Guidelines of the National Conference of Catholic Bishops*. The "Guidelines" that are offered throughout the document are based on liturgical traditions and practices of the Church, a wide range of consultations prior to the publication of BLS, and the collective wisdom and insight of the bishops. With this in mind, BLS has a certain moral authority and is to be given serious consideration when any local Church embarks on a renovation or new church construction project.

The statement by the bishops in the preface to the document gives further explanation of the authority of the document:

> This document has been approved by the bishops of the Latin Church of the United States and issued by the authority of the National Conference of Catholic Bishops on November 16, 2000. *Built of Living Stones* contains many of the provisions of universal law governing liturgical art and architecture and offers pastoral suggestions based upon the experience of the last thirty-five years. The document presents guidelines that can serve as the basis for diocesan bishops to issue further guidelines and directives for their dioceses. Where the document quotes or reiterates norms from liturgical books and the *Code of Canon Law*, those prescriptions are binding on local communities and dioceses.[4]

BLS is not a general legislative decree[5] in itself, but as noted above, it refers to and in some instances reiterates certain aspects in existing legislative documents of the Church. Since the publication of BLS, a number of bishops have in fact issued guidelines and directives that have the nature of particular law[6] for their diocese.

The area of liturgical design and sacred art depends to a great extent on the imagination and spiritual insight of artists and artisans. The Church has never espoused a particular style or expression of liturgical architecture or liturgical art. BLS does not offer blueprints for a church building, dimensions for furnishings, or prescriptions for liturgical art and appointments. Nonetheless, BLS is a significant resource for parishes engaged in the renovation or building of a church

---

4. Ibid., 10.

5. A general legislative decree is one that has the weight of law in and of itself by virtue of the legislative body that promulgates it. The prescriptions of the whole decree are binding on those designated as its subjects, unless otherwise noted in the text. *The General Instruction of the Roman Missal* (GIRM) is such a decree. BLS is a set of guidelines that expresses the clear preferences of the USCCB in matters of liturgical design. The legislative weight of these guidelines is in their similarity with the prescriptions of other documents that are binding (for example, the *Code of Canon Law* and the GIRM). In those instances the legislative document is quoted in the text or referenced in the footnotes.

6. "Particular law" refers to a binding decree that is particular on a certain issue and/or within a certain constituency. For example, BLS states that the diocesan bishop may issue further directives concerning the reservation of the Eucharist (see article 75). If the local ordinary chooses to do that, then the "directives" might state his preference in this matter, or actually require that certain norms be followed. In the latter case this would be particular law in the matter of the reservation of the Eucharist and in that particular diocese. It would not apply to other dioceses. Note that there is a similar issue referenced in article 57 of BLS in the matter of the choice of materials for an altar.

and provides helpful guidelines for determining the appropriateness of style, design, and materials for liturgical furnishings and appointments.

In addition to the guidelines and directives of BLS, pastors, parish committees, architects, liturgical consultants, and all others involved with a church project should be familiar with other documents pertaining to liturgical design. Among those documents to be considered are the GIRM, especially chapters V and VI; the *Rite for the Dedication of a Church and an Altar* (DedCh); the CIC; and the various rituals for the celebration of the sacraments. Several other pertinent documents are listed in the introductory pages of the document. Since the publication of BLS, neither the USCCB nor the Congregation for Divine Worship and Discipline of the Sacraments (CDWDS) has published any additional documents, instructions, or guidelines that have changed the parameters of BLS for the dioceses of the United States.

THEMES AND PRINCIPLES

The liturgical theology of BLS is essentially that of the CSL, and it is echoed in five fundamental principles. First, the liturgy is the meeting place of the whole Communion of Saints, united in Christ as his Body and by Christ through his redemptive act of the Cross. The Church gathered in praise and thanksgiving is joined as one with the saints and angels by its sharing in the priesthood of Jesus Christ.[7] Hence, the Church's liturgy is by its nature a communitarian action: the participation of the faithful is constitutive of the act of worship. BLS makes several references to the principle that the liturgical space is primarily intended to serve the liturgical action of the whole assembly.

Second, "liturgy is the 'participation of the People of God in the "work of God."'"[8] Whether by active participation in the Eucharistic celebration or in quiet prayer before the Blessed Sacrament, the baptized are impelled to live out that relationship in active charity.[9]

Third, the liturgy is the locus of the presence of Christ. Again BLS reiterates the teaching of the CSL. In the liturgical assembly, "Christ's presence is realized in all *the baptized* who gather in his name, in the *word of God* proclaimed in the assembly, in the person of *the priest*, . . . and especially in the *Sacrament of his Body and Blood*."[10]

Fourth, the language of symbol and the importance of signs are seen as vehicles by "which Christians express and deepen their relationship to God."[11] But the signs and symbols of the liturgy must also be regarded as bearers of the "weight of mystery."[12] BLS points out that gestures, words, and actions (for example washing feet, anointing bodies, breaking bread and sharing the cup, and raising arms and imposing hands in blessing) are visible signs by which Christ manifests and accomplishes our sanctification and salvation in the Church.[13]

---

7. See BLS, 15.

8. Ibid., 19.

9. See ibid., 71.

10. Ibid., 22.

11. See ibid., 24.

12. *Environment and Art in Catholic Worship* (EACW), 21.

13. See BLS, 25.

With such importance attached to gestures and objects in the liturgy, it is both logical and critical that the design of such items as altars, ambos, and baptismal fonts, and the use of bread, wine, water, oil, and wax be both generous and honest in order to convey the mystery they express and impart.

Fifth, the Eucharistic celebration is at the "center of the entire Christian life."[14] This theological principle is at the heart of the CSL, and BLS sees it as the fundamental starting point for understanding the demands of liturgical space. It should also be the starting point for liturgical catechesis that informs the educational, formational, and planning efforts in a building or renovation project. The church structure is, in a very real sense, built theology.

Closely related to the liturgical theology expressed in the document, there is an understanding of Church throughout the document. This ecclesiology could be described by five principles. First, the title, *Built of Living Stones*, indicates that the document refers both to the Church as people and the Church as structure. The people of God who gather, as *ecclesia*, do so in a particular time and place.

Second, the action of the Church gathered is a sharing in the exercise of the priestly office of Jesus Christ. The sacred actions of the liturgy are not private events but are the work of the whole Church with Christ the head. Thus, the space should be so designed as to give evidence of a gathered people and not in any way resemble a place for an audience.[15]

Third, BLS states that the whole space, even as it is comprised of various liturgical areas, must be so designed as to reflect the unity of the people of God who share a common Baptism, and worship as one people in the one spirit of Jesus Christ.

Fourth, the Church at worship is made holy through "*ordinary*, perceptible signs of water, oil, bread, and wine", fire, and gestures which are "transformed by *extraordinary* grace."[16] The language of symbol is to be honored and generously expressed in the nobility and quality of the things that are used in the service of the liturgy.

Fifth, there is an important relationship between the Church-as-building, the Church-as-mystery, and the Church-at-prayer. This interrelationship is critical to understanding the purpose of any church building, because "such a house of prayer must be expressive of the presence of God and suited for the celebration of the sacrifice of Christ."[17] It also must be reflective of the community that celebrates there.[18]

THE IMPORTANCE OF THE DOCUMENT

BLS is an official document of the USCCB, and any study or work in the area of liturgical design must acknowledge the nature, authority, and implications of the document. Although BLS is primarily intended as a resource for parishes

---

14. Ibid., 49.
15. See ibid., 51.
16. Ibid., 140.
17. Ibid., 16.
18. See ibid.

contemplating or engaged in a building or renovation project, it is also a worthwhile resource for other situations.

BLS is a pastoral document; it is a reliable and accessible resource for professionals involved with a particular project, as well as for the members of parish committees who might be unfamiliar with the issues and requirements of liturgical design. Even those parishes not planning a project would find this document helpful in evaluating their liturgical space. The various sections and recommendations that pertain to specific liturgical areas (for example, the baptistry), would offer an excellent checklist to assess whether an existing space is as suitable as it could be for the liturgy.

From time to time, parishes may modestly renovate or refurbish their church, replace liturgical furnishings, or commission a new piece of liturgical art. BLS offers good insights and guidelines for all these situations. Artists and architects who seek commissions for their work should also be familiar with the guidelines and directives of BLS. Finally, anyone who has an interest in the liturgical design and arrangement of Catholic churches (for example, seminarians, architectural students, instructors in schools of theology and ministry, and ordinary parishioners) will find this document a good source of information.

IMPLICATIONS FOR LITURGICAL PREPARATION

One of the most important recommendations in BLS is found in article 205: "Collaboration is essential to every architectural project, but it is even more so in architecture at the service of liturgy, for cooperation reflects the very nature of the Body of Christ." The text goes on to say that this collaborative effort is to include the pastor, the members of the parish, the liturgical consultant, the artists, the architect, and the contractors who "should strive to listen to each other with careful attention so that a place of sacred beauty will emerge from their mutual dialogue."

Certainly a primary reason for this collaborative effort is the realization of a church building that is a beautiful and worthy place for the celebration of the liturgies of the Church. But another result is the renewal of the life of the parish community, especially in its liturgical life.

The organizational structure of the document allows a parish to walk through an existing church plan, or to review the plans for a proposed liturgical space, with the lens of the ritual actions that will be celebrated in the renovated or new liturgical space. Such an exercise moves the discussion from the functional aspects of the project to the level of meaning, appropriateness, and inspiration.

CONCLUSION

The building of a new church or the renovation of an existing church is a significant moment in the life of any parish community. It is an opportunity for renewal in the life of the parish; for renewal of its self-understanding as Church; for renewal of its claim to be people of mission and sacrifice; for renewal of its liturgical vibrancy; and for a renewal of its commitment not only to provide a place made of wood and glass, steel and stone, but to be the living stones of faith.

OUTLINE

BUILT OF LIVING STONES:
ART, ARCHITECTURE, AND WORSHIP

GUIDELINES OF THE UNITED STATES CONFERENCE
OF CATHOLIC BISHOPS

PREFACE

§ 1 §   One of the most significant and formative experiences in the life of a parish community is the process of building or renovating a church. As part of that process, parish members are called upon to study the Church's teaching and liturgical theology and to reflect upon their personal pieties, their individual tastes, and the parish history. By bringing together these personal and ecclesial elements in faith and in charity, parishioners help to build a new structure and to renew their parish community.

§ 2 §   The decision-making process and the parish education component that are part of the building experience can assist the parish and its individual members to deepen their sense of Catholic identity. This identity is shaped by the history of the particular parish, by its relationship to other parishes in the local Church known as the diocese, and by its relationship within the communion of local Churches known as the Roman Catholic Church.

§ 3 §   *Built of Living Stones: Art, Architecture, and Worship* is presented to assist the faithful involved in the building or renovation of churches, chapels, and oratories of the Latin Church in the United States. In addition, the document is intended for use by architects, liturgical consultants and artists, contractors, and other professionals engaged in the design and/or construction of these places of worship. The text also may be helpful to those who wish to understand the Catholic Church's tradition regarding church buildings, the arts and architecture. While the suggestions and guidelines within the document have been carefully prepared, they are not exhaustive of the subject matter. They are intended to serve as the basis for decision making at the local level and also can become the foundation for the development of diocesan guidelines and legislation governing liturgical art and architecture.[1]

---

1. Second Vatican Council, *Sacrosanctum Concilium: Constitution on the Sacred Liturgy* [SC] (December 4, 1963), nos. 45–46: "Likewise, by way of advancing the liturgical apostolate, every diocese is to have a commission on the sacred liturgy under the direction of the bishop. Sometimes it may be expedient for several dioceses to form between them one single commission which will be able to promote liturgy by common consultation.

"Besides the commission on the sacred liturgy, every diocese, as far as possible, should have commissions for sacred music and sacred art. These three commissions must harmonize their activities. Indeed it will frequently be advisable to fuse the three of them into a single commission."

§ 4 §   Catholics who live and worship in the United States in the twenty-first century celebrate a liturgy that is the same as that of earlier generations in all its essentials but significantly different in its language, style and form. Recent shifts in the visual arts and in building styles as well as the development of new materials and sound amplification systems have created both opportunities and challenges for those engaged in the building and renovation of places for worship.

§ 5 §   To be able to make specific recommendations about building and renovation projects, parish members need to understand the nature of the liturgy, the space it requires, and the ways in which the physical building can help or hinder worship. Because of the spectrum of ideas, opinions, spiritualities, and personal preferences present in every parish, the assistance of church documents and teachings and of consultants and facilitators is beneficial in the processes of learning and making decisions. With such assistance, parish leaders and members can develop the skills needed for building consensus and resolving conflicts.

§ 6 §   The challenges of building or renovating church buildings increase as the Church grows. The richness of ethnic and cultural groups in the Church in the United States today presents opportunities as we strive to become truly "catholic." The Church seeks to integrate and utilize each culture's strength in accomplishing Christ's mission to bring the Gospel to every person and to proclaim—through all the concerns of daily life—the abiding love and presence of God in the world.[2]

§ 7 §   In 1962 Pope John XXIII convened the Second Vatican Council to help the Church renew its sense of mission. The first of the conciliar documents, *Sacrosanctum Concilium: Constitution on the Sacred Liturgy*, articulated the goals of the Council and, in keeping with those goals, established general principles for the reform and promotion of the sacred liturgy. In addition to mandating that liturgical books and rites be revised,[3] *Sacrosanctum Concilium* called for the revision of legislation governing the material elements involved in the liturgy, particularly the construction of places of worship and altars, the placement of the tabernacle and the baptistry, and the use of images and decoration.[4]

---

2. Second Vatican Council, *Lumen Gentium: Dogmatic Constitution on the Church* [LG] (November 21, 1964), no. 17: "Whatever good lies latent in the religious practices and cultures of diverse peoples, is not only saved from destruction but is also healed, ennobled, and perfected unto the glory of God, the confusion of the devil, and the happiness of man."

Congregation for Divine Worship and the Discipline of the Sacraments, *Inculturation and the Roman Liturgy* [IRL] (1994), no. 18: "So the Liturgy of the church must not be foreign to any country, people or individual, and at the same time it should transcend the particularity of race and nation. It must be capable of expressing itself in every human culture, all the while maintaining its identity through fidelity to the tradition which comes to it from the Lord."

3. SC, no. 25: "The liturgical books are to be revised as soon as possible; from various parts of the world, experts are to be employed and bishops are to be consulted."

4. SC, no. 128: "Along with the revision of the liturgical books, as laid down in Article 25, there is to be an early revision of the canons and ecclesiastical statutes which govern the disposition of material things involved in sacred worship. These laws refer especially to the worthy and well-planned construction of sacred buildings, the shape and construction of altars, the nobility, location, and security of the Eucharistic tabernacle, the suitability and dignity of the baptistery, the proper use of sacred images, embellishments, and vestments. Laws which seem

§ 8 §   In the thirty-five years following the Second Vatican Council, both the Apostolic See and the National Conference of Catholic Bishops have issued documents to implement the provisions of *Sacrosanctum Concilium*, no. 128. In 1977 the Congregation for the Sacraments and Divine Worship issued the revised *Rite of Dedication of a Church and an Altar*. In addition to the norms in the recently revised *General Instruction of the Roman Missal*, pertinent documents have been issued by Vatican congregations concerning the care of the Church's artistic heritage, artists and the arts, and vesture.[5]

§ 9 §   In the United States, the committee statement *Environment and Art in Catholic Worship* was published by the Bishops' Committee on the Liturgy in 1978.[6] This statement has had a profound impact on the building and renovation of parish churches in the United States. Parish communities have studied, discussed and disagreed about the document; many liturgical design consultants have utilized the text in parish education programs; and architects have tried to transform the underlying principles and theology into brick and mortar, stone and glass. Twenty-two years after the publication of *Environment and Art*, the bishops of the United States present a new document on church art and architecture that builds on and replaces *Environment and Art* and addresses the needs of the next generation of parishes engaged in building or renovating churches. *Built of Living Stones* reflects our understanding of the liturgy, of the role and importance of church art and architecture, and of the integral roles of the local parish and the diocese that enter into a building or renovation project.

§ 10 §   This document has been approved by the bishops of the Latin Church of the United States and issued by the authority of the National Conference of Catholic Bishops on November 16, 2000. *Built of Living Stones* contains many of the provisions of universal law governing liturgical art and architecture and offers pastoral suggestions based upon the experience of the last thirty-five years. The document presents guidelines that can serve as the basis for diocesan bishops to issue further guidelines and directives for their dioceses. Where the document quotes or reiterates norms from liturgical books and the *Code of Canon Law*, those prescriptions are binding on local communities and dioceses.

---

less suited to the reformed liturgy are to be brought into harmony with it, or else abolished; and any which are helpful are to be retained if already in use, and introduced where they are lacking. According to the norm of Article 22 of the Constitution, the territorial bodies of bishops are empowered to adapt matters to the needs and customs of their different regions; this applies especially to the material and form of sacred furnishings and vestments."

5. Cf. the Circular Letter *Opera Artis: On the Care of the Church's Historical and Artistic Heritage* [OA] (April 11, 1971), from the Congregation for the Clergy to presidents of the episcopal conferences; the decree *Domus Dei* (1968) on the norms for minor basilicas, from the Congregation of Rites (Consilium); the *Rite of Dedication of a Church and an Altar* [RDCA] (1977) from the Congregation for the Sacraments and Divine Worship; the Instruction *Pontificalis Ritus* (1968) on the simplification of pontifical rites and insignia, from the Congregation of Rites; the Instruction *Ut Sive Sollicite* (1969) on vesture, from the Vatican's Secretariat of State; the Motu Proprio *Inter Eximia Episcopalis* (1978) on the use of the pallium, from Pope Paul VI; and Pope John Paul II's *Letter to Artists* [LA] (April 4, 1999).

6. National Conference of Catholic Bishops' Committee on the Liturgy, *Environment and Art in Catholic Worship* [EACW] (Washington, D.C.: United States Catholic Conference, 1978).

§ 11 § The document begins with a theological reflection on the liturgy and liturgical art and architecture. Since decisions about church art and architecture should always be based upon the theology of the eucharistic assembly and its liturgical action and the understanding of the Church as the house of God on earth, the first chapter is foundational for the chapters that follow. The second chapter outlines the liturgical principles for parish communities to apply when building or renovating liturgical space, and it reviews the spatial demands of the major liturgical celebrations during the year. The third chapter offers suggestions for including art in places of worship and for choosing artists and artistic consultants. The fourth and final chapter describes the practical elements involved in the building or renovation process, including the development of a master plan, the design process, the development of a site plan, and the role of professionals in the process. A section on the special issues involved in the preservation and restoration of artworks and architecture has been included.

CHAPTER ONE
THE LIVING CHURCH

THE LIVING CHURCH: GOD'S BUILDING

§ 12 § God created the universe so that all might have a part in his divine life and be joined in communion with him. Thus did he call forth light from darkness, beauty from chaos, and life from the formless void (Genesis 1:1–23). When all was in readiness, he fashioned Adam and Eve in the divine image and breathed life into them (Genesis 1:24–31) in order to gather all men and women into the great and eternal hymn of praise which is the Church. This is why Christians, from the earliest centuries, could believe that "the world was created for the sake of the Church."[7]

§ 13 § Despite the sin of Adam, God's call to communion perdured. Gradually, he revealed his wish to save humanity "not as individuals without any mutual bonds, but by making them into a people, a people which acknowledges Him in truth and serves Him in holiness."[8] With Abraham and his descendants, God entered into an everlasting covenant. He promised to be their God and claimed them as his own, a holy nation, a people set apart to praise his mighty deeds throughout the ages. Through the waters of death he led his people, Israel, accepting their sacrifices at Sinai through the hands of Aaron and his descendants. "All of these things, however, were done by way of preparation and as a figure of that new and perfect covenant which was to be ratified in Christ . . . .this new covenant in His blood . . . calling together a people made up of Jew and Gentile, making them one, not according to the flesh but in the Spirit."[9]

---

7. United States Catholic Conference-Libreria Editrice Vaticana, *Catechism of the Catholic Church* [CCC] (2000), no. 760.

8. LG, no. 9.

9. Ibid.

§ 14 §   From the altar of the cross Christ accomplished our redemption,[10] forming a holy people, a "temple of God built of living stones, where the Father is worshiped in spirit and in truth."[11] The hymn of praise that Christ places within the heart and on the lips of the Church will be sung at the end of time in all its fullness, when all the members gather at the wedding feast of the Lamb in the heavenly Jerusalem.

§ 15 §   That same hymn is sung today by the Church whenever the liturgy is celebrated. For every time the Church gathers for prayer, she is joined to Christ's priesthood and made one with all the saints and angels, transcending time and space. Together the members worship with the whole company of heaven, "venerating the memory of the saints" and hoping "for some part and fellowship with them"; together they eagerly await Christ's coming in glory.[12] The sacred liturgy is a window to eternity and a glimpse of what God calls us to be.

THE CHURCH BUILDING

§ 16 §   Just as the term *Church* refers to the *living temple*, God's People, the term *church* also has been used to describe "the building in which the Christian community gathers to hear the word of God, to pray together, to receive the sacraments, and to celebrate the eucharist."[13] That building is both the house of God on earth (*domus Dei*) and a house fit for the prayers of the saints (*domus ecclesiae*). Such a house of prayer must be expressive of the presence of God and suited for the celebration of the sacrifice of Christ, as well as reflective of the community that celebrates there.

§ 17 §   The church is the proper place for the liturgical prayer of the parish community, especially the celebration of the Eucharist on Sunday. It is also the privileged place for adoration of the Blessed Sacrament and reservation of the Eucharist for Communion for the sick. Whenever communities have built houses for worship, the design of the building has been of critical importance.[14] Churches

---

10. SC, no. 5: "For it was from the side of Christ as He slept the sleep of death upon the cross that there came forth the wondrous sacrament which is the whole Church."

11. RDCA, ch. 2, no. 1 (International Committee on English in the Liturgy, *Documents on the Liturgy: 1963–1979: Conciliar, Papal and Curial Texts* [DOL] [1982] 547, no. 4369): "This holy people, made one as the Father, Son, and Holy Spirit are one, is the Church, that is, the temple of God built of living stones, where the Father is worshiped in spirit and in truth."

12. SC, no. 8: "In the earthly liturgy, by way of foretaste, we share in that heavenly liturgy which is celebrated in the holy city of Jerusalem toward which we journey as pilgrims, and in which Christ is sitting at the right hand of God, a minister of the sanctuaries and of the true tabernacle . . . ; we sing a hymn to the Lord's glory with all the warriors of the heavenly army; venerating the memory of the saints, we hope for some part and fellowship with them; we eagerly await the Savior, our Lord Jesus Christ, until He, our life, shall appear and we too will appear with Him in glory (cf. Phil. 3:20; Col. 3:4)."

13. RDCA, ch. 2, no. 1 (DOL 547, no. 4369): "Rightly, then, from early times 'church' has also been the name given to the building in which the Christian community gathers to hear the word of God, to pray together, to receive the sacraments, and to celebrate the eucharist."

14. Cf. CCC, no. 2691: "The church, the house of God, is the proper place for the liturgical prayer of the parish community. It is also the privileged place for adoration of the real presence

are never "simply gathering spaces but signify and make visible the Church living in [a particular] place, the dwelling of God" among us, now "reconciled and united in Christ."[15] As such, the building itself becomes "a sign of the pilgrim Church on earth and reflects the Church dwelling in heaven."[16] Every church building is a gathering place for the assembly, a resting place, a place of encounter with God, as well as a point of departure on the Church's unfinished journey toward the reign of God.

§ 18 § Churches, therefore, must be places "suited to sacred celebrations," "dignified," and beautiful.[17] Their suitability for worship is determined by their ability through the architectural design of space and the application of artistic gifts to embody God's initiative and the community's faithful response. Church buildings and the religious artworks that beautify them are forms of worship themselves and both inspire and reflect the prayer of the community as well as the inner life of grace.[18] Conversely, church buildings and religious artifacts that are trivial, contrived, or lack beauty can detract from the community's liturgy. Architecture and art become the joint work of the Holy Spirit and the local community, that of preparing human hearts to receive God's word and to enter more fully into communion with God.[19]

---

of Christ in the Blessed Sacrament. The choice of a favorable place is not a matter of indifference for true prayer."

Cf. RDCA, *Theological Commentary*, no. 6.

15. CCC, no. 1180: "These visible churches are not simply gathering places but signify and make visible the Church living in this place, the dwelling of God with men reconciled and united in Christ."

16. RDCA, ch. 1, no. 2 (DOL 547, no. 4370): "Because the church is a visible building, it stands as a special sign of the pilgrim Church on earth and reflects the Church dwelling in heaven."

Cf. Canon Law Society of America, *Code of Canon Law* [CIC] (1998), c. 1214: "By the term *church* is understood a sacred building designated for divine worship to which the faithful have a right of entry for the exercise, especially the public exercise, of divine worship."

17. RDCA, ch. 2, no. 3 (DOL 547, no. 4371): "The very nature of a church demands that it be suited to sacred celebrations, dignified, and evincing a noble beauty, not merely costly display, and it should stand as a sign and symbol of heavenly realities."

18. Cf. LA, no. 12: "Art must make perceptible, and as far as possible attractive, the world of the spirit, of the invisible, of God. It must therefore translate into meaningful terms that which is in itself ineffable. Art has a unique capacity to take one or other facet of the message and translate it into colors, shapes and sounds which nourish the intuition of those who look or listen. It does so without emptying the message itself of its transcendent value and its aura of mystery."

Cf. LA, no. 16: "Beauty is a key to the mystery and a call to transcendence. It is an invitation to savor life and to dream of the future. That is why the beauty of created things can never fully satisfy. It stirs that hidden nostalgia for God which a lover of beauty like St. Augustine could express in incomparable terms: 'Late have I loved you, beauty so old and so new: Late have I loved you!' (*Confessions* 10:27)."

19. CCC, no. 1098: "The preparation of hearts is the joint work of the Holy Spirit and the assembly, especially of its ministers. The grace of the Holy Spirit seeks to awaken faith, conversion of heart, and adherence to the Father's will. These dispositions are the precondition both for the reception of other graces conferred in the celebration itself and the fruits of new life which the celebration is intended to produce afterward."

It is for this reason that *Sacrosanctum Concilium* (nos. 14–17, and 129) maintains that a firm education in liturgical theology and in the historical development of the arts is central to seminary education.

§ 19 §   Liturgy is "the participation of the People of God in 'the work of God.'"[20] It is the "exercise of the priestly office of Jesus" in which God is worshiped and adored and people are made holy.[21] God begins the work of sanctifying people in time and space and brings that work to completion. Those who respond to God in worship and in service are given the privilege of becoming coworkers in the divine plan.[22]

§ 20 §   The Church marks *time* as holy by setting aside Sunday and by celebrating the liturgical year with its rhythm and seasons. It demonstrates God's reign over all *space* by dedicating buildings to house the Church and its worship. Each Sunday the baptized are challenged to rest from their daily labors, to contemplate the goodness of God, to make present the victory and triumph of Christ's death (SC, no. 6), to enter the joy of the Risen Lord, to receive the life-giving breath of the Spirit, and to commit themselves to serve those in need. Sunday affirms both the primacy of God and the dignity of the person.[23] While the worship of God is not limited to any one place, Christians build churches to shelter the liturgical assembly that praises God and celebrates the sacraments through which the Church is sanctified.

§ 21 §   The liturgy is the perfect expression of the Church, "the summit toward which [all the Church's] activity . . . is directed" and the source of all her power.[24] In the New Testament, the term *liturgy* is intimately connected with the

---

20. Ibid., no. 1069: "The word 'liturgy' originally meant a 'public work' or a 'service in the name of/on behalf of the people.' In Christian tradition it means the participation of the People of God in 'the work of God' (cf. John 17:4). Through the liturgy Christ, our redeemer and high priest, continues the work of our redemption in, with, and through his Church."

The ministerial priest, by the sacred power that he has, forms and rules the priestly people; in the person of Christ he effects the eucharistic sacrifice and offers it to God in the name of all the people. The faithful, indeed by virtue of their royal priesthood, participate in the offering of the Eucharist.

21. SC, no. 7: "Rightly, then, the liturgy is considered as an exercise of the priestly office of Jesus Christ. In the liturgy the sanctification of man is manifested by signs perceptible to the senses, and is effected in a way which is proper to each of these signs; in the liturgy full public worship is performed by the Mystical Body of Jesus Christ, that is, by the Head and His members."

Cf. CIC, c. 834.

22. The *Catechism of Catholic Church*, no. 2567, speaks of God's revelation and prayer as a "covenant drama" that engages the heart and unfolds throughout the whole history of salvation.

23. Pope John Paul II, *Dies Domini: Observing and Celebrating the Day of the Lord* [DD] (May 31, 1998), no. 68: "In order that rest may not degenerate into emptiness or boredom, it must offer spiritual enrichment, greater freedom, opportunities for contemplation and fraternal communion. Therefore, among the forms of culture and entertainment which society offers, the faithful should choose those which are most in keeping with a life lived in obedience to the precepts of the Gospel. Sunday rest then becomes 'prophetic,' affirming not only the absolute primacy of God, but also the primacy and dignity of the person with respect to the demands of social and economic life, and anticipating in a certain sense the 'new heavens' and the 'new earth,' in which liberation from slavery to needs will be final and complete. In short, the Lord's Day thus becomes in the truest sense the day of man as well."

24. SC, no. 10: "Nevertheless the liturgy is the summit toward which the activity of the Church is directed; at the same time it is the fountain from which all her power flows."

proclamation of the Good News and with active charity.[25] Through baptism and confirmation, Christians share in Christ's priesthood, which they exercise through their worship of God and their vocation of service to others. At the Eucharist, Christ calls his members to conversion in the proclamation of the word; he invites them to join with him in offering his perfect sacrifice to the Father; and he sends them forth from liturgy to serve the community in charity. Liturgical participation commits a person to a life of faithful discipleship. "Every liturgical celebration, because it is an action of Christ the priest and of His Body the Church, is a sacred action surpassing all others."[26]

CHRIST'S PRESENCE IN SIGN AND SYMBOL

§ 22* § In the liturgical assembly, Christ's presence is realized[27] in all *the baptized* who gather in his name, in the *word of God* proclaimed in the assembly, in the person of *the priest* through whom Christ offers himself to the Father and gathers the assembly, in *sacramental celebrations,* and especially, in the *Sacrament of his Body and Blood.*[28] In building a house for the Church that is also the house of God on earth, all the expressions of Christ's presence have prominence of place that reflects their proper nature. Among these, the eucharistic species is accorded supreme prominence.[29] From the very beginning of the planning and design

---

25. Cf. Luke 1:23; Acts 13:2; Romans 15:16, 27:2; and Philippians 2:14–17, 25, 30.

26. SC, no. 7: "From this it follows that every liturgical celebration, because it is an action of Christ the priest and of His Body the Church, is a sacred action surpassing all others."

CCC, no. 1070: "In the New Testament the word 'liturgy' refers not only to the celebration of divine worship but also the proclamation of the Gospel and to active charity. In all of these situations it is a question of the service of God and neighbor. In a liturgical celebration, the Church is servant in the image of her Lord, the one 'leitourgos'; she shares in Christ's priesthood (worship), which is both prophetic (proclamation) and kingly service (service of charity)."

27. From the creation of the world, God's presence has been mediated through the very works of his hands (Romans 1:20). With the people of Israel, that presence was seen more clearly and even localized at first in the Tent of Meeting and later in the Temple. These were understood as the place or epiphany of God's glory (the *Shekinah*) (Exodus 40:34–35). In the New Testament, Christ comes to be seen as the complete and definitive epiphany of God's glory (John 1:4; Hebrews 1:3, 10:5–7). The Church, the People of God, is the continued sacramental presence of Christ, and the new church building is the privileged place of this continued epiphany in the ongoing history of salvation.

28. Congregation for Divine Worship and the Discipline of the Sacraments, *General Instruction of the Roman Missal* [GIRM] (2000), no. 27: "At Mass or the Lord's Supper, the people of God are called into unity, with a priest presiding and acting in the person of Christ, to celebrate the memorial of the Lord or Eucharistic sacrifice. For this reason Christ's promise applies supremely to such a local gathering together of the Church: 'Where two or three come together in my name, there am I in their midst' (Matthew 18:20). For at the celebration of Mass, which perpetuates the sacrifice of the cross, Christ is really present in the assembly gathered in his name; he is present in the person of the minister, in his own word, and indeed substantially and permanently under the eucharistic elements."

29. Cf. Pope Paul VI, *Mysterium Fidei: On the Doctrine and Worship of the Eucharist* [MF] (September 3, 1965), no. 39 (DOL 176, no. 1183): "This presence is called the *real presence* not to exclude the other kinds as though they were not real, but because it is real par excellence, since it is substantial, in the sense that Christ whole and entire, God and man, becomes present."

* In the first printing of this text, the article number 23 was missing. However, no text was omitted. To maintain consistency across editions, we are maintaining the original numbering.

process, parishes will want to reflect upon the relationship of the altar, the ambo, the tabernacle, the chair of the priest celebrant, and the space for congregation.

§ 23 § Gestures, language and actions are the *physical, visible* and *public* expressions by which human beings understand and manifest their inner life. Since human beings on this earth are always made of flesh and blood, they not only will and think, but also speak and sing, move and celebrate. These human actions as well as physical objects are also the signs by which Christians express and deepen their relationship to God.[30]

§ 24 § Jesus himself used physical signs to manifest his union with the Father and to reveal his mission to the world. Jesus was baptized in the waters of the Jordan River, he fed the multitudes with bread, healed the sick with his touch, and forgave sinners. He was anointed with oil, he shared a Passover meal with his disciples, and he surrendered his body to death on the cross. Christ, the incarnate one, used material signs to show to humanity the invisible God.[31]

§ 25 § Christ, taking on human flesh, reveals the Father. "No one has ever seen God" (1 John 4:12). The only begotten Son, living in the Father's heart, has revealed him. Indeed, Jesus said, "Whoever sees me sees the one who sent me" (John 12:45). Christ is himself the sacrament of the Father. In his risen glory, he is no longer visible in this world and Leo the Great testifies that "What has been visible of our Savior has passed over into the sacraments": *Quod igitur conspicuum fuit Salvatoris Nostri in sacramenta transivit* (*Sermo.* 74, 2: PL 54, 398). And so washing and anointing, breaking the bread and sharing the cup, raising arms in blessing and imposing hands are *visible* signs by which Christ manifests and accomplishes our sanctification and salvation in the Church.[32] To the central signs and word, the Church adds gestures and material elements such as incense, ashes, holy water, candles and vestments to dispose us for the heavenly gifts of our crucified and Risen Lord and to deepen our reverence for the unceasing mercy and grace that come to us in the Church through the passion and death of Jesus, our Lord.

§ 26 § Just as Christ invited those who heard him to share his personal union with the Father through material signs, so Christ leads the Church through

---

30. Cf. CCC, no. 1146: "In human life, signs and symbols occupy an important place. As a being at once body and spirit, man expresses and perceives spiritual realities through physical signs and symbols. As a social being, man needs signs and symbols to communicate with others, through language, gestures, and actions. The same holds true for his relationship with God."

Cf. GIRM, no. 288: "Churches and other places of worship should therefore be suited to celebrating the liturgy and to ensuring the active participation of the faithful. Further, the buildings and requisites for worship should be truly worthy and beautiful, signs and symbols of heavenly realities."

31. Cf. CCC, no. 1151: "In his preaching the Lord Jesus often makes use of the signs of creation to make known the mysteries of the Kingdom of God. He performs healings and illustrates his preaching with physical signs or symbolic gestures."

32. Cf. CCC, no. 1148; cf. no. 1152: "Since Pentecost, it is through the sacramental signs of his Church that the Holy Spirit carries on the work of sanctification. The sacraments of the Church do not abolish but purify and integrate all the richness of the signs and symbols of the cosmos and of social life. Further, they fulfill the types and figures of the Old Covenant, signify and make actively present the salvation wrought by Christ, and prefigure and anticipate the glory of heaven."

these same signs in the liturgy from the visible to the invisible.[33] As a result, effective liturgical signs have a teaching function and encourage full, conscious, and active participation, express and strengthen faith, and lead people to God. Poorly utilized or minimal signs do not enliven the community's faith and can even diminish active participation.[34] It must likewise be kept in mind that the liturgy and its signs and symbols do not exercise merely a teaching function. They also touch and move a person to conversion of heart and not simply to enlightenment of mind.

LITURGICAL PRINCIPLES FOR BUILDING OR RENOVATING CHURCHES

§ 27 §   The basic liturgical principles for designing and renovating churches today are drawn from the Second Vatican Council and the documents that implemented its decrees.[35] Even though the Church offers no universal blueprint or style for the design of a church, attention to the following principles will ensure that from the beginning, the ritual requirements will receive the priority they deserve in the design process.

§ 28 §   1. *The church building is designed in harmony with church laws and serves the needs of the liturgy.* The liturgical books are the foundational source for those who wish to plan a building well suited for the liturgy. First among these are the prescriptions contained in the fifth chapter of the *General Instruction of the Roman Missal* and the norms in the introduction to the *Rite of Dedication of a Church and an Altar*. Other directives can be found in the various liturgical books and the *Code of Canon Law*.

§ 29 §   Because the church is a house of prayer in which the Eucharist is celebrated and the Blessed Sacrament is reserved, a place where the faithful assemble, and a setting where Christ is worshiped, it should be worthy of prayer and sacred celebration, built in conformity with the laws of the Church, and dignified with noble beauty and intrinsically excellent art.[36] The general plan of the building reflects the Church that Christ gathers there, is expressive of its prayer, fosters the members' participation in sacred realities, and supports the solemn character of the sacred liturgy.

---

33. Cf. SC, no. 59; CCC, no. 1075: "Liturgical catechesis aims to initiate people into the mystery of Christ (It is 'mystagogy.') by proceeding from the visible to the invisible, from the sign to the thing signified, from the 'sacraments' to the 'mysteries.'"

34. Cf. National Conference of Catholic Bishops' Committee on the Liturgy, *Music in Catholic Worship* [MCW] (1983), nos. 6–7.

35. These include the SC, the GIRM, the RDCA, the *Ceremonial of Bishops*, the various sacramental rituals, and the CIC.

36. CCC, no. 1179; Second Vatican Council, *Presbyterorum Ordinis: Decree on the Ministry and Life of Priests* [PO] (December 7, 1965), no. 5; cf. SC, nos. 122–127; GIRM no. 288: "For the celebration of the Eucharist the people of God normally assemble in a church or, if there is none or one that is inadequate for some reason, then in some other place nevertheless worthy of so great a mystery. Churches and other places of worship should therefore be suited to celebrating the liturgy and to ensuring the active participation of the faithful. Further, the buildings and requisites for worship should be truly worthy and beautiful, signs and symbols of heavenly realities."

§ 30 §   The general plan of the building should be such that "in some way it conveys the image of the gathered assembly. It should also allow the participants to take the place most appropriate to them and assist all to carry out their function properly."[37]

§ 31 §   2. *The church building fosters participation in the liturgy.* Because liturgical actions by their nature are communal celebrations, they are celebrated with the presence and active participation of the Christian faithful whenever possible.[38] Such participation, both internal and external, is the faithful's "right and duty by reason of their baptism."[39] The building itself can promote or hinder the "full, conscious, and active participation" of the faithful. Parishes making decisions about the design of a church must consider how the various aspects and choices they make will affect the ability of all the members to participate fully in liturgical celebrations.

§ 32 §   *The design of the church building reflects the various roles of the participants.* Since the liturgical celebration is an action of Christ and the Church, it belongs to the whole Body of the Church.[40] While all the members are called to participate in worship, not all have the same role.[41] From the earliest days of the Church, the Holy Spirit has called forth members to serve in a variety of ministries. That same Spirit continues to call the members to various ministries today and to bestow gifts necessary for the good of the community.[42]

---

37. RDCA, ch. 2, no. 3 (DOL, 547, no. 4371): "The very nature of a church demands that it be suited to sacred celebrations, dignified, evincing a noble beauty, not mere costly display, and it should stand as a sign and symbol of heavenly realities. 'The general plan of the sacred edifice should be such that in some way it conveys the image of the gathered assembly. It should also allow the participants to take the place most appropriate to them and assist all to carry out their function properly.'"

38. CIC, c. 837 § 2: "Inasmuch as liturgical actions by their nature entail a common celebration, they are to be celebrated with the presence and active participation of the Christian faithful where possible."

39. SC, no. 14: "[The] Church earnestly desires that all the faithful be led to that full, conscious, and active participation in liturgical celebrations which is demanded by the very nature of the liturgy. Such participation by the Christian people as 'a chosen race, a royal priesthood, a holy nation, a purchased people' (1 Peter 2:9, cf. 2:4–5), is their right and duty by reason of their baptism."

40. GIRM, no. 294: "The people of God assembled at Mass possess an organic and hierarchical structure, expressed by the various ministries and actions for each part of the celebration. The general plan of the sacred building should be such that in some way it conveys the image of the gathered assembly. Thus it should also allow the participants to take the place most appropriate to them and assist all to carry out their individual functions properly.

"The faithful and the choir should have a place that facilitates their active participation.

"The priest celebrant, the deacon and other ministers have their place in the sanctuary. At the same time, seats for the concelebrants should be prepared. If there is truly a great number of concelebrants, then seats should be arranged in another part of the church, but near the altar.

"Even though all these elements must express a hierarchical arrangement and the diversity of functions, they should at the same time form a deep and organic unity, clearly expressive of the unity of the entire holy people. The character and beauty of the place and all its appointments should foster devotion and show the holiness of the mysteries celebrated there."

41. Cf. SC, nos. 14 and 26; PO, no. 2; LG, no. 28; GIRM, nos. 4, 58, and 60.

42. Cf. 1 Cor 12:27–28.

§ 33 § **The Church** is a holy people, a chosen race, a royal priesthood, whose members give thanks to God and offer the sacrifice of Christ. Together, they take part in the liturgy conscious of what they are doing, with reverence and full involvement. They are instructed by God's word and nourished at the Table of the Lord's Body; they are formed day by day into an ever more perfect unity with God and with each other—they are sent forth for the transformation of society, so that finally God may be all in all. And by offering Christ, "the Victim not only through the hands of the priest but also together with him," they "learn to offer themselves."[43]

§ 34 § **Bishops** "are the high priests, the principal dispensers of the mysteries of God, and the directors, promoters, and guardians of the entire liturgical life" of the particular Church.[44] Therefore, every authentic celebration of the liturgy is directed by the bishop, either in person or through the priests who assist him.[45] Within the process of building or renovating a church, the diocesan bishop has an irreplaceable role and final responsibility. The construction of a new church requires the permission of the bishop, who must consult and determine that the building will contribute to the spiritual welfare of the faithful, and that the parish has the necessary means to build and care for the church.[46]

§ 35 § **Priests** "are consecrated to celebrate divine worship and to sanctify the people."[47] The priest "stands at the head of the faithful people gathered together, presides over its prayer, proclaims the message of salvation, joins the people to himself in offering the sacrifice to God the Father through Christ in the Spirit,

---

43. GIRM, no. 95: "In the celebration of Mass the faithful are a holy people, a chosen people, a royal priesthood: they give thanks to God and offer the Victim not only through the hands of the priest but also together with him and learn to offer themselves. They should endeavor to make this clear by their deep sense of reverence for God and their charity toward brothers and sisters who share with them in the celebration."

44. CIC, c. 835 § 1: "The bishops in the first place exercise the sanctifying function; they are the high priests, the principal dispensers of the mysteries of God, and the directors, promoters, and guardians of the entire liturgical life in the church entrusted to them."

Ibid, c. 838 § 4: "Within the limits of his competence, it pertains to the diocesan bishop in the Church entrusted to him to issue liturgical norms which bind everyone."

45. Cf. GIRM, no. 22; LG, nos. 26 and 28; SC, no. 42: "Because it is impossible for the bishop always and everywhere to preside over the whole flock in his church, he cannot do other than establish lesser groupings of the faithful. Among these, parishes set up locally under a pastor who takes the place of the bishop are the most important: for in a certain way they represent the visible Church as it is established throughout the world.

"Therefore the liturgical life of the parish and its relationship to the bishop must be fostered in the thinking of and practice of both laity and clergy; efforts also must be made to encourage a sense of community within the parish, above all in the common celebration of the Sunday Mass."

46. CIC, c. 1215 §§ 1 and 2: "No church is to be built without the express written consent of the diocesan bishop.

"The diocesan bishop is not to give consent unless, after having heard the presbyteral council and the rectors of the neighboring churches, he judges that the new church can serve the good of souls and that the means necessary for building the church and for divine worship will not be lacking."

47. Ibid., c. 835 § 2: "Presbyters also exercise this function [the sanctifying function]; sharing in the priesthood of Christ and as his ministers under the authority of the bishop, they are consecrated to celebrate divine worship and to sanctify the people."

gives his brothers and sisters the bread of eternal life, and shares in it with them."[48] As the one who presides, he always prays in the name of the Church and of the community gathered together. As the leader and representative of the local parish, the pastor takes the lead in the building process, keeps the local parish in communication with the bishop and other diocesan officials, and helps to draw the parishioners together in the decision-making process.

§ 36 § **A variety of ministries** serve the assembly at the liturgy. First among the ministers is the deacon.[49] Some faithful have been installed in the ministries of lector or acolyte. Others serve as readers, altar servers, extraordinary ministers of Holy Communion, cantors, musicians and sacristans.[50] As members of the Church, each person forms an essential and distinct part of the assembly that is gathered by God in an "organic and hierarchical" way.[51] Each minister, ordained or lay, is called upon to fulfill his or her role and only that role in the celebration of the liturgy.[52]

§ 37 § By its design and its furnishings, the church reflects this diversity of roles. The one who presides, those who proclaim God's word, the ministers of music, those who assist at the altar, and members of the congregation all play an integral part in the public prayer of the Church. The design of the church should reflect the unity of the entire assembly and at the same time ensure that each person is able to exercise his or her ministry in a space that fully accommodates the ritual action called for by that ministry. Careful attention to the placement of the individuals and groups who comprise the liturgical assembly

---

48. GIRM, no. 93: "Within the Church the priest also possesses the power of Holy Orders to offer sacrifice in the person of Christ. He therefore stands at the head of the faithful people gathered together, presides over its prayer, proclaims the message of salvation, joins the people to himself in offering the sacrifice to God the Father through Christ in the Spirit, gives his brothers and sisters the bread of eternal life, and shares in it with them. At the Eucharist he should, then, serve God and the people with dignity and humility; by his bearing and by the way he recites the words of the liturgy he should communicate to the faithful a sense of the living presence of Christ."

49. Ibid., no. 94: "After the priest, in virtue of the sacred ordination he has received, the deacon has first place among those who minister in the celebration of the Eucharist. For the sacred Order of the diaconate has been held in high honor in the Church since the time of the Apostles. At Mass the deacon proclaims the gospel reading, sometimes preaches God's word, announces the intentions of the general intercessions, ministers to the priest, prepares the altar and serves the celebration of the sacrifice, distributes the Eucharist to the faithful, especially under the species of wine, and from time to time gives directions regarding the people's gestures and posture."

50. LG, nos. 26 and 28.

51. GIRM, no. 294: "The people of God assembled at Mass possess an organic and hierarchical structure, expressed by the various ministries and actions for each part of the celebration."

Cf. GIRM, no. 5: "In addition, the nature of the ministerial priesthood puts into its proper light another reality of which much should be made, namely, the royal priesthood of believers. Through the ministry of priests, the people's spiritual sacrifice is brought to completeness in union with the sacrifice of Christ, our one and only Mediator. For the celebration of the Eucharist is the action of the whole Church; in it all should do only, but all of, those parts that belong to them in virtue of their place within the people of God."

52. SC, no. 28: "In liturgical celebrations, whether as a minister or as one of the faithful, each person should perform his role by doing solely and totally what the nature of the things and liturgical norms require of him."

can manifest and enhance their relationship with one another and with the entire body.

§ 38 §   4. *The church building respects the culture of every time and place.* The Roman rite respects cultural differences and fosters the genius and talents of the various races and peoples.[53] This cultural diversity can be expressed in architectural styles, in art forms, and in some instances in the celebration of liturgical rites with appropriate adaptations.

§ 39 §   Just as each local community is different, styles and forms of churches will vary. The New Testament speaks of the upper room where Christ gathered the apostles for the Last Supper and appeared to them after the resurrection, and where the Holy Spirit descended on the Blessed Virgin and the Twelve at Pentecost. After the Lord's ascension, believers gathered in homes for the celebration of the "breaking of the bread."[54] Such homes evolved into "house churches" and became the Christian community's earliest places for worship. The unique forms and architecture of the Roman and Byzantine world provided the Church with an architectural language in the form of the basilica. With its long nave and an apse for the bishop and clergy, the basilica quickly became a standard architectural form for churches of the West. The effect of these architectural forms is still reflected in the structure of our liturgical life today.

§ 40 §   The rich history of Catholic worship space traces a path through every people and place where the liturgy has been offered. Innumerable monasteries, cathedrals and parish churches stand as witnesses to an organic growth of the liturgical and devotional life of the Church throughout the world. Since the Church is not wedded to a single architectural or artistic form, it seeks to engage the genius of every time and place, to craft the finest praise of God from what is available.[55] The rich dialogue between the Church's liturgy, as a singular expression of divine revelation, and a local culture is an essential ingredient in the evangelization of peoples and the celebration of the Roman Catholic liturgy in a given time and place. The liturgy is proclaimed, celebrated and lived in all cultures in such a way that they themselves are not abolished by it but redeemed and fulfilled.[56]

---

53. SC, nos. 37 and 119; CCC, no. 1158: "The harmony of signs (song, music, words, and actions) is all the more expressive and fruitful when expressed in the cultural richness of the People of God who celebrate."

54. Cf. Mark 14:15; Acts 2:42 and 17:16–34.

55. Cf. SC, no. 123; GIRM, no. 289: "At all times, therefore, the Church seeks out the noble support of the arts and welcomes the artistic expressions of all peoples and regions. Even more, the Church is intent on keeping the works of art and the treasures handed down from the past and, when necessary, on adapting them to new needs. It strives as well to promote new works of art that appeal to the contemporary mentality.

"In commissioning artists and choosing works of art that are to become part of a church, the highest artistic standard is therefore to be set, in order that art may aid faith and devotion and be true to the reality it is to symbolize and the purpose it is to serve."

56. Cf. CCC, nos. 1201–1206; Pope John Paul II, *Catechesi Tradendae: On Catechesis in Our Time* [CT] (October 16, 1979), no. 53.

§ 41 §   Inculturation is the incarnation of the Christian message within particular cultures that have their own sense, artistic expressions, vocabulary and grammar, and conceptual frameworks.[57] All ancient and modern evangelizing strategies in art and architecture are acts of inculturation to enable church buildings to proclaim the creative and redemptive meaning of the Gospel in every time and place.

§ 42 §   When the Gospel was first brought to America, it arrived clothed with expressions of European Christian culture and piety. Grateful for these invaluable gifts, the Church in America slowly, and often reluctantly, developed an appreciation for native music, language and art and accepted them for use in the service of the liturgy. Today the Church in the United States is again exploring how to translate the Gospel and to build churches in conversation with complex, secularized cultures that have sometimes rejected religion and attempted their own forms of human transcendence through intricate electronic modes of communication, art, and architecture.[58] Secular cultures in industrial and post-industrial countries have been particularly difficult to evangelize since they often treat human dignity selectively, attempting to control the mystery that animates the human thirst for meaning and purpose, and ignore those who

---

57. Cf. CT, no. 53: "'The term "acculturation" or "inculturation" may be a neologism, but it expresses very well one factor of the great mystery of the Incarnation.' We can say of catechesis, as well as of evangelization in general, that it is called to bring the power of the Gospel into the very heart of culture and cultures. For this purpose, catechesis will seek to know these cultures and their essential components; it will learn their most significant expressions; it will respect their particular values and riches. In this manner it will be able to offer these cultures the knowledge of the hidden mystery and help them to bring forth from their own living tradition original expressions of Christian life, celebration and thought. Two things must however be kept in mind.

"On the one hand the Gospel message cannot be purely and simply isolated from the culture in which it was first inserted (the Biblical world or, more concretely, the cultural milieu in which Jesus of Nazareth lived), nor, without serious loss, from the cultures in which it has already been expressed down the centuries; it does not spring spontaneously from any cultural soil; it has always been transmitted by means of an apostolic dialogue which inevitably becomes part of a certain dialogue of cultures.

"On the other hand, the power of the Gospel everywhere transforms and regenerates. When that power enters into a culture, it is no surprise that it rectifies many of its elements. There would be no catechesis if it were the Gospel that had to change when it came into contact with the cultures.

"To forget this would simply amount to what Saint Paul very forcefully calls 'emptying the cross of Christ of its power' (1 Corinthians 1:17).

"It is a different matter to take, with wise discernment, certain elements, religious or otherwise, that form part of the cultural heritage of a human group and use them to help its members to understand better the whole of the Christian mystery. Genuine catechists know that catechesis 'takes flesh' in the various cultures and milieux: one has only to think of the peoples with their great differences, of modern youth, of the great variety of circumstances in which people find themselves today. But they refuse to accept an impoverishment of catechesis through a renunciation or obscuring of its message, by adaptations, even in language, that would endanger the 'precious deposit' of the faith, or by concessions in matters of faith or morals. They are convinced that true catechesis eventually enriches these cultures by helping them to go beyond the defective or even inhuman features in them, and by communicating to their legitimate values the fullness of Christ."

58. Cf. Pope Paul VI, *Evangelii Nuntiandi: On Evangelization in the Modern World* (December 8, 1975), no. 42; CT, no. 53; Irish Episcopal Commission for Liturgy, *The Place of Worship: Pastoral Directory on the Building and Reordering of Churches* [PW] (1994), no. 3.7.

do not fit their economic or social purpose. The Gospel requires that particular care be taken to welcome into the Church's assembly those often discarded by society—the socially and economically marginalized, the elderly, the sick, those with disabilities, and those with special needs. In building a church, every diocese and parish must wrestle with these and other complex questions raised by the Church's mission to evangelize contemporary cultures.

§ 43 § Parishes in the United States today often find their places of worship shared by people of varied languages and ethnic backgrounds and experience vast differences in styles of public worship and personal devotion. What can sustain Christian communities in this challenge of hospitality is the realization that a pluralism of symbolic, artistic, and architectural expression enriches the community.[59]

§ 44 § 5. *The church building should be beautiful.* The external and internal structure of the church building should be expressive of the dignified beauty of God's holy people who gather there and of the sacred rites they celebrate. Liturgical art and architecture reflect and announce the presence of the God who calls the community to worship and invite believers to raise their minds and hearts to the One who is the source of all beauty and truth. Art or architecture that draws more attention to its own shape, form, texture, or color than to the sacred realities it seeks to disclose is unworthy of the church building.[60]

§ 45 § The Church's great treasury of art and architecture helps it to transcend the limitations of any one culture, region or period of time.[61] The Church is not exclusively identified with the forms of the past, but is ever open to embrace newer forms that nonetheless have grown organically from her rich heritage of artistic expression. Great religious art fosters the life of prayer of contemporary assemblies who, while rooted in prior artistic traditions, hear God's unceasing call to proclaim the reign of Christ in the languages of a particular time and place. Every artistic form that is at once capable of faithfully expressing sacred

---

59. CCC, nos. 1157–1158; cf. SC, no. 119.

60. Cf. LA, no. 6: "Every genuine artistic intuition goes beyond what the senses perceive and, reaching beneath reality's surface, strives to interpret its hidden mystery. The intuition itself springs from the depths of the human soul, where the desire to give meaning to one's own life is joined by the fleeting vision of beauty and of the mysterious unity of things. All artists experience the unbridgeable gap which lies between the work of their hands, however successful it may be, and the dazzling perfection of the beauty glimpsed in the ardor of the creative moment: What they manage to express in their painting, their sculpting, their creating is no more than a glimmer of the splendor which flared for a moment before the eyes of their spirit. . . .

"Every genuine art form in its own way is a path to the inmost reality of man and of the world. It is therefore a wholly valid approach to the realm of faith, which gives human experience its ultimate meaning. That is why the Gospel fullness of truth was bound from the beginning to stir the interest of artists, who by their very nature are alert to every 'epiphany' of the inner beauty of things."

61. Cf. SC, nos. 123 and 129; Congregation of Rites, *Eucharisticum Mysterium: On Worship of the Eucharist* [EM] (May 25, 1967), no. 24 (DOL 179, no. 1253).

realities and serving the Church's liturgical action with the highest quality of the arts can find a home in the Church's house of prayer.[62]

CHAPTER TWO
THE CHURCH BUILDING AND
THE SACRED RITES CELEBRATED THERE

§ 46 §   The church building houses the community of the baptized as it gathers to celebrate the sacred liturgy. By its practical design and beauty it fosters the full, dignified, and graceful celebration of these rites. The primary concern in the building or renovation of a space for worship must be its suitability for the celebration of the Eucharist and other liturgical rites of the Church. Consequently, the fundamental prerequisite for those engaged in the building or renovation of a church is familiarity with the rites to be celebrated there.

§ 47 §   The prayer life of the Church is richly diverse. The eucharistic liturgy, the other sacraments, and the Liturgy of the Hours are sacred actions surpassing all others. The praise and thanksgiving, which are at the heart of the Eucharist, are continued in the celebration of the Liturgy of the Hours. The Liturgy of the Hours is the Church's daily liturgical prayer that expresses the nature of the praying Church and is, itself, a sign of the Church.[63] In addition to their participation in communal prayer, Christ's followers deepen their relationship with God through private prayer, which flows from the liturgy. Thus, the Church encourages popular devotions that "harmonize with the liturgical seasons" and "lead people to [the liturgy]."[64] Besides its primary role of providing a suitable place for the celebration of the liturgical rites, the church building also offers a place to which

---

62. Cf. SC, no. 124: "When churches are to be built, let great care be taken that they be suitable for the celebration of liturgical services and for the active participation of the faithful."

Cf. GIRM, no. 292: "Church decor should seek to achieve noble simplicity rather than ostentation. The choice of materials for church appointments must be marked by concern for genuineness and by the intent to foster instruction of the faithful and the dignity of the place of worship."

Cf. GIRM, nos. 295, 306, and 311–312.

63. Pope Paul VI, *Laudis Canticum* (November 1, 1970) (DOL, 424, no. 3427): "The life of Christ in his Mystical Body also perfects and elevates for each member of the faithful his own personal life, any conflict between the prayer of the Church and personal prayer must be entirely rejected, and the relationship between them strengthened and enlarged. . . . If the prayer of the Divine Office becomes genuine personal prayer, the relation between the liturgy and the whole Christian life also becomes clearer. The whole life of the faithful, hour by hour during the day and night, is a kind of *leitourgia* or public service, in which the faithful give themselves over to the ministry of love toward God and men, identifying themselves with the action of Christ, who by his life and self-offering sanctified the life of all mankind."

64. SC, nos. 12 and 13: "The spiritual life, however, is not confined solely to participation in the liturgy. The Christian is assuredly called to pray with his brethren, but he must also enter into his chamber to pray to the Father in secret (cf. Matthew 6:6); indeed, according to the teaching of the Apostle Paul, he should pray without ceasing (cf. 1 Thessalonians 5:17). . . .

"Popular devotions of the Christian people are warmly commended, provided they accord with the laws and norms of the Church. Such is especially the case with devotions called for by the Apostolic See. . . . Nevertheless these devotions should be so drawn up that they harmonize with the liturgical seasons, accord with the sacred liturgy, are in some fashion derived from it, and lead people to it, since the liturgy by its very nature far surpasses any of them."

individuals may come to pray in the presence of the Blessed Sacrament, and in which groups of the faithful may gather for a rich variety of devotions expressive of the faith life of a given culture, region, or ethnic community.

§ 48 §   This chapter is intended to help a community fulfill its role in designing a place that readily accommodates all these needs. In new construction, parishes usually have several options for various elements of design. Sometimes those options are limited by the space or terrain, or by financial resources. And sometimes, as in the case of renovation, there are additional limits imposed by the existing structure. This chapter reviews the spatial demands of the various liturgical rites and offers principles for choosing among the various options. Many dioceses have developed their own procedures and guidelines for the building and renovation of churches. The principles in this document should guide dioceses in the writing of local directives.

THE EUCHARIST

§ 49 §   The celebration of the Eucharist is the center of the entire Christian life, both for the universal Church and for local faith communities. The other sacraments, like every other ministry of the Church and every work of the apostolate, are linked with the Holy Eucharist and have it as their end.[65] The celebration of the Sunday Eucharist is the appropriate starting point for understanding the demands of space, sound, and visibility made upon a church building. An analysis of these requirements will include attention to the place for the congregation, for the preaching of the word, and for the celebration of the Liturgy of the Eucharist, with special care for the location of the altar, the ambo, and the chairs for the priest celebrant and deacon, as necessary. Considerations about the narthex and the environment of the building flow from the central action of the Eucharist. The celebration of the Easter Vigil and of the Sunday Eucharist are appropriate starting points. In addition, special consideration should be given to the place for the reservation of the Blessed Sacrament.

THE BUILDING: THE PLACE FOR THE LITURGICAL ASSEMBLY
GATHERED AS ONE BODY IN CHRIST

§ 50 §   The church building is a sign and reminder of the immanence and transcendence of God—who chose to dwell among us and whose presence cannot be contained or limited to any single place. Worship is the loving response of God's People to the mystery of God who is with us and who is yet to come. "As visible constructions, churches are signs of the pilgrim church on earth; they are images that proclaim the heavenly Jerusalem, places in which are actualized

---

65. SC, no. 10: "Nevertheless the liturgy is the summit toward which the activity of the Church is directed; at the same time it is the fountain from which all her power flows. For the goal of apostolic works is that all who are made sons of God by faith and baptism should come together to praise God in the midst of His church, to take part in her sacrifice, and to eat the Lord's supper."

the mystery of the communion between man and God."[66] In addition, the church building manifests the baptismal unity of all who gather for the celebration of liturgy and "conveys the image of the gathered assembly."[67] While various places "express a hierarchical arrangement and the diversity of functions," those places "should at the same time form a deep and organic unity, clearly expressive of the unity of the entire holy people."[68]

THE CONGREGATION'S AREA

§ 51 §   The space within the church building for the faithful other than the priest celebrant and the ministers is sometimes called the *nave*. This space is critical in the overall plan because it accommodates a variety of ritual actions: processions during the Eucharist, the singing of the prayers, movement during baptismal rites, the sprinkling of the congregation with blessed water, the rites during the wedding and funeral liturgies, and personal devotion. This area is not comparable to the audience's space in a theater or public arena because in the liturgical assembly, there is no audience. Rather, the entire congregation acts. The ministers of music could also be located in the body of the church since they lead the entire assembly in song as well as by the example of their reverent attention and prayer.

§ 52 §   Two principles guide architectural decisions about the form and arrangement of the nave: (1) the community worships as a single body united in faith, not simply as individuals who happen to find themselves in one place, and the nature of the liturgy demands that the congregation as well as the priest celebrant and ministers be able to exercise their roles in a full and active way; and (2) the priest celebrant and ministers together with the congregation form the liturgical assembly, which is the Church gathered for worship.

---

66. Congregation for Divine Worship, Circular Letter on Concerts in Churches (November 5, 1987), no. 5: "According to tradition as expressed in the rite for the dedication of a church and altar, churches are primarily places where the people of God gather and are 'made one as the Father, the Son and the Holy Spirit are one, and are the church, the temple of God built with living stones, in which the Father is worshiped in spirit and truth.' . . .

"As visible constructions, churches are signs of the pilgrim church on earth; they are images that proclaim the heavenly Jerusalem, places in which are actualized the mystery of the communion between man and God. Both in urban areas and in the countryside, the church remains the house of God and the sign of his dwelling among men. It remains a sacred place, even when no liturgical celebration is taking place."

67. GIRM, no. 294: "The people of God assembled at Mass possess an organic and hierarchical structure, expressed by the various ministries and actions for each part of the celebration. The general plan of the sacred building should be such that in some way it conveys the image of the gathered assembly. Thus it should also allow the participants to take the place most appropriate to them and assist all to carry out their individual functions properly.

"The faithful and the choir should have a place that facilitates their active participation."

68. Ibid.: "Even though all these elements must express a hierarchical arrangement and the diversity of functions, they should at the same time form a deep and organic unity, clearly expressive of the unity of the entire holy people. The character and beauty of the place and all its appointments should foster devotion and show the holiness of the mysteries celebrated there."

§ 53 §   The body of the church is not simply a series of unrelated sections. Rather, each part contributes to the unity of the space by proportion, size, and shape. While various rites are celebrated there, the sense of the nave as a unified whole should not be sacrificed to the need for flexibility.

THE SANCTUARY AREA

§ 54 §   The sanctuary is the space where the altar and the ambo stand, and "where the priest, deacon and other ministers exercise their offices." The special character of the sanctuary is emphasized and enhanced by the distinctiveness of its design and furnishings, or by its elevation.[69] The challenge to those responsible for its design is to convey the unique quality of the actions that take place in this area while at the same time expressing the organic relationship between those actions and the prayer and actions of the entire liturgical assembly. The sanctuary must be spacious enough to accommodate the full celebration of the various rituals of word and Eucharist with their accompanying movement, as well as those of the other sacraments celebrated there.

§ 55 §   The principal ritual furnishings within the sanctuary are the altar on which the eucharistic sacrifice is offered, the ambo from which God's word is proclaimed, and the chair of the priest celebrant. These furnishings should be constructed of substantial materials that express dignity and stability. Their placement and their design again make it clear that although they are distinct entities, they are related in the one eucharistic celebration.

THE ALTAR

§ 56 §   At the Eucharist, the liturgical assembly celebrates the ritual sacrificial meal that recalls and makes present Christ's life, death and resurrection, proclaiming "the death of the Lord until he comes."[70] The altar is "the center of thanksgiving that the Eucharist accomplishes"[71] and the point around which the other rites are in some manner arrayed.[72] Since the Church teaches that "the altar is Christ,"[73] its composition should reflect the nobility, beauty, strength and simplicity of the One it represents. In new churches there is to be only one

---

69. Ibid., no. 295: "The sanctuary is the place where the altar stands, the word of God is proclaimed, and the priest, deacon and other ministers exercise their offices. It should clearly be marked off from the body of the church either by being somewhat elevated or by its distinctive design and appointments. It should be large enough to allow for the proper celebration of the Eucharist which should be easily seen."

70. 1 Corinthians 11:26; cf. Revelation 19:9.

71. GIRM, no. 296: "At the altar the sacrifice of the cross is made present under sacramental signs. It is also the table of the Lord, and the people of God are called together to share in it. The altar is, as well, the center of the thanksgiving that the Eucharist accomplishes."

72. Pope Pius XII, *Mediator Dei: On the Sacred Liturgy* (November 20, 1947), no. 21.

73. RDCA, ch. 4, no. 4 (DOL, 547, no. 4401): "Therefore, the Church's writers have seen in the altar a sign of Christ himself. This is the basis for the saying 'the altar is Christ.'"

altar so that it "signifies to the assembly of the faithful the one Christ and the one Eucharist of the Church."[74]

§ 57 §   The altar is the natural focal point of the sanctuary and is to be "free-standing to allow the [priest] to walk around it easily and Mass to be celebrated facing the people."[75] Ordinarily, it should be fixed (with the base affixed to the floor) and with a table or mensa made of natural stone,[76] since it represents Christ Jesus, the Living Stone (1 Peter 2:4). The pedestal or support for the table may be fashioned from "any sort of material, as long as it is becoming and solid."[77] In the United States it is permissible to use materials other than natural stone for a fixed altar, provided these materials are worthy, solid, properly constructed, and subject to the further judgment of the local ordinary.[78] Parishes building new churches must follow the directives of the diocesan bishop regarding the kind of altar chosen and suitable materials for new altars.

§ 58 §   Although there is no specified size or shape for an altar, it should be in proportion to the church. The shape and size should reflect the nature of the altar as the place of sacrifice and the table around which Christ gathers the community to nourish them. In considering the dimensions of the altar, parishes will also want to ensure that the other major furnishings in the sanctuary are in harmony and proportion to the altar. The mensa should be large enough to accommodate the priest celebrant, the deacon and the acolytes who minister there and should be able to hold *The Sacramentary (The Roman Missal)* and the

---

74.GIRM, no. 303: "In the building of new churches, it is especially important that a single altar be erected which signifies to the assembly of the faithful the one Christ and the one Eucharist of the Church.

"However, in churches already built, when an old altar is already so positioned that it makes the participation of the people difficult, or it is impossible to move it without detriment to its artistic value, then another fixed altar may be erected. It should be artfully made and dedicated according to the rite. The sacred celebrations should be performed upon it alone; and in order that the attention of the faithful not be distracted from the new altar, the old altar should not be decorated in any special way."

75. Ibid., no. 299: "In every church there should ordinarily be a fixed, dedicated altar, which should be freestanding to allow the ministers to walk around it easily and Mass to be celebrated facing the people, which is desirable whenever possible. The altar should occupy its place so that it is truly the center on which the attention of the whole congregation of the faithful naturally focuses. As a rule, the altar is fixed and dedicated."

76. RDCA, ch. 4, no. 9 (DOL, 547, no. 4406): "In accordance with received custom in the Church and the biblical symbolism connected with an altar, the table of a fixed altar should be of stone, indeed of natural stone. But, at the discretion of the conference of bishops, any becoming, solid, and finely wrought material may be used in erecting an altar."

Cf. GIRM, no. 301; CIC, cc. 1235 and 1236a.

77. GIRM, no. 301: "The pedestal or base of the table may be of any sort of material, as long as it is becoming and solid."

Cf. CIC, c. 1236.

78. GIRM, no. 301: "According to the Church's traditional practice and the altar's symbolism, the table of a fixed altar should be of stone and indeed of natural stone. But at the discretion of the Conference of Bishops some other solid, becoming, and well-crafted material may be used. The pedestal or base of the table may be made of any sort of material, as long as it is becoming and solid."

Cf. National Conference of Catholic Bishops, *The Appendix to the General Instruction for the Dioceses of the United States of America* (1975), no. 263.

vessels with the bread and wine. Impact and focal quality are not only related to placement, size or shape, but also especially to the quality of the altar's design and worthiness of its construction. The altar should be centrally located in the sanctuary and the center of attention in the church.

§ 59 §   During the Liturgy of the Eucharist, the altar must be visible from all parts of the church but not so elevated that it causes visual or symbolic division from the liturgical assembly. Methods of elevation can be found that still allow access to the altar by ministers who need wheelchairs or who have other disabilities.

§ 60 §   In the Church's history and tradition, the altar was often placed over the tombs of the saints or the relics of saints were deposited beneath the altar. The presence of relics of saints in the altar provides a witness to the Church's belief that the Eucharist celebrated on the altar is the source of the grace that won sanctity for the saints.[79] The custom of placing small relics of martyrs or other saints in an altar stone and setting this in the mensa has changed since the Second Vatican Council. Relics of martyrs or other saints may be placed *beneath* the altar, as long as the relics are of a size sufficient for them to be recognizable as parts of a human body and that they are of undoubted authenticity. Relics are no longer placed *on* the altar or set into the mensa in an altar stone.[80]

THE AMBO

§ 61 §   The central focus of the area in which the word of God is proclaimed during the liturgy is the *ambo*. The design of the ambo and its prominent placement reflects the dignity and nobility of that saving word and draws the attention of those present to the proclamation of the word.[81] Here the Christian community encounters the living Lord in the word of God and prepares itself

---

79. Cf. RDCA, ch. 4, no. 5 (DOL 547, no. 4402): "[In the words of Saint Ambrose] the triumphant victims come to their rest in the place where Christ is victim: he, however, who suffered for all is on the altar; they who have been redeemed by his sufferings are beneath the altar."

80. RDCA, ch. 4, no. 11c (DOL 547, no. 4408): "A reliquary must not be placed on the altar or set into the table of the altar, but placed beneath the table of the altar, as the design of the altar permits."

81. Congregation for Divine Worship and the Discipline of the Sacraments, *General Introduction to the Lectionary for Mass* [GILM] (1998), no. 32: "There must be a place in the church that is somewhat elevated, fixed, and of a suitable design and nobility. It should reflect the dignity of God's word and be a clear reminder to the people that in the Mass the table of God's word and of Christ's body is placed before them. The place for the readings must also truly help the people's listening and attention during the liturgy of the word. Great pains must therefore be taken, in keeping with the design of each church, over the harmonious and close relationship of the ambo with the altar."

Cf. GIRM, no. 309: "The dignity of the word of God requires the church to have a place that is suitable for proclamation of the word and is a natural focal point for the faithful during the liturgy of the word.

"As a rule the ambo should be stationary, not simply a movable stand. In keeping with the structure of each church, it must be so placed that the ordained ministers and readers may be easily seen and heard by the faithful.

"The readings, responsorial psalm and the Easter Proclamation (*Exsultet*) are proclaimed only from the ambo."

for the "breaking of the bread" and the mission to live the word that will be proclaimed. An ample area around the ambo is needed to allow a gospel procession with a full complement of ministers bearing candles and incense. The *General Introduction to the Lectionary* recommends that the design of altar and ambo bear a "harmonious and close relationship" to one another[82] in order to emphasize the close relationship between word and Eucharist. Since many people share in the ministry of the word, the ambo should be accessible to everyone, including those with physical disabilities.[83]

§ 62 §   Our reverence for the word of God is expressed not only in an attentive listening to and reflection upon the Scripture, but also by the way we handle and treat the Book of the Gospels. The ambo can be designed not only for reading and preaching, but also for displaying the open Book of the Gospels or a copy of the Scriptures before and after the liturgical celebration.[84]

THE CHAIR FOR THE PRIEST CELEBRANT

§ 63 §   The chair of the priest celebrant stands "as a symbol of his [office] of presiding over the assembly and of directing prayer."[85] An appropriate placement of the chair allows the priest celebrant to be visible to all in the congregation. The chair reflects the dignity of the one who leads the community in the person of Christ, but is never intended to be remote or grandiose. The priest celebrant's chair is distinguished from the seating for other ministers by its design and placement. "The seat for the deacon should be placed near that of the celebrant."[86] In the cathedral, in addition to the bishop's chair or *cathedra*, which is permanent, an additional chair will be needed for use by the rector or priest celebrant.[87]

§ 64 §   "The [most appropriate] place for the chair is at the head of the sanctuary and turned toward the people, unless the design of the building or other circumstances [such as distance or the placement of the tabernacle] are an obstacle."[88] This chair is not used by a lay person who presides at a service of the word with Communion or a Sunday celebration in the absence of a priest.

---

82. GILM, no. 32: "Great pains must therefore be taken, in keeping with the design of each church, over the harmonious and close relationship of the ambo with the altar."

83. The elevation of the ambo, an access without steps, and in situations where it seems feasible, an ambo with a top section that is adjustable in height either manually or electrically will enable all to serve as celebrant, lector, and cantor.

84. It has become customary to provide a place for the permanent display of the Scriptures in the sanctuary area. This can be done using the front of the ambo or another kind of pedestal.

85. GIRM, no. 310: "The priest celebrant's chair ought to stand as a symbol of his function of presiding over the assembly and of directing prayer. Thus the best place for the chair is at the head of the sanctuary and turned toward the people, unless the design of the building or other circumstances are an obstacle, for example, if too great a distance would interfere with communication between the priest and the gathered assembly, or if the tabernacle is positioned medially behind the altar. However, anything resembling a throne is to be avoided.

"The seat for the deacon should be placed near that of the celebrant. However the seats for the other ministers should be arranged so that they are clearly distinguished from the seats for clergy and, so that the lay ministers are easily able to fulfill the office assigned to them."

86. Ibid.

87. *Ceremonial of Bishops*, no. 47.

88. GIRM, no. 310.

(Cf. Congregation for Divine Worship, *Directory for Sunday Celebrations in the Absence of a Priest* [1988], no. 40.)

§ 65 § Other chairs may be placed in the sanctuary for the priest concelebrants and other priests present for the celebration in choir dress.

THE BAPTISTRY

§ 66 § The rites of baptism, the first of the sacraments of initiation, require a prominent place for celebration.[89] Initiation into the Church is entrance into a eucharistic community united in Jesus Christ. Because the rites of initiation of the Church begin with baptism and are completed by the reception of the Eucharist, the baptismal font and its location reflect the Christian's journey *through* the waters of baptism *to* the altar. This integral relationship between the baptismal font and the altar can be demonstrated in a variety of ways, such as placing the font and altar on the same architectural axis, using natural or artificial lighting, using the same floor patterns, and using common or similar materials and elements of design.

§ 67 § The location of the baptismal font, its design, and the materials used for its construction are important considerations in the planning and design of the building. It is customary to locate the baptismal font either in a special area within the main body of the church or in a separate baptistry. Through the waters of baptism the faithful enter the life of Christ.[90] For this reason the font should be visible and accessible to all who enter the church building. While the baptistry is proportioned to the building itself and should be able to hold a good number of people, its actual size will be determined by the needs of the local community.

§ 68 § Water is the key symbol of baptism and the focal point of the font. In this water believers die to sin and are reborn to new life in Christ. In designing the font and the iconography in the baptismal area, the parish will want to consider the traditional symbolism that has been the inspiration for the font's design throughout history. The font is a symbol of both tomb and womb; its power is the power of the triumphant cross; and baptism sets the Christian on the path

---

89. Congregation for Divine Worship, *Rite of Christian Initiation of Adults* [RCIA] (1988), General Introduction, no. 25: "The baptistery or the area where the baptismal font is located should be reserved for the sacrament of baptism and should be worthy to serve as the place where Christians are reborn in water and the Holy Spirit. The baptistery may be situated in a chapel either inside or outside the church or in some other part of the church easily seen by the faithful; it should be large enough to accommodate a good number of people. After the Easter season, the Easter candle should be kept reverently in the baptistery, in such a way that it can be lighted for the celebration of baptism and so that from it the candles for the newly baptized can easily be lighted."

90. Ibid., no. 213: "Therefore in the celebration of baptism the washing with water should take on its full importance as the sign of that mystical sharing in Christ's death and resurrection through which those who believe in his name die to sin and rise to eternal life. Either immersion or the pouring of water should be chosen for the rite, whichever will serve in individual cases and in the various traditions and circumstances to ensure the clear understanding that this washing is not a mere purification rite but the sacrament of being joined to Christ."

to the life that will never end, the "eighth day" of eternity where Christ's reign of peace and justice is celebrated.

§ 69 §   The following criteria can be helpful when choosing the design for the font:

1.   *One font that will accommodate the baptism of both infants and adults symbolizes the one faith and one baptism that Christians share.* The size and design of the font can facilitate the dignified celebration for all who are baptized at the one font.

2.   *The font should be large enough to supply ample water for the baptism of both adults and infants.* Since baptism in Catholic churches may take place by immersion in the water, or by infusion (pouring), fonts that permit all forms of baptismal practice are encouraged.[91]

3.   *Baptism is a sacrament of the whole Church and, in particular, of the local parish community.* Therefore the ability of the congregation to participate in baptisms is an important consideration.

4.   *The location of the baptistry will determine how, and how actively, the entire liturgical assembly can participate in the rite of baptism.*

5.   *Because of the essential relationship of baptism to the celebration of other sacraments and rituals, the parish will want to choose an area for the baptistry or the font that visually symbolizes that relationship.* Some churches choose to place the baptistry and font near the entrance to the church. Confirmation and the Eucharist complete the initiation begun at baptism; marriage and ordination are ways of living the life of faith begun in baptism; the funeral of a Christian is the final journey of a life in Christ that began in baptism; and the sacrament of penance calls the faithful to conversion and to a renewal of their baptismal commitment. Placing the baptismal font in an area near the entrance or gathering space where the members pass regularly and setting it on an axis with the altar can symbolize the relationship between the various sacraments as well as the importance of the Eucharist within the life and faith development of the members.

6.   *With the restoration of the* Rite of Christian Initiation of Adults *that culminates in baptism at the Easter Vigil, churches need private spaces where the newly baptized can go immediately after their baptism to be clothed in their white garments and to prepare for the completion of initiation in the Eucharist.* In some instances, nearby sacristies can serve this purpose.

---

91. Ibid.: "Either immersion or the pouring of water should be chosen for the rite, whichever will serve in individual cases and in the various traditions and circumstances to ensure the clear understanding that this washing is not a mere purification rite but the sacrament of being joined to Christ."

Cf. RCIA, *National Statutes for the Catechumenate* (1986), no. 17: "Baptism by immersion is the fuller and more expressive sign of the sacrament and, therefore, provision should be made for its more frequent use in the baptism of adults. The provision of the *Rite of Christian Initiation of Adults* for partial immersion, namely, immersion of the candidate's head, should be taken into account."

§ 70 §   Christ present in the eucharistic species is a treasure the Church has come to cherish and revere over the centuries. The reservation of the Eucharist was originally intended for the communion of the sick, for those unable to attend the Sunday celebration, and as *Viaticum* for the dying. As the appreciation of Christ's presence in the eucharistic species became more developed, Christians desired through prayer to show reverence for Christ's continuing presence in their midst. For Catholics, eucharistic adoration has "an authentic and solid basis, especially because faith in the real presence of the Lord leads naturally to external, public expression of that faith."[92]

§ 71 §   The Second Vatican Council led the Church to a fuller understanding of the relationship between the presence of the Lord in the liturgical celebration of the Eucharist and in the reserved Sacrament, and of the Christian's responsibility to feed the hungry and to care for the poor. As the baptized grow to understand their active participation in the Eucharist, they will be drawn to spend more time in quiet prayer before the Blessed Sacrament reserved in the tabernacle, and be impelled to live out their relationship in active charity. In reverent prayer before the reserved Eucharist, the faithful give praise and thanksgiving to Christ for the priceless gift of redemption and for the spiritual food that sustains them in their daily lives. Here they learn to appreciate their right and responsibility to join the offering of their own lives to the perfect sacrifice of Christ during the Mass[93] and are led to a greater recognition of Christ in themselves and in others, especially in the poor and needy. Providing a suitable place for the reservation of the Blessed Sacrament is a serious consideration in any building or renovation project.

§ 72 §   The general law of the Church provides norms concerning the tabernacle and the place for the reservation of the Eucharist that express the importance Christians place on the presence of the Blessed Sacrament. The *Code of Canon Law* directs that the Eucharist be reserved in a part of the church that is "distinguished, conspicuous, beautifully decorated, and suitable for prayer."[94]

---

92. Congregation for Divine Worship, *Holy Communion and Worship of the Eucharist Outside Mass* [HCWEOM] (1976), no. 5: "The primary and original reason for reservation of the eucharist outside Mass is the administration of viaticum. The secondary reasons are the giving of communion and the adoration of our Lord Jesus Christ present in the sacrament. The reservation of the sacrament for the sick led to the praiseworthy practice of adoring this heavenly food in the churches. This cult of adoration rests upon an authentic and solid basis, especially because faith in the real presence of the Lord leads naturally to external, public expression of that faith."

93. SC, no. 48: "The Church, therefore, earnestly desires that Christ's faithful, when present at this mystery of faith, should not be there as strangers or silent spectators. On the contrary, through a proper appreciation of the rites and prayers they should participate knowingly, devoutly, and actively. They should be instructed by God's word and be refreshed at the table of the Lord's body; they should give thanks to God; by offering the Immaculate Victim, not only through the hands of the priest, but also with him, they should learn to offer themselves too. Through Christ the Mediator, they should be drawn day by day into ever closer union with God and with each other, so that finally God may be all in all."

94. CIC, c. 938 § 2: "The tabernacle in which the Most Holy Eucharist is reserved is to be situated in some part of the church or oratory which is distinguished, conspicuous, beautifully decorated, and suitable for prayer."

It directs that regularly there be "only one tabernacle" in the church.[95] It should be worthy of the Blessed Sacrament—beautifully designed and in harmony with the overall decor of the rest of the church. To provide for the security of the Blessed Sacrament the tabernacle should be "solid," "immovable," "opaque," and "locked."[96] The tabernacle may be situated on a fixed pillar or stand, or it may be attached to or embedded in one of the walls. A special oil lamp or a lamp with a wax candle burns continuously near the tabernacle as an indication of Christ's presence.[97]

§ 73 §   The place of reservation should be a space that is dedicated to Christ present in the Eucharist and that is designed so that the attention of one praying there is drawn to the tabernacle that houses the presence of the Lord. Iconography can be chosen from the rich treasury of symbolism that is associated with the Eucharist.

THE LOCATION OF THE TABERNACLE

§ 74 §   There is a number of possible spaces suitable for eucharistic reservation. The revised *General Instruction of the Roman Missal* states that it is more appropriate that the tabernacle in which the "Blessed Sacrament is reserved not be on the altar on which Mass is celebrated."[98] The bishop is to determine where the tabernacle will be placed and to give further direction. The bishop may decide that the tabernacle be placed in the sanctuary apart from the altar of celebration or in a separate chapel suitable for adoration and for the private prayer of the faithful. In making his determination, the bishop will consider the importance of the assembly's ability to focus on the eucharistic action, the piety of the people, and the custom of the area.[99] The location also should allow for easy access by people in wheelchairs and by those who have other disabilities.

---

95. Ibid., c. 938 § 1: "The Most Holy Eucharist is to be reserved habitually in only one tabernacle of a church or oratory."

96. Ibid., c. 938 § 3: "The tabernacle in which the Most Holy Eucharist is reserved habitually is to be immovable, made of solid and opaque material, and locked in such a way that the danger of profanation is avoided as much as possible."
        Cf. GIRM, no. 314.

97. HCWEOM, no. 11: "According to traditional usage, an oil lamp or lamp with a wax candle is to burn constantly near the tabernacle as a sign of the honor which is shown to the Lord."

98. GIRM, no. 315: "It is more in keeping with its meaning as a sign, that the tabernacle in which the Most Blessed Sacrament is reserved not be on the altar on which Mass is celebrated. Moreover, the tabernacle should be placed, according to the judgment of the diocesan Bishop:
        (a) either in the sanctuary, apart from the altar of celebration, in the most suitable form and place, not excluding on an old altar which is no longer used for celebration;
        (b) or even in another chapel suitable for adoration and the private prayer of the faithful, and which is integrally connected with the church and is conspicuous to the faithful."

99. There has been a shift in directives about the placement of the tabernacle over time. The latest edition of the *General Instruction of the Roman Missal* (2000) alters the earlier directive in GIRM, no. 276, which gave a clear preference for reservation in a separate chapel. GIRM, no. 315, now directs the diocesan bishop to determine the appropriate placement either in the sanctuary (including on the old altar which is no longer used for celebration) or in a separate chapel. It may not be reserved on the altar at which the Eucharist is celebrated.

§ 75 §   In exercising his responsibility for the liturgical life of the diocese, the diocesan bishop may issue further directives regarding the reservation of the Eucharist. Before parishes and their liturgical consultants begin the educational component and the discussion process, it will be important for all those involved to know what specific directives or guidelines the diocesan bishop has issued. Good communication at the first stage of the process will help to avoid confusion or conflict between the parish's expectations, the consultant's experience and diocesan directives.

§ 76 §   The pastor, the parish pastoral council, and the building committee will want to examine the principles that underlie each of the options, consider the liturgical advantages of each possibility, and reflect upon the customs and piety of the parishioners. Many diocesan worship offices assist parishes by facilitating the study and discussion process with the parish. This is also an area where liturgical consultants can be of great assistance to the parish.

THE CHAPEL OF RESERVATION

§ 77 §   The diocesan bishop may direct the parish to reserve the Blessed Sacrament in a chapel separate from the nave and sanctuary but "integrally connected with the church" and "conspicuous to the faithful."[100] The placement and design of the chapel can foster reverence and can provide the quiet and focus needed for personal prayer, and it should provide kneelers and chairs for those who come to pray.

§ 78 §   Some parishes have inaugurated the practice of continuous adoration of the Eucharist. If, for some good reason, perpetual exposition must take place in a parish church, the Congregation for Divine Worship and the Discipline of the Sacraments has directed that this take place in a separate chapel that is "distinct from the body of the church so as not to interfere with the normal activities of the parish or its daily liturgical celebration."[101]

THE TABERNACLE IN THE SANCTUARY

§ 79 §   A special area can be designed within the sanctuary. Careful planning is needed so that the placement chosen does not draw the attention of the faithful away from the eucharistic celebration and its components.[102] In addition, the

---

100. GIRM, no. 315.

101. Cf. Response of the Congregation for Divine Worship and the Discipline of the Sacraments Regarding Perpetual Exposition of the Eucharist published in the June 1995 issue of the National Conference of Catholic Bishops' BCL [Bishops' Committee on the Liturgy] Newsletter, p. 21: "Because perpetual exposition is a devotional practice of a religious community or a pious association, it should normally take place in a chapel of that religious community or association. If for some good reason perpetual exposition must take place in a parish church, it should be in a chapel distinct from the body of the church so as not to interfere with the normal activities of the parish or its daily liturgical celebration. When Mass is celebrated in a chapel where the Blessed Sacrament is exposed, the Eucharist must be replaced in the tabernacle before the celebration of Mass begins."

102. EM, no. 55 (DOL 179, no. 1284): "It is more in keeping with the nature of the celebration [of the Eucharist] that, through reservation of the sacrament in the tabernacle, Christ not be present eucharistically from the beginning on the altar where Mass is celebrated."

placement must allow for a focus on the tabernacle for those periods of quiet prayer outside the celebration of the Eucharist.

§ 80 §   Ordinarily, it is helpful to have a sufficient distance to separate the tabernacle and the altar. When a tabernacle is located directly behind the altar, consideration should be given to using distance, lighting or some other architectural device that separates the tabernacle and reservation area during Mass, but that allows the tabernacle to be fully visible to the entire worship area when the eucharistic liturgy is not being celebrated.

HOLY WEEK AND THE PASCHAL TRIDUUM

§ 81 §   Passion (Palm) Sunday marks the final movement of the Lenten season toward the Triduum. The liturgy of Palm Sunday requires space for a procession that recalls Christ's triumphant entry into Jerusalem (Matthew 21:1–11). For the cathedral church, the additional consideration of elements of the stational (i.e., pontifical) liturgies should be part of the planning. The Paschal Triduum is the heart of the liturgical year. When designing the church, the rites of the Triduum should be reviewed to ensure that planning will provide space for the key elements of the Triduum: an area for the washing of the feet, a location for the Altar of Reposition after the Evening Mass of the Lord's Supper, space for the Veneration of the Cross on Good Friday, a site for the Blessing of the Fire and the Lighting of the Paschal Candle, and space for the catechumens to be baptized and for candidates for admission to full membership to stand if they are admitted at the Vigil.

THE ALTAR OF REPOSITION

§ 82 §   Following the Mass of the Lord's Supper on Holy Thursday, the Blessed Sacrament is carried to a place of reservation. If the Blessed Sacrament is ordinarily reserved in a chapel separated from the central part of the church, the place of repose and adoration will be there.[103] If there is no reservation chapel, then a space for reposition with a tabernacle should be prepared for the occasion.

THE VENERATION OF THE CROSS ON GOOD FRIDAY

§ 83 §   The celebration of the Lord's passion on Good Friday has its particular spatial requirements. After the proclamation of the passion and the General Intercessions, the entire assembly rises to venerate the cross or crucifix.[104] The cross used for the veneration preferably should be of sufficient size to be held easily, carried in procession, and venerated. After the veneration, the cross remains in the sanctuary.

---

103. Congregation for Divine Worship, *Circular Letter Concerning the Preparation and Celebration of the Easter Feasts* [PCEF] (January 16, 1988), no. 49: "For the reservation of Blessed Sacrament, a place should be prepared and adorned in such a way as to be conducive to prayer and meditation; that sobriety appropriate to the liturgy of these days is enjoined, to the avoidance or suppression of all abuses."
104. Ibid.

§ 84 §   In some circumstances parishes may be able to create a permanent place for lighting the Easter fire. In others, the rite may be conducted in the gathering area immediately outside the church. While safety is always an important consideration, a flame to "dispel the darkness and light up the night" is needed to achieve the full symbolism of the fire.[105] In climates and circumstances where weather precludes lighting the fire outdoors, a more limited fire can be enkindled indoors with the proper accommodations for ventilation, for heat and smoke detectors, for local fire regulations, and for surrounding the space with non-combustible materials.

ACCOMMODATING THE LITURGICAL POSTURES OF THE CONGREGATION

§ 85 §   The location set aside for the people will convey their role within the liturgical assembly.[106] The members of the congregation should be able to see the ministers at the altar, the ambo and the chair.

§ 86 §   Since the liturgy requires various postures and movements, the space and furniture for the congregation should accommodate them well.[107] Styles of benches, pews, or chairs can be found that comfortably accommodate the human form. Kneelers or kneeling cushions should also be provided so that the whole congregation can easily kneel when the liturgy calls for it. Parishes will want to choose a seating arrangement that calls the congregation to active participation and that avoids any semblance of a theater or an arena. It is also important that the seating plan provide spaces for an unimpeded view of the sanctuary by people in wheelchairs or with walkers. Experience indicates that space in the front or at the sides of the church is better than in the rear where a standing congregation obscures the view of those seated in wheelchairs at the back of the church.

---

105. PCEF, no. 82: "Insofar as possible, a suitable place should be prepared outside the church for the blessing of the new fire, whose flames should be such that they genuinely dispel the darkness and light up the night."

106. GIRM, no. 294: "The people of God assembled at Mass possess an organic and hierarchical structure, expressed by the various ministries and actions for each part of the celebration. The general plan of the sacred building should be such that in some way it conveys the image of the gathered assembly. Thus it should also allow the participants to take the place most appropriate to them and assist all to carry out their individual functions properly.

"The faithful and the choir should have a place that facilitates their active participation.

"The priest celebrant, the deacon and other ministers have their place in the sanctuary. At the same time, seats for the concelebrants should be prepared. If there is truly a great number of concelebrants, then seats should be arranged in another part of the church, but near the altar.

"Even though all these elements must express a hierarchical arrangement and the diversity of functions, they should at the same time form a deep and organic unity, clearly expressive of the unity of the entire holy people. The character and beauty of the place and all its appointments should foster devotion and show the holiness of the mysteries celebrated there."

107. Ibid., no. 311: "The places for the faithful should be arranged with care so that they are able to take their rightful part in the celebration visually and mentally. As a rule, there should be benches or chairs for their use. But the custom of reserving seats for private persons must be abolished. Especially in newly built churches, however, benches or chairs should be set up in such a way that the people can easily take the postures required during various parts of the celebration and have unimpeded access to receive communion."

§ 87 § There are no universal norms regarding fixed or flexible seating but the diocesan bishop may issue further directives in this area. Many churches have found that a combination of fixed and flexible seating works best to accommodate the various liturgical actions. Ideally, no seat in the nave would be located beyond a point where distance and the lighting level of the sanctuary severely impede the view of and participation in liturgical actions. In earlier periods churches designed for large congregations were limited by engineering constraints. The latest construction and engineering technologies now allow for cost-effective and flexible approaches to designing churches with greater roof spans.

THE PLACE FOR THE PASTORAL MUSICIANS

§ 88 § Music is integral to the liturgy. It unifies those gathered to worship, supports the song of the congregation, highlights significant parts of the liturgical action, and helps to set the tone for each celebration.[108]

§ 89 § It is important to recognize that the building must support the music and song of the entire worshiping assembly. In addition, "some members of the community [have] special gifts [for] leading the [assembly in] musical praise and thanksgiving."[109] The skills and talents of these pastoral musicians, choirs and instrumentalists are especially valued by the Church. Because the roles of the choirs and cantors are exercised within the liturgical community, the space chosen for the musicians should clearly express that they are part of the assembly of worshipers.[110] In addition, cantors and song leaders need visual contact with the music director while they themselves are visible to the rest of the congregation.[111] Apart from the singing of the Responsorial Psalm, which normally occurs at the ambo, the stand for the cantor or song leader is distinct from the ambo, which is reserved for the proclamation of the word of God.

---

108. MCW, no. 23; GIRM, no. 103: "The *schola cantorum* or choir exercises its own liturgical function among the faithful. Its task is to ensure that the parts proper to it, in keeping with the different types of chants, are carried out becomingly and to encourage active participation of the people in the singing. What is said about the choir applies in a similar way to other musicians, especially the organist."

109. National Conference of Catholic Bishops' Committee on the Liturgy, *Liturgical Music Today* (1982), no. 63: "The entire worshiping assembly exercises a ministry of music. Some members of the community, however, are recognized for the special gifts they exhibit in leading the musical praise and thanksgiving of Christian assemblies. These are the pastoral musicians, whose ministry is especially cherished by the Church."

110. GIRM, no. 294: "The people of God assembled at Mass possess an organic and hierarchical structure, expressed by the various ministries and actions for each part of the celebration. The general plan of the sacred building should be such that in some way it conveys the image of the gathered assembly. Thus it should also allow the participants to take the place most appropriate to them and assist all to carry out their individual functions properly.

"The faithful and the choir should have a place that facilitates their active participation."

Ibid., no. 312: "In relation to the design of each church, the *schola cantorum* should be so placed that its character as a part of the assembly of the faithful that has a special function stands out clearly. The location should also assist the exercise of the duties of the *schola cantorum* and allow each member of the choir complete, that is, sacramental participation in the Mass."

111. Cf. MCW, nos. 33–38.

§ 90 § The directives concerning music found in the *General Instruction of the Roman Missal* and the guidance offered by *Music in Catholic Worship and Liturgical Music Today*[112] can assist the parish in planning appropriate space for musicians. The placement and prayerful decorum of the choir members can help the rest of the community to focus on the liturgical action taking place at the ambo, the altar, and the chair. The ministers of music are most appropriately located in a place where they can be part of the assembly and have the ability to be heard. Occasions or physical situations may necessitate that the choir be placed in or near the sanctuary. In such circumstances, the placement of the choir should never crowd or overshadow the other ministers in the sanctuary nor should it distract from the liturgical action.

OTHER RITUAL FURNISHINGS

THE CROSS

§ 91 § The cross with the image of Christ crucified is a reminder of Christ's paschal mystery. It draws us into the mystery of suffering and makes tangible our belief that our suffering when united with the passion and death of Christ leads to redemption.[113] There should be a crucifix "positioned either on the altar or near it, and . . . clearly visible to the people gathered there."[114] Since a crucifix placed *on* the altar and large enough to be seen by the congregation might well obstruct the view of the action taking place on the altar, other alternatives may be more appropriate. The crucifix may be suspended over the altar or affixed to the sanctuary wall. A processional cross of sufficient size, placed in a stand visible to the people following the entrance procession, is another option. If the processional cross is to be used for this purpose, the size and weight of the cross should not preclude its being carried in procession. If there is already a cross in the sanctuary, the processional cross is placed out of view of the congregation following the procession.[115]

---

112. Cf. the section in chapter four of this document on "The Placement of the Organ and Other Musical Instruments."

113. Cf. Congregation for Divine Worship, National Conference of Catholic Bishops, *Book of Blessings* [BB] (1988), no. 1233: "Of all sacred images, the 'figure of the precious, life-giving cross of Christ' is pre-eminent, because it is the symbol of the entire paschal mystery. The cross is the image most cherished by the Christian people and the most ancient; it represents Christ's suffering and victory and at the same time, as the Fathers of the Church have taught, it points to his Second Coming."

114. GIRM, no. 308: "There is also to be a cross, with the figure of Christ crucified upon it, positioned either on the altar or near it, and which is clearly visible to the people gathered together. It is fitting that a cross of this kind, recalling for the faithful the saving passion of the Lord, remain near the altar even outside of liturgical celebrations."

115. Cf. ibid., no. 122: "The cross adorned with the figure of Christ crucified and which has been carried in procession, is placed near the altar so that it may become the altar cross, which ought then to be the only cross used; otherwise it is set aside."

§ 92 §   Candles, which are signs of reverence and festivity, "are to be used at every liturgical service.[116] The living flame of the candle, symbolic of the risen Christ, reminds people that in baptism they are brought out of darkness into God's marvelous light.[117] For the celebration of the Eucharist it is appropriate to carry candles in the entrance procession and during the procession with the Book of the Gospels.[118] At least two candles are placed near the altar in the sanctuary area. If there is a lack of space, they may be placed on the altar. Four or six candles may be used for the celebration of Mass and for exposition of the Blessed Sacrament. If the bishop of the diocese celebrates, seven candles may be used. Candles placed in floor-standing bases or on the altar should be arranged so they do not obscure the view of the ritual action in the sanctuary, especially the action at the altar.

§ 93 §   Candles for liturgical use should be made of a material that provides "a living flame without being smoky or noxious." To safeguard "authenticity and the full symbolism of light," electric lights as a substitute for candles are not permitted.[119]

THE PASCHAL CANDLE

§ 94 §   The paschal candle is the symbol of "the light of Christ, rising in glory," scattering "the darkness of our hearts and minds."[120] Above all, the paschal

---

116. Ibid., no. 307: "Candles are to be used at every liturgical service as a sign of reverence and of the festiveness of the celebration. The candlesticks are to be placed either on or around the altar in a way suited to the design of the altar and the sanctuary. Everything is to be well balanced and must not interfere with the faithful's clear view of what takes place at the altar or is placed on it."

117. 1 Peter 2:9.

118. GIRM, no. 117: "The altar is to be covered with at least one white colored cloth. On or even next to the altar are to be candlesticks with lighted candles, at least two in every celebration, or even four or six, especially if a Sunday Mass or Mass for a holy day of obligation is celebrated, or if the Bishop of the diocese celebrates, then seven candles should be used. There is also to be a cross on or near the altar, with a figure of Christ crucified. However, the candles and the cross adorned with the figure of Christ crucified may be carried in the entrance procession. The *Book of the Gospels*, if distinct from the book of other readings, may be placed on the altar, unless it is carried in the entrance procession."

119. DOL 208, p. 519, note R47, quoting the newsletter of the Congregation for Divine Worship and the Discipline of the Sacraments *Notitiae* 10:80 (1974), no. 4: "Query: Must the lighted candles that are to be placed in candlesticks for the celebration of Mass consist in part of beeswax, olive oil, or other vegetable oil? Reply: The GIRM prescribes candles for Mass 'as a sign of reverence and festiveness' (nos. 79, 269). But it makes no further determination regarding the material of their composition, except in the case of the sanctuary lamp, the fuel for which must be oil or wax (see *Holy Communion and Worship of the Eucharist Outside Mass*, Introduction no. 11). The faculty that the conferences of bishops possess to choose suitable materials for sacred furnishings applies therefore to the candles for Mass. The faculty is limited only by the condition that in the estimation of the people the materials are valued and worthy and that they are appropriate for sacred use. Candles intended for liturgical use should be made of material that can provide a living flame without being smoky or noxious and that does not stain the altar cloths or coverings. Electric bulbs are banned in the interest of safeguarding authenticity and the full symbolism of light."

120. Congregation for Divine Worship, *The Sacramentary* [*The Roman Missal*] (1973, 1985), The Easter Vigil, no. 12.

candle should be a genuine candle, the pre-eminent symbol of the light of Christ. Choices of size, design, and color should be made in relationship to the sanctuary in which it will be placed. During the Easter Vigil and throughout the Easter season, the paschal candle belongs near the ambo or in the middle of the sanctuary. After the Easter season it is moved to a place of honor in the baptistry for use in the celebration of baptisms. During funerals the paschal candle is placed near the coffin as a sign of the Christian's passover from death to life.[121]

THE GATHERING SPACE OR NARTHEX

§ 95 §   The narthex is a place of welcome—a threshold space between the congregation's space and the outside environment. In the early days of the Church, it was a "waiting area" for catechumens and penitents. Today it serves as gathering space and as the entrance and exit to the building. The gathering space helps believers to make the transition from everyday life to the celebration of the liturgy, and after the liturgy, it helps them return to daily life to live out the mystery that has been celebrated. In the gathering space, people come together to move in procession and to prepare for the celebration of the liturgy. It is in the gathering space that many important liturgical moments occur: men and women participate in the Rite of Becoming a Catechumen as they move toward later, full initiation into the Church; parents, godparents and infants are greeted for the celebration of baptism; and Christians are greeted for the last time as their mortal remains are received into the church building for the celebration of the funeral rites.

§ 96 §   In addition to its religious functions, the gathering space may provide access to the vesting sacristy, rooms for choir rehearsal, storage areas, restrooms, and rooms for ushers and their equipment. Adequate space for other gatherings will be an important consideration in planning the narthex and other adjoining areas.

§ 97 §   The doors to the church have both practical and symbolic significance. They function as the secure, steady symbol of Christ, "the Good Shepherd" and "the door through which those who follow him enter and are safe [as they] go in and go out."[122] In construction, design and decoration, they have the ability to remind people of Christ's presence as the Way that leads to the Father.[123] Practically, of course, they secure the building from the weather and exterior dangers, expressing by their solid strength the safe harbor that lies within. The appearance and height of the church doors reflect their dignity and address practical considerations such as the accommodation of the processional cross or banners.

---

121. PCEF, no. 99: "In the celebration of funerals, the paschal candle should be placed near the coffin to indicate that the death of a Christian is one's own passover. The paschal candle should not otherwise be lit or placed in the sanctuary outside the Easter season."

122. BB, no. 1229.

123. Ibid., no. 1216: "It is proper, then, that in construction, design, and decoration church doors should stand as a symbol of Christ, who said, 'I am the door, whoever enters through me will be safe,' and of those who have followed the path of holiness that leads to the dwelling place of God."

THE AREA SURROUNDING THE CHURCH BUILDING

§ 98 §   When constructed and maintained well, the outside of a church can proclaim the Gospel to the city or town in which it is located. Even before the members of the worshiping community enter through the doors of the building, the external environment with its landscaping, artwork, and lighting can contribute to a gracious approach to the place of worship. Creative landscaping that separates the entrance to the church from the parking area as well as well-placed religious art can facilitate the spiritual transition as people move to a sense of communal worship. Appropriate signage can provide information and can offer hospitality and an invitation to enter the space for worship. Walkways with well-designed patterns of stone or other materials subtly contribute to the awareness that believers are about to enter holy ground. When choosing a site for a church, consideration should be given to the possibility of landscaped setback so that the church building is not completely surrounded by the parking lot.

§ 99 §   It is an ancient practice to summon the Christian people to the liturgical assembly or to alert them to important happenings in the local community by means of bells. The peal of bells is an expression of the sentiments of the People of God as they rejoice or grieve, offer thanks or petition, gather together and show outwardly the mystery of their oneness in Christ.

THE ROLE OF THE CHURCH BUILDING IN OTHER LITURGICAL RITES

§ 100 §   The church building is the space for the celebration of the other sacraments, in addition to the Eucharist. While preserving the primary focus upon the eucharistic assembly and the unity and integrity of the building as a whole, the design of the church must also accommodate the needs of these rites.

THE RITES OF INITIATION

§ 101 §   Through the waters of baptism Christians are buried with Christ and rise to a new life with him. They are made sharers of God's own life and members of Christ's Body, the Church, and they are regenerated and cleansed of sin. In confirmation the seal of the Holy Spirit is set upon them, and their initiation is completed through their participation in the Eucharist. The specific spatial needs for the celebration of baptism and the Eucharist are addressed in the earlier sections of this chapter.

HOLY ORDERS

§ 102 §   In the sacrament of holy orders, the ministry of word and sacrament is established and fulfilled. The sacrament is most often celebrated in the cathedral but may also be celebrated in the parish church. Planning should include space for the prostrations and the key liturgical actions such as the imposition of hands, the anointing, and the handing over of the vessels.

THE RITE OF PENANCE OR RECONCILIATION

§ 103 §   In the sacrament of penance, God forgives sins and restores broken relationships through the ministry of the Church. The Rite of Penance does not describe the place for the celebration of the sacrament except to say that it be in the space "prescribed by law."[124] The *Code of Canon Law* designates a church or an oratory as "the proper place" for the celebration of the sacrament of penance[125] and requires a screen or fixed grille between penitent and confessor to ensure the anonymity of those who wish it.[126] Canon 964 further directs conferences of bishops to issue more specific norms. The bishops of the United States have directed that the place for sacramental confession be visible and accessible, that it contain a fixed grille, and that it allow for confession face-to-face for those who wish to do so.[127]

§ 104 § By its design, furnishings, and location within the church building, the place for reconciliation can assist penitents on the path to contrition and sorrow for sin and to proclaim their reconciliation with God and the community of faith.

§ 105 § In planning the reconciliation area, parishes will want to provide for a sound-proof place with a chair for the priest and a kneeler and chair for the penitent. Since the rite includes the reading of Scripture, the space should also include a Bible.[128] Appropriate artwork, a crucifix symbolic of Christ's victory over sin and death, icons or images reflective of baptism and the Eucharist, or Scriptural images of God's reconciling love help to enhance the atmosphere of prayer. Warm, inviting lighting welcomes penitents who seek God's help, and some form of amplification as well as braille signs can aid those with hearing or visual disabilities. Additional rooms or spaces will be needed as confessional areas for communal celebrations of penance, especially in Advent and Lent.

THE RITE OF MARRIAGE

§ 106 § The Rite of Christian Marriage contains no directives about the spatial requirements for the celebration. Instead, the ritual focuses upon the consent given by the bride and the groom, the ambo from which the word of God is proclaimed, and the altar at which the couple share the Body and Blood of Christ within a nuptial Mass.

---

124. Congregation for Divine Worship, *Rite of Penance* [OP] (1974), no. 12: "The sacrament of penance is celebrated in the place and location prescribed by law."
125. CIC, c. 964 § 1: "The proper place to hear sacramental confessions is a church or oratory."
126. Ibid., c. 964 § 2: "The conference of bishops is to establish norms regarding the confessional: it is to take care, however, that there are always confessionals with a fixed gate between penitent and the confessor in an open place so that the faithful who wish to can use them freely."
127. Complementary legislation approved at the November 1999 meeting of the NCCB: "The National Conference of Catholic Bishops, in accord with the prescriptions of canon 964 and the approved liturgical rite, hereby decrees the following norms governing the place for sacramental confessions: Provision must be made for a place for sacramental confessions which is clearly visible, truly accessible, and which provides a fixed grille between the penitent and confessor. Provision must also be made for those instances when the penitent wishes to confess face-to-face."
128. OP, no. 17: "Then the priest, or the penitent himself, may read a text of holy Scripture, or this may be done as part of the preparation for the sacrament. Through the word of God the Christian receives light to recognize his sins and is called to conversion and to confidence in God's mercy."

§ 107 §   The options within the Rite of Marriage provide for a procession of the priest and ministers to the door of the church to greet the wedding party, followed by an entrance procession, or the entrance of the wedding party and movement down the aisle to meet the priest celebrant at the altar. Some planners have experimented with seating arrangements that eliminate a center aisle in favor of two side aisles. Although this plan can be very useful by allowing the congregation to face the altar and the priest celebrant directly, it challenges parishes to plan how they will provide for entrance processions and recessionals, especially during wedding processions when all wish to have equal visual access to the wedding party.

§ 108 §   If it is the custom to have the bride and groom seated in the sanctuary, then the design of the sanctuary should be spacious enough to allow an arrangement of chairs and kneelers that does not impinge upon the primary furniture in the sanctuary. Many ethnic groups and local churches have additional customs for the celebration of marriage that can be honored and accommodated when they are in keeping with the spirit of the liturgy.

THE RITE OF ANOINTING OF THE SICK

§ 109 §   The Rite of Anointing and Pastoral Care of the Sick provides for the communal celebration of the sacrament in a parish church or chapel. As noted earlier[129] the church building must be accessible to those with disabilities, including those in wheelchairs and those who must travel with a breathing apparatus. Since many of those to be anointed may be unable to approach the priest, the parish will want to provide an area where the priest is able to approach persons with disabilities with ease and grace. Often this is possible in a section of the church that has flexible rather than fixed seating.

CHRISTIAN FUNERALS

§ 110 §   The *Order of Christian Funerals* rites mark the final stage of the journey begun by the Christian in baptism. The structure of the current rites dates back to "Christian Rome where [there were] three 'stages' or 'stations' [during the funeral rite] joined by two processions": the first from the home of the deceased to the church and the second from the church to the place of burial.[130] While the current rite preserves the procession to the church by the mourners who

---

129. Cf. additional sections in this document on accessibility, pp. 464, 465, 466, 469, 472, 476, 478, 479, 481, 506, 507, 508, 512, 515, and 517.

130. Congregation for Divine Worship, International Committee on English in the Liturgy, *Order of Christian Funerals* [OCF] (1985, 1989), no. 42: "Processions continue to have special significance in funeral celebrations, as in Christian Rome where funeral rites consisted of three 'stages' or 'stations' joined by two processions. Christians accompanied the body on its last journey. From the home of the deceased the Christian community proceed to the church singing psalms. When the service in the church concluded, the body was carried in solemn procession to the grave or tomb. During the final procession the congregation sang psalms praising the God of mercy and redemption and antiphons entrusting the deceased to the care of the angels and saints. The funeral liturgy mirrored the journey of human life, the Christian pilgrimage to the heavenly Jerusalem."

accompany the deceased, a funeral cortege of automobiles is more common than a procession on foot in most places in the United States.

§ 111 § Because the faith journey of the deceased began in baptism, it is appropriate that there be a physical association between the baptismal font and the space for the funeral ritual. "In the act of receiving the body, the members of the community acknowledge the deceased as one of their own, as one who was welcomed in baptism and who held a place in the assembly."[131] With the baptismal symbols of water, light, and the pall, the mourning community prepares for the "liturgy in which it asks for a share in the heavenly banquet promised to the deceased and to all who have been [baptized in Christ]."[132]

§ 112 § In designing the seating configuration, parishes will want to consider the size and placement of the casket and the paschal candle during funerals as well as the presence of the cremated remains when cremation has taken place before the funeral Mass. Good planning will ensure that doors and aisles are wide enough for pall bearers to carry a coffin easily.

§ 113 § The permission to celebrate the funeral Mass in the presence of the cremated remains necessitates a dignified place on which the remains can rest during the Mass.[133] To avoid ritual use of makeshift carriers or other inappropriate containers, parishes may wish to obtain a well-designed urn or ceremonial vessel and stand to hold the cremated remains during the vigil and funeral.

§ 114 § The funeral rites permit the celebration of the vigil for the deceased in the church.[134] If this is the practice, it is appropriate to wake the body in the baptistry or gathering area or in another dignified area of the church that will not interfere with the normal liturgical life of the parish.

---

131. Ibid., no. 131: "Since the church is the place where the community of faith assembles for worship, the rite of reception of the body at the church has great significance. The church is the place where the Christian life is begotten in baptism, nourished in the eucharist, and where the community gathers to commend one of its deceased members to the Father. The church is at once a symbol of the community and of the heavenly liturgy that the celebration of the liturgy anticipates. In the act of receiving the body, the members of the community acknowledge the deceased as one of their own, as one who was welcomed in baptism and who held a place in the assembly. Through the use of various baptismal symbols the community shows the reverence due to the body, the temple of the Spirit, and in this way prepares for the funeral liturgy in which it asks for a share in the heavenly banquet promised to the deceased and to all who have been washed in the waters of rebirth and marked with the sign of faith."
132. Ibid.
133. Cf. OCF, Appendix 2, regarding the indult for the United States and the ritual directives governing the presence of the cremated remains at the funeral Mass, and the reverent disposition of the cremated remains.
134. OCF, no. 55: "The vigil may be celebrated in the home of the deceased, in the funeral home, parlor or chapel of rest, or in some other suitable place. It may also be celebrated in the church, but at a time well before the funeral liturgy, so that the funeral liturgy will not be lengthy and the liturgy of the word repetitious."

THE LITURGY OF THE HOURS

§ 115 § The Liturgy of the Hours is the public, daily prayer of the Church. Recognizing the importance of the Liturgy of the Hours in the life of the Church,[135] many parishes are rediscovering the spiritual beauty of the Hours and are including Morning or Evening Prayer in their daily liturgical life. Although there are no specific spatial requirements for the celebration of the Hours, the focal points of the celebration are the word of God and the praying assembly. An area of flexible seating can facilitate the prayer of a smaller group divided into alternating choirs. The importance of music in public celebrations of the Hours suggests that the place designated for their celebration should provide access to necessary equipment for musicians, particularly cantors and instrumentalists who accompany the singing community.

SUNDAY CELEBRATIONS IN THE ABSENCE OF A PRIEST

§ 116 § The celebration of the Eucharist is the norm for Sunday assemblies. However, a decrease in the number of priests makes this difficult or impossible on a weekly basis in some communities. When the celebration of Mass on a Sunday is not possible in a given parish and the people have no reasonable alternatives, the diocesan bishop can permit the celebration of the Liturgy of the Word or the Liturgy of the Hours or one of these combined with a communion service.[136] When a community gathers for a Sunday celebration in which a priest is not present, the deacon who presides leads the community's prayer from the presidential chair in the sanctuary.[137] A lay person who presides leads the prayer from a chair placed outside the sanctuary.[138]

---

135. Congregation for Divine Worship, *General Instruction of the Liturgy of the Hours* (February 2, 1971), no. 20 (DOL, 426, no. 3450): "The liturgy of the hours, like other liturgical services, is not a private matter but belongs to the whole Body of the Church, whose life it both expresses and affects."

136. Cf. National Conference of Catholic Bishops' Committee on the Liturgy, *Sunday Celebrations in the Absence of a Priest: Leader's Edition* (1993), no. 14: "It is the responsibility of the diocesan bishop, after having received the advice of the diocesan presbyteral council and, if appropriate, other consultative bodies, to decide whether Sunday celebrations in the absence of a priest should be held on an occasional or regular basis in his diocese. He is to set out general and particular norms for such celebrations. They are to be held only when and where approved by the bishop and only under the pastoral ministry of a priest who has the responsibility for the particular community."

137. Ibid., no. 19: "When a deacon presides at a Sunday celebration in the absence of a priest, he acts in the usual manner in regard to the greetings, the prayers, the gospel reading and homily, the giving of communion, and the dismissal and blessing. He wears the vestments proper to his ministry, that is, the alb with stole, and, as circumstances suggest, the dalmatic. He uses the presidential chair."

138. Ibid., no. 24: "The layperson wears vesture that is suitable for his or her function or the vesture prescribed by the bishop. A layperson does not use the presidential chair."

Cf. Congregation for Divine Worship, *Directory for Sunday Celebrations in the Absence of a Priest* (1988), no. 40.

§ 117 §   The consecrated oil of chrism for initiation, ordination and the dedication of churches, as well as the blessed oils of the sick and of catechumens, are traditionally housed in a special place called an ambry or repository.[139] These oils consecrated or blessed by the bishop at the Mass of Chrism deserve the special care of the community to which they have been entrusted.[140] The style of the ambry may take different forms. A parish church might choose a simple, dignified, and secure niche in the baptistry or in the wall of the sanctuary or a small case for the oils. Cathedrals responsible for the care of a larger supply of the oils need a larger ambry. Since bright light or high temperatures can hasten spoilage, parishes will want to choose a location that helps to preserve the freshness of the oil.

THE RITE OF DEDICATION OF A CHURCH AND AN ALTAR

§ 118 §   In addition to containing the rituals of dedication, the *Rite of Dedication of a Church and an Altar* contains liturgies for laying the cornerstone, for commencing work on the building of a church, for dedication of a church already in use, and for the blessing of a church and an altar.[141] These rituals serve as a foundational resource for those engaged in designing and building churches. Just as the initiation of a person into the Christian community occurs in stages, so the construction of church building unfolds over a period of time. Rites are celebrated at the beginning of the building process "to ask God's blessing for the success of the work and to remind the people that the structure built of stone will be a visible sign of the living Church, God's building which is formed of the people themselves."[142] At the conclusion of the construction, the church is dedicated to God with a solemn rite.[143] Familiarity with this rite and the context of prayer that it offers will help to prevent the building project from degenerating into a purely pragmatic or functional enterprise.

---

139. BB, no. 1125: "The oils used for the celebration of the sacraments of initiation, holy orders, and the anointing of the sick according to ancient tradition are reverently reserved in a special place in the church. This repository should be secure and be protected by a lock."

140. CIC, c. 847 § 2: "The pastor is to obtain the holy oils from his own bishop and is to preserve them diligently with proper care."

141. RDCA, ch. 5, no. 1 (DOL 547, no. 4428): "Since sacred edifices, that is, churches, are permanently set aside for the celebration of the divine mysteries, it is right for them to receive a dedication to God. This is done according to the rite in chapters two and three [of the *Rite of Dedication of a Church and an Altar*] for dedicating a church, a rite impressive for its striking ceremonies and symbols.

   "Private oratories, chapels, or other sacred edifices set aside only temporarily for divine worship because of special conditions, more properly receive a blessing, according to the rite [found in chapter 5 of *the Rite of Dedication of a Church and an Altar*]."

142. Ibid., ch. 1, no. 1 (DOL 547, no. 4361): "When the building of a new church begins, it is desirable to celebrate a rite to ask God's blessing for the success of the work and to remind the people that the structure built of stone will be a visible sign of the living Church, God's building that is formed of the people themselves."

143. Ibid., ch. 2, no. 2 (DOL 547, no. 4370): "When a church is erected as a building destined solely and permanently for assembling the people of God and for carrying out sacred functions, it is fitting that it be dedicated to God with a solemn rite, in accordance with the ancient custom of the Church."

§ 119 § Since the celebration of the Eucharist on the new altar after it has been solemnly anointed, incensed, covered, and lighted, is at the heart of the dedication ritual,[144] a new or renovated church is, as far as possible, not used for the celebration of the sacraments until after the Rite of Dedication has taken place. To celebrate the rite after the altar has been in use is anti-climactic and can reduce the rite to empty symbolism.[145] Use of a temporary altar in the period before the dedication is a viable alternative that can help to heighten anticipation of the day of dedication when the new altar will receive the ritual initiation that solemnly prepares it for the celebration of the central mystery of our faith.

§ 120 § When the people of the parish community gather to dedicate their new church building or to celebrate its renovation, they will have made many decisions, balanced a variety of needs, and overcome a multitude of challenges. As the diocesan bishop celebrates the Rite of Dedication and receives the church from his people,[146] the connection between the diocesan Church and the parish community is particularly evident.

§ 121 § The Rite of Dedication provides that the walls of the church may be anointed with sacred chrism in four or twelve places depending on the size and design of the structure. These points can be marked by crosses made from stone, brass, or another appropriate material or carved into the walls themselves. A bracket for a small candle should be affixed to the wall beneath each of these crosses.[147] The candles in these brackets are then lighted during the ritual lighting at the dedication, on anniversaries of the dedication, and on other solemn occasions.

THE LITURGICAL YEAR: SEASONAL DECORATIONS

§ 122 § During the liturgical year the Church unfolds the whole mystery of Christ, from his incarnation and birth through his passion, death, and resurrection to his ascension, the day of Pentecost, and the expectation of his coming

---

144. Ibid., ch. 2, no. 15 (DOL 547, no. 4383): "The celebration of the eucharist is the most important and the one necessary rite for the dedication of a church."

145. Ibid., ch. 3, no. 1 (DOL 547, no. 4396): "In order to bring out fully the symbolism and the significance of the rite, the opening of a new church and its dedication should take place at one and the same time. For this reason, as was said before, care should be taken that, as far as possible, Mass is not celebrated in a new church before it is dedicated (see chapter two, nos. 8, 15, 17).

"Nevertheless in the case of the dedication of a church where the sacred mysteries are already being celebrated regularly, the rite set out in this chapter must be used."

Cf. RDCA, ch. 4, no. 13 (DOL 547, no. 4410): "Since an altar becomes sacred principally by the celebration of the Eucharist, in fidelity to this truth the celebration of Mass on a new altar before it has been dedicated is to be carefully avoided, so that the Mass of dedication may also be the first eucharist celebrated on the altar."

146. Ibid., ch. 2, no. 33: "At the threshold of the church the procession comes to a halt. Representatives of those who have been involved in the building of the church (members of the parish or of the diocese, contributors, architects, workers) hand over the building to the bishop, offering him according to place and circumstances either the legal documents for possession of the building, or the keys, or the plan of the building, or the book in which the progress of the work is described and the names of those in charge of it and the names of the workers are recorded."

147. Ibid., ch. 2, no. 22 (DOL 547, no. 4390): "Beneath each cross a small bracket should be fitted and in it a small candlestick is placed, with a candle to be lighted."

in glory. In its celebration of these mysteries, the Church makes these sacred events present to the people of every age.[148]

§ 123 § The tradition of decorating or not decorating the church for liturgical seasons and feasts heightens the awareness of the festive, solemn, or penitential nature of these seasons. Human minds and hearts are stimulated by the sounds, sights, and fragrances of liturgical seasons, which combine to create powerful, lasting impressions of the rich and abundant graces unique to each of the seasons.

§ 124 § Plans for seasonal decorations should include other areas besides the sanctuary. Decorations are intended to draw people to the true nature of the mystery being celebrated rather than being ends in themselves. Natural flowers, plants, wreaths and fabric hangings, and other seasonal objects can be arranged to enhance the primary liturgical points of focus. The altar should remain clear and free-standing, not walled in by massive floral displays or the Christmas crib, and pathways in the narthex, nave, and sanctuary should remain clear.

§ 125 § These seasonal decorations are maintained throughout the entire liturgical season. Since the Christmas season begins with the Vigil Mass on Christmas Eve and ends with the Baptism of the Lord, the placement and removal of Christmas decorations should coincide with these times. Since the Easter season lasts fifty days, planning will encompass ways to sustain the decor until the fiftieth day of Pentecost.

§ 126 § In the course of the liturgical year, the feasts and memorials of Our Lady and of saints with special significance for the parish afford opportunities to show devotion by adorning their images with tasteful floral arrangements or plants.

§ 127 § Fabric art in the form of processional banners and hangings can be an effective way to convey the spirit of liturgical seasons, especially through the use of color, shape, texture, and symbolic form. The use of images rather than words is more in keeping with this medium.

§ 128 § Objects such as the Advent wreath,[149] the Christmas crib,[150] and other traditional seasonal appointments proportioned to the size of the space and to the other furnishings can enhance the prayer and understanding of the parish community.

---

148. SC, no. 102: "Holy Mother Church is conscious that she must celebrate the saving work of her divine spouse by devoutly recalling it on certain days throughout the course of the year. Every week, on the day which she has called the Lord's Day, she keeps the memory of His resurrection. In the supreme solemnity of Easter she also makes an annual commemoration of the resurrection, along with the Lord's blessed passion.

"Within the cycle of a year, moreover, she unfolds the whole mystery of Christ, not only from his incarnation and birth until his ascension, but also as reflected in the day of Pentecost, and the expectation of a blessed hoped-for return of the Lord.

"Recalling thus the mysteries of redemption, the Church opens to the faithful the riches of the Lord's powers and merits, so that these are in some way made present at all times, and the faithful are enabled to lay hold of them and become filled with saving grace."

149. Cf. BB, no. 1512.

150. Ibid., no. 1544.

§ 129 § The use of living flowers and plants, rather than artificial greens, serves as a reminder of the gift of life God has given to the human community. Planning for plants and flowers should include not only the procurement and placement but also the continuing care needed to sustain living things.

THE CHURCH BUILDING AND POPULAR DEVOTIONS

§ 130 § Throughout history and among widely differing cultures, a rich heritage of popular devotions honoring Christ, the Blessed Virgin Mary, and the saints has developed in the Church. Popular devotions "express and nourish the spirit of prayer"[151] and are to be encouraged when they are in conformity with the norms of the Church and are derived from and lead to the liturgy.[152] Like the liturgy, devotions are rituals. They can involve singing, intercession, thanksgiving, and common postures.

§ 131 § Devotional prayer is another way for people to bring the very personal concerns of life to God and to ask the intercession of the saints and of other members of the Christian community. Sacred images are important not only in liturgical prayer but also in devotional prayer because they are sacramentals that help the faithful to focus their attention and their prayer. The design of the church building can do much to foster devotions and to ensure that they enhance and reinforce rather than compete with the liturgical life of the community.

THE STATIONS OF THE CROSS

§ 132 § The Stations of the Cross originated early in the history of the Church. It was the custom of the faithful to follow the way walked by Christ from Pilate's house in Jerusalem to Calvary. As time went on, pilgrims to the holy city desired to continue this devotion when they returned home. In the fourteenth century when the Franciscans were entrusted with the care of the holy places in Jerusalem they promoted the use of images depicting the Lord's Way of the Cross.

§ 133 § Whether celebrated by a community or by individuals, the Stations of the Cross offers a way for the faithful to enter more fully into the passion and death of the Lord and to serve as another manifestation of the pilgrim Church on its homeward journey. Traditionally the stations have been arranged around

---

151. Congregation for Bishops, *Directory on the Pastoral Ministry of Bishops* (1974), no. 91: "A healthy zeal for promoting liturgical life carries with it the desire to preserve, foster and even spread those exercises of piety which express and nourish the spirit of prayer. This is especially true if they are redolent of holy scripture and the sacred liturgy, have originated in the hearts of saints or have for a long time witnessed to the traditional faith and piety."
152. SC, no. 13: "Popular devotions of the Christian people are to be warmly commended, provided they accord with the laws and norms of the Church. Such is especially the case with devotions called for by the Apostolic See.

"Devotions proper to individual churches also have a special dignity if they are conducted by mandate of the bishops in accord with customs or books lawfully approved.

"Nevertheless these devotions should be so drawn up that they harmonize with the liturgical seasons, accord with the sacred liturgy, are in some fashion derived from it, and lead the people to it, since the liturgy by its very nature far surpasses any of them."

the walls of the nave of the church, or, in some instances, around the gathering space or even the exterior of the church, marking the devotion as a true journey.[153]

§ 134 §   The Stations enjoy a long tradition. In recent times some parishes have clustered the stations in one place. While such an arrangement may be expedient, it is not desirable because it eliminates space for movement, which characterizes this devotion as a "way" of the cross.

SACRED IMAGES

§ 135 §   Reflecting the awareness of the Communion of Saints, the practice of incorporating symbols of the Trinity and images of Christ, the Blessed Mother, the angels, and the saints into the design of a church creates a source of devotion and prayer for a parish community and should be part of the design of the church.[154] Images can be found in stained glass windows, on wall frescoes and murals, and as statues and icons. Often these images depict scenes from the Bible or from the lives of the saints and can be a source of instruction and catechesis as well as devotion. Since the Eucharist unites the Body of Christ, including those who are not physically present, the use of images in the church reminds us that we are joined to all who have gone before us, as well as to those who now surround us.

§ 136 §   In choosing images and devotional art, parishes should be respectful of traditional iconography when it comes to the way sacred images are recognized and venerated by the faithful. However, they also should be mindful that the tradition is not limited to literal images. While Mary is the mother of Jesus, she is also an icon of the Church, a disciple of the Lord, a liberated and liberating woman. She is the Immaculate Conception, patroness of the United States, and Our Lady of Guadalupe, patroness of all America. Other symbols such as the crucifix, icons, or images of patron saints depicted in various ways can also draw us into the deeper realities of faith and hope as they connect us to the stories behind the image.[155]

§ 137 §   The placement of images can be a challenge, especially when a number of cultural traditions are part of a single parish community and each has its own devotional life and practices. Restraint in the number and prominence of sacred images[156] is encouraged to help people focus on the liturgical action that is celebrated in the church. Separate alcoves for statues or icons can display a variety

---

153. Often churches have images as well as the crosses that mark the fourteen or fifteen stations. While the depictions of the passion are desirable, only the crosses are needed. The images that accompany the crosses are optional.

154. Cf. BB, no. 1258: "The Church encourages the devout veneration of sacred images by the faithful, in order that they may see more deeply into the mystery of God's glory. For that glory has shown in the face of Christ and is reflected in his saints, who have become 'light in the Lord.'"

155. Cf. BB, no. 1258, quoting the Second Council of Nicea, Act. 7, as cited in Mansi 13, 378 and Denzinger-Schoenmetzer, no. 601: "For the faithful such images recall our Lord and the saints whom they depict, but they also in some way lead the faithful back to the Lord and the saints themselves. 'The more often we gaze on these images, the quicker we who behold them are led back to their prototypes in memory and in hope.'"

156. SC, no. 125: "The practice of placing sacred images in churches so that they may be venerated by the faithful is to be firmly maintained. Nevertheless their number should be

of images through the year. Some parishes designate an area as the shrine for an image that is being venerated on a given day or for a period of time, such as the image of a saint on his or her feast day.

§ 138 § It is important that the images in the church depict saints for whom devotion currently exists in the parish. It is particularly desirable that a significant image of the patron of the church be fittingly displayed, as well as an image of Mary, the Mother of God, as a fitting tribute to her unique role in the plan of salvation. As time passes and demographics change, saints who were once the object of veneration by many parishioners may at another time be venerated by only a few. When this happens, these images could be removed, provided sensitivity is shown with regard to the piety of the faithful and the impact on the building.

CONCLUSION

§ 139 § In this chapter, the liturgical actions of the Church provide the guidelines for the building of a church. There must be space for the variety of the community's prayer, which extends from the primary worship of the Eucharist to popular devotions. The complex balance of all these factors and of the people who participate in them is the most important dimension for the education, planning, and execution of a building plan for a community. The following chapter will reflect upon the use of the arts and the importance of planning for their proper placement early in the design process.

CHAPTER THREE
THE WORK OF OUR HANDS:
ART AND ARTISTS ASSISTING THE CHURCH AT PRAYER

§ 140 § When God's people gather for prayer, the most intimate and all-embracing aspect of their life together occurs: the moment when they touch, taste, smell, hear, see, and share those hidden realities that would otherwise remain imperceptible. Together they adore the holiness of God and give expression to the unceasing life God has given them. God nourishes them as a community and makes them holy through the use of *ordinary* perceptible signs of water, oil, bread, and wine, transformed by *extraordinary* grace. The *place* where God gathers this people powerfully draws them more deeply into communion and expresses in beauty God's profound holiness. This is the place that prompts them to recognize the divine image in which they have been created, now restored in Christ. "For from the greatness and the beauty of created things their original author, by analogy, is seen."[157]

§ 141 § Throughout the history of the Church, a dynamic tension has existed between the continuity of traditional artistic expression and the need to articulate the faith in ways proper to each age and to diverse cultures. In every age the

---

moderate and their relative locations should reflect right order. Otherwise they may create confusion among the Christian people and promote a faulty sense of devotion."
157. Wisdom 13:5; cf. 13:3.

Church has attempted to engage the best contemporary artists and architects to design places of worship that have sheltered the assembly and disclosed the presence of the living God. In the past, dialogue between the Church and the artist has yielded a marriage of faith and art, producing sublime places of prayer, buildings of awe-inspiring, transcendent beauty, and humble places of worship that, in their simplicity, inspire a sense of the sacred.

THE ROLE OF RELIGIOUS ART

§ 142 § In the Christian community's place of prayer, art evokes and glorifies "the transcendent mystery of God—the surpassing invisible beauty of truth and love visible in Christ."[158] Therefore the "Church entrusts art with a mediating role, analogous, we might say, to the role of the priest or, perhaps better, to that of Jacob's ladder descending and ascending. Art is meant to bring the divine to the human world, to the level of the senses, then, from the spiritual insight gained through the senses and the stirring of the emotions, to raise the human world to God, to his inexpressible kingdom of mystery, beauty, and life."[159]

§ 143 § Art chosen for the place of worship is not simply something pretty or well made, an addition to make the ordinary more pleasant. Nor is the place of worship a museum to house artistic masterpieces or artistic models. Rather, artworks truly belong in the church when they are worthy of the place of worship and when they enhance the liturgical, devotional, and contemplative prayer they are inspired to serve.

§ 144 § The central image of Christianity is the cross, calling to mind the passion, resurrection, and Christ's final coming in glory. Every work of Christian art or architecture shares in this image and embraces the ambiguities of suffering and death, healing and resurrection, recognizing that "by his wounds we are healed." Such art draws from the mystery of redemption a unique power to provoke and invite the world more deeply into the mysteries of our faith.

§ 145 § Likewise, Christian art is also a product of "spontaneous spiritual joy" that challenges believers to complete the reign of God for which they hope.[160] Born from an ecstatic love of God, Christian beauty proclaims something new and original, manifesting itself as an echo of God's own creative act.

---

158. CCC, no. 2502; cf. CCC, nos. 1156–1162; SC , no. 122: "The fine arts are considered to rank among the noblest expressions of human genius. This judgment applies especially to religious art and to its highest achievement, which is sacred art. By their very nature, both of the latter are oriented to God's boundless beauty, for this is the reality which these human efforts are trying to express in some way. To the extent that these works aim exclusively at turning men's thoughts to God persuasively and devoutly, they are dedicated to the cause of His greater honor and glory."
159. Pope Paul VI, Address to the Pontifical Commission for Sacred Art in Italy (December 17, 1969) (DOL 540, no. 4324).
160. Cf. CCC, nos. 2500–2503, 2513.

§ 146 § Authentic art is integral to the Church at prayer[161] because these objects and actions are "signs and symbols of the supernatural world"[162] and expressions of the divine presence. While personal tastes will differ, parish committees should utilize the criteria of quality and appropriateness in evaluating art for worship. *Quality* is perceived only by contemplation, by standing back from things and really trying to see them, trying to let them speak to the beholder. *Quality* is evident in the honesty and genuineness of the materials that are used, the nobility of the form embodied in them, the love and care that goes into the creation of a work of art, and the personal stamp of the artist whose special gift produces a harmonious whole, a well-crafted work.

§ 147 § *Quality* art draws the beholder to the Creator, who stands behind the artist sharing his own creative power, for the "divine Artist passes on to the human artist a spark of his own surpassing wisdom."[163] This is true of music, architecture, sculpture, painting, pottery making, textiles, and furniture making, as well as other art forms that serve the liturgical environment. The integrity and energy of a piece of art, produced individually by the labor of an artist, is always to be preferred above objects that are mass-produced. Similarly, in the construction of new church buildings, there is no standard pattern for church art nor should art and architectural styles from any particular time or culture be imposed arbitrarily upon another community. Nonetheless, the patrimony of sacred art and architecture provides a standard by which a parish can judge the worthiness of contemporary forms and styles.

§ 148 § *Appropriateness* for liturgical action is the other criterion for choosing a work of art for church. The quality of *appropriateness* is demonstrated by the work's ability to bear the weight of mystery, awe, reverence, and wonder that

---

161. SC, no. 122: "The fine arts are considered to rank among the noblest expressions of human genius. This judgment applies especially to religious art and to its highest achievement, which is sacred art. By their very nature, both of the latter are oriented to God's boundless beauty, for this is the reality which these human efforts are trying to express in some way. To the extent that these works aim exclusively at turning men's thoughts to God persuasively and devoutly, they are dedicated to the cause of His greater honor and glory."

162. OA, no. 1 (DOL 541, no. 4327): "Works of art, the most exalted expressions of the human spirit, bring us closer and closer to the divine Artisan and with good reason are regarded as the heritage of the entire human family.

"The Church has always held the ministry of the arts in the highest esteem and has striven to see that 'all things set apart for use in divine worship are truly worthy, becoming, and beautiful, signs and symbols of the supernatural world.' The Church through the centuries has also safeguarded the artistic treasures belonging to it."

163. LA, no. 1: "God therefore called man into existence, committing to him the craftsman's task. Through his 'artistic creativity' man appears more than ever 'in the image of God,' and he accomplishes this task above all in shaping the wondrous 'material' of his own humanity and then exercising creative dominion over the universe which surrounds him. With loving regard, the divine Artist passes on to the human artist a spark of his own surpassing wisdom, calling him to share in his creative power. Obviously, this is a sharing which leaves intact the infinite distance between the Creator and the creature, as Cardinal Nicholas of Cusa made clear: 'Creative art, which it is the soul's good fortune to entertain, is not to be identified with that essential art which is God himself, but is only a communication of it and a share in it.'"

the liturgical action expresses and by the way it serves and does not interrupt the ritual actions that have their own structure, rhythm, and movement. Since art is revelatory, a gift from God, a truly beautiful object stretches "beyond what the senses perceive and, reaching beneath reality's surface, strives to interpret its hidden mystery." Nonetheless, there is always the chasm between "the work of [the artist's] hands" and the "dazzling perfection" glimpsed in God's creative moment.[164] Art that is used in worship must therefore evoke wonder at its beauty but lead beyond itself to the invisible God. Beautiful, compelling artworks draw the People of God into a deeper awareness of their lives and of their common goals as a Christian community as well as of their roles and responsibilities in the wider world.[165] Art that fulfills these qualities is art *worthy* of the Christian assembly.

§ 149 § Worthy art is an essential, integral element in the sacred beauty of a church building. Through skilled use of proportion, shape, color, and design, art unifies and helps to integrate the place of worship with the actions of worship. Artistic creations in the place of worship inspire contemplation and devotion. Sculpture, furnishings, art-glass, vesture, paintings, bells, organs, and other musical instruments as well as windows, doors, and every visible and tactile detail of architecture possess the potential to express the wholeness, harmony, and radiance of profound beauty.

THE ARTIST WITHIN THE CHRISTIAN COMMUNITY

§ 150 § When artists are called upon to serve the Christian community, there is an "ethic," a "spirituality of artistic service."[166] Breadth of imagination enables

---

164. Ibid., no. 6: "Every genuine artistic intuition goes beyond what the senses perceive and, reaching beneath reality's surface, strives to interpret its hidden mystery. The intuition itself springs from the depths of the human soul, where the desire to give meaning to one's own life is joined by the fleeting vision of beauty and of the mysterious unity of things. All artists experience the unbridgeable gap which lies between the work of their hands, however successful it may be, and the dazzling perfection of the beauty glimpsed in the ardour of the creative moment: What they manage to express in their painting, their sculpting, their creating is no more than a glimmer of the splendor which flared for a moment before the eyes of their spirit."

165. Second Vatican Council, *Gaudium et Spes: Pastoral Constitution on the Church in the Modern World* (December 7, 1965), no. 62: "Literature and the arts are also, in their own way, of great importance to the life of the Church. For they strive to probe the unique nature of man, his problems, his experiences as he struggles to know and perfect both himself and the world. . . .

"Let the Church also acknowledge new forms of art which are adapted to our age and are in keeping with the characteristics of various nations and regions. Adjusted in their mode of expression and conformed to liturgical requirements, they may be introduced into the sanctuary when they raise the mind to God.

"In this way the knowledge of God can be better revealed. Also, the preaching of the gospel can become clearer to man's mind and show its relevance to the conditions of human life."

166. LA, no. 4: "The particular vocation of individual artists decides the arena in which they serve and points as well to the tasks they must assume, the hard work they must endure and the responsibility they must accept. Artists who are conscious of all this know too that they must labor without allowing themselves to be driven by the search for empty glory or the craving for cheap popularity, and still less by the calculation of some possible profit for themselves. There is therefore an ethic, even a 'spirituality' of artistic service, which contributes in its way to the life and renewal of a people. It is precisely this to which Cyprian Norwid seems to allude in declaring that 'beauty is to enthuse us for work, and work is to raise us up.'"

artists to communicate deep meaning and powerful religious sentiment with grace and sensitivity. This gift from God is combined with refined educated talents that execute elegantly crafted objects for the good of the community and the glory of God. Like the gift of prophecy, religious imagination is a power through which the Holy Spirit can move and speak. As a result, artists do not always confirm comfortable piety but, like the prophets of old, they may confront God's people with their faults and sins and they challenge the community's injustice and lack of love. "Even when they explore the darkest depths of the soul or the most unsettling aspects of evil, artists give voice in a way to the universal desire for redemption."[167]

§ 151 § Artists respond to the demands of art, actualizing in aesthetic form their ideas, feelings, and intentions so that when artists activate their imagination, their intentions and inner life are expressed in their work. In working with a parish, artists will also express the intentions, faith, and life of that community. A truly worthy and beautiful artwork can transform the artist and the community for which it is intended. The dialogue with God that an artwork mediates can persuade and invite; however, it does not force its meanings upon individuals or communities.

§ 152 § Artists willing to accept commissions destined for a place of worship must be respectful and supportive of the doctrines, beliefs, and liturgical practices of the Church. They also should be knowledgeable about the traditional iconography and symbolism of Christian art. Artists who are genuinely in search of meaning in their work and in their lives will find a homeland for their souls since, in the realm of Christianity, the most vital personal and social questions are posed. Not only does the Bible provide a rich inventory of themes and ideas, but also artists who have envisioned these stories and images have offered unique perspectives on the heart of revelation itself and "this partnership has been a source of mutual spiritual enrichment."[168]

§ 153 § A commission for a church or for worship affords artists an opportunity to join their creative gifts to those in a long history of artists who have placed

---

167. Ibid., no. 10.

168. Ibid., no. 13: "The church therefore needs art. But can it also be said that art needs the church? The question may seem like a provocation. Yet, rightly understood, it is both legitimate and profound. Artists are constantly in search of the hidden meaning of things, and their torment is to succeed in expressing the world of the ineffable. How then can we fail to see what a great source of inspiration is offered by that kind of homeland of the soul that is religion? Is it not perhaps within the realm of religion that the most vital personal questions are posed, and answers both concrete and definitive are sought?

"In fact, the religious theme has been among those most frequently treated by artists in every age. The church has always appealed to their creative powers in interpreting the Gospel message and discerning its precise application in the life of the Christian community. This partnership has been a source of mutual spiritual enrichment. Ultimately, it has been a great boon for an understanding of man, of the authentic image and truth of the person.

"The special bond between art and Christian revelation has also become evident. . . . It remains true, however, that because of its central doctrine of the incarnation of the Word of God, Christianity offers artists a horizon especially rich in inspiration. What an impoverishment it would be for art to abandon the inexhaustible mine of the Gospel!"

their talents at the service of God and who have enriched the Church's treasury of sacred art and architecture. "All artists who, in view of their talents, desire to serve God's glory in holy Church should ever bear in mind that they are engaged in a kind of sacred imitation of God the Creator, and are concerned with works destined for use in Catholic worship and for the edification, devotion, and religious instruction of the faithful."[169]

§ 154 § The Church needs art and artists to communicate Christ's message, and artists need the Church to inspire their investigations of the material world, their own inner lives, and the fabric of the community. Before an artist is selected, the parish will want to carefully consider and evaluate the artist and his or her work with the assistance of those best qualified to advise the community. Once a community has chosen artists to assist them in worship, they should give the necessary direction and then trust those they have selected. Artists deserve the independence appropriate to their gifts.

THE SPECIAL REQUIREMENTS OF LITURGICAL ART

§ 155 § In order to create art that truly serves the liturgy, the artist must have an understanding of and reverence for the liturgy. There is both a distinction and a connection between devotional art and that designed for public liturgy. Liturgical arts are integrally related to the sacraments of the Church while devotional arts are designed to enrich the spiritual life of the community and the personal piety of its members. As the devotions of the Church are derived from the liturgy and lead to it,[170] so devotional art must be in harmony with the liturgy, respect its nature, and draw people to its celebration. "The primary norm is that sacred art be functional, that is, the felicitous expression of what the liturgy is meant to be, the worship of God and the language of the community at prayer."[171] Parishes will want both liturgical and devotional art.

§ 156 § Prominent among Christian devotions is piety directed to Mary, the Mother of God. Since the earliest days of the Church, God's People have grown in their love of Mary as their mother, given to them by Jesus on the cross. Venerated and loved, invoked and imitated, she is a model for Christian faith, a support and refuge in time of need, and an eschatological image of what the Church hopes to become.[172] Although this devotion differs essentially from the prayer of adoration directed to Christ, to the Spirit, and to the Father, it is one that is deeply imbedded in the hearts of Catholics.

---

169. SC, no. 127.
170. Ibid., no. 13.
171. Pope Paul VI, Address to participants in a national congress of diocesan liturgical commissions of Italy (January 4, 1967) (DOL 539, no. 4319).
172. LG, no. 66: "The Church has endorsed many forms of piety toward the Mother of God, provided they were within the limits of sound and orthodox doctrine. These forms have varied according to the circumstances of time and place and have reflected the diversity of native characteristics and temperament among the faithful. While honoring Christ's Mother, these devotions cause her Son to be rightly known, loved, and glorified, and all His commands observed."

§ 157 § The special and unique dignity of the Mother of God has been expressed in the devotional art of the Church. Artists have painted her image in wondrously meditative fashion as a "sign of sure hope and solace for the pilgrim People of God."[173] At the same time, veneration of Mary, like that of all other devotions, leads clearly to the worship of her Son. The location, style, and importance of Marian images in the church demonstrate the intimate connection she has with the eucharistic liturgy of Christ, as well as its distinctions.

THE INTEGRATION OF ART WITHIN THE LITURGICAL SETTING

§ 158 § The role of the Church is to educate artists in the appropriate relationships between their personal approach to art and the needs of the liturgy. The role of artists is to explore the powerful personal resonances that exist between sacred art, interior devotion, and the public life of the community. An essential ingredient for a successful marriage between the artistic needs of the Church and the creative talent of the artist is the ability to collaborate. Artists must cultivate the capacity to work with the leaders and people of the local community and within the frameworks established by the universal Church if they are to have the opportunity to use their talents to fashion beautiful objects that will enliven the worship of the community.

§ 159 § Artists who collaborate with architects and liturgical consultants need to make an honest assessment of several key elements, attending to the way the objects will be placed within the building, how the works will be integrated with the architecture of the church and with its local setting, and the ways the Christian community moves within its space.

§ 160 § Attention should also be given to the way artistic objects influence acoustics and other functional elements within the building and, at the same time, to the ways in which various elements, especially lighting, may affect the objects. In addition, consideration must be given to how easily an object can be cleaned and maintained.

MATERIALS OF THE ARTIST

§ 161 § Artists bridge the worlds of the visible and the mysterious invisible. They focus upon items with specific shapes, sizes, weights, densities, colors, forms, and textures. At the same time, they utilize materials that struggle to express ideas and concepts, visions and imaginative constructions. Even as they

---

173. Ibid., no. 68: "In the bodily and spiritual glory which she possesses in heaven, the Mother of Jesus continues in this present world as the image and first flowering of the Church as she is to be perfected in the world to come. Likewise, Mary shines forth on earth, until the day of the Lord shall come (cf. 2 Peter 3:10), as a sign of sure hope and solace for the pilgrim People of God."

nourish the senses with beauty, they also disclose the "transcendent value" and the "aura of mystery" in the Christian message.[174]

§ 162 § Artists choose materials with integrity because they will endure from generation to generation, because they are noble enough for holy actions, and because they express what is most respected and beautiful in the lives and cultures of the community. Materials, colors, shapes, and designs that are of short-lived popularity are unworthy. In addition to eliminating unsuitable materials, artists and communities should be cautious and discerning about promoting features closely identified with the values and attitudes of any class, ethnic or age group to the exclusion of others in the community.

§ 163 § Similarly, artworks consisting of technological and interactive media, such as video and other electronically fabricated images, may also be appropriate for sacred purposes. Subject to the same criteria of suitability as other sacred art, technologically produced works of art can point toward sacred realities even though they do not possess the more enduring form, color, texture, weight, and density found in more traditional sacred art.

VESSELS AND VESTMENTS SUITABLE FOR THE LITURGY

§ 164 § As in the case of styles of architecture, there is no particular style for sacred furnishings for the liturgy.[175] Sacred vessels may be in "a shape that is in keeping with the culture of each region, provided each type of vessel is suited to the intended liturgical use and is clearly distinguished from [utensils] designed

---

174. LA, no. 12: "In order to communicate the message entrusted to her by Christ, the church needs art. Art must make perceptible, and as far as possible attractive, the world of the spirit, of the invisible, of God. It must therefore translate into meaningful terms that which is in itself ineffable. Art has a unique capacity to take one or other facet of the message and translate it into colors, shapes and sounds which nourish the intuition of those who look or listen. It does so without emptying the message itself of its transcendent value and its aura of mystery.

"The church has need especially of those who can do this on the literary and figurative level, using the endless possibilities of images and their symbolic force. Christ himself made extensive use of images in his preaching, fully in keeping with his willingness to become, in the incarnation, the icon of the unseen God.

"The church also needs musicians. How many sacred works have been composed through the centuries by people deeply imbued with the sense of the mystery! The faith of countless believers has been nourished by melodies flowing from the hearts of other believers, either introduced into the liturgy or used as an aid to dignified worship. In song, faith is experienced as vibrant joy, love and confident expectation of the saving intervention of God.

"The church needs architects, because she needs spaces to bring the Christian people together and celebrate the mysteries of salvation. After the terrible destruction of the last world war and the growth of great cities, a new generation of architects showed themselves adept at responding to the exigencies of Christian worship, confirming that the religious theme can still inspire architectural design in our own day. Not infrequently these architects have constructed churches which are both places of prayer and true works of art."

175. GIRM, no. 325: "As in the case of the building of churches, the Church welcomes the artistic style of every region for all sacred furnishings and accepts adaptations in keeping with the genius and traditions of each people, provided they fit the purpose for which the sacred furnishings are intended.

"In this matter as well, the concern is to be for the noble simplicity that is the perfect companion of genuine art."

for every day use."[176] Materials used for sacred vessels such as the chalice and paten should be worthy, solid, and durable, and should not break easily. Chalices and cups used for the distribution of the Precious Blood should have bowls made of nonabsorbent material. Vessels made from metal are gilded on the inside if the metal ordinarily rusts. The vestments worn by ministers symbolize the ministers' functions and add beauty to the celebration of the rites. "In addition to traditional materials, natural fabrics proper to the [local area] may be used for making vestments; . . . The beauty and nobility of a vestment should derive from its material and design rather than from lavish ornamentation."[177]

§ 165 § Conferences of bishops may make further determinations regarding the appropriate style and material for sacred vessels and vestments to be used in the celebration of the liturgy.[178] Likewise, the diocesan bishop can make further determinations regarding the suitability of the materials or the design for vessels and vestments, and, in cases of doubt, he is the judge of what is appropriate in this regard.[179]

THE DISPOSITION OF WORKS OF ART
NO LONGER NEEDED FOR SACRED USE

§ 166 § Sacred art that is no longer useful or needed or that is simply worn out and beyond restoration deserves to be treated with respect. To ensure the protection of worn or used sanctuary furnishings, vessels, vesture, and other liturgical artifacts, many diocesan bishops have issued directives about their proper disposition when they are no longer suitable for worship. In addition, with the closing or merging of parishes, vessels and vestments can be available for the use of other parishes and missions. In disposing of such artifacts pastors should consult the diocesan worship office or chancery to learn what directives or procedures are in effect.

---

176. Ibid., no. 332: "The artist may fashion the sacred vessels in a shape that is in keeping with the culture of each region, provided each type of vessel is suited to the intended liturgical use and is clearly distinguished from those designed for every day use."

177. Ibid., nos. 343–344: "In addition to the traditional materials, natural fabrics proper to the region may be used for making vestments; artificial fabrics that are in keeping with the dignity of the liturgical service and the person wearing them may also be used. The Conference of Bishops will be the judge in this matter.

"The beauty and nobility of a vestment should derive from its material and design rather than from lavish ornamentation. Representations on vestments should consist only of symbols, images, or pictures portraying the sacred. Anything out of keeping with the sacred is to be avoided."

178. Ibid., no. 329: "In accord with the judgment of the Conference of Bishops, in acts confirmed by the Apostolic See, sacred vessels may be made even from other solid materials which, in the common estimation of the region are regarded as noble e.g., ebony or other hard woods as long as such materials are suited to sacred use. In such cases, preference is always to be given to materials that do no break easily or deteriorate. Materials intended for all vessels which hold the Eucharistic bread such as the plate, ciborium, theca, monstrance or others of this kind should be likewise suitable to sacred use."

Cf. SC, no. 128.

179. Cf. National Conference of Catholic Bishops, *The Appendix to the General Instruction for the Dioceses of the United States* (1975), nos. 288 and 305.

§ 167 § In addition, bishops have exercised their responsibility as stewards of the Church's artistic resources by encouraging pastors and diocesan personnel to consult with experts and to create an inventory of historic churches and of objects in any church that have artistic or historical value. Such inventories are most helpful when they carefully itemize and list each entry's value and note any changes to the objects since they were acquired.[180] Usually two copies are made so that one can be kept at the local parish and the other in the diocesan curia, both as a historical record and for insurance purposes. In some cases, copies are sent to the Vatican library if this is appropriate.

§ 168 § Objects of great artistic or historical value or those donated to the Church through a vow may not be sold without special permission of the Holy See.[181] When such objects are not to be sold but disposed of in some other way, the diocesan bishop should be contacted so that the concerns of donors and the requirements of canon law are fulfilled.

§ 169 § Every community knows that, if its house of prayer is to radiate the beauty of divine presence, effort and sacrifice will be required. Besides appropriate remuneration for the work of its artists, the community must show its respect for these works by maintaining and preserving them as the years pass. In doing so, they encourage those with artistic aptitudes to continue to serve the community and in this way build up and support a local community of artists worthy of liturgical work. A covenant is established linking artists and congregations, an "alliance between art and the life of religion" through which may be heard an artistic voice "that love inspires and that inspires love."[182]

---

180. OA, no. 3 (DOL 541, no. 4330): "Each diocesan curia is responsible for measures to ensure that, in conformity with the norms set by the local Ordinary, rectors of churches, after consultation with experts, prepare an inventory of places of worship and of the contents that are of artistic or historical importance. This is to be an itemized inventory that lists the value of each entry. Two copies are to be drawn up, one to be kept by the church and the other by the diocesan curia. It would be well for another copy to be sent by the curia to the Vatican Library. This inventory should include notations on changes that have taken place in the course of time."
    Since the publication of *Opera Artis*, the Pontifical Commission for the Cultural Goods of the Church was established in 1993 to oversee the artistic and historic patrimony of the Church. The current president is Archbishop Francesco Marchisano.
181. CIC, c. 1292 § 2: "The permission of the Holy See is also required for the valid alienation of goods whose value exceeds the maximum amount, goods given to the Church by vow, or goods precious for artistic or historical reasons."
182. Pope Paul VI, Address to the Pontifical Commission for Sacred Art in Italy (December 17, 1969) (DOL 540, no. 4326): "This leads us to conclude by encouraging you to act in such a way that, under the aegis of the liturgy, that is, divine worship, a bond of union, an alliance, will be reestablished between modern art and the life of religion. This should contribute to restore to art its two greatest and most characteristic values. The first is beauty, perceptible beauty (*id quod visum placet*: a beauty grasped in the integrity, proportion, and purity of the work of art; ST 1a, 39.1). The second is that indefinable but vibrant value, the artistic spirit, the lyrical experience in the artist that is reflected in his work. The alliance between art and the life of religion will also succeed in giving again to the Church, the Bride of Christ, a voice that love inspires and that inspires love.
    "There is a second concluding point to which Vatican Council II attributes particular importance. Before anticipating a new epiphany for sacred art, as though it could spontaneously give itself a new birth and new creativity, we must take pains with the formation of artists. As always we must begin with the education of the person (see SC art. 127)."

CHAPTER FOUR
BUILDING A CHURCH: PRACTICAL CONSIDERATIONS

§ 170 §   Having reflected upon the nature and purpose of a church, having reviewed the activities that take place within the worship space, and having considered the role and importance of the arts as part of the act of worship, we here address the actual task of building. This chapter examines the practical considerations such as who should collaborate in building the church, how to develop a master plan, what kind of educational process will be most helpful for parishes, and how to work with the relevant professionals.

§ 171 §   Churches are built to be legacies to a community's faith. Every parish community hopes that its space for worship will endure long after those who now pray there have joined the Messianic Banquet. Liturgical education is primary in the development of any parish's plans for the future, since the building is an embodiment of the Church's transmission of the Gospel. If built wisely and well, the building itself will evangelize the descendants of its builders.

THE MASTER PLAN

§ 172 §   As part of its stewardship efforts, each parish should have a master plan for the current and future allocation and augmentation of its resources. The master plan contains the statement of the parish vision and priorities, the long-range general plan for parish buildings and properties, and the outline for the allocation of financial and personnel resources.

§ 173 §   The parish mission statement and its list of priorities can serve as the basis for making decisions about resources and projects. In addition to the mission statement, the master plan includes a current inventory of buildings and property; a site plan; an analysis of the current condition of significant items that impact budget, plans, and priorities; and regularly updated reports on the parish's financial assets and projections for future growth, or the amortization of debts as well as maintenance and replacement data on major items such as furnaces, roofs, elevators, and other items of capital outlay.

§ 174 §   Since planning is affected by many events, a regularly updated report on area demographics, population trends, and planned growth and development by the municipality's planning office that could affect parish property and the surrounding area is an important part of the data in the plan. The assessment of potential items of major liability or sources of income are also part of this long-range plan. The decision to build a church or to renovate an existing worship space is made within the framework of the master plan.

BEGINNING THE PROCESS

§ 175 §   The construction or renovation of a church building is a complex task that demands prayer and reflection, technical expertise and study. A building or renovation project is not the work of the pastor alone, nor is it that of a building committee. Rather, it is an act of faith that belongs to and engages the entire community. To be successful, a building project must be rooted in a proper understanding of the Church and of worship that becomes the point of reference for all future decision making. Creating and articulating this shared vision is a key element of the process.

§ 176 § Deepening a sense of ownership for the project involves taking the time to educate the parish, to listen to the people's concerns, and to discuss the vision and values at stake in such a project. The time devoted to communication and education will help make the later stages of the process move more smoothly and will ensure that the relationships among parish members are strengthened rather than strained by the project.

§ 177 § Since no single pastor or parish possesses the totality of expertise or vision required to execute a project of such great scope, the congregation and clergy will need to recognize the areas of their own competence, the role of the diocesan bishop and diocesan personnel, and their limits beyond which the assistance of experts will be required. Respect and appreciation for the competence of others in their respective fields is essential for good teamwork.

THE ROLE OF THE APOSTOLIC SEE AND THE DIOCESAN CHURCH

§ 178 § The Apostolic See has provided guidance for designing places of worship that is necessary and invaluable for the local community. In constructing or renewing a place of worship, it is the bishop who, in his role of fostering and governing the liturgy, must assume primary responsibility and authority for the regulation and direction of such projects.[183] As the *Code of Canon Law* states, "No church is to be built without the express written consent of the diocesan bishop . . . .after having heard the presbyteral council and the rectors of the neighboring churches."[184] Therefore, the building or renovation of a place for worship is a project that belongs to the local parish and the whole diocesan Church.[185] Care must be exercised by the pastor and parish to consult with diocesan personnel from the earliest stages of the discernment process through the completion of the work. The diocesan liturgical commission or diocesan commission on liturgy and art assists with liturgical education and the development of the liturgical and artistic components of the building's design. Some dioceses

---

183. Cf. GIRM, no. 387; SC, no. 124: "Ordinaries, by the encouragement and favor they show to art which is truly sacred, should strive after noble beauty rather than mere extravagance. This principle is to apply also in the matter of sacred vestments and appointments.

"Let bishops carefully exclude from the house of God and from other sacred places those works of artists which are repugnant to faith, morals, and Christian piety, and which offend true religious sense either by distortion of forms or by lack of artistic worth, by mediocrity or by pretense.

"When churches are to be built, let great care be taken that they be suitable for the celebration of liturgical services and for the active participation of the faithful."

184. CIC, c. 1215 §§ 1 and 2.

185. GIRM, no. 291: "All who are involved in the construction, restoration, and remodeling of churches are to consult the diocesan commission on liturgy and liturgical art. However, the diocesan Bishop is to use the counsel and help of this commission whenever it comes to laying down norms on this matter, approving plans for new buildings, and making decisions on the more important issues."

have additional building offices or similar agencies to help parishes with the selection of architects, engineers, and building contractors, and to provide valuable information about those who have successfully served the Church in the past. In the early stages of the project, the parish needs to be in communication with the appropriate diocesan office or commission in developing the budget for the project and the financial plan, since these require the approval of the bishop and his financial advisors. This document is designed to assist diocesan bishops in developing local norms and procedures to guide parishes in church design and construction and to provide knowledgeable advisors for the local parish, especially in the complex areas of engineering and construction.

§ 179 § In some dioceses the first step in any building or renovation process is a meeting of the pastor, the architect, and possibly, the liturgical consultant with the diocesan bishop or his representative to discuss any diocesan parameters. Such early consultation can prevent confusion and unrealistic expectations or diversions later.

THE ROLE OF THE PARISH COMMUNITY

THE ASSESSMENT OF NEED

§ 180 § The entire parish is an integral part of the needs assessment and the development of priorities, which are the first steps of a process that will lead to a decision about building, renovating, and expending parish resources. While some decisions in the process will be made by committees, the decision and the design should never become the exclusive project of a small select group.

§ 181 § When a parish is determining the need for a new church or for the renovation of an existing church, a thorough self-study and educational program is part of the needs assessment process. In that study the parish community reflects upon what it is, and what it hopes for in a new or renovated church. This is essential to enable the community to give direction to the architect and other professionals who will design the building.

ROLES WITHIN THE PARISH

THE PASTOR

§ 182 § The pastor is vital to the building or renovation of a parish church. The pastor shepherds the community through the various and often lengthy stages of discernment and planning and works with the finance committee in fulfilling his responsibility for the fiscal dimensions of the project. He must open channels of communication with the entire parish so that all voices may be heard. A clear initial presentation on the scope of the project and frequent updates on the progress of the work, especially any alterations to initial plans, coupled with displays of the architect's renderings, floor plans, and scale models help to involve parishioners as part of the project from beginning to end. With the help of the staff and others in the parish, the pastor arranges for the parish self-study, the liturgical education of parishioners, and the preparation of the building committee as it begins discernment. The pastor is also the connection and communication link with the diocese throughout the process. In the final analysis, decisions concerning every facet of the building program from beginning to end remain with the pastor, in conformity with diocesan regulations. Wisdom, however, requires that the pastor consult broadly with the congregation, the parish staff, the parish pastoral council, the parish liturgy committee, and the parish finance council, as well as with liturgical and architectural experts and experienced diocesan personnel.

THE PARISH BUILDING COMMITTEE

§ 183 § Depending on the organization of the parish, a building committee will be formed that will have significant responsibility for the consultation and educational components as well as for the oversight of the actual building or renovation process. In selecting this committee, the pastor will search for parishioners whose skills and knowledge will contribute to the project. Engineers, architects, artists, interior designers, contractors, and individuals with experience in construction can be of great assistance in overseeing the work to be done. As professionals who have a vested interest in the life of the parish but who are not financially or materially engaged in the process, they can assist with the development of realistic plans and can also provide an ongoing objective evaluation of the work as it progresses.

§ 184 § In addition to having professionals and people with a broad range of experience on the committee, the pastor will want to ensure that the committee is representative of the parish by choosing members of various ages and viewpoints and some liaisons from key parish committees. When all views are heard in the discussion phases, better decisions are likely to be made and a greater sense of ownership will result.

THE PARISH PASTORAL COUNCIL, THE PARISH WORSHIP COMMITTEE, AND THE FINANCE COUNCIL

§ 185 § Each of the key parish committees oversees the various aspects of parish life and continues to work during this major parish activity. As the building or renovation project progresses, these parishioners contribute to its development through membership on existing parish committees or on newly formed committees entrusted with specific tasks. The parish pastoral council can assist the pastor with the general oversight of pastoral activity in the parish and represents the concerns of the parishioners. The parish worship committee can contribute its expertise in keeping the liturgical needs in the forefront of the discussion. The finance council has a significant role with regard to sources and limits of funding, debt amortization, and financial campaigns. Areas that might be addressed by other committees include furnishings, seating arrangements, the chapel of reservation, devotional items, interior and exterior artwork, and landscaping design.

§ 186 § However, it is essential that members of these committees approach their tasks from an informed perspective and stay in constant communication with other committees to ensure a well-informed team and a coordinated project. While the professional experience of people related to a building project is valuable, care must be taken that these professionals familiarize themselves with the special requirements of the liturgy related to their area of competence. In many instances, the initial work of the committees will be to gain knowledge of the church's liturgical practices as they relate to their task. As the project develops, these committees may be called upon to provide an ongoing, informed review of plans from their areas of expertise.

THE PARISH SELF-STUDY

§ 187 § By their design and construction, church buildings serve the rites of the Church and the devotion of the people, fostering their encounter with God who dwells in all holiness,[186] and reflecting the faith of the people and the culture in which they live. Ideally the church building will be designed so that it also responds to the local environment. While the church building belongs to the Church, its visual aspects belong to its neighbors. In addition, there must be a concern for the impact of the building on its natural surroundings; that is, the site on which it will be located and the resources available there.

§ 188 § Parishioners may have some sense of the history of the parish, but it is helpful to sharpen the common knowledge of church members at the beginning of the project. This review can consider the origins of the parish; its evolving identity within the local community; and the social, political, economic, and religious elements that have shaped its life. Among other things, the parish will want to reflect on the cultures represented in its members, the geographical and historical factors that have contributed to its development, significant aspects of the community's liturgical and devotional life, and changes that have already taken place in the building in which its members worship.

§ 189 § During the study it may be helpful to invite parishioners to contribute photographs of weddings, first communions, baptisms, and other sacramental and seasonal events. These photos, arranged chronologically, can provide graphic evidence of the changes that the church building has already undergone. The

---

186. SC, no. 122: "Very rightly the fine arts are considered to rank among the noblest expressions of human genius. This judgment applies especially to religious art and to its highest achievement, which is sacred art. By their very nature both of the latter are related to God's boundless beauty, for this is the reality which these human efforts are trying to express in some way. To the extent that these works aim exclusively at turning men's thoughts to God persuasively and devoutly, they are dedicated to God and to the cause of His greater honor and glory.

"Holy Mother Church has therefore always been the friend of the fine arts and has continuously sought their noble ministry with the special aim that all things set apart for use in divine worship should be truly worthy, becoming, and beautiful, signs and symbols of heavenly realities. For this purpose, too, she has trained artists. In fact, the Church has, with good reason, always reserved the right to pass judgment upon the arts, deciding which of the works of artists are in accordance with faith, piety, and cherished traditional laws, and thereby suited to sacred use.

"The Church has been particularly careful to see that sacred furnishings worthily and beautifully serve the dignity of worship, and has welcomed those changes in materials, style, or ornamentation which the progress of the technical arts has brought with the passage of time.

"Therefore it has pleased the Fathers to issue the following decrees on these matters."

archives of local and diocesan newspapers also can provide material that will help in piecing together the story of the parish over the years.

§ 190 § As part of the self-study, the parish will want to develop a process for liturgical education. While the actual content will vary from one parish to another, parishioners need to learn more about the liturgy, which is the heart of the Church's life, and about their participation in the liturgy, which is the "primary and indispensable source" of the "true Christian spirit."[187] In addition, they need to understand the intrinsic relationships between the Eucharist and the other sacraments, the Liturgy of the Hours, the liturgical year, and the building that houses these celebrations. After reflecting on the basics of liturgy, the assembly can learn about the ways in which architectural elements, the placement and design of liturgical objects, and the choice of floor plans can encourage, control, or hinder liturgical actions. Full and active participation will be greatly affected by the appropriate architectural expression of faith for a particular community. The liturgical consultant chosen by the parish often develops and directs this education process. In other instances diocesan offices can provide assistance and resources in this area.

PRIORITIES AND STEWARDSHIP OF RESOURCES

§ 191 § Since the building of a place of worship has serious financial implications, wise stewardship of resources demands that the parish establish liturgical, spiritual, artistic, and social priorities upon which financial decisions rest. However, the cost of an item is not the only consideration in planning for construction and renovation. Every faith community, even the financially poorest, is called to use all the powers of human ingenuity at its disposal to provide beautiful, uplifting, and enriching places of worship that also serve basic human needs.

§ 192 § Building a beautiful church is itself an act of worship because beauty is a reflection of God and "a call to transcendence."[188] All church buildings and their contents should mirror divine beauty, which is not to be confused with

---

187. Ibid., no. 14: "In the restoration and promotion of the sacred liturgy, this full and active participation by all the people is the aim to be considered before all else; for it is the primary and indispensable source from which the faithful are to derive the true Christian spirit. Therefore, through the needed program of instruction, pastors must zealously strive to achieve in it all their pastoral work.

"Yet it would be futile to entertain any hopes of realizing this goal unless the pastors themselves, to begin with, become thoroughly penetrated with the spirit and power of the liturgy, and become masters of it. It is vitally necessary, therefore, that attention be directed, above all, to the liturgical instruction of the clergy. Therefore this most sacred Council has decided to enact as follows."

188. LA, no. 16: "Beauty is a key to the mystery and a call to transcendence. It is an invitation to savor life and to dream of the future. That is why the beauty of created things can never fully satisfy. It stirs that hidden nostalgia for God which a lover of beauty like St. Augustine could express in incomparable terms: 'Late have I loved you, beauty so old and so new: late have I loved you!'

"Artists of the world, may your many different paths all lead to that infinite Ocean of beauty where wonder becomes awe, exhilaration, unspeakable joy."

lavish display. Whatever the style of architecture adopted, extravagant expenditures on the construction of a church should be avoided in light of the obligation to share the resources of the earth in an equitable manner. However, compromises in cost should not compromise the durability, stability, and structural soundness of the building. Balancing the social needs of the local faith community with their duty to worship God through beauty affects the equation of design and execution. Beauty also can be found in simplicity of shape; in humble, honest materials; in the creative use of light, water, and sound; in elegant design; and in worthy religious art.

SURVEYING EXISTING CHURCHES

§ 193 § Before people make architectural and liturgical decisions, they need some experience of the broad spectrum of architectural designs already in new and renovated churches. People's preferences are often determined by things with which they are familiar. Visits to a variety of churches can help them to develop a store of images that they can evaluate and consider as potential options for the building project in their own parish.

§ 194 § Although the visits should not be confined to the work of architects or liturgical consultants under consideration for their project, people will want to visit churches that demonstrate the candidates' work. Gaining knowledge of a professional's previous work, whether religious or secular, is indispensable to the process of selecting the architect.

§ 195 § When actual site visits are not possible, slides, videos, and other visual aids can expand the experience of those preparing for the building or renovation of a church. Liturgical and construction offices within the diocese also can be invaluable resources in advising parish building committees of recent or exemplary projects in the local area.

THE ROLE OF PROFESSIONALS

§ 196 § In deciding to employ professionals, and in hiring specific people, the parish must be aware of any diocesan directives and requirements for contracts and licenses and is encouraged to utilize the expertise of diocesan staff with experience in this area. Doing so can help to avert serious financial and legal difficulties for the parish and major time delays. Because the architect is the contracted professional responsible for the development of the building's design, it is appropriate that other professionals serve as consultants to the architect. It is also crucial that all professionals chosen have the expertise to fulfill the particular tasks needed and that a clear description of their roles and responsibilities be developed and agreed upon before they actually begin the work.

§ 197 § Normally, engaging the skills of professionals with experience in the lighting of churches, acoustical design and sound transmission, and design is preferable to selecting vendors of equipment or accepting the "good will" services of individuals who may have some knowledge but who lack the requisite qualifications to design and install elements suitable for a church. Both the scale of the building and the demands of the liturgy require varied solutions that differ from those suitable for domestic or smaller-scale projects.

THE ARCHITECT

§ 198 § The architect, the primary agent of design, has an essential role in the building or renovation project. In choosing an architect, the parish will look for someone whose designs will embody the mysteries of the faith expressed and lived in the liturgical assembly. In addition to having the skills and exercising the appropriate standard of care required of a professional architect, those chosen to design church buildings should be able to

1. *Create an environment by the use of space, sound, and visual aspects that will facilitate and encourage liturgical celebrations and the active participation of the faithful.*[189]

2. *Give visual expression to aspects of doctrine and spirituality that words alone cannot adequately express, employing in their own designs, and requiring in those of others hired by them, the highest artistic standards for the inspiration, devotion, and religious formation of believers.*[190]

3. *Draw attention to and protect the significant treasures of the Church's architectural and artistic heritage, whenever possible.*

4. *Be collaborative and willing to participate in the dialogue essential to the development of a building program that will fulfill the needs of the local Church.*

5. *Be sensitive to the financial realities of the parish and work within its budget.*

THE LITURGICAL CONSULTANTS

§ 199 § The construction of a church building cannot be undertaken without proper professionals in a variety of fields. When a parish begins to undertake the building or renovation of a liturgical space, the parish building committee should obtain the services of specialists in liturgical design. lt is the responsibility of the liturgical consultant to assist the pastor, the staff, and the entire parish with continuing education about the importance, role, and value of worship, and the impact of the church building upon worship.

§ 200 § The liturgical consultant also works with the architect. Some architects are *liturgical* architects. They possess, in addition to their architectural

---

189. GIRM, no. 288: "For the celebration of the Eucharist, the people of God normally assemble in a church or, if there is none or one that is inadequate for some reason, then in some other place nevertheless worthy of so great a mystery. Churches and other places of worship should therefore be suited to celebrating the liturgy and to ensuring the active participation of the faithful. Further, the buildings and requisites for worship should be truly worthy and beautiful, signs and symbols of heavenly realities."

190. Ibid., no. 289; SC, no. 127: "All artists who, in view of their talents, desire to serve God's glory in holy Church, should ever bear in mind that they are engaged in a kind of sacred imitation of God the Creator and are concerned with works destined for use in Catholic worship and for the edification, devotion, and religious instruction of the faithful."

credentials, artistic insights and formal liturgical education that equip them to engage in liturgical design. However, this is not always the case. The liturgical consultant(s) selected by the parish work(s) with the architect and other members of the design team from the earliest stages of the process to help them apply the principles and norms of liturgical design to the practical and liturgical needs of the parish being served. This includes examining the acoustics, the flow and movement for processions, appropriate styles for liturgical celebrations, the inter-relationships within the Eucharist as well as the relationship of the Eucharist with the other sacraments, and all the elements required by the Church's liturgy. In addition, the consultant may have expertise in design and can help to coordinate the design and fabrication of appropriate furniture and other objects to be used during liturgical services, as well as the liturgical art to be placed within the church.

THE CONTRACTOR

§ 201 § Parishes will search for contractors who exhibit skills appropriate to the scope and significance of the project and who are properly licensed and insured. Candidates should demonstrate their ability to finance and to fulfill their commitments completely and on time and should exhibit skills in the areas of management, supervision, building technology, and construction methods and procedures. They also should have a record of good labor relations supported by positive benefit practices that are consonant with and reflective of the Church's teachings on social justice. Most dioceses keep careful records of the competence, working methods, completion practices, and fiscal responsibility of the contractors who have worked on church buildings in the diocese to assist parishes with the competitive bidding process. This information can be readily available to the pastor and the parish building committee.

COMPENSATION AND PROFESSIONAL STANDARDS

§ 202 § Excellent designs can be brought to beautiful completion only by competent and trustworthy professionals. These professionals have a right to compensation that matches the expectations of the outstanding competence and expertise demanded of them. A major and continuing educational effort is required among believers in order to restore respect for competence and expertise in all the arts and to cultivate a desire for their best use in public worship. The Church needs in its service professional people with the appropriate qualifications. The community must be willing to budget and expend resources for appropriate professionals so that the criteria for good liturgical art and sound building practices can be met.

§ 203 § The architects, liturgical consultants, artists, contractors, and all others engaged in the project should be held to a high professional standard of care and to the observance of the social teaching of the Church. Because they are, in part, responsible for the stewardship of the resources of the parish, all who are engaged in the project must be worthy of the trust of the community.

§ 204 § Volunteers and donors of contributed services and in-kind gifts are valuable assets in any parish building project. However, these individuals and their contributions must be held to the same standard of skill, quality, and appropriateness that is required of services and objects procured through conventional methods. As a parish utilizes contributed services, it will be important to work with diocesan personnel to ensure that all legal and insurance requirements are met.

COLLABORATION

§ 205 § Collaboration is essential to every architectural project, but it is even more so in architecture at the service of liturgy, for cooperation reflects the very nature of the Body of Christ. The members of the parish community along with their pastor, the liturgical consultant, the artist, the architect, and the contractor are all called to a collaborative effort, whose goal is to summon forth the finest expressions of faith within their means. Mutual trust and openness are central components of the collaborative effort. The parish, represented by its pastor and committees, the architect and liturgical design consultant, the artist, and the contractors should strive to listen to each other with careful attention so that a place of sacred beauty will emerge from their mutual dialogue.

THE DESIGN OF THE CHURCH AND ITS SURROUNDINGS: SPECIAL CONCERNS

THE SITE PLAN

§ 206 § The unity of God's People is both expressed and brought about in the gathering of the eucharistic assembly.[191] Since the church building is fundamentally a place where God and his gathered people meet, care should be exercised in designing the entire complex of site and church building so that it will serve this *gathering* of the faithful that is essential to liturgical worship.[192]

§ 207 § The design of the area surrounding the church can integrate trees, shrubs and flowers with places for outdoor gathering and for quiet meditation. While there is no maintenance-free landscaping, it is possible to keep landscape care at a manageable level by using indigenous and low-maintenance plants that can withstand dry conditions without requiring excessive watering.

§ 208 § The outdoor paths that lead to the church building should be welcoming and free of barriers, especially to persons with disabilities. In the design of these paths, consideration should be given not only to groups and individuals coming to Sunday Eucharist but also to the arrival and departure of special groups such as the wedding party or the mourners who accompany the deceased's body at a funeral.

§ 209 § In suburban and rural parishes, the building approach must ordinarily provide access for pedestrians as well as for those who arrive by automobile. The

---

191. LG, no. 11: "Strengthened anew at the holy table by the Body of Christ, they manifest in a practical way that unity of God's People which is suitably signified and wondrously brought about by this most awesome sacrament."

192. SC, no. 10: "Nevertheless the liturgy is the summit toward which the activity of the Church is directed; at the same time it is the fountain from which all her power flows. For the goal of apostolic works is that all who are made sons of God by faith and baptism should come together to praise God in the midst of His Church, to take part in her sacrifice, and to eat the Lord's supper."

building site can be designed so that all who approach are helped to make the transition from everyday life to the celebration of the mysteries of faith. Parking lots and passenger drop-off areas can be convenient yet unobtrusive. Sensitive design of vehicular approaches, parking sites, and walkways coupled with appropriate landscaping make it possible to accommodate the automobile without allowing it to dominate the site. Weather considerations will influence the arrangement and the choices made by the local parish.

§ 210 § Paths provided for those approaching on foot, especially paths that lead to the principal gathering space outside the building, should receive special attention. The space at which these paths converge should be welcoming and hospitable, drawing together those who assemble for worship and providing for those who wish to linger in conversation with one another after liturgical services. Pavement patterns, borders, and configurations; shrines containing images in sculpture, mosaic, or other art media; as well as planters and outdoor benches help with the passage from the mundane to the sacred action of worship.

ACCESSIBILITY

§ 211 § Every person should be welcomed into the worshiping assembly with respect and care. It was the prophet Isaiah who announced the Lord's message: "For my house shall be called a house of prayer for all peoples."[193] The bishops of the United States have stated that "it is essential that all forms of the liturgy be completely accessible to persons with disabilities, since these forms are the essence of the spiritual tie that binds the Christian community together."[194] Further direction is given by Pope John Paul II, who has called the Church to the full integration of persons with disabilities into family, community, and Church, and to overcome "the tendency to isolate, segregate and marginalize [those with disabilities]."[195] When buildings present barriers to the full and active participation of all, the Body of Christ is harmed.

§ 212 § Special attention should be given to individuals with visual or hearing impairments, to those who have difficulty walking or who are in wheelchairs, and to the elderly with frailties. In addition to ramps, elevators, braille signs, and special sound systems that can be accessed by those who need assistance, staircases should have at least one railing. If the sanctuary is elevated by steps, an unobtrusively placed ramp with a hand rail should be provided to make it possible for everyone to have access to the sanctuary.[196]

---

193. Is 56:7.
194. United States Catholic Conference, *Pastoral Statement of the U.S. Catholic Bishops on Persons with Disabilities* (1978), p. 6.
195. Pope John Paul II, *Devoted to the Handicapped* (March 4, 1981), I, 4. In *The Pope Speaks* 26:2 (Summer 1981), p. 160.
196. In addition to eliminating architectural barriers, other forms of assistance should be available to persons with disabilities (for example, providing listening devices, providing places for signing/interpretation, using printed texts and captioned audiovisual materials, installing visual emergency alarms, and making available special telephones for use by persons with hearing difficulties).

§ 213 § The planning process should include consultation with persons with various disabilities and the use of an accessibility inventory[197] to ensure a careful review of potential or existing architectural barriers. All new construction and renovation work must fully integrate the demands of the liturgy with current laws, codes, and ordinances for persons with disabilities.

§ 214 § Older places of worship can be especially challenging because of the obstacles they present to persons with disabilities. In the renovation of older buildings, special provisions must be made to harmonize the requirements for accessibility with the architectural integrity of the building and with the norms for the proper celebration of liturgy. Adaptations to existing buildings can be expensive, but failure to make the community's places of worship accessible will exact a far more costly human and ecclesial toll. The goal is always to make the entire church building accessible to all of God's People.

THE CHOICE OF BUILDING MATERIALS

§ 215 § A church building is a lasting expression of a faith community's life. Because the church building is destined to endure, parishes and the professionals who assist them should ensure that the components of the building, especially the building materials, are sturdy and substantial enough to stand the test of time. While traditional building materials have served the Church well in the past, more recently developed materials and building techniques might better serve a contemporary structure. In all instances, the building that is designed for an extended life will need fine, durable materials. The use of materials available locally and of designs that are expressive of local culture can be an advantage to parishes.

§ 216 § Faithful stewardship of the earth's resources demands that the Church be a partner in the development of a sustainable architecture. Materials, construction methods, and procedures that are toxic to the environment or that are wasteful of the earth's resources should be avoided. Providing heating, ventilating, air conditioning, and lighting systems that are energy efficient is financially sound practice and, at the same time, environmentally responsible. It is an exercise in parish stewardship.

CHANGE ORDERS AND MODIFICATIONS

§ 217 § During the construction phase of the process, the pastor and building committee may find the need to modify the original plan. Because modifications involve additional costs, parishes will want to anticipate as many situations as possible before plans are finalized and contracts are signed.

§ 218 § If the need for modifications becomes apparent at a later stage, the procedures should be clear to all involved. It is helpful to

1. *Specify that the pastor is to communicate any change orders to the architect, who acknowledges them in writing.*

---

197. Cf. *Accessibility Inventory* from the National Office of Persons with Disabilities. This is available also in the January 2000 *Environment and Art Newsletter* from Liturgy Training Publications.

2.   *Specify that the acknowledgment is to state the additional cost involved.*

3.   *Specify that the pastor and/or someone specifically authorized by the pastor is/are the only one(s) designated to sign the change orders approving the additional expenditure.*

4.   *Specify that the architect is responsible for communicating with the contractor or subcontractors regarding the changes.*

BUILDING MAINTENANCE

§ 219 § The design process will include planning for the long-term and short-term maintenance of the new or renovated building. The beauty and utility of a place of worship can be sustained only by an ongoing, careful attention to its upkeep through regular maintenance. Therefore, funds for both general maintenance and capital improvements should be anticipated in every future parish budget.

§ 220 § Durability and maintenance expenses are critical factors in the selection of building materials and of the mechanical, electrical, and plumbing systems. Decisions made on the basis of short-term economy can be very costly when viewed from the perspective of long-term expenses. A well-thought-out plan for maintenance that includes a financial component is necessary in the case of existing structures. In addition, special attention may be needed when the maintenance of historical buildings is at issue.

SOUND IN THE PLACE OF WORSHIP

§ 221 § Silence is the ground of all prayer. From contemplative silence emerge the sung and spoken prayer of the entire assembly and the prayers and proclamations of the various ministers. Liturgical celebrations call for the clear transmission of the sung and spoken responses of the liturgical assembly, as well as of the words of the individual ministers such as the priest celebrant, the deacon, the readers, and the cantor and leader of song. In addition, the space should provide an environment for instrumental music that supports the assembly's song and worship.

§ 222 § The first consideration in providing quality sound transmission is the acoustic design of the building. The interior surfaces such as the walls, the floor, and the ceiling affect the transmission of sound, as do design features like the ceiling height, the shape and construction of rooms, and the mechanical systems such as heating and cooling units and lighting fixtures. The sound-deadening tiles so vital to noise reduction in gymnasiums and other public buildings will be used rarely in a church and only with professional advice to reduce or eliminate outside noise. Soft surfaces such as carpets, rugs, and large fabric wall hangings absorb sound, while hard surfaces such as stone, tile, glass, and metals reflect it. A combination of sound-absorbing and sound-reflecting surfaces properly applied and used in correct proportion provides the kind of system needed for a worship space.

§ 223 § Acoustical engineers can help parishes design a building capable of the natural transmission of sound; they also can be of great assistance in the renovation of existing buildings.

§ 224 § Another aspect of an effective audio environment is the electronic amplification system, which can augment the natural acoustics and can help to remedy problems that cannot be solved in other ways. Planners also should consider provisions for sound in the nave, in the sanctuary, and in adjacent spaces such as the gathering area and the space around the baptismal font. Accommodations should be made for people with special hearing needs.

§ 225 § Providing for the amplification of the proclaimed and sung word and for instrumental and choral music is a complex task that demands the skills and experience of experts in the field of acoustical design. Choosing local vendors who do not possess the requisite skills to understand the complex needs of the liturgical assembly may prove to be a serious, even costly liability.

THE PLACEMENT OF THE ORGAN AND OTHER MUSICAL INSTRUMENTS

§ 226 § Musical instruments, especially the pipe organ, have long added to the beauty and prayerfulness of Catholic worship.[198] Planning sufficient space for the organ and other instruments that may be used to accompany the assembly's prayer is an important part of the building process. This includes the design of the organ casework, if such is used, or the placement of the pipes of large instruments. An acoustical specialist and musicians working together can arrive at a placement that allows the pipes to be seen and heard well without becoming a distraction or competing with the other artwork and iconography. The placement of the organ also must ensure that the instrumentalists have a clear visual connection with the director of music and, if necessary, with the cantor or leader of song.

§ 227 § Some instruments are used only occasionally for more solemn and festive occasions. For this reason there is need for flexibility in the arrangement of the space allotted for music so that there will be adequate room to accommodate them when they are included in the worship services.

LIGHTING THE PLACE OF WORSHIP

§ 228 § Light is a powerful symbol for the followers of Christ who is the "light shining in the darkness" and whose image is seen in the sun and in the paschal candle whose flame is "divided but undimmed."[199] In addition to its theological

---

198. SC, no. 120: "In the Latin Church the pipe organ is to be held in high esteem, for it is the traditional musical instrument, and one that adds a wonderful splendor to the Church's ceremonies and powerfully lifts up man's mind to God and to heavenly things.

"But other instruments also may be admitted for use in divine worship, with the knowledge and consent of the competent territorial authority, as laid down in Articles 22, § 2; 37 and 40. This may be done, however, only on condition that the instruments are suitable for sacred use, or can be made so, that they accord with the dignity of the temple, and truly contribute to the edification of the faithful."

199. Cf. Congregation for Divine Worship, *The Sacramentary* [*The Roman Missal*] (1973, 1985), Easter Proclamation (*Exsultet*).

symbolism, light takes on pastoral, aesthetic, and practical import in the construction of churches. Careful planning enables parishes to choose options that make maximum use of the natural light, which can be supplemented by artificial sources.

§ 229 § Professionals can make planners aware of the ways in which fixtures shield glare, of the manner in which specific lamp types render color, and of the noise level of ballasts in some fixtures. If a church building is to foster the worship of those who gather there, it must first meet minimum standards of hospitality, which means that those gathered for worship will be able to see as well as to hear one another. In the design of the lighting scheme for a church, the highest priority should be given to the ability of the worshipers to see both the faces of those with whom they gather as the Body of Christ and the faces of those who minister to them.

§ 230 § In addition, lighting can aesthetically enhance the architectural and artistic components of the building and its appointments. Lighting for Sunday Mass differs from lighting required for a baptism or for times when the church is open for private prayer. What is appropriate for the chapel of reservation may not be effective in the nave, and what works in the sanctuary at the priest celebrant's chair may not be helpful for the reader or the priest at the altar. Lighting engineers can suggest appropriate options to ensure the light production that will best serve the liturgy. Additional practical considerations include the cost and efficiency of various types of lamping, the ease or difficulty of replacing burnt-out bulbs, possible computerization, and the ease of use and flexibility of the system to meet the needs of a variety of liturgical situations.[200]

§ 231 § Planning the building's lighting includes both the exterior and the interior of the building. Illumination of pathways and entries is not only a matter of safety but also of aesthetic enhancement. In keeping with good stewardship, using lighting generated by solar power is ecologically responsible, and it is an effective form of exterior lighting to be considered.

§ 232 § Building codes require that exit signs, fire alarm strobes, fire alarm pull boxes, annunciator panels, and fire extinguisher cabinets be located in "conspicuous places." Timely planning can help to reconcile these required elements with liturgical, devotional, and artistic focal points. It is the responsibility of the architect to work with all design and engineering consultants to ensure that conflicts are avoided and that smoke-detecting devices are calibrated so that candle smoke and incense do not set off fire alarms.[201]

§ 233 § Provisions for electronic media should be incorporated into the initial design of a new building. These should fit into the architectural design and

---

200. A dimmer can provide for flexibility of the lighting fixtures and can help to reduce energy consumption.

201. As with the case of selecting professionals to design and install sound systems, normally the skills of a professional with experience in the lighting of churches should be preferred over the "good will" services of someone who may have some knowledge of electricity and domestic lighting but who lacks the requisite qualifications to design and install lighting suitable for a church.

should be made inconspicuous. Consideration should be given to the effect of light on projected images.

SACRISTIES

§ 234 § Well-designed, well-equipped, and well-organized sacristies contribute to the smooth function of the liturgy and to the maintenance and preservation of vesture, vessels, linens, and other liturgical appointments. Since the Second Vatican Council, most new churches and some renovated structures provide a vesting sacristy near the entrance to the church adjacent to the gathering space so that the entrance procession can proceed directly from the sacristy into the gathering space and down the aisle to the altar. The vesting sacristy provides storage space for vestments as well as a place where the vestments of the day can be arranged by the sacristan. A restroom, or at least a wash basin with running water, and a full-length mirror can be helpful additions to this area. If the vesting sacristy is located in the rear of the church, it is helpful to have an additional work sacristy that offers easy access to the altar located near the sanctuary. This sacristy would contain the *sacrarium* (see below) and another basin deep enough to fill tall vases with water. It could contain locked cabinets for items of special value and storage for sacred vessels, altar cloths and other linens, candles and candle stands, and vases, containers, and plant stands. In addition, the work sacristy should be equipped for the laundering and care of church linens. If fabric art in the form of hangings or banners is used in the church, it will be desirable to include a storage area with rods over which these fabrics can be hung so that they do not become wrinkled or damaged from improper storage.

SECURITY ISSUES

§ 235 § Distressing though it may be, the contemporary reality compels the Church to be mindful also of security issues for the church building. This is appropriate not only for the sake of securing items and treasures within the church building but it is also equally important for the safety of the faithful. It is unfortunate that so many churches today must be locked, thus preventing the faithful from entering for prayer and meditation except at specific times. Investigation should be made regarding the possibility of securing the items inside the church in such a way as to allow the faithful greater access to this house of prayer.

THE SACRARIUM

§ 236 § The sacristy near the sanctuary will usually contain the *sacrarium*, the special sink used for the reverent disposal of sacred substances. This sink has a cover, a basin, and a special pipe and drain that empty directly into the earth, rather than into the sewer system. After Mass, when the vessels are rinsed and cleansed, the water is poured into the sacrarium so that any remaining particles that might be left will not be poured into the sewer but will go directly into the earth. When the purificators and corporals are rinsed before being washed, the water is disposed of in the sacrarium. The sacrarium also can be used to discard old baptismal water, leftover ashes, and the previous year's oils, if they are not burned.

§ 237 § In addition, if any of the Precious Blood is accidentally spilled during Mass, it is carefully wiped up and the area is washed. The water from this process also should be poured down the sacrarium. Reverence for sacred things continues even after they are no longer useful in the liturgy.

SPECIAL ISSUES IN THE RENOVATION OF CHURCHES

§ 238 § When a parish constructs a new building, there are many options available for responding to the liturgical needs and balancing the values involved. When a parish is renovating an existing worship space, the building itself may limit some of the design possibilities and constrain the parish to choose between options that are less than ideal. In making compromises demanded by the limits of the existing space, it is important for the parish to continue to work with professionals to consider all the possible options and to make the choice that will best serve the requirements of the liturgy and the other parish priorities.

ALTERATION OF HISTORIC STRUCTURES

§ 239 § Over time, as public expressions of worship change, there is a consequent shift in the demands on the physical space used for the Church's liturgy. In accord with the norms of the liturgical reform, it is sometimes necessary to alter historic structures that pose a challenge.[202] In projects of this kind, a delicate balance can be achieved through a selection of designs and appointments that respect and protect the Church's ancient artistic heritage and, at the same time, effectively serve the requirements of contemporary worship.

RENOVATION OF CHURCHES

§ 240 § When renovation of a church is to be undertaken or when it becomes necessary to raze an old church, special care is needed. A church that has served its people over many years will not easily be relinquished, especially by those with deep roots in the parish. In this type of project, parish involvement in the assessment of need and in subsequent planning is especially critical. Although consultation allows opposition to emerge more quickly than it otherwise might, in the final analysis it is better that all points of view be heard and dealt with in an atmosphere of respect and collaboration than that they be left unvoiced to fester for the future.

§ 241 § There will always be some members of a community who will find it difficult, if not impossible, to relinquish their past church, but an open assessment of the local needs, coupled with education about the liturgical rites, can go far toward drawing a parish together in support of the work to be done. In

---

202. OA, no. 4 (DOL 541, no. 4331): "Mindful of the legislation of Vatican Council II and of the directives in the documents of the Holy See, bishops are to exercise unfailing vigilance to ensure that the remodeling of places of worship by reason of the reform of the liturgy is carried out with the utmost caution. Any alterations must always be in keeping with the norms of the liturgical reform and may never proceed without the approval of the commissions on sacred art, on liturgy, and, when applicable, on music, or without prior consultation with experts. The civil laws of the various countries protecting valuable works of art are also to be taken into account."

principle, the community deserves to hear how the renovation will enhance their ability to pray with solemnity, beauty, and dignity.

§ 242 § It is also important in situations such as these for respect to be shown for the existing building and its appointments so as to preserve as much of the original worthy fabric as possible. When the project involves a renovation, materials such as marble and wood paneling, as well as other artifacts or furnishings, often can be refurbished and incorporated into the new design, provided they are of requisite quality. Informing the parish of the efforts being made in this regard may make the adjustment to the new worship space less difficult, if not more appealing.

§ 243 § There are times, however, when the materials are no longer suitable, either because they are worn or because they no longer serve the needs of the liturgy. In such cases, pastors and committees need to consult with the diocesan worship office or the chancery regarding any policies governing the disposal of such items. In recent years there have been examples of religious artifacts and sacred vessels appearing at auctions and on websites for purchase with seemingly no consideration of their purpose or significance.

§ 244 § Finally, when a church interior is to be gutted or torn down, celebrating a final Mass to mark the closing of the church building is appropriate. Perhaps the most appropriate ritual would be the final celebration of Mass in the church, followed by a procession in which the people journey to either the new place of worship or to the place that will serve them temporarily until the necessary work on the new or renewed space for worship is finished.

THE ALTAR

§ 245 § In the construction of new churches, there should be only one altar to signify the one Eucharist and the one Lord, Jesus Christ, who gathers the community at the one Table of his Body and Blood. However, in renovating an existing church, when the position of the old altar hinders the people's participation, or if "it is impossible to move it without detriment to its artistic value, then another fixed altar may be erected" in the church. This new altar is the one on which the liturgy should be celebrated.[203]

§ 246 § It is usually better to avoid attaching individual names to specific appointments, furnishings, or works of art within the church. While allowing people to pay for these objects may be an easy fund-raising solution, it can lead to future problems when there may be need to remove or alter the memorialized object.

---

203. GIRM, no. 303: "However, in churches already built, when an old altar is already so positioned that it makes the participation of the people difficult, or it is impossible to move it without detriment to its artistic value, then another fixed altar may be erected. It should be artfully made and dedicated according to the rite. The sacred celebrations should be performed upon it alone; and in order that the attention of the faithful not be distracted from the new altar, the old altar should not be decorated in any special way."

§ 247 § In an earlier chapter, the issue of the location of the tabernacle was covered. The structure of the existing building will determine some of the options the parish is able to consider. In exercising his responsibility for the liturgical life of the diocese, the diocesan bishop may issue specific directives regarding the reservation of the Eucharist and the placement of the tabernacle. Again, the pastor, the parish pastoral council, and the building committee will need to review all existing diocesan norms and then carefully examine the principles that underlie each of the options, weigh the liturgical advantages of each possibility, and reflect upon the customs and piety of the parishioners before making a recommendation on the placement of the tabernacle. The location also should allow for easy access by people in wheelchairs and by those who have other disabilities. Diocesan worship offices can assist parishes by facilitating the study and discussion process regarding the placement of the tabernacle and other significant issues involved in the renovation of a church. This is an area where liturgical consultants also can be of great assistance to the parish.

§ 248 § In most churches built before 1969, the tabernacle was situated on the main altar. At the close of the Second Vatican Council, when parishes were able to celebrate the liturgy facing the congregation, many pastors installed movable altars somewhere in front of the existing altar, and they used the former altar as the place for the reservation of the Blessed Sacrament.

§ 249 § In renovating a church designed in another time period, a parish has an opportunity to consider other locations for the tabernacle. Care must be taken to ensure that the area set aside for the reservation of the Eucharist is worthy and distinguished. The place for eucharistic reservation and its furnishings should never be temporary, makeshift, or difficult to find.

§ 250 § In some renovated churches it is possible to remove older altars and tabernacles. When there are good reasons for not removing the altar, an alternate site for the tabernacle may still be considered. In some churches an area that previously housed a side altar or some devotional space might be an appropriate space for reservation, assuming that it meets the other requirements set forth in the *General Instruction of the Roman Missal*. In other situations, the only appropriate place for reservation will be in the sanctuary itself and on the former main altar. In these instances, a balance must be sought so that the placement of the tabernacle does not draw the attention of the faithful away from the eucharistic celebration and its components.[204] On the other hand, the location must provide for a focus on the tabernacle during those periods of quiet prayer outside the celebration of the Eucharist.

---

204. EM, no. 55 (DOL 179, no. 1284): "It is more in keeping with the nature of the celebration [of the Eucharist] that, through reservation of the sacrament in the tabernacle, Christ not be present eucharistically from the beginning on the altar where Mass is celebrated. That presence is the effect of the consecration and should appear as such."

§ 251 § Ordinarily, there should be a sufficient distance to separate the tabernacle and the altar. When a tabernacle is located directly behind the altar, consideration should be given to using distance, lighting, or some other architectural device that separates the tabernacle and reservation area during Mass but that allows the tabernacle to be fully visible to the entire worship area when the eucharistic liturgy is not being celebrated.

§ 252 § When a place is chosen for the tabernacle and the former tabernacle can be removed from an existing altar without damaging the altar or the setting, this will be beneficial and will help to prevent confusion among the faithful.

PRESERVATION OF THE ARTISTIC HERITAGE OF THE CHURCH

§ 253 § The coexistence of past and present called for in renovating and restoring church art and architecture is not without rich, multilayered, and successful precedent. "The Church is intent on keeping the works of art and the treasures handed down from the past and, when necessary, on adapting them to new needs."[205] In many parishes, even those whose churches are not considered historically, architecturally, or artistically significant, it is possible to find worthy works of art such as art-glass, furnishings, wood and marble structures, and musical instruments that are of aesthetic and artistic value. Parishes, therefore, are encouraged to undertake an assessment of their artistic works and furnishings to determine their value. The architect, artist, and liturgical consultant, as well as diocesan personnel, are indispensable collaborators in discerning works that are considered part of the sacred heritage of the Church's art. "Many people have made unwarranted changes in places of worship under the pretext of carrying out the reform of the liturgy and have thus caused the disfigurement or loss of priceless works of art."[206]

§ 254 § "Care should be taken against destroying the treasures of sacred art in the course of remodeling churches." When it is necessary to relocate or remove artistic pieces in the interest of the liturgical reform, they can be appropriately cared for and placed in a location "befitting and worthy of the works themselves."[207] Sacred art that at one time appropriately served liturgy and devotion but that is

---

205. GIRM, no. 289: "The Church is intent on keeping the works of art and the treasures handed down from the past and, when necessary, on adapting them to new needs. It strives as well to promote new works of art that appeal to the contemporary mentality.

"In commissioning artists and choosing works of art that are to become part of a church, the highest artistic standard is therefore to be set, in order that art may aid faith and devotion and be true to the reality it is to symbolize and the purpose it is to serve."
206. OA, no. 5 (DOL 541, no. 4327).
207. EM, no. 24 (DOL 179, no. 1253): "Care should be taken against destroying treasures of sacred art in the course of remodeling churches. On the judgment of the local Ordinary, after consulting experts and, when applicable, with the consent of other concerned parties, the decision may be made to relocate some of these treasures in the interest of the liturgical reform. In such a case this should be done with good sense and in such a way that even in their new locations they will be set up in a manner befitting and worthy of the works themselves."

less capable of functioning in that capacity must still be accorded respect and must never be put to secular or "profane use."[208]

§ 255 § Each diocese is strongly encouraged to record and protect the cultural heritage of the faithful. Where possible, a diocesan repository or museum can properly preserve and make available the rich heritage of the local Church. Every renovation project should include a careful photographic and videographic documentation of the building as it evolves.

§ 256 § As custodians of the Church's sacred heritage, architects, artists, and clergy must be educated in the appreciation of sacred art and in its purposes within liturgy. The priests' leadership often will provide the initial inspiration to communities seeking to build new churches, to design new liturgical art, or to renovate existing worship spaces. The Second Vatican Council was particularly clear in its teaching on this issue:

> "Clerics are to be taught about the history and development of sacred art and about the sound principles on which the productions of its works must be grounded. In consequence they will be able to appreciate and preserve the Church's treasured monuments and be in a position to offer good advice to artists who are engaged in producing works of art."[209]

CONCLUSION

§ 257 § Church architecture embodies the Gospel and awakens true liturgical piety in all believers, drawing them into the life of the Triune God.[210] The eucharistic piety around which churches are built is always Trinitarian, Christological, Scriptural, and communal, and builds upon the Church's liturgical tradition *lex orandi, lex credendi*. Without such well-grounded liturgical piety, the church building will lack the essentials for which it was constructed. The most technically brilliant architecture can lack a Christian soul if it does not house a community with the mind and heart of Christ.

§ 258 § Decisions about what is considered appropriate Christian art, while they should be informed by expert taste and opinion, are best made after consultation with the whole liturgical assembly under the leadership of the pastor. When the Church's buildings and artworks engender a contemplative attitude toward God's creation, Christ's redemption of history, and the gifts of the Holy Spirit, they proclaim her faith in visible signs and evangelize the neighborhood, the city, and the nation. Non-believers point to them as stunning examples of

---

208. OA, no. 6 (DOL 541, no. 4333): "When it is judged that any such works are no longer suited to divine worship, they are never to be given over to profane use. Rather they are to be set up in a fitting place, namely, in a diocesan or interdiocesan museum, so that they are accessible to all who wish to look at them. Similarly, ecclesiastical buildings graced by art are not to be treated with neglect even when they no longer are used for their original purpose. If they must be sold, buyers who can take proper care of them are to be given preference (see CIC 1187)."
209. Congregation for Seminaries and Universities, *Doctrina et Exemplo* (December 25, 1965), no. 60 (DOL 332, no. 2731), quoting SC, no. 129.
210. Cf. CCC, nos. 1079–1109.

art as well as mysterious, public symbols of Christian piety. Without a meditative dimension, Christian architecture risks reducing the mystery of divine presence to either social action or to a comfortable domesticity.

§ 259 § Prayer and liturgy both arise from communities of faith and, at the same time, help to create those communities. The eucharistic assembly enters into a dialogue initiated by God and continued among brothers and sisters. Without a commitment to the building of community, a parish may create a church building that is architecturally refined but stark and oppressively distant.

§ 260 § The process of building a church calls the People of God to the unfinished business of the community; it alerts the eucharistic assembly to the fact that complacency is destructive and that Christ's redemption of the universe is incomplete until God is truly all in all. Without the prophetic challenge of the Holy Spirit, church buildings could be merely triumphalistic monuments, a confirmation of comfortable opinions. The Spirit's prophetic gift reminds the assembly of the poor in the midst of plenty, of the homeless living on the streets, and of the abused and battered whose faces can be so easily avoided. These members of the Communion of Saints must be welcome at the Table of the Lord, and their concerns and needs must guide all building decisions. "What makes a church different from any other building is not its form or shape but rather how it facilitates for a particular community of believers a regular unfolding of the Christian mystery, the eternal divine plan for humanity as revealed in the person of Jesus Christ."[211] Eucharistic assemblies, housed in church buildings, have Jesus Christ at their center. He is the Word spoken by divine mystery, the beloved Son of the Father, the head of the community of believers, and the prophet who challenges and inspires them to live for God and neighbor. Every church built for the People of God unfolds his presence.

§ 261 § A characteristic of Christians is how they love one another even while they meet the challenge of building a new place for worship. It may be difficult and the fabric of the assembly may fray and even tear. But the Spirit's work in the assembly of God's People encourages cooperation so that each can perform a task for the building up of the Body of Christ. During a building process, the community works together with the diocese and with the universal Church as another way of building up the Church with the "living stones" from which God's assembly is made. If the community looks upon its work with the eyes of faith, then it can be assured that God will bring the good work to completion.

---

211. PW, Introduction.

FULFILLED
IN
YOUR HEARING

THE HOMILY IN THE SUNDAY ASSEMBLY

BISHOPS' COMMITTEE ON
PRIESTLY LIFE AND MINISTRY

NATIONAL CONFERENCE OF CATHOLIC BISHOPS
FEBRUARY 15, 1982

AN OVERVIEW OF *FULFILLED IN YOUR HEARING: THE HOMILY IN THE SUNDAY ASSEMBLY*

Rev. Thomas J. Scirghi, SJ

The document *Fulfilled in Your Hearing: The Homily in the Sunday Assembly* (FYH) restores the proper dignity to the role of liturgical preaching. Some readers may be surprised by the opening line taken from the Conciliar document, *Presbyterorum ordinis*, "The primary duty of priests is the proclamation of the Gospel of God to all." We might think of the priest's primary duty as the celebration of the sacraments or his pastoral care. However, here we are reminded of the Apostle Paul, who said, "Faith comes from what is heard."[1] It is the Word of God, proclaimed and preached, that leads people to the Church and the sacraments.

FYH was published in 1982 by the subcommittee on Priestly Life and Ministry for the National Conference of Catholic Bishops (NCCB). It was commissioned by this subcommittee in 1979. Its principal author was Rev. William Skudlarek, OSB, who was well qualified for this role. He earned a doctorate in Homiletics from Princeton Theological Seminary and he is the author of *The Word in Worship*, a study of liturgical preaching. This is the subject of FYH: preaching during the Sunday liturgy of the Eucharist. Its purpose is to provide a basis for discussion among bishops, priests, and the congregation. In this sense, FYH is an instructional document with the goal of improving the quality of preaching throughout the Roman Catholic Church in the United States. While preaching extends beyond the Sunday worship and the doors of the Church, the bishops chose to focus on the preaching of the priest in the Eucharist. However, all of the faithful are encouraged to read the document so that they may contribute to the renewal of preaching.

The discussion flows in four parts. The first three adhere to the three points of the classic triangle of public speaking found in Aristotle's *Rhetoric*: the listener, the speaker, and the message. Part four provides a "homiletical method" of preparation.

THE ASSEMBLY

"Who are the listeners?" The bishops chose to begin with the assembly because the preacher must know his audience if he is to tell them what they need to hear. They begin here also because the "church is the visible sacrament of the saving unity to which God calls all people."[2] We are reminded of the fourfold presence of Christ in the Eucharist as explained in the *Constitution on the Sacred Liturgy* (CSL): Christ is present in the Eucharistic species, in the Word, in the minister, and in the gathering who pray and sing together. And just as the

---

1. Romans 10:17.
2. *Fulfilled in Your Hearing: The Homily in the Sunday Assembly* (FYH), 5.

preacher will exegete the Scripture of the day to uncover new meaning from an ancient text, so too he exegetes the congregation. He wonders about their concerns, their needs, their questions, and ultimately how they will hear the message in a new way. The preacher must appreciate the diversity of the assembly: men and women, young and old, wealthy and poor, highly educated and barely literate, the ethnic mix, and of course, the devout and those who came under duress.[3] While this diversity is apparent, the preacher should focus on our unity, which is our hope in Jesus Christ.[4] The preacher helps to reveal the presence of the divine around us, pointing to signs in the lives of the faithful so that they will find new reason to praise God. In the words of the prophet Isaiah, "The Lord God has given me the tongue of a teacher, / that I may know how to sustain the weary with a word."[5]

THE PREACHER

"What does the assembly want from their preacher?" The people are listening for a person of faith.[6] This section raises the question, where does the preacher stand in relation to the congregation? Indeed, the people are not listening for a brilliant theologian or an eloquent orator (and certainly not a stand-up comic); they are listening for a prayerful person. In turn, the preacher must be a good listener. He must listen to the Lord with his personal prayer time, allowing the Holy Spirit to inspire him.[7] Rather than beginning what can I say about the text, he needs to ask, what does the text say to me? John of the Cross writes in *The Ascent of Mount Carmel*, "Preaching is more a spiritual practice than a vocal one. . . . It has no force save for the interior spirit."[8]

The practice of listening continues from personal prayer to Scripture study, mining the text for its historical and cultural background, the material needed to appreciate the passage within its context. For this task the preacher needs the tools of the trade, such as Scripture commentaries and other reference works. Since the publication of FYH, many of these tools can now be found on the Internet.

The preacher listens to the Lord in prayer and study. He also listens to the community who gathers on Sunday, as well as to the surrounding culture. An appreciation for culture is no mere luxury but is necessary for professional development.[9] The preacher should have regular contact with the classical culture of literature, art, and music, and be familiar with the popular culture of television, film, and pop music. He also must be conversant with the concerns of the day, such as politics and economics. Recall the well-worn adage that when preparing to preach, the preacher should have a Bible in one hand and a newspaper in the other.

---

3. See ibid., 8.
4. See ibid., 9.
5. Isaiah 50:4.
6. See FYH, 39.
7. See ibid., 22.
8. *The Ascent of Mount Carmel*, book III, chapter 45, no. 2.
9. See FYH, 32.

"What is the purpose of the Homily?" Briefly stated, the Homily interprets the lives of the faithful in light of the story of salvation that is proclaimed in the Scriptures. (Notice how many times the word "interpret" appears in this section.) For this interpretation, the preacher asks two questions. First, what is the human situation to which these texts were originally addressed? Second, what is the human situation to which they speak today?[10]

The preacher is advised also to follow the structure of the Lectionary in the selection of texts. Sometimes the texts are chosen because they correspond to a particular feast or season, so he interprets the text in light of the occasion. Usually, however, they are arranged according to the principle of *lectio continua*, following the order of a book of the Bible. For example, the Church reads the Gospel according to Matthew in sequence during Year A. In preparing to preach, then, it will be helpful to think of the Sunday text as one episode within a series, rather than as a discrete unit.

Once again, taking the time for preparation is essential. The preacher must enter into an "incubation period," in which he should read, reflect, research, and then stand back to allow the text to dwell in his unconscious.[11] This incubation period may prove helpful especially for some of the greatest challenges to the preacher, namely struggling to find a new idea for a familiar text, such as the parable of the prodigal son, or dealing with a text which may seem inappropriate for a particular occasion. Nevertheless, through the dialogue of the ancient text with the current human situation, a new interpretation may arise. The story remains the same, but those who will hear it again have changed and may hear it anew. So the preacher asks, "How will they hear it this time?" In other words, "How will the Scriptures help to interpret their lives today?"

As we learn that the purpose of the Homily is to interpret the lives of the faithful, we also learn what it is not. The Homily should not be used to teach new information or to change behavior. The authors cite studies from communication experts explaining that, given the brevity of a Homily, liturgical preaching is a poor means to impart new information. This is true for public speaking in general. Of course, some instruction on Scripture and doctrine is appropriate, as well as moral exhortation, but this should be presented with an eye toward recognizing God's active presence in their lives that prepares them for Christian witness in the world.[12] Likewise, the preacher should respect the limits of the Homily and not expect it to do everything. Instead, the Homily may open doors for further exploration, encouraging the faithful to gather in groups for Bible study, spiritual renewal, young adult catechesis, and so on.[13]

HOMILETIC METHOD

The fourth part addresses the question, how should a preacher prepare? Obviously there is no one method of preparation for everyone to use; however, everyone

---

10. See ibid., 54.
11. Ibid., 55.
12. See ibid., 43.
13. See ibid., 72.

needs a method, that is, a plan to return to regularly. In other words, the "incubation period" should be structured as "a regular pattern of activity."[14] In this part many of the points already mentioned are collected and organized into a method of preparation. It shows FYH to be a practical document. Some of the key points are as follows.

First, the preacher should read all four Scripture texts; this includes the Responsorial Psalm. When the document was first published, it was common for the Psalm of the day to be replaced with a song containing a similar message. One reason for this was that at the time musical settings for each of the Psalms were not readily available. This is no longer the case, so there is no good reason to make a substitution. Besides, to omit the Psalm disrupts the flow of the Liturgy of the Word. This text is called the "Responsorial Psalm" for a reason: it is the peoples' response to having heard the First Reading. In preparing to preach, the preacher should imagine who in the First Reading is speaking the Psalm. Also, the Psalm is intended to be sung. A spoken Psalm has the dulling effect of a song that is recited. (Imagine reciting the "Star Spangled Banner" at a ballgame.)

Second, as mentioned earlier, the preacher is advised to use commentaries and other sources, but he should not turn to them immediately. Rather, he should allow the Scripture to speak to him first and to form his own interpretation. The commentaries can then help to shape the message rather than to determine it.[15]

Third, there is an element of performance to preaching. It is not simply a matter of what is said, but how it is spoken that will either aid or impede the preaching. The preacher should choose carefully his words and tone of voice, and ask himself, "Does this sound natural?" Adopting a "preacher's voice" or an elaborate vocabulary for the moment will lead some listeners to doubt the authenticity of the messenger and the message. Also, we are reminded that preaching is embodied; in other words, the whole body communicates. Speakers send signals through facial expression, eye contact, hand gestures, and vocal tone. All of these play a powerful part in oral communication. Preachers should not think of themselves as merely talking heads.

Fourth, the document recommends forming Homily preparation groups. These are weekly meetings of the preacher with several parishioners or a group of priests. They meet, preferably early in the week, to discuss the Scriptures for the following Sunday. One task recommended for the preparation group, which is sorely neglected but would prove very helpful, is evaluation of the preaching. Preachers need feedback from their listeners both on the content and the style. Was the content clear? Was the Good News heard and was there a message to carry home? Did the style of presentation direct or distract the listeners? Once again, the preacher must be a listener, and this means listening to the feedback of the assembly. Perhaps it is a sign of a priestly people to contribute to their preaching in this way.

A LOOK AHEAD

FYH has provided a good beginning for the renewal of preaching in the Roman Catholic Church. At this time, the bishops of the United States are planning to

---

14. Ibid., 82.
15. See ibid., 90.

publish a new document on preaching, not to replace the current one, but to expand upon it in order to address some contemporary issues. One of these issues concerns preaching within different cultures, including Latin American, African American, and Asian American congregations. Perhaps another issue to address is the role of lay preaching and to ask if there is room for occasional preaching by a lay ecclesial minister. The American bishops continue to call out for more effective preaching. For this reason, FYH deserves a careful reading.

OUTLINE

FULFILLED IN YOUR HEARING

THE HOMILY IN THE SUNDAY ASSEMBLY

INTRODUCTION

"The primary duty of priests is the proclamation of the Gospel of God to all." These clear, straightforward words of the Second Vatican Council (*Decree on the Ministry and Life of Priests*, #4) may still come as something of a surprise to us. We might more spontaneously think that the primary duty of priests is the celebration of the Church's sacraments, or the pastoral care of the People of God or the leadership of a Christian community. Yet the words of the document are clear: the proclamation of the Gospel is primary. The other duties of the priest are to be considered properly presbyteral to the degree that they support the proclamation of the Gospel.

"Proclamation" can cover a wide variety of activities in the church. A life of quiet faith and generous loving deeds is proclamation; the celebration of the Eucharist is the proclamation "of the death of the Lord until he comes." But a key moment in the proclamation of the Gospel is preaching, preaching which is characterized by "proclamation of God's wonderful works in the history of salvation, that is, the mystery of Christ, which is ever made present and active within us, especially in the celebration of the liturgy" (Constitution on the Sacred Liturgy, #35, 2).

The *Decree on the Ministry and Life of Priests* is especially clear in relating the ministry of preaching to that of the celebration of the sacraments. Since these sacraments are sacraments of faith, and since "faith is born of the Word and nourished by it," the preaching of the Word is an essential part of the celebration of the sacraments. This is especially true in the celebration of the Eucharist, the document goes on to note, for "in this celebration the proclamation of the death and resurrection of the Lord is inseparably joined both to the response of the people who hear, and to the very offering whereby Christ ratified the New Testament in His blood."

This intimate link between preaching and the celebration of the sacraments, especially of the Sunday Eucharist, is what we intend to address in this document on preaching. We recognize that preaching is not limited to priests. Deacons are also ordained ministers of the Word. Indeed, the proclamation of the Word of God is the responsibility of the entire Christian community by virtue of the sacrament of baptism. Moreover, we recognize that preaching is not limited to the Eucharist, and we are pleased to support the ways in which more and more Catholics are celebrating the power of God's Word in evangelistic gatherings, in the catechumenate, and in groups devoted to the study of the Bible and to prayer. We also recognize that for the vast majority of Catholics the Sunday homily is the normal and frequently the formal way in which they hear the Word of God proclaimed. For these Catholics the Sunday homily may well be the most decisive factor in determining the depth of their faith and strengthening the level of their commitment to the church.

The focus of this document, therefore, will be the Sunday homily, and even more specifically, the homily preached by the bishop or priest who presides at the celebration of the Eucharist. Again, we recognize that there are occasions when the homily may be preached by someone other than the presider, by a deacon serving in the parish or a guest priest preacher, for example. Yet, in terms of common practice and of liturgical norm, the preaching of the homily belongs to the presiding minister. (See *The General Instruction of the Roman Missal*, #42: "The homily should ordinarily be given by the celebrant.") The unity of Word and Sacrament is thus symbolized in the person of the presiding minister of the Eucharist.

While this document is addressed specifically to priests who have a pastoral ministry that involves regular Sunday preaching, we hope that all who are concerned with effective proclamation of the Gospel will find it helpful. This document may also prove useful in the preparation for and continuing formation of permanent deacons as ministers of the Word.

We propose that this document be used as a basis of discussion among priests and bishops, and by priests with members of their congregations. In such sharing of personal experiences, of expectations and frustrations, and by mutual support, we find hope for a renewal of preaching in the church today.

I. THE ASSEMBLY

[1] Jesus came to Nazareth where he had been reared, and entering the synagogue on the sabbath as he was in the habit of doing, he stood up to do the reading. When the book of the prophet Isaiah was handed him, he unrolled the scroll and found the passage where it was written:

"The spirit of the Lord is upon me;
  therefore he has anointed me.
He has sent me to bring glad tidings to the poor,
  to proclaim liberty to captives,
Recovery of sight to the blind
  and release to prisoners,
To announce a year of favor from the Lord."

Rolling up the scroll he gave it back to the assistant and sat down. All in the synagogue had their eyes fixed on him. Then he began by saying to them, "Today this Scripture passage is fulfilled in your hearing." All who were present spoke favorably of him; they marveled at the appealing discourse which came from his lips. (Lk 4:14–22a)

[2] These verses from the fourth chapter of the Gospel of Saint Luke present us with a picture of Jesus as reader and homilist in the synagogue at Nazareth.

He stands up to read the lesson from the prophet which was placed at the end of the service. He then draws on this passage to speak to the here-and-now situation. All who listened to him were favorably impressed.

[3]   The three major elements of liturgical preaching are all here: the preacher, the word drawn from the Scriptures, and the gathered community. Each element is essential and each must be considered carefully if we are to understand the challenge and the possibilities of liturgical preaching.

[4]   We believe that it is appropriate, indeed essential, to begin this treatment of the Sunday homily with the assembly rather than with the preacher or the homily, and this for two principal reasons. First of all we can point to the great emphasis which communication theorists place on an accurate understanding of the audience if communication is to be effective. Unless a preacher knows what a congregation needs, wants, or is able to hear, there is every possibility that the message offered in the homily will not meet the needs of the people who hear it. To say this is by no means to imply that preachers are only to preach what their congregations want to hear. Only when preachers know what their congregations want to hear will they be able to communicate what a congregation needs to hear. Homilists may indeed preach on what they understand to be the real issues, but if they are not in touch with what the people think are the real issues, they will very likely be misunderstood or not heard at all. What is communicated is not what is said, but it is what is heard, and what is heard is determined in large measure by what the hearer needs or wants to hear.[1]

[5]   Contemporary ecclesiology provides a second and even more fundamental reason for beginning with the assembly rather than with the preacher or the homily. *The Dogmatic Constitution on the Church* describes the church as the mystery of God's saving will, given concrete historical expression in the people with whom he has entered into a covenant. This church is the visible sacrament of the saving unity to which God calls all people. "Established by Christ as a fellowship of life, charity, and truth, the church is also used by Him as an instrument for the redemption of all, and is sent forth into the whole world as the light of the world and the salt of the earth" (#9). The church, therefore, is first and foremost a gathering of those whom the Lord has called into a covenant of peace with himself. In this gathering, as in every other, offices and ministries are necessary, but secondary. The primary reality is Christ in the assembly, the People of God.

[6]   This renewed understanding of the church is gradually becoming consciously present in the words and actions of the Catholic people. By means of their involvement in diocesan and parish organizations, their sharing in various forms of ministry, and their active participation in the liturgy, they are beginning to experience what it means to say that the people are the church and the church are people.

---

1. The material on "audience analysis" is voluminous. Access to the most up-to-date studies can be found by consulting the bibliographies of recent books on speech communication. Such materials frequently describe various methods for determining with some accuracy the interest and abilities of an audience.

[7]   Obviously the development we are speaking of is not uniform. But it is clear that the parish in which the priest acts in an arbitrary manner, in which virtually all active ministry—liturgical, educational, and social—is in the hands of the clergy and religious, and in which the laity do little more than attend Mass and receive the sacraments, is no longer the norm. Such a drastic change in the practices and self-consciousness of the Catholic congregation is bound to have significant consequences for the content and style of preaching that takes place in the Sunday Eucharistic assembly.

To preach in a way that sounds as if the preacher alone has access to the truth and knows what is best for everyone else, or that gives the impression that there are no unresolved problems or possibility for dialogue, is to preach in a way that may have been acceptable to those who viewed the church primarily in clerical terms. In a church that thinks and speaks of itself as a pilgrim people, gathered together for worship, witness, and work, such preaching will be heard only with great difficulty, if at all.

THE IDENTITY OF THE ASSEMBLY

[8]   The Eucharistic assembly that gathers Sunday after Sunday is a rich and complex phenomenon. Even in parishes that are more or less uniform in ethnic, social, or economic background, there is great diversity: men and women, old and young, the successes and the failures, the joyful and the bereaved, the fervent and the halfhearted, the strong and the weak. Such diversity is a constant challenge to the preacher, for our words can all too easily be heard as excluding one or the other segment of the congregation. We may not mean to ignore the presence of women when we say "Jesus came to save all men," but if exclusion is heard, then exclusion is communicated, whether intended or not.

[9]   While the diversity of every assembly is a factor that needs to be taken seriously by the preacher, and all the more so when the diversity cuts across racial, ethnic, economic, and social lines, this diversity should not blind us to another, even greater reality: the unity of the congregation. This assembly has come together because its members have been baptized into the one body of Christ and share a common faith. This faith, though rooted in a common baptismal identity, is expressed in ways that extend from the highest levels of personal appropriation and intellectual understanding to the most immature forms of ritualism and routine. And yet, to a greater or lesser degree, it is faith in Jesus Christ that is common to all the members of a community gathered for Eucharist.

[10]   To say that a community shares a common faith is to say that its members have a common way of interpreting the world around them. For the Christian community, the world is seen and interpreted as the creation of a loving God. Although this world turned away from God through sin, God reached out again and again to draw the world to himself, finally sending his own Son in human flesh. This Son expressed the fullness of the Father's love by accepting death on the cross. The Father in turn glorified his Son by raising him from the dead and making him the source of eternal life for all who believe. Believers witness to the presence and word of Jesus in the world and are a continuing sign of the

Kingdom of God, which is present both in and through Jesus, and still to come to its fullness through the power of the Holy Spirit.

[11]   In very broad outline this is the common faith that binds together the Christian community gathering for worship. No individual in the community would very likely express the faith in quite these words. Some might find it difficult to express their faith in any words at all. They do not possess the background of theology to enable them to do so. We might say, therefore, that one of the principal tasks of the preacher is to provide the congregation of the faithful with words to express their faith, and with words to express the human realities to which this faith responds. Through words drawn from the Scriptures, from the church's theological tradition, and from the personal appropriation of that tradition through study and prayer, the preacher joins himself and the congregation in a common vision. We can say, therefore, that the homily is a unifying moment in the celebration of the liturgy, deepening and giving expression to the unity that is already present through the sacrament of baptism.

THE PREACHER AS MEDIATOR OF MEANING

[12]   The person who preaches in the context of the liturgical assembly is thus a mediator, representing both the community and the Lord. The assembly gathers for liturgy as a community of faith, believing that God has acted in human history and more particularly, in their own history. The community gathers to respond to this living and active God. They may also gather to question how or whether the God who once acted in human history is still present and acting today. They may wonder how this God, whom the Scriptures present as so powerful and so loving, can be experienced in lives today that seem so broken and meaningless. How can parents believe in a God who raises the dead to life when their daughter has just been killed in a car accident? How can a family hope in a God who leads his people out of slavery into freedom when they are trapped in an inflationary spiral in which costs increase and the buying power of their salaries diminishes? How can young people join with the angels and saints in praise of the glory of God when they are struggling with the challenges of establishing their own identities and their relationship to family and friends?

[13]   The preacher represents this community by voicing its concerns, by naming its demons, and thus enabling it to gain some understanding and control of the evil which afflicts it. He represents the Lord by offering the community another word, a word of healing and pardon, of acceptance and love. Like humans everywhere, the people who make up the liturgical assembly are people hungry, sometimes desperately so, for meaning in their lives. For a time they may find meaning in their jobs, their families and friends, their political or social causes. All these concerns, good and valid as they are, fall short of providing ultimate meaning. Without ultimate meaning, we are ultimately unsatisfied. If we are able to hear a word which gives our lives another level of meaning, which interprets them in relation to God, then our response is to turn to this source of meaning in an attitude of praise and thanksgiving.

[14]   The community that gathers Sunday after Sunday comes together to offer God praise and thanksgiving, or at least to await a word that will give a meaning to their lives and enable them to celebrate Eucharist. What the preacher can do best of all at this time and in this place is to enable this community to celebrate by offering them a word in which they can recognize their own concerns and God's concern for them.

[15]   The preacher acts as a mediator, making connections between the real lives of people who believe in Jesus Christ but are not always sure what difference faith can make in their lives, and the God who calls us into ever deeper communion with himself and with one another. Especially in the Eucharistic celebration, the sign of God's saving presence among his people, the preacher is called to point to the signs of God's presence in the lives of his people so that, in joyous recognition of that presence, they may join the angels and saints to proclaim God's glory and sing with them their unending hymn of praise.

II. THE PREACHER

[16]   We began our treatment of the Sunday homily by looking first to the assembly that gathers to celebrate the liturgy of the Eucharist. Such a beginning could be interpreted to mean that the importance of the ordained priesthood is not what it used to be. Nothing could be further from the truth. The priesthood of the faithful and the ordained ministerial priesthood although distinct are not opposed to one another. In fact, they stand or fall together. To the degree that we give full weight to the priesthood of all the baptized, to that degree do we see the full importance and significance of the ordained priesthood. To the degree that we downplay the importance of the priesthood of the faithful, to that degree is the ordained priesthood diminished.

[17]   The community gathered to worship is a priestly people, men and women called to offer God worship. If this community is conscious of its dignity, then those it calls to service in positions of leadership will be able to recognize their dignity as well. We think of the priest as the representative of Christ. This way of thinking is true, as long as we remember that one represents Christ by representing the church, for the church is the fundamental sacrament of Christ. Moreover, it is the church, through its bishops, that calls individuals to presbyteral ministry in the church.

PASTORAL ROLE OF THE PREACHER

[18]   Preachers who are conscious of their representative role strive to preach in a way that indicates they know and identify with the people to whom they are speaking. Their preaching is pastoral, displaying a sensitive and concerned knowledge of the struggles, doubts, concerns, and joys of the members of a local community.

[19]   To be in touch with the cares and concerns, needs and good fortunes of the assembly does not mean that the preacher has to answer questions or solve problems in every homily. There will be occasions when nothing we can say will do

anything to change a situation. We cannot raise a dead daughter to life; our words will not stop inflation or lower unemployment. What our words can do is help people make connections between the realities of their lives and the realities of the Gospel. We can help them see how God in Jesus Christ has entered and identified himself with the human realities of pain and of happiness.

LISTENING AND PRAYING

[20] In order to make such connections between the lives of the people and the Gospel, the preacher will have to be a listener before he is a speaker. Listening is not an isolated moment. It is a way of life. It means openness to the Lord's voice not only in the Scriptures but in the events of our daily lives and in the experience of our brothers and sisters. It is not just *my* listening but *our* listening together for the Lord's word to the community. We listen to the Scriptures, we listen to the people, and we ask, "What are they saying to one another? What are they asking of one another?" And out of that dialogue between the Word of God in the Scriptures and the Word of God in the lives of his people, the Word of God in preaching begins to take shape.

[21] Attentive listening to the Scriptures and to the people is, in essence, a form of prayer, perhaps the form of prayer most appropriate to the spirituality of the priest and preacher. There is nothing more essential than prayerful listening for effective preaching, a praying over the texts which seeks the light and fire of the Holy Spirit to kindle the *now* meaning in our hearts. A week of daily meditation on the readings of the following Sunday is not too much time to spend in preparation for the preaching we are called to do on the Lord's Day. Such regular preparation will allow us not only to savor the word in prayer but also to incorporate the experiences of a full week into our preparation.

[22] Such extended, prayerful preparation is so important for preaching because it helps us reach the moment of inspiration, an inspiration that has affinities to poetic inspiration but is more. We ask for and expect the real movement of the Holy Spirit in us and in the assembly. If the words of Scripture are divinely inspired, as we believe them to be, then divine inspiration must be at work when those words are made alive and contemporary to the believing community in and through our ministry.

[23] The preacher is thus called, above all, to be prayerful. The prayer we speak of is not prayer alongside of preparation for preaching, or over and above this preparation, but the very heart and center of the preparation itself. Unless the Word of God in the Scriptures is interiorized through prayerful study and reflection, it cannot possibly sustain the life-giving, love-generating words that preachers want to offer their people. Preachers then are called to a prayerful dwelling with their people and to a prayerful dwelling with the texts of Scripture knowing them and allowing themselves to be known by them.

[24] This dwelling with the Scriptures and with the people which is the necessary prelude to effective preaching points to the necessity for certain pastoral skills and academic knowledge, both of which the modern seminary offers its

candidates for priesthood, but which need continual updating and refining. We speak here of the skills of understanding and communicating with people, and of the knowledge required for the accurate and relevant interpretation of Scriptural texts.

INTERPRETING THE SCRIPTURES

[25] Let us begin with the second requirement first, since that is somewhat easier to describe. The interpretation of texts is the science of hermeneutics, and in order to accomplish its end, hermeneutics relies first of all on exegesis. For exegesis to be done at the highest professional level, the exegete must have knowledge of the original languages, access to the tools of textual criticism, extensive historical and archeological background, a comprehensive knowledge of the development of biblical faith, and a familiarity with the history of the theological interpretation of texts in both the synagogue and the Christian churches. Obviously few preachers have the training or access to the resources for exegesis of this kind.

[26] Exegesis for preaching need not always be done at the highest professional level. Our seminary training and our continuing education provide us with tools and resources to tap the best of contemporary exegesis in a fruitful way. Even a smattering of Hebrew and Greek is helpful in capturing the flavor or nuances of certain words. An acquaintance with the methods of scriptural scholarship enables us to understand, for example, why the sayings of Jesus can appear in such different contexts, and therefore with such different meanings, in the Gospels. Or again, knowing how the biblical author used a particular passage as a building block in a larger literary context can help us appreciate how the church of succeeding ages found it important to set the passage in contemporary contexts, a task which is ours in the liturgical celebration today.

[27] It is hard to imagine that a person who has as his primary duty the proclamation of the Gospel to all would be without the basic tools and methods that help to ensure an accurate understanding of this Gospel. Surely every preacher ought to have a basic library to turn to in the preparation of homilies. A good Bible dictionary will help in picturing the background of a passage; a concordance will locate other passages that are related; a "theological" dictionary of Scripture will trace ideas that recur through Old and New Testaments; Gospel parallels will set similar texts that occur in more than one Gospel side by side. Standard commentaries on the major books of the Bible that appear in the lectionary should also be ready at hand, as well as exegetical commentaries based on the lectionary itself.

[28] The texts of Scripture from which our preaching flows are not locked in antiquity. They are texts which have nourished the church's life throughout all its history, sustaining it in times of trial, calling it back to fidelity in times of weakness and opening up new possibilities when it seemed immobilized by the weight of human traditions.

[29] The history of the interpretation of the Scriptures is part of the contemporary meaning of the Scriptures. The way they have been preached, the liturgical

expressions they have generated, the prayer they have nourished, the magisterial statements they have inspired, the theological systems they have fostered, even the heresies they have occasioned, expand and deepen the way the Scriptures speak to us today.

[30] It is the faith of the church that the preacher must proclaim, not merely his own. Consequently, the more familiar the preacher is with the history of scriptural interpretation and the development of the church's doctrine, the more capable he is of bringing that word into dialogue with the contemporary situation. Church doctrine is nourished by profound meditation upon the inspired Word, the exegesis of the fathers, conciliar documents and the teaching of the Magisterium. Therefore, the qualified preacher will lead his people to ever greater unity of faith among themselves as well as with prior generations of believers.

[31] It is somewhat more difficult to speak of what is involved in the understanding of people and how the priest/preacher can prepare himself for this demand of his office. Surely part of the rationale of the requirement that students in theological seminaries have a background in the liberal arts, with an emphasis on philosophy, is that familiarity with the leading ideas, movements, and personalities of human civilization (or at least of Western civilization) will enable preachers to engage in a critical dialogue with contemporary culture, recognizing what is conformable with the Gospel, challenging that which is not. The great artistic and literary achievements of a culture are surely a privileged means of access to the heart and mind of a people.

[32] Regular and sustained contact with the world's greatest literature or with its painting, sculpture, and musical achievements can rightfully be regarded by preachers not simply as a leisure-time activity but as part of their ongoing professional development. The same can be said of attention to modern entertainment media—television, film, radio—or to the theater. Dramatic presentations that deal sensitively with significant human issues can provide a wealth of material for our reflection and our preaching, both in its content and in its form.

[33] If preachers are to know and understand their congregations today, some familiarity with popular forms of entertainment may also be necessary. We need not spend whole afternoons watching soap operas, memorizing baseball statistics, or listening to the latest hit albums. Yet if we are totally unaware, or give the impression that we are unaware of the activities and interests to which people devote a good deal of their leisure time, energy, and money, it will be difficult for us to make connections between their lives and the Gospel, or to call them to fuller, richer, and deeper levels of faith response.

[34] Finally, preachers need to devote some time and energy to understanding the complex social, political, and economic forces that are shaping the contemporary world. Watching the evening news on television or scanning the headlines of the daily paper may be a beginning but it is not enough. Preachers need exposure to more serious and sustained commentary on the contemporary world, the kind of exposure that can be gained through a program of reading or through conversation with people who are professionally involved in such areas as business,

politics, or medicine. Without this kind of informed understanding of the complex world we live in, preaching too easily degenerates into platitudes of faith, meaningless broadsides against the wickedness of the modern world, or into an uncritical affirmation of the wonderful advances that have taken place in modern times.

[35]   To have a comprehensive knowledge of the social, political and economic forces shaping the contemporary world, while at the same time specializing in scriptural exegesis and theology and being pastorally competent may well appear to be an overwhelming, even impossible, expectation to lay on any one person. The point to be made here, however, is not that preachers must know everything, but rather that there is no limit to the sources of knowledge and insight that a preacher can draw upon. There are many avenues which lead toward a deeper understanding of the human condition. Some will travel more easily down the avenue of the social sciences, others down the avenue of literature and the arts, others down the avenue of popular culture. What ultimately matters is not which avenue we take, but what we take with us as we travel.

[36]   As long as we carry the Word of God with us, a word that we have allowed to touch on our own lives in prayer and reflection, and as long as we speak that word in language and images that are familiar to the dwellers of the particular avenue we are traveling, the Word of God will be preached, and the possibility of faith and conversion will be present.

THE LIMITATIONS OF THE PREACHER

[37]   It may be good to close this section with a word of caution. While preachers, like other people, cannot be expected to know everything, they are easily tempted to give the impression that they do. As one perceptive critic put it, preachers in their pulpits are people who speak ten feet above contradiction. The Word of God which we are called to proclaim is a divinely inspired Word, and therefore an authoritative and unfailing Word. But we who are limited and fallible possess no guarantee that our understanding of this Word—or of the human situation—is without error and therefore relevant and binding.

[38]   Preachers accept their limitations not by making the pulpit a sounding board for their personal doubts, anxieties or problems, but by offering people a Word which has spoken to their lives and inviting these people to think and ponder on that Word so that it might speak to their lives as well. A recent poster says it well: "Jesus came to take away our sins, not our minds." What preachers may need to witness to more than anything else is the conviction that authentic, mature faith demands the hard struggle of thinking and choosing. What the Word of God offers us is a way to interpret our human lives, a way to face the ambiguities and challenges of the human condition, not a pat answer to every problem and question that comes along.

[39]   Some years ago a survey was taken among a group of parishioners. They were asked what they hoped to experience during a sermon. When the results were in, the answer was clear. What the majority wanted was simply to hear a person

of faith speaking. Ultimately, that's what preaching is all about, not lofty theological speculation, not painstaking biblical exegesis, not oratorical flamboyance. The preacher is a person speaking to people about faith and life.

III. THE HOMILY

[40] The Sunday Eucharist is a privileged point of encounter between a local Christian community and its priest. Within this Eucharistic celebration the homily is a moment when this encounter can be especially intense and personal. We want now to look at the nature and function of this form of preaching, to relate it to the issues we have already raised in speaking of the assembly and the preacher, and finally to suggest a method for building and preaching the homily.

THE HOMILY AND FAITH

[41] Like all preaching, the homily is directed to faith. As Paul writes, "But how shall they call on him in whom they have not believed? And how can they believe unless they have heard of him? And how can they hear unless there is someone to preach?" (Romans 10:14). Some preaching is directed to people who have not heard the Gospel and is meant to lead them to an initial acceptance of Jesus Christ as Savior. Other forms of preaching are directed to a deeper understanding of the faith or to its ethical implications.

[42] The homily is preaching of another kind. It may well include evangelization, catechesis, and exhortation, but its primary purpose is to be found in the fact that it is, in the words of the Second Vatican Council, "a part of the liturgy itself" (*Constitution on the Sacred Liturgy*, #52). The very meaning and function of the homily is determined by its relation to the liturgical action of which it is a part. It flows from the Scriptures which are read at that liturgical celebration, or, more broadly, from the Scriptures which undergird its prayers and actions, and it enables the congregation to participate in the celebration with faith.

[43] The fact that the homily is addressed to a congregation of believers who have gathered to worship indicates that its purpose is not conversion from radical unbelief to belief. A homily presupposes faith. Nor does the homily primarily concern itself with a systematic theological understanding of the faith. The liturgical gathering is not primarily an educational assembly. Rather the homily is preached in order that a community of believers who have gathered to celebrate the liturgy may do so more deeply and more fully—more faithfully—and thus be formed for Christian witness in the world.[2]

---

2. While the homily is not the same as catechetical instruction, as Pope Paul VI makes clear in his apostolic exhortation *Evangelii nuntiandi* (nos. 43 and 44), the homily can certainly be a means of catechesis for Christian communities. The homilist who preaches from the Scriptures as these are arranged in the lectionary over a three-year cycle of Sundays and feasts will certainly deal with all the major truths of the faith. It will still be necessary, however, to provide educational opportunities in and through which the faithful can reflect more deeply on the meaning of these truths and on their concrete contemporary implications for Christian life. In the early church such a systematic presentation of the truths of the faith was given to the newly baptized in the post-baptismal preaching known as mystagogy.

[44] To say that preaching, the homily included, is directed to faith is another way of saying that preaching is involved in the task of interpretation. "Faith" can be defined as a way of seeing or interpreting the world. The way we interpret the world, in turn, determines the way we relate to it. For example, if we believe that a particular race or class of people are our enemies, we will relate to them with suspicion and hostility. A friendly gesture will be interpreted not as a genuine sign of good will but as a ruse to get us to lower our guard. On the other hand, if we believe that a group of people are our friends, we will tend to excuse even a hostile gesture with the explanation that there must have been some mistake: they didn't recognize us or we have misinterpreted their gesture. Our "faith" in the way things are has led us to live in the world in a way that corresponds to what we believe about it.

[45] The Christian interprets the world not as a hostile and evil place, but as a creation of a loving God who did not allow it to destroy itself, but sent his Son to rescue it. The Christian response to the world, then, is one of acceptance and affirmation—along with the recognition that it is still awaiting its full redemption.

[46] One of the most important, and most specifically human, ways in which faith is communicated to individuals and communities is through language. The way we speak about our world expresses the way we think about it and interpret it. One of the reasons we speak about our world at all is to share our vision of the world with others. The preacher is a Christian specially charged with sharing the Christian vision of the world as the creation of a loving God. Into this world human beings unleashed the powers of sin and death. These powers have been met, however, by God through his Son Jesus Christ, in whom he is at work not only to restore creation, but to transform it into a new heaven and a new earth.

FAITH LEADING TO A RESPONSE

[47] When one hears and accepts this vision of the world, this way of interpreting reality, a response is required. That response can take many forms. Sometimes it will be appropriate to call people to repentance for the way they have helped to spread the destructive powers of sin in the world. At other times the preacher will invite the congregation to devote themselves to some specific action as a way of sharing in the redemptive and creative word of God. However, the response that is most general and appropriate "at all times and in every place" is the response of praise and thanksgiving (Eucharist).

[48] When we accept the good news that the ultimate root and source of our being is not some faceless Prime Mover, not a merciless judge, but a prodigally loving Father who calls us to share in his love and to spread it to others, we sense that it is indeed right to give him thanks and praise.

Although we have received this good news, believed in it, and sealed our belief in the sacrament of baptism, we need to rediscover the truth of it again and again in our lives. Our faith grows weak, we are deceived by appearances, overwhelmed by suffering, plagued by doubt, anguished by the dreadful silence of God. And yet we gather for Eucharist, awaiting a word that will rekindle the spark of faith and enable us to recognize once again the presence of a loving God in our lives. We come to break bread in the hope that we will be able to do so with hearts burning. We come expecting to hear a Word from the Lord that will again help us to see the meaning of our lives in such a way that we will be able to say, with faith and conviction, "It is right to give him thanks and praise."

[49] The preacher then has a formidable task: to speak from the Scriptures (those inspired documents of our tradition that hand down to us the way the first believers interpreted the world) to a gathered congregation in such a way that those assembled will be able to worship God in spirit and truth, and then go forth to love and serve the Lord. But while the task is formidable, it is not impossible, especially if one goes about it with purpose and method.

THE HOMILY AND THE LECTIONARY

[50] The homily is not so much *on* the Scriptures as *from* and *through* them. In the Roman Catholic tradition, the selection of texts to be read at the Eucharistic liturgy is normally not left to the preacher, but is determined ahead of time and presented in the form of a lectionary. The basic purpose of a lectionary is two-fold: to ensure that the Scripture texts appropriate to a feast or season are read at that time, and to provide for a comprehensive reading of the Scriptures. Thus, we find in the lectionary two principles guiding the selection of texts: the the-matic principle (readings chosen to correspond to the "theme" of a feast or sea-son), and the *lectio continua* principle (readings taken in order from a book of the Bible which is being read over a given period of time).

[51] In the section of the lectionary entitled "Masses for Various Occasions," we find the thematic principle at work in a way that corresponds more closely to what some liturgical planners refer to as the theme of a liturgy: e.g., readings appropriate for Christian unity, or for peace and justice. Such thematic liturgies have their place, as the lectionary title indicates, on various or special occasions, rather than at the regular Sunday liturgy.[3]

[52] It is to these given texts that the preacher turns to prepare the homily for a community that will gather for the Sunday liturgy. Since the purpose of the homily is to enable the gathered congregation to celebrate the liturgy with faith, the preacher does not so much attempt to explain the Scriptures as to interpret the human situation through the Scriptures. In other words, the goal of the liturgical preacher is not to interpret a text of the Bible (as would be the case in teaching a Scripture class) as much as to draw on the texts of the Bible as they are presented in the lectionary to interpret peoples' lives. To be even more pre-cise, the preacher's purpose will be to turn to these Scriptures to interpret peo-ples' lives in such a way that they will be able to celebrate Eucharist—or be

---

3. A fuller description of the principles guiding the choice of readings can be found in the introduction to the lectionary. These principles should be familiar to all preachers, for a knowledge of how and why passages of Scripture are assigned to certain times and feasts provides an important key to the liturgical interpretation of those readings in preaching.

reconciled with God and one another, or be baptized into the Body of Christ, depending on the particular liturgy that is being celebrated.[4]

[53]   To preach from the Scriptures in this way means that we have to "get behind them," as it were. We have to hear these texts as real words addressed to real people. Scholarly methods of interpreting Scripture can help us do this by putting us in touch with the life situations that originated these texts, or by making us more aware of the different ways language can function as a conveyer of meaning. But scholarly methods are not enough. As we emphasized in the second chapter, the preacher needs to listen to these texts meditatively and prayerfully.

[54]   As preachers we go to the Scriptures saying, "What is the human situation to which these texts were originally addressed? To what human concerns and questions might these same texts have spoken through the Church's history? What is the human situation to which they can speak today? How can they help us to understand, to interpret our lives in such a way that we can turn to God with praise and thanksgiving?" Only when we approach the Scriptures in this way do they have any possibility of becoming a living word for us and for others.

[55]   Such prayerful listening to the text demands time, not just the time of actual reading and praying and studying but, just as importantly, the time of standing back and letting the text dwell in our unconscious mind. This period of "incubation," as it is often called, is essential to all human creative effort. It is especially important for the homilist when reflecting upon texts which have become overly familiar, or which seem inappropriate for a given situation. With the use of a lectionary, the readings assigned for a particular day may seem to have little to say to a specific congregation at a specific time in its life. However, if the text and the actual human situation are allowed to interact with one another, a powerful interpretative word of faith will often emerge. But for this to happen we need to dwell with the text and allow it to dwell with us. Only then will the text reveal new meaning to us, a new and fresh way of interpreting and speaking about our world.[5]

THE HOMILY, THE CONGREGATION, AND HOMILY SERVICES

[56]   If the homily must be faithful to the Scriptures for it to be the living Word of God, it must also be faithful to the congregation to whom this living Word of God is addressed. The homily will be effective in enabling a community to worship God with praise and thanksgiving only if individuals in that community recognize there a word that responds to the implicit or explicit questions of their lives.

[57]   There are many ways in which priests get to know their congregations and allow themselves to be known by them: involvement with parish organizations, individual and family counseling, social contacts, visits to the sick and the bereaved, planning for weddings and baptisms, the sacrament of reconciliation, and, equally

---

4. Cf. *Lectionary for Mass.* English translation of the Second *Editio-Typica* (1981) no. 24 prepared by International Commission on English in the Liturgy.

5. Ibid. no. 8–10.

as important, simply being with people as a friend and member of the community. The preacher will be able to draw on all these contacts when he turns to the Scriptures to seek there a Word from the Lord for the lives of his people.

[58] This pastoral dimension of the homily is the principal reason why some homily services, especially those that do little more than provide ready-to-preach homilies, can actually be a hindrance to effective preaching. Since the homily is integrally related to the liturgy, and since liturgy presupposes a community that gathers to celebrate it, the homily is by definition related to a community. Homily services can be helpful in the interpretation of scriptural texts (though generally not as much as some basic exegetical resources) and give some ideas on how these texts can be related to contemporary human concerns. But they cannot provide individual preachers with specific indications of how these texts can be heard by the particular congregations to whom they will preach.

[59] Homily services can provide valuable assistance to the preacher when they are concerned to relate the interpretation of the lectionary texts to the liturgical season in which they appear, and when they are attentive to the *lectio continua* principle of the lectionary. They may also be helpful in suggesting some possibilities for the development of a homily, or in providing suitable examples and illustrations. The primary help that a good homily service will offer is to make available to the preacher recent exegetical work on the specific texts that appear in the lectionary and to indicate some ways in which this biblical word can be heard in the present as God's Word to his people. They can never replace the homilist's own prayer, study, and work.

THE HOMILY AND THE LITURGY OF THE EUCHARIST

[60] A homily is not a talk given on the occasion of a liturgical celebration. It is "a part of the liturgy itself." In the Eucharistic celebration the homily points to the presence of God in people's lives and then leads a congregation into the Eucharist, providing, as it were, the motive for celebrating the Eucharist in this time and place.[6]

[61] This integral relation of the homily to the liturgy of the Eucharist which follows the liturgy of the word has implications for the way in which the homily is composed and delivered. In the first place, the homily should flow quite naturally out of the readings and into the liturgical action that follows. To set the homily apart by beginning or ending it with a sign of the cross[7], or by delivering it in a style that is totally different from the style used in the rest of the

---

6. Ibid. no. 24.

7. With regard to the sign of the cross before and after the homily, the Congregation for the Sacraments and Divine Worship gave the following official *responsum* in 1973:

Query: Is it advisable to invite the faithful to bless themselves before or after the homily, to address a salutation to them, for example, "Praised be Jesus Christ"? Reply: It all depends on lawful local custom. But generally speaking it is inadvisable to continue such customs because they have their origin in preaching *outside Mass*. The homily is *part* of the liturgy; the people have already blessed themselves and received the greeting at the beginning of Mass. It is better, then, not to have a repetition before or after the homily. Source: *Notitiae* 29 (1973) 178.

liturgy, might only reinforce the impression that the homily is simply a talk given on the occasion of a liturgical gathering, one that could just as well be given at another time and in another context.

[62] Although the preaching of the homily properly belongs to the presiding minister of the Eucharistic celebration, there may occasionally be times when it is fitting for someone else, priest or deacon, to preach. On these occasions the integral relation of the homily to the rest of the liturgy will be safeguarded if the preacher is present and actively involved in the whole of the liturgical celebration. The practice of having a preacher slip in to read the Gospel and preach the homily, and then slip out again, does not do justice to the liturgical integrity of the homily.

HOMILETIC STYLE

[63] As regards the structure and style of the homily, we can take a lead from the use of the Greek word *homileo* in the New Testament.[8] While the etymology of the word suggests communicating with a crowd, its actual use in the New Testament implies a more personal and conversational form of address than that used by the classical Greek orator. The word is employed in reference to the conversation the two disciples engaged in on their way to Emmaus (Luke 24:14) and of the conversation Antonius Felix, Procurator of Judea, had with Paul when the latter was held prisoner in Caesarea (Acts 24:26). The New Testament usage suggests that a homily should sound more like a personal conversation, albeit a conversation on matters of utmost importance, than like a speech or a classroom lecture. What we should strive for is a style that is purposeful and personal, avoiding whatever sounds casual and chatty on the one extreme or impersonal and detached on the other.

[64] One of the ways we can move toward a more personal style of address in our homilies is by the way we structure them. Many homilies seem to fall into the same three-part pattern: "In today's readings . . . This reminds us . . . Therefore let us . . ." The very structure of such homilies gives the impression that the preacher's principal purpose is to interpret scriptural texts rather than communicate with real people, and that he interprets these texts primarily to extract ethical demands to impose on a congregation. Such preachers may offer good advice, but they are rarely heard as preachers of good news, and this very fact tends to distance them from their listeners.

---

8. *Keryssein,* "To proclaim," is the word most frequently used for preaching in the New Testament. The word "presupposes that the preachers are heralds who announce simply that which they are commissioned to announce, not in their own name, but by the authority of the one who sends them" (John L. McKenzie, *Dictionary of the Bible,* p. 689). Although the practice of first-century Jewish synagogues may have included explanations and applications of the Scriptures as part of the regular service, the New Testament itself does not use a specific technical word to describe the kind of preaching we refer to as a "homily," that is, the exposition of a text of scripture which takes place in and as a part of a liturgical celebration. The word *homileo* does appear in the New Testament, and its usage there can provide a way to understand a homiletic approach to preaching as distinguished from preaching addressed to unbelievers *(kerygma).*

[65]   Another way of structuring the homily, and one that is more in keeping with its function of enabling people to celebrate the liturgy with deepened faith, is to begin with a description of a contemporary human situation which is evoked by the scriptural texts, rather than with an interpretation or reiteration of the text. After the human situation has been addressed, the homilist can turn to the Scriptures to interpret this situation, showing how the God described therein is also present and active in our lives today. The conclusion of the homily can then be an invitation to praise this God who wills to be lovingly and powerfully present in the lives of his people.[9]

[66]   The point of the preceding paragraph is not to substitute a new straight jacket for an old one. There is no one correct form for the homily. On occasion it may be a dramatic and engaging story, on another a well-reasoned exposition of a biblical theme showing its relevance to the contemporary situation, or the liturgical day, feast or season. It might also take the form of a dialogue between two preachers or involve the approved local use of visual or audio media. Ideally, the form and style will be determined by the form and style of the Scriptures from which it flows, by the character of the liturgy of which it is a part, and by the composition and expectations of the congregation to which it is addressed, and not exclusively by the preference of the preacher.

[67]   Whatever its form, the function of the Eucharistic homily is to enable people to lift up their hearts, to praise and thank the Lord for his presence in their lives. It will do this more effectively if the language it uses is specific, graphic, and imaginative. The more we can turn to the picture language of the poet and the storyteller, the more we will be able to preach in a way that invites people to respond from the heart as well as from the mind.

THE LIMITS AND POSSIBILITIES OF LITURGICAL PREACHING

[68]   But isn't all this too limited a view of preaching? Does it really respond to the needs of the people? Doesn't regular Sunday preaching have to take into account the ignorance of the Scriptures on the part of large numbers of Catholics, even those who participate regularly in the Sunday Eucharist, and deal in some systematic way with the fundamentals of the faith? Is there not a crying need for regular and sustained teaching about the moral imperatives that flow from an acceptance of the Good News? What about all those times when people's lives are shattered, when they simply are psychologically incapable of offering God praise and thanks, when it seems they have nothing to be thankful for? How do we speak to all the people in our congregations who have yet to hear the basic Gospel message calling them to faith and conversation, or who may even need a form of preaching that heightens their sensitivity to basic human realities and in this way readies them for the hearing of the Gospel?

---

9. The continuing ability of Scripture texts to speak to situations that are temporally and culturally distinct from those to which they were originally addressed is one way in which the canonicity of the Scriptures continues to be affirmed by the church. The canon is, in fact, composed of those writings which the church considers too important to forget because they address issues which are present in every generation, albeit in different garb and guises.

[69] In the last analysis the only proper response to these questions is a pastoral one. Priests will have to decide what form of preaching is most suitable for a particular congregation at a particular time. We would simply like to make two points here. First of all, social science research contends that the oral presentation of a single person is not a particularly effective way to impart new information or to bring about a change in attitude or behavior. It is, however, well suited to make explicit or to reinforce attitudes or knowledge previously held. The homily, therefore, which normally is an oral presentation by a single person, will be less effective as a means of instruction and/or exhortation than of interpretation—that is, as a means of enabling people to recognize the implications, in liturgy and in life, of the faith that is already theirs.

[70] The second point to be made is that the liturgical homily, which draws on the Scriptures to interpret peoples' lives in such a way that they can recognize the saving presence of God and turn to him with praise and thanksgiving, does not exclude doctrinal instruction and moral exhortation. Such instruction and exhortation, however, are here situated in a broader context, namely, in the recognition of God's active presence in the lives of the people and the praise and thanksgiving that this response elicits.[10]

[71] It may very well be that what God is doing in the life of a congregation at some particular moment is asking them to change in a way that is demanding and disorienting. The homily can be one way of helping to bring about that change, and it can still lead to a response of praise and thanksgiving by showing that our former way of life, comfortable as it may have been, was a way that led to death, while the new way, with all of its demands and difficulties, is a way that leads to life.

[72] But even though the liturgical homily can incorporate instruction and exhortation, it will not be able to carry the whole weight of the Church's preaching. There will still need to be special times and occasions for preaching that addresses human values in such a way as to dispose the hearers to be open to the Gospel of Jesus Christ, preaching intended to bring the hearers to an inner conversion of heart, and preaching intended to instruct the faithful in matters of doctrine or morality. These three kinds of preaching—sometimes referred to as pre-evangelization, evangelization, and catechesis—can be found today in evangelistic gatherings, the adult catechumenate, youth ministry programs, spiritual renewal programs, Bible study groups and many forms of religious education.

---

10. In the Apostolic Exhortation, *On Catechesis in Our Time*, 1979, #48, Pope John Paul II observes, "Respecting the specific nature and proper cadence of this setting [i.e., liturgy, especially the Eucharistic assembly], the homily takes up again the journey of faith put forward by catechesis and brings it to its natural fulfillment. At the same time it encourages the Lord's disciples to begin anew each day their spiritual journey in truth, adoration and thanksgiving. Accordingly, one can say that catechetical teaching, too, finds its source and fulfillment in the eucharist, within the whole circle of the liturgical year.

"Preaching, centered upon the Bible texts, must then in its own way make it possible to familiarize the faithful with the whole of the mysteries of the faith and the norms of Christian living. . . ." Cf. also: *Sharing the Light of Faith*, An Official Commentary on the National Catechetical Directory for Catholics of the United States, 1981, p. 54, Office of Publishing Services, USCC, Washington, D.C.

[73]   The homily can complement all these forms of preaching by attending more specifically to what it is to accomplish. Such would be to show how and where the mystery of our faith, focused upon by that day's Scripture readings, is occurring in our lives. This would bring the hearers to a more explicit and deepened faith, to an expression of that faith in the liturgical celebration and, following the celebration, in their life and work.

[74]   But is it really possible to create this readiness for praise and thanksgiving in congregations as large and diverse as those in which many of us minister? In these congregations some people will be feeling a sense of loss because of a recent bereavement; some facing marital difficulties; some having problems adjusting emotionally to school, job, home or community; some struggling with a deep sense of guilt stemming from their inability to deal maturely with their sexuality, or because of their addiction to drugs or alcohol. Others in our congregations will be struggling with the relevance of the Gospel to oppressive economic structures, to world peace, or to the many forms of discrimination in our society. Is it really possible to say to these people, "Look at the way in which God is present in your lives and turn to him with praise and thanksgiving?"

[75]   Obviously, it will not always be easy to do this. And we will never be able to do it, at least not with any honesty and integrity, if we have not recognized the active presence of God in our own lives, as broken and shattered as they may be, and out of that brokenness affirm that it is still good to praise him and even to give him thanks. We need to remember in situations like this that our celebration of the Eucharist is done in memory of Jesus Christ who, *on the night before he died*, turned to God and praised and thanked him out of the very depths of his distress. Praise and thanksgiving, therefore, do not automatically imply the presence of euphoria.

[76]   We can and must praise God even when we do not feel like it, for praise and thanksgiving are rooted in and grow out of faith, not feeling, a faith which interprets this world by saying that in spite of appearances often to the contrary, our God is a loving God. It is for this reason that even at the time of death, we celebrate a Eucharist, because we believe that for his faithful ones life is changed, not, as appearances would seem to indicate, taken away.

[77]   The challenge to preachers then is to reflect on human life with the aid of the Word of God and to show by their preaching, as by their lives, that in every place and at every time it is indeed right to praise and thank the Lord.

IV. HOMILETIC METHOD

[78]   Every art is based on a theory and a method, and preaching is no exception. Some artists, it is true, work solely from inspiration. They do not know why or how they do what they do. Consequently, they are incapable of passing their insight on to others. But they have a method nonetheless, and if their work is lasting, their method will sooner or later be uncovered by interpreters and critics of their work.

[79]   Artists who are conscious of their method are in a much more advantageous position than those who are not. They are able to channel and direct their work more easily, can work more efficiently within time constraints, and can adapt their method to changed circumstances and demands. They know what they are doing and how they go about doing it, and they can pass this information on to others who might like to learn from them.

[80]   Ultimately, individual preachers will have to develop their own method for moving from the Scriptures to the homily, learning from their own successes and failures, as well as from other preachers through whose words they have heard the Word of God. The description of a method for building the homily that follows is not intended as—nor could it possibly be—a foolproof system for producing outstanding homilies week after week. Rather it provides a model that includes the major components of the creative process (data gathering, incubation, insight, communication) and does so within the framework of a week.

[81]   This method also respects the understanding of the homily that is central to this document: a scriptural interpretation of human existence which enables a community to recognize God's active presence, to respond to that presence in faith through liturgical word and gesture, and beyond the liturgical assembly, through a life lived in conformity with the Gospel.

[82]   The most important feature of any method is precisely that it be methodical, that is, orderly and regular. In the preparation of the homily, as in other creative endeavors, the total amount of time we spend preparing may be less important than our observance of a regular pattern of activity spread out over a certain period of time. Doing the same thing each day for the same amount of time is often a condition for success, whether this be in study, in prayer, in writing, or in artistic achievement. A regular daily pattern of activity for the preparation of the Sunday homily is likewise often the key factor in effective preaching over the long term.

[83]   Each of us called to the regular ministry of preaching needs to determine just what part of each day of the week is going to be devoted to the preparation of the Sunday homily. The time we spend each day need not be lengthy, but it needs to be determined ahead of time and be held sacred. Schedules, of course, are always to be adjusted for emergencies, but unless we determine in advance that a particular time is going to be used for a particular purpose, and stick to it, it is all too easy to have our entire day filled with appointments and meetings which we felt we could not turn down or postpone because "we had nothing special planned."

[84]   One final preliminary remark. The method that follows describes a process that extends over a week's time. Some form of "remote preparation" is also in order. Such preparation could take the form of reading a recent work on the theology of the particular Synoptic Gospel that will be the "Gospel of the Year" or spending some time planning a unified sequence of homilies for a particular liturgical season.

[85]   One of the reasons our preaching is less effective than it could be is that we have not taken seriously enough the *lectio continua* principle of our lectionary. We preach each Sunday's homily as if it had no connection with what preceded or what will follow. It should be possible, and indeed it would emphasize a sense of continuity and identity in the congregation, if from time to time our homilies would end on a "to be continued" note.

READING, LISTENING, PRAYING

[86]   The preparation for a Sunday homily should begin early in the week whenever possible, even on Sunday evening. The first step is to read and reread the texts for the liturgy. Frequently the texts will be familiar, so it is important for us to do everything we can to make this reading as fresh as possible. Read the texts aloud; read them in several versions; if we read and understand Greek or Hebrew, we might try to read them in the original. Even if our knowledge of these languages is minimal, we may find ourselves becoming aware of nuances and connections that can easily be missed if we rely entirely on translations.

[87]   At this point in the preparation process it is helpful, indeed almost essential, to read the texts in context—that is, to read them from the Bible rather than from the lectionary only. In reading and rereading the texts, continue to read all four of them (Gospel, Old Testament, Psalm, New Testament), even if a decision has been made about which text will become the focus of the homily. It is not necessary for a homily to tie together all the readings. Indeed, for the Sundays throughout the year, when the New Testament lesson is chosen without reference to the Old Testament or the Gospel, attempts to impose some kind of thematic unity can be quite artificial. Nonetheless, the reading of the texts side by side, even if they are unrelated to one another, can often prompt new and rich insights into the "now" meaning of the Scriptures.

[88]   Read the texts with pen in hand, jotting down any and all ideas. Keep in mind that what we are listening for is a Word from the Lord, a Word which can be heard as good news. We will be all the more disposed to hear and receive such a word if our reading is a prayerful, attentive listening to the text of the Scriptures. Try to read the text without asking "What does it mean?" Approach it humbly, dwell with it, and let it speak for itself.

STUDY AND FURTHER REFLECTION

[89]   One of the major temptations of students when they are assigned a paper is immediately to run to the "experts." The same temptation afflicts preachers. All too often our preparation for a homily consists of looking up the lessons, reading them over quickly, and then turning to a commentary or a homily service to find out what they mean and what we might be able to say about them. By so doing we block out the possibility of letting these texts speak to us and to the concerns we share with a congregation.

[90]   Another danger in going to the commentaries too early is that we program ourselves for preaching which, in content and style, is academic rather than existential. We look for information about the texts that we can pass on to our hearers. We think of the text as a container of a hidden meaning that we have to discover and pry loose with the appropriate tools, rather than as a word spoken directly to us by the Lord. This approach to the text leads to preaching that is a word about something rather than a word, God's Word, to someone.

[91]   The process of personal reflection and interpretation, therefore, should go on for a couple of days without the aid of commentaries. We are our own interpreters first of all, and then when we do turn to the professional exegetes, we do so for the purpose of checking out the accuracy of our own interpretation. We will frequently receive new insights and ideas from the professionals, and these will be helpful to us. If we have allowed the texts to speak to us directly, we will be much better prepared to speak a word that is expressive of our own faith and in touch with the concerns of our people. We will also be able to better recognize and use the insights the professional exegetes give us.

LETTING GO

[92]   Sometime in the middle of the preparation process we should allow ourselves to step back from the work we are doing and give free reign to the subconscious processes of our minds. At times we will find that our preparation has brought us to a roadblock. A passage may make no sense to us. It may even scandalize us. We may want to ignore it, but it will not go away. The more we wrestle with it, the more troublesome it becomes. The words of Jesus about love for enemies fly in the face of our natural inclination for retribution; his words about selling possessions and giving them to the poor contradict our instinctive sense of the necessity for prudent stewardship. Paul's teaching that sin and death entered the world through one man seems to contradict everything we hold about individual, personal freedom and responsibility. We sense a real tension between the Word of God and the human situation.

[93]   When this happens we have one of the best signs that we are on to something vital. The Word of God may in fact be challenging our faith, calling us to conversion, to a new vision of the world. This period can be a difficult one, for we can feel that we are being asked to give up a way of looking at and dealing with the world which has served us well and with which we have grown comfortable. At a time like this we need to let go in order to allow the Holy Spirit to work within us and lead us to a deeper and richer faith.

DRAFTING

[94]   A time for writing should be scheduled at least two days before the preaching of the homily in order to provide ample time for alterations. Knowing that there will be opportunity to rework the homily will do much to save us from writer's block. At this stage we need not be concerned with matters of style, or even with making sure that the homily is tightly reasoned and well constructed. The point is simply to begin getting ideas down on paper so that we will have something to work with.

[95] It is quite possible that we will come to this stage of preparation still not having any idea—any new and fresh idea, that is—of what we are going to say. We may simply feel empty and without inspiration. Begin writing anyway, for the very act of writing often unleashes a flow of ideas that will be new, fresh, and exciting. It is often at this point of initial writing that the difficult text suddenly opens up its meaning and provides a new, a richer understanding of how God is present in our lives. At this point, too, the two readings which had seemed so totally unrelated may suddenly come together and illuminate one another. When something like this happens (sometimes referred to as the moment of insight, or the "aha" experience), we may well have the central idea for our homily.

[96] So, at this point, simply write. Jot down words, phrases, unrelated sentences. Think of sketching the homily, or of working on an outline, rather than writing out a text. In fact, it is better not to put the ideas in too fixed a form at this point, for we may find that it then becomes difficult to alter them. Don't stop to think of the best way to say something; don't go back and cross out words and phrases because they don't sound right. There is time for that later. Let the pen or the typewriter simply go, even though we are sure that we will not use anything we are putting down on paper. The very act of writing is a way of calling to the surface the ideas and the words that will in fact be the stuff of which our homilies are made.

REVISING

[97] The revising stage is one of the most important and the one that is too easily omitted for lack of time. To revise is frequently to cut: the good but extraneous material that surfaced in the jotting down stage of preparation; the technical theological terms and jargony "in" words that creep into our vocabularies; the use of the non-specific "this" or "it" at the beginning of sentences; the moralistic "therefore let us" or "we should" which we so easily resort to in winding up the homily; the references to "he" and "men" when the words are meant to include everyone; the vague generalities that can be replaced with specific incidents or examples.

[98] The time for revising is also the time to arrange the material in the order best suited to gain, and hold, people's attention and to invite them to a response of faith in God's Word. In the sketching stage a story may have occurred to us which exemplified perfectly the human situation being addressed by the Word of God. Bring that story up front. Use it as the opening so that people are able to identify with the situation right from the beginning. Beginning the homily with "in today's Gospel . . ." or words to that effect, risks losing the attention of the congregation right at the beginning for they will not have been given any indication of why they should be interested in what was said in today's Gospel.

[99] The time of revising is also the time to make sure that the homily does in fact have a central, unifying idea, and that this idea is clearly stated and repeated throughout the homily. We need not repeat the idea in the same words all the time, but we need to come back to it several times. People will inevitably drift in and out, no matter how good the preacher is. The restatement of the central

idea is a way of inviting people back into the homily again if they happen to have been distracted from what we were saying.

[100] Finally, the time for revising is the time to make sure that the homily is fashioned not simply as a freestanding talk, but as an integral part of the liturgical action. Does the conclusion in any way lead people into the liturgy that follows? Have we spoken the Word of God in such a way that God has become more present in people's lives and they are enabled to be drawn more fully into the act of worship for which they have gathered? Remember that a homily is not a talk given on the occasion of a liturgical celebration, but an integral part of the liturgy. Just as a homily flows out of the Scriptures of the Liturgy of the Word, so it should flow into the prayers and actions of the Liturgy of the Eucharist which follows.

PRACTICING

[101] After revising the homily, practice it. Repeat it several times to become familiar with what has to be said and how to say it. Practice it aloud and ask if that is really "me" speaking. Does it sound natural, or have I introduced words and phrases that sounded good when I jotted them down but are not suited to oral communication? It may be helpful to preach the homily to a friend or co-worker or to use an audio/video tape recorder. Can I say to that person without embarrassment what I intend to say to the congregation? Do I really believe what I am saying, or have I hidden behind some conventional expression of piety or theology that I would probably not use in any other situation?

PREACHING

[102] Our emphasis on the importance of writing in the preparation of a homily does not in any way imply that homilies should normally be read. Writing is a means to arrive at good organization, clarity of expression, and concreteness. Whether or not we actually take a manuscript to the pulpit with us will depend on a number of things: the nature of the gathering (very formal or more informal); how familiar we are with our own material; how apprehensive we feel about forgetting something essential.

[103] Sometimes we know what we are going to say so well, and are so enthused about it that a manuscript would only get in the way or distract us. On the other hand, there may be times when we are sure that our message will be clearer and more forceful if we have the text with us. As long as we have something to say, as long as we are saying it, and as long as we establish and maintain rapport with the congregation, we may be able to preach quite effectively from a text.

[104] In general, it is much better to speak from notes or an outline—or without any written aids at all, for such a way of preaching enables us to enter more fully into direct, personal contact with a congregation. If we feel we must take the text with us, be familiar enough with the material so that instead of reading it, we can simply have it present as an aid to our memory.

[105] In preaching, as in all forms of communication, remember that it is the whole person who communicates. Facial expression, the tone of voice, the posture of the body are all powerful factors in determining whether a congregation will be receptive to what we have to say. If, as we preach, we remember that in carrying out this ministry we are showing our love, and God's, for the people, we will more easily avoid a delivery that sounds affected ("churchy") or impersonal.

THE HOMILY PREPARATION GROUP

[106] An effective way for preachers to be sure that they are addressing some of the real concerns of the congregation in the homily is to involve members of that congregation in a homily preparation group. One way to begin such a group is for the preachers to invite four or five people they trust and can work with easily to join them for an hour at the beginning of the week. In a parish setting it is advisable to have one of the members drop out after four weeks and invite someone else to take his or her place. Similarly, a second will drop out after the fifth week, so that after eight weeks or so they will be working with a new group of people.

[107] A homily preparation group can also be formed by gathering the priests in the rectory, the parish staff, priests from the area, priest and ministers, or a priests' support group. The presence of members of the congregation in a group is especially helpful in raising issues that are of concern to them and which the homily may be able to address. Groups that involve only clergy or parish staff members can also be a rich source of insight into the ways in which the Scriptures point to the continuing presence of God in human history.

[108] After the group has gathered and spent a few minutes quieting down, the following steps can be followed:

1. *Read the passages* (15 minutes). Begin with the Gospel, then the Old Testament, Psalm, and New Testament. As one of the participants reads the passages slowly, the others listen and jot down images, words or phrases that strike them.

2. *Share the words* (10 minutes). This is not a time for discussion but simply an opportunity for each person to share the words or phrases which resonated and fired the imagination. As this sharing is going on, the homilist may pick up some recurring words and phrases. He may be surprised to hear what parts of the Scriptures are being highlighted. These responses are already a sign of the concerns, questions and interests that are present in the lives of the congregation.

3. *Exegete the texts* (10 minutes). One of the members of the group presents a short exegesis of the texts. The task is not to bring to the discussion everything that could be said, but to make a special effort to determine what concrete human concerns the author was addressing when the text was written. What questions were there to which these words were at least a partial answer? When dealing with the Gospel passage, one way to answer this question is to show how other evangelists treated the same materials.

4. *Share the good news* (10 minutes). What good news did the first listeners hear in these accounts? What good news does the group hear? Where is God's promise, power and influence in our personal story present in the readings?

5. *Share the challenge these words offer us* (10 minutes). What is the doubt, the sin, the pain, the fracturing in our own lives which the passage touches? To what form of conversion do these words call us? In responding to these questions, the group may resort to generalities. By gentle persuasion and personal example the homilist can encourage the group to speak personally and with examples.

6. *Explore the consequences* (5 minutes). What difference can the good news make in my life? What happens if the scriptural good news is applied to contemporary bad news? Can my life be changed? Can the world be transformed if people believe in the good news and begin acting according to it? These are questions to which final answers cannot be given. They demand prayer and reflection.

7. *Give thanks and praise* (5 minutes). Conclude with a brief prayer of thanksgiving for God's saving Word .

Working with a homily preparation group will help to ensure two things: that the homilist hears the proclamation of the good news in the Sunday Scripture readings as it is heard by the people in the congregation; and secondly, that the preacher is able to point in concrete and specific ways to the difference that the hearing of this good news can make in the lives of those who hear it. When the preacher spends time with the congregation, struggling with how the Word touches real life, the possibility of this homily striking a listener as "talking to me" increases. The Word of God then achieves that for which it was sent. Preacher and listener, responding together, are nourished by the Word of God and drawn to praise the God who has again given a sign of his presence and power.

THE NON-NEGOTIABLES OF HOMILY PREPARATION

[109] As we mentioned at the beginning of this chapter, there is no one way to prepare a homily, nor does a particular method work the same way all the time for the same person. But no matter what the method, there are certain elements in the preparation of the homily which cannot be omitted if our preaching over the long term is going to be scripturally sound and pastorally relevant. We may be able to "wing it" on occasion, but to try to sustain a weekly ministry of preaching with little more than a glance at the lectionary and the quick consultation of a homily service is to attempt the impossible.

[110] Effective preaching—that is, preaching that enables people to hear the Word of God as good news for their lives and to respond accordingly—requires time and serious work. Unless we are willing to accept the drudgery that is a part of preaching, as it is of all creative work, we will not know the joy of having the Scriptures come alive for us, nor the profoundly satisfying experience of sharing that discovery with others.

[111] To conclude this chapter on homiletic method we would point to what we consider to be the non-negotiable elements of effective preaching:

1. *Time.* The amount of time will vary from preacher to preacher. However, the importance of the ministry of preaching demands that a significant amount of time be devoted to the homily each week, and ideally, that this time be spread out over the entire week.

2. *Prayer.* All preaching flows from faith to faith. It is only through prayer that faith is nourished.

3. *Study.* Without continuing study, stagnation sets in and preaching becomes insipid. Preachers have a professional responsibility to continue their education in the areas of Scripture, theology, and related disciplines. They might well make a book on preaching part of their regular reading program.

4. *Organization.* Much preaching suffers from lack of direction and the absence of a central, controlling idea. The writing and revising of homilies helps to ensure that there is a point to what we preach.

5. *Concreteness.* Another common fault of preachers is their tendency to speak in vague generalities or to use technical theological language. Once again, writing and revising helps to ensure that homilies are concrete and specific.

6. *Evaluation.* In public discourse we easily fall back on familiar ideas and set patterns of speech. More often than not, we are unaware of such tendencies and need the feedback of others to alert us to them.

EPILOGUE: THE POWER OF THE WORD

[112] The pulpit of St. Stephen's Cathedral in Vienna displays an elaborate handrail in which are carved a detailed series of ugly, mythical creatures. The open mouths and oversized snouts of the beasts are there to remind the preacher of his inadequacies as he ascends the stairs. At the very top of the handrail, carved into the pillar that separates the stairs from the open, circular pulpit, stands a dog, jaws open, barking down at the ominous figures. The hellish beasts are not to enter the sacred place. The preacher has been enjoined to leave his sinful self behind as he prepares to speak God's Word.

[113] The medieval artisan has captured in stone the inner tension of all of us who dare to preach. We are aware that the words we speak are human words, formed through reflection both on the Scriptures and on our personal experience of the needs of our community. Looking into the faces of the people who sit before us, we see those who are holier, more intelligent, and more creative. And yet they wait for us to speak, to preach, to proclaim and witness to the presence of God among us. Our theology tells us that the words we speak are also God's Word. "What we utter is God's wisdom, a mysterious, a hidden wisdom" (1 Cor 2:7).

[114] We dare to utter that sacred Word because we once heard the voice of Mystery who spoke to Isaiah: "Whom shall I send? Who will go for us?" And we answered with Isaiah, "Here I am; send me" (Is 6:8). With Jeremiah we trust that

the Lord will place his words in our mouths, despite our youth or age, our ignorance and our inadequacies (Jer 1:6–9). Even when we fall on our faces, the promise of Ezechiel is there, that a voice will speak to us and a spirit enter into us and set us again on our feet (Ezek 2:1–3). We believe that the Word we speak is the Word God intends to have an effect upon the world in which we live.

> For just as from the heavens the rain and snow come
> And do not return there till they have watered the earth,
> making it fertile and fruitful,
> Giving seed to him who sows and bread to him who eats,
> So shall my word be that goes forth from my mouth;
> It shall not return to me void, but shall do my will,
> achieving the end for which I sent it. (Is 55:10–11)

[115] We too stand in sacred space, aware of our personal inadequacy, yet willing to share how the scriptural story has become integrated into our thoughts and actions while we walked among those who turn their faces toward us. The words we speak are human words describing how God's action has become apparent to us this week. Is it any wonder then that excitement and tension fill us in the moments before we preach? With a final deep breath may we also breathe in the Spirit of God who will animate our human words with divine power.

APPENDIX

[116] This document on preaching has dealt mainly with what the individual preacher can do to improve the quality of the Sunday homily. In conclusion, we offer some recommendations for steps that can be taken on the national, diocesan, and parish levels to foster more effective preaching.

NATIONAL

[117] 1. A doctoral program in homiletics to prepare teachers of preaching should be established with diocesan support, perhaps at the Catholic University of America.

2. Seminaries, especially at the theologate level, are urged to emphasize preaching as a priority (cf. *Program of Priestly Formation*, 3rd Edition, Chapter III, Art. 2, Homiletics).

DIOCESAN

[118] 1. Programs to improve preaching skills should be established at the diocesan or regional level.

2. Programs for the study and deeper understanding of Scripture and preaching theology should also be established.

3. A Center for Preaching Resources should be founded in each diocese by the diocesan office for worship or continuing education, or by the seminary.

4. The Bishop(s) of the diocese should model the nature and purpose of the homily in preaching. They should not accept more preaching engagements per day than allow for preparation.

5. Criteria for the granting of faculties to preach should be clearly formulated and followed.

6. Continuing development of good preaching should be supported by the diocese through the granting of time and funding.

PARISH

[119] 1. A resource center should be established within each parish to assist preachers and lectors in fulfilling their ministry.

2. Groups to help preachers prepare and evaluate their homilies should be formed.

3. When there are several preachers in a parish, their preparation for preaching should be coordinated.

4. Readers should be trained in the effective proclamation of Scripture and provided opportunities to grow in their understanding of it.

5. Job descriptions for priests should be evaluated in order to highlight the importance and provide adequate time for preparation of the ministry of preaching.

6. Some record should be kept of the themes of each Sunday's homily in order to bring the parish community into contact with the major facets of our faith each year, and to avoid undue emphasis on one truth at the expense of others.

[120] At all levels, national, diocesan and parish, bishops and priests are urged to invite religious and laity to read this document so as to assist, encourage and support priests in efforts toward a renewal of preaching in the church.

SUNDAY CELEBRATIONS
IN THE
ABSENCE OF A PRIEST
INTRODUCTION

APPROVED BY THE UNITED STATES CONFERENCE
OF CATHOLIC BISHOPS
NOVEMBER 2003

RITUAL BOOK PUBLISHED BY
THE UNITED STATES CONFERENCE OF CATHOLIC BISHOPS
2007, EMENDED 2012

AN OVERVIEW OF *SUNDAY CELEBRATIONS IN THE ABSENCE OF A PRIEST: INTRODUCTION*

Michael R. Prendergast

When the latest ritual edition of *Sunday Celebrations in the Absence of a Priest* (SCAP) was originally published in 2007, the "Introduction" included 117 articles which more than doubled the *praenotonda* of the 1994 edition of the ritual book.[1] No typical edition (that is to say, an edition of this ritual text published in Latin) of SCAP exists; rather, it was a ritual book that grew from a pastoral need: Catholic parishes without the luxury of a priest to celebrate Sunday Mass with the community. The 1988 Roman document, *Directory for Sunday Celebrations in the Absence of a Priest*, was issued at the request of several bishops' conferences. The purpose of the directory is to offer guidance and norms for real circumstances requiring a Sunday celebration in the absence of a priest. This text is found in "Appendix IV" of the current ritual book. In 1991 the United States Bishops' Committee on the Liturgy (BCL) issued the document, *Gathered in Steadfast Faith*. This document provides detailed information about the role of the local bishop; guidance for the selection, training, commissioning, and ongoing formation of leaders of prayer; and general principles that apply to Sunday celebrations in the absence of a priest. The document suggests collaboration with parishes faced with these celebrations and the need for training programs for the "administration of communion to the sick and viaticum to the dying, in preaching (when specifically designated), in the exposition of the holy Eucharist, in those rites from the *Order of Christian Funerals*, which, on occasion, they may be required to lead, and in other liturgical and devotional services."[2] This text is found in appendix V of the current ritual book.

The *Directory, Gathered in Steadfast Faith*, and the *praenotanda* ("Introduction") to the bilingual edition of *Sunday Celebrations in the Absence of a Priest: Leaders Edition* (2007, 2012) all uphold the importance of the community gathering on Sunday, the Lord's Day, even when no priest is present to celebrate the Eucharist. This is the central focus of the legislation and the ritual texts. Every liturgical assembly is called to gather on Sunday. "The revised edition of *Sunday Celebrations in the Absence of a Priest* is offered not as particular law, but as an approved resource of the USCCB Committee on the Liturgy, and may be used in the dioceses of the United States under the direction of the diocesan bishop."[3]

---

1. The 2007 edition of *Sunday Celebrations in the Absence of a Priest* (SCAP) was emended and republished in 2012 to reflect the changes in the English translation of the third edition of *The Roman Missal* (RM). These changes include: before the proclamation of the Gospel and as part of the final blessing, the deacon says "The Lord be with you," and the people respond "And with your spirit"; the texts of the Nicene and Apostles' Creeds have been changed to reflect the translation now found in the Order of Mass.

2. *Gathered in Steadfast Faith* (GSF), 30.

3. SCAP, Foreword.

The "Introduction" to the ritual includes 117 articles of instruction. The first section, "Sunday and Its Observance," alerts us to the venerable tradition of the assembly gathering on Sunday, participating in the Paschal Mystery under the guidance of the Holy Spirit.[4] In the second section of SCAP, we see that the principal need for these services is due to the shortage of priests in certain areas.[5] Where faith communities are served by a nonresident priest, whenever he does visit a community the Mass and the sacraments should be celebrated.[6] In circumstances where the faithful cannot gather with a community the family, as the domestic church, should devote itself to prayer.[7] An important instruction of the "Introduction" says, "Any confusion . . . between this kind of liturgical assembly and a Eucharistic celebration must be carefully avoided . . . [and] increase the desire of the faithful to . . . participate in the celebration of the Eucharist."[8] This raises questions about how we celebrate Sunday Eucharist in our faith communities. The documentation suggests that good celebration of the Eucharist is what those who cannot attend Sunday Mass should desire or long for.

Normally only one such celebration may occur in a given community in the course of a weekend.[9] The ritual encourages the consecrated hosts to be renewed often.[10] While the Church has traditionally reserved the Eucharistic species for *Viaticum* (Communion to the sick and dying) and prayer in the presence of the Blessed Sacrament, we have a new reality: reserving the Eucharist for distribution at a Sunday liturgy where a priest is not present. This is frequently called a "Communion service." These services are often celebrated on weekdays in several different pastoral settings. However the ritual book that we have is for use only on Sundays and Holydays of Obligation. For communities that celebrate a Communion service on weekdays, the ritual text *Holy Communion and Worship of the Eucharist Outside of Mass* (HCWEOM) is used. This text has undergone a revision by the United States bishops to bring it into closer conformity with the ritual text for Sunday; as of this date this revision is still awaiting confirmation from the Holy See.

In light of the most recent legislation from *The General Instruction of the Roman Missal* (GIRM), "it is most desirable that the faithful, just as the Priest himself is bound to do, receive the Lord's Body from hosts consecrated at the same Mass and that, in the cases where this is foreseen, they partake of the chalice (cf. no. 283), so that even by means of the signs Communion may stand out more clearly as participation in the sacrifice actually being celebrated."[11] It is imperative that the practice of communicating the Sunday assembly with hosts consecrated at a previous celebration of the Eucharist come to an end. This practice has led some to question the difference between Sunday Eucharist and a Sunday celebration in the absence of a priest, because the people receive from

---

4. See SCAP, 1–5.

5. See ibid., 7.

6. See ibid., 12.

7. See ibid., 11.

8. Ibid., 16.

9. See ibid., 15.

10. See ibid., 22.

11. *The General Instruction of the Roman Missal* (GIRM), 85.

the tabernacle's supply at both celebrations. If current pastoral practice continues, it will lead to a greater divide between the faithful's understanding of what it means to fully participate in the sacrifice of the Mass. The problem, it seems, goes much deeper than merely being able to understand the distinction between the two celebrations, although we have in many cases successfully catechized the faithful on the revisions of the liturgical reform. There remains a critical area of weakness: enabling the faithful to understand better and articulate and signify in action what the Church does when it celebrates the Eucharist.

When the presbyter is absent, so is the connection to the bishop; that is why the "Introduction" to the ritual book calls on the local ordinary to appoint lay leaders of prayer to lead these celebrations in the absence of a priest or deacon. In the "Introduction," the section entitled "Offices and Ministries" tells us that the local ordinary oversees these celebrations and issues appropriate guidelines for use within the local Church.[12] In the article regarding the role of the pastor we find this profound statement: "communities . . . will come to realize that their liturgical assembly on Sunday is not a liturgical assembly 'without a Priest,' but a liturgical assembly 'in the absence of a Priest,' or, better still, a liturgical assembly 'in expectation of a Priest.'"[13]

The next three articles are devoted to the role of the deacon and his function in leading the celebrations, and notes that "he acts in the usual manner in regard to the greetings, the prayers, the Gospel reading and homily, the giving of Holy Communion, and the dismissal and blessing."[14] The deacon does not sit in the chair reserved for the priest, but sits in another chair "as a symbols that the community awaits the presence of the Priest."[15] Five full articles are devoted to the role of the layperson who leads these celebrations. "In the absence of both a Priest and a Deacon, upon the request and recommendation of the pastor, the Bishop may appoint lay persons . . ."[16] The laypersons minister in virtue of their Baptism and delegation and are chosen by the way in which they live out their lives in relationship to the Gospel.[17]

Lay leaders of prayer are appointed by the bishop for a definite period of time and are commissioned in a liturgical celebration using the "Order for the Blessing of Those Who Exercise Pastoral Service," which is found in the *Book of Blessings* (BB), chapter 27. The lay leader ensures the presence of lectors and readers, cantors, servers, and other liturgical ministers, and is to remember that their function is "not so much as an honor but as a responsibility and, above all, as a service to their brothers and sisters."[18] Eight articles are devoted to the role of preaching, which suggests the importance of this responsibility that is entrusted to a lay leaders of prayer[19] and a nod to their role in leading the celebration.[20] Article 38 instructs that the "lay leaders of prayer should be well trained to lead

---

12. See SCAP, 18–20.
13. Ibid., 21.
14. Ibid., 24.
15. Ibid.
16. Ibid., 26.
17. Ibid., 27.
18. Ibid., 30.
19. Ibid., 31–34.
20. See ibid., 35–38.

the liturgical rites found in the ritual book." These would include, but are not limited to, the rites that may be led by a lay leader of prayer found in the *Rite of Baptism for Children* (RBC); *Rite of Christian Initiation of Adults* (RCIA); *Pastoral Care of the Sick* (PCS); *Order of Christian Funerals* (OCF); the nonsacramental penitential celebrations in appendix II of *Rite of Penance*; the *Rite of Marriage* (RMarr), which allows for a lay leader to witness the marriage of a couple when a priest or deacon is not available; and the blessings found in the BB.

Twenty-one articles are devoted to the "Forms the Sunday Celebration May Take."[21] Catholic bishops of the United States recommend a celebration of the Liturgy of the Hours and the Liturgy of the Word with or without the distribution of Holy Communion. The Canadian Bishops recommend a service of the Word without the distribution of Holy Communion. The difficulty with celebrating the Liturgy of the Hours is that most people are unfamiliar with this official ritual prayer of the Church. The United States Bishops' Conference and the task force that created the revised ritual wanted to ensure that these celebrations would not look "too much like Mass." The documents from Rome and those of the United States Bishops stated that these celebrations should be careful not to resemble Mass, yet the prayers used in the 1994 ritual were lifted directly from *The Sacramentary*. Especially problematic was the Prayer after Communion which contained sacrificial language (at a Communion service there is no sacrifice). These prayers have been removed from the current ritual. When Holy Communion is distributed during the celebration of the Hours or Liturgy of the Word, an Act of Thanksgiving follows. The Act of Thanksgiving takes the form of a psalm, canticle, hymn, litany, or prayer.[22] Fifty-one articles are devoted to "Preparations for the Sunday Celebration";[23] the Liturgical Year[24] with articles concerning the Sacred Paschal Triduum; encouraging communities to join a neighboring parish for the three days; and, when this is not possible, to "gather as family, that is, the domestic Church, or in small faith communities and thus unite themselves in prayer to the universal church."[25] SCAP devotes the remaining articles to the "Importance of Singing"[26] and the importance of "Sacred Silence."[27]

SCAP will continue to be used—perhaps even more frequently in places where the priesthood shortage continues to be extreme. Sometime after the fourth century, some people abstained from Holy Communion on the grounds of awe and unworthiness; they attended the sacrifice of the Mass but did not partake in the meal. The phenomena of SCAP has left us with the opposite: people participating in the meal but not attending the sacrifice.

---

21. See ibid. 39–51.
22. See ibid., 51 and 59.
23. See ibid., 66–67.
24. See ibid., 68–108.
25. Ibid., 95.
26. Ibid., 109–111.
27. Ibid., 117.

OUTLINE

SUNDAY CELEBRATIONS
IN THE ABSENCE OF A PRIEST

INTRODUCTION

SUNDAY AND ITS OBSERVANCE

1 "By a tradition handed down from the apostles which took its origin from the very day of Christ's resurrection, the Church celebrates the paschal mystery every eighth day; with good reason this, then, bears the name of the Lord's day or Sunday."[1]

2 The New Testament and the Fathers of the Church give ample evidence that for the early Church Sunday was the "Lord's Day." For it was on Sunday that the Lord conquered sin and death and rose to new life. In our own time, the Second Vatican Council has reminded us: "For on this day Christ's faithful should come together into one place so that, by hearing the word of God and taking part in the eucharist, they may call to mind the passion, the resurrection, and the glorification of the Lord Jesus, and may thank God who 'has begotten them again, through the resurrection of Jesus Christ from the dead, unto a living hope' (1 Peter 1:3)."[2]

3 The complete liturgical celebration of Sunday is characterized by the gathering of the faithful to manifest the Church, not simply on their own initiative but as called together by God, that is, as the people of God in their organic structure, presided over by a Priest, who acts in the person of Christ. Through the celebration of the Liturgy of the Word the assembled faithful are instructed in the Paschal Mystery by the Scriptures which are proclaimed and which are then explained in the Homily by a Priest or Deacon. And through the celebration of the Liturgy of the Eucharist, by which the Paschal Mystery is sacramentally effected, the liturgical assembly participates in the very sacrifice of Christ.[3]

4 Pastoral catechesis on the importance of Sunday should emphasize that the sacrifice of the Mass is the only true actualization of the Lord's Paschal

---

1. Vatican Council II, Constitution on the Liturgy *Sacrosanctum Concilium* (hereafter, *SC*), no. 106, http://www.vatican.va/archive/hist_councils/ii_vatican_council/documents/vat-ii _const_19631204_sacrosanctum-concilium_en.html. See also Appendix, Declaration of the Second Vatican Ecumenical Council on Revision of the Calendar, no. 2, in Daughters of St. Paul, *The Sixteen Documents of Vatican II and the Instruction on the Liturgy* (Boston: St. Paul Editions, 1966), p. 56.

2. *Directory for Sunday Celebrations in the Absence of a Priest*, no. 8; see *SC*, no. 106.

3. See *Directory*, no. 12.

Mystery[4] and is the most complete manifestation of the Church: "Hence the Lord's day is the original feast day, and it should be proposed to the piety of the faithful and taught to them. . . . Other celebrations, unless they be truly of greatest importance, shall not have precedence over the Sunday which is the foundation and kernel of the whole liturgical year."[5]

5   In the Sunday liturgical assembly, as also in the life of the Christian community, the faithful should experience active participation as well as the opportunity to be renewed spiritually under the guidance of the Holy Spirit.[6]

SUNDAY CELEBRATIONS IN THE ABSENCE OF A PRIEST

6   There have been and still are many of the faithful in the United States for whom, because of the lack of a priest or some other serious reason, participation in the Mass is not possible.[7]

7   In addition, because of the shortage of priests in certain areas, priests must celebrate Mass several times on Sundays in many widely scattered churches.[8] They are to be commended for their dedication and pastoral zeal.

8   "When it is difficult to have the celebration of Mass on a Sunday in a parish church or in another community of Christ's faithful, the diocesan Bishop together with his Priests should consider appropriate remedies. Among such solutions will be that other Priests be called upon for this purpose, or that the faithful transfer to a church in a nearby place so as to participate in the Eucharistic mystery there."[9]

9   "All Priests, to whom the Priesthood and the Eucharist are entrusted for the sake of others, should remember that they are enjoined to provide the faithful with the opportunity to satisfy the obligation of participating at Mass on Sundays. For their part, it is the right of the lay faithful, barring a case of real impossibility, that no Priest should ever refuse either to celebrate Mass for the people or to have it celebrated by another Priest if the people otherwise would not be able to satisfy the obligation of participating at Mass on Sunday or the other days of precept."[10]

---

4. See Paul VI, Address to the Bishops of central France (26 March 1977): AAS 69 (1977) 465: "Furthermore, the goal should always be to have the sacrifice of the Mass celebrated since this is the only authentic actualization of the Lord's paschal mystery" (tr., *The Pope Speaks* 22:2 [1977]: 134); see John Paul II, Apostolic Letter *Dies Domini* (31 May 1998).

5. *SC*, no. 106.

6. See *Directory*, no. 15.

7. See ibid., no. 2; see *Codex Iuris Canonici*, 1983 (hereafter, *CIC*), can. 1248 §2.

8. See ibid., no. 5.

9. Congregation for Divine Worship and the Discipline of the Sacraments, Instruction *Redemptionis Sacramentum*, On Certain Matters to Be Observed or Be Avoided Regarding the Most Holy Eucharist (hereafter, *RS*): Liturgy Documentary Series 15 (Washington, DC: United States Conference of Catholic Bishops [USCCB], 2004), no. 162.

10. Ibid., no. 163.

10   In circumstances in which there is no reasonable opportunity to provide for the celebration of Mass, local bishops may judge it necessary to provide for other Sunday celebrations in the absence of a priest, so that in the best way possible the weekly gathering of the faithful can be continued and the Christian tradition regarding Sunday preserved.[11]

11   When on a particular Sunday even this kind of celebration is not possible, the faithful are strongly urged to devote themselves to prayer "for a suitable time either individually or with the family or, if possible, with a group of families."[12]

12   Even when a Priest is not available to celebrate Mass on a Sunday, it may be possible to schedule Mass sometime during the week, when he could be present. While this celebration does not take the place of the Sunday Mass, the faithful should be encouraged to attend whenever possible.

13   "All Deacons or lay members of Christ's faithful who are assigned a part in such celebrations by the diocesan Bishop should strive to keep alive in the community a genuine hunger for the Eucharist, so that no opportunity for the celebration of Mass will ever be missed, also taking advantage of the occasional presence of a Priest who is not impeded by Church law from celebrating Mass."[13]

CONDITIONS FOR HOLDING SUNDAY CELEBRATIONS IN THE ABSENCE OF A PRIEST

14   When a Priest cannot be present for the celebration of Mass on the Lord's Day, it is of paramount importance that the parish or mission community still come together to celebrate the resurrection of the Lord. Even so, however, "it is unthinkable on the Lord's Day to substitute for Holy Mass, either ecumenical celebrations of the word or services of common prayer with Christians from the. . . Ecclesial Communities or even participation in these Communities' liturgical celebrations."[14] If, in the judgment of the diocesan bishop, it is not practical or possible for the community to participate in the celebration of Mass in a church nearby,[15] they should assemble for Sunday worship in their own community under the leadership of the person whom the bishop and pastor have designated to lead them in prayer. In such a case the celebration takes one of the forms found in this ritual.

15   Before Sunday celebrations in the absence of a priest are begun, it should be explained to the faithful that although these celebrations substitute for the Sunday celebration of the Eucharist, they should not be regarded as the ideal

---

11. See ibid., no. 164.

12. *Directory*, no. 32; see CIC, can. 1248 §2.

13. *RS*, no. 164.

14. Pope John Paul II, Encyclical Letter *Ecclesia de Eucharistia* (Washington, DC: USCCB, 2003), no. 30; cf. also Pontifical Council for the Promotion of Christian Unity, Directory for the Application of the Principles and Norms on Ecumenism, *La recherché de l'unité* (25 March 1993), no. 115: AAS 85 (1003) 1039–1119, here 1085.

15. See *Directory*, no. 18.

solution to present circumstances nor as a surrender to mere convenience.[16] These celebrations are held within communities that await a Priest and these solutions must be considered merely temporary. There should normally be only one liturgical assembly of this kind in each place on any given Sunday. One of these services may never be held in a location where Mass has been celebrated that weekend.[17] Because of the emphasis on Sunday as the Lord's Day, such liturgical assemblies should be held on Sunday.

16   Any confusion in the minds of the faithful between this kind of liturgical assembly and a Eucharistic celebration must be carefully avoided. These celebrations should increase the desire of the faithful to be present at and participate in the celebration of the Eucharist.[18]

17   To this end, the faithful need to be led to an understanding that the Eucharistic Sacrifice cannot take place without a priest, even though the reception of Holy Communion which they receive in this kind of liturgical assembly is closely connected with the sacrifice of the Mass, but not equal to it. This serves as an urgent reminder for prayers that those whom God has called to the priesthood will respond generously.[19]

OFFICES AND MINISTRIES

BISHOP

18   Such services should be occasional. It is the responsibility of the diocesan bishop, after having received the advice of the diocesan presbyteral council and, if appropriate, other consultative bodies, to decide how often Sunday celebrations in the absence of a priest will be celebrated. He should be sensitive if there is an increasing shortage of priests as well as to the increasing demands made upon them. He is to set out general and particular norms for such celebrations. They are to be held only when and where approved by the bishop and only under the pastoral ministry of a priest who has the responsibility for the particular community.[20]

19   Before the Bishop decides on having such Sunday celebrations, he should consider the possibility of recourse to priests, even religious priests, who are not directly assigned to the care of souls. At the same time, he should consider the frequency of Masses in the various parishes and churches of the diocese with a view toward freeing a priest to celebrate Mass with a community without its

---

16. See Paul VI, Address to the Bishops of Central France (26 March 1977): AAS 69 (1977): "Our judgment is that you should proceed along this line but with discernment and without multiplying this kind of assembly as though it were the best solution and the last chance" (tr., *The Pope Speaks* 22:2 [1977]: 134).

17. See *Directory*, no. 21.

18. See ibid., no. 22.

19. See ibid., no. 23.

20. See ibid., no. 24.

own priest.[21] The preeminence of the celebration of the Eucharist, particularly on Sunday, over other pastoral activities is to be respected.[22]

20   The bishop should appoint a delegate or a special committee to ensure that the lay ministers who will lead the liturgical assembly are properly instructed and that these celebrations are carried out correctly. He is also to see to it that the people of the parish or community receive the necessary instruction. However, the bishop's concern should always be that the faithful involved have the opportunity to participate in the celebration of the Eucharist as often as possible, and at least several times a year.[23]

PASTOR

21   The pastor has the responsibility of informing the bishop about the need for such celebrations in the area under his pastoral care, to prepare the faithful for them, to visit them during the week, and at a convenient time to celebrate the sacraments with them, particularly the sacrament of penance. In this way the communities involved will come to realize that their liturgical assembly on Sunday is not a liturgical assembly "without a priest," but a liturgical assembly "in the absence of a priest," or, better still, a liturgical assembly "in expectation of a priest."[24]

22   When Mass cannot be celebrated, the pastor will see to it that frequent opportunities are provided for giving Holy Communion. He is also to see to it that there is a celebration of the Eucharist in due time in each community. The consecrated hosts are to be renewed often and kept in the tabernacle.[25]

DEACON

23   As a minister of the Word, who also has a responsibility for the sacraments, the deacon is called in a special way to lead these Sunday assemblies. Since the deacon has been ordained for the nurture and increase of the People of God, it belongs to him to lead the prayers, to proclaim the Gospel, to preach the homily, and to give Holy Communion.[26] When a deacon is available, he leads the celebration.

24   When a deacon presides at a Sunday celebration in the absence of a priest, he acts in the usual manner in regard to the greetings, the prayers, the Gospel reading and homily, the giving of Holy Communion, and the dismissal and blessing. He wears the vestments proper to his ministry, that is, the alb with stole

---

21. See ibid., no. 25; see SC Rites, Instruction *Eucharisticum mysterium* (25 May 1967), no. 26: AAS 59 (1967) 555: *Furrow* 18 (July 1967): 384–418.

22. See ibid., no. 25

23. See ibid., no. 26.

24. Ibid., no. 27.

25. See ibid., no. 28.

26. See ibid., no. 29; see Paul VI, Motu Proprio *Ad pascendum* (15 August 1972), no. 1: AAS 64 (1972) 534 (tr., *The Pope Speaks* 17:3 [1972]: 234–235).

and the dalmatic.[27] Leaving the priest's chair vacant, he uses a chair other than the priest's as a symbol that the community awaits the presence of the Priest.

25   The Deacon is to be assisted by other ministers who will proclaim the Scriptures other than the Gospel, assist him in the distribution of Holy Communion, if needed, sing the Psalms and other songs, provide instrumental music, and prepare the place for the celebration.[28]

LAYPERSON[29]

26   It is not appropriate for any member of the lay faithful to be seen as presiding over the celebration in the same way as a priest or deacon.[30] However, in the absence of both a priest and a deacon, upon the request and recommendation of the pastor, the bishop may appoint lay persons, who may be religious, as lay leaders of prayer, who are entrusted with the care of preparing and directing these celebrations. They would be responsible for leading the prayers and, when it is to be included in the celebration, with distributing Holy Communion.

27   All ministers carry out their responsibilities in virtue of their baptism and the delegation of the diocesan bishop.[31] Lay leaders of prayer are to be chosen in view of the consistency of their way of life with the Gospel and in the expectation of their being acceptable to the community of the faithful. The appointment of such ministers is made by the bishop for a definite time. Their appointment is to be made known to the community by means of a liturgical celebration in which prayers are offered to God on behalf of those appointed. The Order for the Blessing of Those Who Exercise Pastoral Service contained in the *Book of Blessings* may be used for this purpose.[32] It is appropriate to engage seminarians in this ministry when they are available.

28   All other roles in the celebration should be distributed among lectors, cantors, servers, and other liturgical ministers.[33]

29   The pastor is to see to the suitable and continuous instruction of these laypersons and to assist them in the preparation of worthy celebrations.[34]

30   The laypersons appointed as lay leaders of prayer should regard the office entrusted to them not so much as an honor but as a responsibility and, above all, as a service to their brothers and sisters under the authority of the pastor.[35] They "should do all of, but only, those parts which pertain to his office by the

---

27. See *RS*, no. 125: "The proper vestment of the Deacon is the dalmatic, to be worn over an alb and stole. In order that the beautiful tradition of the Church may be preserved, it is praiseworthy to refrain from exercising the option of omitting the dalmatic."

28. See ibid., no. 40.

29. In a worship context, the term "lay minister" refers to all non-ordained, whether religious or lay person.

30. See *RS*, no. 165.

31. See CIC, can. 230 §3.

32. See The Roman Ritual, *Book of Blessings* (hereafter, *BB*), Part VI, ch. 60.

33. See *RS*, nos. 165–166.

34. See *Directory*, no. 30.

35. See ibid., no. 27; see CIC, can. 230 §3.

nature of the rite and the principles of liturgy."[36] They should carry out their office with sincere devotion and the decorum demanded by such a responsibility and rightly expected of them by God's people.[37]

PREACHING

31   The local bishop bears the responsibility for moderating the entire ministry of the Word in each local church. Preaching is an essential ministry and should be taken seriously by those who have been duly delegated by the bishop. Church law itself gives all the ordained the faculty to preach, and the homily, within the celebration of the Eucharist, is reserved to the priest or deacon.[38]

32   With the permission of the bishop, a lay person may be chosen to preach in the absence of a priest or a deacon.[39] The diocesan bishop therefore should issue norms concerning the preaching ministry which are to be observed by all the faithful of that diocese.[40]

33   Those who preach, when properly delegated, should preserve a diligence in prayer, commitment to the study of Scripture, growth in faith, and careful preparation.

34   Those designated for lay preaching must have completed a process of discernment with the pastor or pastoral administrator responsible for the pastoral care of the faith community. They must also complete the program for training, certification, and commissioning provided for by the local diocese. Formation in the ministry of lay preaching includes thorough familiarity with the documents issued by the USCCB and legislation issued by the USCCB as complementary to Canon 766.[41]

35   The leader of prayer who is a not a deacon uses the special form in this ritual for the blessing, does not use words that are proper to a priest or deacon, and omits those rites, gestures, and texts that are too readily associated with the Mass and which might give the impression that the layperson is ordained.

36   The layperson wears vesture that is suitable for his or her function or the vesture prescribed by the bishop.[42] A layperson as well as the deacon does not

---

36. *SC*, no. 28.

37. See *Directory*, no. 31; see *SC*, no. 29.

38. See ibid.; see CIC, can. 767 §1; cf. Pontifical Commission for the Authetic Interpretation of the Code of Canon Law (26 May 1987): AAS 79 (1987) 1249.

39. See CIC, can. 766.

40. See ibid., can. 772 §1, and the Complementary Legislation for Canon 767 of the *Code of Canon Law*: *BCL Newsletter* 37 (December 2001): 49.

41. See Complementary Legislation for Canon 767 of the *Code of Canon Law* and *Fulfilled in Your Hearing: The Homily in the Sunday Assembly* (Washington, DC: USCCB, 1982).

42. See The Roman Ritual, *Holy Communion and Worship of the Eucharist Outside Mass* (hereafter *HCWEOM*), no. 20 (Washington, DC: USCCB, 1976); and the *General Instruction of the Roman Missal* (hereafter *GIRM*), Liturgy Documentary Series 14 (Washington, DC: USCCB, 2011), no. 339: "In the Dioceses of the United States of America, acolytes, altar servers, readers, and other lay ministers may wear the alb or other appropriate and dignified clothing."

use the priest's chair, as a symbol that the community awaits the presence of a priest. In fact, the leadership of this prayer is best done from among the faithful. Since the altar is the table of sacrifice and of the paschal banquet, its only use in one of these celebrations is for the Rite of Communion.

37   The leader of prayer is always to be assisted by other ministers who will proclaim the Scriptures, assist in the distribution of Holy Communion, sing the psalms and other songs, provide instrumental music, and prepare the place for the celebration.[43]

38   Lay leaders of prayer should be well trained to lead the liturgical rites found in the ritual book.[44]

FORMS THE SUNDAY CELEBRATION MAY TAKE

39   A common feature of the liturgical rites provided for the Sunday celebration in the absence of a Priest is the proclamation of the Word of God. The aim of this provision is that the riches of Sacred Scripture and of the Church's prayer be amply provided to the faithful gathered on Sundays in various ways even apart from Mass. For the faithful should not be deprived of the readings that are read at Mass in the course of a year, nor of the prayers of the liturgical seasons.[45]

40   A second provision of the services which follow is the distribution of Holy Communion. Although the faithful cannot share in the actual celebration of the Mass, they nevertheless may be fed at the table of the Lord and be spiritually united to the community from which the holy Eucharist was brought to the Sunday celebration.

According to circumstances, it may not always be possible to have the distribution of Holy Communion during the Sunday celebration. When this is the case, those present should be made to realize that, nevertheless, Christ is present in the gathered liturgical assembly of the Church and in the Scriptures that are proclaimed.[46]

41   In the dioceses of the United States, the bishops have decided that Holy Communion is permitted, though not required during such celebrations. The diocesan bishop may decide if Holy Communion is to be distributed during Sunday celebrations in the absence of a priest.[47]

---

43. See *Directory*, no. 40.

44. In addition, these ministers should be well versed in the administration of communion to the sick and viaticum to the dying; in the exposition of the Holy Eucharist; in those rites from the *Order of Christian Funerals*, which on occasion they may be required to lead; and in other liturgical and devotional services. See *Gathered in Steadfast Faith*, no. 30, in *Sunday Celebrations in the Absence of a Priest*, Liturgy Documentary Series 10 (Washington, DC: USCCB, 1996).

45. See *Directory*, no. 19.

46. See *SC*, no. 7.

47. See *RS*, no. 166.

42   The first form given for the Sunday celebration in the absence of a priest is that of Morning or Evening Prayer from the *Liturgy of the Hours*.[48] For "when the people are invited to the *Liturgy of the Hours* and come together in unity of heart and voice, they show forth the Church in its celebration of the mystery of Christ."[49] Holy Communion may be given at the end of either Morning or Evening Prayer.[50]

43   Those responsible for the preparation and celebration of Morning or Evening Prayer should be familiar with the *General Instruction of the Liturgy of the Hours*[51] as well as the structure and contents of the *Liturgy of the Hours*.[52]

44   The texts provided for Morning Prayer (nos. 118–151) and Evening Prayer (nos. 152–185) are given as a common form and by way of example. The texts proper to each Sunday contained in the *Liturgy of the Hours* may always be used.

45   Music is an essential part of the divine office and should be a part of the celebration as often as possible. The amount of singing and the type of music used will depend on the musical resources that are available and the abilities of the members of the gathered assembly to sing.

46   Morning and Evening Prayer both have the same structure in this ritual and the following elements:

Introductory Rites—These rites (Introduction and Hymn) serve to form the gathered faithful into a community and for them to dispose themselves for the celebration.

Psalmody—The singing or recitation of Psalms and scriptural canticles, along with their respective antiphons and optional Psalm-prayers, permits the liturgical assembly to join its praise and thanksgiving to God to that of Christ, who is our great high priest and advocate.

Liturgy of the Word—The proclamation of the Scriptures to those gathered in faith brings them the message of the good news of salvation and redemption in Christ. The response of the liturgical assembly to the Word of God is a combination of intercession (Intercessions) for the needs of the Church and the world and thanksgiving (Canticle of Zechariah or Canticle of Mary) for God's goodness to us.

[*Communion Rite*—The liturgical assembly unites itself to the Paschal Mystery of Christ in Holy Communion. It is also a sign and expression of the liturgical assembly's union with those who are able to celebrate the Eucharist on that particular day.]

---

48. See the *Liturgy of the Hours* (hereafter *LOTH*) (New York: Catholic Book Publishing Company, 1975–1976).

49. *General Instruction of the Liturgy of the Hours* (hereafter, *GILH*), Liturgy Documentary Series 5 (Washington, DC: USCCB, 2002), no. 22.

50. See *Directory*, no. 33.

51. See *LOTH*.

52. See ibid.

Act of Thanksgiving—The faithful praise the glory and mercy of God and give thanks for the celebration of Sunday. When combined with the distribution of Communion, the canticles are recited after Communion.

Concluding Rite—After having heard the Word of God (and having been nourished by the Body of Christ in Holy Communion), the liturgical assembly listens to brief announcements, takes up a monetary collection, is encouraged to pray for vocations to the priesthood, exchanges the sign of peace, and goes forth with God's blessing to live the Christian life.

LITURGY OF THE WORD

47   Among the forms of celebration found in liturgical tradition when Mass is not possible, a celebration of the Word of God may be celebrated.[53] This celebration may be concluded by Eucharistic Communion, when possible. In this way the faithful can be nourished by both the Word of God and the Body of Christ. "By hearing the Word of God the faithful learn that the marvels it proclaims reach their climax in the paschal mystery, of which the Mass is a sacramental memorial and in which they share by communion."[54] Further, in certain circumstances the Sunday celebration may be combined with the celebration of baptism, marriage, or blessings in ways that are suited to the needs of each community.[55]

48   The order to be followed in this form of the Sunday celebration consists of the celebration of the Word of God and may also include the giving of Holy Communion. Nothing that is proper to Mass, and particularly the presentation of the gifts and the Eucharistic prayer, is to be inserted into the celebration.[56]

49   The texts of the prayers and readings for each Sunday, Solemnity, or feast of the Lord are taken from the *Roman Missal*[57] and the *Lectionary for Mass*.[58] This allows the faithful to follow the cycle of the liturgical year and pray and listen to the Word of God in communion with the other communities of the Church.[59] The prayers from the *Roman Missal* are contained in Appendix III of this ritual.

50   Those who are responsible for the preparation and celebration of this form of the Sunday celebration should be familiar with the principles found in the *General Instruction of the Roman Missal* and the Introduction of the *Lectionary for Mass*.

51   The following is an outline of the elements of the celebration:

Introductory Rites—The purpose of these rites is to form the gathered faithful into a community and for them to dispose themselves for the celebration.

---

53. See *SC*, no. 35, 4.
54. *HCWEOM*, no. 26.
55. See *Directory*, no. 20.
56. See ibid., no. 40.
57. See *The Roman Missal*.
58. See *Lectionary for Mass* (New York: Catholic Book Publishing Company, 1998).
59. See *Directory*, no. 36.

Liturgy of the Word—God speaks to his people, to disclose to them the mystery of redemption and salvation; the people respond through the profession of faith and the Prayer of the Faithful.

[*Communion Rite*—This rite is an expression and accomplishment of communion with Christ and with his members in the whole Church and especially with those who on this same day take part in the Eucharistic sacrifice.]

Act of Thanksgiving—God is blessed for his great glory and thanks is given for the celebration of Sunday.

Concluding Rites—The blessing and dismissal point to the connection existing between the liturgy and the Christian life.[60]

INDIVIDUAL PARTS OF ALL SUNDAY CELEBRATIONS

INTRODUCTORY RITES

52   The introductory rites gather the members of the local community and unite them to other liturgical assemblies throughout the world. This is expressed by participation in the song of the introductory rites and in the opening prayer. The deacon or lay leader of prayer should always begin the rite by using the text provided, which reminds all present that this celebration is conducted in the absence of a priest.

PSALMODY

53   The singing of psalms is included in every Sunday celebration. Psalmody lies at the core of Morning and Evening Prayer. By the use of the psalms the Church unites the praise of the Church on earth to that of the saints. The responsorial psalm in the liturgy of the Word allows the liturgical assembly to respond to the Word of God and reflect upon it.

LITURGY OF THE WORD

54   Normally there are three readings as at the Sunday Mass. The first reading is followed by a responsorial psalm, and the second reading is followed by the Gospel acclamation.

55   The first two readings are proclaimed by two lectors, when possible. The Gospel is proclaimed by the leader of prayer. A layperson omits the greeting, "The Lord be with you," before the Gospel.

56   In order that the gathered assembly may retain the Word of God, there should be an explanation of the readings or a period of silence for reflection on what has been heard.

57   The Prayer of the Faithful follows the established series of intentions as is indicated in Appendix I.[61] Particular intentions for the whole diocese proposed

---

60. See ibid., no. 41.
61. See *GIRM*, nos. 69–71.

by the bishop are always to be included. Intentions for vocations to sacred orders, for the bishop, and for the pastor should be included in the Prayer of the Faithful.[62]

ACT OF THANKSGIVING

58   At the celebration of Morning and Evening Prayer from the *Liturgy of the Hours*, thanksgiving is expressed by the use of the Canticle of Zechariah for Morning Prayer and the Canticle of Mary for Evening Prayer. When combined with the distribution of Holy Communion, the canticles are recited after the reception of Communion, as an Act of Thanksgiving.

59   At a celebration of a Liturgy of the Word, the Act of Thanksgiving is part of the communal response to the Word of God, and when Holy Communion is distributed it is an expression of gratitude when Holy Communion is received.

While no. 45 of the *Directory for Sunday Celebrations in the Absence of a Priest* provides several positions for the thanksgiving, the United States Conference of Catholic Bishops has determined that it should take place in the following manner:

In a Liturgy of the Word, after the Prayer of the Faithful, the leader of prayer invites all to an Act of Thanksgiving, in which the faithful praise the glory and mercy of God. This can be done by use of a psalm (for example, Psalms 100, 113, 118, 136, 147, 150), a hymn (for example, the *Gloria*), a canticle (for example, the Canticle of Mary), a litany, or a prayer. All stand, and the deacon or lay leader of prayer, facing in the same direction as the gathered assembly, leads the Act of Thanksgiving.

Additional texts for the Act of Thanksgiving in Word services are given in Appendix II. It should be noted that when a Liturgy of the Word is celebrated with Holy Communion, the Act of Thanksgiving takes place after Holy Communion is received.

In order to avoid all confusion between the Eucharistic prayer of the Mass and the prayer of thanksgiving used in these Sunday celebrations, these prayers of thanksgiving are not to take the form of a Eucharistic prayer or preface.[63]

COMMUNION RITE

60   The faithful are to be frequently reminded that even when they receive Holy Communion outside Mass they are united to the Eucharistic sacrifice, but the rite of reception of Holy Communion is not the same as participating in the sacrifice itself.[64] Communion may be received only under the form of bread, as the consecrated wine is not reserved except for the communion of the sick.[65]

61   Hosts consecrated at the last Mass celebrated in the place where the liturgical assembly gathers may be used. Before the Lord's Prayer, the deacon or lay

---

62. See ibid., no. 69.
63. See ibid., no. 45.
64. See *Directory*, no. 46.
65. See *HCWEOM*, no. 11.

leader of prayer goes to the place where the Blessed Sacrament is reserved, genuflects, takes the ciborium containing the body of the Lord, and places it on the altar.[66] The deacon or lay leader of prayer then returns to his or her chair and introduces the Lord's Prayer. After the Lord's Prayer, the deacon or lay leader of prayer goes to the altar for the invitation to Holy Communion.[67]

62   The Lord's Prayer is always recited or sung by all, even if there is to be no communion. After communion, "a period of silence may be observed or a psalm or song of praise may be sung."[68]

63   The deacon or lay leader of prayer reverently consumes the Body of Christ. Then the deacon or lay leader of prayer and other extraordinary ministers of Holy Communion, if needed, take a ciborium with the Eucharist and go to the communicants.

CONCLUDING RITE

64   Before the end of the celebration, announcements or notices relating to the life of the parish or the diocese are read.[69] The collection of monetary gifts of the liturgical assembly may also be done at this time.

65   The community is then invited to pray for vocations to the priesthood and exchange the sign of peace before being sent forth in mission to the world.

PREPARATIONS FOR THE SUNDAY CELEBRATION

66   The deacon or lay leader of prayer or some other person should see to the preparation of the church or place where the celebration will take place. The following preparations are made:

The *Lectionary* is placed on the ambo before the celebration.

The *Book of the Gospels* is prepared beforehand and placed on the altar. When Morning or Evening Prayer or a Liturgy of the Word is celebrated without the distribution of Holy Communion, lighted candles may be placed near the ambo.

The decorations of the church or place of celebration should be in accord with the liturgical season being celebrated.

When Holy Communion is given in a church or oratory, a corporal is to be placed on the altar, which is already covered with a white cloth. When Holy Communion is given in other places, a suitable table is to be prepared and covered with a white cloth. Lighted candles are placed on or near the altar or table.[70]

---

66. See ibid., no. 47.

67. Letter from the Congregation for Divine Worship and the Discipline of the Sacraments (24 April 1991), Prot. N. CD 6/90.

68. *HCWEOM*, no 37.

69. *Directory*, no. 49.

70. See *HCWEOM*, no. 19.

67   In preparing the celebration the pastor, together with the appointed Deacons and/or laypersons, should take due account in arranging the celebration according to the options given in the rite suited to the number of those who will take part in the celebration, the ability of the leader of prayer of the liturgical assembly and other ministers, and the kind of instruments available for the music.[71]

THE LITURGICAL YEAR

68   When planning music, art, and environment for Sunday celebrations the season and feasts of the liturgical year should shape choices.

69   When planning the liturgical space, care should be taken not to obscure the rich symbols of the altar, ambo, priest's chair, and baptismal font.

70   The Sunday readings may not be changed since they are an integral part of the celebration of the liturgical year which celebrates the mysteries of the Incarnation and Redemption. When baptism or marriage is celebrated within the context of the ritual, a reading from the rite of baptism or marriage may be used in accordance with the Introduction of each.

THE SEASON OF ADVENT

71   Advent begins the cycle of time known as the liturgical year. It is a season of hope and preparation. It begins with Evening Prayer I of the First Sunday of Advent and ends on December 24, before Evening Prayer I of Christmas.[72]

72   Advent has a two-fold character: as a season of remembrance that directs our mind and heart to await Christ's second coming at the end of time; and as a season to prepare for Christmas when Christ's first coming to us is remembered. It is not principally a penitential time but is considered a time of joyful expectation.[73]

73   Violet or purple is used in Advent. Rose may be used, when it is the practice, on *Gaudete* Sunday (Third Sunday of Advent).

74   The *Gloria* as an Act of Thanksgiving is not sung or recited during this season, except on solemnities or feasts.

THE SEASON OF CHRISTMAS

75   Next to the yearly celebration of the paschal mystery, the Church holds most sacred the memorial of Christ's birth and early manifestations. This is the purpose of the Christmas season.[74]

---

71. See *Directory*, no. 37.

72. See *Universal Norms on the Liturgical Year and the General Roman Calendar* (hereafter, *UNLY*), in the GIRM, no. 40.

73. See ibid., no. 39.

74. See ibid., no. 32.

76   The Christmas season begins with Evening Prayer I of Christmas and concludes with the feast of the Baptism of the Lord, which recalls the opening of Jesus' public mission and ministry to the world.[75]

77   The Sunday within the octave of Christmas is celebrated as the feast of the Holy Family.[76]

78   The octave of Christmas, January 1, is celebrated as the Solemnity of Mary, Mother of God.

79   Epiphany is celebrated on the Sunday between January 2 and January 8. Epiphany means manifestation, or the appearance of Jesus to the world. The proclamation of the date of Easter may follow the homily or preaching.

80   If the Christmas manger or Nativity scene is placed in the church, it must not be placed in the presbyterium.[77] It should not displace or overshadow the signs of the Lord's real presence in word, sacrament, liturgical assembly, and ministers. It may be blessed during the Vigil of Christmas or at another more suitable time, e.g., during a celebration of the Word of God or during a Service of Lessons and Carols.

81   The Office of Readings may be celebrated with the people as an extended Vigil of Christmas.

82   White is the color of the Christmas Season (although gold may also be used).[78]

THE SEASON OF LENT

83   Lent has a double character: baptismal and penitential. It is during this time that the catechumens and faithful are prepared to celebrate the paschal mystery.[79]

84   The season of Lent begins on Ash Wednesday and concludes before the Evening Mass of the Lord's Supper on Holy Thursday.[80]

85   The alleluia is not sung or said from the beginning of Lent until the Easter Vigil. It is replaced by other verses as acclamations before the Gospel.[81]

86   During Lent the altar should not be decorated with flowers. The *Gloria* is not sung or recited, and the music should reflect the sincere simplicity of the spirit of the season; the playing of the organ and musical instruments is allowed only to support the singing except for *Laetare* Sunday (Fourth Sunday), solemnities, and feasts.

---

75. See ibid., no. 33.
76. See ibid., no. 35.
77. See *BB*, nos. 1542–1544.
78. See *RS*, no 127.
79. See *SC*, no. 109.
80. See *UNLY*, no. 28.
81. See ibid.

87   Lent is the time of purification and enlightenment for the elect. The elect participate in several rituals during this season, marking significant moments in their journey toward baptism:

- The Rite of Sending Catechumens for Election and Candidates for recognition by the bishop is celebrated on the First Sunday of Lent.

- The scrutinies are celebrated on the Third, Fourth and Fifth Sundays of Lent.

88   Violet or purple is used during the Sundays of Lent. Rose may be used, when it is the practice, on *Laetare* Sunday (Fourth Sunday of Lent).

HOLY WEEK

89   Holy Week has as its purpose the remembrance of Christ's passion, beginning with his Messianic entrance into Jerusalem.[82]

PASSION SUNDAY (PALM SUNDAY)

90   The community may celebrate Christ's entry into Jerusalem to accomplish his paschal mystery by a procession or solemn entrance. The essence of the procession or solemn entrance is that the whole community join in the procession.

91   Red is used on Passion Sunday (Palm Sunday).

TRIDUUM

92   At the very heart of the liturgical year is the celebration of the Triduum. This is one single liturgy that unfolds over the course of three days. It is the solemn celebration of the suffering, death, and resurrection of the Lord Jesus.

93   It begins with the Mass of the Lord's Supper and reaches its high point in the Easter Vigil and culminates with Evening Prayer on Easter Sunday.

94   Diocesan bishops and pastors should encourage communities without a resident priest to join neighboring communities for these three days. Even though this presents difficulties, every effort must be made to respect the integrity of the Paschal Triduum. Therefore, smaller communities should assemble with a larger community to celebrate the Paschal Triduum.

95   Those physically unable to join the larger community are encouraged to gather as family, that is, the domestic Church, or in small faith communities and thus unite themselves in prayer to the universal church.

EASTER

96   The season of Easter is celebrated for fifty days, until the solemnity of Pentecost.

---

82. See ibid., no. 31.

97   On Easter Sunday the rite of the renewal of baptismal promises may be repeated after the homily or preaching. When appropriate, water blessed elsewhere at an Easter Vigil should be used in a sprinkling rite led by a deacon or lay person, following the renewal of baptismal promises. The creed is omitted.

98   When possible it is suggested that Evening Prayer be celebrated on Easter Sunday.

99   During the Easter Season, at the end of Night Prayer, and, customarily, in place of the *Angelus*, the *Regina Coeli* is sung or said. The paschal candle, a symbol of the presence of the risen Christ among the people of God, remains in the sanctuary near the altar or ambo from the Easter Vigil through Evening Prayer on Pentecost Sunday. Its use is encouraged at all liturgical celebrations. In those parishes and missions in which no Easter Vigil is celebrated, a paschal candle blessed at another Easter Vigil may be used.

100   White or gold is the color of the Easter season.[83]

ASCENSION

101   The Solemnity of the Ascension is celebrated on the fortieth day after Easter, but in many provinces of the United States the observance of this Solemnity has been transferred to the seventh Sunday of Easter. Clarification on this can be obtained from diocesan pastoral centers.

PENTECOST

102   The celebration of an extended Vigil on the eve of Pentecost is encouraged.

103   Red is the color for the solemnity of Pentecost.

ORDINARY TIME

104   In addition to the above seasons there are thirty-three or thirty-four weeks in the course of the year, which form the cycle known as "Ordinary Time."[84]

105   When a solemnity, or a feast of the Lord, or the Commemoration of All the Faithful Departed falls on a Sunday in Ordinary Time, these celebrations take precedence over the Sunday liturgy. The first Sunday after Pentecost is the solemnity of the Holy Trinity. The following Sunday is the solemnity of The Most Holy Body and Blood of Christ; and Friday of the following week is the solemnity of the Sacred Heart. The solemnity of Christ the King is celebrated on the last Sunday of Ordinary Time.

106   Ordinary Time enables the Church to appreciate more fully the ministry and message of Christ. The *Lectionary for Mass* provides a semi-continuous reading of the Synoptic Gospels on the Sundays of Ordinary Time in such a way

---

83. See *RS*, no. 127.
84. See *UNLY*, nos. 58–59.

that, as the Lord's life and preaching unfold, the teaching proper to these Gospels is presented.[85]

107   Although there are times when a solemnity falls on a Sunday, by its very nature, Sunday excludes the permanent assignment of any other celebrations to the day.[86]

108   Green is the color for Ordinary Time.

IMPORTANCE OF SINGING

109   Singing is a necessary and integral part of the liturgical celebration.[87] Sung prayer is another dimension of our faith expression.[88] Singing by the ministers and people should always be a part of the Sunday celebration and holy days of obligation.[89] The singing of the acclamations, responses, Psalmody, antiphons, songs, and hymnody are normative for the full, conscious, and active participation when the Church gathers for ritual prayer.[90]

110   For Sunday celebrations in the absence of a priest, hymns and acclamations accompany the ritual action. They include, in order of importance: the acclamation before the Gospel, a hymn, responsorial psalm, communion processional chant, the Lord's Prayer, and the Act of Thanksgiving. Other possibilities might include the response to the intercessions and a closing song or choral anthem of the day.

111   When the Liturgy of the Hours is celebrated the following are usually sung: the psalms and canticles with their antiphons, the hymn, the intercessions, and the Lord's Prayer. Furthermore, the selection of liturgical music is guided by the liturgical year and the *Lectionary*. Attention should be given to the numerous musical settings for the hymns, psalms, and canticles that are available.

THE LITURGICAL ACTION OF THE GATHERED ASSEMBLY

112   The Church encourages those gathered for worship to participate fully in the liturgical celebration. Music fosters this participation. Its function is "ministerial"; it must serve and never dominate thus reducing the liturgical assembly to mere silent spectators or listeners.[91]

113   In the planning and preparation of celebrations in the absence of a Priest, musicians and those who prepare the celebrations should follow the guidelines

---

85. See *Introduction to the Lectionary for Mass, Second Typical Edition*, Liturgy Documentary Series 1 (Washington, DC: USCCB, 1998), no. 105.
86. See *UNLY*, no. 6.
87. See *SC*, no. 112.
88. See *Sing to the Lord: Music in Divine Worship* (hereafter *SL*), Pastoral Liturgy Series 4 (Washington, DC: USCCB, 2008), no. 5.
89. See *GIRM*, no. 40.
90. See *SC*, no. 30.
91. See *SL*, no. 28, and *SC*, no. 48.

on the use of sacred music of *Musicam sacram, Music in Catholic Worship*, and *Liturgical Music Today*.[92]

114   The role of the musician as servant of the liturgical action is to facilitate the sung prayer of the gathered community. A full complement of music ministers including cantor, psalmist, instrumentalist, and choir is encouraged for the celebration.

115   By uniting our voices in sung prayer, regardless of the style of music, the choice of instruments, or the focus of celebration, we proclaim and share our faith so that Christ may grow among us all.[93]

116   The musical choices for these celebrations are guided by a threefold judgment: musical, liturgical, and pastoral.[94] Thus a careful review should be given to the text of hymns and songs used in the celebration. Texts, especially communion songs, often speak of the action of the Eucharist and the eating and drinking of both the body and blood of Christ. Texts of this nature should not be used in Sunday celebrations in the absence of a priest. Nonetheless, a song for the Communion Rite would ideally reflect the Eucharistic mystery of Christ's presence in the holy sacrament. Likewise, the pastoral judgment calls for sensitivity to the "age, culture, language, and education of a given liturgical assembly."[95]

SACRED SILENCE

117   Sacred silence is an important element of all good liturgical celebrations. It is to be observed at appropriate times; it is recommended that silence be observed in the church, in the sacristy, in the vesting room and in adjacent areas. The ministers of music, as well as the deacon or lay leader of prayer, are to model the sacred silence for the gathered community.

---

92. See Instruction *Musicam sacram*, On Music in the Liturgy (5 March 1967): AAS 60 (1967) 300–320; ibid., and *Liturgical Music Today* (Washington, DC: USCCB, 1982).
93. See *SL*, no. 5.
94. See *SL*, no. 126.
95. *SL*, no. 132.

DIRECTORY
FOR
SUNDAY CELEBRATIONS
IN THE
ABSENCE OF A PRIEST

SACRED CONGREGATION FOR DIVINE WORSHIP
JUNE 2, 1988

AN OVERVIEW OF THE *DIRECTORY FOR SUNDAY CELEBRATIONS IN THE ABSENCE OF A PRIEST*

Michael R. Prendergast

In response to a growing phenomenon of communities unable to celebrate the Sunday Eucharist, by the call of several conferences of bishops to the Holy See, and at the request of Pope John Paul II, the Sacred Congregation for Divine Worship published the *Directory for Sunday Celebrations in the Absence of a Priest* (DSCAP), in 1988. "The fundamental point of the entire *Directory* is to ensure, in the best way possible and in every situation, the Christian celebration of Sunday. This means remembering that the Mass remains the proper way of celebrating Sunday, but also means recognizing the presence of important elements even when Mass can not be celebrated."[1]

The *Directory* is divided into three major sections. The first section is devoted to a summary of the meaning of Sunday. This summary is rooted in article 106 of the *Constitution on the Sacred Liturgy* (CSL): "By a tradition handed down from the apostles which took its origin from the very day of Christ's resurrection, the Church celebrates the paschal mystery every eighth day; with good reason this, then, bears the name of the Lord's Day or Sunday."[2] The celebration of the Mass of Sunday, the Lord's Day, is central to the life of the Church and the life of the parish; it is the sacrament of unity that builds up the Body of Christ. The second section of the *Directory* lays out the conditions that are necessary for a local Church (diocese) to schedule celebrations in the absence of a priest and addresses the collaborative nature that is necessary between the laity and pastors. The third section of the *Directory* provides a description of the rite for Sunday celebrations of the Word and the Liturgy of the Hours with or without the distribution of Holy Communion. The entire *Directory* is only 50 articles in length.

The *Directory* recognizes the need for previously unforeseen pastoral arrangements to be made in order for the community to assemble on Sunday. The Roman document, in recognizing the importance of the Sunday assembly as essential to the continuing life of the Church, provides guidelines for the decisions that must be made in regard to such celebrations taking place. The *Directory* leaves the task of determining the criteria and procedures of these celebrations to the bishop of each diocese. The *Directory* is not intended "to encourage, much less facilitate unnecessary or contrived Sunday assemblies without the celebration of the eucharist. The intent rather is simply to guide and to prescribe what should be done when real circumstances require the decision to have a Sunday celebration in the absence of a priest."[3]

---

1. Sacred Congregation for Divine Worship, Prot. 691/86.
2. *Directory for Sunday Celebrations in the Absence of a Priest* (DSCAP), 8; quoting the *Constitution on the Sacred Liturgy* (CSL), 106.
3. Sacred Congregation for Divine Worship, Prot. 691/86.

For a number of reasons (such as the unavailability of a priest) there will be occasions when the celebration of the Eucharist will not be possible. On such occasions, in order to maintain the vitality of parishioners' faith and strengthen their parish life, the diocesan bishop, together with his priests and deacons, must find ways to help the faithful gather for Sunday celebration.

The directory affirms the following values:

1) the preservation of the Christian tradition of Sunday, the Lord's Day;
2) the celebration of the Eucharist as the central, constitutive element in the life of the Church;
3) the differences between the celebration of the Eucharist and the Sunday celebration in the absence of a priest;
4) the importance of the weekly local gathering of the faithful;
5) the affirmation of the priesthood of the faithful and lay ministries;
6) the presence of the Lord when the community gathers;
7) the presence of the Lord when his Word is proclaimed and preached;
8) the urgency of fostering and praying for vocations to the priesthood.

The document names the reality of a lack of priests;[4] upholds the role of catechists;[5] encourages families or small groups to gather on Sunday;[6] acknowledges the challenges in mission territories;[7] and gives the responsibility of each conference of bishops to create norms, adapted to the culture and conditions of their people when the local Church gathers in the absence of a priest.[8]

In chapter 1, the *Directory* upholds the principal requisites for the Sunday assembly of the faithful: The people of God in their organic structure manifest the Church, "presided over by a priest, who acts in the person of Christ."[9] At the center of the Church is the Paschal Mystery proclaimed through Scripture and broken open by the priest or deacon.[10] At the heart of the gathered Church is the celebrations of sacrifice of the Mass, where the Paschal Mystery is expressed and is offered by the priest "in the name of the entire Christian people."[11] The *Directory* speaks to the Lord's Day as "a sign of the divine transcendence over all human works, and not simply a day off from work."[12] It speaks of Sunday as a day that is to "stand out in today's culture as a sign of freedom and consequently a day established for the well-being of the human person."[13]

Chapter 2 of the *Directory* first encourages the faithful to attend the celebration of the Eucharist "in a place nearby."[14] The *Directory* uphold the primacy of the celebration of the Word of God saying that celebrations in the absence

---

4. See DSCAP, 2.
5. See ibid., 3.
6. See ibid., 4.
7. See ibid., 6.
8. See ibid., 7.
9. Ibid., 12, a.
10. Ibid., 12, b.
11. Ibid., 12, c.
12. Ibid., 14.
13. Ibid., 16.
14. Ibid., 18.

of a priest may "be combined with the celebration of one or more of the sacraments and especially of the sacramentals."[15] The *Directory* takes great care to ensure that adequate catechesis be provided about the nature of this type of liturgical assembly. It also tells us these celebrations are not to be held for "mere convenience"[16] on Sundays where Mass has already been celebrated, or in place of the Vigil Mass of Saturday, "even if the Mass is celebrated in a different language."[17] It finally states that no more than one celebration in the absence of priest be held on a Sunday.

The *Directory* speaks to the role of the bishop, the pastor, deacons, and laypersons who exercise their office "in the absence of ministers."[18] Citing the *Constitution on the Sacred Liturgy* laypersons are reminded in the *Directory* that they "should do all of, but only, those parts which pertain to . . . [their] office."[19] Finally this chapter upholds the tradition of the domestic Church at prayer,[20] the call to celebrate the Liturgy of the Hours,[21] and the role of the Holy Spirit whose power calls us to "enter into communion with Christ and with the Church, his living body."[22]

Chapter 3 speaks of the order of the celebration. The *Directory* cautions that nothing proper to the celebration of the Mass "is to be inserted in the celebration" especially "the presentation of the gifts and the eucharistic prayer."[23] The readings from the *Lectionary for Mass* (LM) are to be used,[24] and the leaders of prayers are referred to as "animators."[25] The deacon's role is explained, and deacons are reminded that they use "a chair other than the priest's as a symbol that the community awaits the presence of a priest."[26] Three full articles are devoted to the role of the lay leader whom the *Directory* says "acts as one among equals"[27] and reminds the lay leader that they do not "use words that are proper to a priest or deacon."[28] Finally, the *Directory* explains that the leader of prayer "wears vesture that is suitable for his or her function or the vesture prescribed by the bishop."[29] Like the deacon, the lay leader does not sit in the presidential chair, and the chair that they do use is to be placed "outside the sanctuary."[30] The *Directory* then lists an outline of the elements of the celebration:

- Introductory Rites
- Liturgy of the Word

---

15. Ibid., 20.
16. Ibid., 21.
17. Ibid., 21.
18. Ibid., 31, quoting the *Code of Canon Law* (CIC), § 3. See also SCAP, 27–31.
19. Ibid., 31, quoting CSL, 28.
20. See ibid., 32.
21. See ibid., 33.
22. Ibid., 34; quoting the *General Instruction of the Liturgy of the Hours*, 258.
23. Ibid., 35.
24. See ibid., 36.
25. Ibid., 37.
26. Ibid., 38.
27. Ibid., 39; see also 37 and 40.
28. Ibid.
29. Ibid., 40.
30. Ibid.

- Thanksgiving
- Communion Rite
- Concluding Rites[31]

It should be noted that this order of celebration has been slightly altered with the 2007 edition of SCAP.[32] The Act of Thanksgiving no longer follows the Liturgy of the Word, but rather the Communion Rite. The *Directory* offers expanded notes on each of these sections of the outline of the celebration. Some highlights include the role of the lay leader and preaching (because the Homily is reserved to a priest or deacon, the *Directory* suggests that the leader of prayer read the Homily prepared by the priest or deacon), but leaves this matter to be considered by the "conference of bishops."[33] The Prayer of the Faithful (the Universal Prayer) should include "intentions for vocations to sacred orders."[34] When the faithful receive Communion outside of Mass they are to be reminded that they are "united to the eucharistic sacrifice"[35] and that the Lord's Prayer is recited or sung by all "even if there is to be no Communion."[36] The Concluding Rites include a Sign of Peace, the collection, announcements, and a final blessing.[37]

The *Directory* concludes with a quote from an address to French bishops by Pope John Paul II given on the occasion of their *ad limina* visit in 1987:

> All Christians must share the conviction that they cannot live their faith or participate—in the manner proper to them—in the universal mission of the Church unless they are nourished by the eucharistic bread. They should be equally convinced that the Sunday assembly is a sign to the world of the mystery of communion, which is the eucharist.[38]

Let us continue to pray for an increase to vocations, so that all may be fed at the Eucharistic table.

---

31. See ibid., 41, a-e.
32. In 2012 the USCCB issued a revised ritual text which corresponds to the English translation of the third edition of *The Roman Missal*.
33. Ibid., 43.
34. Ibid., 44.
35. Ibid., 46.
36. Ibid., 48.
37. See ibid., 48–49.
38. Ibid., 50.

OUTLINE

DIRECTORY FOR SUNDAY CELEBRATIONS IN THE ABSENCE OF A PRIEST

PREFACE

1   From the day of Pentecost, after the coming of the Holy Spirit, the Church of Christ has always faithfully come together to celebrate the paschal mystery on the day called "the Lord's Day" in memory of the Lord's resurrection. In the Sunday assembly the Church reads in all the Scriptures those things that concern Christ[1] and celebrates the eucharist as the memorial of the death and resurrection of the Lord until he comes.

2   But a complete celebration of the Lord's Day is not always possible. There have been and still are many of the faithful for whom "because of the lack of a priest or some other serious reason, participation in the eucharistic celebration is not possible."[2]

3   In some regions, after their first evangelization, the bishops have put catechists in charge of gathering the faithful together on Sunday and, in the form of a devotional exercise, of leading them in prayer. In such cases the number of Christians grew and they were scattered in so many and such widely separated places that a priest could not reach them every Sunday.

4   In other places the faithful were completely blocked from gathering on Sunday, either because of the persecution of Christians or because of other severe restrictions of religious freedom. Like the Christians of old, who held fast to the Sunday assembly even in the face of martyrdom,[3] the faithful today, even when deprived of the presence of an ordained minister, also strive to gather on Sunday for prayer either within a family or in small groups.

5   On other grounds today, namely, the scarcity of priests, in many places not every parish can have its own eucharistic celebration each Sunday. Further, for various social and economic reasons some parishes have many fewer members. As a consequence many priests are assigned to celebrate Mass several times on Sunday in many, widely scattered churches. But this practice is regarded as not always satisfactory either to the parishes lacking their own pastor or to the priests involved.

---

1. See Luke 24:17.
2. *Codex Iuris Canonici*, 1983 (hereafter, CIC), can. 1248 §2.
3. See *Acta Martyrum Bytiniae*, in D. Ruiz Bueno, *Acttas de los Martires*, Biblioteca de Autores Cristianos (hereafter, BAC) 75 (Madrid, 1951), 973.

6   In some local Churches, then, because of the conditions indicated, the bishops have judged it necessary to arrange for other Sunday celebrations in the absence of a priest, so that in the best way possible the weekly gathering of the faithful can be continued and the Christian tradition regarding Sunday preserved.

It is by no means unusual, particularly in mission territories, for the faithful themselves, aware of the importance of the Lord's Day and with the help of catechists and religious, to gather to listen to the word of God, to pray, and, in some cases, even to receive Holy Communion.

7   The Congregation for Divine Worship has considered these matters, reviewed the documents already published by the Holy See,[4] and acceded to the wishes of the conferences of bishops. Therefore the Congregation regards it as opportune to recall elements of the teaching on the meaning of Sunday, to lay down the conditions for the lawfulness of such celebrations in dioceses, and to provide guidelines for carrying out such celebrations correctly.

It will be the responsibility of the conferences of bishops, as circumstances suggest, to determine these norms in greater detail, to adapt them to the culture and conditions of their people, and to report their decisions to the Apostolic See.

CHAPTER I
SUNDAY AND ITS OBSERVANCE

8   "By a tradition handed down from the apostles which took its origin from the very day of Christ's resurrection, the Church celebrates the paschal mystery every eighth day; with good reason this, then, bears the name of the Lord's Day or Sunday."[5]

9   Evidence of the gathering of the faithful on the day which the New Testament itself already designates as the Lord's Day[6] appears explicitly in documents of the first and second centuries.[7] Outstanding among such evidence is the testimony of Saint Justin: "On this day which is called Sunday, all who live in the cities or in the country gather together in one place."[8] But the day of gathering for Christians did not coincide with the day of rest in the Greek or Roman calendar and therefore even the gathering on this day was a sign to fellow citizens of the Christians' identity.

---

4. See SC Rites, Instruction *Inter Oecumenici* (26 September 1964), no. 37: *Acta Apostolicae Sedis* (hereafter; AAS) 56 (1964) 884–885: in Daughters of St. Paul, *The Sixteen Documents of Vatican II and the Instruction on the Liturgy* (Boston: St. Paul Editions, 1966), 72. See also CIC, can. 1248 §2.

5. Vatican Council II, Constitution on the Liturgy *Sacrosanctum Concilium* (hereafter, SC), no. 106, http://www.vatican.va/archive/hist_councils/ii_vatican_council/documents/vat-ii _const_19631204_sacrosanctum-concilium_en.html. See also Appendix, Declaration of the Second Vatican Ecumenical Council on Revision of the Calendar, no. 2, in Daughters of St. Paul, p. 56.

6. See Revelation 1:10. See also John 20:19, 26, Acts 20:7–12, 1 Corinthians 16:2, Hebrews 10:24–25.

7. See *Didache* 14, 1: F.X. Funk, ed., *Doctrina duodecim Apostolorum* (1887), 42.

8. St. Justin, *Apologia* I, 67: PG 6, 430.

10   From the earliest centuries pastors had never failed to counsel their people on the need to gather together on Sunday. "Because you are Christ's members, do not scatter from the church by not coming together . . . do not neglect your Savior or separate him from his members. Do not shatter or scatter the Body of Christ. . . . "[9] Vatican Council II recalled this teaching in the following words: "For on this day Christ's faithful should come together into one place so that, by hearing the word of God and taking part in the Eucharist, they may call to mind the passion, the resurrection, and the glorification of the Lord Jesus, and may thank God who 'has begotten them again, through the resurrection of Jesus Christ from the dead, unto a living hope'" (1 Peter 1:3).[10]

11   Saint Ignatius of Antioch pointed out the importance of the Sunday celebration for the life of the faithful: "Christians no longer observe the sabbath day, but live according to the Lord's Day, on which our life was restored through Jesus Christ and his death."[11]

In their "sense of the faith" *(sensus fidelium)* the faithful, now as in the past, have held the Lord's Day in such high regard that they have never willingly omitted its observance even in times of persecution or in the midst of cultures alien or hostile to the Christian faith.

12   The following are the principal requisites for the Sunday assembly of the faithful:

a.   the gathering of the faithful to manifest the Church, not simply on their own initiative but as called together by God, that is, as the people of God in their organic structure, presided over by a priest, who acts in the person of Christ;

b.   their instruction in the paschal mystery through the Scriptures that are proclaimed and that are explained by a priest or deacon;

c.   the celebration of the eucharistic sacrifice, by which the paschal mystery is expressed, and which is carried out by the priest in the person of Christ and offered in the name of the entire Christian people.

13   Pastoral efforts should have this aim above all that the sacrifice of the Mass on Sunday be regarded as the only true actualization of the Lord's paschal mystery[12] and as the most complete manifestation of the Church: "Hence the Lord's day is the original feast day, and it should be proposed to the piety of the faithful and taught to them. . . . Other celebrations, unless they be truly of greatest

---

9. *Didascalia Apostolorum* 2, 59, 1–3: F.X. Funk, ed., *Didascalia et Constitutiones Apostolorum* (1905), vol. 1, p. 170.

10. SC, no. 106.

11. St. Ignatius of Antioch, *Ad Magnesios* 9, 1: EX. Funk, ed., *Didascalia et Constitutiones Apostolorum* (1905), vol. 1, p. 199.

12. See Paul VI, Address to bishops of Central France (26 March 1977): MS 69 (1977) 465: "Furthermore, the goal should always be to have the sacrifice of the Mass celebrated since this is the only authentic actualization of the Lord's paschal mystery" (tr., *The Pope Speaks* 22:2 [1977]: 134).

importance, shall not have precedence over the Sunday which is the foundation and kernel of the whole liturgical year."[13]

14   Such principles should be set before the faithful and instilled in them right from the beginning of their Christian formation, in order that they may willingly fulfill the precept to keep this day holy and may understand why they are brought together for the celebration of the eucharist by the call of the Church[14] and not simply by their personal devotion. In this way the faithful will be led to experience the Lord's Day as a sign of the divine transcendence over all human works, and not simply a day off from work; in virtue of the Sunday assembly they will more deeply perceive themselves to be members of the Church and will show this outwardly.

15   In the Sunday assembly, as also in the life of the Christian community, the faithful should find both active participation and a true spirit of community, as well as the opportunity to be renewed spiritually under the guidance of the Holy Spirit. In this way, too, they will be protected against the attractions of sects that promise relief from the pain of loneliness and a more complete fulfillment of religious aspirations.

16   Finally, pastoral effort should concentrate on measures which have as their purpose "that it may become in fact a day of joy and freedom from work."[15] In this way Sunday will stand out in today's culture as a sign of freedom and consequently as a day established for the well-being of the human person, which clearly is a higher value than commerce or industrial production.[16]

17   The word of God, the eucharist, and the ministry of the priest are gifts that the Lord presents to the Church, his Bride, and they are to be received and to be prayed for as divine graces. The Church, which possesses these gifts above all in the Sunday assembly, thanks God for them in that same assembly and awaits the joy of complete rest in the day of the Lord "before the throne of God and before the Lamb."[17]

CHAPTER II
CONDITIONS FOR HOLDING SUNDAY CELEBRATIONS IN THE ABSENCE OF A PRIEST

18   Whenever and wherever Mass cannot be celebrated on Sunday, the first thing to be ascertained is whether the faithful can go to a church in a place nearby to participate there in the eucharistic mystery. At the present time this solution is to be recommended and to be retained where it is in effect; but it

---

13. SC, no. 106.

14. See SC Rites, Instruction *Eucharisticum mysterium* (25 May 1967), no. 25: AAS 59 (1967) 555; *Furrow* 18 (July 1967): 384–418.

15. SC, no. 106.

16. See "Le sens du dimanche dans une societé pluralists Reflexions pastorals de la Conference des eveques du Canada," *La Documentation Catholique*, no. 1935 (1987), pp. 273–276.

17. Revelation 7:9.

demands that the faithful, rightly imbued with a fuller understanding of the Sunday assembly, respond with good will to a new situation.

19   The aim is that the riches of Sacred Scripture and of the Church's prayer be amply provided to the faithful gathered on Sundays in various ways even apart from Mass. For the faithful should not be deprived of the readings that are read at Mass in the course of a year, nor of the prayers of the liturgical seasons.

20   Among the forms of celebration found in liturgical tradition when Mass is not possible, a celebration of the word of God is particularly recommended,[18] and also its completion, when possible, by eucharistic Communion. In this way the faithful can be nourished by both the word of God and the Body of Christ. "By hearing it they learn that the marvels it proclaims reach their climax in the paschal mystery of which the Mass is a sacramental memorial and in which they share by communion."[19] Further, in certain circumstances the Sunday celebration can be combined with the celebration of one or more of the sacraments and especially of the sacramentals and in ways that are suited to the needs of each community.

21   It is imperative that the faithful be taught to see the substitutional character of these celebrations, which should not be regarded as the optimal solution to new difficulties nor as a surrender to mere convenience.[20] Therefore a gathering or liturgical assembly of this kind can never be held on a Sunday in places where Mass has already been celebrated or is to be celebrated or was celebrated on the preceding Saturday evening, even if the Mass is celebrated in a different language. Nor is it right to have more than one liturgical assembly of this kind on any given Sunday. Because of the celebration of Sunday, as the Lord's Day, this liturgical assembly should take place on Sunday.

22   Any confusion between this kind of assembly and a eucharistic celebration must be carefully avoided. Assemblies of this kind should not take away but rather increase the desire of the faithful to take part in the celebration of the eucharist, and should make them more eager to be present at the celebration of the eucharist.

23   The faithful are to understand that the eucharistic sacrifice cannot take place without a priest and that the eucharistic Communion which they may receive in this kind of assembly is closely connected with the sacrifice of the Mass. On that basis the faithful can be shown how necessary it is to pray that God will "give the Church more priests and keep them faithful in their love and service."[21]

---

18. See SC, no. 35, 4.

19. The Roman Ritual. *Holy Communion and Worship of the Eucharist Outside Mass* (hereafter, *HCWEOM*) (Washington, DC: USCCB, 1976), no. 26.

20. See Paul VI, Address to bishops of Central France (26 March 1977): AAS 69 (1977): "Our judgment is that you should proceed along this line but with discernment and without multiplying this kind of assembly as though it were the best solution and the last chance" (tr., *The Pope Speaks* 22:2 [1977]: 134).

21. *The Roman Missal*, Masses and Prayers for Various Needs and Occasions, 1. For the Church, and 9. For Priestly Vocations, prayer over the gifts.

24   It belongs to the diocesan bishop, after hearing the council of priests, to decide whether Sunday assemblies without the celebration of the eucharist should be held on a regular basis in his diocese. It belongs also to the bishop, after considering the place and persons involved, to set out both general and particular norms for such celebrations. These assemblies are therefore to be conducted only in virtue of their convocation by the bishop and only under the pastoral ministry of the pastor.

25   "No Christian community, however, is built up unless it has its basis and center in the celebration of the most Holy Eucharist."[22] Therefore before the bishop decides on having Sunday assemblies without celebration of the eucharist, the following in addition to the status of parishes (see no. 5) should be considered: the possibility of recourse to priests, even religious priests, who are not directly assigned to the care of souls and the frequency of Masses in the various parishes and churches.[23] The preeminence of the celebration of the eucharist, particularly on Sunday, over other pastoral activities is to be respected.

26   Either personally or through his representatives the bishop will, by an appropriate catechesis, instruct the diocesan community on the causes requiring provision of these celebrations, pointing out the seriousness of the issue and urging the community's support and cooperation. The bishop is to appoint a delegate or a special committee to see to it that these people receive the necessary instruction. But the bishop's concern is always to be that several times a year the faithful involved have the opportunity to participate in the celebration of the eucharist.

27   It is the duty of the pastor to inform the bishop about the opportuneness of such celebrations in his territory, to prepare the faithful for them, to visit them during the week, and at a convenient time to celebrate the sacraments for them, particularly the sacrament of penance. In this way the communities involved will come to realize that their assembly on Sunday is not an assembly "without a priest," but an assembly "in the absence of a priest," or, better still, an assembly "in expectation of a priest."

28   When Mass cannot be celebrated, the pastor is to ensure that Holy Communion be given. He is also to see to it that there is a celebration of the eucharist in due time in each community. The consecrated hosts are to be renewed often and kept in a safe place.

29   As the primary assistants of priests, deacons are called in a special way to lead these Sunday assemblies. Since the deacon has been ordained for the nurture and increase of the people of God, it belongs to him to lead the prayers, to proclaim the gospel, to preach the homily, and to give Holy Communion.[24]

---

22. Vatican Council II, Decree on the Ministry and Life of *Priests Presbyterorum ordinis*, no. 6, http:// www.vatican.va/archive/hist_ councils/ii_ vatican_council/documents/vat-ii_decree _19651207_presbyterorum-ordinis_en.html.

23. See SC Rites, Instruction *Eucharisticum mysterium* (25 May 1967), no. 26: AAS 59 (1967) 555: *Furrow* 18 (July 1967): 384–418.

24. See Paul VI, Motu proprio *Ad pascendum* (15 August 1972), no. 1: AAS 64 (1972) 534: *The Pope Speaks* 17:3 (1972): 234–235.

30   In the absence of both a priest and a deacon, the pastor is to appoint lay-persons, who are to be entrusted with the care of these celebrations, namely, with leading the prayers, with the ministry of the Word, and with giving Holy Communion.

Those to be chosen first by the pastor are readers and acolytes who have been duly instituted for the service of the altar and of the word of God. If there are no such instituted ministers available, other laypersons, both men and women, may be appointed; they can carry out this responsibility in virtue of their baptism and confirmation.[25] Such persons are to be chosen in view of the consistency of their way of life with the Gospel and in the expectation of their being acceptable to the community of the faithful. Appointment is usually to be for a definite time and is to be made known publicly to the community. It is fitting that there be a celebration in which prayers are offered to God on behalf of those appointed.[26]

The pastor is to see to the suitable and continuous instruction of these laypersons and to prepare with them worthy celebrations (see Chapter III).

31   The laypersons appointed should regard the office entrusted to them not so much as an honor but as a responsibility and above all as a service to their brothers and sisters under the authority of the pastor. For theirs is not a proper office but a suppletory office, since they exercise it "where the need of the Church suggests in the absence of ministers."[27]

Those who are appointed to such an office "should do all of, but only, those parts which pertain to his office by the nature of the rite and the principles of liturgy."[28] They should carry out their office with sincere devotion and the decorum demanded by such a responsibility and rightly expected of them by God's people.[29]

32   When on a Sunday a celebration of the word of God along with the giving of Holy Communion is not possible, the faithful are strongly urged to devote themselves to prayer "for a suitable time either individually or with the family or, if possible, with a group of families."[30] In these circumstances the telecast of liturgical services can provide useful assistance.

33   Particularly to be kept in mind is the possibility of celebrating some part of the *Liturgy of the Hours*, for example, morning prayer or evening prayer, during which the Sunday readings of the current year can be inserted. For "when the people are invited to the *Liturgy of the Hours* and come together in unity of heart and voice, they show forth the Church in its celebration of the mystery of Christ."[31] At the end of such a celebration Holy Communion may be given (see no. 46).

---

25. See CIC, can. 230 §3.

26. See The Roman Ritual, *Book of Blessings* (hereafter, *BB*), ch. 4, I, B.

27. CIC, can. 230 §3.

28. SC, no. 28.

29. See SC, no. 29.

30. CIC, can. 1248 §2.

31. *General Instruction of the Liturgy of the Hours* (hereafter, GILH), Liturgy Documentary Series 5 (Washington, DC: USCCB, 1983), no. 22.

34   "The grace of the Redeemer is not lacking for individual members of the faithful or entire communities that, because of persecution or a lack of priests, are deprived of celebration of the eucharist for a short time or even for a long period. They can be moved by a deep desire for the sacrament and be united in prayer with the whole Church. Then when they call upon the Lord and raise their minds and hearts to him, through the power of the Holy Spirit they enter into communion with Christ and with the Church, his living body . . . and therefore they receive the fruits of the eucharist."[32]

CHAPTER III
ORDER OF CELEBRATION

35   The order to be followed in a Sunday celebration that does not include Mass consists of two parts, the celebration of the word of God and the giving of Holy Communion. Nothing that is proper to Mass, and particularly the presentation of the gifts and the eucharistic prayer, is to be inserted into the celebration. The order of celebration is to be arranged in such a way that it is truly conducive to prayer and conveys the image not of a simple meeting but of a genuine liturgical assembly.

36   As a rule the texts for the prayers and readings for each Sunday or solemnity are to be taken from *The Roman Missal* and the *Lectionary for Mass*. In this way the faithful will follow the cycle of the liturgical year and will pray and listen to the word of God in communion with the other communities of the Church.

37   In preparing the celebration the pastor together with the appointed laypersons may make adaptations suited to the number of those who will take part in the celebration, the ability of the leaders of prayer (animators), and the kind of instruments available for the music and the singing.

38   When a deacon presides at the celebration, he acts in accord with his ministry in regard to the greetings, the prayers, the gospel reading and homily, the giving of Holy Communion, and the dismissal and blessing. He wears the vestments proper to his ministry, that is, the alb with stole, and, as circumstances suggest, the dalmatic. He uses a chair other than the priest's as a symbol that the community awaits the presence of a priest.

39   A layperson who leads the assembly acts as one among equals, in the way followed in the liturgy of the hours when not presided over by an ordained minister, and in the case of blessings when the minister is a layperson ("May the Lord bless us . . ."; "Let us praise the Lord . . ."). The layperson is not to use words that are proper to a priest or deacon and is to omit rites that are too readily associated with the Mass, for example, greetings—especially "The Lord be with you"—and dismissals, since these might give the impression that the layperson is a sacred minister.[33]

---

32. Congregation for the Doctrine of the Faith, *Epistle . . . on certain questions regarding the minister of the eucharist* (6 August 1983): MS 75 (1983) 1007.
33. See *GILH*, no. 258; see also *BB*, nos. 48, 119, 130, 181.

40   The lay leader wears vesture that is suitable for his or her function or the vesture prescribed by the bishop.[34] He or she does not use the priest's chair, but another chair prepared outside the sanctuary.[35] Since the altar is the table of sacrifice and of the paschal banquet, its only use in this celebration is for the rite of Communion, when the consecrated bread is placed on it before Holy Communion is given.

Preparation of the celebration should include careful attention to a suitable distribution of offices, for example, for the readings, the singing, etc., and also to the arrangement and decoration of the place of celebration.

41   The following is an outline of the elements of the celebration.

a.   Introductory rites. The purpose of these is to form the gathered faithful into a community and for them to dispose themselves for the celebration.

b.   Liturgy of the word. Here God speaks to his people, to disclose to them the mystery of redemption and salvation; the people respond through the profession of faith and the Prayer of the Faithful.

c.   Thanksgiving. Here God is blessed for his great glory (see no. 45).

d.   Communion rites. These are an expression and accomplishment of communion with Christ and with his members, especially with those who on this same day take part in the eucharistic sacrifice.

e.   Concluding rites. These point to the connection existing between the liturgy and the Christian life.

The conference of bishops, or the individual bishop himself, may, in view of the conditions of the place and the people involved, determine more precisely the details of the celebration, using resources prepared by the national or diocesan liturgical committee, but the general structure of the celebration should not be changed unnecessarily.

42   In the introduction at the beginning of the celebration, or at some other point, the leader of prayer should make mention of the community of the faithful with whom the pastor is celebrating the eucharist on that Sunday and urge the assembly to unite itself in spirit with that community.

43   In order that the participants may retain the word of God, there should be an explanation of the readings or a period of silence for reflection on what has been heard. Since only a pastor or a deacon may give a homily,[36] it is desirable that the pastor prepare a homily and give it to the leader of prayer of the assembly to read. But in this matter the decisions of the conference of bishops are to be followed.

---

34. See *HCWEOM*, no. 20.
35. See *GILH*, no. 258.
36. See CIC, cann. 766–767.

44   The Prayer of the Faithful is to follow an established series of intentions.[37]

Intentions for the whole diocese that the bishop may have proposed are not to be omitted. There should also often be intentions for vocations to sacred orders, for the bishop, and for the pastor.

45   The thanksgiving may follow either one of the ways described here.

After the Prayer of the Faithful or after Holy Communion, the leader of prayer invites all to an act of thanksgiving, in which the faithful praise the glory and mercy of God. This can be done by use of psalm (for example, Psalms 100, 113, 118, 136, 147, 150), a hymn (for example, the Gloria), a canticle (for example, the Canticle of Mary), or a litanic prayer, together recite the thanksgiving.

1.   Before the Lord's Prayer, the leader of prayer of the assembly goes to the tabernacle or other place where the eucharist is reserved and, after making reverence, places the ciborium with the holy eucharist on the altar. Then while kneeling before the altar he or she together with all the faithful sing or recite a hymn, psalm, or litany, which in this case is directed to Christ in the eucharist.

2.   But this thanksgiving is not in any way to take the form of the eucharistic prayer, the texts of the prefaces or eucharistic prayers from *The Roman Missal* are not to be used, and all danger of confusion is to be removed.

46   For the Communion rite the provisions given in *The Roman Ritual* for distributing Holy Communion outside Mass are to be observed.[38] The faithful are to be frequently reminded that even when they receive communion outside Mass they are united to the eucharistic sacrifice.

47   For communion, if at all possible, bread consecrated that same Sunday in a Mass celebrated elsewhere is used; a deacon or layperson brings it in a ciborium or pyx and places it in the tabernacle before the celebration. Bread consecrated at the last Mass celebrated in the place of assembly may also be used. Before the Lord's Prayer the leader of prayer goes to the tabernacle or place where the eucharist is reserved, takes the vessel with the body of the Lord, and places it upon the altar, then introduces the Lord's Prayer—unless the act of thanksgiving mentioned in no. 45.2 is to take place at this point.

48   The Lord's Prayer is always recited or sung by all, even if there is to be no communion. The sign of peace may be exchanged. After communion, "a period of silence may be observed or a psalm or song of praise may be sung."[39] A thanksgiving as described in no. 45.1 may also take place here.

49   Before the conclusion of the assembly, announcements or notices related to the life of the parish or the diocese are read.

---

37. See *General Instruction of the Roman Missal* (hereafter, *GIRM*), Liturgy Documentary Series 2 (Washington, DC: USCCB, 2003), nos. 45–47.

38. See HCWEOM, ch. 1.

39. Ibid., no. 37.

50   "Too much importance can never be attached to the Sunday assembly, whether as the source of the Christian life of the individual and of the community, or as a sign of God's intent to gather the whole human race together in Christ.

"All Christians must share the conviction that they cannot live their faith or participate—in the manner proper to them—in the universal mission of the Church unless they are nourished by the eucharistic bread. They should be equally convinced that the Sunday assembly is a sign to the world of the mystery of communion, which is the eucharist."[40]

On 21 May 1988 this Directory, prepared by the Congregation for Divine Worship, was approved and confirmed by Pope John Paul II, who also ordered its publication.

Office of the Congregation for Divine Worship, Solemnity of the Body and Blood of Christ, 2 June 1988.

Paul Augustin Cardinal Mayer, OSB
Prefect

Virgilio Noé
Titular Archbishop of Voncaria
Secretary

---

40. John Paul II, Address to the bishops of France on the occasion of their *ad limina* visit (27 March 1987).

GATHERED IN
STEADFAST FAITH:
STATEMENT OF
THE BISHOPS' COMMITTEE
ON THE LITURGY ON SUNDAY WORSHIP
IN THE ABSENCE OF A PRIEST

APPROVED BY THE NATIONAL CONFERENCE OF CATHOLIC BISHOPS
ADMINISTRATIVE COMMITTEE
MARCH 20, 1990

AN OVERVIEW OF *GATHERED IN STEADFAST FAITH: STATEMENT OF THE BISHOPS' COMMITTEE ON THE LITURGY ON SUNDAY CELEBRATIONS IN THE ABSENCE OF A PRIEST*

Michael R. Prendergast

Gathered in Steadfast Faith is the 1990 statement of the Bishops' Committee on the Liturgy (now the Bishops' Committee on Divine Worship) on Sunday worship in the absence of a priest. The 1983 *Code of Canon Law*, articulating the tradition of the Church, states that the faithful are obliged to participate in the Mass on Sundays,[1] while it also states that if it is impossible for the faithful to participate in the Mass due to the lack of a minister, or for some other grave cause, the obligation to participate in Mass no longer exists. However, if a Catholic can easily participate at Mass in another parish without great inconvenience, one is obliged to do so. Yet, if this is not possible, it is highly recommended that the faithful participate at the Liturgy of the Word if it is celebrated in the parish church.[2] Thus, when Mass is not possible and a parish offers a Liturgy of the Word, and with, when possible, the distribution of Holy Communion, the *Code* allows Catholics to follow the Church's recommendation to sanctify Sunday in some other way.

Gathered in Steadfast Faith was prepared in response to the *Directory for Sunday Celebrations in the Absence of a Priest*, issued by the Congregation for Divine Worship on June 2, 1988. The statement is "meant to assist diocesan bishops, who are faced with the unavoidable reality of Sunday assemblies deprived of the celebration of Mass."[3] Bishops of the United States issued the statement as a response to a present need in the Church while calling to mind the prayer of the Good Shepherd, "Ask the master of the harvest to send out laborers for his harvest."[4] Nearly 20 percent of Catholic parishes in the United States are without a resident priest, and so the shortage of priests to serve full-time is an ever growing concern.

INTRODUCTION

The introductory articles to *Gathered in Steadfast Faith* place the current reality of the priest shortage in the context of the beginning of the Catholic Church in North America where "priests found it necessary to divide their presence among a circuit of fledgling parishes."[5] The phenomena of fewer priests is a call for both "new approaches in the discernment and nurturing of vocations to the

---

1. See *Code of Canon Law*, 1247.
2. See ibid, 1248 § 2.
3. *Gathered in Steadfast Faith* (GSF), 9.
4. Ibid., quoting Matthew 9:38 and Luke 10:2.
5. Ibid., 1.

priesthood" and "reflection upon the mystery of the Church and the role of all the baptized in its mission."[6] The document affirms a common baptismal priesthood which "provides impetus for the Catholic people of God to gather in solemn liturgical assembly . . . on the Lord's Day . . . [for] the celebration of the eucharist."[7] The bishops speak of common celebrations of Morning or Evening Prayer from the Liturgy of the Hours or a Liturgy of the Word with or without the distribution of Holy Communion. The document recognizes "that alternative liturgical celebrations cannot truly substitute for the Eucharistic sacrifice" and the document goes on to state that "assemblies without the presence of a priest are to be encouraged to look forward to the celebration of the Eucharist."[8]

CHAPTER 1

The document offers six articles on the importance and tradition of Sunday as the day of the Lord. The document includes references to the tradition of gathering on Sunday from sacred Scripture (Matthew 28:1, Mark 16:2, Luke 24:1, John 20:1, I Corinthians 16:2 and Revelation 1:10) and from the writings of the early Church including those of Saint Ignatius of Antioch and the Didache.[9] The document contains a lengthy exposition on Sunday by Justin Martyr and refers to the writing from the Didascalia and Tertullian that affirms Sunday as "a day of joy, [where] no one was allowed to fast or to kneel."[10] The history of the Church upholds the tradition of Sunday as "indispensable, and no other day of the week can be substituted for it."[11]

CHAPTER 2

Sunday as the preeminent day for the celebration of the Eucharist is affirmed and the document quotes Saint John Chrysostom who said "to abstain from this meal is to separate oneself from the Lord: the Sunday meal is that which we take in common with the Lord and with the brothers and sisters."[12]

CHAPTER 3

Sunday celebrations when a priest cannot be present uphold the importance of communities gathering on Sunday when "it is not practical or possible for the community to participate in the celebration of Mass in a church nearby."[13] The person designated to lead these celebrations is to be delegated by the bishop "in consultation with the pastor."[14] When God's holy people gather on the Lord's Day and celebrate the Liturgy of the Word, intercede for the Church and the world, and sing God's praises they "encourage one another in the life of grace,"[15]

---

6. Ibid., 3.
7. Ibid., 6.
8. Ibid., 8.
9. Ibid., 10–11.
10. Ibid., 13.
11. Ibid., 15.
12. Ibid., 17.
13. Ibid., 18.
14. Ibid.
15. Ibid., 19.

and this "contributes to the building up of the faith of its members."[16] The document speaks of the importance of these Sunday assemblies as occasions for "nurturing vocations to the priesthood and diaconate."[17] When the community gathers it contributes "to the preservation of programs of catechetical instruction, the care of the sick and of persons with disabilities and small gatherings for study, prayer and witness . . . even in the absence of a priest . . . [these] ecclesial communities judged by the bishops to be viable, independent faith communities."[18] The bishops remind us of the liturgical renewal following the Council that "have rightly reinforced the understanding that the Eucharist is both essential and central to the lives of the faithful."[19] Referring to the presence of Christ in the Eucharist as "real par excellence"[20] the document references the other modes of Christ's presence in liturgical celebrations including the "liturgical assembly of believers [which] is of particular importance"[21] and the presence of Christ in the Word "since it is he himself who speaks when the holy Scriptures are read in the Church."[22] Christ is also present in the person of the minister: the bishop, priest, and deacon. Given the fact that one of the reasons deacons are ordained is for "leading the prayer of the liturgical assembly"[23] the document encourages the diocesan bishop to "give preference to the appointment of deacons as presiding ministers at Sunday worship in the absence of a priest."[24] Since the layperson is to be appointed by the bishop for the responsibility of leading worship in the absence of a priest or deacon they do so "by virtue of that common priesthood which each Christian shares through baptism and confirmation."[25] This section concludes with reference to the importance of reserving "the consecrated elements for the communion to the sick and viaticum for the dying, and for the adoration of the faithful."[26]

CHAPTER 4

The diocesan bishop in consultation with the local pastor appoints a deacon or "another person, lay or religious"[27] to lead the various rites found in SCAP. These leaders of prayer are those who "exhibit a living appreciation for Scripture, a deep reverence for the Eucharist, an active prayer life, an exemplary moral life, a spirit of cooperation with the laity and clergy . . . [and] an acceptance by the members of the community."[28] The training of these leaders should include study of the sacramental and prayer life of the Church, a theology of ministry, the Scriptures, formation in preaching, a knowledge of the Liturgy of the Hours, "a familiarity

---

16. Ibid.
17. Ibid., 20.
18. Ibid., 21.
19. Ibid., 22.
20. Ibid., 22; quoting *Mysterium fide*, 39.
21. Ibid., 23.
22. Ibid., 24; quoting the *Constitution on the Sacred Liturgy*, 7.
23. Ibid., 26.
24. Ibid.
25. Ibid., 27.
26. Ibid., 28.
27. Ibid., 29.
28. Ibid., 32.

with the Lectionary for Mass, the Roman Missal, and other liturgical books, and a practicum in liturgical presidency."[29] The commissioning of the leader by the bishop of his appointed delegate "bestows a mandate for leadership in a specific community . . . [and] it is recommended that a brief letter from the bishop be read to the community of the newly commissioned minister on the first Sunday that ministers leads . . . Sunday worship."[30]

CHAPTER 5

The general principles of liturgical prayer which apply to Sunday celebration in the absence of a priest focus on the Paschal Mystery which is "at the center of all Christian worship"[31] and the liturgical year "which shapes the liturgy on any given Lord's day."[32] The saving plan of God unfolds over the course of the liturgical year and is "illumined further by the Scripture readings . . . [and the announcement] of the paschal mystery must be related to the living, human experience of a specific group of people at a particular time and place."[33] The document calls for the celebration to be prepared carefully and for the leader to use the official ritual texts found in *Sunday Celebrations in the Absence of a Priest* and the *Lectionary for Mass*. The leader of prayer is to lead the parts of the celebration particular to their role while employing a "full complement of trained and prepared ministers."[34]

Since *Sing to the Lord: Music in Divine Worship* has replaced *Music in Catholic Worship* and *Liturgical Music Today* the new document should be consulted.[35] The importance of "the moments of sung prayer which belong to the whole assembly" should be considered first "since the liturgy is an action of the whole assembly."[36] Finally this chapter addresses the importance of silence,[37] the environment for worship,[38] and movement, gesture, and posture.[39]

CHAPTER 6

This chapter includes two options for Sunday prayer: the structure of Sunday celebrations in the absence of a priest can take the form of Morning or Evening Prayer[40] and the Liturgy of the Word.[41] The readings from the Lectionary are to be used and "whenever possible a sung responsorial psalm should follow the first reading."[42] Three full articles are devoted to the role of the Homily and preaching noting that "for deacons, and for those lay persons who may be delegated to

---

29. Ibid., 35.
30. Ibid., 36–37.
31. Ibid., 40.
32. Ibid., 41.
33. Ibid., 42–43.
34. Ibid., 46.
35. See ibid., 47.
36. Ibid., 48.
37. See ibid., 49.
38. See ibid., 50.
39. See ibid., 51.
40. See ibid., 53.
41. See ibid., 54.
42. Ibid., 55.

preach within the Lord's Day assembly, a diligence in prayer, commitment to the study of Scripture, growth in faith, and preparation are required."[43] The final section of this chapter address the placement of candles in the celebration[44] and the possible delegation by the bishop for lay leaders to "impart any of the blessings given in the *Book of Blessings* which are not reserved to a bishop, priest, or deacon."[45]

CHAPTER 7

Catechesis about Sunday celebrations in the absence of a priest must take place. Particular attention is given to the preparation of the community before these celebrations occur,[46] the "meaning of the Mass . . . the difference between the distribution of Holy Communion outside Mass and the celebration of Mass . . . [and that] the expression that a layperson or a deacon is 'celebrating Mass' is to be studiously avoided."[47] Finally, the document reminds us that Christians who receive Communion outside of Mass "are closely united with the sacrifice which perpetuates the sacrifice of the cross."[48]

CONCLUSION

The document concludes by noting that these celebrations are "only a temporary measure;"[49] however, the bishops are "convinced that in the present circumstances providing Sunday celebrations under the leadership of a deacon or designated layperson is the best response to the phenomenon of the 'priestless Sunday.'"[50]

---

43. Ibid.
44. See ibid.
45. Ibid.
46. See ibid., 56.
47. Ibid., 57.
48. Ibid., 58; quoting *Holy Communion and Worship of the Eucharist Outside Mass*, 15.
49. Ibid., 62.
50. Ibid., 63.

OUTLINE

GATHERED IN STEADFAST FAITH:
STATEMENT OF THE BISHOPS' COMMITTEE ON THE LITURGY ON SUNDAY WORSHIP IN THE ABSENCE OF A PRIEST

INTRODUCTION

1   When the Catholic Church was just beginning to take root in North America, it often happened that only on an occasional Sunday could the new communities expect to gather for the celebration of the Mass. Priests found it necessary to divide their presence among a circuit of fledgling parishes. As a result, Catholic families in those communities would stay at home on other Sundays for family devotions, private prayer, festive meals, and the observance of the Sunday rest.

2   Today an increasing number of Catholic communities throughout the United States are faced with a similar reality: the necessity of observing Sunday, of keeping holy the Lord's Day, without the liturgical leadership of their priest. In many dioceses, large parishes which formerly had several priests may now have only one; parishes which once had a resident pastor are now served by a priest traveling from a nearby community; areas that once had large Catholic populations, e.g., inner cities, are now experiencing population shifts; people are moving to different regions of the country, but they are not bringing clergy with them; some parishes have been and will continue to be combined with neighboring ones.

3   This situation, while being a serious problem facing the Church, is also a cause for reflection upon the mystery of the Church and the role of all the baptized in its mission. It raises the possibility of creative solutions in the redistribution of ordained priests within and among dioceses and of new approaches in the discernment and nurturing of vocations to the priesthood.

4   Until such new approaches bear fruit, there will continue to be priests in certain areas of the country who must celebrate Mass several times on Sundays in many widely scattered churches in order to serve the needs of the faithful. These priests are to be commended for their dedication and pastoral zeal.

5   It is the entire Church which the New Testament refers to as "'a chosen race, a royal priesthood, a holy nation, a people of his own, so that you may announce the praises' of him who called you out of darkness into his wonderful light" (1 Pt 2:9). Through baptism all Christians are called to holiness and are commissioned for Christian service to the Church and to the world. Through baptism all participate in the paschal mystery of the Lord's dying and rising; all

are called to continual conversion, ever-stronger discipleship, abundant life, and unfailing hope.

6   The common priesthood of all the baptized provides impetus for the Catholic people of God to gather in solemn liturgical assembly for worship on the Lord's Day, normally with the celebration of the eucharist. Likewise, when the community of believers is deprived of priests and therefore unable to celebrate the eucharist, the bishop should make provisions that will enable it to assemble on Sunday in order to be strengthened in faith through various liturgical celebrations. Such communities may celebrate Morning or Evening Prayer from the *Liturgy of the Hours* or have a Celebration of the Liturgy of the Word, all of which may include the distribution of Holy Communion, reserved for this purpose.

7   This statement of the Bishops' Committee on the Liturgy acknowledges a growing need for these celebrations. At the same time, the Committee wishes to reaffirm the constant teaching of the Church concerning the primacy of Sunday, its intimate connection with the celebration of the eucharist, and the constitutive nature of the ministerial priesthood for the life of the Church. The statement affirms that the Church is by its nature sacramental, and that the full Eucharistic celebration is the fount and summit of the life of the Church.[1] It also addresses the many modes of Christ's presence in the community, the Sunday liturgical assembly as a visible gathering of the Church, and the need for well-prepared and reverently celebrated liturgical prayer.

8   In addition, this statement presents several points for the consideration of those communities which, because of the absence of priests, are unable to have the celebration of Mass on Sunday. It recognizes that alternative liturgical celebrations cannot truly substitute for the Eucharistic sacrifice, for it is in the Eucharistic celebration that "the entire Church recognizes and gives expression to itself"[2] But when necessity demands that the Sunday liturgy take another form, it is to be structured in the best way possible while being made clear to all that it is not the Mass. In addition, assemblies without the presence of a priest are to be encouraged to look forward to the celebration of the Eucharist; one way of helping to insure this is through good celebrations of other forms of liturgical prayer until such assemblies may once again celebrate the Eucharist each Sunday.

9   This statement has been prepared in light of the *Directory for Sunday Celebrations in the Absence of a Priest*, issued by the Congregation for Divine Worship on June 2, 1988. It is meant to assist diocesan bishops, who are faced with the unavoidable reality of Sunday assemblies deprived of the celebration of Mass. The statement is seen as providing for a present need, while never forgetting the plea of the Good Shepherd, "Ask the master of the harvest to send out laborers for his harvest" (Mt 9:38; Lk 10:2).

---

1. See Vatican Council II, *Constitution on the Liturgy* (*Sacrosanctum Concilium*) (hereafter *SC*) (4 December 1963), art. 10; the English translation is from *Documents on the Liturgy 1965–1979: Conciliar, Papal, and Curial Texts* (hereafter *DOL*) (Collegeville, MN: The Liturgical Press, 1982), 1, no. 10.

2. Congregation for Divine Worship, circular letter *Eucharistiae participationem* (27 April 1973), no. 11 [*DOL* 248, no. 1985].

I. THE TRADITION OF SUNDAY, THE DAY OF THE LORD

10   From its earliest days the Christian faithful have assembled for corporate worship on the Lord's Day. It was on the "first day of the week," according to the Jewish calendar; that Christ rose from the dead and appeared to and was present with his disciples (see Mt 28:1, Mk 16:2, Lk 24:1, Jn 20:1). No doubt it was for this reason that Christ's followers met on the first day of each week for common and, almost certainly, Eucharistic worship. Saint Paul presumed this weekly gathering of the Church (1 Cor 16:2).

11   For Christians the earliest term for Sunday was "the first day of the week." That was soon replaced by "the Lord's Day" (see Rv 1: 10; Ignatius, *Letter to the Magnesians* 9: 1; *Didache* 14: 1), a term which was used along side of the customary civil designation of "the day named after the sun," that is, "Sunday." In about 150 A.D. Justin Martyr wrote concerning the activity on this day:

> And on the day called Sunday there is a meeting in one place of those who live in cities or the country, and the memoirs of the apostles or the writings of the prophets are read as long as time permits . . . Then we all stand up together and offer prayers. And, as said before, when we have finished the prayer, bread is brought, and wine and water, and the president similarly sends up prayers and thanksgivings to the best of his ability, and the congregation assents, saying the Amen; the distribution, and reception of the consecrated (elements) by each one, takes place and they are sent to the absent by the deacons . . . We all hold this common gathering on Sunday, since it is the first day, on which God transforming darkness and matter made the universe, and Jesus Christ our Savior rose from the dead on the same day.[3]

12   Keeping the Lord's Day by coming together for the weekly liturgical assembly was regarded as essential in the life of a Christian, even in times of persecution: "We have to celebrate the Lord's Day. It is our rule. . . . We could not live without celebrating the Lord's Day," the martyrs of Abitina asserted.[4]

13   For Christians Sunday was always a day of joy;[5] no one was allowed to fast[6] or to kneel.[7] It became a day of rest after 321 A.D. when Constantine closed the law courts and stopped people from working on that day. Under Constantine Sunday became the Christian festival of the Roman Empire.

---

3. Justin Martyr (ca. AD 150), 1 *Apology* 67:3–7. English translation by Edward Rochie Hardy, from *Early Christian Fathers*, edited by Cyril C. Richardson (New York: Macmillan Publishing Co. Inc., 1970), p. 287.

4. *Bibliographica hagiographica latina*, no. 7492, in Peter G. Cobb, "The History of the Christian Year," in *The Study of Liturgy*, ed. by Cheslyn Jones, Geoffrey Wainwright, and Edward Yarnold (New York: Oxford University Press, 1978), p. 405.

5. See *Didascalia* 21; see Cobb, p. 405.

6. See Tertullian, *On the Crown* 3; see Cobb, p. 405.

7. See Tertullian, *On Prayer* 23; Canon 20 of the Council of Nicaea; see Cobb, p. 405.

14   In their observance of the Lord's Day the early Christians realized their identity and mission. In their Eucharistic celebrations they strengthened their faith, steadied themselves for further worship and service in society, helped to liberate themselves from the manifold pressures of an isolating and alienating existence, and readied themselves again to become more clearly the life and the leaven of the world.[8]

15   This weekly celebration of Christians remains as a "sign" of the salvific reality of the new creation that began with the resurrection of Christ. As a feast of the Christian liturgical assembly, a day of Eucharistic celebration, and a day of Christian anticipation of what is to come, Sunday is indispensable, and no other day of the week can be substituted for it.[9]

II. SUNDAY, THE PREEMINENT DAY FOR THE EUCHARIST

16   Whenever the Christian community gathers to celebrate the Eucharist, it shows forth the death and resurrection of the Lord in the hope of his glorious coming.[10] "In the Mass we have the high point of the work that in Christ God accomplishes to sanctify us and the high point of the worship that in adoring God through Christ, his Son, we offer to the Father."[11] By entering into the Eucharistic action, the community enters into the sharing of the body and blood of Christ, for "the sharing of the body and blood of Christ does nothing less than transform us into what we receive."[12] By sharing in the Eucharistic body and blood of Christ, the Church becomes the body of Christ in the world, and by

---

8. These effects flowing from the Sunday celebration have not always been adequately perceived or appreciated by Catholic Christians. In the middle ages the Church found it necessary to impose a law which commanded the observance of Sunday through participation in the Mass and by abstinence from all unnecessary work. Such a law remains to this day (see 1983 *Code of Canon Law* [hereafter *CIC*], canon 1247. It should be noted, however, that canon 1248 recognizes that at times participation in the eucharist is impossible either because no priest is available or for some other grave cause. In such cases, "it is specially recommended that the faithful take part in the liturgy of the word if it is celebrated in the parish church or in another sacred place according to the prescriptions of the diocesan bishop, or engage in prayer for an appropriate amount of time personally or in a family or, as occasion offers, in groups of families.") Thus the faithful have the duty of regularly taking part in Sunday worship not merely because of a legal precept, but as an expression of the virtue of religion, of gratitude and love for God, and in witness to those who do not know the Lord. In their catechesis on Sunday celebrations in the absence of a priest, diocesan bishops should insure proper instruction on the precept of participating in Mass on Sundays and holy days of obligation and the obligations of those who are unable to do so because of the lack of a priest or some other grave circumstance.

9. See Joint Synod of the Dioceses of the Federal Republic of Germany, Resolution on the Liturgy (21 November 1975), no. 2.1. Typescript copy.

10. See Sacred Congregation of Rites, instruction *Eucharisticum mysterium* [hereafter *EM*] (25 May 1967), no. 25 [*DOL* 179, no. 1254].

11. Congregation for Divine Worship, *General Instruction of the Roman Missal* [hereafter *GIRM*], 4th ed. (27 March 1975), no. 1 [*DOL* 208, no. 1391].

12. Leo the Great, "Sermon 63," in *EM*, no. 7 [*DOL* 179, no. 1236], see also Vatican Council II, *Dogmatic Constitution on the Church—Lumen Gentium* (21 November 1964), art. 26 [*DOL* 4, no. 146].

being united to Christ, the head of the Church, the members of his body are united to one another.

17   Saint John Chrysostom, when speaking of the central importance of the Eucharist in the life of the Christian, declared, "To abstain from this meal is to separate oneself from the Lord: the Sunday meal is that which we take in common with the Lord and with the brothers and sisters."[13] The Eucharist, then, is a celebration of communion, of union with the Lord Jesus and with his Body, the Church, that unites and transforms both the individual and the community.

III. SUNDAY CELEBRATIONS WHEN A PRIEST CANNOT BE PRESENT

18   When a priest cannot be present for the celebration of Mass on the Lord's Day, it is of paramount importance that the parish or mission community still come together to celebrate the resurrection of the Lord.[14] If in the judgment of the diocesan bishop it is not practical or possible for the community to participate in the celebration of Mass in a church nearby,[15] they should assemble for Sunday worship in their own community under the leadership of the person the bishop, in consultation with the pastor, has designated to lead them in prayer. In such a case the celebration may take one of the forms given in the *Sunday Celebrations in the Absence of a Priest: Leader's Edition:* Morning or Evening Prayer or a Celebration of the Liturgy of the Word, all of which may include the distribution of Holy Communion.

19   By continuing to gather on the Lord's Day to hear God's word and reflect on it, to make intercession for the Church and the world, to sing God's praises, and to encourage one another in the life of grace,[16] the community expresses and develops itself as Church. It contributes to the building up of the faith of its members; it gives glory to God.

20   The faith of a Catholic Christian is normally lived in the context of a parish community; for it is there that faith is nourished and celebrated. Thus, even when the Sunday Eucharist is not available, the community's gathering for worship preserves the sanctity of the Lord's Day, helps them to remain in the habit of assembling on Sunday, and prepares them for the time when there will be a priest to lead the community in the Sunday Eucharist.[17] These Sunday assemblies also

---

13. In *Epist. 1 ad Cor. Hom.* 27, in Cobb, p. 405.

14. Although, in certain circumstances, it may be the pastoral decision of the diocesan bishop to close a parish or combine one or more parishes or communities into a new parish or community with a common church or other place for the Sunday celebration of the eucharist, this document is concerned with, circumstances where parishes or communities continue, but without the regular weekly celebration of Mass on Sunday.

15. See Congregation for Divine Worship, *Directory for Sunday Celebrations in the Absence of a Priest* (hereafter *Directory*) (2 June 1988), no. 18.

16. See *CIC*, canon 1248, par. 2.

17. See Canadian Conference of Catholic Bishops, "Sunday Liturgy: When Lay People Preside," *National Bulletin on Liturgy* 14 (May/June 1981), pp. 102–103.

provide opportunities within the community for nurturing vocations to the priesthood and diaconate and for continual prayer for vocations to the ordained ministries of the Church.

21   These Sunday celebrations will also contribute to the preservation of programs of catechetical instruction, the care of the sick and of persons with disabilities, and small gatherings for study, prayer and witness in the community. The community is less likely to grow in faith—or even sustain its faith—if the Sunday liturgical assembly disperses in various directions. Therefore, no effort should be spared in helping foster the celebration of faith, particularly on Sunday—even in the absence of a priest in those ecclesial communities judged by the bishop to be viable, independent faith communities.

22   The thought of Roman Catholics gathering for Sunday worship without the celebration of the Mass is altogether new for most. The years of liturgical renewal since the Second Vatican Council have rightly reinforced the understanding that the Eucharist is both essential and central to the lives of the faithful. For it is in the Eucharistic action that the Church encounters Christ in a preeminent way and through a variety of modes:

> First, he is present in the very assembly of the faithful, gathered together in his name; next, he is present in his word, with the reading and explanation of Scripture in the church; also in the person of the minister; finally, and above all, in the Eucharistic elements. In a way that is completely unique, the whole and entire Christ, God and man, is substantially and permanently present in the sacrament. This presence of Christ under the appearance of bread and wine "is called real, not to exclude other kinds of presence as though they were not real, but because it is real par excellence."[18] Yet throughout the ages Christians have believed that Christ is present in other liturgical celebrations in the ways indicated above.

23   Divine Revelation continually underscores the Church's understanding that Christ is present in the liturgical assembly of the faithful,[19] especially when it gathers in prayer.[20] Christ manifests himself in the words and gestures of the liturgical assembly as it listens and responds to the proclamation of God's Word and as it gathers around the altar to give thanks and praise and receive the body and blood of Christ.[21] Among the symbols of the liturgy the liturgical assembly of believers is of particular importance.[22]

18. Congregation for Divine Worship, *Holy Communion and Worship of the Eucharist Outside Mass* (hereafter *HCWEOM*) (21 June 1973), General Introduction, no. 6 [*DOL* 279, no. 2198]. The internal reference in this quotation is from the encyclical of Paul VI, *Mysterium fidei* (3 September 1965), no. 39 [*DOL* 176, no. 1183].

19. See Ephesians 2: 15–23; 3:9–10; 3:19; 5:18.

20. See Matthew 18:20; 1 Corinthians 5:4.

21. See Bishops' Committee on the Liturgy, National Conference of Catholic Bishops, *Environment and Art in Catholic Worship*, 1978, no. 29.

22. See ibid., no. 28.

24   It is likewise Catholic belief that Christ is truly present in the Word, "since it is he himself who speaks when the holy Scriptures are read in the Church."[23] Thus the Church has always revered sacred Scripture even as it has revered the Body of the Lord, because, above all in the liturgy, it never ceases to receive the Bread of Life from the table both of God's Word and of Christ's Body and Blood.[24] The Second Vatican Council likened the Bible to a fountain of inner renewal within the community of God's people, and directed that in the revision of liturgical celebrations there should be more reading from Scripture.[25] Thus it is seen that by means of the Scriptures proclaimed and explained within the liturgy "God is speaking to his people, opening up to them the mystery of redemption and salvation, and nourishing their spirit; Christ is present to the faithful through his own word."[26]

25   The ordained ministers of the Church have the responsibility of presiding over the prayer which builds up the Church. Through the minister the voice of Christ himself calls, invokes, challenges, proclaims, and encourages. This manifestation of Christ, of course, is most clearly seen in the bishop or priest who presides at the Eucharist. By virtue of priestly ordination, he acts in the person of Christ when he prays, presides over the liturgical assembly, and speaks on behalf of all present.[27]

26   Through ordination the deacon also has the responsibility of leading the prayer of the liturgical assembly, since he "has been ordained for the nurture and increase of the people of God."[28] For this reason, all things being equal, the diocesan bishop should give preference to the appointment of deacons as presiding ministers at Sunday worship in the absence of a priest.

27   Likewise a layperson who has been appointed by the bishop may be given the responsibility of leading worship in the absence of a priest or deacon. Although not ordained, a layperson so designated leads the prayer of a community by virtue of that common priesthood which each Christian shares through baptism and confirmation.[29]

28   Finally, and above all, Christ is uniquely present in the Eucharistic elements under the appearances of bread and wine at each celebration of the Eucharist. This presence continues even after the celebration has concluded. The Church accordingly reserves the consecrated elements for the communion of the sick and viaticum for the dying, and for the adoration of the faithful. The reservation of the sacrament of Christ's body and blood also makes it possible for communities without a priest to receive Holy Communion when Mass cannot be celebrated; this practice is to be encouraged. The Eucharist is reserved under the

23. *SC*, art. 7 [*DOL* 1, no. 7].
24. See Vatican Council II, *Dogmatic Constitution on Divine Revelation—Dei Verbum* (18 November 1965), art. 21 [*DOL* 24, no. 224].
25. See *SC*, art. 35 [*DOL* 1, no. 35].
26. *GIRM*, no. 33 [*DOL* 208, no. 1423].
27. See *SC*, art. 33 [*DOL* 1, no. 33].
28. *Directory*, no. 29.
29. See *Directory*, no. 30.

form of the consecrated bread, except in those circumstances where the sick are able to receive communion only under the form of the consecrated wine (see *Pastoral Care of the Sick*, no. 74). The pastor should see that the Eucharist is brought at least weekly to the community from the parish or other community where the Eucharist has been celebrated. This will serve to strengthen the bonds between the community without a priest, its pastor, and the other communities where the Eucharist is celebrated.

IV. THE LEADER OF PRAYER AT A SUNDAY CELEBRATION IN THE ABSENCE OF A PRIEST

29   When the Sunday Mass cannot be celebrated because there is no assigned priest or because the priest is legitimately unavailable, the diocesan bishop, in consultation with the pastor, may appoint a deacon or, if necessary, another person, lay or religious, to lead one of the several liturgical rites provided in *Sunday Celebrations in the Absence of a Priest: Leader's Edition*. If desired, the bishop may determine a specific term for this appointment, and its renewal may be subject to review.

30   Those so chosen for this ministry should be trained to lead each of these liturgical rites: Morning Prayer, Evening Prayer, and the Celebration of the Liturgy of the Word, all of which may include the distribution of Holy Communion. In addition, especially when these ministers also serve as the pastoral administrators of parishes, they should be well versed in the administration of communion to the sick and viaticum to the dying, in preaching (when specifically designated), in the exposition of the holy Eucharist, in those rites from the *Order of Christian Funerals* which, on occasion, they may be required to lead, and in other liturgical and devotional services.

SELECTION

31   Each diocese should establish its own procedures for the selection of suitable candidates for formation in leading the Sunday liturgical assembly in worship. Pastoral insight must be exercised in the selection of those to be trained and commissioned to serve in such a capacity.

32   Those chosen for this ministry should not merely be "volunteers," but persons who exhibit a living appreciation for Scripture, a deep reverence for the Eucharist, an active prayer life, an exemplary moral life, a spirit of cooperation with the laity and clergy of the particular community, an acceptance by the members of the community, an active involvement in the pastoral life of the community, and both a strong desire and ability to foster participation by lay people as members of the worshiping liturgical assembly and in other liturgical roles. The cultural makeup and linguistic needs of the liturgical assembly should also be considered in the selection of candidates.

33   Moreover, the candidates should demonstrate the necessary skills for public speaking which will enable them to be heard and understood in a liturgical setting, as well as the requisite sense of presence that is called for in movement

and gesture in prayer. Finally, there should be evidence of the persons' commitment to this ministry, of their availability to exercise it, and of their willingness and ability to integrate within a solid spirituality the exercise of this ministry with personal and family obligations.

34   In parishes and missions where Sunday celebrations in the absence of a priest may be required on a regular basis, e.g., bi-weekly or monthly, it is recommended that a minimum of two candidates receive formation in exercising the ministry of leading Sunday celebrations.

TRAINING

35   Each candidate for the role of leader should complete the program of training and formation required by the diocese. This training will help the candidate to learn what the ministry requires with respect to knowledge of the Church's faith and tradition, as these are expressed in its worship life, and what the leadership of the local assembly in the expression of its faith requires. The training sessions should include a study of the sacramental and prayer life of the Church and its sources and spirituality, the theology of ministry, formation in the Scriptures and in the ministry of preaching, the Liturgy of the Hours, the rite of Holy Communion outside Mass, the liturgical year, devotions in the life of the Church, a familiarity with the *Lectionary for Mass*, the *Roman Missal*, and other liturgical books, and a practicum in liturgical presidency.

COMMISSIONING

36   Upon completion of the course of formation, the bishop or his delegate should commission the new ministers. The "Order for the Blessing of Those Who Exercise Pastoral Service," contained in the American edition of the *Book of Blessings*, might be used or adapted. (Deacons, by their ordination, are ordinary ministers of the Eucharist and have received the commission to preside at Christian worship. However, it may on occasion be possible to include them in a service led by the bishop or his delegate which bestows a mandate for leadership in a specific community, while, at the same time, acknowledging that they are ordained ministers of the Church.) The initial designation to function in this ministry should be established for a specific place and period of time, after which, upon a favorable evaluation of an individual's service, the bishop's appointment may be renewed.

37   The commissioning rite may be celebrated in the parish church of the candidates. However, when candidates from several parishes are commissioned by the bishop at the cathedral church, it is appropriate that members of their communities be present at the commissioning along with the clergy, and the family and friends of the candidates. In such cases, it is recommended that a brief letter from the bishop be read to the community of the newly commissioned minister on the first Sunday that minister leads the community's Sunday worship.

CONTINUING FORMATION

38   Those who exercise the role of leading Sunday celebrations in the absence of a priest bear a responsibility for continued personal growth in the Lord through

prayer and study beyond the formation period itself. If their ministry is not to become routine and perfunctory, they will need to root themselves ever more deeply in the mystery of life in Christ. Of special value will be retreats and days of recollection, parish adult education programs, and workshops sponsored by the diocese that address the needs of sacred worship. The reading of periodicals and books on liturgy and prayer, and the study of Scripture will also serve to nourish not only these ministers but also those they serve. Parishes would do well to make such periodicals available to all who exercise liturgical ministries on their behalf.

V. GENERAL PRINCIPLES OF LITURGICAL PRAYER WHICH APPLY TO SUNDAY CELEBRATIONS IN THE ABSENCE OF A PRIEST

39   Several fundamental principles concerning liturgical prayer provide assistance in correctly understanding the nature of Sunday celebrations in the absence of a priest. These principles must be kept in mind when planning the celebrations.

PROCLAMATION OF THE PASCHAL MYSTERY

40   "Themes" are never arbitrarily to be imposed on the liturgy. Rather the assembly's Sunday worship always flows from four interrelated liturgical factors. Foremost among them is the understanding that at the center of all Christian worship is the proclamation of the paschal mystery: the Good News of God's marvelous plan whereby the scattered children of God have been gathered together in love through the life, death and resurrection of Jesus Christ.

41   The second factor which shapes the liturgy on any given Lord's Day is the liturgical year. The Sundays and seasons of Advent, Christmas, Lent, Easter, and Ordinary Time and the other elements of liturgical time (sunrise and sunset, vigils and octaves and particular festivals) provide the setting through which the community gains an understanding of the meaning and celebrates a particular facet of the mystery of God's love in Jesus Christ.

42   God's saving plan, unfolded in the course of the Church's year, is illumined further by the Scripture readings assigned in the *Lectionary for Mass*. Through the appointed Scripture readings of the *Lectionary* the Church reaches a more specific statement of the Good News by which the members are spiritually nourished.

43   Finally, this proclamation of the paschal mystery must be related to the living, human experience of a specific group of people at a particular time and place. In light of this factor the leader of prayer and all who prepare the liturgy should mold the explanation of the Scriptures, the Prayer of the Faithful, the choices made among prayer texts where options are provided, the selection of music, and the composition of introductions to the needs of the worshiping community.[30]

---

30. See *SC*, art. 35.3 [*DOL* 1, no. 35]; *GIRM*, nos. 11 and 13 [*DOL* 208, nos. 1401 and 1403].

44   In order to insure that the Sunday celebration be done as well as possible, care should be taken to prepare carefully all the elements of the celebration: the ministers, the liturgical texts, the actions and gestures, the music, the liturgical environment, and the assembly itself. This should be done in collaboration with the parish or community liturgical committee.

LITURGICAL TEXTS

45   The *Liturgy of the Hours*, the *Roman Missal*, the *Lectionary for Mass*, *Holy Communion and Worship of the Eucharist outside Mass*, and the other approved ritual books offer a variety of prayers, readings, and other texts for Sunday celebrations in the absence of a priest. In order to assist ministers, the National Conference of Catholic Bishops has prepared *Sunday Celebrations in the Absence of a Priest: Leader's Edition*, a ritual book composed of texts taken from the above mentioned sources. On Sundays and solemnities no substitutions should be made for the readings given in the *Lectionary* and the Prayer of the Day (used as the opening prayer or the concluding prayer) since these have been chosen with the whole Church in mind.[31] But whenever optional texts are provided, the leader and those who assist in preparing for the celebration should make use of the options allowed. These options might include the choice of particular readings and presidential prayers, etc. However, the basic structure of the rite itself should not be changed or adapted, even by the leader. "Liturgical services are not private functions but are celebrations of the Church."[32]

MINISTERS

46   In addition to the leader a full complement of trained and prepared ministers should participate in each celebration: readers, musicians, cantors, choir, acolytes, ministers of hospitality (ushers), and any other ministers required for the celebration. "In liturgical celebrations each one, minister or layperson, who has an office to perform, should do all of, but only, those parts which pertain to that office by the nature of the rite and the principles of liturgy."[33] Hence, the leader should not assume the roles and function of other ministers.

MUSIC

47   The musical principles given in the introductions to the various rites of the Church, as well as those provided by the Committee on the Liturgy of the National Conference of Catholic Bishops, such as *Music in Catholic Worship* (1972; revised edition, 1983) and *Liturgical Music Today* (1982), are to be applied to Sunday celebrations in the absence of a priest. At a celebration of the Liturgy of the Hours, the principle of progressive solemnity should guide the choice of sung settings of the various elements.[34] Similarly, the musical requirements for celebrations of the Word and the distribution of Holy Communion are similar to those for the celebration of the Eucharist, except for those elements of the

---

31. See *GIRM*, nos. 11 and 332 [*DOL* 208, no. 1401 and 1722].
32. *SC*, art. 26 [*DOL* 1, no. 26].
33. Ibid., art. 28 [*DOL* 1, no. 28].
34. See *General Instruction of the Liturgy of the Hours*, nos. 273–277 [*DOL* 426, nos. 3703–3707].

Mass which are not included (i.e., the preparation of the altar and the gifts, the Eucharistic prayer, and the breaking of the bread).

48   Since the liturgy is an action of the whole assembly, the first attention of leaders and music planners should be given to the moments of sung prayer which belong to the whole assembly, namely, the entrance song, the responsorial psalm, the gospel acclamation, and, when communion is distributed, the communion song. After that music has been planned, with special attention to seasonal and particular needs, other congregational, choral, vocal, or instrumental music may be chosen. In particular circumstances the use of music in more than one language may be appropriate. All musical choices, including the manner in which the music will be performed, must serve the shape and dynamics of the entire liturgy, as well as its basic structure.

SILENCE

49   Silence serves as a positive and necessary element within the structure of worship. It is important because it provides the community with the opportunity for personal reflection. A period of silence should be observed after the invitations to prayer, i.e., "Let us pray," the Scripture readings, and the communion song.[35]

THE ENVIRONMENT FOR WORSHIP

50   A carefully prepared environment will convey the message and spirit of celebration to the community as it enters the area for worship. Vesture, lighting, the effective use of colors, candles, live plants, an attractive *Lectionary* and *Book of Gospels* (when available), candles at the proclamation of the Gospel (when judged appropriate)—all have a great effect on the mood of the celebration. Attention should also be given to the cultural life, religious symbols, and artistic expressions of a particular community. Whenever possible, attempts should be made to integrate them into the liturgical environment.

MOVEMENT, GESTURE, AND POSTURE

51   The words and music of the community's prayer should be balanced and focused by attention given to movement, gesture, and posture. The care with which these bodily elements of worship are approached by those who prepare the liturgy, the leader of prayer, the other ministers, and the entire assembly, will affect the prayer of all present.

VI. THE STRUCTURE OF SUNDAY CELEBRATIONS IN THE ABSENCE OF A PRIEST

52   Two options are provided for Sunday worship in the absence of a priest: the celebration of Morning or Evening Prayer from the *Liturgy of the Hours,* or the celebration of the Liturgy of the Word, all of which may include the distribution of Holy Communion.

---

35. See *SC*, art. 30 [*DOL* 1, no. 30]. *GIRM*, nos. 23, 56, and 121 [*DOL* 208, nos. 1413, 1446, and 1511].

53   Morning Prayer and Evening Prayer both have the same structure and the following elements:

Introductory Rites—These rites (Invitatory and Hymn) serve to gather the faithful into a worshiping community.

Psalmody—The singing or recitation of psalms and scriptural canticles, along with their respective antiphons and optional psalm–prayers, permits the assembly to join its praise and thanksgiving to God to that of Christ, who is our great high priest and advocate.

Liturgy of the Word—The proclamation of the Scripture readings assigned in the *Lectionary for Mass* brings to those gathered in faith the message of the good news of salvation and redemption in Christ. The response of the assembly to the Word of God is a combination of thanksgiving (Canticle of Zechariah or Canticle of Mary) for God's goodness to us, and of intercession (Intercessions) for the needs of the Church and the world.

Communion Rite—The assembly unites itself to the paschal mystery of Christ in Holy Communion. The reception of communion is also a sign and expression of the assembly's union with those who are able to celebrate the Eucharist on that particular day. If Holy Communion is not distributed, this portion of the rite is omitted.

Concluding Rite—After having heard the Word of God (and having been nourished by the body and blood of Christ in Holy Communion), the assembly is sent forth with God's blessing to live the Christian life.

LITURGY OF THE WORD

54   When the Sunday celebration takes the form of a celebration of the Liturgy of the Word, it includes the following elements:

Introductory Rites—The purpose of these rites is to form the gathered faithful into a community and to dispose them for the celebration.

Liturgy of the Word—God speaks to his people through the Scripture readings assigned in the *Lectionary for Mass*, disclosing to them the mystery of redemption and salvation; the people respond through the profession of faith and the Prayer of the Faithful.

Thanksgiving—The community blesses God for the gift of redemption in Christ.

Communion Rite—This rite is an expression and accomplishment of communion with Christ and with his members, especially with those who on this same day take part in the Eucharistic sacrifice. If Holy Communion is not distributed, this portion of the rite is omitted.

Concluding Rites—The blessing and dismissal point to the connection existing between the liturgy and the Christian life.

55   In either form of the Sunday celebration the following particular points should be kept in mind by those responsible for planning the celebration and by the leader.

a.   The person who leads the community at a Sunday celebration in the absence of a priest, whether a deacon or layperson, is called the "leader."

b.   The leader may be vested in lay clothing or religious habit, a well-designed alb, or other suitable vesture according to diocesan policy. The use of the stole and dalmatic is reserved to deacons.

c.   Laypersons are to avoid all things proper to a priest or deacon. They do not use the greeting before the Gospel ("The Lord be with you") or any of the other greetings designated for a deacon or priest. Nor do they use the priestly or diaconal forms of blessing. *Sunday Celebrations in the Absence of a Priest: Leader's Edition* provides proper forms of blessing for laypersons. When giving a blessing, a layperson does not make the sign of the cross over the people.

d.   The chair used by a layperson must be different from the presidential chair used by a priest and normally it should be placed outside the presbyterium in close proximity to the assembly. The ambo is reserved for the Liturgy of the Word. The altar is used only when the Eucharist is placed on it before the distribution of Holy Communion, if it is included in the celebration.

e.   The readings assigned in the *Lectionary* for a particular Sunday, solemnity or feast are always to be used. On occasions when there are no assigned readings or when a selection is provided, the minister may choose appropriate readings. On Sundays and solemnities three readings are used, as at Mass. Whenever possible a sung responsorial psalm should follow the first reading.

f.   The preaching of a homily is part of most liturgical rites and is, by its very definition, reserved to a priest or deacon.[36] However, the bishop may allow a layperson who is properly trained to explain the Word of God at Sunday celebrations in the absence of a priest or deacon and at other specified occasions.[37]

The pastor may provide a text for the leader to read,[38] or if the bishop has authorized the leader to preach, the minister preaches in his/her own words. It is essential that when the leader is to preach, the text should be prepared well in advance.

Preaching, an irreplaceable ministry for explaining the Scriptures and applying them to the here-and-now of a particular gathering, is a task to be taken seriously by those who have been duly delegated by the bishop.

---

36. See *CIC*, canon 767, 1.

37. See ibid., canon 766.

38. In some circumstances it may be desirable for the pastor to send a recorded message or homily to the community.

When one preaches in the name of the Church, the great public work of Christ is continued. For deacons, and for those laypersons who may be delegated to preach within the Lord's Day assembly, a diligence in prayer, commitment to the study of Scripture, growth in faith, and preparation are required.[39]

g.   Candles may be used in the entrance procession or placed near the ambo. When the distribution of Holy Communion concludes the celebration, candles are lighted at the altar before the Sacrament is brought to it from the place of reservation.

h.   A layperson, delegated by the bishop, may impart any of the blessings given in the *Book of Blessings* which are not reserved to a bishop, priest, or deacon.

VII. CATECHESIS

56   It is essential that before Sunday celebrations in the absence of a priest are begun in a particular community there be a period of thorough catechesis on the importance of Sunday worship, the reasons for having these celebrations, and the need for prayer and other means of encouragement for more vocations to the priesthood. It is especially important that the community be assisted in deepening its understanding of the importance of the sacramental worship of the Church and its ordained ministry, lest, in time, Sunday worship in the absence of a priest come to be seen as normative.

57   Catechesis directed to the Sunday assembly should clearly state the Church's teaching on the meaning of the Mass as found in the *General Instruction of the Roman Missal*.[40] The catechesis should explain the very nature of the Eucharist and the difference between the distribution of Holy Communion outside Mass and the celebration of Mass. Because of this difference, only a bishop or priest may preside at the Eucharist, while a deacon, acolyte, or other specially designated minister may distribute Holy Communion.[41] Although a celebration of the Liturgy of the Word followed by the rite for the distribution of Holy Communion outside Mass parallels in a general fashion the structure of the Mass—introductory rites, celebration of the Word of God, reception of Holy Communion, and concluding rite—the essential element of the full Eucharistic action, the Eucharistic prayer and the usual rites for preparing the altar and the gifts of bread and wine, are not included. Reception of communion at such a liturgical celebration is from the reserved sacrament consecrated at an earlier celebration of Mass, particularly a Mass celebrated the same day (or preceding evening). Thus, in referring to these Sunday celebrations, the expression that a layperson or a deacon is "celebrating Mass" is to be studiously avoided.

---

39. See the statement of the Bishops' Committee on Priestly Life and Ministry, *Fulfilled in Your Hearing* (Washington, DC: USCC, 1982), which offers a brief yet thorough introduction to the task and method of preaching.

40. See *GIRM*, Introduction and chapter 1 [*DOL* 208, nos. 1376–1396].

41. See *HCWEOM*, no. 17 [*DOL* 266, no. 2095].

58   When due to necessity Christians receive communion outside of Mass, "they are closely united with the sacrifice which perpetuates the sacrifice of the cross."[42] The sacred species themselves are reserved in Catholic churches for sharing communion, especially with the sick, and viaticum with the dying, and for that worship of the Eucharist which flows from the Mass. It is always the celebration of the Eucharist itself which is at once the origin and the goal of the reverence which is shown the Eucharist outside the Mass.[43]

CONCLUSION

59   The preparation of this statement and *Sunday Celebrations in the Absence of a Priest: Leader's Edition* has been a major project for the Bishops' Committee on the Liturgy. The Committee wishes to thank all those who assisted in this work and is especially appreciative of all the bishops who cooperated in the survey it conducted in 1987.

60   The task group that was established by the Liturgy Committee to prepare these documents quickly learned of the complexity of the problem on both the theological and pastoral levels. It also discovered that proposed solutions did not really deal with the root problem. The primary need for having Sunday celebrations in the absence of a priest is the lack of a sufficient number of priests or, at least, an inequitable distribution of priests so that some regions of the country have large numbers of priests and others are forced to place several parishes under a single pastor. Until a solution is found for the lack of a sufficient number of priests, the need for Sunday celebrations in the absence of a priest will continue and, according to the survey conducted by the Bishops' Committee on the Liturgy in 1987, the need will increase at least through the next several years.

61   On the positive side, it is clear that Sunday celebrations under the leadership of a deacon or layperson will enable a community to continue to worship and be nourished by the Word of God and the Eucharist. Such celebrations allow Catholics to take responsibility for prayer and worship in the absence of their own priest, a responsibility that flows from their baptism and confirmation.

62   However, at best these celebrations are only a temporary measure. The community is deprived of the celebration of the Eucharist, and Holy Communion is separated from the Mass. There is a danger of a return to the situation of the past in which the Mass was seen only as a means for providing consecrated hosts for communion. The positive effects of the liturgical reform and renewal which have affirmed the Mass as the fount and summit of the Church's life are endangered by the practical need for these celebrations. Another danger which may arise is the acceptance of the notion of the Church as a local community with little or no direct connection to the diocese and the universal Church. It can easily lead to a sense of self-sufficiency that sees little or no need for ordained ministers. The challenge that faces the Church is to insure that parishes and

---

42. *HCWEOM*, no. 15 [*DOL* 266, no. 2093].
43. See *EM*, no. 3 [*DOL* 179, no. 1232].

other communities that do not have a priest remain closely connected to the life of the diocese, and that Mass be celebrated in them as frequently as possible.

63   The Bishops' Committee on the Liturgy is convinced that in the present circumstances providing Sunday celebrations under the leadership of a deacon or designated layperson is the best response to the phenomenon of the "priest-less Sunday." These celebrations enable communities gathered in steadfast faith to hear and respond to God's Word, to be strengthened and nourished by the body and blood of Christ, and to continue to do the work of Christ in the world. However, it remains for the entire Church to continue to work and pray for more laborers for the harvest, more shepherds for the sheep. The Church has faced similar problems in the past and with a faith, filled hope now looks to the future and to the continuing renewal of all the People of God.

GLOSSARY
Rev. Msgr. Patrick R. Lagges

Apostolic Constitution: A document issued by the Roman Pontiff that "constitutes" something (establishing a diocese, instituting laws, defining doctrine, etc.). It is one of the most solemn declarations of the Church.

Apostolic Exhortation: A document issued by the Roman Pontiff that is "exhortative" in nature. It is not primarily legislative. Apostolic exhortations are often issued after a synod of bishops has addressed an issue of pastoral importance for the Church. An apostolic exhortation can be issued to the whole Church or to a portion of the Church.

Apostolic Letter issued *motu proprio*: A document issued by the Roman Pontiff "on his own initiative (*motu proprio*)." This type of document is primarily legislative, and sets forth norms for the entire Church.

Apostolic See: The Roman Pontiff, along with the various offices that assist him in the leadership of the Church.

Authentic Interpretations: A document containing an authoritative interpretation of a law whose meaning was previously unclear, or extending a law to cover a situation that was not explicit in the law. Because it is a legislative document, it can only be issued by someone with legislative power. Authentic interpretations are given by the Pontifical Council for Legislative Texts. In the past, they were given by the Pontifical Commission for the Interpretation of the Second Vatican Council or by the Consilium for Liturgy.

Circular Letter: A document, issued by an office of the Roman Curia, which usually explains certain procedural matters in the Church. It is not legislative because the offices of the Curia do not possess legislative authority. Circular letters are more along the lines of guidelines that ought to be followed when carrying out certain aspects of Church life. The use of circular letters has increased in recent years.

Commission: An office of the Roman Curia, usually designated a "Pontifical Commission." At the present time, there are Pontifical Commissions for the Cultural Heritage of the Church, for Sacred Archaeology, for Latin America, and for the Vatican City State, as well as the Pontifical Biblical Commission and the International Theological Commission.

Committee: An office of the Roman Curia, usually designated a "Pontifical Committee." At the present time, there are Pontifical Committees for the International Eucharistic Congresses and for the Historical Sciences.

Conference of Bishops: A grouping of bishops of a nation or a certain territory, established by the Holy See, which jointly exercises certain pastoral functions within its territory. The Conference of Bishops possesses teaching authority under certain conditions, legislative authority as specified in the *Code of Canon Law* (CIC), and some executive authority. The conference is not an intermediary institution between the Holy See and the individual diocesan bishops, and cannot interfere in the diocesan bishop's power of governance in his diocese. The norms issued by the conference of bishops are binding throughout the territory. Norms binding in the United States can be found on the website of the United States Conference of Catholic Bishops at www.usccb.org.

Congregations: An office of the Holy See that assists the Roman Pontiff in day-to-day Church operations. They are part of the Roman Curia. Congregations are not primarily legislative, but can be given legislative authority by the Roman Pontiff in specific instances. They are governed by their own special law, at present the apostolic constitution, *Pastor Bonus*. Currently, there are Congregations for the Doctrine of the Faith; for the Oriental Churches; for Divine Worship and the Discipline of the Sacraments; for the Causes of Saints; for Bishops; for the Evangelization of Peoples; for the New Evangelization; for the Clergy; for Institutes of Consecrated Life and Societies of Apostolic Life; and for Catholic Education.

Council: A gathering of particular Churches. Councils can be ecumenical (for all the bishops of the Church); plenary (consisting of all the particular Churches within the territory of a conference of bishops); or provincial (consisting of all the particular Churches of the same ecclesiastical province). Plenary and provincial councils are legislative in nature and can establish norms for their particular territory.

Curia: The administrative offices of the universal or particular Church. They assist the Roman Pontiff or the diocesan bishop in the day-to-day governance of the Christian faithful who have been entrusted to his care. They are not legislative in nature.

Customary Law: A law introduced into a community by a custom that is not contrary to divine law or forbidden by law, and which has been observed for thirty continuous and complete years.[1] Canon 27 refers to custom as "the best interpreter of laws."

Declaration: A statement from one with executive authority concerning the proper way to carry out a law—in which case it would be akin to a general executory decree, an instruction, a precept, or other singular administrative decree—or a statement from one with legislative authority concerning an authentic interpretation or modification of the law. It could also be a statement from an ecclesiastical authority that an automatic penalty has been incurred. Declarations were not specified in the 1983 CIC.

Decretal Letter: A solemn pronouncement of the Roman Pontiff, usually concerned with the beatification or canonization of saints. They are not generally legislative in nature.

Dicastery: Another name for one of the Roman Curial offices. In practical terms, *dicastery* is most often used as a synonym for the Roman Congregations rather than Commissions, Committees, or Tribunals.

---

1. See *Code of Canon Law* (CIC), § 23–28.

Diocesan Bishop: A bishop who has been entrusted with a portion of the people of God as their proper pastor. The diocesan bishop possesses all of the legislative, executive, and juridical authority needed to carry out his office, although he does so with the assistance of other members of the faithful, who are sometimes referred to as the diocesan curia. When the law specifies that the diocesan bishop can do something, it refers only to him, and not to others who may have delegated authority (vicar general, judicial vicar, episcopal vicars, vicars forane, deans, etc.). Ecclesiastical territories that are not dioceses are pastored by territorial prelates, territorial abbots, apostolic vicars, or apostolic prefects who are equivalent to diocesan bishops. A diocese that is vacant may also be pastored by an apostolic administrator.

Diocesan Synod: A gathering within a diocese of the bishops, diocesan priests, members of religious institutes, and the faithful. The synod assists the diocesan bishop with the pastoral care of the diocese. The synod usually results in particular law, although it is the bishop alone who is the legislator.

Directory: A form of general executory decree that determines how a law ought to be applied or that urges the observance of a law. There are directories, for example, on ecumenism and on the pastoral ministry of bishops. A directory is not a law in itself, but it explains how to carry out the law.

Disciplinary Decree: A document that indicates how something is to be done in the Church. As such, it indicates the "discipline" that is to be followed in carrying out Church functions. It is distinguished from a "penal decree," which imposes a penalty on someone for an offense.

Dispensation: A relaxation of a merely ecclesiastical law in a particular case for a spiritual purpose. Laws stating how something or some action is constituted are not subject to dispensation. While the diocesan bishop can generally dispense from disciplinary laws in the Church, he cannot dispense from laws that establish a penalty or that describe a procedure. In addition, the dispensation from some laws is reserved to the Holy See.

Ecclesiastical Authority: The person who has responsibility for governance in a particular case or in all cases. It is always necessary to determine who has the authority to act in a particular situation.

General Decree: A provision made by one with legislative authority for a community that is capable of receiving laws. For example, a diocesan bishop would establish particular law (policies, procedures, or protocols) for his diocese by means of a general decree.

General Executory Decree: A provision made by one with executive authority that more precisely determines the way laws are to be observed or that urges their observance. A directory is a type of general executory decree.

Holy See: Another name for the Apostolic See; namely, the Roman Pontiff and the offices that assist him in the leadership of the Church.

Indult: A singular administrative act that grants an individual or group something beyond what is stated in a law. Indults are sometimes granted to individual countries or regions to celebrate liturgical ceremonies in a certain way.

Instruction: A document issued by one with executive authority that clarifies what is contained in the law and determines the methods to be used in observing the law. The *General Instruction of the Roman Missal* is a good example of an instruction.

Liturgical Law: Generally refers to a body of law that is contained in the rites themselves or various directories, instructions, or particular law. For the most part, the CIC does not define the rites themselves. The individual ritual editions, particularly their *praenotandae,* ought to be consulted.

Local Ordinary: A term used for one who has executive authority over a certain territory. In addition to the Roman Pontiff and the diocesan bishop, local ordinaries include vicars general and episcopal vicars. The vicar general has authority over the whole territory, while the episcopal vicar has authority over either the whole territory or a part of the territory, depending on the decree appointing him. Religious superiors have authority over certain groups of persons and would not be considered "local ordinaries."

Norms: A document issued by one with executive authority that more precisely determines how laws are to be carried out in the Church. Norms must always be reconciled to the actual laws that they seek to explain or clarify. When their meaning is unclear, the laws on which they are based ought to be consulted.

Notification: A document issued by one with executive authority, which usually serves as a reminder of something contained in the law, or explains more clearly the meaning of a law.

Ordinary: A term used for one who has executive authority over a certain territory or a certain group of people. In addition to the Roman Pontiff and the diocesan bishop, ordinaries include the vicar general, the episcopal vicars, and the major superiors of clerical religious institutes and societies of apostolic life or pontifical right.

Papal Address: A talk given by the Roman Pontiff about an element of Church teaching, practice, or legislation. Papal addresses are not considered legislative in nature, but they indicate the thinking of the Roman Pontiff on various matters of importance to the Church.

Papal Allocution: A particular form of papal address that is usually more formal than a simple talk and is usually directed toward one of the dicasteries of the Holy See.

Papal Nuncio: The representative of the Roman Pontiff for the Church in a particular country, whose task is to strengthen the bond of unity between the Holy See and the Churches of that country. If there are no diplomatic relations between the Holy See and the civil state in a country, the papal representative is called the "apostolic delegate."

Particular Law: Laws established for a particular group of people, such as a diocese. They are sometimes referred to as "policies," "guidelines," "procedures," or "protocols," although these terms can sometimes be misleading.

Plenary Council: A gathering of all the churches of an individual conference of bishops. The council provides for the pastoral needs of the people of God within the territory of the conference, particularly those concerning "the increase of faith, the organization of common pastoral action, and the regulation of morals and of the common ecclesiastical discipline which is to be observed, promoted, and protected."[2] A plenary council is legislative in nature, with the bishops having deliberative vote and the clergy and laity having consultative vote. The Councils of Baltimore in the United States were plenary councils.

Praenotanda: The introductory section to a ritual established for the Church. It provides essential information about the nature of the ritual and how to carry it out.

Privilege: A favor given to an individual or group of individuals. It could be in the form of an indult or other type of singular administrative act, or it could be a centenary or immemorial privilege that has always existed for the individual or group.

Promulgation: The act of making a law public and assigning a date when it will become effective. If no date is assigned for a law to take effect, and the law is issued by the Holy See, the effective date is three months after it has been promulgated; if the law is issued by another entity, the effective date is one month after it has been promulgated. Laws issued by the Holy See are generally promulgated in the *Acta Apostolicae Sedis*, but could be promulgated in another forum.

Province: A grouping of dioceses or ecclesiastical territories for pastoral purposes. The province is headed by an archbishop, who is also called the *metropolitan*. He does not have any governing authority over the other bishops of the province, but exercises vigilance over the faith and ecclesiastical discipline within the province; he reports to the Roman Pontiff if there are any difficulties in these areas.

Provincial Council: A gathering of all the churches within an ecclesiastical province which is concerned with the pastoral care of the faithful within a certain territory. It is legislative in nature, with the bishops having deliberative vote and the clergy and laity having consultative vote.

Recognitio: The required approval given by the Holy See to legislative acts of the conference of bishops. The *recognitio* guarantees that the legislation does not harm the unity of the Church. It is an act of executive authority, with the legislative authority coming from the conference of bishops.

Recourse: The process used when there is disagreement over an action. The person who disagrees with the action has ten days to ask that the decision be changed. Church law recommends that such disputes be settled through conciliation,

---

2. Canon 445.

mediation, or arbitration, but also provides for recourse to the person's hierarchical superior should attempts at conciliation fail.

Region: A grouping of provinces, requested by the conference of bishops and established by the Holy See, to promote the pastoral good of a larger portion of the faithful within a certain territory.

Regulation: Similar to a norm, a regulation specifies how a law is to be carried out. Regulations are issued by those who possess executive authority, and must be harmonized with existing legislation.

Rescript: A singular administrative act, giving a decision or making provision for a particular case. Dispensations, privileges, and other favors are examples of rescripts.

Responses: A document that provides an answer to a specific question that has been posed to one of the dicasteries of the Holy See. Recent responses concerned the invalidity of Baptism in the Church of Jesus Christ of Latter Day Saints and the inability of deacons to celebrate the Sacrament of the Anointing of the Sick.

Rubric: A form of liturgical law that indicates how a rite is to be performed. It gets its name from the fact that these instructions were usually written in red within the ritual, giving rise to the phrase, "Read the black; do the red."

Singular Decree: A singular administrative act that contains a decision or makes provision in a particular case, not necessarily in response to a request. Like all decrees, it should be made in writing, and only after the person with executive authority issuing the decree has gathered the necessary information and heard those whose rights could be injured.[3]

Singular Precept: A singular administrative act which directly and legitimately orders an individual or a group of individuals to do something or to refrain from or avoid doing something. It should be issued in writing, and only after the person with executive authority issuing the precept has gathered the necessary information and heard those whose rights could be injured.[4]

Special Law: A law given for specific situations. For example, the laws concerning canonizations and concerning the dissolution of marriages could be considered special law. It differs from particular law, in that a special law is not given to a particular group of people, but generally covers special processes in the Church.

Synod of Bishops: A gathering of bishops from different regions of the world that meets periodically to foster greater unity between the Roman Pontiff and the bishops; to assist the Roman Pontiff with their counsel regarding faith, morals, and ecclesiastical discipline; and to consider questions pertaining to the activity of the Church in the world. The synod of bishops is not a legislative body. After listening to the counsel of the bishops, the Roman Pontiff usually issues an apostolic exhortation on the topic of the synod, which represents the counsel of the bishops throughout the world.

---

3. See Canon 50.
4. Ibid.

Universal Law: Law that is given for the entire Church. It could be contained in the CIC or in the rites of the Church. It binds all the members of the Church, and must be made known to them through publication in some form.

Vatican II Documents: The sixteen official documents of the Second Vatican Council. They are divided into three categories:

Constitutions, which are called either dogmatic (on the Church and on Divine Revelation) or pastoral (on the Church in the Modern World) or simply a Constitution (on the Sacred Liturgy), without any particular explanation for the differing titles;

Decrees on the Instruments of Social Communication, on Ecumenism (two documents), on the Eastern Catholic Churches, on the Bishop's Pastoral Office, on Priestly Formation, on the Renewal of Religious Life, on the Apostolate of the Laity, on the Ministry and Life of Priests, and on the Church's Missionary Activity;

Declarations on the Relationship of the Church to Non-Christian Religions and on Religious Freedom.

INDEX

References are to articles or section numbers of individual documents that are included in *The Liturgy Documents, Volume 1: Fifth Edition*. For a list of abbreviations of document names, see pages x–xi. Because of space constraints, citations are limited. See also the detailed outlines which precede each document.

LAY MINISTERS
CSL 28–29; GIRM 43, 50, 95–107, 112,
133, 139, 169, 335, 339; BLS 36;
SCAP 26–30; *See also individual
ministerial roles by name*

LECTIONARY
GIRM 61, 62, 118, 120, 128, 349, 355, 358,
359, 362

LECTOR
GIRM 98, 99, 101; RS 44; STL 115, 160;
BLS 36

LENT
absence of a priest: SCAP 83–88
character of: CSL 109–10; UNLY 27–31
liturgies of: GIRM 53, 62, 66, 305, 313,
346, 354, 355, 372, 373, 374, 380;
LM 25, 60, 67, 69, 97
See also Ash Wednesday

LIGHTING
GIRM 316; BLS 228–33

LITANIES
LM 14, 17, 20–22, 23, 56, 89–90; STL 146

LITURGICAL TIME
GIRM 47, 48, 62, 81, 131; GSF 41

LITURGICAL YEAR
nature of: CSL 102, 107–11; UNLY 1–2,
17–44; BLS 20, 81
role of Sunday in: CSL 106; UNLY 4–7,
16; *See also Sunday*
role of weekdays in: GIRM 66, 354, 355,
358, 363, 365, 375–77, 381
seasons of: CSL 107–10; UNLY 18–42;
BLS 122–29
solemnities, feasts, and memorials:
GIRM 11, 13, 40, 53, 55, 115, 305, 313,
346, 354, 357; UNLY 8–15, 59
*See also individual days and seasons
by name*

LITURGY OF THE EUCHARIST
consecration: GIRM 3, 11, 43, 79, 147,
150, 151, 179, 218, 275, 276, 324, 331
offertory and preparation of the gifts:
GIRM 2, 5, 30, 33, 43, 72–79, 93, 96,
140, 144, 146, 214, 215, 221, 222, 227,
230, 233, 276, 277, 363, 365
music for: STL 172–97
relationship of to Liturgy of the Word:
CSL 56; FYH 60–62

LITURGY OF THE HOURS
CSL 83–85, 89–101; UNLY 3; BLS 115;
DD 27; STL 230–40; SCAP 42–46;
GSF 53

LITURGY OF THE WORD
absence of a priest: SCAP 47–51; GSF 54
elements and nature of: CSL 24; LM 1–37
offices and ministries in: LM 38–57
readings during: GIRM 24, 29, 31, 33, 37,
43, 44, 55–60, 65, 67, 94, 99, 101, 102,
109, 130–35, 171–76, 194–96, 212, 260,
262, 273–77, 309, 352, 355, 357–62, 367,
369, 370, 385, 390, 391, 395; LM 17, 23,
36, 74, 93–110
relationship of to Liturgy of the
Eucharist: CSL 56; FYH 60–62
music for: STL 152–171

MARRIAGE, SACRAMENT OF
CSL 77–78; BLS 106–8; STL 216–24

MARY, SAINT
(BLESSED VIRGIN MARY)
CSL 103; GIRM 275, 346, 355, 375, 378;
UNLY 8, 15; BLS 126, 130, 135–38,
156–57; DD 78, 86; EE 7, 53, 55

MASSES, SPECIAL TYPES OF
Chrism Masses: GIRM 4, 199, 203, 204
Masses for the Dead: GIRM 381, 385
Masses for Various Needs: GIRM 347,
355, 371, 373, 376
ritual Masses: CSL 67; GIRM 15, 347, 359,
371, 372, 377
Votive Masses: GIRM 347, 355, 371, 375,
376

MEMORIALS
GIRM 354, 355, 357, 363, 376, 381;
UNLY 8–15

MISSALS
GIRM 1, 2, 6–10, 15, 25, 31, 43, 48, 73, 87,
90, 111, 118, 139, 147, 163, 170, 179, 190,
198, 215, 218, 256, 306, 363, 364, 368,
386, 389, 390, 394, 398, 399

MISSION
DD, 45; EE 22, 27, 28, 60; RS 13, 29;
LM 98; STL 46; BLS 6, 7, 25, 41, 61, 173;
SCAP 65, 76; DSCAP 50; GSF 3, 14, 18

MUSIC, LITURGICAL
absence of a priest: GSF 47–48
Alleluia: GIRM 37, 43, 62, 63, 64, 131,
132, 175, 212, 261; UNLY 28; LM 28
Blessing and Sprinkling of Holy Water:
STL 147
chants: CSL 116–17; GIRM 24, 37, 41,
43–44, 47, 48, 50, 52, 55, 62, 74, 86, 87,
103, 104, 121, 124, 131–32, 139, 142,
159, 175, 261, 366–67, 370, 390
Communion song: GIRM 87, 269
composers of: CSL 121; STL 81–85

ABOUT THE AUTHORS

Authors are listed in the order in which their articles appear in this publication.

Rev. Michael S. Driscoll, PHD, STD, is a presbyter of the Diocese of Helena and an associate professor of sacramental theology and liturgy at the University of Notre Dame. Besides having a theoretical appreciation of the liturgy, he is actively involved in pastoral practice: he has worked as choir director of the Cathedral of St. Helena and as a liturgical consultant across the country. He is the founding director of the graduate program in sacred music and the undergraduate minor in liturgical music ministry at the University of Notre Dame. He is the current president of the Catholic Academy of Liturgy and is past president of the North American Academy of Liturgy.

Rev. Msgr. Richard B. Hilgartner, STD, STL, is the executive director of the Secretariat of Divine Worship at the United States Conference of Catholic Bishops (USCCB). A priest of the Archdiocese of Baltimore, he has worked in parish ministry and campus ministry, and has also taught theology and homiletics. He holds an STL in liturgical and sacramental theology from the Pontifical Athenaeum of San Anselmo in Rome, and is currently pursuing an STD in liturgical studies at The Catholic University of America.

Joyce Ann Zimmerman, CPPS, PHD, STD, is the director of the Institute for Liturgical Ministry in Dayton, Ohio; adjunct professor of liturgy at the Athanaeum of Ohio; a liturgical consultant; frequent speaker and facilitator of workshops on liutrgy, spirituality, and other related topics; and an award-winning author of numerous books and articles on liturgy and spirituality.

Rev. Msgr. Joseph DeGrocco, DMIN, a priest of the Diocese of Rockville Centre, is pastor of Our Lady of Perpetual Help Church in Lindenhurst, New York. He served as professor of liturgy and director of liturgical formation at the Seminary of the Immaculate Conception in Huntington, New York from 2003–2012 and continues to teach as adjunct professor. He holds a master of arts degree in theology (liturgical studies) from the University of Notre Dame, and a doctorate in ministry from the Seminary of the Immaculate Conception. Msgr. DeGrocco is the author of *A Pastoral Commentary on the General Instruction of the Roman Missal*, the *Dictionary of Liturgical Terms*, *The Church at Worship: Reflections on Celebrating Liturgy in Parishes Today* (tentative title, pending publication), the "Roman Missal" sections of the 2014 *Sourcebook for Sundays, Seasons, and Weekdays*, and is a regular contributor to the "Q & A" column in *Pastoral Liturgy* (all from Liturgy Training Publications). A member of the Diocesan Liturgical Commission, he also writes about liturgical topics in *The Long Island Catholic* newspaper, and can be seen on television throughout the country as host of the award-winning show *Divine Intervention*.

Jason J. McFarland, MMUS, PHD, is a scholar of music and liturgy, and a frequent presenter at academic conferences and workshops on liturgical music and theology. He is a member of the North American Academy of Liturgy, Societas Liturgica, the Catholic Theological Society of America, and the National Association of Pastoral Musicians. Jason has authored articles and reviews in *Pastoral Music, Catholic Studies,* and the *Proceedings of the North American Academy of Liturgy* (2012). His book *Announcing the Feast: The Entrance Song in the Mass of the Roman Rite* was published by Liturgical Press in 2011. Jason sang as a member of the professional choir at the Basilica of the National Shrine of the Immaculate Conception from 1997–2011. For the past six years Jason has worked as the Assistant Editor at the International Commission on English in the Liturgy (ICEL), where he was involved in the preparation of the new edition of *The Roman Missal,* and has been a lecturer in Liturgical Studies at The Catholic University of America. From 2012–2014, he will be working as a university professor in China. His home parish is St. Joseph the Workman, Huntimer, South Dakota.

Christoher Carstens, MA, MA (LS) holds a BA from the Oratory of St. Philip in Toronto, an MA in Philosophy from the University of Dallas, and an MA (Liturgical Studies) from The Liturgical Institute. He is currently the Director of the Office of Sacred Worship for the Diocese of LaCrosse, Wisconsin, where he serves as Coordinator of Pontifical Liturgies, liturgical coordinator for the Permanent Deacon formation program, and diocesan Director of RCIA. He is an adjunct faculty member at the Liturgical Institute and a frequent presenter in liturgical conferences and parish education. He is a member of the Society for Catholic Liturgy and is married with five children. Mr. Carstens is one of the presenters of the *Mystical Body, Mystical Voice* program for understanding the English-language texts of the third edition of *The Roman Missal.*

Rev. Daniel J. Merz, SLD, a priest of the Diocese of Jefferson City, MO, completed doctoral studies in liturgy at the Pontifical Institute of Liturgy in Rome in 2011. He has been an associate pastor, chairman of the Diocesan Liturgical Commission, seminary professor and formator, dean of students, and vice-rector. His published works include popular and scholarly articles on the liturgy, and he co-authored the *Essential Presidential Prayers and Texts* (LTP) with Abbot Marcel Rooney, OSB. He currently works as the associate director for the Divine Worship Secretariat at the USCCB.

Mary Elizabeth Sperry, MA, holds a master's degree in liturgical studies from The Catholic University of America. She has worked for the USCCB since 1994 in the Secretariat for the Liturgy, USCCB Publishing, and the Department of Communications. She is the author of *Bible Top Tens* and *Ten: How the Commandments Can Change Your Life* (both 2012). Her articles have appeared in *The Liguorian, Emmanuel Magazine, Today's Parish Minister,* and other publications. She has been interviewed about the Bible on National Public Radio, CBS Radio, NBC News, the *Drew Mariani Show,* and *Seize the Day.*

Corinna Laughlin, PhD, is the director of liturgy for St. James Cathedral in Seattle. She also serves on the Liturgical Commission for the Archdiocese of Seattle. She co-authored *The Liturgical Ministry Series: Guide for Sacristans* and *The Liturgical Ministry Series: Guide for Servers* (both LTP), and is a frequent contributor to *Sourcebook for Sundays, Seasons, and Weekdays: The Almanac for Parish Liturgy.* Corinna has also written articles for *Pastoral Liturgy, Today's Liturgy, Ministry & Liturgy,* and *AIM.* She holds a doctorate in English from the University of Washington and a bachelor's degree in English from Mount Holyoke College.

Steven R. Janco, MCM, STL, DMin, is Director of the Rensselaer Program of Church Music and Liturgy at Saint Joseph's College in Rensselaer, Indiana, which offers summer study leading to master's degrees in church music and pastoral liturgy, as well as a number of three-day intensives—including its long-standing Gregorian Chant Institute. A composer of liturgical music, his published works include three Mass settings written for the texts of the Roman Missal, third edition. He has had articles and reviews published in a number of liturgy and liturgical music journals. He is a member of the North American Academy of Liturgy, the Catholic Academy of Liturgy, the National Association of Pastoral Musicians, and the National Association for Lay Ministry. He is also a life member of the Hymn Society in the United States and Canada and has served on the Society's Executive Committee.

Rev. J. Philip Horrigan, STB, MED, MTH, DMin, is a presbyter of the Archdiocese of Kingston, Ontario, Canada. As a pastor he was responsible for starting a new parish and leading a parish through a new church building project. He served as the director of the Department of Art and Architecture, Office for Divine Worship, Archdiocese of Chicago (1997–2009). He acted as a resource/consultant for those parishes involved in building or renovation projects. He is an independent liturgical design consultant on several projects in Canada and the United States. He is a frequent speaker at conferences and workshops on topics related to the building and renovation of liturgical spaces; the liturgical environment; and the history, documents, and components of liturgical design. His particular interest is understanding and exploring the relationship between ritual space and ritual event.

Rev. Thomas J. Scirghi, SJ, THD, is associate professor of theology at Fordham University, specializing in liturgical and sacramental theology. He has taught homiletics at the Weston Jesuit School of Theology and the Jesuit School of Theology at Berkeley. He also has presented workshops on preaching for clergy and laity throughout the United States. He preaches regularly at the Fordham University Church.

Michael R. Prendergast, MTS, MA, is a seasoned pastoral musician and liturgist with experience at the parish, cathedral, and diocesan levels. He is a frequent speaker and clinician for conferences, dioceses, and parishes. He has edited and authored numerous books and articles, including *The Liturgical Ministry Series: Guide for Liturgy Committees* (LTP), co-authored with Paul Turner. Michael holds advanced degrees in theological studies and liturgy. Michael is coordinator of liturgy at St. Andrew Church in Portland, Oregon; an instructor in the Lay Ministry Formation program for the Archdiocese of Portland; and an instructor in the theology department at the University of Portland. He is also a team member for the North American Forum on the Catechumenate. Michael is founder and executive director of Sacred Liturgy Ministries, a liturgical consulting firm; find out more at www.sacredliturgyministries.

Rev. Msgr. Patrick R. Lagges, JCD, PHD, is a presbyter of the Archdiocese of Chicago. He is currently chaplain and director of Calvert House, the Catholic center at the University of Chicago, and director of the Hesburgh Sabbatical Program at Catholic Theological Union. His articles have been published in *Studia canonica*, *The Jurist*, *Proceedings of the Canon Law Society of America*, *Fidelium iuris*, *CLSA Advisory Opinions*, *The Liguorian*, *Catechumenate*, and *Marriage and Family*. Canon Law studies were done at St. Paul University, Ottawa, Ontario, Canada, where he received a doctorate in canon law.